D0576283

HOMELAND SECURITY

An Introduction to Principles and Practice

Second Edition

HOMELAND SECURITY

An Introduction to Principles and Practice

Second Edition

Charles P. Nemeth, JD, PhD, LLM

CRC Press
Taylor & Francis Group
Boca Raton London New York

CRC Press is an imprint of the
Taylor & Francis Group, an **informa** business

CRC Press
Taylor & Francis Group
6000 Broken Sound Parkway NW, Suite 300
Boca Raton, FL 33487-2742

Printed in the United States of America on acid-free paper
Version Date: 20121008

International Standard Book Number: 978-1-4665-1090-6 (Hardback)

Library of Congress Cataloging-in-Publication Data

Nemeth, Charles P., 1951-
Homeland security : an introduction to principles and practice / Charles P. Nemeth. -- 2nd ed.
p. cm.
Includes bibliographical references and index.
ISBN 978-1-4665-1090-6 (hbk. : alk. paper)
1. United States. Dept. of Homeland Security. 2. National security--United States. 3. Terrorism--United States--Prevention. I. Title.

HV6432.4.N46 2013
363.340973--dc23 2012039335

Visit the Taylor & Francis Web site at
http://www.taylorandfrancis.com

and the CRC Press Web site at
http://www.crcpress.com

*To Lt. Stephen Charles Nemeth, a marine and a gentleman—
the type of man who protects the nation and its homeland and
the type of son and man that impresses each and every day.*

To St. Thomas Aquinas who remarked:

Nothing hinders one act from having two effects, only one of which is intended, while the other is beside the intention. Now moral acts take their species according to what is intended, and not according to what is beside the intention, since this is accidental as explained above. Accordingly the act of self-defense may have two effects, one is the saving of one's life, the other is the slaying of the aggressor. Therefore this act, since one's intention is to save one's own life, is not unlawful, seeing that it is natural to everything to keep itself in "being," as far as possible.

Summa Theologica II-II, Question 64, Article 7

Contents

Preface xv

Acknowledgments xix

Introduction xxi

Author xxiii

CHAPTER 1 — The Idea and Origin of Homeland Security 1

1.1 Introduction 2
1.2 Threats to the Homeland: Twentieth-Century Military Movements 2
1.3 Threats to the Homeland: The Cold War Experience 7
1.4 Threats to the Homeland: Revolution, Riot, and Rightful Demonstration 15
1.4.1 Domestic Terrorism: Pre-9/11 17
1.4.2 International Terrorism: Pre-9/11 23
1.5 Conclusion 25
Keywords 26
Discussion Questions 27
Practical Exercises 27
Notes 28

CHAPTER 2 — Terror, Threat, and Disaster Post-9/11: A New Paradigm of Homeland Security. 29

2.1 Introduction. 30
2.2 The Genesis of DHS. 31
2.3 DHS: 2001–2003 36
2.3.1 Evolution and Change in DHS 38
2.4 Reorganization and Evolution of DHS: 2003–2012 43
2.4.1 The Office of the Secretary of DHS. 45
2.4.2 DHS Directorates 49
2.4.2.1 Directorate for National Protection and Programs 49
2.4.2.2 Directorate for Science and Technology. 51
2.4.2.3 Directorate for Management 52
2.4.3 DHS Offices 52
2.4.4 Agencies Swept into DHS. 54
2.4.4.1 U.S. Coast Guard. 56
2.4.4.2 U.S. Secret Service. 59
2.4.4.3 Federal Protective Service 61
2.4.4.4 Federal Law Enforcement Training Center 61
2.4.5 Advisory Panels and Committees. 65
2.5 Conclusion 68
Keywords 68
Discussion Questions 69
Practical Exercises. 70
Notes 70

CHAPTER 3 — Homeland Security Law, Regulations, and Budgeting 73

3.1 Introduction. 74
3.2 Homeland Security Law, Regulations, and Executive Orders. 74
3.2.1 Executive Order 13228: The Origin of DHS 74
3.2.2 Executive Order 12231: Protection of Infrastructure. 74
3.2.3 Executive Order 13493 of January 22, 2009 79
3.2.4 Executive Order 13567 of March 7, 2011 80
3.2.5 Homeland Security Act of 2002 80
3.2.5.1 The Homeland Security Act and Posse Comitatus. 82
3.2.6 USA Patriot Act. 83
3.2.7 Specialized Laws 85
3.2.7.1 The REAL ID Program. 86
3.2.7.2 Office of US-VISIT 88
3.2.7.3 Chemical Facilities 90
3.2.7.4 Invention and Technology: The SAFETY Act 91

3.3 Budgeting, Finance, and Funding in Homeland Security..............92
3.3.1 Budget Year: 2003..............94
3.3.2 Budget Year: 2004..............95
3.3.3 Budget Year: 2005..............102
3.3.4 Budget Year: 2006..............109
3.3.5 Budget Year: 2007..............114
3.3.6 Budget Year: 2008..............118
3.3.7 Budget Years: 2009–2010..............123
3.3.8 Budget Years: 2011–2012..............125
3.4 Conclusion..............133
Keywords..............133
Discussion Questions..............134
Practical Exercises..............135
Notes..............135

CHAPTER 4 — Risk Management, Threats, and Hazards 139

4.1 Introduction..............140
4.2 Risk Management..............140
4.2.1 The Nature of Risk..............141
4.2.2 Risk Assessment..............143
4.2.3 CARVER+Shock Assessment Tool..............148
4.3 Threats and Hazards..............151
4.3.1 The Concept of Threat and Hazard..............151
4.3.2 Weapons of Mass Destruction..............156
4.3.2.1 Nuclear..............156
4.3.2.2 Radiological..............162
4.3.2.3 Biological..............165
4.3.2.4 Chemical..............173
4.3.2.5 Improvised Explosive Devices..............185
4.4 Computer Security and Information Infrastructure..............187
4.4.1 National Cyber Security Division..............192
4.4.2 US-CERT: Computer Emergency Response Team..............194
4.5 The Private Sector and Homeland Security..............198
4.6 Conclusion..............204
Keywords..............206
Discussion Questions..............207
Practical Exercises..............208
Notes..............209

CHAPTER 5 — **Training and Exercises in Homeland Security 213**

5.1 Introduction 214
5.2 Office of Grants and Training 215
5.3 Center for Domestic Preparedness 221
5.4 Emergency Management Institute 222
5.5 Homeland Security Exercise and Evaluation Program 225
5.6 Lessons Learned: Best Practices (LLIS.gov) 228
5.7 Community Emergency Response Teams 231
5.8 National Incident Management System 232
5.9 Conclusion 241
Keywords 245
Discussion Questions 248
Practical Exercises 248
Notes 249

CHAPTER 6 — **DHS Challenges: National vs. State and Local, National Security vs. Homeland Security 251**

6.1 Introduction 252
6.2 Challenge of National Policy at the State and Local Levels 254
 6.2.1 Structure at the State Level 254
 6.2.2 Structure at the Local Level 268
  6.2.2.1 Fusion Centers 269
 6.2.3 Funding and Local Initiatives 271
6.3 Fine Line of National and Homeland Security 273
 6.3.1 Department of Defense and Homeland Security 277
 6.3.2 Intelligence Gathering and Sharing 280
  6.3.2.1 Office of Naval Intelligence 281
  6.3.2.2 Air Force Intelligence 281
  6.3.2.3 U.S. Marine Corps 284
  6.3.2.4 U.S. Army 285
 6.3.3 Specialized Military/Defense Units Dedicated to Homeland Security 287
  6.3.3.1 National Maritime Intelligence Center 287
  6.3.3.2 National Reconnaissance Office 288
  6.3.3.3 Weapons of Mass Destruction Civil Support Teams 288
  6.3.3.4 Center for Combating Weapons of Mass Destruction and the Defense Threat Reduction Agency 290
6.4 Conclusion 291
Keywords 293
Discussion Questions 293

Practical Exercises..........294
Notes..........294

CHAPTER 7 — **FEMA, Response, and Recovery..........297**

7.1 Historical Foundation for FEMA..........298
7.1.1 Federal Emergency Management Agency: Pre-9/11..........298
7.1.2 Federal Emergency Management Agency: Post-9/11..........299
7.2 FEMA and Preparedness..........303
7.2.1 Role of Mitigation in the Preparedness Model..........309
7.3 FEMA Response and Recovery..........319
7.3.1 National Response Framework..........321
7.4 Conclusion..........326
Keywords..........326
Discussion Questions..........327
Practical Exercises..........327
Notes..........327

CHAPTER 8 — **Intelligence..........331**

8.1 Introduction..........332
8.2 Intelligence..........332
8.3 Terror, Threats, Disaster, and Intelligence Agencies..........335
8.3.1 Federal Bureau of Investigation..........337
8.3.1.1 Joint Terrorism Task Forces..........340
8.3.1.2 National Security Branch..........343
8.3.1.3 Analysis of Intelligence..........346
8.3.2 Central Intelligence Agency..........347
8.3.2.1 Directorate of Intelligence..........350
8.3.2.2 Office of Clandestine Services..........351
8.3.2.3 Directorate of Science and Technology..........351
8.3.2.4 Office of Support..........352
8.3.3 Office of the Director of National Intelligence..........352
8.3.3.1 National Counterterrorism Center..........355
8.3.3.2 Office of the National Counterintelligence Executive..........356
8.3.3.3 National Intelligence Council..........358
8.3.4 Defense Intelligence Agency..........360
8.4 Conclusion..........363
Keywords..........364
Discussion Questions..........364
Practical Exercises..........365
Notes..........366

CHAPTER 9 — Border Security, U.S. Citizenship, and Immigration Services...... 369

9.1 Introduction....370
9.2 U.S. Customs and Border Protection....370
9.2.1 Border Protection....373
9.2.1.1 Secure Border Initiative....374
9.2.1.2 CBP Air and Marine....379
9.2.2 CBP and the Facilitation of Trade and Commerce....381
9.2.2.1 Cargo....382
9.3 U.S. Citizenship and Immigration Services....388
9.3.1 Project Shield America Initiative....390
9.3.2 Fugitive Operations Program....392
9.3.3 Cornerstone Initiative....393
9.3.4 Cyber Crimes Center....394
9.3.5 US-VISIT Program....397
9.4 Conclusion....398
Keywords....400
Discussion Questions....400
Practical Exercises....401
Notes....401

CHAPTER 10 —Transportation Security.... 403

10.1 Introduction....404
10.2 Transportation Security Administration....404
10.2.1 Federal Air Marshals....410
10.2.2 Federal Flight Deck Officers....411
10.2.3 Law Enforcement Officers Flying Armed....411
10.2.4 TSA's Canine Explosive Detection Unit....412
10.2.5 Risk Management Programs....413
10.2.6 TSA Technology and Innovation....414
10.2.6.1 Trace Portals....414
10.2.6.2 Millimeter Wave/Advanced Imaging Technology....415
10.2.6.3 Biometrics....417
10.3 Maritime Security....420
10.3.1 National Strategy for Maritime Security....422
10.3.2 Other Maritime Plans....423
10.3.2.1 National Plan to Achieve Maritime Domain Awareness....424
10.3.2.2 Maritime Transportation System Security Plan....424
10.3.3 DHS: Borders and Marine Division....424
10.3.4 Role of the Coast Guard in Maritime Security....426

10.3.4.1 Emergency Safety. 427
10.3.4.2 Security and Law Enforcement 430
10.3.4.3 Cargo and Ports. 435
10.4 Rail and Mass Transit. 443
10.4.1 Representative Security Programs for Rail and Transit. 449
10.4.1.1 Amtrak 450
10.4.1.2 CSX: The Freight Line. 451
10.4.1.3 SEPTA: Rail Mass Transit 455
10.5 Conclusion 457
Keywords 464
Discussion Questions 464
Practical Exercises. 465
Notes 466

CHAPTER 11 — Homeland Security and Public Health 469

11.1 Introduction. 470
11.2 Water. 470
11.3 Agriculture and Food 474
11.3.1 Strategic Partnership Program on Agroterrorism 483
11.3.2 Infectious Animals 485
11.3.3 Infectious Diseases and Bioterrorism. 489
11.3.3.1 Project BioShield 493
11.3.3.2 National Pharmaceutical Stockpile. 495
11.3.3.3 National Select Agent Registry Program 496
11.4 Pandemic Threats 497
11.4.1 Planning and Response 500
11.5 Conclusion 507
Keywords 511
Discussion Questions 511
Practical Exercises. 512
Notes 512

CHAPTER 12 — The Future of Homeland Security. 515

12.1 Introduction. 515
12.2 Growth without Reason 518
12.3 Curbing Expansionism in Mission 520
12.4 The Merits of Decentralization 523
12.5 The Rise of Technology. 525
12.6 The Need for a New Way of Thinking—Jump Out of the Box 530
Notes 531

Appendix A: United States Department of Homeland Security: Homeland Security Advisory Council Charter 533

Appendix B: Definitions. 539

Appendix C: Biological Incident Annex 559

Appendix D: Suggested Protective Measures 573

Appendix E: CDC Reporting Form for Loss, Release, or Theft of Agents or Toxins 595

Index 601

Preface

This is a book about the very complex and highly bureaucratic world of Homeland Security. It is a humble attempt to give order to a mighty colossus of agencies and personnel dedicated to the protection of the homeland. At the commencement of this project, I never envisioned the "bigness" of the undertaking—the interweaving and entangling roles of people and departments and the sweep of the endeavor. Homeland Security, by any measure, is a massive enterprise that gets larger by the moment. Much of the growth arises from our understanding of things—what was once mostly a TSA/aircraft threat evolved into a multidimensional operation. While surely aircraft and passengers remain, the book makes plain that just about everything in life has a homeland quality to it. Whether it is food or water, military or private-sector justice, or the border on land or sea, the task of protecting the homeland is a work in progress. Homeland Security extends its influence to all sectors of the economy, the business and corporate world, law enforcement and military branches, as well as communities, towns, and cities.

Chapter 1 provides a foundational look at how our present system emerged by looking at the history of security threats in the American experience. In particular, the chapter considers how the Cold War period shaped our present policy on the homeland front and, just as importantly, how domestic forms of terrorism edify the DHS mindset and mentality. The protesters of the 1970s tell us much about the motive and method of terrorists as does the KKK Klansman, the spy engaged in espionage, and the anti-government zealot seeking to topple the established order. This pre-9/11 perspective is critical to any contemporary understanding of the homeland system.

Chapter 2 sees the world in the prism of events leading up to 9/11 and the subsequent evolution of policy and practice after these cataclysmic events. It is clear that a security outlook existed before 9/11, although that vision would be forever altered after the attack on the Twin Towers. Soon after these horrid events, the reaction of government and policymakers was to erect an agency and systematic response to these types of tragedies. The chapter zeroes in on the original version of the Department of Homeland Security (DHS) and its subsequent evolution and change. The DHS of 2002 was subject to many forces as leaders continuously sought more effective means of domestic protection. From 2003 and onward, diverse governmental entities were swept into the environs of DHS, from the Coast Guard to the Secret Service. Exactly how those adjustments and alterations came about and how these actions impacted the safety of our nation is closely scrutinized.

Chapter 3 stresses the legal basis and foundation for DHS. Exactly what laws, executive orders, and rulemaking made DHS possible? What is the primary legislation that enabled DHS? What other acts or laws govern homeland practice? Specific coverage includes the Patriot Act and the Homeland Security Act as well as specialized promulgations that deal with identity, chemical facilities, and safety practice. The chapter also highlights the budgetary commitment of lawmakers entrusted with the defense of a nation. From 2001 to 2009, budgets reflect the urgency of policymakers and the central mission of DHS. The genealogy of the budget is keenly reviewed since the DHS's emphasis will shift and move dependent on new threats or a better understanding of earlier homeland principles.

The nature of risk and threat is fully examined in Chapter 4. What is risk? What is a threat? How is risk defined and calculated? What types of risk and threat exist—merely nuclear, biological, and chemical? Other coverage includes risk measuring systems such as CARVER. The chapter expends considerable energy evaluating and distinguishing the world of threats and risk. Threats take many forms, including man-made and natural varieties. Special attention is given to biological and chemical threats, including plague, ricin, nerve agents, and dirty bombs. Finally, the chapter highlights how computer breaches are a new form of security risk in the world of Homeland Security and how US-CERT and the National Cyber Security Division address these issues.

Chapter 5 introduces the reader to the world of training and preparatory exercises for the homeland professional. Within DHS resides a major infrastructure of offices dedicated to the funding and actual training for Homeland Security eventualities. Offices such as the Grants and Training, the Homeland Security Exercise and Evaluation Program (HSEEP), the Emergency Management Institute (EMI), and the Center for Domestic Preparedness are fully examined. Past security practices are evaluated within the DHS Lessons Learned program, which stores experiences and results from homeland protection policy and practice. The chapter ends with a comprehensive look at NIMS—the National Incident Management System, which provides guidance and an operational methodology for hospitals, educational institutions, and other entities seeking to prevent threats.

Chapter 6 assesses the operational demands evident in the world of Homeland Security. More specifically, the chapter gauges how states and localities, which are considered the frontline of Homeland Security, can work compatibly with federal policymakers. A highly successful example of this cooperative mentality can be discovered in the funding mechanism for homeland grants and training allotments as well as the regional Fusion Centers that feed state and local information to the larger federal system. In addition, the chapter evaluates the fine line between civilian homeland function and that historically and contemporaneously assumed by the nation's military infrastructure. How do the various offices of intelligence in the military model share with DHS? Are the agencies and functions properly aligned? The chapter ends with a look at specialized entities and agencies that support the role and work of states and localities as these governmental authorities seek to advance the mission of DHS.

Chapter 7 targets the Federal Emergency Management Agency (FEMA) in both the pre- and post-9/11 world. Of all the agencies undergoing a transformation in mission and purpose since 9/11, none has been as dramatic as FEMA. FEMA has transformed itself from an agency dedicated to natural disaster to one concerned about the functions and tactics of response and recovery. The chapter examines the National Response Framework that provides protocol steps in the event of natural or man-made disasters and poses many examples of the agency's educational and mitigation function that prevents the full effect of disasters.

Chapter 8 delves into the world of intelligence. Aside from its definition and methodology, the stress is on the agencies and entities entrusted with intelligence analysis. Special attention is given to the FBI and its Joint Terrorism Task Forces and the CIA, whose various Directorates aid DHS in its overall mission. The CIA's Directorates on Intelligence, Clandestine Activities, Science and Technology, and Support make major contributions to intelligence practice in the world of Homeland Security. On top of this, the chapter provides a summary review of the Defense Intelligence Agency and its intelligence functions and the role of the Office of the Director of National Intelligence that seeks to be a central repository for intelligence gathering across all government agencies.

The subject of border security, immigration, and U.S. citizenship compose the bulk of Chapter 9. At the border, there are many challenges and corresponding methodologies to control access. Way beyond fencing alone, the newly developed Customs and Border Patrol (CBP) tackles myriad tasks involving violations of our border integrity. By air and boat, by foot and vehicle, the CBP tracks and traces encroachments. The CBP's involvement with cargo and containers is featured. The last portion of the chapter deals with citizenship and immigration issues, including an assessment of Project Shield, the US-VISIT program, and the Cornerstone Initiative.

The vast expanse of homeland practice in the airline industry comprises a major portion of Chapter 10. In immediate reaction to the Twin Towers attack, DHS set about to establish a series of programs and protocols involving both personnel and equipment. The Transportation Security Agency (TSA) is the center of the activities. Added to their functions would be the federal air marshals, armed officers aboard flights, and the federal flight deck officer program. Using specialized equipment, such as trace portals and biometrics, TSA has been advancing technology across its many duties and responsibilities. How Homeland Security practices play out in the maritime world receives considerable attention. From emergency to safety practice, from cargo to ports, the chapter deals with the diverse functions of the U.S. Coast Guard—a crucial player in the world of maritime security. Lastly, the chapter covers how real and mass transit systems must be attentive to homeland demands and features both national, regional, and local rail systems.

The interplay between public health and Homeland Security is the chief aim of Chapter 11. Terrorists' threats are meaningful as to the world's food and water supply. So, too, are the potential harms that can arise from contaminated livestock and poultry. Second, infectious diseases pose an extraordinary threat to the community from a security perspective. How DHS stores antidotes and other medical remedies receives serious attention. A close examination of the National Pharmaceutical Stockpile is part of the chapter's approach, and how a pandemic might impact both individuals and the collective is fully critiqued. Planning documents that address pandemic threats are provided.

The final chapter of the book summarizes a few of the challenges inherent in the task and the natural bureaucracy that emerges in the war on terror. DHS clearly is a work in progress and already has a lively history of change. Some examples of this critical inquiry are: Does DHS grow rationally? Does the mission of DHS match its organizational structure? Has DHS become overly bureaucratic, politically correct, and out of touch? Are the practices of DHS too centralized? Has technology been effectively integrated into the practices of DHS? Are policymakers in DHS too entrenched to think creatively, or is there a need to think outside normal channels?

In the end, I have tried to capture the structure and intent of DHS. The question of what DHS really is may be more metaphysical than we think. All of us can concur on its intent—to make the nation safe. But although we are sure of its intent, it may take a generation or two before we really understand how to shape and construct DHS. Indeed, DHS is an idea on not only a righteous path but also the beginnings of a solid foundation.

Acknowledgments

The sheer volume of DHS material and content makes this a project that heavily depends on others. To be sure, I could not have authored this alone. Instead, I was heavily dependent on the skill and acumen of colleagues.

To Hope Haywood, my thanks again. I cannot envision being ever able to coordinate this maze of concepts and ideas. While I may clearly know the subject matter, I cannot or could not know how to orchestrate it. This is a God-given skill. I am happy to see her recent appointment as assistant director of the Institute of Law and Public Policy—a place her many talents so sorely needs.

To CRC Press, I appreciate the opportunity. Editor Mark Listewnik has been professional and very enlightened. I have never met an editor so intensely engaged.

I am also fortunate to have found a recent position at John Jay College of Criminal Justice as chair of Security, Fire and Emergency Management. Few would argue the extraordinary place that John Jay is, but more need to know how supportive the John Jay environment is when it comes to scholarship. President Jeremy Travis and Provost Jane Bowers are forever encouraging and supportive.

At home, my blessings simply cannot be counted, for it is family that drives most of what I do. If I leave any legacy to my spouse and closest friend, Jean Marie, and my seven children, it is that their father loved them.

Charles P. Nemeth, JD, PhD, LLM
Chair and Professor, Security, Fire and Emergency Management

Introduction

The term "Homeland Security" is of recent invention. For the bulk of this nation's glorious history, the view that security was inexorably and inevitably tied to the homeland itself was a foreign notion. Surely, the nation always had a continuous interest in the protection of its borders from invasion, and just as assuredly, the nation and its states were perpetually concerned with the protection of the citizenry from natural disasters. To be certain, the idea that government has an obligation to protect and safeguard the citizenry is nothing new under the sun. Yet despite this penchant for safeguarding the general population, protection of the homeland took on a very different meaning in the year 2001. The world changed in more ways than we could have ever envisioned as the attacks on the Twin Towers and the Pentagon unfolded.

From September 11, 2001, onward, the world will perceive the idea, the notion of security, and the homeland in a unique and very different way. Homeland Security will be referred to as a "New National Calling."[1] In *Securing the Homeland: Strengthening the Nation*, President George W. Bush exhorts the citizenry to remember this new vocation:

> The higher priority we all now attach to homeland security has already begun to ripple through the land. The Government of the United States has no more important mission than fighting terrorism overseas and securing the homeland from future terrorist attacks. This effort will involve major new programs and significant

> reforms by the Federal government. But it will also involve new or expanded efforts by State and local governments, private industry, non-governmental organizations, and citizens. By working together we will make our homeland more secure.[2]

Before 9/11, terrorism was surely one of many variables considered in the planning and implementation of national security. After 9/11 it became the predominant and preeminent criteria in the war on terror and a national fixation in most facets of the public domain.

Notes

1. President George W. Bush, *Securing the Homeland: Strengthening the Nation* (Washington, DC: U.S. Government Printing Office, 2002), 3.
2. Bush, *Securing the Homeland*, 3.

Author

Charles P. Nemeth, chair and professor of Security, Fire and Emergency Management at John Jay College, New York, has spent the vast majority of his professional life in the study and practice of law and justice, the role of private-sector justice in a free society, and the ethical demands on justice professionals. A recognized expert on ethics and the legal system, appellate legal practice and private-sector justice, he also is a prolific writer, having published numerous texts and articles on law and justice throughout his impressive career. His most recent works include these titles: *Private Security and the Investigative Process* (CRC Press, 2010); *Private Security and the Law*, 4th Edition (Elsevier, 2012); *Aquinas and King: A Discourse on Civil Disobedience* (Carolina Academic Press, 2010); *Aquinas and Crime* (St. Augustine's Press, 2009); *Criminal Law* (Prentice Hall, 2003; CRC Press, 2011); *Law & Evidence: A Primer for Criminal Justice, Criminology, Law, and Legal Studies* (Prentice Hall, 2001; Jones and Bartlett, 2010); *Aquinas in the Courtroom* (Greenwood and Praeger Publishing, 2001); *Private Sector and Public Safety: A Community Based Approach* (Prentice Hall, 2005); *The Prevention Agency* (California University of Pennsylvania Press—Institute for Law and Public Policy, 2005); and *The Paralegal Resource Manual* (McGraw-Hill, 2008).

An educator for more than 30 years, Dr. Nemeth's distinctive career is a blend of both practice and theory. A member of the Pennsylvania, New York, and North

Carolina bars, Dr. Nemeth has extensive experience in all aspects of criminal and civil practice.

His previous academic appointments include Niagara University (1977–1980), the University of Baltimore (1980–1981), Glassboro State College (1981–1986), Waynesburg College (1988–1998), the State University of New York at Brockport (1998–2003), and California University of Pennsylvania (2000–2012). He is a much sought-after legal consultant for security companies on the trend of privatization, and he is a recognized scholar on issues involving law and morality and how ethics relates to the professions.

Chapter 1

The Idea and Origin of Homeland Security

Objectives

1. To identify major twentieth and twenty-first century events, both domestic and international, that have formed the United States' current policy position on Homeland Security.
2. To comprehend that war, by its very nature, its military tactics and strategies and governmental policies, relies on forms of terror to meet its goals.
3. To analyze the effect the Cold War had on shaping Americans' notions of terror and understand the evolution of government's policy responses.
4. To describe the domestic events of the turbulent 1960s and 1970s to shed light on the country's response to domestic terrorism, as well as gain an understanding of the unique motivations of the domestic terrorist.
5. To differentiate the motives of the international terrorist from the domestic terrorist and comprehend that although the methods may be the same, the motivations differ.
6. To explain the unique motivations of the jihadist by exploring attacks against U.S. military targets and discover the motivations leading up to the events of 9/11.

7. To evaluate specific international terror incidents against U.S. installations prior to 9/11 to gain an understanding of the jihadist mentality that led up to the terror attacks against the Twin Towers and the Pentagon.
8. To identify specific domestic terror attacks, such as those perpetuated by Timothy McVeigh and Ted Kaczynski, in light of the effect these types of attacks have on national security policy.

1.1 Introduction

The concept of a threat to the homeland has historically taken many shapes. Terror and the terrorist are not new phenomena—they are a construction of the ages, seen throughout history in various guises. In recent years, the country has focused on domestic security and preventing acts of terrorism. Couple this perspective with a predictable national desire to protect one's homeland, and nothing here is unexpected. What is of greater utility in the discussion of security of the homeland will be how we arrived at our current position. Specifically, what did we do before the jihadist? What types of terror attacks did America experience? What motivated the terrorist? For example, the Ku Klux Klansman is hardly a jihadist, although his methods may be just as dastardly. How do we reconcile that difference? What of the military dictator, the tyrant, the leader who leads his country to ruin and grounds his enterprise on hate, such as the Third Reich. This too is terror by any reasonable definition. Terror is nothing new. The acts of the terrorist have been with us since the dawn of recorded history. It is important to keep this in context in our interpretation of history. This chapter traces a whole host of acts and movements in the twentieth century that preceded the events of 9/11. All of the examples covered illuminate how and why terrorists do what they do. All of these illustrations, from the military machine that oppresses people and states, to the Weathermen that sabotage government installations, help to bring perspective to the discussion. When one scrutinizes the diversity of these acts and approaches, one can better understand the landscape of modern terrorism in a post-9/11 world.

1.2 Threats to the Homeland: Twentieth-Century Military Movements

While much can be written about the nature of threat and violence throughout U.S. history, it would appear that the best place to start in order to understand modern day terrorism is the twentieth century—a century with complex conflicts and territorial challenges. From World War I to World War II (WWII), the concept of threats to the homeland was largely the result of country-to-country conquests, political disagreements, and imperial empire building. For example, the Third Reich's move into the Polish frontier, in the name of reclamation of Aryan races under the thumb of Polish authorities, is a land grab with eugenic flavor. This is a very different kind of threat than that currently considered by the Department of Homeland Security. Yet these wars and conflicts serve as an appropriate backdrop for how any nation seeks to maintain its territorial integrity. In a sense, the planes attacking the World Trade Center buildings were an assault on the country's sovereignty not unlike the way the German troops crossed into the Sudetenland (Figure 1.1).

The means and motivation are clearly different, though the net effect is not completely dissimilar. The Nazi onslaught of WWII was, in a sense, the largest whole-scale terror campaign ever inflicted on a continent (Figure 1.2).

Aside from this illegal and unjustified sweep of countries, Germany culminated its terror by implementing its Final Solution, its programs of extermination for Jews and all forms of resisters, for the mentally disabled, the old and infirmed, for Catholic priests and Lutheran ministers. More than 6 million human beings perished under the crush of an evil state (Figure 1.3).

That the Nazi regime engaged in deliberate, intentional threats against whole races, ethnic types, and classification of citizens is a self-evident conclusion when the historical record is scratched just a little. The systematic extermination program was the subject of endless meetings and conferences, though admittedly the Nazi leaders were quite effective in removing the paper trail. In 1942, at what was billed as the Wannsee Conference, the leadership of the SS, the Nazi and other aligned government entities, met to discuss the efficacy and corresponding efficiencies of mass extermination.

FIGURE 1.1 German troops goose step through Warsaw, Poland, during the 1939 invasion that saw Poland fall within 3 weeks. The invasion caused Britain and France to declare war on Germany. (National Archives, image 200-SFF-52.)

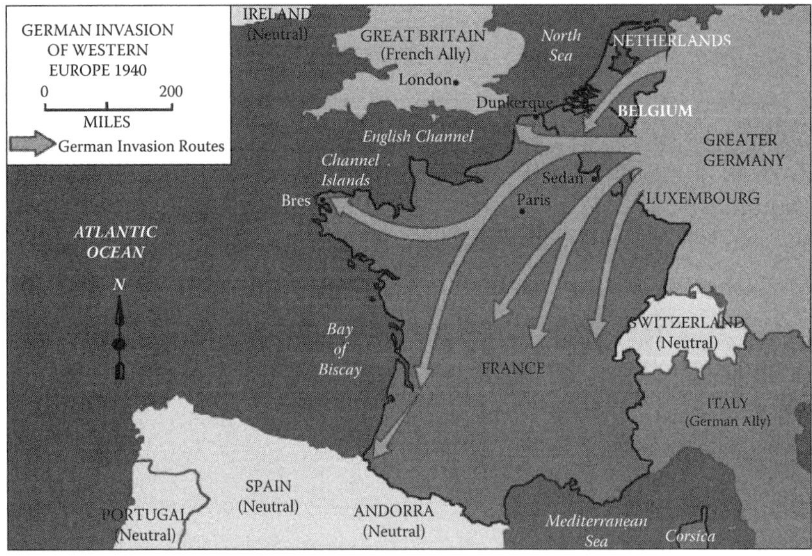

FIGURE 1.2 From Poland to Stalingrad, from Holland to Northern Africa, the propaganda of the Third Reich was a campaign that terrorized the entire civilized world.

FIGURE 1.3 A survivor stokes smoldering human remains in a crematorium oven that is still lit, Dachau, Germany, April 29–May 1, 1945. (Courtesy of the U.S. Holocaust Museum, Washington, DC.)

FIGURE 1.4 Reinhard Heydrich, chief of the SD (Security Service) and Nazi governor of Bohemia and Moravia. Place uncertain, 1942. (National Archives and Records Administration, College Park, MD.)

Leading the charge calling for the physical extermination of millions was SS officer Reinhard Heydrich (Figure 1.4).

The bureaucratic apparatus was coupled by legions of resources, from transportation to the building of crematoria. The task of moving millions of people to their own deaths requires extraordinary efforts by the Captains of industry. Consider the complexities of rail movement alone as portrayed in Figure 1.5.

Similar arguments about Japanese imperialism can be posited, and for good cause. The Japanese intent was to dominate and rule the world using means far outside the mainstream of modern warfare. Survivors of Japanese occupation in the Philippines or of Japan's own concentration camps tell a story of brutality and degradation that seems inexplicable when one considers the modern democratic state of Japan. The notorious Unit 731 on the Japanese mainland witnessed forced sterilization, castration, live burial, vivisection, mutilation, and mass experimentation (Figure 1.6).

Internet Exercise: Visit the National Archives collection, which catalogs Japanese war crimes in WWII at http://www.archives.gov/iwg/japanese-war-crimes/select-documents.pdf.

None of these atrocities can be adequately covered in a text on homeland security, although it is critical that the reader understands that war, by its

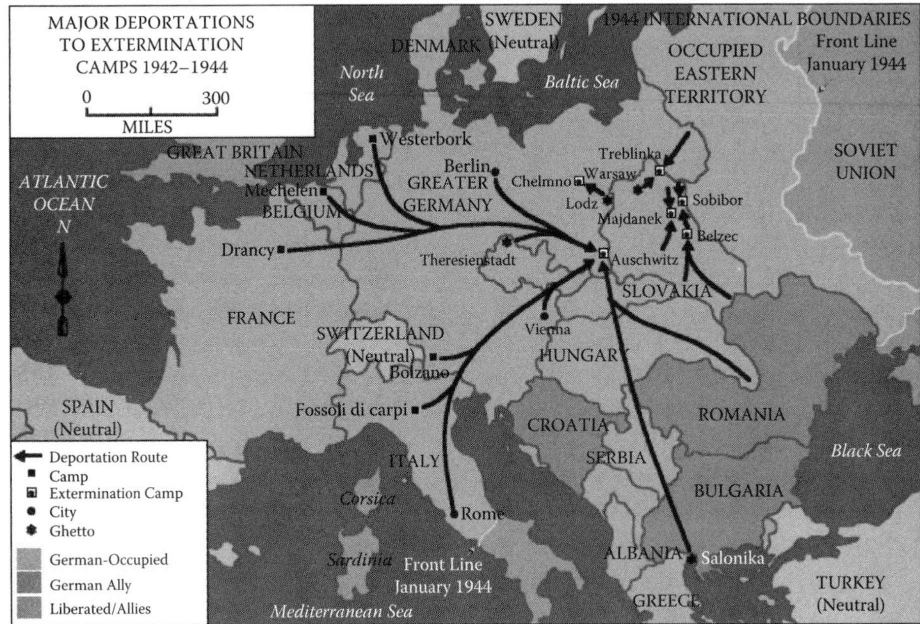

FIGURE 1.5 The Germans attempted to disguise their intentions, referring to deportations as "resettlement to the east." The victims were told they were to be taken to labor camps, but in reality, from 1942 onward, deportation for most Jews meant transit to killing centers and then death. (US Holocaust Memorial Museum at http://www.ushmm.org/wlc/en/media_nm.php?ModuleId=10005372&MediaId=362.)

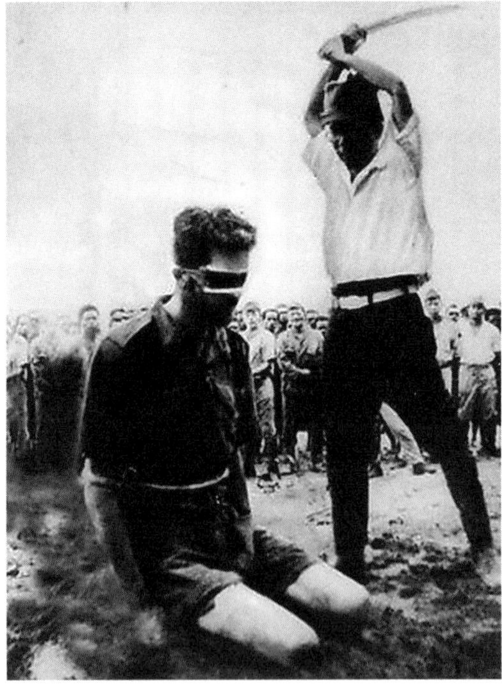

FIGURE 1.6 Camp 731 beheading an American POW. (Courtesy of the University of Minnesota, Center for the Study of Holocaust and Genocide Studies.)

very nature, depends upon terror to some extent. Whether it is the summary execution of civilians and prisoners of war or the indiscriminate bombing of wholesale populations, terror is both an end and a by-product of war. Much of what we witness in the terror battlefield today connects its heritage to the makings and doings of war. By way of illustration, Saddam Hussein thought Joseph Stalin—one of history's most remarkable figures—was to be envied and copied in approach. In this way, a look at twentieth-century conflicts can illuminate the rationale behind the tactics used by terrorists.

1.3 Threats to the Homeland: The Cold War Experience

At the end of the conflagration known as WWII, another conflict of a very different sort emerged—the Cold War. As the victors of WWII set out to fashion a new Europe and continental framework, the Allies saw the world in distinct and sometimes incompatible ways. For sure, Britain and the United States shared the core values of freedom and democratic, republican principles. Contrasted by that was the starkly divisive approach of our Russian ally, whose Trotskyite–Leninist revolutionary mindset was fundamentally at odds with Western ideals. The Russian mindset directly struck at the heart of free societies. At the end of the war, during the Potsdam Convention, Russia's expansionist desires clearly won the day (Figure 1.7).

FIGURE 1.7 Churchill, Truman, and Stalin during the Potsdam Convention. (Courtesy of the Truman Library.)

Dividing up countries such as Germany and replacing free democratic or monarchical countries such as Poland and Hungary with a Soviet-style socialist model, the Russian Bear flexed extraordinary muscle immediately after the end of the conflict. Concession after concession was made to the Soviet demand, much to the distress of Winston Churchill.

In response, Churchill ultimately sounded a clarion call for halting the expansion of the Soviet empire in one of his finest speeches.[1]

> I have a strong admiration and regard for the valiant Russian people and for my wartime comrade, Marshal Stalin. There is deep sympathy and goodwill in Britain—and I doubt not here also—toward the peoples of all the Russias and a resolve to persevere through many differences and rebuffs in establishing lasting friendships.
>
> It is my duty, however, to place before you certain facts about the present position in Europe.
>
> From Stettin in the Baltic to Trieste in the Adriatic an iron curtain has descended across the Continent. Behind that line lie all the capitals of the ancient states of Central and Eastern Europe. Warsaw, Berlin, Prague, Vienna, Budapest, Belgrade, Bucharest and Sofia; all these famous cities and the populations around them lie in what I must call the Soviet sphere, and all are subject, in one form or another, not only to Soviet influence but to a very high and in some cases increasing measure of control from Moscow.

Internet Exercise: To read Churchill's entire speech, titled "The Sinews of Peace," visit http://www.nato.int/docu/speech/1946/S460305a_e.htm.

By 1946, Churchill knew full well that a geopolitical shift was underway. In appealing to the United States, he urged its government to consider its many sacrifices of men and material and to envision a world where an "iron curtain" would split the free from the oppressed. The legacy of the sacrifice must amount to more than an iron wall between the totalitarian and the democratic. But this is exactly what was unfolding and with frightening speed—a new world order divided in two and directly at odds with one another. Hence, a new war emerged—one not fought on the battlefield but in the sphere of territorial conquest and subliminal and direct attempts to destroy either side. This is the stuff of the Cold War, and it escalated very quickly. The United States quickly recognized these expansionist motivations.

Internet Exercise: Read President Harry Truman's Secretary of State Keenan's letter to General George C. Marshall for his prescient commentary on an upcoming Cold War at www.trumanlibrary.org. Click on *Documents* in the Main Menu, then *Cold War* under "Online Documents," click on

Documents. Locate the January 29, 1946 Telegram from George Kennan to James Byrnes.

The Cold War is not an illusory war by any means, but one with significant military and political consequences. By 1947, the Soviet Union commenced the construction of the Berlin Wall—separating the East from the West and trapping East Berlin in a dark, communist world. Ever the expansionist, the Soviet Union boldly expanded its sphere of influence into countries like Iran.

In the wake of these actions, President Harry Truman discerned a meaningful and bona fide threat to free peoples. As a result, he made plain that the United States would not sit idly by while Soviet aggression spread throughout the world. In 1947, Truman enunciated what is now known as the Truman Doctrine. With the Truman Doctrine, President Truman established that the United States would provide political, military, and economic assistance to all democratic nations under threat from external or internal authoritarian forces. The Truman Doctrine effectively reoriented U.S. foreign policy, guiding it away from the usual stance of withdrawal from regional conflicts not directly involving the United States, to one of possible intervention in faraway conflicts.

Internet Exercise: Read President Truman's diary, written in 1947, to get some sense of the threat the country was experiencing at the time: http://www.trumanlibrary.org/diary/index.html.

In light of the Soviet Union developing an atomic bomb in 1949, the doctrine was never more important to fend off threats to our national security. See Figure 1.8 for a timeline of the Cold War to the point of Soviet nuclear power.

1945–1946: Creation of Eastern European People's Republics
1946: George Kennan's Long Telegram and the Policy of Containment
1946: Churchill's Iron Curtain Speech
1946: Soviet Troops in Iran
1947: Truman Doctrine
1947: U.S. Efforts to Control Atomic Energy
1947: Marshall's Offer of Economic Assistance
1948–1949: Berlin Airlift
1949: North Atlantic Treaty Organization
1949: Creation of the Two Germanys
1949: Soviet Atomic Bomb

FIGURE 1.8 Timeline of the Cold War: 1945–1949.

With the emergence of the Cold War, relations between the Western nations and the Soviet Union spiraled in a downward fashion for years to come. The first major test of this tension was manifest in the Berlin Airlift of 1948–1949 where supplies for beleaguered Germans were dropped daily over objections from Soviet officials who had set up blockades to thwart delivery of much needed supplies. The Soviets also closed roads and forbade movement from one sector of the city of Berlin to the other. The Western edge of Berlin largely remained in American/British hands, while the smaller northeastern portion of Germany remained Soviet. The Soviets were figuratively choking the people of Berlin. United States' C-47s began a mass supply line to overcome this obstacle. The planes flew in three major corridors toward the city (Figure 1.9).

When the Soviet Union entered into a treaty with China, the geopolitical framework of the world stood on its historic head. As Soviet expansionism marched onward, the United States felt obliged to "save" free peoples or, when the nations were not all that free, to keep the flow of communism to a bare minimum.

Throughout the 1950s the problems associated with the Cold War simply worsened. Nuclear proliferation, uprisings in Soviet-dominated countries, human rights violations without precedent, and a host of other evils heaped upon unwilling populations—all signify the tragedy and worst elements of communism in practice. The major events of the Cold War during the 1950s are outlined in Figure 1.10.

FIGURE 1.9 Berlin Airlift at Templehof Airport. (Courtesy of the Truman Library.)

1950: Sino–Soviet Treaty
1950: NSC-68
1950–1953: Korean War
1952: U.S. Hydrogen Bomb
1953: Stalin's Death
1953: Soviet Hydrogen Bomb
1954: Atomic Energy Act
1955: Creation of the Warsaw Pact
1955: Austrian State Treaty
1955: Big Four Geneva Summit
1956: Twentieth Congress of Soviet Communist Party
1956: Polish Uprising
1956: Suez Crisis
1956: Hungarian Uprising
1957–1958: Sputnik and the Space Race
1958: Suspension of Nuclear Tests
1958: Khrushchev's Berlin Demands
1959: Khrushchev Visits the United States
1959: Khrushchev–Eisenhower Meeting at Camp David
1959: Antarctic Treaty

FIGURE 1.10 Timeline of the Cold War: 1950–1959.

Of course, the Truman Doctrine was cited in the Korean War, the Cuban Missile Crisis, and the Vietnam War. When President Kennedy confronted the Soviet government for its dispatch of long-range missiles to Cuba (Figure 1.11), the justification was the containment theory, the right of the Western hemisphere to be safe from this corrupt hegemony, and the insistence of Harry Truman that free peoples need not tolerate this political oppression.

Each of these unofficial wars were, at least in a legislative sense, efforts to contain the "threat" of communist takeover. Throughout the 1960s, 1970s, and into the early 1980s, the two opposing giants in the Soviet and American systems remained entrenched. Nuclear proliferation continued unabated. A lack of trust and cooperation remained standard operating procedures. Spy agencies, such as the CIA and the KGB, spent most of their energy engaged in the activities and efforts of the Cold War.

When President Richard Nixon visited China in 1972 (Figure 1.12), a tectonic shift occurred in the Cold War. Nixon had brilliantly undercut the Sino–Soviet cooperation that appeared impenetrable for so many generations. Nixon made possible a new vision of cooperation on missile deployment, cultural exchange, and foreign relations.

FIGURE 1.11 U-2 reconnaissance photo showing concrete evidence of missile assembly in Cuba. Shown here are missile transporters and missile-ready tents where fueling and maintenance took place. (Courtesy of the CIA.)

From this point forward, the Soviet system would be isolated and internally suffering from decades of misplaced investment in the military model over any other benefit for its people. The Soviet system was crumbling from within. By the time of President Ronald Reagan, the time was ripe for an end to the intolerable Cold War (Figure 1.13).

Reagan was an unabashed believer in the American way of life. He showed diplomacy in the background of negotiations and protocol, but publically there was no greater critic of the Soviet system. On March 8, 1983, he labeled the Soviet state an "evil empire"—critics charged him with sensationalism. Those who supported Reagan felt he was defending the notion of freedom, believing that any government that dominated and oppressed its people was unjust in the eyes of history and its people. He was a strong proponent for the elimination of communism and, in particular, the Soviet-style system.

Prescient in his position on Soviet-style communism and his belief that it would ultimately fall, he remarked:

> In the 1950s, Khrushchev predicted: "We will bury you." But in the West today, we see a free world that has achieved a level of prosperity and well-being

FIGURE 1.12 President and Mrs. Nixon visit the Great Wall of China and the Ming tombs, February 24, 1972. (Courtesy of the National Archives.)

FIGURE 1.13 Ronald Reagan at the Brandenburg Gate, Germany, June 12, 1987. (Courtesy of the Ronald Reagan Library.)

> unprecedented in all human history. In the Communist world, we see failure, technological backwardness, declining standards of health, even want of the most basic kind—too little food. Even today, the Soviet Union still cannot feed itself. After these four decades, then, there stands before the entire world one great and inescapable conclusion: Freedom leads to prosperity. Freedom replaces the ancient hatreds among the nations with comity and peace. Freedom is the victor.
>
> And now the Soviets themselves may, in a limited way, be coming to understand the importance of freedom. We hear much from Moscow about a new policy of reform and openness. Some political prisoners have been released. Certain foreign news broadcasts are no longer being jammed. Some economic enterprises have been permitted to operate with greater freedom from state control.[2]

Reagan was often labeled a dreamer, an idealist lacking common sense, and worst of all, an "actor." However, while no administration is perfect, he was consistent in his approach. Ultimately, it was his interpersonal skill and relationship with Mikhail Gorbachev that set the stage for much that followed, among other things, the fall of the Berlin Wall and, subsequently, an end to the Cold War. The threats that had generated so much fear were replaced with cautious friendship. There is something to be learned from this episode in history. Just as the Russians were deemed the ultimate threat to the United States then, so too is the terrorist extremist currently considered the most immediate threat.

To be sure, both have been at the forefront of our national security over the years. What we do know is that enemies are not permanent stations. They are subject to change. Experts at the time would never have imagined the United States and Russia having closer ties and working together. Yet the two countries have taken many diplomatic strides though it is too early to tell with the current political leaders in Russia with the reemergence of Vladimir Putin. Putin is often referred to as Russia's strongman and he works arduously to develop this caricature amongst his countrymen.[3] Putin has been vocal and transparent in many of his efforts to consolidate power although it is not the nation once ruled by the KGB but a populace that has tasted some element of a free society. The mass demonstrations of December 2011 say much about a Russian political system evolving (Figure 1.14).

While only time will tell in the matter of Russian political processes, it is a safe bet that once the citizenry experiences a bit of freedom, there is no going back. The prospects for Russian–U.S. relations are a safer bet than once imagined. Perhaps we can hope to mend relations with certain parts of the Middle East, where there is tension or anti-U.S. sentiment, in the same fashion.

FIGURE 1.14 Demonstrators hold Russian opposition flags during a rally against election fraud in Moscow, Saturday, December 24, 2011. (Massive Russian Protest Poses Growing Challenge to Putin. James Brooke, Voice of America website: http://www.voanews.com/english/news/europe/—New-Anti-Election-Fraud-Protests-Begin-in-Moscow—136180068.html.)

1.4 Threats to the Homeland: Revolution, Riot, and Rightful Demonstration

There is little doubt that the concept of terror resounded across the American landscape from the nineteenth century onward.[4] From the Black Panthers to the Ku Klux Klan (KKK), from the Workers Party to communist agitators, from Students for a Democratic Society (SDS) to the Weathermen of the Vietnam Era, the concept of terror against governing authority was entrenched into the political and social fabric of these organizations (Figure 1.15).

The internal, urban violence of the 1960s, triggered and prompted by generations of inequality and injustice, caused law enforcement not only to challenge their historic reactions to public protest, but also to see that "enemies" or protagonists of the government may actually be operating from a higher moral plane. The protest could also not be universally condemned because some were plainly justified. Certainly, the entire movement sparked by Dr. Martin Luther King Jr. challenged the status quo of police power and the re-mediation of injustice. Then too, those operating without moral

FIGURE 1.15 Public protest against the Vietnam War. (U.S. Marshal's Service, "History," U.S. Marshals and the Pentagon Riot of October 21, 1967, http://www.usmarshals.gov/history/civilian/1967a.htm.)

advantage—groups such as the KKK or the SDS—posed real and meaningful threats against the internal security of the country by their egregious actions. In a sense, both lawful and unlawful protests shaped how the justice model reacted to protest and terror.

For example, during the Nixon era, ordinary citizens were perceived as troublemakers and seditionists for any protest to the policies of the president. Much has been written about the insular and almost paranoid perceptions of Nixon insiders as that government sought to squelch public protest concerning the war in Vietnam.[5]

Enemies of the state came in many shapes and sizes, some deserved and others not. In the midst of this era, the FBI posted its list of groups that were allegedly anti-American in design.[6] During this exceptionally turbulent time, politicians, government officials and law enforcement professionals perceived events as a threat to our democratic process.

Internet Exercise: Read about the Weatherman, a subversive antiwar, antigovernment, and anticapitalist entity active all through the late 1960s–1980s at http://www.pbs.org/independentlens/weatherunderground/movement.html.

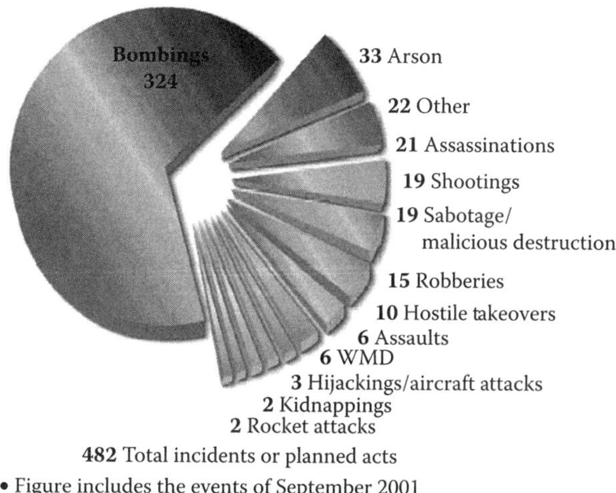

FIGURE 1.16 Amount of terroristic activities by type of event, 1980–2001.

Throughout the centuries, even until the present day, we can see that terror is a tool for those wishing to maintain the status quo as well as those wishing revolution. Hence, it is imperative to remember that American justice policy has had an historic understanding and relationship with terror throughout most of its history. These acts of terror can be broken down into two essential categories: international and domestic.

Since the early 1960s, the threat of terror has sought to disrupt world economies, overthrow political structures, annihilate religious competitors, and assault value systems considered antagonistic to a perverted worldview. For most of the past 60 years, terror has been on the radar screen. Figure 1.16[7] lays out the full scope of terror activities, from bombings to the use of weapons of mass destruction.

1.4.1 Domestic Terrorism: Pre-9/11

Domestic terrorism is considered that which is perpetrated by U.S. nationals and not the product of fringe Islamic extremists or jihadists. Terrorists can equally come from disenfranchised citizens, hate groups, or other extreme wings within the country. There have been some consistent players in terror activities across the American landscape, and surely the KKK fits the bill of consistency. Political upheaval and radical social change by any means whatsoever appropriately describe the KKK. For the KKK, terror was central to the mission of the rabid segregationist and promoter of inequality. Historic harassment and lynchings have been replaced by slick media and membership campaigns. Their official website, the "Official Knights Party of the KKK"[8] chastises those who see cross burnings as acts of terror and refers to the burnings as a theological exhortation. Regardless of the terrorist's mindset or rationale, history makes clear the motivation behind the tactics.

> The cross lighting ceremony is another example of how the national media distorts the Klan image. They purposely use the word "burn" because of the negative image that is conjured up in the minds of many people. To them it is a desecration, a desire to destroy the cross. And any attempt by hoodlums to use the lighted cross as a symbol of hate or a threat is strictly NOT advocated by The Knights. These acts are cowardly and counterproductive and are usually the actions of folks who watch too much late night television or Hollywood movies. Serious patriotic men and women never lower themselves to use the sacred cross in such a manner!
>
> And we should also point out that often "cross burnings" or other types of threatening actions including graffiti are often the acts of disturbed blacks, Asians, non-white Hispanics, homosexuals, or Jews who use the publicity for fund raising, to bolster sought after legislation, or even insurance scams!
>
> The Knights definitely does not burn the cross, but we do light the cross. The lighted cross of The Knights is no different than the average church that has a lighted cross either on top or in front of their church building. The light of the cross symbolizes the Light of Christ dispelling darkness and ignorance. It is the fire of the cross that reminds us of the cleansing "fire" of Christ that cleanses evil from our land. The fiery cross is a symbol that has long been popular with the Christian faith, for example the Methodist denomination uses the fiery cross as their symbol.
>
> In fact, it is because the founder of the Klan of the 1920's was a Methodist minister that the Klan adopted the practice. The lighted cross was not used until that time and was most certainly NOT used during the reconstruction period following the civil war!
>
> We don't burn the cross, we Light the cross. We recognize that Christ is the light of the world.
>
> The lighted cross is a symbol of freedom—freedom from sin—freedom from tyranny. When a Klansman or Klanswoman participates in a cross lighting ceremony they are making a public declaration to Jesus Christ of their continued commitment to the Christian faith.
>
> From The Official website of The Knights Party, USA, "The Christian Cross lighting Ceremony," http://www.kkk.bz/cross.htm

Domestic terror before the events of 9/11 occurred in a somewhat narrower or localized model in that the motive for attack was often not on a global scale. Just as the Klansman cares little beyond his or her myopic racism, the student radical, wishing the overthrow of the military complex, cannot see things in global terms. The student radical concludes that a group or a few assembled might wish to publicize their claims in every imaginable way—violence among its approaches. This was the stuff of the

FIGURE 1.17 Weather Underground leaders John Jacobs (center) and Terry Robbins (right) at the Days of Rage protest march, Chicago, October 1969.

Weathermen—they found banks a legitimate and moral target for destruction in order that a war may end (Figure 1.17).

These operatives see the world in more myopic terms since it is the foundation of their movement that unites them and drives their relationship. In no sense does one justify the actions of the Black Panther or the Weathermen. This merely demonstrates a differing worldview exists when compared to the jihadist who ultimately desires the radical reconstruction of the entire planet while imposing a particular religious ideology and zealotry.

1975 TERRORISM FLASHBACK: STATE DEPARTMENT BOMBING

01/29/04

Twenty-nine years ago Thursday, an explosion rocked the headquarters of the U.S. State Department in Washington, DC. No one was hurt, but the damage was extensive, impacting 20 offices on three separate floors. Hours later, another bomb was found at a military induction center in Oakland, California, and safely detonated. A domestic terrorist group called the Weather Underground claimed responsibility. Remember them?

Who were these extremists? The Weather Underground—originally called the Weathermen, taken from a line in a Bob Dylan song—was a small, violent offshoot of the Students for a Democratic Society (SDS), created in the turbulent 1960s to promote social change.

When the SDS collapsed in 1969, the Weather Underground stepped forward, inspired by communist ideologies and embracing violence and crime as a way to protest the Vietnam War, racism, and other left-wing aims. "Our intention is to disrupt the empire ... to incapacitate it, to put pressure on the cracks," claimed the group's 1974 manifesto, Prairie Fire. By the next year, the group had claimed credit for 25 bombings and would be involved in many more over the next several years.

The Chase. The FBI doggedly pursued these terrorists as their attacks mounted. Many members were soon identified, but their small numbers and guerilla tactics helped them hide under assumed identities. In 1978, however, the Bureau arrested five members who were plotting to bomb a politician's office. More were arrested when an accident destroyed the group's bomb factory in Hoboken, New Jersey. Others were identified after two policemen and a Brinks' driver were murdered in a botched armored car robbery in Nanuet, New York.

Success for the FBI/NYPD Task Force. Key to disrupting the group for good was the newly created FBI-New York City Police Anti-Terrorist Task Force. It brought together the strengths of both organizations and focused them on these domestic terrorists. The task force and others like it paved the way for today's Joint Terrorism Task Forces—created by the Bureau in each of its field offices to fuse federal, state, and local law enforcement and intelligence resources to combat today's terrorist threats.

By the mid-1980s, the Weather Underground was essentially history. Still, several of these fugitives were able to successfully hide themselves for decades, emerging only in recent years to answer for their crimes. Once again, it shows that grit and partnerships can and will defeat shadowy, resilient terrorist groups.

One of the more notable domestic terror attacks against the United States was the 1993 attack on New York City's World Trade Center (Figure 1.18).

The boldness of the World Trade Center bombing shocked the intelligence community. The sophistication of the plan, the potential for extreme damage and destruction, and the symbolism of the target itself attested to the determination of the terrorist movement long before 9/11.[9]

Presently, terror finds root in the ideology of religious fanaticism and the jihad. Previously, terror was grounded in the ideology of politics and social movements. When the Communist Workers Party clamored for change, its advocacy dealt with the evils of excessive capitalism and the real need for collectivism in the distribution of goods and services. When the Black Panther Party set off violent action, it did so with a political revolution in mind and the whole-scale redress and payback for injustice based on race. Neither of these arguments can justify the violence that these groups offer up, but both groups attest to the dramatically different mindset when compared to the extreme and very radical Islamic fundamentalists who flew planes into the Twin Towers.

FIGURE 1.18 Investigators going through the rubble following the 1993 bombing of the World Trade Center.

Terrorism on the domestic front can be driven by diverse motivations. Race hatred, white supremacy, protests against governmental policy, and an inordinate desire to subvert and undermine the nature of the democratic state are just a few of the rationales employed. Timothy McVeigh's bombing of the federal building in Oklahoma City manifests the disproportionate dislike and distrust of government in any sense and the extreme alienation and isolation that certain terrorists seem to experience in light of the democratic process. That government may or may not be too intrusive cannot provide a sufficient justification for murder, but the level of distrust and flat-out antagonism toward government is a growing phenomenon in select quarters.

Ted Kaczynski (aka the Unabomber) also reflects this loner, antigovernment tradition of the terrorist. In his "manifesto," Kaczynski railed against most aspects of modern life, industrialization, the loss of freedom, and the invasiveness of government. Kaczynski's arrest, one of the FBI's most successful apprehensions, was celebrated and recollected in 2008.[11]

The array of terror groups include those advocating radical change involving racist ideologies, economic overthrow of existing governmental structures, and ideologies relating to the environment and animal rights. These groups are capable of inflicting extraordinary damage to the country,

FBI 100: THE UNABOMBER

04/24/08

Part 4 of our history series commemorating the FBI's 100th anniversary in 2008

How do you catch a twisted genius who aspires to be the perfect, anonymous killer—who builds untraceable bombs and delivers them to random targets, who leaves false clues to throw off authorities, who lives like a recluse in the mountains of Montana and tells no one of his secret crimes?

That was the challenge facing the FBI and its investigative partners, who spent nearly two decades hunting down this ultimate lone wolf bomber.

The man that the world would eventually know as Theodore Kaczynski came to our attention in 1978 with the explosion of his first, primitive homemade bomb at a Chicago university. Over the next 17 years, he mailed or hand delivered a series of increasingly sophisticated bombs that killed three Americans and injured 24 more. Along the way, he sowed fear and panic, even threatening to blow up airliners in flight.

In 1979, an FBI-led task force that included the ATF and U.S. Postal Inspection Service was formed to investigate the "UNABOM" case, code-named for the University and Airline Bombing targets involved. The task force would grow to more than 150 full-time investigators, analysts, and others. In search of clues, the team made every possible forensic examination of recovered bomb components and studied the lives of victims in minute detail. These efforts proved of little use in identifying the bomber, who took pains to leave no forensic evidence, building his bombs essentially from "scrap" materials available almost anywhere. And the victims, investigators later learned, were chosen randomly from library research.

We felt confident that the Unabomber had been raised in Chicago and later lived in the Salt Lake City and San Francisco areas. This turned out to be true. His occupation proved more elusive, with theories ranging from aircraft mechanic to scientist. Even the gender was not certain: although investigators believed the bomber was most likely male, they also investigated several female suspects.

The big break in the case came in 1995. The Unabomber sent us a 35,000 word essay claiming to explain his motives and views of the ills of modern society. After much debate about the wisdom of "giving in to terrorists," FBI Director Louis Freeh and Attorney General Janet Reno approved the task force's recommendation to publish the essay in hopes that a reader could identify the author.

After the manifesto appeared in the *Washington Post* and the *New York Times*, thousands of people suggested possible suspects. One stood out: David Kaczynski described his troubled brother Ted, who had grown up in Chicago, taught at the University of California at Berkeley (where two of the bombs had been placed), then lived for a time in Salt Lake City before

FIGURE 1.19 Ted Kaczynski's cabin in the mountains of Montana.

settling permanently into the primitive 10′ × 14′ cabin that the brothers had constructed near Lincoln, Montana (Figure 1.19).

Most importantly, David provided letters and documents written by his brother. Our linguistic analysis determined that the author of those papers and the manifesto were almost certainly the same. When combined with facts gleaned from the bombings and Kaczynski's life, that analysis provided the basis for a search warrant.

On April 3, 1996—a dozen years ago this month—investigators arrested Kaczynski and combed his cabin (Figure 1.20). There, they found a wealth of bomb components; 40,000 handwritten journal pages that included bomb-making experiments and descriptions of Unabomber crimes; and one live bomb, ready for mailing.

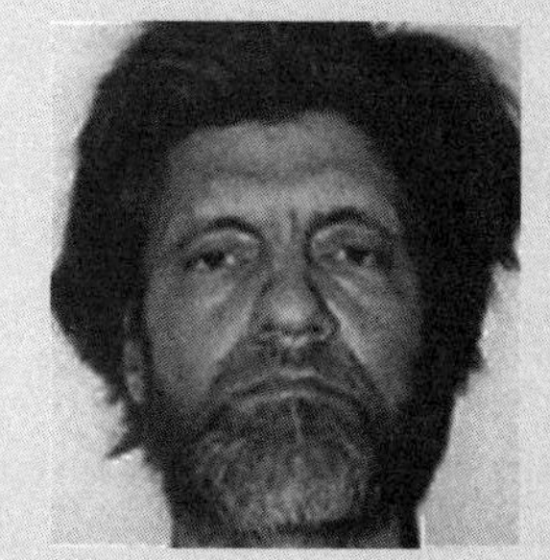

FIGURE 1.20 Ted Kaczynski, aka "The Unabomber."

Kaczynski's reign of terror was over. His new home, following his guilty plea in January 1998: an isolated cell in a "Supermax" prison in Colorado.[10]

and must remain on the radar screen of those entrusted with the security of the United States and its citizens.

1.4.2 International Terrorism: Pre-9/11

Just as in the United States, the international community had experienced a series of attacks from various constituencies. One of the more notable overseas terror attacks against the United States was at the Marine base in Beirut, Lebanon, in 1983, where 241 servicemen lost their lives (Figure 1.21).

FIGURE 1.21 The aftermath of the attack on the Marine base in Lebanon. (Source: U.S. Army.)

The attack in Lebanon, in a secure military environment, made plain the tenacity of the terrorist and the willingness of this enemy to tackle any target no matter how formidable. This attack sent a vivid reminder to the government and military alike that terrorism was a growing and very dangerous reality.

During the 1980s, organized terrorist groups that we have come to know only too well—Al Qaeda, Hamas, and Hezbollah—gained foundational and organizational support from wide quarters in both a political and an economic sense. By the 1990s, Osama bin Laden had amassed a network of terrorists eager to carry out attacks.

In Yemen and Somalia, Bin Laden funded, planned, and orchestrated acts that killed and injured a number of U.S. soldiers. Eighteen Special Forces members were attacked and killed in Somalia in 1993. In 1996, Bin Laden set out to attack the Khobar Towers in Saudi Arabia, where 19 American airmen died. In August 1998, Bin Laden and Al Qaeda bombed the embassies of Kenya and Tanzania, which resulted in death and injury of thousands of innocents. Al Qaeda and Bin Laden were getting even bolder as time progressed, carrying out a direct attack on a U.S. warship—the USS *Cole*—in Yemen in 2000 (Figure 1.22). Using a small boat as a suicide projectile, Al Qaeda operatives displayed unparalleled methods in carrying out their attack.

None of these events occurred in a vacuum, but rather as a progressive series of events that eventually culminated in the single largest attack by a foreign enemy on American soil. Each attack displayed an evolving

FIGURE 1.22 The USS *Cole* suffered the loss of 17 crewmen and represented the first attack against a naval vessel of the United States in nearly 25 years.

aggressiveness toward America, each attack employed a variety of tactics to keep the defenders off guard, and each attack manifested an increasing fanaticism in the Islamic extremist world. Succinctly, 9/11 did not occur out of the blue. Terror has a progressive history.

1.5 Conclusion

The concepts of terror and the terrorist have a long and perpetual history on both the domestic and international fronts. Terrorists have always been with us in one way or the other. In this short survey, the reader learns the events and conditions that led up to our present definition of terror. The chapter commences with a look at how war, military tactics and strategy, and aligned governmental policy frequently employ terror tactics. Then, the reader is exposed to how the Cold War mentality shaped our perceptions about terror and subterfuge and weighed and evaluated how government policy can be influenced by events and conditions that can alter once repressive regimes into more open societies. The chapter then shifts to terrorism as it existed previous to 9/11. The American experience has long had vestiges of terror in its social fabric. Special attention is given to the KKK, the Weathermen, the Black Panthers, and the SDS, as well as newly developing and ever-evolving groups espousing hatred. Terrorism, pre-9/11, was rooted in differing motivations ranging from racism to a desire for change and revolution.

By the 1990s, the face of terrorism adopted a virulent form of antigovernment sentiment in the likes of Ted Kaczynski and Timothy McVeigh. Each had more than an axe to grind and sought to destroy what he perceived as a corrupt culture and government. In addition, pre-9/11 there was the rise of Islamic jihadists who carried out a number of international attacks, most coordinated by Osama bin Laden and others who followed him.

Hijackings, terror in the skies, embassy bombings, kidnapping of American personnel, and attacks on naval targets became commonplace events of terror. All of this culminates in the catastrophe of 9/11—events and circumstances that still are overwhelmingly shocking and tragic. More particularly, the chapter looks at the attacks on the USS *Cole* and the Marine post in Lebanon.

As a direct result of 9/11, the missions of multiple U.S. agencies would undergo exceptional reorientation. In addition, these same agencies would become part of the newly constructed agency—the Department of Homeland Security.

Keywords

Al Qaeda
Allies
Berlin Wall
Black Panthers
Cold War
Communism
Cuban missile crisis
Domestic terrorism
Final Solution
Hamas
Harry S. Truman
Hezbollah
Homeland security
Human rights
Imperialism
Iron Curtain
Islamic fundamentalism
Jihad
Joseph Stalin
Korean War
Ku Klux Klan
Mikhail Gorbachev
Nikita Khrushchev
Nuclear proliferation
Osama bin Laden
Potsdam Convention
Religious fanaticism
Richard Nixon
Ronald Reagan
Saddam Hussein
Sino-Soviet
Socialism
Socialist Workers Party
Students for a Democratic Society
Ted Kaczynski
Terror

Terrorist
Third Reich
Timothy McVeigh
Truman Doctrine
Vietnam War
Weathermen
Winston Churchill

Discussion Questions

1. When one evaluates the past 50 years of terrorist activities, what threats or trends can be discovered? Is there a commonality of purpose or type?
2. Why do terrorists so often choose embassies as targets?
3. In what way are Timothy McVeigh and Osama bin Laden the same?
4. Compare and contrast domestic and international terrorism. Point out the differences.
5. What are the motivations of terrorists groups in the pre-9/11 world compared to the post-9/11 world?
6. How can war be an instrument of terror?
7. Is it fair to argue that the United States engaged in terror during any of its war campaigns?
8. What does the Cold War teach us about the transient nature of the terror threat?
9. Was the Cold War threat different than the USS *Cole* threat?
10. Is the aim of the Unabomber similar to Osama bin Laden?

Practical Exercises

1. Find out whether or not a revolutionary group such as the Aryan Brotherhood or the KKK still operates in your area.
2. Are you aware of any paramilitary organizations that train in your region?
3. What type of terror prevention programs does your area have in rooting out domestic terrorists?
4. Contact your local police chief. Ask whether or not he or she sees any real threats from local groups that might engage in terrorist activity.
5. Visit the Truman or Reagan Library online for a virtual tour.

Notes

1. W. S. Churchill, The Sinews of Peace, North American Treaty Organization, http://www.nato.int/docu/speech/1946/S460305a_e.htm (accessed March 3, 2009).
2. President R. L. Reagan, *Tear Down That Wall*, http://www.reaganlibrary.com/reagan/speeches/speech.asp?spid=25 (accessed March 4, 2009).
3. E. D. Johnson, Putin and Putinism, *The Slavonic and East European Review*, 89(3) (2011): 788–790.
4. For an interesting analysis of the Ku Klux Klan as it rationalized its hatred with the fervor of false patriotism, see P. D. Brister, Patriotic enemies of the state: A cross comparison of the Christian Patriot Movement and the 1920's Ku Klux Klan, *The Homeland Security Review*, 4 (2010): 173.
5. R. Perlstein, *Nixonland: America's Second Civil War and the Divisive Legacy of Richard Nixon, 1965–1972* (New York: Simon & Schuster, 2008).
6. G. R. Stone, review of *Spying on Americans: Political Surveillance from Hoover to the Huston Plan*, by Athan Theoharis, *Reviews in American History*, 8(1) (March 1980): 134–138. For a full analysis of how the Weathermen worked, see Federal Bureau of Investigation, "Weathermen Underground Summary Dated 8/20/76," http://foia.fbi.gov/weather/weath1a.pdf.
7. Federal Bureau of Investigation, *Terrorism 2000–2001*, Publication 0308 (Washington, DC: U.S. Government Printing Office, 2004), 16.
8. Official website of the Knights Party, United States, http://www.kkk.bz.
9. U.S. Fire Administration, *The World Trade Center Bombing: Report and Analysis*, ed. W. Manning (Washington, DC: U.S. Government Printing Office, 1993), 15. For a comparison of the 1993 emergency reaction with that of 2001, see R. F. Fahy, G. Proulx, A comparison of the 1993 and 2001 evacuation of the World Trade Center, *Proceedings of the 2002 Fire Risk & Hazard Assessment Research Application Symposium* (Fire Protection Research Foundation, Quincy, MA), 111–117. For a close look at how World Center bombings caused extraordinary upheaval from a social, behavioral and health perspective, see R. E. Adamsa, J. A. Boscarinoa, S. Galeac, Social and psychological resources and health outcomes after the World Trade Center disaster, *Social Science & Medicine*, 62 (2006): 176–188, http://www.sciencedirect.com/science/article/pii/S027795360500239X.
10. Federal Bureau of Investigation, Headline Archives, *The Unabomber*, http://www.fbi.gov/page2/april08/unabomber_042408.html.
11. Federal Bureau of Investigation, Headline Archives, *The Unabomber*, http://www.fbi.gov/page2/april08/unabomber_042408.html.

Chapter 2

Terror, Threat, and Disaster Post-9/11

A New Paradigm of Homeland Security

Objectives

1. To analyze the events of 9/11 and understand the effect they had on the American population's psyche in relation to domestic security.
2. To appraise the effectiveness of the immediate response by government agencies to the events of September 11, 2001.
3. To describe the shortcomings of the lack of information exchange between various government agencies prior to 9/11 and analyze the influence the lack of communication had on the day's events.
4. To outline the new strategies and tactics that the safety community developed for mitigation and prevention of terrorism immediately following 9/11.
5. To describe the initial formation of the Department of Homeland Security (DHS), its structure, and policy approach, mission, and goals.
6. To explain the structural changes that have taken place in DHS since its inception.
7. To summarize the DHS's hierarchy, major players, and various advisory committees.
8. To list the various directorates and offices of DHS and discuss their mission and responsibilities.

2.1 Introduction

To say the world changed on September 11, 2001, is an extraordinary understatement. As the air assault on the Twin Towers and the Pentagon unfolded, both government agencies and the general populace watched in stunned silence. Even today, it is difficult to fathom the full and sweeping implications of such an attack. Dual plane attacks on the Twin Towers of the World Trade Center are almost impossible to fathom. Yet this is exactly what occurred. Radical Islamic extremists perpetrated the most deadly attack carried out on U.S. soil (Figure 2.1).[1]

The damage in New York's financial district was catastrophic. Not only was the loss of life at staggering proportions, but the economic impact on the New York metropolitan area and the country was significant (Figures 2.2 through 2.4).

Notions of security would be forever challenged and altered. Ideas of safety within America's borders would now be doubted.

FIGURE 2.1 Terrorists aboard Flight #77 that crashed into the Pentagon on September 11, 2001. (American Airlines #77 Boeing 8.10 a.m. Departed Dulles for Los Angeles 9.39 a.m. Crashed into Pentagon.)

FIGURE 2.2 Twin Towers rubble after the collapse. (www.whitehouse.gov.)

2.2 The Genesis of DHS

Confidence in our ability to withstand or detect attacks was severely undermined by the events of 9/11. The attacks against American soil were sweeping in scope and left the public safety and law enforcement communities stunned. How could planes be hijacked and crashed into the financial district of one of the largest American cities? How could the walls of the Pentagon be breached? How could a plane crash in rural Pennsylvania represent a thwarted bid to attack the White House (Figure 2.5)?

The complexity of the undertaking manifests a well-prepared and very determined enemy. The timeline of the attacks says much about the complexity of these events (see Figure 2.6).[2]

It is impossible to measure the complete impact these events had upon the American psyche, the former invincibility of our home soil, and the pronounced reexamination of our entire approach to law enforcement and the overall security of a nation[3] (Figure 2.7).

As one illustration, the FBI, while historically concerned about the potential random acts of terrorists, had to shift into a more intense scrutiny of the terrorist impact on our way of life. The National Commission on 9/11 was attuned to this strategic shift when it wrote:

> Collection of useful intelligence from human sources was limited. By the mid-1990s senior FBI managers became concerned that the bureau's statistically driven performance system had resulted in a roster of mediocre sources. The FBI did not have a formal mechanism for validating source reporting,

FIGURE 2.3 National Guard members at Twin Towers disaster site. (www.fema.gov.)

nor did it have a system for adequately tracking and sharing such reporting, either internally or externally. The "wall" between criminal and intelligence investigations apparently caused agents to be less aggressive than they might otherwise have been in pursuing Foreign Intelligence Surveillance Act (FISA) surveillance powers in counterterrorism investigations. Moreover, the FISA approval process involved multiple levels of review, which also discouraged agents from using such surveillance. Many agents also told us that the process for getting FISA packages approved at FBI headquarters and the Department of Justice was incredibly lengthy and inefficient. Several FBI agents added that, prior to 9/11, FISA-derived intelligence information was not fully exploited but was collected primarily to justify continuing the surveillance. The FBI did not dedicate sufficient resources to the surveillance or translation needs of counterterrorism agents. The FBI's surveillance personnel were more focused on counterintelligence and drug cases. In fact, many

FIGURE 2.4 The Pentagon after the fires were extinguished. (www.fema.gov.)

FIGURE 2.5 United Flight 93 in Shanksville, Pennsylvania. (www.fema.gov.)

field offices did not have surveillance squads prior to 9/11. Similarly, the FBI did not have a sufficient number of translators proficient in Arabic and other languages useful in counterterrorism investigations, resulting in a significant backlog of untranslated FISA intercepts by early 2001. FBI agents received very little formalized training in the counterterrorism discipline. Only 3 days of the 16-week new agent's course were devoted to national security matters, including counterterrorism and counterintelligence, and most subsequent counterterrorism training was received on an *ad hoc* basis or "on the job." Additionally, the career path for agents necessitated rotations between headquarters and the field in a variety of work areas, making it difficult for agents

8:00 a.m.—American Airlines Flight 11, Boeing 767 with 92 people on board, takes off from Boston's Logan International Airport for Los Angeles.
8:14 a.m.—United Air Lines Flight 175, Boeing 767 with 65 people on board, takes off from Boston's Logan airport for Los Angeles.
8:21 a.m.—American Airlines Flight 77, Boeing 757 with 64 people on board, takes off from Washington Dulles International Airport for Los Angeles.
8:40 a.m.—Federal Aviation Administration notifies North American Aerospace Defense Command's Northeast Air Defense Sector about suspected hijacking of American Flight 11.
8:41 a.m.—United Air Lines Flight 93, Boeing 757 with 44 people on board, takes off from Newark International Airport for San Francisco.
8:43 a.m.—FAA notifies NORAD's Northeast Air Defense Sector about suspected hijacking of United Flight 175.
8:46 a.m.—American Flight 11 crashes into north tower of World Trade Center.
9:03 a.m.—United Flight 175 crashes into south tower of World Trade Center.
9:08 a.m.—FAA bans all takeoffs nationwide for flights going to or through New York airspace.
9:17 a.m.—FAA closes down all New York City-area airports.
9:21 a.m.—All bridges and tunnels into Manhattan closed.
9:24 a.m.—FAA notifies NORAD's Northeast Air Defense Sector about suspected hijacking of American Flight 77.
9:26 a.m.—FAA bans takeoffs of all civilian aircraft.
9:31 a.m.—In Sarasota, FL, President Bush calls crashes an "apparent terrorist attack on our country."
9:40 a.m. (approx.)—American Flight 77 crashes into Pentagon.
9:45 a.m.—FAA orders all aircraft to land at nearest airport as soon as practical. More than 4500 aircraft in air at the time. This is the first time in U.S. history that nationwide air traffic is suspended.
9:48 a.m.—U.S. Capitol and White House's West Wing evacuated.
9:57 a.m.—President Bush leaves Florida.
9:59 a.m.—South tower of World Trade Center collapses.
10:07 a.m. (approx.)—United Flight 93 crashes in a field in Shanksville, PA, southeast of Pittsburgh.
10:28 a.m.—North tower of World Trade Center collapses.
10:50 a.m.—New York's primary elections, scheduled for Sept. 11, are postponed.
10:56 a.m.—Palestinian leader Yasser Arafat speaks in Gaza: "First of all, I am offering my condolences, the condolences of the Palestinian people, to their American President, President Bush, to his government, to the American people, for this terrible time. We are completely shocked, completely shocked. Unbelievable."
11:00 a.m.—New York City Mayor Rudolph W. Giuliani orders the evacuation of lower Manhattan south of Canal Street.
11:04 a.m.—The United Nations is fully evacuated.
12:04 p.m.—Los Angeles International Airport, the destination of three of the hijacked airplanes, is closed and evacuated.
12:15 p.m.—San Francisco International Airport, the destination of United Airlines Flight 93, which crashed in Pennsylvania, is closed and evacuated.
12:30 p.m.—The FAA says 50 flights are in U.S. airspace, but none are reporting any problems.
1:04 p.m.—From Barksdale Air Force base in Louisiana, Bush announces U.S. military on high-alert worldwide: "Make no mistake: The United States will hunt down and punish those responsible for these cowardly acts."
1:37 p.m.—Bush leaves Barksdale for Offutt Air Force Base, near Omaha, NE.
2:51 p.m.—Navy dispatches missile destroyers to New York, Washington.
3:07 p.m.—Bush arrives at U.S. Strategic Command at Offutt Air Force Base in Nebraska.
4:36 p.m.—Bush leaves Offutt Air Force Base aboard Air Force One to return to Washington.
5:25 p.m.—The empty, 47-story 7 World Trade Center collapses.
7:00 p.m.—Bush arrives at the White House.
8:30 p.m.—Bush addresses nation and vows to "find those responsible and bring them to justice."

FIGURE 2.6 Chronology of the key events of September 11, 2001 (all times Eastern).

FIGURE 2.7 Workers in the rubble of the Twin Towers. (www.fema.gov.)

> to develop expertise in any particular area, especially counterterrorism and counterintelligence. We were told that very few FBI field managers had any counterterrorism experience, and thus either were not focused on the issue or did not have the expertise to run an effective program.[4]

Aside from a lack of coordination and interagency cooperation, the events of 9/11 make plain that an actual wall did exist between the varied agencies of government. The CIA did not share with the FBI, the state and local police did not communicate readily, and jurisdictional and turf issues often influenced policy making in the pre-9/11 world. "The absence of coordination and collaboration in the area of information and intelligence sharing contributed to the surprise of the attack."[5] After 9/11, it was blatantly obvious that walls had to be torn down and new infrastructures and agencies created upon a cooperative mentality. In general, law enforcement and emergency management authorities have to see the world in a post-9/11 prism fully recognizing that what once was effective is now ineffectual in cases of mass terror. "There are significant changes not only in the daily lives of the American people but also in the function of the country's emergency management system."[6] In matters of command, communication, deployment, planning, and dispatch, traditional agencies were challenged in ways never before envisioned. Nothing in the status quo could have operationally prepared these professionals for a post-9/11 world. And in a sense, that is exactly what the emergency, military, and law enforcement community has been doing since 9/11—searching out the best approach and adapting to the new reality. As law enforcement and fire personnel perished in the rubble of the Twin Towers and civilians in the airplanes plummeted to their deaths, the knowledge base of traditional safety was turned on its head.

Soon after 9/11, law enforcement and intelligence agencies developed and learned new strategies and tactics for prevention and mitigation. Soon after, the safety community began to reevaluate long established practices in light of this tragedy. From September 11, 2001, an extraordinary series of new approaches was implemented, many of which were implemented by a new DHS. Right from the start, state, local, and federal services rattled the cages of ordinary bureaucratic practices. Getting to the implementation of DHS did not happen overnight but evolved from a series of policy steps. From that tragic day until the following year, government moved at lightning speed as evidenced by the actions during the month of September in the chart in Figure 2.8.[7]

Not only was a new department erected, but so too a new policy and definitional approach. The term *Homeland Security* encompasses much of the emergency, military, and law enforcement sector once dedicated to a variety of relevant responsibilities to the defense of a nation. DHS makes every effort to unify the diverse functions of responsibilities of a homeland in need of protection. DHS is one department chosen over myriad others because DHS is:

- One department whose primary mission is to protect the American homeland
- One department to secure our borders, transportation sector, ports, and critical infrastructure
- One department to synthesize and analyze homeland security intelligence from multiple sources
- One department to coordinate communications with state and local governments, private industry, and the American people about threats and preparedness
- One department to coordinate our efforts to protect the American people against bioterrorism and other weapons of mass destruction
- One department to help train and equip for first responders
- One department to manage federal emergency response activities
- More security officers in the field working to stop terrorists and fewer resources in Washington managing duplicative and redundant activities that drain critical homeland security resources[8]

2.3 DHS: 2001–2003

Any conception of a government agency dedicated to the protection of the homeland takes time to develop and implement. The evolution of a governmental structure, responsible for maintaining homeland safety and security, is both complex and ever changing. Since 2001, the face and internal

September 11

- America attacked
- Department of Defense begins combat air patrols over U.S. cities
- Department of Transportation grounds all U.S. private aircraft
- FEMA activates Federal Response Plan
- U.S. Customs goes to Level 1 alert at all border ports of entry
- HHS activates (for the first time ever) the National Disaster Medical System, dispatching more than 300 medical and mortuary personnel to the New York and Washington, DC areas, dispatching one of eight 12-h emergency "push packages" of medical supplies, and putting 80 Disaster Medical Assistance Teams nationwide and 7000 private sector medical professionals on deployment alert
- Nuclear Regulatory Commission advises all nuclear power plants, nonpower reactors, nuclear fuel facilities, and gaseous diffusion plants go to the highest level of security. All complied
- President orders federal disaster funding for New York
- FEMA deploys National Urban Search and Rescue Response team
- FEMA deploys US Army Corp of Engineers to assist debris removal

September 12

- FEMA deploys emergency medical and mortuary teams to NY and Washington
- FAA allows limited reopening of the nation's commercial airspace system to allow flights that were diverted on September 11 to continue to their original destinations

September 13

- President orders federal aid for Virginia
- Departments of Justice and Treasury deploy Marshals, Border Patrol, and Customs officials to provide a larger police presence at airports as they reopen

September 14

- President proclaims a national emergency (Proc. 7463)
- President orders ready reserves of armed forces to active duty
- FBI releases list of nineteen suspected terrorists

September 17: Attorney General directs the establishment of 94 Anti-Terrorism Task Forces, one for each United States Attorney Office

September 18

- President signs authorization for Use of Military Force bill
- President authorizes additional disaster funding for New York

September 20: President addresses Congress, announces creation of the Office of Homeland Security and appointment of Governor Tom Ridge as director

September 21: HHS announces that more than $126 million (part of $5 billion the President released for disaster relief) is being provided immediately to support health services provided in the wake of the attacks

September 22: President signs airline transportation legislation, providing tools to assure the safety and immediate stability of our Nation's commercial airline system, and establish a process for compensating victims of the terrorist attacks

September 25: The first of approximately 7200 National Guard troops begin augmenting security at 444 airports

September 27: The FBI releases photographs of 19 individuals believed to be the 9/11 hijackers

FIGURE 2.8 Administration Homeland Security action during September 2001.

bureaucratic attributes of DHS have undergone birth and rebirth, change and reincarnation. The DHS of 2001 was a very different animal than the DHS of today. There have been growing pains in the development of the agency, its mission, and structure. Despite these challenges, DHS has maintained a unique and surprising adaptability in its changing programs, mission, and structure in its short existence.

MISSION

We will lead the unified national effort to secure America. We will prevent and deter terrorist attacks and protect against and respond to threats and hazards to the nation. We will secure our national borders while welcoming lawful immigrants, visitors, and trade (U.S. DHS One Team, One Mission, Securing Our Homeland—U.S. DHS Strategic Plan (2008)).

Strategic Goals

Awareness—Identify and understand threats, assess vulnerabilities, determine the potential impact, and disseminate timely information to our homeland security partners and the American public.

Prevention—Detect, deter, and mitigate threats to our homeland.

Protection—Safeguard our people and their freedoms, critical infrastructure, property, and the economy of our Nation from acts of terrorism, natural disasters, or other emergencies.

Response—Lead, manage, and coordinate the national response to acts of terrorism, natural disasters, or other emergencies.

Recovery—Lead national, state, local, and private sector efforts to restore services and rebuild communities after acts of terrorism, natural disasters, or other emergencies.

Service—Serve the public effectively by facilitating lawful trade, travel, and immigration.

Organizational Excellence—Value our most important resource, our people. Create a culture that promotes a common identity, innovation, mutual respect, accountability, and teamwork to achieve efficiencies, effectiveness, and operational synergies—U.S. DHS, Securing Our Homeland: U.S. DHS Strategic Plan (2004).

2.3.1 Evolution and Change in DHS

While safety and security issues are permanent national concerns, the examination of how to predict and prevent threats to the national homeland took on added importance after 9/11. On the front burner was how to take existing governmental agencies and deploy them in the fight against terrorism. On the side burner was the nagging question of whether or not the front burner was competent enough to generate the necessary heat and intensity to be successful in this new undertaking. In choosing to erect a new government agency in DHS, both President George W. Bush and Congress agreed that the "changing nature of the threats facing America requires a new government structure against the invisible enemies that can strike with a wide variety of weapons."[9] Creating a new agency could be argued as strictly political—giving the general public a sense of action and aggressive posturing against America's enemies, although this characterization would be unfair. The previous patchwork of aligned and even competing government agencies was obvious. Even the 9/11 Commission critiqued the lack of information sharing and turf games between competing agencies.

> The agencies cooperated, some of the time. But even such cooperation as there was is not the same thing as joint action. When agencies cooperate, one defines the problem and seeks help with it. When they act jointly, the problem and options for action are defined differently from the start. Individuals from different backgrounds come together in analyzing a case and planning how to manage it.
>
> In our hearings we regularly asked witnesses: Who is the quarterback? The other players are in their positions, doing their jobs. But who is calling the play that assigns roles to help them execute as a team?[10]

The drive toward a new agency was rooted in a host of compelling rationales. Unity of purpose and mission was surely at the forefront. The "one" agency mindset represented a significant change of ethos for the intelligence community. No longer would the CIA, FBI, NSA, and NORAD see themselves as individual players in the fight against terrorism, but instead part of the collective and simultaneously unified effort to detect and prevent harm to the homeland. DHS refers to these shifts in operational mentality as an "evolution of the paradigm"[11]—a movement away from the decentralized to a totally centralized approach in the management of threat. DHS would be the centerpiece of these efforts.

Not long after 9/11, Congress and the President, working swiftly and in concert, moved passage of the *Homeland Security Act of 2002*.[12] The act seeks to minimize the threat of another 9/11 and poses its mission in broad terms. Part of the act lays out the mission of DHS.

The primary mission of the department is to:

- Prevent terrorist attacks within the United States;
- Reduce the vulnerability of the United States to terrorism;
- Minimize the damage, and assist in the recovery, from terrorist attacks that do occur within the United States;
- Carry out all functions of entities transferred to the department, including by acting as a focal point regarding natural and man-made crises and emergency planning;

- Ensure that the functions of the agencies and subdivisions within the department that are not related directly to securing the homeland are not diminished or neglected except by a specific explicit act of Congress;
- Ensure that the overall economic security of the United States is not diminished by efforts, activities, and programs aimed at securing the homeland; and
- Monitor connections between illegal drug trafficking and terrorism, coordinate efforts to sever such connections, and otherwise contribute to efforts to interdict illegal drug trafficking.[13]

The act further compartmentalizes the agency into four main areas of responsibility, namely border and transportation; emergency preparedness and response; chemical, biological, radiological, and nuclear countermeasures; and information analysis and infrastructure protection. The organization chart of DHS in 2008,[14] shown in Figure 2.9, portrays those with crucial responsibility for DHS.

The significance of these categories cannot be overemphasized. In border and transportation, DHS assumed control over security services relating to our borders, territorial waters, and transportation systems. Immigration and Naturalization, Customs, Coast Guard, and animal protection issues are now DHS functions.

In emergency preparedness and response there was a complete merger of FEMA operations into DHS. FEMA, as will be discussed in Chapter 7, became an organization dedicated not only to natural disaster, but also to man-made events. Federal interagency emergency programs were subsumed into DHS as well as critical response units relating to nuclear and pharmaceutical events.

In matters involving prevention of chemical, radiological, and nuclear terror, DHS plays a central, coordinating role. Efforts here would be one of centralization and coordination of diverse department activities across the spectrum of government agencies. Guidelines regarding weapons of mass destruction were rapidly promulgated.

In the area of intelligence and threat analysis, DHS acts as a central repository for information pertaining to threats to the homeland. Data from traditional intelligence organizations such as the CIA, FBI, NSA, INS, and DEA are catalogued and disseminated as needed. DHS now works closely with the FBI's Office of Intelligence.

As for infrastructure, DHS is responsible for the evaluation and protection of the country's primary infrastructure, including food and water systems, health and emergency services, telecommunications, energy, chemical and defense industries, and common carrier transportation. Issues of infrastructure continue to be pressed by both the executive and legislative branch. Since roads, bridges, tunnels, and other access points are not part of the infrastructure equation, President Obama has sought to designate homeland funding to

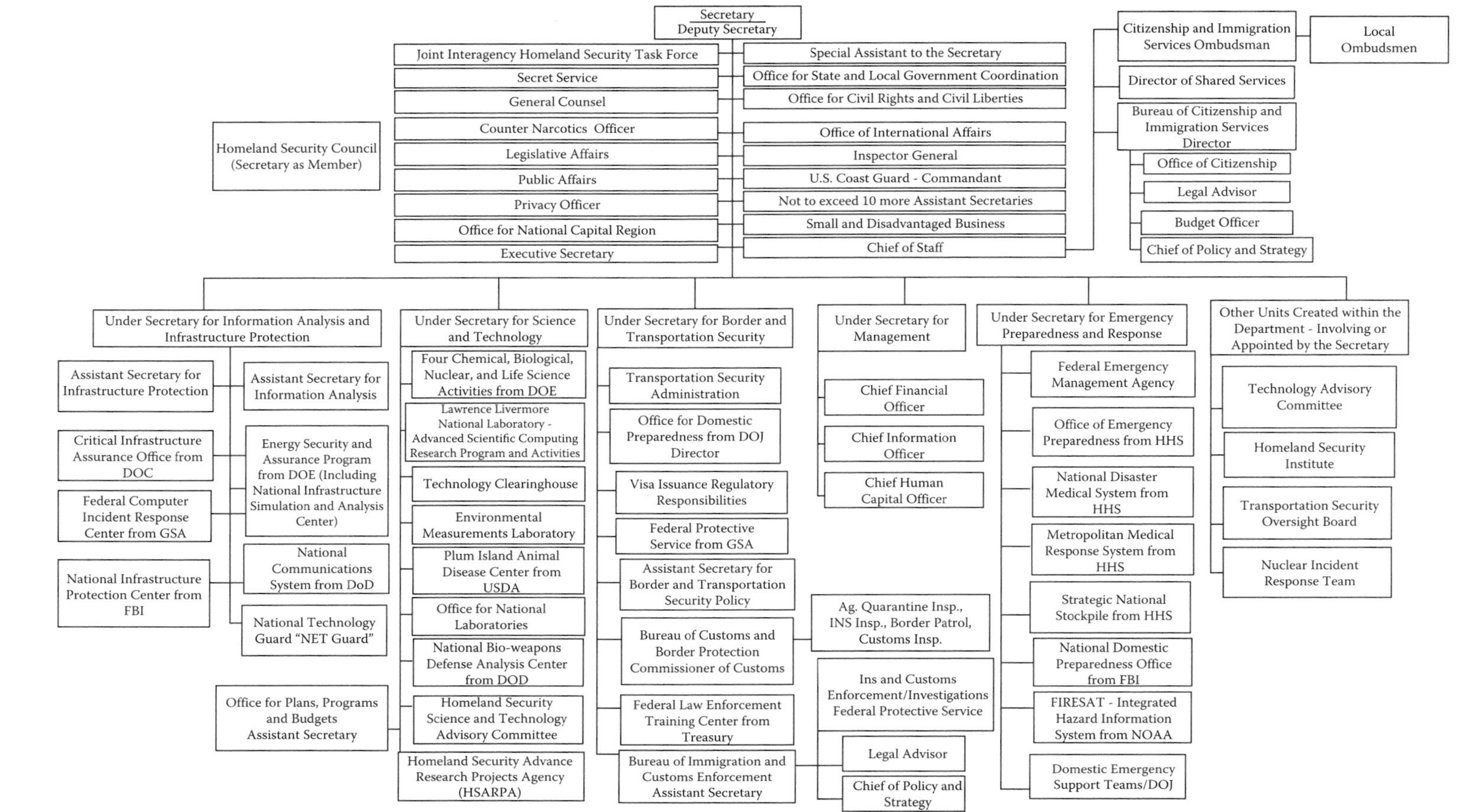

FIGURE 2.9 DHS organizational chart in 2008.

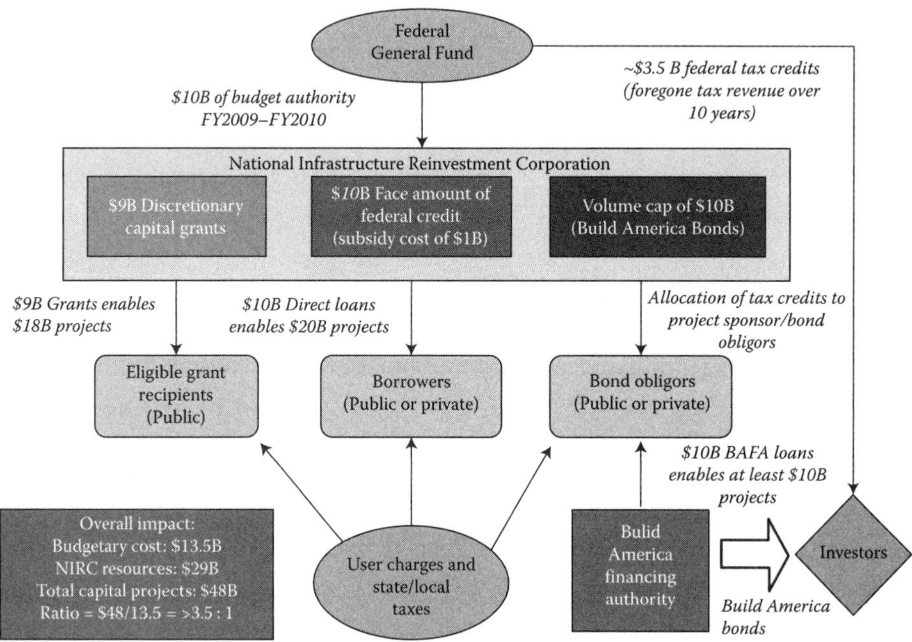

FIGURE 2.10 National infrastructure bank: slowly taking shape. (From NIRC draft legislation summary.)

its maintenance and repair. In 2009, President Obama suggested the creation of a "National Infrastructure Reinvestment Corporation"—a quasi-public entity with funding assurances from the private market. See Figure 2.10.

Given budget realities, the NIRC has yet to take shape. In December 2010, the president issued a Proclamation naming the month "Critical Infrastructure Protection Month,"[15] but this effort did not advance his cause.

DHS continues to correctly dabble and identify infrastructure[16] with various programs such as:

- Workshops on Aging Technology
- Rapid Visual Screening Tools for Buildings and Tunnels
- Collapse Mitigation
- Building Design Training Programs

Internet Exercise: See the many resources DHS makes available in the matter of infrastructure at http://www.dhs.gov/files/programs/scitech-bips-tools.shtm.

Finally, DHS of 2003 extended its program reach to state, local, and private sector justice agencies. One of the hallmarks of DHS is the cultivation of governmental, both inter- and intra-agency, cooperation. DHS saw the essential need for mutual trust and respect between competing agencies so that the mission of DHS might be implemented. DHS erected an "intergovernmental affairs office" to coordinate the numerous initiatives emanating from the agency. Figure 6.3 in Chapter 6 contains contact information for state offices dedicated to the affairs of homeland security.

In time, these external constituencies will take on added importance for DHS. Structurally, DHS will have to adapt and evolve to serve these varied interests.

The Homeland Security Act of 2002 also mandated:

> Not later than 60 days after enactment, of a reorganization plan regarding two categories of information concerning plans for the DHS ("the Department" or "DHS"):
>
> - The transfer of agencies, personnel, assets, and obligations to the Department pursuant to this Act.
> - Any consolidation, reorganization, or streamlining of agencies transferred to the Department pursuant to this Act.[17]

Internet Resource: For the complete text of the Homeland Security Act of 2002, see http://www.dhs.gov/xlibrary/assets/hr_5005_enr.pdf.

2.4 Reorganization and Evolution of DHS: 2003–2012

In accordance with the act, DHS looks internally and externally for structural changes within the agency and the merger of agencies from outside. The task of DHS is to foster the unified culture of prevention and information sharing so needed in the fight against terrorism. DHS is many things to many entities and, in the final analysis, a clearinghouse as well as an operational center for policy on homeland safety and security. DHS minimally

- Prevents terrorist attacks within the United States
- Reduces America's vulnerability to terrorism
- Minimizes the damage and oversees the recovery from attacks that do occur[18]

The current structure of DHS is charted in Figure 2.11.

Over its short life span, DHS has evolved vigorously, at least in a programmatic sense, but has taken to a slow mode of structural change. From 2008 to the present, the structure of DHS displays only minor internal and administrative differences. For example, the National Cyber Security Center no longer stands side by side with the Federal Law Enforcement Center and Domestic Nuclear Detection Office but has been merged into the DHS Directorate on Science and Technology. Replacing the National Cyber Security Center, as a stand-alone office, is "Intergovernmental Affairs." For the remainder, the 2008 version of DHS is identical to that promulgated

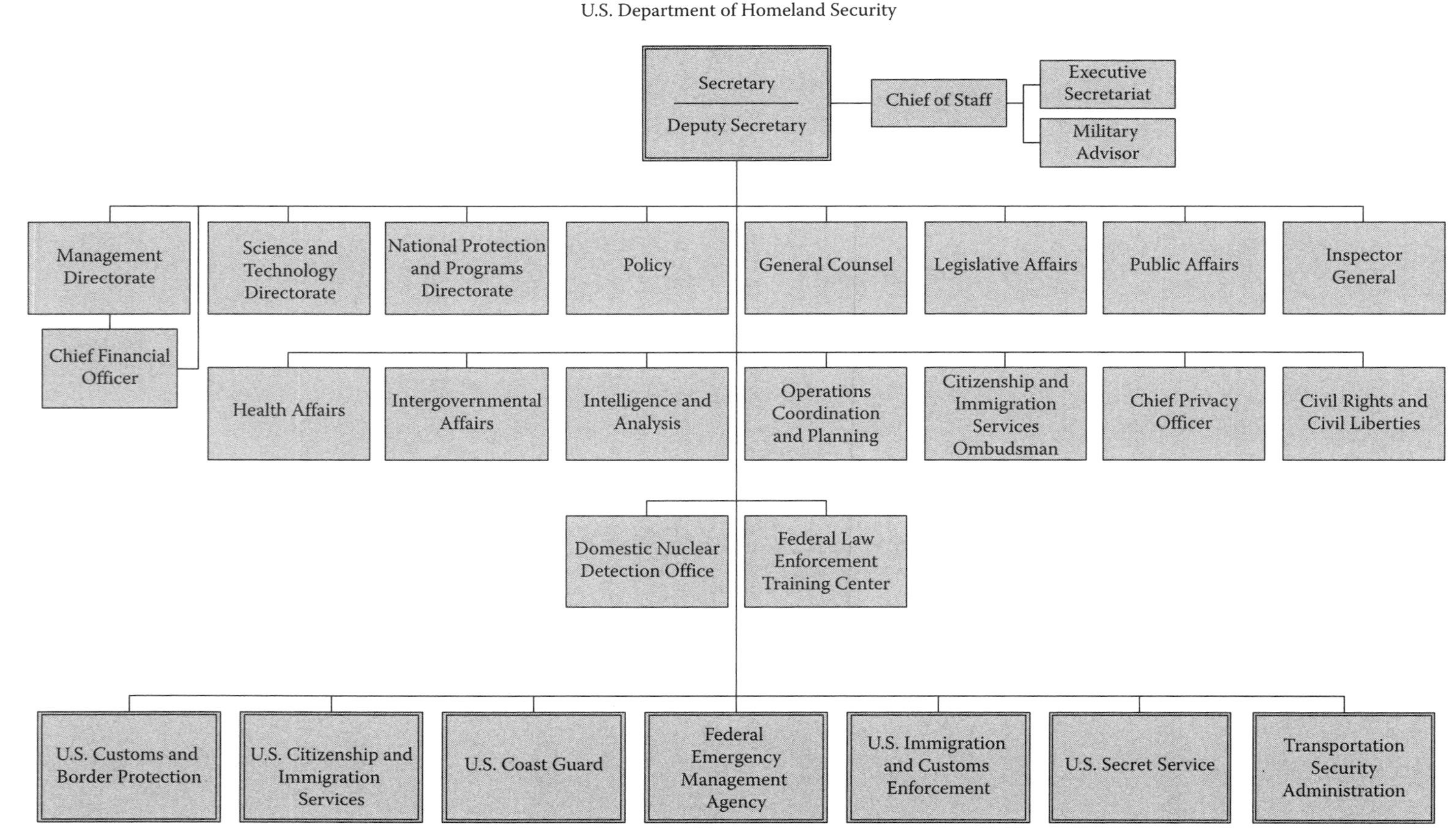

FIGURE 2.11 DHS organizational chart as of April 1, 2012.

in 2001. Given the previous "sweeps" of agencies and personnel, it is likely the prudent course which assures stability. Even so, there are many legislators and policymakers who have urged some significant consolidation and merger of task and function at DHS and budget realities may force that issue in the very near future.[19]

2.4.1 The Office of the Secretary of DHS

Within DHS, the organizational structure of the Office of the Secretary was altered under the provisions of the act. The secretary of homeland security oversees and provides leadership in all facets of the homeland defense and protection.

During its early history, the secretary was former Pennsylvania governor Thomas Ridge (Figure 2.12).

Secretary Ridge is largely lauded for his skill and demeanor during the turbulent initial days of DHS. His reputation for integrity, consensus building, and political skill is well deserved.

After Secretary Ridge, leadership of DHS was provided by former prosecutor and judge, Michael Chertoff (Figure 2.13).

Secretary Chertoff was a tireless advocate for his department. His six-point agenda for DHS, developed and announced in July 2005, ensures that the department's policies, operations, and structures are aligned in the best way to address the potential threats—both present and future—that face the United States. The agenda for DHS includes these tenets

- Increase overall preparedness, particularly for catastrophic events.
- Create better transportation security systems to move people and cargo more securely and efficiently.
- Strengthen border security and interior enforcement and reform immigration processes.

FIGURE 2.12 Thomas Ridge, the first secretary of DHS.

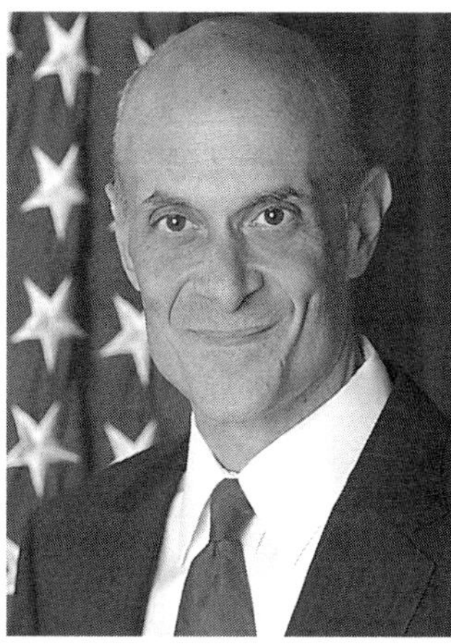

FIGURE 2.13 Michael Chertoff.

- Enhance information sharing with our partners.
- Improve DHS financial management, human resource development, procurement, and information technology.
- Realign the DHS organization to maximize mission performance.

With the election and swearing in of Barack Obama, the 44th president of the United States, a new homeland security secretary was selected and appointed. Janet Napolitano (Figure 2.14) was sworn in on January 21, 2009, as the third secretary of DHS.

Napolitano's homeland security background is extensive. As U.S. attorney, she helped lead the domestic terrorism investigation into the Oklahoma City bombing. As Arizona attorney general, she helped write the law to break up human smuggling rings. As governor of Arizona, she implemented one of the first state homeland security strategies in the country, opened the first state counterterrorism center, and spearheaded efforts to transform immigration enforcement. She has also been a pioneer in coordinating federal, state, local, and bi-national homeland security efforts, and presided

FIGURE 2.14 Janet Napolitano, the third secretary of Homeland Security.

over large-scale disaster relief efforts and readiness exercises to ensure well-crafted and functional emergency plans.

As the first woman to head up the new agency, the DHS chief's tenure has been marked by such notable events as the Christmas Day Bomber on December 25, 2009; the shooting attack and assassination attempt on House Representative Gabrielle Giffords and others in Arizona on January 8, 2011; the shooting in a movie theater in Aurora, Colorado, on July 20, 2012; the Sandy Hook Elementary School shooting in Newtown, Connecticut, on December 14, 2012; as well as the Occupy Movement. These are in addition to numerous domestic terrorist plots in various stages that have been thwarted by U.S. intelligence agencies within DHS. These events and phenomenon, as well as the various plots, have obviously influenced the focus of the agency. The secretary's most recent platform has emphasized an increased need for utilities security, including SCADA systems that control utilities, and the need for increased vigilance and expertise in the area of cybersecurity across both the public and private sectors.

Napolitano's tenure as DHS chief has not been without controversy. These include various reports of wasteful spending by DHS, certainly something that many government agencies are not immune to. In addition, civil liberties groups have decried the continued use of TSA pat downs and imaging technologies—which some argue are too invasive—in airport security screening.[20] (See Figure 2.15.)

In the wake of the Christmas Day Bomber in 2009, the secretary had to backtrack from statements that "the system worked" to concede that the system, in fact, did not work. This is due to the fact that Umar Farouk Abdulmutallab was allowed to board the plane with explosives and make it

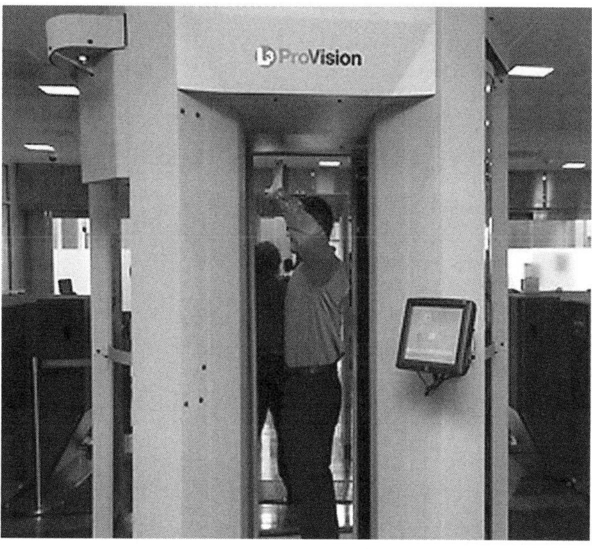

FIGURE 2.15 Advanced imaging technology (AIT) in use by TSA. (www.tsa.gov.)

all the way to Detroit before his underwear bombing device failed to detonate properly. Reports also indicate that the United States had received intelligence, prior to the attack attempt, in reference to a Nigerian national based in Yemen planning a possible attack.

Another notable event, through no fault of Secretary Napolitano's, has been the disclosure of the failed "Fast and Furious" operation, conducted from 2006 to 2011, in which over 1,600 firearms that were sold to dealers ultimately made their way into the hands of Mexican traffickers. The intent was to track the weapons and reveal key figures in the Mexican cartel hierarchy. The operation, however, was a failure in that, not only did authorities not track the movement of guns, according to reports, but those guns have been directly linked to over 200 deaths in Mexico. While this originated under the watch of Attorney General Eric Holder—out of the Bureau of Alcohol, Tobacco, and Firearms (ATF) and not DHS—it was perceived as a black-eye moment for the Obama administration that tested the public's trust of government operations in the name of security, not to mention an increasingly tense relationship with Mexico. If anything, the operation emphasized the importance of border security in the south and the need to stem the increasing threat of violence spilling over the border from Mexico, albeit not in a wholly positive way.

Despite these controversies and the increasing range of threats and challenges, Secretary Napolitano continues to lead the department on new initiatives in areas that certainly demand the country's and her reporting agencies' attention.

Within DHS, the secretary orchestrates a complex bureaucracy, like most in federal and state service. Many DHS functions are operational and legal in design. Presently, the following departments directly answer to the secretary of DHS:

- Privacy Office—Balances and implements privacy laws relevant to DHS action.
- Office of the Inspector General—Audits, investigates, and inspects practices and protocols of DHS.
- Office of Civil Rights and Civil Liberties—Delivers legal and policy advice to management at DHS as to practice and constitutional implications.
- Citizenship and Immigration Services Ombudsman—Resolves individual and employer disputes regarding immigration practices.
- Office of Legislative Affairs—Liaison with congressional leaders, staff, and the executive branch.
- Office of General Counsel—Staff of 1700 lawyers working in Office of the Secretary as well as the various departments and divisions of DHS.

Other offices include Public Affairs, Military Advisor's Office, Counter Narcotics Enforcement, and the Executive Secretariat.

2.4.2 DHS Directorates

In the reorganization phase, DHS clearly articulated its internal structure by establishing various departments within the department. At various stages in 2005 until the present, directorates were implemented and then, in some cases, were later abolished. To say that DHS is a dynamic bureaucracy is an understatement. At face value, the directorates reflect the stress of the agency—what it wishes to primarily focus upon. Before 2005, during reorganization, directorates were established in:

- Border and transportation security
- Emergency preparedness and response
- Information analysis and infrastructure protection

By 2007, each of these directorates was abolished and the respective obligations and duties transferred to other departments within DHS. Presently, there are three directorates at DHS.

2.4.2.1 Directorate for National Protection and Programs

The Directorate for National Protection and Programs deals with risk and physical and virtual threats and dedicates itself to the analysis, identification, and elimination of risk whether man made or natural in design. The Directorate covers risk from a definitional, operational, and personnel perspective and stresses best practices to protect infrastructure and human capital.

The Directorate oversees the activities of the FPS which is a law enforcement entity dedicated to the safety and risk reduction at federal installations. See Figure 2.16.

With more than 2000 officers, and in coordination with a host of contract security firms, the FPS provides security at courthouses, federal buildings, and installations as well as conduct facility assessments and special events protection. The FPS will conduct criminal investigations if required.

FIGURE 2.16 FPS logo.

Internet Resource: Find out about the many careers in FPS service at http://www.dhs.gov/xabout/careers/gc_1271345939265.shtm.

The Directorate's Office of Cyber security and Communications is entrusted with assuring the integrity of governmental and private communications system in order that these systems are free from cyber vulnerabilities. The Directorate is broken into three major sectors:

1. National Communications Systems
2. National Cyber-Security Division
3. Office of Emergency Communication

The Directorate plays a crucial role in training and simulation for governmental and private officers entrusted with communication and cyber responsibilities. Its "Cyber Storm" exercise provides a bi-annual opportunity to test and confirm the integrity of communication and cyber designs. See Figure 2.17.

Cyber Storm participants perform the following activities:

- Examine organizations' capability to prepare for, protect from, and respond to cyber attacks' potential effects.
- Exercise strategic decision making and interagency coordination of incident response(s) in accordance with national level policy and procedures.
- Validate information-sharing relationships and communications paths for collecting and disseminating cyber incident situational awareness, response, and recovery information.
- Examine means and processes through which to share sensitive information across boundaries and sectors without compromising proprietary or national security interests.

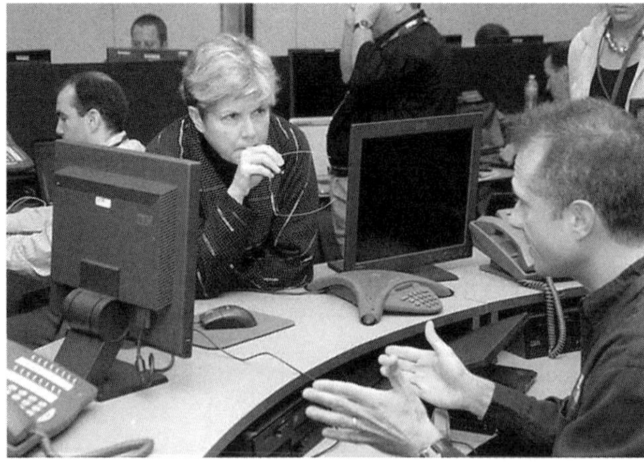

FIGURE 2.17 DHS Cyber Storm participants, September 2010. (www.dhs.gov.)

Central to the Directorate's overall mission is protection of the infrastructure which includes but is not limited to the power grid, food and water supplies, national monuments, transportations systems, and chemical facilities.

Infrastructure sectors include:

- Agriculture and food
- Banking and finance
- Chemical
- Commercial facilities
- Critical manufacturing
- Dams
- Defense industrial base
- Drinking water and water treatment systems
- Emergency services
- Energy
- Government facilities
- Information technology
- National monuments and icons
- Nuclear reactors, materials, and waste
- Postal and shipping
- Public health and healthcare
- Telecommunications
- Transportation systems

The National Protection and Programs Directorate needs to analyze these critical forms of infrastructure to determine potential threats and vulnerability, management and mitigation of identified risks to same and be just as adept in the coordination of agency response in the event of threat. Covered later in this chapter will be the protocol and methodology of infrastructure analysis. Much of what state, local, and federal authorities do in response to infrastructure threat is derived from the Directorate's research results and recommended best practices.

A myriad of other functions are assumed by the National Protection and Programs Directorate and will be encountered throughout the remainder of this chapter. Special offices precisely deal with matters of risk analysis, assessment, and management as well as the emerging statistical and quantitative discipline of risk analytics. The Directorate oversees the US-VISIT program which will be covered in a later section.

2.4.2.2 Directorate for Science and Technology

The role of science and technology in the world of homeland security is patently obvious. As government agencies and localities deal with shrinking budgets, the efficiency and efficacy of its practices take on added importance. The Science and Technology Directorate plays a key role in the development of all forms of technology useful to homeland defense. It serves a variety of broader functions such as being a clearinghouse for technology practices and equipment, especially as to design and engineering; it tests and evaluates the compatibility and interoperability of diverse technologies used across the various states and weighs and assesses the primary needs of the nation's first responder requirements for technology.

The Directorate encompasses nearly a dozen divisions including:

- Borders and Maritime Security
- Chemical and Biological
- Command Control and Interoperability
- Explosives
- Human Factors/Behavioral Sciences
- Infrastructure
- Geophysical[21]

The Directorate also engages technology in specific situations such as border and maritime, chemical and biological defense, explosive mitigation, and the cyber security threats. Amongst many other activities, the Directorate plays a key role in science and technology development at the college and university level and coordinates a wide array of research and disseminates funds for technological and scientific innovation.

Internet Resource: Discover the many activities of the Office of University Programs at http://www.dhs.gov/xabout/structure/editorial_0555.shtm.

2.4.2.3 Directorate for Management

The Directorate for Management is the administrative arm of DHS where traditional functions of personnel, finance, and capital and procurement requirements are dealt with as well as the acquisition and maintenance of DHS properties. The Directorate is responsible for budget development and oversight. With more than 200,000 employees in DHS, the Management Directorate takes on a major undertaking in the matter of human and physical capital. See Figure 2.18 for the organizational chart of the Directorate.

2.4.3 DHS Offices

At the office level, DHS further differentiated task and function by the following:

- Office of Policy—Formulates and coordinates DHS policy and program.
- Office of Health—Deals with medically related incidents.

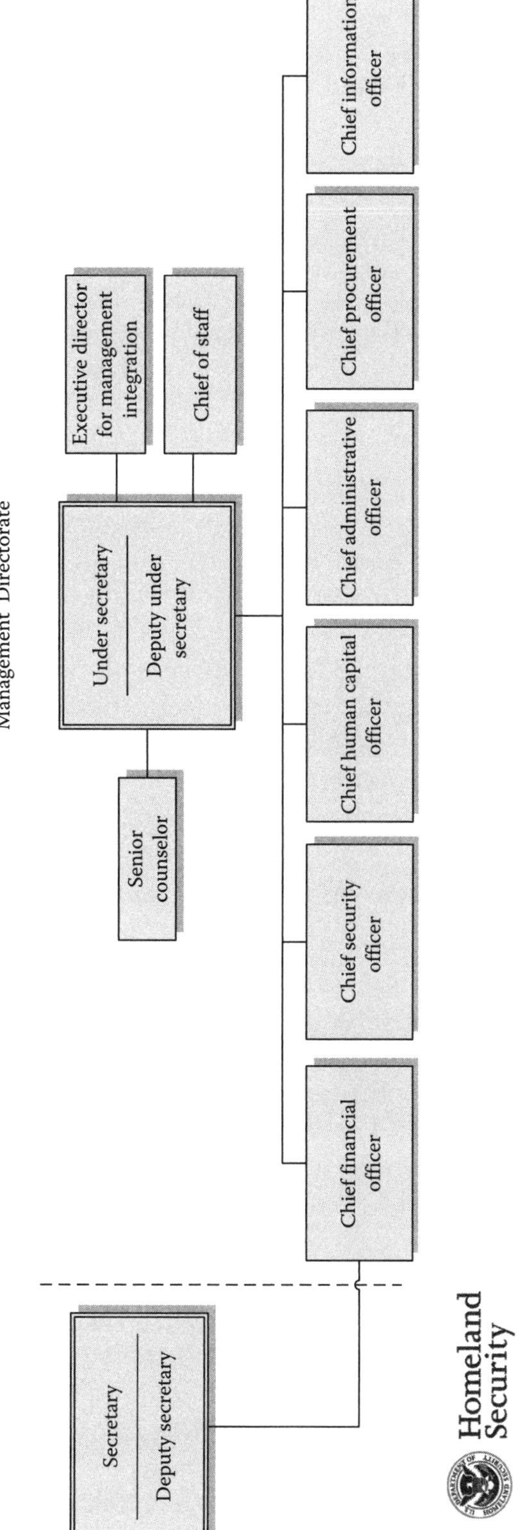

FIGURE 2.18 Management Directorate organizational chart.

- Office of Intelligence and Analysis—Assesses and analyzes information and data regarding threat.
- Office of Operations Coordination—Monitors and coordinates homeland security activities and programs in the 50 states, in 50 major urban areas, in conjunction with law enforcement partners.

2.4.4 Agencies Swept into DHS

After 2003 a host of external agencies were also swept into DHS during the reorganization phase:

- Federal Law Enforcement Training Center (FLETC)—The premier center for professional law enforcement training located in Glencoe, Georgia.
- U.S. Customs and Border Protection (CBP)—The agency primarily responsible for the security of our borders.
- U.S. Citizenship and Immigration Services—Administers the immigration and naturalization adjudication.
- U.S. Immigration and Customs Enforcement (ICE)—The investigative arm of DHS that identifies and classifies threats at the borders.
- U.S. Coast Guard—Protection of nation's ports and waterways.
- FEMA—Manages hazards and threats and responds thereto.
- U.S. Secret Service—Protection of the president, vice president, and other high-level officials; investigates financial crimes.
- Transportation Security Agency (TSA)—Protects nation's transportation systems.
- Domestic Nuclear Detection Office—Coordinates threat response related to nuclear materials.

The intent was to combine, blend, and synthesize appropriate agency's functions with the appropriate office. For the most part, DHS has remained largely intact since these radical days of reorganization in 2003–2004. It was not only an administrative sweep that took place when these agencies moved from familiar locale to the DHS setting. For both DHS and the incoming agency, a change of outlook and culture was required. By change one means that a new prioritization of agency function had to occur; the former agency had to inculcate, acclimate, and become part of a new mission and mindset. In governmental life span, this is a difficult order to fulfill. Even so, it appears that DHS has done a fairly good job integrating so much in such an expeditious fashion.

To truly appreciate these cultural and administrative shifts, one need only look to the moves from one agency to another (Table 2.1).

In DHS, these moves are simply unrivaled in the history of the government—the movement can only be termed radical in scope. Sweeping moves, from so many governmental agencies, are not the stuff of government personality, whether it is local, state, or federal.

TABLE 2.1 Agency Relocations within DHS

Original Agency (Department)	Current Agency/Office
The U.S. Customs Service (Treasury)	U.S. Customs and Border Protection—Inspection, border, and ports of entry responsibilities U.S. Immigration and Customs Enforcement—Customs law enforcement responsibilities
The Immigration and Naturalization Service (Justice)	U.S. Customs and Border Protection—Inspection functions and the U.S. Border Patrol U.S. Immigration and Customs Enforcement—Immigration law enforcement: detention and removal, intelligence, and investigations U.S. Citizenship and Immigration Services—Adjudications and benefits programs
The Federal Protective Service	U.S. Immigration and Customs Enforcement
The Transportation Security Administration (Transportation)	Transportation Security Administration
Federal Law Enforcement Training Center (Treasury)	Federal Law Enforcement Training Center
Animal and Plant Health Inspection Service (part) (Agriculture)	U.S. Customs and Border Protection—Agricultural imports and entry inspections
Office for Domestic Preparedness (Justice)	Responsibilities distributed within FEMA
The Federal Emergency Management Agency (FEMA)	Federal Emergency Management Agency
Strategic National Stockpile and the National Disaster Medical System (HHS)	Returned to Health and Human Services, July, 2004
Nuclear Incident Response Team (Energy)	Responsibilities distributed within FEMA
Domestic Emergency Support Teams (Justice)	Responsibilities distributed within FEMA
National Domestic Preparedness Office (FBI)	Responsibilities distributed within FEMA
CBRN Countermeasures Programs (Energy)	Science and Technology Directorate
Environmental Measurements Laboratory (Energy)	Science and Technology Directorate
National BW Defense Analysis Center (Defense)	Science and Technology Directorate
Plum Island Animal Disease Center (Agriculture)	Science and Technology Directorate
Federal Computer Incident Response Center (GSA)	US-CERT, Office of Cybersecurity and Communications in the National Programs and Preparedness Directorate

continued

TABLE 2.1 (continued) Agency Relocations within DHS

Original Agency (Department)	Current Agency/Office
National Communications System (Defense)	Office of Cybersecurity and Communications in the National Programs and Preparedness Directorate
National Infrastructure Protection Center (FBI)	Dispersed throughout the department, including Office of Operations Coordination and Office of Infrastructure Protection
Energy Security and Assurance Program (Energy)	Integrated into the Office of Infrastructure Protection
U.S. Coast Guard	U.S. Coast Guard
U.S. Secret Service	U.S. Secret Service

In the final analysis, such shifts and mergers were essential to any notion of a "single roof" for homeland security. While many of these former agencies and offices will be covered in other portions of this chapter, this section will highlight four significant structural shifts into DHS.

2.4.4.1 U.S. Coast Guard

The placement of the U.S. Coast Guard (USCG) into DHS was considered a radical shift by many, but upon close inspection, it makes perfect sense. Historically the Coast Guard's dedication to safety and security in our waterways and coastline makes the agency the perfect complement to DHS (Figure 2.19).

FIGURE 2.19 U.S. Coast Guard approaching a cargo ship.

The mission of the USCG is (www.uscg.mil/top/missions/):

- *Maritime Safety*: Eliminate deaths, injuries, and property damage associated with maritime transportation, fishing, and recreational boating.
- *Maritime Security*: Protect America's maritime borders from all intrusions by (a) halting the flow of illegal drugs, aliens, and contraband into the United States through maritime routes; (b) preventing illegal fishing; and (c) suppressing violations of federal law in the maritime arena.
- *Maritime Mobility*: Facilitate maritime commerce and eliminate interruptions and impediments to the efficient and economical movement of goods and people, while maximizing recreational access to and enjoyment of the water.
- *National Defense*: Defend the country as one of the five U.S. armed services. Enhance regional stability in support of the National Security Strategy, utilizing the Coast Guard's unique and relevant maritime capabilities.
- *Protection of Natural Resources*: Eliminate environmental damage and the degradation of natural resources associated with maritime transportation, fishing, and recreational boating.

Long considered a military operation, as one of the five traditional branches in the military complex, the Coast Guard increasingly evolved into a safety and law enforcement organization as well as a military command. How the Coast Guard contributes to the defense of the country is quite evident in its homeland security functions, which include (www.uscg.mil/top/mission/defense.asp):

- Protect ports, the flow of commerce, and the marine transportation system from terrorism.
- Maintain maritime border security against illegal drugs, illegal aliens, firearms, and weapons of mass destruction.
- Ensure that we can rapidly deploy and resupply our military assets, both by keeping Coast Guard units at a high state of readiness, and by keeping marine transportation open for the transit assets and personnel from other branches of the armed forces.
- Protect against illegal fishing and indiscriminate destruction of living marine resources, prevention and response to oil and hazardous material spills—both accidental and intentional.
- Coordinate efforts and intelligence with federal, state, and local agencies.

With its extraordinary infrastructure of maritime resources, its skill in detection and prevention of crime on the seas and waterways, and its technical superiority in a host of operations, the USCG has been called upon to be a major player in the fight against terrorism (Figure 2.20).

Its flexibility of vision is what makes it a key component of a national strategy. Vice Admiral Vivien Cream of the U.S. Coast Guard rightfully argues:

> The need to protect the homeland in the context of the "long war" against terrorism has been a key force for change in the Coast Guard. Although our initial response to this new terrorism threat temporarily drained resources from other mission areas, we have worked to restore the maritime safety and security mission balance. Congress and the administration have provided critical funding support. New and more capable assets have been added, and all of our resources present a multi-mission capability that can instantly and flexibly surge from search and rescue, to restoration of our ports and waterways, to response to avert threat to our homeland security.[22]

The transition, of course, has not been without its share of challenges. The Coast Guard has a variety of masters to answer to. The sheer volume of coverage, in both task and geography, is daunting. "With 95,000 miles of coastline and close to 360 ports of entry, the United States is challenged daily with monitoring maritime safety, securing national borders and the global supply chain, and protecting natural resources,"[23] the Coast Guard labors under heavy demands. The Coast Guard has undergone a "fundamental reordering,"[24] which requires it to be an "instrument of national security."[25]

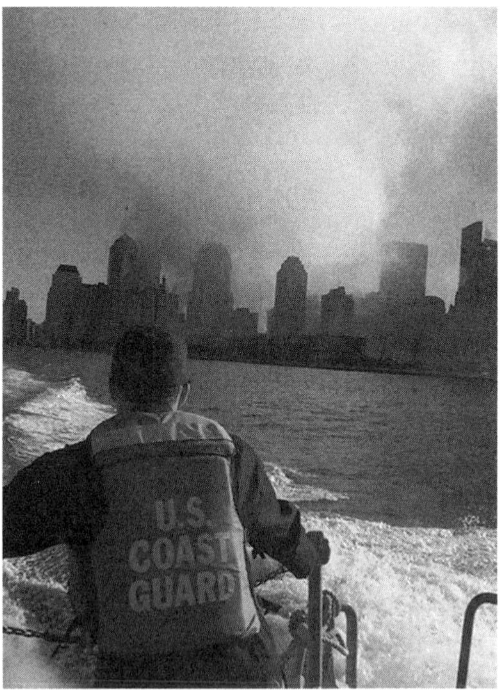

FIGURE 2.20 Coast Guard officer approaching the Twin Towers disaster site.

2.4.4.2 U.S. Secret Service

Given how threat and attack targets are often high-profile political figures, the decision to move Secret Service under the roof of DHS is mission consistent.

The Secret Service (Figure 2.21) is entrusted with the protection of these figures:

- The president, the vice president (or other individuals next in order of succession to the Office of the President), the president-elect, and vice president-elect.
- The immediate families of the above individuals.
- Former presidents and their spouses for their lifetimes, except when the spouse remarries. In 1997, congressional legislation became effective limiting Secret Service protection to former presidents for a period of not more than 10 years from the date the former president leaves office.
- Children of former presidents until age 16.
- Visiting heads of foreign states or governments and their spouses traveling with them, other distinguished foreign visitors to the United States, and official representatives of the United States performing special missions abroad.
- Major presidential and vice presidential candidates, and their spouses, within 120 days of a general presidential election.
- Other individuals as designated per executive order of the president.
- National Special Security Events, when designated as such by the secretary of DHS.

The Secret Service also deals with counterfeiting and select federal crimes not aligned to homeland security issues. Its investigations unit

FIGURE 2.21 U.S. Secret Service agents on duty.

deals with identity crimes such as access device fraud, identity theft, false identification fraud, bank and check fraud, telemarketing fraud, telecommunications fraud (cellular and hard wire), computer fraud, fraud targeting automated payment systems and teller machines, direct deposit fraud, and investigations of forgery. For homeland purposes the protection unit assumes a central role.

Two areas where the Secret Service orchestrates protective services are in major events and threat assessment. In the first instance, major events, the Secret Service coordinates agencies and their respective resources when a significant public event, involving protected persons, takes place. In this case, the secretary of DHS designates the event as a National Special Security Event (NSSE). The Secret Service assumes its mandated role as the lead agency for the design and implementation of the operational security plan. The NSSE is coordinated in cooperation with its established partnerships with law enforcement and public safety officials at the local, state, and federal levels.

A second integral contribution of the service is the development and operational oversight of the National Threat Assessment Center. See Figure 2.22.

The center focuses its research and activities on the protection of public figures, the creation and implementation of best practices in the protection thereof, and recommendations on how best to serve potential targets of threat. The center directs its attention chiefly to:

- Research on threat assessment and various types of targeted violence
- Training on threat assessment and targeted violence to law enforcement officials and others with protective and public safety responsibilities
- Information sharing among agencies with protective or public safety responsibilities
- Programs to promote the standardization of federal, state, and local threat assessment and investigations involving threats

Internet Resource: For best practices in the prevention of threat to public targets, see http://www.ustreas.gov/usss/ntac/ntac_threat.pdf.

FIGURE 2.22 National Threat Assessment Center logo.

2.4.4.3 Federal Protective Service

Once a part of the General Service Administration, the FPS is the law enforcement and security force that protects federal buildings and installations. In the reorganization of DHS, the agency was moved to Immigration and Customs Enforcement (ICE). The ICE is under the supervision of DHS. The FPS provides security services in all federal buildings, including office buildings, courthouses, border stations, and warehouses. FPS services include but are not limited to:

- Providing a visible uniformed presence in our major Federal buildings
- Responding to criminal incidents and other emergencies
- Installing and monitoring security devices and systems
- Investigating criminal incidents
- Conducting physical security surveys
- Coordinating a comprehensive program for occupants' emergency plans
- Presenting formal crime prevention and security awareness programs
- Providing police emergency and special security services during natural disasters such as earthquakes, hurricanes, and major civil disturbances—as well as during man-made disasters, such as bomb explosions and riots

The FPS also takes a lead role in the assurance that federal buildings and installations are rid of security problems and that the design, operation, and layout of facilities are best conducive to safe security practices. In each facility, the FPS sets up a Building Security Committee that conducts a vulnerability assessment of each facility.

The FPS administers a program for lost and missing children in federal installations called Code Adam Alert. See Figure 2.23.

Internet Resource: For a copy of the FPS brochure *Making Buildings Safe*, see http://www.gsa.gov/gsa/cm_attachments/GSA_DOCUMENT/fps_making_buildings_safe_R25Z74_0Z5RDZ-i34K-pR.pdf.

2.4.4.4 Federal Law Enforcement Training Center

Just as it was wise to relocate the Coast Guard and Secret Service to DHS, it makes eminent sense to move the federal government's premier training agency under the same roof (Figures 2.24 and 2.25).

FLETC has assumed a central role in the training of law enforcement professionals across the United States. From every jurisdiction, justice professionals benefit from the expertise and cutting-edge subject matter relevant to homeland security (Figure 2.26).

The Federal Law Enforcement Training Center is located in Glynco, Georgia, with satellite facilities in Washington, DC; Jacksonville, Florida;

CODE★ADAM★ALERT
To help protect children in federal facilities, the U.S. General Services Administration with the Federal Protective Service, has adopted the "Code Adam" Program. These are the steps to follow when an alert is announced that a child is missing.
Step 1 Obtain a detailed description of the child:
• Name, age, gender, and race
• Weight, height, hair and eye color
• Describe what the child is wearing, specifically the color and type of clothing including shoe color and style.
Step 2 Report information about the missing child to the Federal Protective Service or security guards on duty. If no security guard, contact on-site facility manager or delegated official. They will activate the "Code Adam" alert to all building tenants. Also, place a courtesy call to local police (911) to report missing child.
Step 3 Security officials will conduct a search of the building. Tenants might be asked to assist with the search. Please cooperate with security.
Step 4 If the child is found with someone other than Parent or Guardian, use reasonable efforts to delay the departure of the person accompanying the child, but do not put yourself or others at risk. If possible, notify security officials and describe the identity of the person accompanying the child.
Step 5 When a child is found, bring child to security officials or on-site facility manager. They will reunite child with Parent or Guardian. Security personnel will cancel "Code Adam" alert. If child is not found, security officials or on-site facility manager will contact local police again reporting any additional information.
GSA
NATIONAL CENTER FOR MISSING & EXPLOITED CHILDREN
CODE★ADAM

FIGURE 2.23 Code Adam alert flyer.

Charleston, South Carolina; Artesia, New Mexico; and Cheltenham, Maryland. The strategic goals of FLETC are:

- Provide training that enables our partners to accomplish their missions
- Foster a high-performing workforce
- Provide mission-responsive infrastructure
- Optimize business practices

FIGURE 2.24 Federal Law Enforcement Training Center in Glynco, Georgia.

FIGURE 2.25 FLETC training exercise.

See Figure 2.27 for an organization chart of the Federal Law Enforcement Training Center hierarchy.

Each facility provides a wide array of training opportunities. Those more appropriately applicable to homeland security are:

Antiterrorism Intelligence Awareness Training Program (AIATP)
Commercial Vehicle Counterterrorism Training Program (CVCTP)
Computer Network Investigations Training Program (CNITP)
Covert Electronic Surveillance Program (CESP)

FIGURE 2.26 Trainee in gear ready for an exercise at the Federal Law Enforcement Training Center.

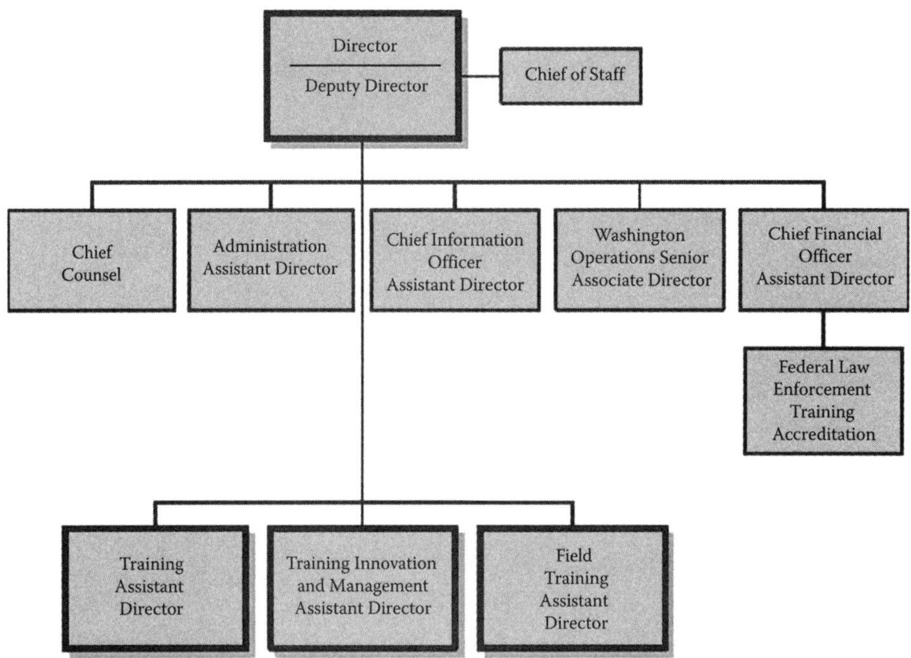

FIGURE 2.27 Federal Law Enforcement Training Center organizational chart.

Covert Electronic Tracking Program (CETP)
Crisis Management Training Program (CMTP)
Critical Incident Response Training Program (CIRTP)
Critical Infrastructure Key Resource Protection Qualification Training Program (CIKRTP)
Critical Infrastructure Protection Training Program (CIPTP)
Cyber Counterterrorism Investigations Training Program (CCITP)
Domestic Terrorism and Hate Crimes Training Program (DTHCTP)
Intelligence Analyst Training Program (IATP)
Intelligence Awareness for Law Enforcement Executives Training Program (IALEETP)
International Banking and Money Laundering Training Program (IBMLTP)
Internet Investigations Training Program (IITP)
Internet Protocol Camera Program (IPCP)
Introductory Intelligence Analyst Training Program (IIATP)
Operations Security for Public Safety Agencies Counterterrorism Training Program (OPSACTP)
Seaport Security Antiterrorism Training Program (SSATP)
Suicide Bomber Mitigation Training Program (SBMTP)
Vehicle Ambush Countermeasures Training Program (VACTP)
Weapons of Mass Destruction Training Program (Level I) (WMDTP L1—Operations—Core NFPA 472.5)
Weapons of Mass Destruction Training Program (Level II) (WMDTP L2—Technician)

FLETC dedicates a large portion of its training to terrorism and counterterrorism. An entire certification program exists for those seeking this specialized knowledge. FLETC delivers state-of-the-art training in advanced topics relevant to homeland security, including:

- Cyber terrorism training
- Critical infrastructure training
- Antiterrorism intelligence

Internet Resource: For a full catalog of courses, see http://www.fletc.gov/training/cotp.pdf/view.

2.4.5 Advisory Panels and Committees

One of the recurring themes in DHS operations is the agency's willingness to work with external authority—both public and private. The Council is more than mere formality but an essential contributor to the integrity of the homeland effort. So integral is the Council considered to the mission of DHS, that the body is statutorily required to report its recommendations every 4 years. Reports from May 27, 2010 urge the agency to "define and operationalize the strategic framework; to delineate roles and responsibilities" with a keener eye and to measure DHS Mission with "measurable outcomes ... and targets to drive alignment of the Department's priorities, structures, systems and resources."[26]

The report intends to serve as a critique of DHS using the combined wisdom of the Committee as outside, objective observers. The aim is for the Council to turn a critical and pragmatic eye to DHS programs and offer recommendations for improvement and to curtail initiatives that may be redundant, or not properly vetted, to avoid unnecessary bureaucracy within the department.

The Council wisely calls for the aggressive integration and melding of state and local governmental authorities, working side by side with federal entities in law enforcement, the intelligence community, the agency also seeks input and professional participation by other suitable means. One avenue erects and establishes a body of government leaders, scholars, and practitioners that give advice to DHS. Some of the more prominent panels are:

- Homeland Security Advisory Council (HSAC)—Advice and recommendations on homeland practices.
- National Infrastructure Advisory Council—Advice on information systems for both the public and private sector.
- Homeland Security Science and Tech Advisory Committee—Independent scientific advice for planning purposes within DHS.
- Critical Infrastructure Partnership Advisory Council—Coordinates state, local, tribal, and federal reporting on critical infrastructure protection.
- Interagency Coordinating Council on Emergency Preparedness and Individuals with Disabilities—Group that reviews DHS practices and recommendations in light of disability.
- Task Force on New Americans—Supports immigrants in the learning of language and American culture.

Current members of the Homeland Security Advisory Council are a Who's Who of distinguished citizens.

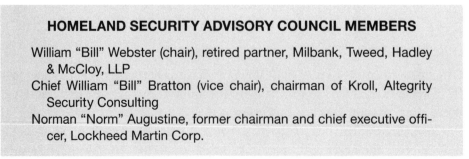

HOMELAND SECURITY ADVISORY COUNCIL MEMBERS

William "Bill" Webster (chair), retired partner, Milbank, Tweed, Hadley & McCloy, LLP

Chief William "Bill" Bratton (vice chair), chairman of Kroll, Altegrity Security Consulting

Norman "Norm" Augustine, former chairman and chief executive officer, Lockheed Martin Corp.

Leroy "Lee" Baca, sheriff, Los Angeles County
Richard "Dick" Cañas, security consultant
Kenneth "Chuck" Canterbury, president, Fraternal Order of Police
Jared "Jerry" Cohon, president, Carnegie Mellon University
Ruth David, president and chief executive officer, ANSER (Analytic Services, Inc.)
Manny Diaz, senior partner, Lydecker Diaz
Mohamed Elibiary, Foundation, founder, Lone Star Intelligence, LLC
Clark Kent Ervin, director, Homeland Security Program, The Aspen Institute
Ellen Gordon, associate director, Naval Postgraduate School, CHDS
Lee H. Hamilton, director, the Center on Congress at Indiana University
Raymond Kelly, police commissioner, City of New York
John Magaw, self-employed, Domestic and International Security Consultant
Bonnie Michelman, director of Police, Security and Outside Services at Massachusetts General Hospital and instructor at Northeastern University's College of Criminal Justice
Jeff Moss, chief security officer, Internet Corporation for Assigned Names and Numbers (ICANN)
Martin O'Malley, governor, State of Maryland
Sonny Perdue, former governor, State of Georgia
Harold Schaitberger, general president, International Association of Firefighters
Joe Shirley Jr., former president, The Navajo Nation
Lydia W. Thomas, trustee, Noblis, Inc.
Frances Fragos Townsend, senior vice president—Worldwide Government, Legal and Business Affairs, MacAndrews & Forbes Holdings Inc.
Chuck Wexler, executive director, Police Executive Research Forum
John "Skip" Williams, provost and vice president for Health, The George Washington University

For the charter that established the HSAC, see Appendix A.

DHS also relies upon specialized committees that deal with topics of significant interest to the agency. Presently these committees are designated as senior advisory committees, an example being referenced below.

Other areas of expertise are solicited in private sector justice, secure borders, state and local officials, and the academe. These committees issue reports and recommendations to the secretary as needed.

Internet Resource: For an example of a committee report dealing with secure borders, visit http://www.dhs.gov/xlibrary/assets/hsac_SBODACreport508-compliant_version2.pdf.

Since 2011, under the leadership of President Barack Obama, the Advisory Council has been asked to erect a Task Force on Secure Communities. The initiative gives special attention to the problem of illegal immigration and how it impacts community safety.

Internet Resource: Visit the Task Force's Draft Recommendations on how to secure border towns directly suffering from the problems and challenges of illegal immigration at http://www.dhs.gov/xlibrary/assets/hsac-task-force-on-secure-communities.pdf.

2.5 Conclusion

Chapter 2 began with a review of the events of September 11, 2001, and a discussion of the immediate responses of various federal agencies. The lack of coordination, cooperation, and information sharing between federal agencies was discussed as a contributing factor to the attacks. The strategies and tactics developed as a result, namely, the creation of DHS and its many directorates and committees, were next introduced.

DHS was created to be a flexible entity, one that can change to reflect national security needs at any given time. This is apparent due to the fluctuation in the organization's structure in its first 8 years of being. The text next turned to the initial formation of the department, from 2001 to 2003, its strategic goals and mission, and initial policy formulation. The *Homeland Security Act of 2002* established the department itself, outlined its powers, main areas of responsibility, and authority. Its early evolution and early department mergers were presented.

As with any bureaucratic entity, change is inevitable, and this was never more apparent than in the major reorganization of DHS between 2003 and 2008. The text next highlighted the first three secretaries of DHS and the agency's various directorates and offices and their corresponding responsibilities. During this major reorganization phase many government agencies were swept under DHS's mantle and partially or, in some cases, completely reorganized. The four major agency reorganizations, the Coast Guard, Secret Service, FPS, and FLETC, were analyzed in depth. Finally, DHS's advisory panel and committee structure was explained.

Keywords

Agency culture
Border security
Bureaucracy
Central Intelligence Agency
Coast Guard
Counterterrorism
Critical infrastructure
Customs and Border Protection
Department of Homeland Security
Directorate

Domestic Nuclear Detection Office
Drug Enforcement Administration
Emergency management
Federal Aviation Administration
Federal Bureau of Investigation
Federal Emergency Management Agency
FLETC
Hijack
Homeland Security Act of 2002
Illegal aliens
Immigration and Customs Enforcement
Infrastructure
Intelligence
Intelligence sharing
Interagency cooperation
Law enforcement
Maritime security
Mitigation
National Commission on 9/11
National defense
National Security Agency
National Threat Assessment Center
Natural disaster
NORAD
Pentagon
Prevention
Protective services
Public safety
Secret Service
Security survey
Targeted violence
Threat analysis
Threat assessment
Transportation Security Administration
U.S. Citizenship and Immigration Services
Vulnerability assessment
Weapons of mass destruction

Discussion Questions

1. How would you rate the federal government response to 9/11 as compared to more recent disasters such as Hurricane Katrina and Hurricane Sandy?
2. Why did an agency for homeland security evolve?
3. What alternatives to DHS are possible?
4. What is the most striking difference between DHS 2003 and DHS today?
5. Does DHS have a political edge? Does DHS reflect who is in power?
6. Which agencies might be arguably misplaced in DHS?
7. How do lay people and lay organizations impact DHS?

Practical Exercises

1. Visit DHS's website and access the pages regarding the three directorates. List the programs and offices that each directorate supervises.
2. Review the list of agencies that were swept into DHS during the reorganization. Can you think of a better plan or reorganization? Does the current organization make sense from an operational perspective?
3. Visit the U.S. Coast Guard's website. Find out about MARSEC levels.
4. Visit the U.S. Secret Service's website and locate information on the National Threat Assessment Center. Find out about their current major research projects.
5. Visit the FPS section of the ICE website. Locate current job vacancies and familiarize yourself with the requirements for hire by the FPS.

Notes

1. Federal Bureau of Investigation, Press room, *9/11 Investigation (PENTTBOM)*, http://www.fbi.gov/pressrel/penttbom/aa77/77.htm.
2. FOXNews.com, News Archive, *Timeline: Sept. 11, 2001*, http://www.foxnews.com/story/0,2933,62184,00.html.
3. For an interesting look into the cultural shifts in the intelligence community as it evaluated terrorism see T. A. Gilly, Deconstructing terrorism: Counter-terrorism's trajectory for the 21st century, *The Homeland Security Review*, 5 (2011): 5.
4. National Commission on Terrorist Attacks upon the United States, Tenth Public Hearing, Law Enforcement, Counterterrorism, and Intelligence Collection in the United States prior to 9/11, Staff Statement No. 9, April 13, 2004, 8, http://govinfo.library.unt.edu/911/staff_statements/staff_statement_9.pdf.
5. R. Ward et al., *Homeland Security: An Introduction* (Cincinnati: Anderson Publishing Co., 2006), 57.
6. Bullock, Homeland Security, 23.
7. President G. W. Bush, *The Department of Homeland Security* (Washington, DC: U.S. Government Printing Office), 19–23 June 2002, http://www.whitehouse.gov/deptofhomeland/sect8.html or http://www.whitehouse.gov/deptofhomeland/book.pdf.
8. Bush, Department Homeland Security, 1, http://www.whitehouse.gov/deptofhomeland/sect1.html.
9. Bush, Department Homeland Security, 1, http://www.whitehouse.gov/deptofhomeland/sect1.html.
10. *The 9/11 Commission Report: Final Report of the National Commission on Terrorist Attacks upon the United States*, Official Government Edition (Washington, DC: U.S. Government Printing Office, July 22, 2004), 400.
11. Homeland Security Council, National Strategy for Homeland Security (October 2007), 3, http://www.whitehouse.gov/infocus/homeland/nshs/2007/sectionII.html or http://www.whitehouse.gov/infocus/homeland/nshs/NSHS.pdf.
12. Homeland Security Act of 2002, U.S. Code 6 (2002), § 101.

13. Homeland Security Act of 2002, U.S. Code 6 (2002), § 101 (b).
14. U.S. Department of Homeland Security Organization Chart, http://www.dhs.gov/xlibrary/assets/dhs-orgchart.pdf (2012).
15. Presidential Proclamation: Critical Infrastructure Protection Month, Nov. 30, 2010.
16. Congressional Research Service, Critical Infrastructures: Background, Policy and Implementation (July 2011).
17. Homeland Security Act of 2002, U.S. Code 6 (2002), § 1502.
18. Office of Homeland Security, The National Strategy for Homeland Security (June 16, 2002), vii, http://www.whitehouse.gov/homeland/book/sect1.pdf or http://www.whitehouse.gov/homeland/book/nat_strat_hls.pdf.
19. The Federal News Radio reports that support for consolidation is growing in the U.S. Senate. See: http://www.federalnewsradio.com/?nid=108&sid=2545915.
20. See Ben Forer, TSA Full-Body Scanners: No More Naked Images, ABCnew.com, July 21, 2011, at http://abcnews.go.com/Travel/Travel/tsa-full-body-scanners-naked-images/story?id=14125474.
21. See Department of Homeland Security website, Science and Technology Resources, at http://www.dhs.gov/files/scitech.shtm.
22. Vivien Crea, The U.S. coast guard: A flexible force for national security, *Naval War College Review*, 60 (Winter 2007): 15–23.
23. T. Allen, New threats, new challenges: The coast guard's new strategy, *Proceedings*, 133 (March 2007): 74.
24. B. B. Stubbs, U.S. coast guard annual review, *Proceedings*, 133 (May 2007): 84.
25. Stubbs, *Proceedings*, 84; See also *The US Coast Guard of the 21st Century*, www.uscg.mil/history/articles/21stcentury.pdf.
26. Department of Homeland Security, Homeland Security Advisory Council, Quadrennial Review Advisory Committee: Final Report 8–9 (May 27, 2010).

Chapter 3

Homeland Security Law, Regulations, and Budgeting

Objectives

1. To identify the major laws, regulations, and executive orders that form and govern the Department of Homeland Security (DHS).
2. To analyze Executive Order 13228, which created DHS, and Executive Order 12231, which focuses on the national infrastructure and its protection.
3. To summarize the provisions of the Homeland Security Act of 2002.
4. To describe the USA Patriot Act, its provisions, and authority.
5. To comprehend the various specialized laws that govern certain operations within DHS, such as the REAL ID Program, US-VISIT, the SAFETY Act, and the like.
6. To explain the reasoning behind budgeting priorities in DHS and why the priorities fluctuate from year to year.
7. To compare the changes in allotments and priorities in DHS budgets from the agency's inception to the present.
8. To predict where future allotments in DHS budgets may change and why.

3.1 Introduction

Exactly how the affairs of DHS are managed is an ongoing and very vibrant topic. The power of DHS emanates from the legal authority that initiated its existence. Laws, regulations, and executive orders enable the agency so that it might carry out its aim and purpose. Many laws touch upon the functions of homeland defense, such as in matters of privacy, arrest, search, and wire-tap, while other laws establish centers of research, operational funds for new initiatives or primer for a new directive. Funding for DHS is just as important. Without money, the agency would have no life whatsoever. How Congress and the President eventually agree to fund DHS is an annual responsibility. From another management perspective, DHS needs to evaluate how it interacts with other governmental authorities—namely, state and local entities; this is a perpetual policy concern and consideration for DHS. If anything is certain, it is that DHS needs to collaborate at every governmental level. Just as importantly, DHS will need to work closely and cooperatively with private sector justice as well, since private sector justice is the country's fastest-growing arm in the criminal justice body. Privatization is a reality that must be factored in as DHS manages its affairs.

3.2 Homeland Security Law, Regulations, and Executive Orders

The power of DHS is derived from its legal authority. Soon after the September 11, 2001, attacks, President George W. Bush sought to establish an agency dedicated to the protection of the homeland. The speed with which these promulgations occurred not only can impress but also manifests the urgency of these tragic events.

3.2.1 Executive Order 13228: The Origin of DHS

By executive order dated October 11, 2001, the President calls for the establishment of DHS, lays out its mission, categorizes its purpose and aim, and sets an early tone for how this agency will develop. See Figure 3.1.

3.2.2 Executive Order 12231: Protection of Infrastructure

Shortly thereafter, President Bush issued another executive order that focused on the nation's infrastructure. Given the recent events, the President, as well as Congress, was rightfully concerned about the country's infrastructure of transportation, water, energy and power plants, and other essential components of the American way of life. At the time, there were serious, very legitimate concerns about these facilities. Executive Order 12231 (Figure 3.2), signed October 16, 2001, dealt directly with infrastructure.

EXECUTIVE ORDER: ESTABLISHING THE OFFICE OF HOMELAND SECURITY AND THE HOMELAND SECURITY COUNCIL

By the authority vested in me as President by the Constitution and the laws of the United States of America, it is hereby ordered as follows:

Section 1. Establishment. I hereby establish within the Executive Office of the President an Office of Homeland Security (the "Office") to be headed by the Assistant to the President for Homeland Security.

Section 2. Mission. The mission of the Office shall be to develop and coordinate the implementation of a comprehensive national strategy to secure the United States from terrorist threats or attacks. The Office shall perform the functions necessary to carry out this mission, including the functions specified in section 3 of this order.

Section 3. Functions. The functions of the Office shall be to coordinate the executive branch's efforts to detect, prepare for, prevent, protect against, respond to, and recover from terrorist attacks within the United States.

a. National Strategy. The Office shall work with executive departments and agencies, state and local governments, and private entities to ensure the adequacy of the national strategy for detecting, preparing for, preventing, protecting against, responding to, and recovering from terrorist threats or attacks within the United States and shall periodically review and coordinate revisions to that strategy as necessary.
b. Detection. The Office shall identify priorities and coordinate efforts for collection and analysis of information within the United States regarding threats of terrorism against the United States and activities of terrorists or terrorist groups within the United States. The Office also shall identify, in coordination with the Assistant to the President for National Security Affairs, priorities for collection of intelligence outside the United States regarding threats of terrorism within the United States.
    i. In performing these functions, the Office shall work with federal, state, and local agencies, as appropriate, to:
        A. Facilitate collection from state and local governments and private entities of information pertaining to terrorist threats or activities within the United States;
        B. Coordinate and prioritize the requirements for foreign intelligence relating to terrorism within the United States of executive departments and agencies responsible for homeland security and provide these requirements and priorities to the Director of Central Intelligence and other agencies responsible collection of foreign intelligence;
        C. Coordinate efforts to ensure that all executive departments and agencies that have intelligence collection responsibilities have sufficient technological capabilities and resources to collect intelligence and data relating to terrorist activities or possible terrorist acts within the United States, working with the Assistant to the President for National Security Affairs, as appropriate;
        D. Coordinate development of monitoring protocols and equipment for use in detecting the release of biological, chemical, and radiological hazards; and
        E. Ensure that, to the extent permitted by law, all appropriate and necessary intelligence and law enforcement information relating to homeland security is disseminated to and exchanged among appropriate executive departments and agencies responsible for homeland security and, where appropriate for reasons of homeland security, promote exchange of such information with and among state and local governments and private entities.
    ii. Executive departments and agencies shall, to the extent permitted by law, make available to the Office all information relating to terrorist threats and activities within the United States.

FIGURE 3.1 Executive order establishing DHS.

c. Preparedness. The Office of Homeland Security shall coordinate national efforts to prepare for and mitigate the consequences of terrorist threats or attacks within the United States. In performing this function, the Office shall work with federal, state, and local agencies, and private entities, as appropriate, to:
   i. Review and assess the adequacy of the portions of all Federal emergency response plans that pertain to terrorist threats or attacks within the United States;
   ii. Coordinate domestic exercises and simulations designed to assess and practice systems that would be called upon to respond to a terrorist threat or attack within the United States and coordinate programs and activities for training federal, state, and local employees who would be called upon to respond to such a threat or attack;
   iii. Coordinate national efforts to ensure public health preparedness for a terrorist attack, including reviewing vaccination policies and reviewing the adequacy of and, if necessary, increasing vaccine and pharmaceutical stockpiles and hospital capacity;
   iv. Coordinate Federal assistance to state and local authorities and nongovernmental organizations to prepare for and respond to terrorist threats or attacks within the United States;
   v. Ensure that national preparedness programs and activities for terrorist threats or attacks are developed and are regularly evaluated under appropriate standards and that resources are allocated to improving and sustaining preparedness based on such evaluations; and
   vi. Ensure the readiness and coordinated deployment of Federal response teams to respond to terrorist threats or attacks, working with the Assistant to the President for National Security Affairs, when appropriate.

d. Prevention. The Office shall coordinate efforts to prevent terrorist attacks within the United States. In performing this function, the Office shall work with federal, state, and local agencies, and private entities, as appropriate, to:
   i. Facilitate the exchange of information among such agencies relating to immigration and visa matters and shipments of cargo; and, working with the Assistant to the President for National Security Affairs, ensure coordination among such agencies to prevent the entry of terrorists and terrorist materials and supplies into the United States and facilitate removal of such terrorists from the United States, when appropriate;
   ii. Coordinate efforts to investigate terrorist threats and attacks within the United States; and
   iii. Coordinate efforts to improve the security of United States borders, territorial waters, and airspace in order to prevent acts of terrorism within the United States, working with the Assistant to the President for National Security Affairs, when appropriate.

e. Protection. The Office shall coordinate efforts to protect the United States and its critical infrastructure from the consequences of terrorist attacks. In performing this function, the Office shall work with federal, state, and local agencies, and private entities, as appropriate, to:
   i. Strengthen measures for protecting energy production, transmission, and distribution services and critical facilities; other utilities; telecommunications; facilities that produce, use, store, or dispose of nuclear material; and other critical infrastructure services and critical facilities within the United States from terrorist attack;
   ii. Coordinate efforts to protect critical public and privately owned information systems within the United States from terrorist attack;
   iii. Develop criteria for reviewing whether appropriate security measures are in place at major public and privately owned facilities within the United States;
   iv. Coordinate domestic efforts to ensure that special events determined by appropriate senior officials to have national significance are protected from terrorist attack;
   v. Coordinate efforts to protect transportation systems within the United States, including railways, highways, shipping, ports and waterways, and airports and civilian aircraft, from terrorist attack;
   vi. Coordinate efforts to protect United States livestock, agriculture, and systems for the provision of water and food for human use and consumption from terrorist attack; and

FIGURE 3.1 (continued) Executive order establishing DHS.

   vii. Coordinate efforts to prevent unauthorized access to, development of, and unlawful importation into the United States of, chemical, biological, radiological, nuclear, explosive, or other related materials that have the potential to be used in terrorist attacks.

f. Response and Recovery. The Office shall coordinate efforts to respond to and promote recovery from terrorist threats or attacks within the United States. In performing this function, the Office shall work with federal, state, and local agencies, and private entities, as appropriate, to:
   i. Coordinate efforts to ensure rapid restoration of transportation systems, energy production, transmission, and distribution systems; telecommunications; other utilities; and other critical infrastructure facilities after disruption by a terrorist threat or attack;
   ii. Coordinate efforts to ensure rapid restoration of public and private critical information systems after disruption by a terrorist threat or attack;
   iii. Work with the National Economic Council to coordinate efforts to stabilize United States financial markets after a terrorist threat or attack and manage the immediate economic and financial consequences of the incident;
   iv. Coordinate Federal plans and programs to provide medical, financial, and other assistance to victims of terrorist attacks and their families; and
   v. Coordinate containment and removal of biological, chemical, radiological, explosive, or other hazardous materials in the event of a terrorist threat or attack involving such hazards and coordinate efforts to mitigate the effects of such an attack.

g. Incident Management. The Assistant to the President for Homeland Security shall be the individual primarily responsible for coordinating the domestic response efforts of all departments and agencies in the event of an imminent terrorist threat and during and in the immediate aftermath of a terrorist attack within the United States and shall be the principal point of contact for and to the President with respect to coordination of such efforts. The Assistant to the President for Homeland Security shall coordinate with the Assistant to the President for National Security Affairs, as appropriate.

h. Continuity of Government. The Assistant to the President for Homeland Security, in coordination with the Assistant to the President for National Security Affairs, shall review plans and preparations for ensuring the continuity of the Federal Government in the event of a terrorist attack that threatens the safety and security of the United States Government or its leadership.

i. Public Affairs. The Office, subject to the direction of the White House Office of Communications, shall coordinate the strategy of the executive branch for communicating with the public in the event of a terrorist threat or attack within the United States. The Office also shall coordinate the development of programs for educating the public about the nature of terrorist threats and appropriate precautions and responses.

j. Cooperation with State and Local Governments and Private Entities. The Office shall encourage and invite the participation of state and local governments and private entities, as appropriate, in carrying out the Office's functions.

k. Review of Legal Authorities and Development of Legislative Proposals. The Office shall coordinate a periodic review and assessment of the legal authorities available to executive departments and agencies to permit them to perform the functions described in this order. When the Office determines that such legal authorities are inadequate, the Office shall develop, in consultation with executive departments and agencies, proposals for presidential action and legislative proposals for submission to the Office of Management and Budget to enhance the ability of executive departments and agencies to perform those functions. The Office shall work with state and local governments in assessing the adequacy of their legal authorities to permit them to detect, prepare for, prevent, protect against, and recover from terrorist threats and attacks.

l. Budget Review. The Assistant to the President for Homeland Security, in consultation with the Director of the Office of Management and Budget (the "Director") and the heads of executive departments and agencies, shall identify programs that contribute to

FIGURE 3.1 (continued) Executive order establishing DHS.

the Administration's strategy for homeland security and, in the development of the President's annual budget submission, shall review and provide advice to the heads of departments and agencies for such programs. The Assistant to the President for Homeland Security shall provide advice to the Director on the level and use of funding in departments and agencies for homeland security-related activities and, prior to the Director's forwarding of the proposed annual budget submission to the President for transmittal to the Congress, shall certify to the Director the funding levels that the Assistant to the President for Homeland Security believes are necessary and appropriate for the homeland security-related activities of the executive branch.

GEORGE W. BUSH
THE WHITE HOUSE,
October 8, 2001.

FIGURE 3.1 (continued) Executive order establishing DHS.

By the authority vested in me as President by the Constitution and the laws of the United States of America, and in order to ensure protection of information systems for critical infrastructure, including emergency preparedness communications, and the physical assets that support such systems, in the information age, it is hereby ordered as follows:

Section 1. Policy.

a. The information technology revolution has changed the way business is transacted, government operates, and national defense is conducted. Those three functions now depend on an interdependent network of critical information infrastructures. The protection program authorized by this order shall consist of continuous efforts to secure information systems for critical infrastructure, including emergency preparedness communications, and the physical assets that support such systems. Protection of these systems is essential to the telecommunications, energy, financial services, manufacturing, water, transportation, health care, and emergency services sectors.
b. It is the policy of the United States to protect against disruption of the operation of information systems for critical infrastructure and thereby help to protect the people, economy, essential human and government services, and national security of the United States, and to ensure that any disruptions that occur are infrequent, of minimal duration, and manageable, and cause the least damage possible. The implementation of this policy shall include a voluntary public–private partnership, involving corporate and nongovernmental organizations.

Section 2. Scope. To achieve this policy, there shall be a senior executive branch board to coordinate and have cognizance of Federal efforts and programs that relate to protection of information systems and involve:

a. Cooperation with and protection of private sector critical infrastructure, state and local governments, critical infrastructure, and supporting programs in corporate and academic organizations;
b. Protection of Federal departments, and agencies, critical infrastructure; and
c. Related national security programs.

Section 3. Establishment. I hereby establish the "President's Critical Infrastructure Protection Board" (the "Board").

FIGURE 3.2 Executive order on critical infrastructure protection.

Internet Resource: For final administrative rules on the protection of infrastructure, see http://a257.g.akamaitech.net/7/257/2422/01jan20061800/edocket.access.gpo.gov/2006/06-7378.htm.

The Executive branch's view of infrastructure has been heightened over the term of President Barack Obama. In matters of funding and operational priorities, President Obama has repeatedly emphasized the interconnectedness of our infrastructure assets and urges agencies to prioritize the protection of our infrastructure in a more holistic way. By Presidential Proclamation 8607, President Obama declared that December 2010 was "Critical Infrastructure Protection Month" and noted that infrastructure is "essential to the security, economic welfare, public health and safety of the United States."[1]

3.2.3 Executive Order 13493 of January 22, 2009

Soon after his installation as President, Barack Obama reiterated his long-held view that the Guantanamo facility and its interrogation practices should be ended. In early 2009, he issued an order setting up a Commission to end the status quo and seek transfer and other disposition of those residing in the facility. This promise was quite controversial. The Order posed in part:

Review of Detention Policy Options

> By the authority vested in me as President by the Constitution and the laws of the United States of America, in order to develop policies for the detention, trial, transfer, release, or other disposition of individuals captured or apprehended in connection with armed conflicts and counterterrorism operations that are consistent with the national security and foreign policy interests of the United States and the interests of justice, I hereby order as follows:
>
> Section 1. Special Interagency Task Force on Detainee Disposition.
>
> (a) Establishment of Special Interagency Task Force. There shall be established a Special Task Force on Detainee Disposition (Special Task Force) to identify lawful options for the disposition of individuals captured or apprehended in connection with armed conflicts and counterterrorism operations.[2]

The sum and substance of this decree was to find ways to end Guantanamo operations. However, while the president promised this policy during his first presidential campaign and in the early days of his administration, the decree has not been realized. By 2011, his position on Guantanamo was reversed. In January of that year he signed the Defense Authorization Bill, essentially restricting the transfer of Guantanamo prisoners to other countries and the U.S. mainland. President Obama further clarified his position on Guantanamo in March 2011 when he signed Executive Order 13567.

3.2.4 Executive Order 13567 of March 7, 2011

Disposing of some of the world's most suspect figures in the underbelly of terrorism can be quite a challenge. President Obama, after nearly 26 months in office essentially reverses himself on the closure of Guantanamo Bay by an order calling for periodic review and assessment of the prison's inhabitants.

The more pertinent part of the Order declares:

> Section 1. Scope and Purpose.
>
> a. The periodic review described in section 3 of this order applies only to those detainees held at Guantanamo on the date of this order, whom the interagency review established by Executive Order 13492 has (i) designated for continued law of war detention; or (ii) referred for prosecution, except for those detainees against whom charges are pending or a judgment of conviction has been entered.
>
> b. This order is intended solely to establish, as a discretionary matter, a process to review on a periodic basis the executive branch's continued, discretionary exercise of existing detention authority in individual cases. It does not create any additional or separate source of detention authority, and it does not affect the scope of detention authority under existing law. Detainees at Guantanamo have the constitutional privilege of the writ of habeas corpus, and nothing in this order is intended to affect the jurisdiction of Federal courts to determine the legality of their detention.
>
> c. In the event detainees covered by this order are transferred from Guantanamo to another U.S. detention facility where they remain in law of war detention, this order shall continue to apply to them.
>
> Section 2. Standard for Continued Detention. Continued law of war detention is warranted for a detainee subject to the periodic review in section 3 of this order if it is necessary.[3]

At Section 2 of the Order, the President makes plain that continued detention is within the discretionary authority of the United States under law of war principles. President Obama has been severely critiqued for essentially maintaining the policy of former George Bush. "The American Civil Liberties Union has been less than kind about the determination holding the decree shameful."[4]

3.2.5 Homeland Security Act of 2002

At the congressional level, there was nothing but cooperation during the early stages of homeland security policy. By November 2002, Congress had passed the Homeland Security Act of 2002. The act was a comprehensive response to terror threats at every level. A summary of the act's provisions is outlined in its table of contents (Figure 3.3).

TITLE I—DEPARTMENT OF HOMELAND SECURITY		
	Sec. 101.	Executive department; mission.
	Sec. 102.	Secretary; functions.
	Sec. 103.	Other officers.
TITLE II—INFORMATION ANALYSIS AND INFRASTRUCTURE PROTECTION		
	Sec. 201.	Under Secretary for Information Analysis and Infrastructure Protection.
	Sec. 202.	Functions transferred.
	Sec. 203.	Access to information.
	Sec. 204.	Information voluntarily provided.
TITLE III—CHEMICAL, BIOLOGICAL, RADIOLOGICAL, AND NUCLEAR COUNTERMEASURES		
	Sec. 301.	Under Secretary for Chemical, Biological, Radiological, and Nuclear Countermeasures.
	Sec. 302.	Functions transferred.
	Sec. 303.	Conduct of certain public health-related activities.
	Sec. 304.	Military activities.
TITLE IV—BORDER AND TRANSPORTATION SECURITY		
	Sec. 401.	Under Secretary for Border and Transportation Security.
	Sec. 402.	Functions transferred.
	Sec. 403.	Visa issuance.
TITLE V—EMERGENCY PREPAREDNESS AND RESPONSE		
	Sec. 501.	Under Secretary for Emergency Preparedness and Response.
	Sec. 502.	Functions transferred.
	Sec. 503.	Nuclear incident response.
	Sec. 504.	Definition.
	Sec. 505.	Conduct of certain public health-related activities.
TITLE VI—MANAGEMENT		
	Sec. 601.	Under Secretary for Management.
	Sec. 602.	Chief Financial Officer.
	Sec. 603.	Chief Information Officer.
TITLE VII—COORDINATION WITH NON-FEDERAL ENTITIES; INSPECTOR GENERAL; UNITED STATES SECRET SERVICE; GENERAL PROVISIONS		
Subtitle A—Coordination with Non-Federal Entities		
	Sec. 701.	Responsibilities.
Subtitle B—Inspector General		
	Sec. 710.	Authority of the Secretary.
Subtitle C—United States Secret Service		
	Sec. 720.	Functions transferred.
Subtitle D—General Provisions		
	Sec. 730.	Establishment of human resources management system.
	Sec. 731.	Advisory committees.
	Sec. 732.	Acquisitions; property.
	Sec. 733.	Reorganization; transfer.

FIGURE 3.3 Table of contents of the *Homeland Security Act of 2002*.

	Sec. 734.	Miscellaneous provisions.
	Sec. 735.	Authorization of appropriations.
TITLE VIII—TRANSITION		
	Sec. 801.	Definitions.
	Sec. 802.	Transfer of agencies.
	Sec. 803.	Transitional authorities.
	Sec. 804.	Savings provisions.
	Sec. 805.	Terminations.
	Sec. 806.	Incidental transfers.
TITLE IX—CONFORMING AND TECHNICAL AMENDMENTS		
	Sec. 901.	Inspector General Act.
	Sec. 902.	Executive Schedule.
	Sec. 903.	United States Secret Service.
	Sec. 904.	Coast Guard.
	Sec. 905.	Strategic National Stockpile and smallpox vaccine development.
	Sec. 906.	Select agent registration.
	Sec. 907.	National Bio-Weapons Defense Analysis Center.

FIGURE 3.3 (continued) Table of contents of the *Homeland Security Act of 2002*.

The act lays out a national blueprint for homeland security and delineates the areas of vital national interest: borders; information and infrastructure; chemical, biological, and nuclear threats; and emergency preparedness and response. The act has been subject to various revisions over the last 6 years regarding critical infrastructure, financial reporting and accountability problems, as well as various privacy clarifications. The act is a work in progress by any measure.

3.2.5.1 The Homeland Security Act and Posse Comitatus

An often overlooked section of the Homeland Security Act makes reference to the *Posse Comitatus Act of 1878*. The Posse Comitatus Act, passed June 18, 1878, essentially outlines limits on the federal government's use of military forces for purposes of law enforcement. Section 886 of the Homeland Security Act refers to Posse Comitatus:

> SEC 886(b) SENSE OF CONGRESS.—Congress reaffirms the continued importance of section 1385 of title 18, United States Code, and it is the sense of Congress that nothing in this Act should be construed to alter the applicability of such section to any use of the Armed Forces as a posse comitatus to execute the laws.[5]

Section 1385 of title 18 is the reference to Posse Comitatus and, per November 11, 2002 remarks for then-President George W. Bush, essentially the

Homeland Security Act and Section 886(b) "does not purport to alter, modify, or otherwise affect the Posse Comitatus Act or judicial interpretations of that Act, and the executive branch shall construe this provision accordingly."[6]

This becomes relevant and creates an interesting debate, however, as on October 1, 2002, just past the one-year anniversary of 9/11, United States Northern Command (USNORTHCOM, or simply, NORTHCOM) was created. A Unified Combatant Command (UCC) of the U.S. military, meaning it has multiple branches of the military under a single command, its purpose is to provide command and control of Department of Defense (DoD) homeland defense efforts and to coordinate defense support of civil authorities. In recent years, there has been a growing debate among politicians, and government policymakers and scholars over what role, if any, the U.S. military should take in domestic operations. Though not exempt when deployed under federal service, The National Guard is exempt during peacetime or when specifically called upon by state governors during crisis and disaster situations. The Coast Guard too is likewise exempt from Posse Comitatus.

Since its creation, NORTHCOM has aided in counter-drug operations as well as in response to Hurricane Katrina, multiple California and Colorado wildfires, as well as other similar regional domestic natural disaster events. It remains to be seen what the ultimate policy on and role of NORTHCOM will be in responding to natural disasters or mass civil disturbances in future.

3.2.6 USA Patriot Act

One of the most controversial pieces of legislation that arose from the turbulent post-9/11 period was the Patriot Act. The Patriot Act was developed out of the belief that our intelligence had been so poor prior to the attacks. It sought to remediate the perceived failures in intelligence and ensure such an attack would never occur again. Patriot Act proposals, swiftly drafted, were just as quickly signed and executed by President Bush on October 26, 2001. Given the intensity of the times, it is not surprising that a bill of this import found formal approval in so short a span. The times influenced the aggressive nature of the bill. A thumbnail sketch of the act displays this inclination to expand or alter historic restrictions:

- Information sharing—The Act liberalizes the sharing of intelligence information and removes most historical barriers to said sharing. Critics argue that the data will be used by other agencies for unrelated purposes or improper reasons.
- Roving wiretaps—The Act permits the jurisdictional grant of one wiretap order that works or roves in multiple jurisdictions. Given the

transiency of terrorists, and the difficulties of dealing with diverse jurisdictions, the policy makes sense. Critics claim it will lead to an open-ended form of electronic surveillance.

- Foreign intelligence and wiretaps—The act liberalizes the grant and extent of this activity. New standards for use have been enacted. Critics claim this will lead to abuse.
- Sneak and peek warrants—In criminal parlance, "exigent" circumstances have always permitted law enforcement to search a house without a warrant. The act permits quick searches, without notification, of a suspected terrorist place of abode under an "any crime" provision. Critics note that the historic standard of these types of searches relates to loss of evidence or other exigency.
- Material support—The act expands the definition of support to include advice and counsel. Historically "material" support related to economic or planning support that was central to the plot and plan. The idea of how one can support has been expanded. Critics claim this violates free speech.

The Patriot Act was reauthorized in 2006 despite significant controversy.[7] See Figure 3.4.

One of the act's most formidable allies was DHS. DHS publicly advocated for passage of the reauthorization since it had amassed concrete examples of how effective the act had been in the apprehension of terrorists and

FIGURE 3.4 President George W. Bush is joined by House and Senate representatives as he signs H.R. 3199, USA Patriot Improvement and Reauthorization Act of 2005, Thursday, March 9, 2006, in the East Room of the White House. (White House photo by Eric Draper.)

prevention of terror. In December 2005, DHS exhorted Congress to finish up its business relative to the act by noting:

> The Department of Homeland Security (DHS) benefits significantly from the USA Patriot Act and urges the United States Congress to reauthorize this proven tool in the global war on terror. The Patriot Act breaks down barriers to information sharing, enabling law enforcement and intelligence personnel to share information that is needed to help connect the dots and disrupt potential terror and criminal activity before they can carry out their plots. The broad information sharing provisions better enables U.S. Customs and Border Protection to screen international visitors and determine whether an apprehended alien presents a threat to security or public safety.[8]

Internet Resource: To see the more important changes in the reauthorization bill, go to http://www.govtrack.us/congress/bill.xpd?bill=h109-3199&tab=summary.

During 2010–2011, the Patriot Act was reauthorized although the debate was spirited and highly contentious on both sides of the aisle. The dissent even crossed party lines as liberals construed the broad sweep of police powers too unchecked while conservatives concerned about the constitutional implications reached similar conclusions.[9] In particular, the "roving wiretaps" provision, whereby investigators seeks court orders which allow changing phone number follow-ups without court scrutiny, was a stumbling block. The Act reiterated its three-part requirement when seeking the court order, namely:

- Establishing probable cause that the target of the surveillance is a foreign power or agent of a foreign power
- Probable cause that the device is being used or about to be used by a foreign power or agent of a foreign power
- That the actions of the target may have the effect of blocking their identification[10]

The reauthorized Act also retained the more liberal and flexible standard when seizing the business records of a suspected terrorist and instead of the historic "specific and articulable facts" requirement a court could issue an order based on a "relevancy standard."[11]

3.2.7 Specialized Laws

Aside from the broader legislation and regulations covering the world of homeland security, there are myriad other laws and rules promulgated on behalf of or by administrative agencies and departments entrusted with functions in homeland protection.

3.2.7.1 The REAL ID Program

Concerns over the legitimacy and integrity of driver's licenses resulted in the promulgation of a new DHS program—REAL ID.[12] The program sets minimal standards for the issuance of driver's licenses, including:

- Information and security features that must be incorporated into each card
- Proof of identity and U.S. citizenship or legal status of an applicant
- Verification of the source documents provided by an applicant
- Security standards for the offices that issue licenses and identification cards

Eventually, there is an integration of other ID triggers such as social security and birth certificates, but at this stage, the driver's license has yet to be systematically governed. Critics of the Act claim it devises a national identity card program, but this criticism seems somewhat inaccurate. The provisions of the act reaffirm the preeminence of state governments in the matter of issuance and oversight. DHS posts a Q&A piece that deals with common misconceptions regarding REAL ID, shown in Figure 3.5.

Myth: REAL ID creates a national identification (ID) card

Fact: REAL ID simply sets minimum standards so that the public can have confidence in the security and integrity of driver's licenses and identification cards issued by all participating states and jurisdictions.

States and jurisdictions will maintain their ability to design and issue their own unique driver's licenses and identification cards. Each state and jurisdiction will continue to have flexibility with regard to the design and security features used on the card. Where REAL ID details the minimum data elements that must be included on the face of the card, most states and jurisdictions already include all or almost all of these data elements on their cards.

REAL ID identification documents will not be the only form of documentation accepted by the federal government or any other entity. You can still present another form of acceptable identification such as a US passport, military ID, or government identification badge. If you do not have another form of acceptable documentation, however, you may experience delays at the airport due to the requirement for additional security screening.

Myth: REAL ID creates a national database of personal information

Fact: REAL ID requires that authorized DMV officials have the capability to verify that an applicant holds only one valid REAL ID. REAL ID does not grant the Federal Government or law enforcement greater access to DMV data, nor does it create a national database.

States will continue to manage and operate databases for driver's license and identification card issuance.

REAL ID does not create a national database or require additional personal information on your driver's license than is already required by most states. It simply verifies the documents an applicant presents at the DMV to confirm the individual's identity and ensure that each individual has only one valid REAL ID.

Personally identifiable information, beyond the minimum information necessary to appropriately route verification queries, will not be stored.

FIGURE 3.5 REAL ID myths and facts.

Myth: REAL ID will diminish privacy

Fact: The REAL ID final rule calls on states to protect personal identity information. It requires each state to develop a security plan and lists a number of privacy and security elements that must be included in the plan.

The DHS Privacy Office has also issued Best Practices for the Protection of Personally Identifiable Information Associated with State Implementation of the Real ID Act, which provides useful guidance to states on how to address the privacy and security of information related to REAL ID.

The REAL ID Act will not allow motor vehicle driver's data to be made available in a manner that does not conform to the Driver's Privacy Protection Act. Furthermore, with REAL ID, DMV employees will be subject to background checks, a necessary step to protect against insider fraud, just one of the vulnerabilities to a secure licensing system. These steps raise the bar for state DMVs beyond what was previously required.

DHS recognizes the importance of protecting privacy and ensuring the security of the personal information associated with implementation of the REAL ID Act.

Myth: DHS is creating a "hub" in order to gain access to Department of Motor Vehicle (DMV) information

Fact: An electronic verification hub will be designed to facilitate connectivity between the states and data owners to ensure that people applying for a REAL ID are who they say they are. The Federal Government will not gain greater access to DMV information as a result. Only authorized DMV officials and law enforcement will have access to DMV records.

REAL ID requires state DMVs to verify an applicant's identity document, date of birth, Social Security Number, residence and lawful status, as well as ensure that each individual has only one valid REAL ID. For example, the electronic verification hub will facilitate the state-to-state exchange of information to check for duplicate registrations in multiple states, therefore limiting the ability for persons to obtain multiple licenses for fraudulent purposes.

While DHS has pledged to fund the development and deployment of the hub, states will continue to manage and operate databases for driver's license and identification card issuance. DHS and the states will work together to ensure that security measures are in place to prevent unauthorized access or use of the information. Personally identifiable information, beyond the minimum information necessary to appropriately route verification queries, will not be stored.

Myth: REAL ID is an unfunded mandate

Fact: To date, approximately $90 million in dedicated grant funds have been offered by DHS to assist states with REAL ID implementation. This includes approximately $40 million in Fiscal Year (FY) 2006 and $50 million in FY 2008. An additional 20% of State Homeland Security Grant funds are discretionary and can be used for this purpose as well.

The President's Fiscal Year 2009 budget request includes up to $150 million in grants for states to implement REAL ID (up to $110 million from National Security and Terrorism Prevention Grants and again, 20% of the State Homeland Security Grants).

DHS requested $50 million in Fiscal Year 2009 appropriated funds for the establishment of a state-owned and operated verification system. Furthermore, DHS cut the total costs to states by more than $10 billion from an original estimate of $14.6 billion to approximately $3.9 billion, a 73% reduction. States will continue to have discretionary authority to use up to 20% of their Homeland Security Grant funds for REAL ID implementation.

In order to focus the first phase of enrollment on those persons who may present the highest risk, DHS outlined an age-based enrollment approach to REAL ID allowing other individuals to be phased-in later. Phased-in enrollment eases the burden on states to re-enroll their entire driver's license and identification card population by providing additional time to accommodate the re-enrollment process.

FIGURE 3.5 (continued) REAL ID myths and facts.

Even DHS fosters an ambivalent and less than supportive view of the program due to costs and implementation challenges. In its Inspector General report, DHS remarked:

> Potentially high costs pose a significant challenge to states in their efforts to implement REAL ID. Specifically, state officials considered REAL ID implementation costs prohibitive because of requirements such as the reenrollment of all current driver's license and identification card holders and the new verification processes. Further, state officials in 17 of the 19 states we contacted indicated they needed more timely guidance from DHS to estimate the full cost of implementing REAL ID. State officials also said that REAL ID grants did not sufficiently mitigate the costs, and they viewed communication of grant information by DHS as ineffective.[13]

With nearly a decade of legislative life, the REAL ID program has yet to fully materialize on a state-by-state level. Implementation results have been dramatically mixed. By 2011, only 11 states had completely implemented the program.[14]

> Pace and commitment still differ among the states, but there is a noteworthy reduction in discussion as states are finding out implementation, on the whole, is not as expensive as they thought and is achievable. States like Maryland and Delaware, once committed, have completed implementation of the 18 benchmarks needed to fulfill material compliance with the law within a year for only twice the grant monies provided by the federal government. Extrapolated out, that puts total costs for implementing these key 18 REAL ID benchmarks in a range from $350 million to $750 million, an order of magnitude less than estimated previously. And with metrics in place, the story of REAL ID's value in securing against fraud is beginning to take shape as not simply theory, but reality.[15]

The card design requirements are estimated at 1.1 billion dollars.[16] See Figure 3.6 for an overview of state-by-state implementation.

While compliance dates have been extended twice now, it appears unlikely that most states will ever be compliant with the diverse requirements of the Act. Critics have also called into question the constitutionality of this sort of federalized oversight in the matter of national identity.[17]

3.2.7.2 Office of US-VISIT

The office of U.S. Visitor and Immigrant Status Indicator Technology (US-VISIT) resides in DHS and was established to track the entry and exit of travelers to the United States by biometric means—digital fingerprints and photographs. The guiding principles of US-VISIT are:

Driver License Security Implementation: System Connectivity and Grant Allocation by Jurisdiction

Jurisdiction	REAL ID Benchmarks Met to Date -18 by May 11, 2011 -all enrolled by 2017[1]	CDLIS[2] & NDR Commercial DL and Nat'l Driver Registry (problem driver)	SSOLV[3] (SSN check)	SAVE[4] (lawful presence required) *ID expires at end of authorized stay	EVVE[5] (digitized vital records) *DMV checks EVVE records	Grant Allocation FY08 ($79.875 mil.)[6]	Grant Allocation FY09 Part I ($48.575 mil.)[7]	Grant Allocation FY10 Part II ($48.000 mil.)	Total Grant Allocation to Date ($176.45 mil.) [total expenditure to comply with 18 benchmarks]
Alabama	18 + compliance mark	✓	✓	✓*	✓	$500,000	$1,060,774	$1,098,276	$2,209,050 [$15,061,141][8]
Alaska	7	✓	✓	✓		0[9]	$600,000	N/A	$600,000
American Samoa[10]	9					$300,000	$600,000	$651,877	$1,551,877
Arizona	12 (+1 partial)	✓	✓	✓*	✓ (partial)[11]	$2,721,110	$1,060,774	$1,098,276	$4,880,160
Arkansas	17	✓	✓	✓*	✓	$891,887	$755,987	$800,677	$2,448,551
California	11 (+3 partial)	✓	✓	✓*	✓[11]	$3,200,000	$1,648,250	$1,656,999	$6,505,249
Colorado	18	✓	✓	✓*	✓ (partial)[11]	$1,169,678	$755,987	$800,677	$2,726,342
Connecticut	17	✓	✓	✓	✓	$1,901,846	$755,987	$800,677	$3,458,510
Delaware	18 + compliance mark	✓	✓	✓*		$500,000	$600,000	$651,877	$1,751,877 [$3,075,000][12]
District of Columbia	14	✓	✓	✓*		$500,000	$600,000	$651,877	$1,751,877
Florida	18 + compliance mark	✓	✓	✓*		$3,750,926[13]	$1,648,250	$1,656,999	$7,056,175 [$945,030][14]
Georgia	15	✓	✓	✓*		$2,478,043	$1,060,774	$1,098,276	$4,637,093
Guam	5				✓ (partial)[11]	$300,000	$600,000	$651,877	$1,551,877
Hawaii	3 (+2 partial)	✓	✓	✓[11]	✓	$470,000	$755,987	$800,677	$2,026,664
Idaho	13 (+3 partial)	✓	✓	✓*		0	$755,987	$800,677	$1,556,664
Illinois	9 (+ 9 partial)	✓	✓	✓		$2,307,808	$1,648,250	$1,656,999	$5,613,057
Indiana	18 + compliance mark	✓	✓	✓*	✓ (partial)[11]	$3,149,637[15]	$1,060,774	$1,098,276	$5,308,687
Iowa	18	✓	✓	✓*	✓*	$1,211,326	$755,987	$800,677	$2,767,990 [$2,093,000][16]
Kansas	18 + compliance mark	✓	✓	✓	✓	$925,026	$755,987	$800,677	$2,481,690
Kentucky	18	✓	✓	✓*	✓	$1,003,087[17]	$755,987	$800,677	$2,559,751
Louisiana	9 (+4 partial)	✓	✓	✓*		0	$1,060,774	$1,098,276	$2,159,050
Maine	8 (+3 partial)	✓	✓	✓*		$1,023,911	$755,987	$800,677	$2,580,575
Maryland	18	✓	✓	✓*[11]		$1,138,000	$755,987	$800,677	$2,694,664 [$5,872,000][18]
Massachusetts	6 (+2 partial)	✓	✓	✓	✓ (partial)[11]	$1,609,635	$1,060,774	$1,098,276	$3,768,685
Michigan	12	✓	✓[11]	✓*	✓ (partial)[11]	$2,495,000	$1,060,774	$1,098,276	$4,654,050
Minnesota	11	✓	✓[11]	✓*	✓	$694,060	$755,987	N/A	$1,450,047
Mississippi	18	✓	✓	✓	✓[11]	$17,718,424[19]	$755,987	$800,677	$19,275,088
Missouri	13 (+2 partial)	✓	✓	✓*	✓	$548,293	$755,987	$800,677	$2,104,957
Montana	9[20]	✓	✓	✓*	✓	0	$600,000	N/A	$600,000
Nebraska	16 (+2 partial)	✓	✓	✓		$687,188	$755,987	$800,677	$2,243,852
Nevada	17	✓	✓	✓*		$2,893,607[21]	$755,987	$800,677	$4,450,271
New Hampshire	11 (+4 partial)	✓	✓	✓		0	$755,987	$800,677	$1,556,664
New Jersey	9	✓	✓	✓*	✓[11]	$1,287,489	$1,060,774	$1,098,276	$3,446,539
New Mexico	10 (+3 partial)	✓	✓			$500,000	$755,987	$800,677	$2,056,664
New York	16	✓	✓	✓	✓ (NYC only)	$2,255,748	$1,648,250	$1,656,999	$5,560,997
North Carolina	12 (+2 partial)	✓	✓	✓*		$1,799,000	$1,060,774	$1,098,276	$3,958,050
North Dakota	15	✓	✓	✓*	✓*	$500,000	$600,000	$651,877	$1,751,877
Northern Mariana Islands	N/A				✓[11]	0	$600,000	$651,877	$1,251,877
Ohio	13	✓	✓	✓*	✓[11]	$1,200,000	$1,060,774	$1,098,276	$3,359,050
Oklahoma	8[20]	✓	✓[11]	✓*	✓	0	$755,987	N/A	$755,987
Oregon	13	✓	✓	✓	✓[11]	$1,169,678	$755,987	$800,677	$2,726,342
Pennsylvania	13	✓	✓	✓*	✓ (partial)[11]	$2,042,800	$1,060,774	$1,098,276	$4,201,850
Puerto Rico	13					$300,000	$600,000	$651,877	$1,551,877
Rhode Island	9	✓	✓	✓	✓[18]	$500,000	$600,000	$651,877	$1,751,877
South Carolina	13 (+1 partial)	✓	✓	✓*		$500,000	$755,987	$800,677	$2,056,664
South Dakota	18 + compliance mark	✓	✓	✓*	✓*	$300,000	$600,000	$651,877	$1,551,877
Tennessee	14	✓	✓	✓*		$694,060	$755,987	$800,677	$2,250,724
Texas	10 (+3 partial)	✓	✓	✓*		$3,200,000	$1,648,250	$1,656,999	$6,505,249
US Virgin Islands	4					$300,000	$600,000	$651,877	$1,551,877
Utah	18 + compliance mark	✓	✓	✓*[11]	✓	$1,006,418	$755,987	$800,677	$2,563,082
Vermont	9 (+5 partial)	✓	✓	✓*		$500,000	$600,000	$651,877	$1,301,877
Virginia	5 (+ 10 partial)	✓	✓	✓*		$2,660,252	$1,060,774	$1,098,276	$4,819,302
Washington	9[20]	✓	✓			0	$1,060,774	$1,098,276	$2,159,050
West Virginia	14	✓	✓	✓*		$500,000	$755,987	$800,677	$2,056,664
Wisconsin	14	✓	✓	✓*		$2,071,063[22]	$755,987	$800,677	$3,627,727[23]
Wyoming	17	✓	✓	✓*		$500,000	$600,000	$651,877	$1,751,877

FIGURE 3.6 Driver's license security implementation: system connectivity and grant allocation by jurisdiction.

- Enhance the security of U.S. citizens and visitors
- Facilitate legitimate travel and trade
- Ensure the integrity of the U.S. immigration system
- Protect the privacy of visitors to the United States

The use of biometrics represents the cutting edge of identity assurance. By using unique physical characteristics, the agency can zero in on identity in a highly dependable way. US-VISIT uses biometric information to

- Check a person's biometrics against a watch list of known or suspected terrorists, criminals, and immigration violators.
- Check against the entire database of all of the fingerprints DHS has collected since US-VISIT began to determine if a person is using an alias and attempting to use fraudulent identification.
- Check a person's biometrics against those associated with the identification document presented to ensure that the document belongs to the person presenting it and not someone else.

Presently, the office is proposing a series of protocols for visitation. Upon a person's entry into the United States, a Customs and Border Protection officer uses inkless, digital finger scanners to scan both the left and right index finger of the person. The officer also takes a digital photograph.

Internet Resource: See the DHS instructional guidance for visitors at http://www.dhs.gov/xlibrary/assets/usvisit/US-VISIT_Updated_Entry_StepxStep.pdf.

3.2.7.3 Chemical Facilities

DHS has been actively involved in the oversight of chemical facilities due to their capacity to inflict widespread damage. Antiterrorism standards must be integrated in the design, plan, and operational security of designated chemical facilities. Congress, in passage of the 2007 Homeland Security reauthorization,[18] applies these standards because of the inherent risk to these facilities. DHS defines the risk as:

- The consequence of a successful attack on a facility (consequence)
- The likelihood that an attack on a facility will be successful (vulnerability)
- The intent and capability of an adversary in respect to attacking a facility (threat)

DHS establishes risk-based performance standards for the security of the country's chemical facilities. Covered chemical facilities are required to:

- Prepare security vulnerability assessments, which identify facility security vulnerabilities

- Develop and implement site security plans, which include measures that satisfy the identified risk-based performance standards

Internet Resource: To see full coverage of the chemical facilities administrative regulations, go to http://www.dhs.gov/xlibrary/assets/chemsec_appendixafinalrule.pdf.

DHS publishes both a list of chemical products of significant interest to the country and a list of assessment tools to ensure compliance.[19] Chemical facilities are construed as infrastructure.

3.2.7.4 Invention and Technology: The SAFETY Act

One of the Homeland Security Act of 2002's best kept secrets was its desire to promote innovation in antiterrorism efforts. Innovation in technology is always a risky business. When the potential legal liabilities are added to the process of invention, such as being open to lawsuit, the inventor is less aggressive. The *Support Antiterrorism by Fostering Effective Technologies Act of 2002 (SAFETY Act)*[20] provides a safe harbor for the inventor and the product developer.

Internet Resource: For a PowerPoint presentation on the Act, see Protecting you, Protecting U.S.: SAFETY Act, May 2011, at http://www.stmarytx.edu/ctl/content/SAFETY_Act_Davidson.pdf.

It also provides a certification process whereby DHS approves a product for usage in the fight against terrorism. See Figure 3.7.

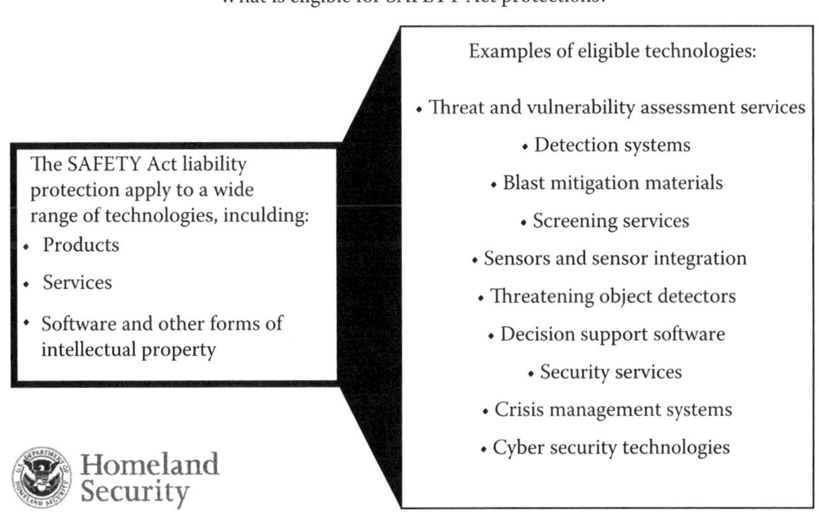

FIGURE 3.7 Technologies protected by the SAFETY Act.

As of 2012, hundreds of products and services have been approved. Here are some recent examples:

July 27, 2011—ASIS International provides ASIS International Certification, a certification process for security personnel, including Certified Protection Professional, Professional Certified Investigators, and Physical Security Professionals. This Designation will expire on August 31, 2016.

August 26, 2011—Mistral Security, Inc. provides its Blast Containment Receptacles, which are trash receptacles designed to absorb the blast energy and resist fragments of an explosive device concealed within the receptacle (the "Technology"). This renewed Designation and Certification will expire on September 30, 2016.

March 15, 2012—Ahura Scientific, Inc. provides FirstDefenderRMTM and FirstDefenderRMXTM. The Technology consists of two separate hand-held devices designed to identify various chemical substances using Raman spectroscopy. The Technology also includes user guides and training. This Designation and Certification will expire on March 31, 2017.

To be an approved seller or certified developer of antiterrorism technology, the party has to register. The process commences in a fairly simple way. See the registration document in Figure 3.8.

Internet Resources: For a full applicant guide, see https://www.safetyact.gov/DHS/SActHome.nsf/EFE2AA2BAA658F9E852573940007AC7E/$FILE/SA + AppKit.pdf.

3.3 Budgeting, Finance, and Funding in Homeland Security

Allocation of funds for operations depends on a multiplicity of factors. The age and history of a department influence funding. So too do the level of political importance and social and cultural demand for a particular service or program. Priorities in budgeting are guided by many forces.[21] In the very short life of DHS, we have witnessed a radical evolution and an equally radical budgetary maturation. In less than 8 years, DHS will grow exponentially in matters of budget. In each of those years, while its numbers will grow, it will decide on a new and hopefully improved allocation formula. From 2003 forward, Congress and the executive branch will look closely at how best to serve up these precious funds. What will be patently obvious is that the investment in homeland security has not been cheap.

The initial step in applying for the liability protections available under the SAFETY Act or for requesting a Pre-Application Consultation is to register with OSAI. Registration can be done electronically at the SAFETY Act website (http://www.safetyact.gov). You can also register by mail, using the forms included in this kit, or you can download an electronic copy of the form, complete it, and mail in the electronic document on a compact disc. Mailed registrations (hard copy or CD) should be sent to:

U.S. Department of Homeland Security
ATTN: Office of SAFETY Act
Implementation
245 Murray Lane, Building 410
Washington, DC 20528

Remember that physical mail sent to DHS is screened and processed, which may delay the Department's response to your submission. Registering with OSAI does not commit you to any further actions. The purpose of Registration is to establish an official point of contact for the Department to use in its interactions with you concerning your Technology and to create a unique identification number for you as a potential seller. This identifier will help the Department track and maintain your application. The SAFETY Act application process is designed to be flexible and to involve ongoing dialogue with the Applicant. Appropriate "points of contact" will facilitate this dialogue. The Applicant's point of contact may be any person you desire to coordinate your application and may include counsel, a representative of management, a technical expert or any other person you consider appropriate for this purpose.

(Registration Form on following page)

REGISTRATION AS A SELLER OF ANTITERRORISM TECHNOLOGY

ACTION

R1. Purpose of Registration *(choose one)*:
Initial Registration
Updated or Corrected Registration Information

REGISTRATION DATA

R2. Seller Name:
R3. Data Universal Numbering System (DUNS) Number (if available):
____
R4. North American Industry Classification System (NAICS) Code (if available):

POINT-OF-CONTACT INFORMATION

R5. Primary Point of Contact:
Name: ____
Address: ____
State/Province: ____________ Country: _____________ ZIP/Mail Code: _____________
Telephone No.: ____________ Fax No.: _____________ E-mail: ____________________
E-mail Communication Authorized? Yes No

R6. Secondary Point of Contact (*optional*):
Name: ____
Address: ____
State/Province: ____________ Country: _____________ ZIP/Mail Code: _______________
Telephone No.: ____________ Fax No.: _____________ E-mail: ______________________
E-mail Communication Authorized? Yes No

FIGURE 3.8 Registration as a seller of antiterrorism technology.

Instructions for Completing Registration Form:

ACTION

Item R1. Purpose of Registration

If your company or business unit has not previously registered with OSAI, check "Initial registration." A company may file more than one registration; certain companies may wish to file multiple registrations if it has multiple business units selling dissimilar types of Technologies. As a rule, the entity that sells the Technology is the entity that should register.

If you are updating or correcting previous registration information, check "Updated or Corrected Registration Information." OSAI strongly encourages you to keep your registration information up to date. In particular, be sure to notify OSAI of any changes in contact information.

REGISTRATION DATA

Item R2. Seller Name

Enter the legal name of your organization. If there will be business affiliates who will also be "sellers" of the Technology, please enter their legal names.

Item R3. Data Universal Numbering System (DUNS) Number

If your company has a nine-digit DUNS number, enter it here. If your company does not have a DUNS number, you do not need to provide one.

Item R4. North American Industry Classification System (NAICS) Code

NAICS Codes can be found in the official 2002 US NAICS Manual North American Industry Classification System—United States, 2002, available from the National Technical Information Service, (800) 553-6847 or (703) 605-6000), or directly from http://www.census.gov/epcd/www/naics.html.

POINT-OF-CONTACT INFORMATION

Item R5. Primary Point of Contact

Enter the name of the individual who will serve as the primary point of contact for interactions between your organization and OSAI. Provide a business address and telephone information for this person. OSAI prefers not to use personal or home contact information unless no other contact information is available. Include area codes and any non-US country codes in telephone and fax numbers. If you wish to permit OSAI to correspond with this individual by e-mail, enter a valid e-mail address in the space provided.

The Applicant's point of contact may be any person you desire to coordinate your application and may include counsel, a representative of management, a technical expert or any other person you consider appropriate for this purpose.

Item R6. Secondary Point of Contact

Enter the name and contact information for an alternate point of contact in your organization. OSAI will attempt to contact this person only if it is unable to reach the primary point of contact identified in item R5.

FIGURE 3.8 (continued) Registration as a seller of antiterrorism technology.

3.3.1 Budget Year: 2003

Since budgets are prepared a year in advance, the events of 9/11, happening close to the end of 2001, would make any 2002 budget a factual impossibility. At best, the funds earmarked for homeland security in early 2002 would strictly be supplemental in design. Add to this the fact that DHS had yet to become a complete department with cabinet status, and the budget for FY

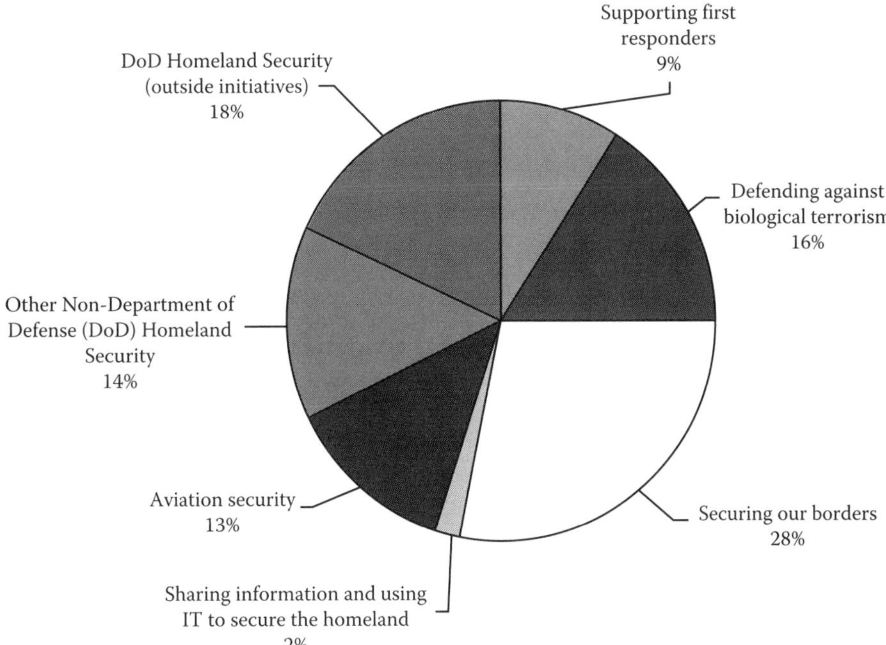

FIGURE 3.9 DHS budget allotments by activity. (George W. Bush, *Securing Our Homeland: Strengthening Our Future* (June 2001).)

2002 was nothing more than a hodgepodge of supplemental additions to existing agencies. By March 2003, the initial allocations were targeted for:

- Supporting first responders
- Defending against bioterrorism
- Securing America's borders
- Using twenty-first-century technology to secure the country

See Figure 3.9.

The lack of a centralized cabinet-level agency is obvious as money is distributed during this budget cycle. Departments such as FEMA and Justice, Health and Human Services and Energy, all share some portion of these homeland funds. In the 2003 budget cycle, the diversity of agencies participating will foretell the natural growing pains of an agency soon to be in the forefront. See Figure 3.10.

3.3.2 Budget Year: 2004

By mid-2003, the idea of a cabinet-level agency for homeland security had come to fruition. Like any new agency of government, special allotments, as start-up costs, so to speak, were issued. In addition, during the reorganization

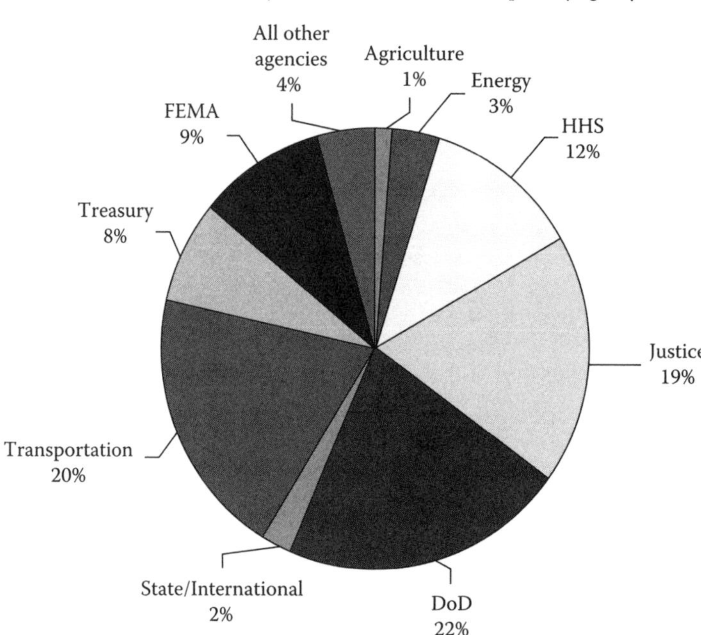

FIGURE 3.10 DHS budget allotments by agency. (George W. Bush, *Securing Our Homeland: Strengthening Our Future* (June 2001).)

phase of 2003, a host of agencies and departments, such as the Coast Guard and Secret Service, were merged into DHS. Hence, operational budgets must reflect these costs of operation. By late 2003 and into 2004, there was a cabinet mentality emerging in matters of homeland security. Yet despite this developing culture, there were a series of adjustments, both structurally and fiscally, that DHS had to go through. The Office of Management and Budget charted this truncated approach by displaying how agencies and their functions often mix and merge together. See Figure 3.11.[22]

Here, we witness how historic governmental entities, such as DoD and FEMA, the FBI and the Coast Guard, would continue historic contributions to the protection of the homeland. In time, more and more of these bifurcated functions coalesced into DHS. By 2004, DHS had centered its attention on four areas of responsibility:

- Border and transportation security—Encompasses airline security and inspection of cargo at points of entry into the United States to prevent unwanted individuals or weapons from entering the country.
- Domestic counterterrorism—Consists largely of federal law enforcement and investigative activities that center on identifying and apprehending terrorists. Primary responsibility for those activities rests with the Department of Justice's Federal Bureau of Investigation (FBI).

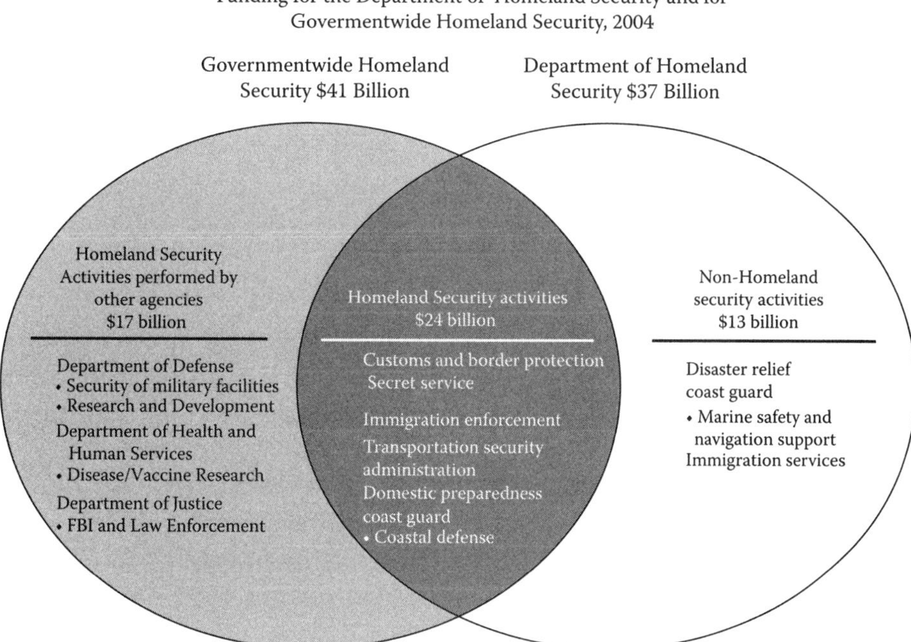

FIGURE 3.11 DHS funding and aligned governmental agency funding. (Congressional Budget Office.)

- Protection of critical infrastructure and key assets—Includes ensuring the physical security of national landmarks and critical infrastructure (e.g., bridges and power plants) as well as the physical security of federal buildings and installations. The DoD receives the largest share of funding for this purpose.
- Defense against catastrophic threats—Entails efforts to prevent terrorists from obtaining weapons of mass destruction (chemical, biological, or nuclear) and activities to mitigate the effects of such weapons if they are used. The Department of Health and Human Services (HHS) carries out most of those tasks.

With full department status, 2004 saw an extraordinary operational infusion. At the same time, the department stressed certain core values in its mission. Budgetary allotments mirrored these values, which were:

- Securing the nation's borders and transportation systems
- Securing the nation's ports and ensuring safety in our waters
- Improving information analysis and infrastructure protection
- Advancing and harnessing science and technology
- Preparing for and responding to national emergencies
- Improving immigration services
- Other DHS activities and support

FIGURE 3.12 U.S. Coast Guard's Deepwater logo.

As for border and transportation, DHS doubled the budget from the previous year, which largely reflected the cache of new employees—approximately 60,000 individuals were hired. Many of these employees were sent directly to the nation's airports to carry on the business of the Transportation Security Agency (TSA). Training funds were also widely disseminated to ensure a "same page" mentality among all agencies and departments, as well as state and local contributors responsible for homeland security.

As for ports and waterways, the emphasis was the same—to launch and support DHS initiatives. New maritime safety and security teams were developed; seed money for a maritime 911 was provided and multimillions given to the Coast Guard to shore up and increase its aging fleet. See Figure 3.12.

In the area of emergency response, the 2004 budget initiated the merger of FEMA and DHS, expanding and redefining the nature of disaster. From this budgetary cycle forward, DHS would see terror and hurricane from an identical prism. Billions were made available to develop a national stockpile for drugs, vaccines, and other medical supplies.

DETAILED INFORMATION ABOUT THE STOCKPILE: HELPING STATE AND LOCAL JURISDICTIONS PREPARE FOR A NATIONAL EMERGENCY

An act of terrorism (or a large-scale natural disaster) targeting the U.S. civilian population will require rapid access to large quantities of pharmaceuticals and medical supplies. Such quantities may not be readily available unless special stockpiles are created. No one can anticipate exactly where a terrorist will strike and few state or local governments have the resources to create sufficient stockpiles on their own. Therefore, a national stockpile has been created as a resource for all.

In 1999 Congress charged the HHS and the Centers for Disease Control and Prevention (CDC) with the establishment of the National Pharmaceutical Stockpile (NPS). The mission was to provide a re-supply of large quantities of essential medical materiel to states and communities during an emergency within 12 hours of the federal decision to deploy.

The Homeland Security Act of 2002 tasked DHS with defining the goals and performance requirements of the SNS program, as well as managing the actual deployment of assets. Effective on 1 March 2003, the NPS became the Strategic National Stockpile (SNS) Program managed jointly by DHS and HHS. With the signing of the BioShield legislation, the SNS Program was returned to HHS for oversight and guidance. The SNS Program works with governmental and nongovernmental partners to upgrade the nation's public health capacity to respond to a national emergency. Critical to the success of this initiative is ensuring capacity is developed at federal, state, and local levels to receive, stage, and dispense SNS assets. See Figure 3.13.

The SNS is a national repository of antibiotics, chemical antidotes, antitoxins, life-support medications, IV administration, airway maintenance supplies, and medical/surgical items. The SNS is designed to supplement and resupply state and local public health agencies in the event of a national emergency anywhere and at any time within the U.S. or its territories.

The SNS is organized for flexible response. The first line of support lies within the immediate response 12-h Push Packages. These are caches of pharmaceuticals, antidotes, and medical supplies designed to provide rapid delivery of a broad spectrum of assets for an ill-defined threat in the early hours of an event. These Push Packages are positioned in strategically located, secure warehouses ready for immediate deployment to a designated site within 12 h of the federal decision to deploy SNS assets.

If the incident requires additional pharmaceuticals and/or medical supplies, follow-on vendor managed inventory (VMI) supplies will be shipped to arrive within 24–36 h. If the agent is well defined, VMI can be tailored to provide pharmaceuticals, supplies, and/or products specific to the suspected or confirmed agent(s). In this case, the VMI could act as the first option for immediate response from the SNS Program.

FIGURE 3.13 A national repository of life-saving pharmaceuticals and medical materiel.

To advance the use of science and technology in the fight against terrorism, the 2004 budget proposed a sevenfold increase over the previous year. The key emphasis was the detection of radiological, chemical, nuclear, and biological threats. A total of $137 million was earmarked for detection systems in points of entry and within the transportation infrastructure, and $365 million was allotted for the detection and prevention of biological

FIGURE 3.14 National Biodefense Analysis and Countermeasures Center.

attacks and the implementation of a new department exclusively dedicated to these tasks—the National Biodefense Analysis and Countermeasures Center (NBACC). See Figure 3.14.

Internet Resource: Read a recent report on the progress, successes, and struggles in the development of the NBACC at http://www.fas.org/sgp/crs/homesec/RL32891.pdf.

ABOUT NATIONAL BIODEFENSE ANALYSIS AND COUNTERMEASURES CENTER

National Biodefense Analysis and Countermeasures Center

The gross space, or entire footprint of the facility, is expected to be about 160,000 square feet. This includes administrative areas, BSL-2, -3, and -4 laboratory spaces, air-handling equipment space, security controls, and other supporting features. NBACC expects to employ 120 researchers and support staff.

NBACC Interim Capability

An interim capability for the NBFAC has been established in partnership with the FBI and the U.S. Army at the U.S. Army Medical Research Institute of Infectious Diseases (USAMRIID). The BTCC supports risk assessment and threat characterization research in other established government and nongovernmental laboratories, including USAMRIID.

The NBACC facility is located at Fort Detrick, Maryland.

Safety Measures

The National Biodefense Analysis and Countermeasures Center will employ state-of-the-art biosafety procedures and equipment to prevent biological material from escaping into the environment. Rigorous safeguards protect those who work in the laboratory and the surrounding community.

Once construction is complete, the NBACC facility will feature proven safeguards, applying time-tested rigorous design standards, special safety equipment, and exacting operating procedures to govern all research.

These standards, equipment, and procedures have been demonstrated to provide the highest level of safety in existing laboratories elsewhere at Fort Detrick and throughout the United States.

The security of the NBACC facility will be safeguarded through strict control access at all times for those working in the laboratory facility. To gain access to select agents, individuals must complete an in-depth background investigation and demonstrate competency in safety and security equipment and procedures, in accordance with both DHS regulations and federal law.

By locating the NBACC facility at Fort Detrick, the Department leverages the security provided by the U.S. Army military garrison with bio containment-specific capabilities to create a controlled, secure environment.

In the area of information sharing and analysis and infrastructure protection, the DHS budget of 2004 funded shared databases, provided essential mechanisms for shared intelligence, and erected a 24/7 intelligence and warning system. The 2004 budget delivered funds to states and localities to develop partnerships and information-sharing systems as well as finances to establish compatible communication systems. The budget provided the necessary funds to create the Homeland Security Advisory Warning System. See Figure 3.15.

Finally, the 2004 budget recognized the dramatic need for improved immigration services. In particular, the budget fully recognized the negative impacts caused by chronic and continuous backlogs.

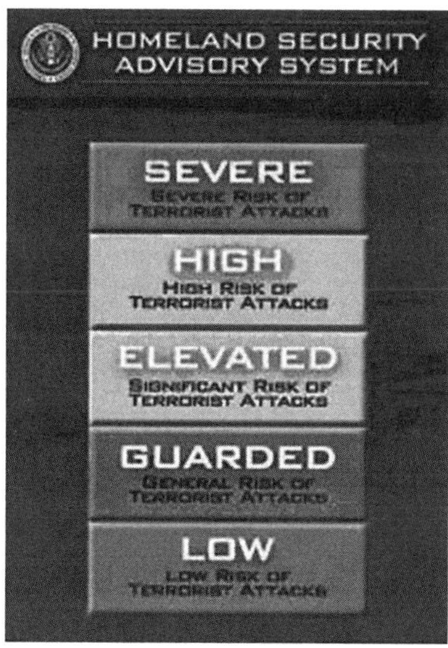

FIGURE 3.15 Levels of the Homeland Security Advisory System.

FIGURE 3.16 The Homeland Security Advisory Warning System was replaced by the National Terrorism Advisory System (NTAS).

By 2011, however, the National Advisory System, the color coded version posted, was scrapped in favor of National Terrorism Advisory System (NTAS). See Figure 3.16.

This new system provides timely, detailed information to the public, government agencies, first responders, airports and other transportation hubs, and the private sector about terrorist threats. See Figure 3.17[23] for a sample Alert format.

Finally, the 2004 budget recognized the dramatic need for improved immigration services. In particular, the budget fully recognized the negative impacts caused by chronic and continuous backlogs.

Internet Resource: For the documentary side of the immigration application, see http://www.uscis.gov/portal/site/uscis/menuitem.eb1d4c2a3e5b9ac89243c6a7543f6d1a/?vgnextoid=db029c7755cb9010VgnVCM10000045f3d6a1RCRD&vgnextchannel=db029c7755cb9010VgnVCM10000045f3d6a1 RCRD.

3.3.3 Budget Year: 2005

Expenditures for homeland defense reflected the growth and priorities of the agency. Now in its second full year of operation, DHS, aside from support for agency and its structure, targeted specific activities and honed its purpose. What is undeniably certain is that growth in the budget continued unabated.[24] See Figure 3.18.

As each year passes the department searches for best practices and discerns where the threat is most imminent. By 2005, DHS stressed ports and maritime security, streamlined preparedness models, enhanced bio-defense practices by increased use of science and technology, as well as provided sufficient funding for the training of first responders at the state and local levels.

Maritime concerns clearly took center stage in 2005 with the budget addressing numerous initiatives associated with port and shipping safety and security. Some examples worth noting are:

- The Container Security Initiative (CSI), which focuses on prescreening cargo before it reaches our shores. The first phase of CSI focused on implementing the program at the top 20 foreign ports, which ship approximately two-thirds of the containers to the United States.

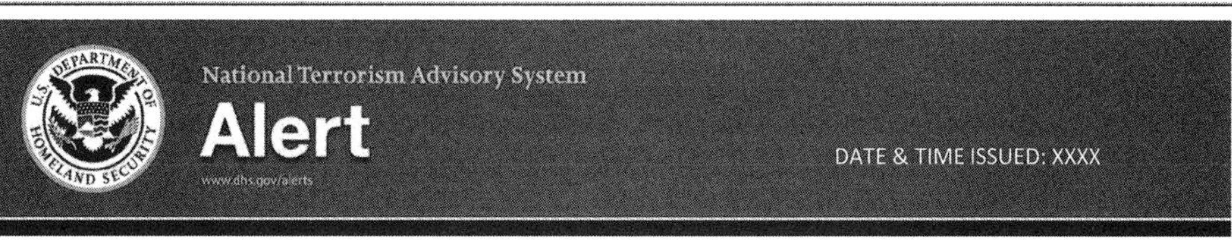

SUMMARY

The Secretary of Homeland Security informs the public and relevant government and private sector partners about a potential or actual threat with this alert, indicating whether there is an "imminent" or "elevated" threat.

DURATION

An individual threat alert is issued for a specific time period and then automatically expires. It may be extended if new information becomes available or the threat evolves.

DETAILS

- This section provides more detail about the threat and what the public and sectors need to know.
- It may include specific information, if available, about the nature and credibility of the threat, including the critical infrastructure sector(s) or location(s) that may be affected.
- It includes as much information as can be released publicly about actions being taken or planned by authorities to ensure public safety, such as increased protective actions and what the public may expect to see.

AFFECTED AREAS

- This section includes visual depictions (such as maps or other graphics) showing the affected location(s), sector(s), or other illustrative detail about the threat itself.

HOW YOU CAN HELP

- This section provides information on ways the public can help authorities (e.g. camera phone pictures taken at the site of an explosion), and reinforces the importance of reporting suspicious activity.
- It may ask the public or certain sectors to be alert for a particular item, situation, person, activity or developing trend.

STAY PREPARED

- This section emphasizes the importance of the public planning and preparing for emergencies before they happen, including specific steps individuals, families and businesses can take to ready themselves and their communities.
- It provides additional preparedness information that may be relevant based on this threat.

STAY INFORMED

- This section notifies the public about where to get more information.
- It encourages citizens to stay informed about updates from local public safety and community leaders.
- It includes a link to the DHS NTAS website http://www.dhs.gov/alerts and http://twitter.com/NTASAlerts

If You See Something, Say Something™. Report suspicious activity to local law enforcement or call 911.

The National Terrorism Advisory System provides Americans with alert information on homeland security threats. It is distributed by the Department of Homeland Security. More information is available at: www.dhs.gov/alerts. To receive mobile updates: www.twitter.com/NTASAlerts

If You See Something Say Something™ used with permission of the NY Metropolitan Transportation Authority.

FIGURE 3.17 Sample DHS National Terrorism Advisory System alert.

Phase II expands the program to additional ports based on volume, location, and strategic concerns. Phase III further increases security at the highest-risk ports. The three core elements of CSI are:

- Identify high-risk containers. Automated targeting tools are used to identify containers that pose a potential risk for terrorism, based on advance information and strategic intelligence.

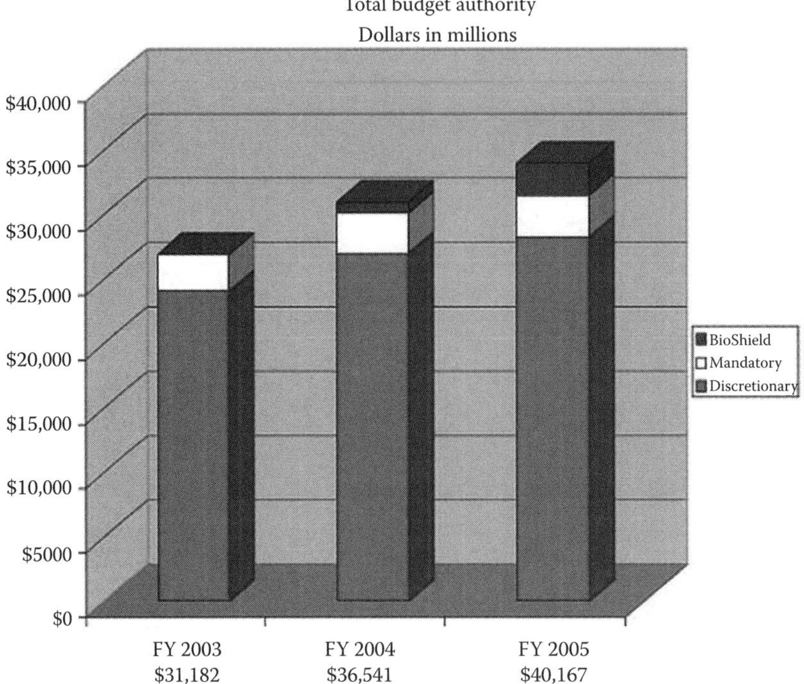

FIGURE 3.18 DHS funding 2003–2005.

- Prescreen and evaluate containers before they are shipped. Containers are screened as early in the supply chain as possible, generally at the port of departure.
- Use technology to prescreen high-risk containers to ensure that screening can be done rapidly without slowing down the movement of trade. This technology includes large-scale x-ray and gamma ray machines and radiation detection devices.

- The Customs Trade Partnership Against Terrorism (C-TPAT), which began in November 2001, is another essential cargo security effort. C-TPAT focuses on partnerships all along the entire supply chain, from the factory floor, to foreign vendors, to land borders and seaports.
- Customs and Border Protection (CBP) targeting systems aid in identifying high-risk cargo and passengers. The budget included an increase of $20.6 million for staffing and technology acquisition to support the National Targeting Center, trend analysis, and the automated targeting systems (Figure 3.19).
- The US-VISIT Program's first phase is being deployed at 115 airports and 14 seaports. US-VISIT expedites the arrival and departure of legitimate travelers, while making it more difficult for those intending to do us harm to enter our nation.

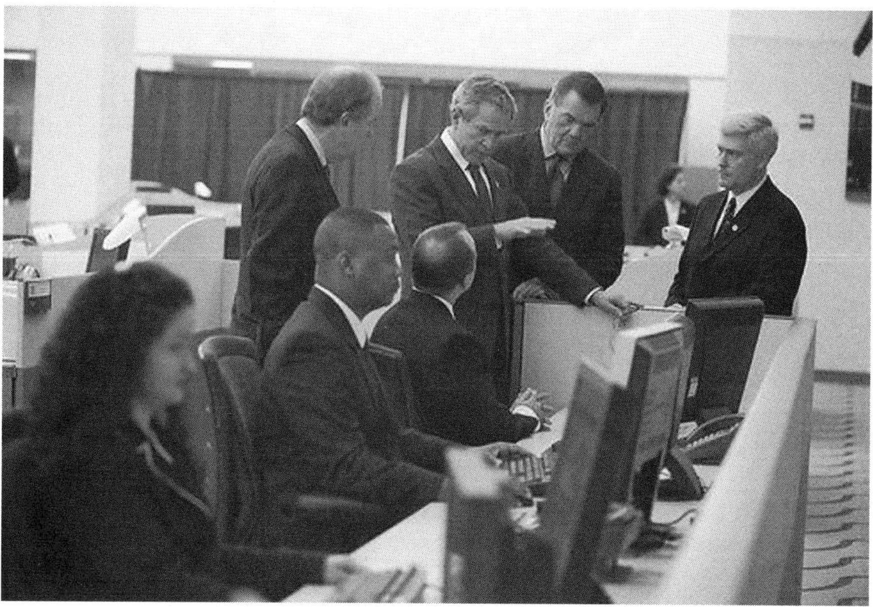

FIGURE 3.19 President George W. Bush tours the National Targeting Center (NTC) in Reston, Virginia, February 6, 2004. The NTC is part of Homeland Security's Bureau of Customs and Border Protection, and the center provides analytical research support for counterterrorism efforts.

- Radiation detection monitors screen passengers and cargo coming into the United States. The budget includes $50 million for the next generation of screening devices (Figure 3.20).
- Aerial surveillance and sensor technology increases the effectiveness of the more than 12,000 Border Patrol agents deployed along the northern and southern borders, and supports other missions, such as drug interdiction (Figure 3.21).

FIGURE 3.20 A radiation monitor at the entrance of a port. (Courtesy of International Atomic Energy Agency.)

FIGURE 3.21 Cargo ship at sea.

On the biodefense front, DHS advanced a mix of technology with proven practices in the fight against terrorism. Project BioShield purchased and collected essential vaccines and medications in the event of a biological attack. Particular emphasis was given to vaccines for smallpox and Anthrax exposure. In addition, just as in the nuclear theater, DHS expended millions developing and installing monitoring equipment that detects biological threats (Figure 3.22).

In the area of preparedness, the 2005 budget developed and implemented the National Incident Management System (NIMS) program and corresponding systems (Figure 3.23). NIMS is a program for all critical infrastructures and provides agencies, hospitals, and justice facilities with a plan of action that protects the facility and prevents attacks. In most jurisdictions, legislation now requires that staff and managers be educated in NIMS practices. NIMS trains and certifies both the personnel and agency.

In the information and infrastructure protection, the budget reflected increased concerns over cyber terrorism (Figure 3.24). Expending nearly $68 million on the National Cyber Security Division—a center that identifies and analyzes cyber vulnerability—the 2005 budget appreciated the extraordinary implications of threats in the virtual world.

Cyber security threats generally fall into the following categories:

- Attempts (either failed or successful) to gain unauthorized access to a system or its data, including PII-related incidents (link to the below description)
- Unwanted disruption or denial of service
- The unauthorized use of a system for processing or storing data

FIGURE 3.22 Example of a monitoring system installed at a port where cargo containers are unloaded. (www.whitehouse.gov.)

- Changes to system hardware, firmware, or software characteristics without the owner's knowledge, instruction, or consent

The budget also delivered funding to develop threat assessment tools for infrastructure protection. Strategic assessments of threats to the country's critical infrastructures and key assets, including 168,000 public water systems, 300,000 oil and natural gas production facilities, 4000 offshore platforms, 278,000 miles of natural gas pipelines, 361 seaports, 104 nuclear power plants, 80,000 dams, and tens of thousands of other potentially critical targets across 14 diverse critical infrastructure sectors, are a central aim of the budget.

The 2005 budget contributed more than just funding to the vision and plan of homeland security. Just as critically, the budget tied budgetary practices to general principles of accountability and assessment. In other words, the budget evaluated the efficacy of the disbursement in light of present strategic directions, future ambition of the departments, and overall accountability. As such, the budget became performance driven. Referring to a loop, the 2005 budget seeks to tie disbursement to effectiveness, as charted below in Figure 3.25.

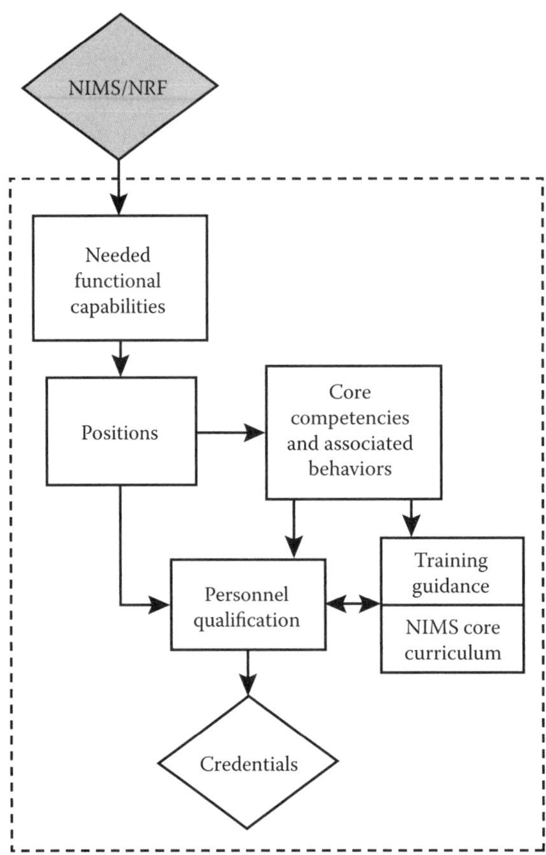

FIGURE 3.23 DHS, National Incident Management System (NIMS): Five-year NIMS training plan: National Integration Center (NIC), Incident Management Systems Integration (IMSI) Division, 4.

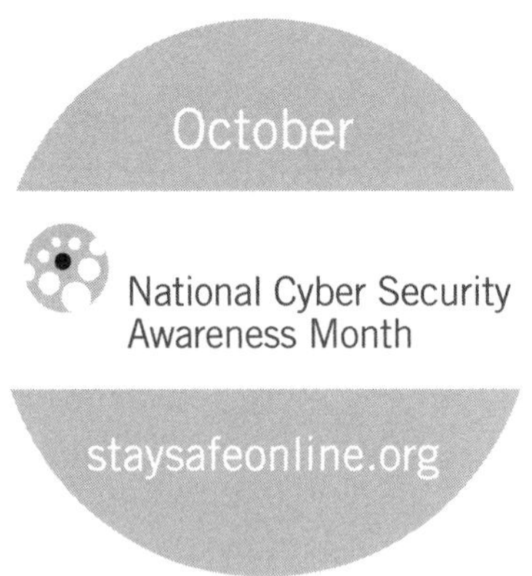

FIGURE 3.24 October is National Cyber Security Awareness Month.

FIGURE 3.25 Department of Homeland Security: performance budget overview FY 2005, at 3.

The goals and mission of DHS are evaluated in light of budgetary disbursement,[25] an example of which is shown in Figure 3.26.

3.3.4 Budget Year: 2006

Expenditures for homeland security continue the upward trek in the year 2006. When compared to 2005, the amount allotted for homeland protection is up 7%.[26] See Figure 3.27.

As each year passes, DHS expends more and more of its energy measuring and evaluating the effectiveness of its programs. In addition, it assesses all of its practices in light of changing demands and new detectable threats. To illustrate, the budget established the Domestic Nuclear Detection Office (DNDO), which seeks to detect and report efforts to acquire and deploy nuclear materials. The strategic objectives of the DNDO are:

- Develop the global nuclear detection and reporting architecture
- Develop, acquire, and support the domestic nuclear detection and reporting system
- Fully characterize detector system performance before deployment

Performance Goal: Establish a fully capable Command, Control, Operations, and Information Exchange System.

Measure: Percentage increase in time efficiency of issuance of information and warning advisories.	Fiscal Year	FY 2003	FY 2004	FY 2005
	Target	None	Baseline	Increase by 10%
	Actual	None	t.b.d.	t.b.d.
Program: Homeland Security Operations Center	$ Thousands	None	$20,878	$36,212
Lead Organization: Information Analysis and Infrastructure Protection Directorate	FTE	None	None	8

Performance Goal: Increase time efficiency of issuance of information and warnings advisories by fifty percent.

Measure: Time efficiency of issuance of information and warning advisories	Fiscal Year	FY 2003	FY 2004	FY 2005
	Target	None	Baseline	Increase by 10%
	Actual	None	t.b.d.	t.b.d.
Program: Information & Warning Advisories	$ Thousands	None	$79,314	$93,056
Lead Organization: Information Analysis and Infrastructure Protection Directorate	FTE	None	None	202

Performance Goal: Reduction of "general" warnings as compared to "at risk" warnings by sixty percent from 2003 levels.

Measure: Reduction of general warnings, as compared to "at risk" warnings	Fiscal Year	FY 2003	FY 2004	FY 2005
	Target	None	Baseline	20%
	Actual	None	t.b.d.	t.b.d.
Program: Infrastructure Vulnerability & Risk Assessment	$ Thousands	None	$95,173	$85,033
Lead Organization: Information Analysis and Infrastructure Protection Directorate	FTE	None	None	85

FIGURE 3.26 Performance goals for DHS.

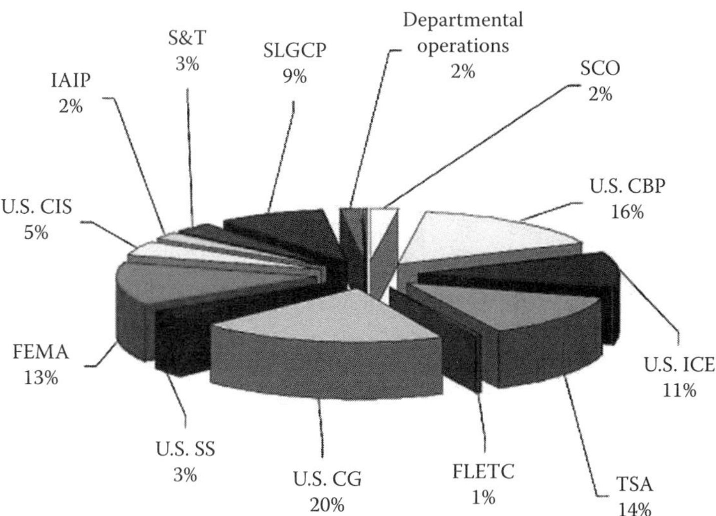

FIGURE 3.27 DHS budgetary lines 2006.

- Establish situational awareness through information sharing and analysis
- Establish operation protocols to ensure detection leads to effective response
- Conduct a transformational research and development program
- Establish the National Technical Nuclear Forensics Center to provide planning, integration, and improvements to USG nuclear forensics capabilities

The budget additionally consolidated a host of research, development, and testing offices into the Science and Technology Directorate. In the area of border security the line items recognize the increasing importance of safety and security at the country's geographic borders. Substantial funding for weapons of mass destruction (WMD) detection equipment became available, as well as the institution of America's Shield Initiative, which employs electronic surveillance equipment at our borders. Long-range radar technology, which detects and intercepts aircraft illegally entering the United States, received support as well.

The 2006 budget is generous in the area of law enforcement by supporting a host of initiatives, including:

- The Armed Helicopter for Homeland Security Project—A project to provide the Coast Guard with more firepower.
- Federal Air Marshal Service—$689 million for increased safety in the air.

FIGURE 3.28 U.S. Coast Guard at work. (U.S. Navy photo by Kelly Newlin.)

- Response boats, cutters—Increased budgeting for Coast Guard upgrades (Figure 3.28).
- Flight deck and crew training in self-defense.

The budget recognized the need for assistance to first responders by erecting the Office of State and Local Government Coordination and Preparedness (SLGCP). In the area of communications and first response, the Office of Interoperability and Compatibility will fund emergency systems to ensure compatible communication systems. As unbelievable as it may seem, emergency responders often cannot talk to some parts of their own agencies—let alone communicate with agencies in neighboring cities, counties, or states. DHS instituted the SAFECOM program, which plans and implements interoperability solutions for data and voice communications. Interoperability will succeed when the following five elements are achieved:

- Gain leadership commitment from all disciplines (e.g., EMS, fire rescue response, and law enforcement)
- Foster collaboration across disciplines through leadership support
- Interface with policymakers to gain leadership commitment and resource support
- Use interoperability solutions regularly

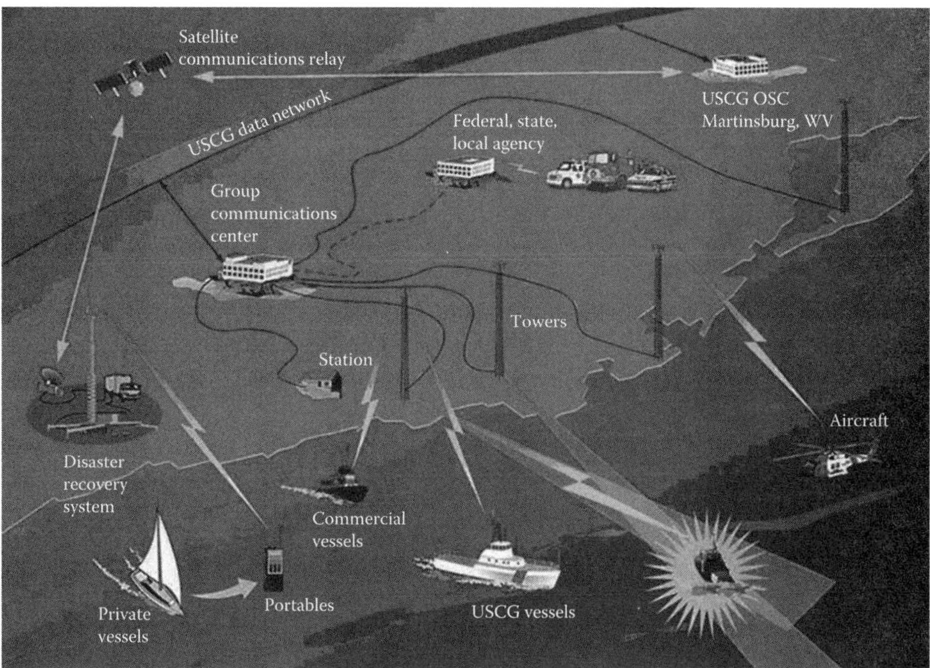

FIGURE 3.29 Rescue 21.

- Plan and budget for ongoing updates to systems, procedures, and documentation

Communication upgrades are in store for the U.S. Coast Guard. Rescue 21 will replace aging and often cumbersome equipment for Coast Guard service. See Figure 3.29.

How it works

- A call for help is sent
- Direction finding (DF) equipment from one or more high sites computes the direction from which the signal originated, or line of bearing (LOB)
- Distress audio and the LOB are sent to the closest Ground Center(s)
- Appropriate resources are dispatched to respond immediately—even across regional boundaries[27]

Other programs emphasized in the 2006 budget include internal funding for more efficient DHS operation, including human resources, information sharing, electronic data capability, high-speed operational connectivity, and sufficient funding to operate the Homeland Security Operations Center (HSOC) (Figure 3.30).

Internet Resource: To evaluate the 2006 budget in light of performance, visit http://www.dhs.gov/xlibrary/assets/Budget_PBO_FY2006.pdf.

FIGURE 3.30 The Homeland Security Operations Center. (www.whitehouse.gov.)

3.3.5 Budget Year: 2007

As DHS entered its fourth year of department status, it was clear that it continued to strive for efficiency in both an internal and an external sense. DHS is well aware that being prepared has much to do with prevention and mitigation of disaster in any form. To anticipate terror or plan for natural disaster forces the department to target its resources and focus its efforts on that is yet to happen. In this sense, the department is becoming a proactive, rather than strictly reactionary, entity.

In the world of preparedness, the 2007 budget expended a good deal of investment. Millions were directed to the National Preparedness Integration Program, a historic FEMA responsibility involving catastrophic planning, emergency communication improvements, and command and control alignment. FEMA received $29 million to reinforce its readiness, mitigation, response, recovery, and national security programs under the initiative Strengthen Operational Capability. Upgrades to the Emergency Alert System (EAS) were also provided. EAS is an integral part of the public alert and warning system in the United States. It provides the president and other authorized federal, state, and local officials the capability to transmit an emergency message to the public during disasters or crises. The national EAS, regulated by the Federal Communications Commission (FCC), is administered by DHS through the Federal Emergency Management Agency.

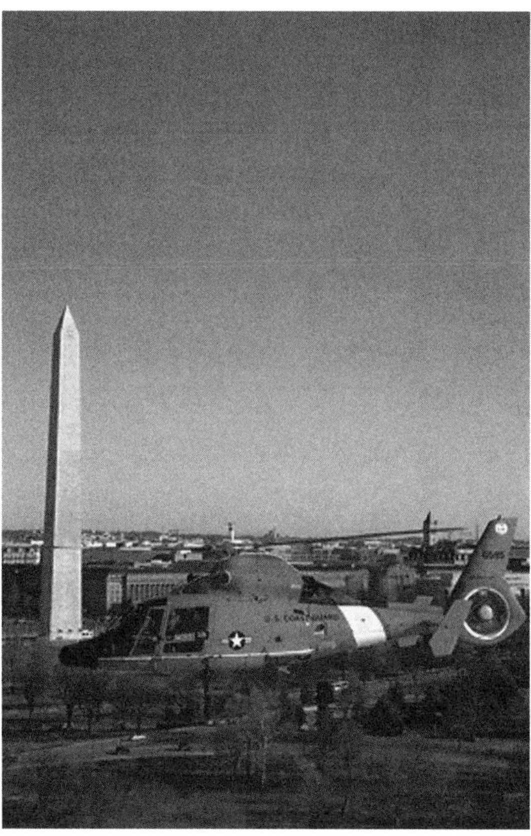

FIGURE 3.31 An HH65 Coast Guard helicopter passes by the Washington Monument during a National Capital Region Air Defense training mission.

Internet Resource: For a comprehensive critique of the EAS system, see http://www.gao.gov/new.items/d07411.pdf.

The Coast Guard received $60 million to enhance its National Capital Region Air Defense program (Figure 3.31).[28]

Border security and reform of the immigration process continued to see substantial support in the budgetary process up to and including 2007. Cutting-edge technology was employed across the borders by use of electronic surveillance. Coupled with technology and surveillance was an infusion of funds, some $459 million, to hire and train 3000 new border agents (Figure 3.32).

Additional fencing, detention beds, and work location and employment verification programs were included in the 2007 budget as well.

Maritime and cargo continued to be a forefront concern in the budgetary process in matters of homeland security in the year 2007. The use of technology continued to be heavily supported when it came to the detection of explosives, nuclear materials, and WMD (Figure 3.33).

At America's ports, the threat that may emerge from cargo is a story likely to be told in the future. Law enforcement cannot inspect all of the cargo

FIGURE 3.32 U.S. Border Patrol on Duty.

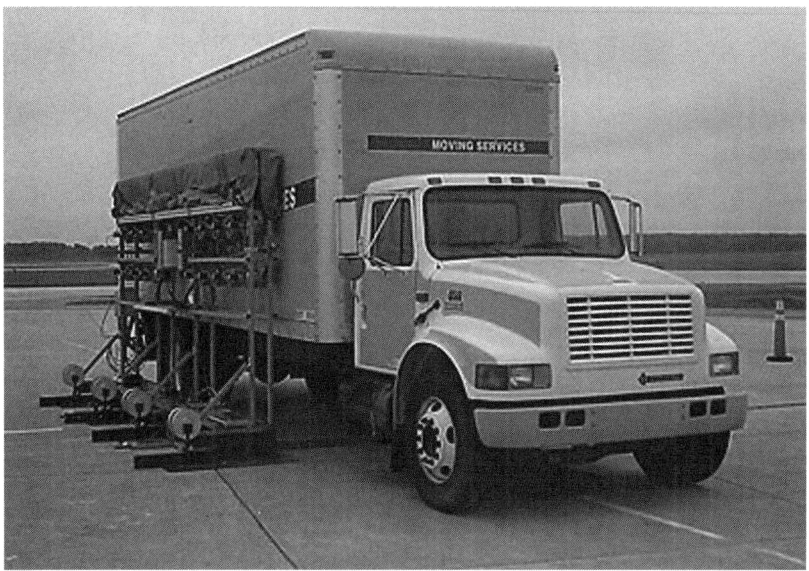

FIGURE 3.33 Explosive detection system.

that enters our ports since manual inspection would be ludicrous given the sheer volume of incoming goods. Advanced radiography is considered a sensible solution to inspecting the millions of cargo containers that enter the American shore each and every year. The 2007 budget funds Cargo Advanced Automated Radiography Systems.[29] See Figure 3.34.

Information sharing takes a preeminent position in the 2007 budget. In the world of IT infrastructure, DHS stressed the common and reliable e-mail

FIGURE 3.34 Radiographic image of a truck.

systems, the centralization of data centers, the modernization of desktops and workstations, and the update of voice, video, and wireless infrastructure. Nearly $50 million was geared to the Office of Intelligence and Analysis and the Operations Directorate, where threat information is analyzed and disseminated and other information pertinent to homeland threat sent to all partners and governmental entities. Of particular interest in 2007 was the Secure Border Initiative. The goals of the initiative are:

- More agents to patrol our borders, secure our ports of entry, and enforce immigration laws
- Expanded detention and removal capabilities to eliminate "catch and re-lease" once and for all
- A comprehensive and systemic upgrading of the technology used in controlling the border, including increased manned aerial assets, expanded use of UAVs, and next-generation detection technology
- Increased investment in infrastructure improvements at the border—providing additional physical security to sharply reduce illegal border crossings
- Greatly increased interior enforcement of our immigration laws—including more robust work site enforcement

The initiative's focus on fencing is quite a challenge; from autos and trucks to pedestrians, the erection of a border fence across the continental United States is a project in the making (Figure 3.35).

Finally, DHS will continue to infuse funds into its own internal operations in order that it might be an agency for the twenty-first century. Special disbursements for human services and procurements were made.

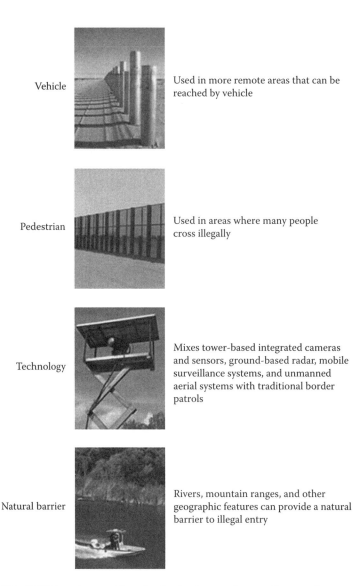

FIGURE 3.35 DHS barrier and border techniques. (www.dhs.gov.)

3.3.6 Budget Year: 2008

In its fifth year of operation, DHS had had sufficient time to examine its practices, to weigh and assess the effectiveness of its plan and operation, and to act and react to existing and novel challenges. What is plain is that budgets continue to rise and threats manifest an uncanny capacity to evolve. DHS needs to stay sharp and always on the offense to fend off a very dangerous world. Congress and the president seem to appreciate the financing demand DHS naturally entails. Since its inception, the budget has matured.[30] See Figure 3.36.

The mission of DHS stays firm and resolute in this budgetary process—first and foremost, to protect the country from danger and threat. Another

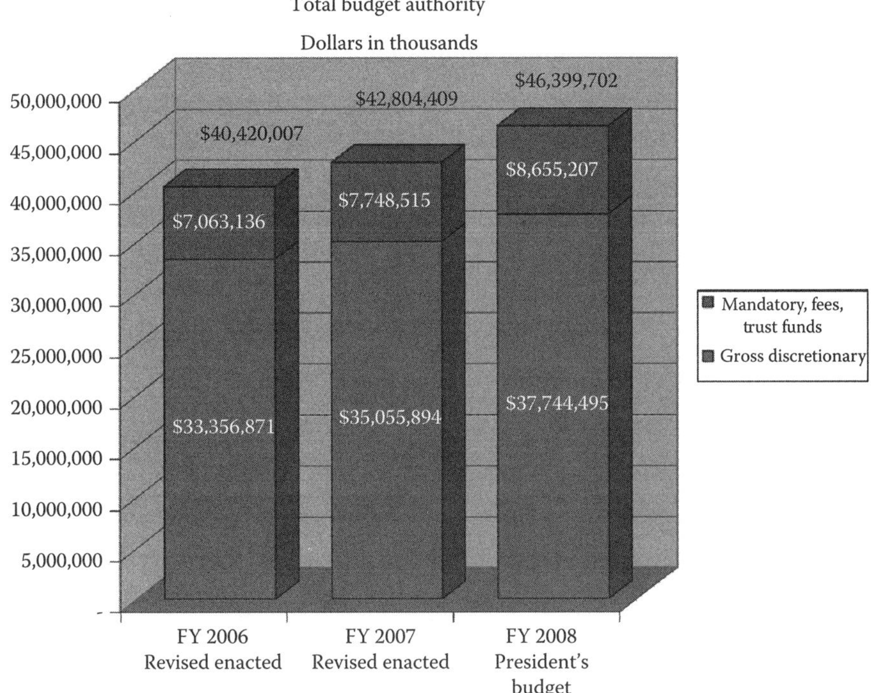

FIGURE 3.36 Budget growth: 2006–2008.

3000 Border Patrol agents were added during this cycle. The Transportation Security Administration saw increased funding for explosives detection, document processes, and the new identification programs.

Border protection received strong support in the 2008 budget. SBInet, a program instituted under the Secure Border Initiative, will provide form and structure to the 6000 miles of border in need of protection. The goal of this program, by technology, infrastructure, staffing, and response resource, is the integration of border protection into a single comprehensive border security suite for the department. U.S. Customs and Border Protection (CBP) will serve as executive agent for the department's SBInet program (Figure 3.37).

The goals of SBInet are:

- Ensure border security by providing resources and capabilities to gain and maintain control for the nation's borders at and between the points of entry
- Lead the development and deployment of a common operating picture (COP)
- Provide responsible acquisition management

Foreign visitors will be subject, depending on location of entry, to biometric screening or other advanced fingerprint imprint analysis (Figure 3.38).

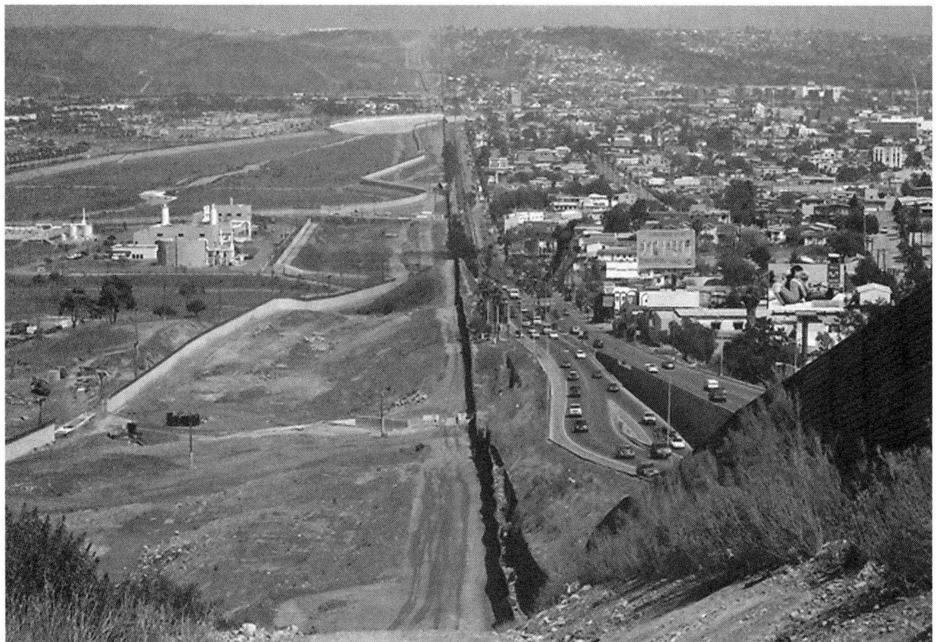

FIGURE 3.37 U.S.–Mexico border. Mexico is on the right.

FIGURE 3.38 A biometric fingerprint device. (Courtesy of CRT Computers.)

Included in the budget were funds to launch the Secure Flight system. Secure Flight will match limited passenger information against government watch lists to identify known and suspected terrorists, prevent known and suspected terrorists from boarding an aircraft, facilitate legitimate passenger air travel, and protect individual privacy. Secure Flight will:

- Identify known and suspected terrorists
- Prevent individuals on the No Fly List from boarding an aircraft
- Identify individuals for enhanced screening
- Facilitate passenger air travel by providing a fair, equitable, and consistent matching process across all aircraft operators

At our commercial ports and points of entry, the 2008 budget demonstrated innovation at the technological level. Advanced spectroscopic portal systems will scan and screen 98% of incoming containers at the end of the

Raytheon

Advanced Spectroscopic Portal (ASP)

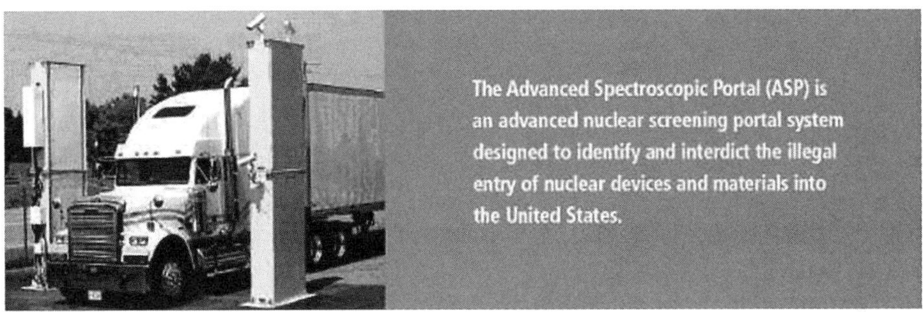

The Advanced Spectroscopic Portal (ASP) is an advanced nuclear screening portal system designed to identify and interdict the illegal entry of nuclear devices and materials into the United States.

Benefits

Critical defense tool for the Department of Homeland Security (DHS) and the Domestic Nuclear Detection Office (DNDO)

Senses nuclear materials at various points of entry into the United States, as well as other locations such as domestic checkpoints and rail lines

Capable of screening cars, trucks, cargo containers and mail

Modular architecture allows system to be mounted in several configurations

Multiple detector types ensure high gamma and neutron sensitivity over full range of usage conditions

Designed to minimize false alarms that would unnecessarily impede the flow of border traffic and commerce

System incorporates advanced threat identification algorithms

Designed to Counter Nuclear Threat

Covert nuclear attack is the foremost threat facing the United States today. The safety of the nation depends upon its ability to design and field systems to detect and interdict smuggled nuclear weapons and materials. For this reason, the ASP is a high-priority program within DHS and a key component of DNDO and other federal national nuclear detection initiatives to meet homeland security needs. By enhancing the country's early detection capabilities, ASP detectors address the threat of radiological dispersal devices, improvised nuclear devices or a nuclear weapon being used by terrorists inside the United States.

Upgrade Over Current Detector Portals

Since Sept. 11, 2001, the Bureau of Customs and Border Protection has deployed nearly 600 first-generation Radiation Portal Monitors at manned ports of entry, international mail and express consignment courier facilities, land border crossings, airports and seaports. As a point of reference, DHS reports that 360,000 vehicles, 5,100 trucks and containers, 2,600 aircraft, and 600 vessels cross into the United States at more than 600 points of entry every day.

Built with available technology, these first-generation Radiation Portal Monitors are unable to distinguish between legitimate naturally occurring radioactive materials such as fertilizer and bananas that are not harmful, and illicit materials that pose a threat. These situations necessitate secondary screening, which is manpower intensive and slows the flow of commerce. Therefore, a more discriminating primary screening system — the ASP — is needed.

FIGURE 3.39 Raytheon's advanced spectroscopic portal.

FIGURE 3.40 Secure freight initiative in Hamburg, Germany.

budget cycle. Raytheon delivered the first prototype and portal for commercial use in 2006. See Figure 3.39.

The Secure Freight program (Figure 3.40) received its start-up costs of $15 million in the 2008 budget. Secure Freight screens foreign containers bound for U.S. ports for radiological and nuclear risk. Containers are screened before leaving a foreign port. DHS and the Department of Energy will partner with international terminal operators, ocean carriers, and host governments.

Containers arriving at participating seaports overseas will be scanned with both nonintrusive radiographic imaging and passive radiation detection equipment placed at terminal arrival gates. Sensor and image data gathered regarding containers inbound to the United States will be encrypted and transmitted near real time to the National Targeting Center operated by DHS's Customs and Border Protection.

As for infrastructure, the 2008 budget heartily supported a continuation of the Domestic Nuclear Detection Office and established an Office of Innovation in the Directorate of Science and Technology. The S&T Directorate is the intellectual arm of DHS and a place of innovation and invention. Partnering with the private sector, national laboratories, universities, and other government agencies, the office promotes the use of high technology in support of homeland security.

The budget allotted a significant increase for chemical site security programs.

Internet Resource: Find out about the registration process for chemical facilities at http://www.dhs.gov/xprevprot/programs/gc_1169501486179.shtm.

From the vantage point of emergency preparedness, DHS works hard to finalize the acculturation of FEMA. FEMA has been an agency under siege since the days of Katrina, and it has taken heartfelt introspection and diligence to reset the agency moorings. The consolidation of FEMA into DHS caused further consternation for personnel. As a result, FEMA revisited its vision and overall mission and, upon completion, was given an additional $100 million to carry out these adjusted aims. FEMA will zero in on these activities:

- Incident management
- Hazard mitigation
- Operational planning
- Disaster logistics
- Service to disaster victims
- Public disaster communication
- Continuity programs

More than $3.2 billion was made available for state and local preparedness training. A total of $3.2 billion was allotted for state and local preparedness expenditures as well as assistance to firefighters. The Homeland Security Grants, Infrastructure Protection, Assistance to Firefighters, and PSIC Grant programs fund activities necessary to support the National Preparedness Goal and related national doctrine, such as the National Incident Management System (NIMS), National Response Plan (NRP), and the National Infrastructure Protection Plan (NIPP). Funds requested through these programs will (1) provide critical assistance to state and local homeland security efforts, (2) support resources available through other federal assistance programs that center on first responder terrorism preparedness activities, and (3) deliver support to all state and local first responder organizations (Figure 3.41).

Finally, the 2008 budget financed internal operations with the hope of improved efficiency at DHS. Funds were directed to internal oversight of personnel, further consolidation of duplicate functions and offices, a permanent Office of Chief Procurement, and increased funding for oversight and audit provided by the Office of the Inspector General.

3.3.7 Budget Years: 2009–2010

Not surprisingly, increased allocations for DHS activities continue their upward march. While it is not difficult to anticipate increasing expenditures for homeland security, it is not as simple to predict where portions of money will go for innovation or changed focus. To be sure, DHS will always have an operational side. Then too, DHS will most likely continue the bulk of its initiatives. Government can change, but the likelihood of radical change or whole-scale change is very remote. For 2009 and 2010,

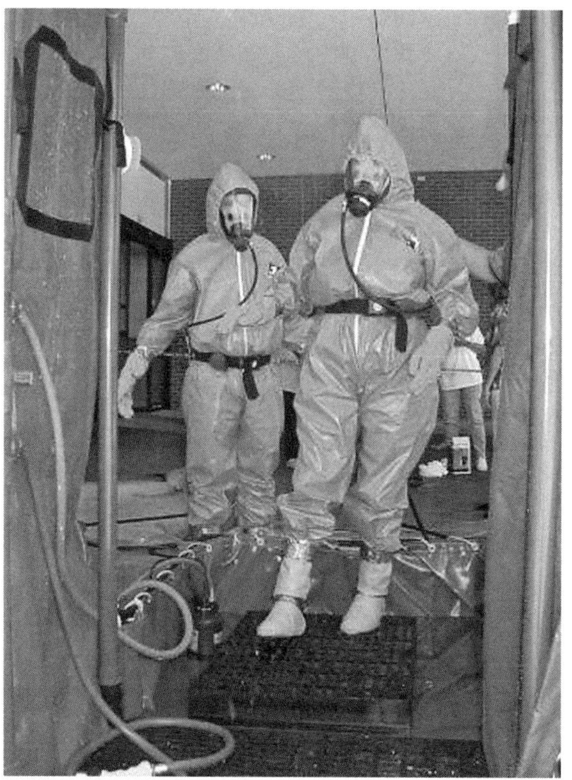

FIGURE 3.41 CBRN response drill.

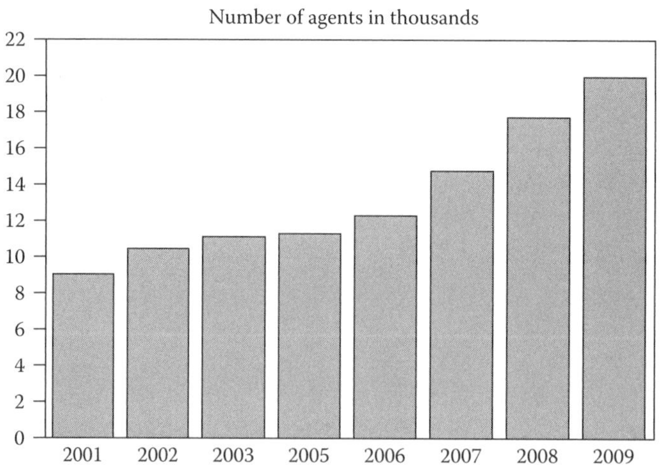

FIGURE 3.42 Border Patrol staffing, 2001–2009. (www.white.gov/omb/budget/fy2009/homeland.html.)

FIGURE 3.43 E-Verify logo.

DHS stayed true to its basic mission. Some of the proposed highlights were:

- Aggressive increase in Border Patrol—2200 new agents and further funding for Secure Flight (Figure 3.42).
- TSA Funds for ID programs and crew vetting as well as a new program that tracks international students.
- An automated, electronic system of worker verification, E-Verify. See Figure 3.43.
- $10 million in increased funding for FLETC relating to border enforcement.
- Increased funding for the U.S. Secret Service for equipment that detects WMD and other attack.
- IED research.

3.3.8 Budget Years: 2011–2012

Two forces were at work in the budgets posed by DHS officials and adopted or under legislative consideration. First, for the first time in its administrative life, there is actually discussion of better efficiencies and trimmed funding for DHS.[31] Across the governmental horizon, there is bleeding in federal overspending- and each agency is being asked to cull where it can. For example, DHS is required to conduct due diligence on its payments to vendors to assure proper amounts and reduce duplication in payments.[32] DHS is required to make public and publish incorrect payments. A few examples of high-dollar overpayments are charted at Figure 3.44.[33]

DHS continues its high-level emphasis on technology as a tool of efficiency. At the same time, despite the technological advances, the agency continues to splurge on employees and increased staff across various departments. What is clear is that budgets are moving across a relative flat-line—at least in a governmental sense. From 2010 to 2011, the department dips $118,000,000 in funds, though the proposed 2012 budget seeks an increase of those losses. See Figure 3.45[34] for a 3-year comparison.

Over the same 3-year period, one can glean some targeted spending as well as some de-emphasis. The proposed 2012 budget reduces funding to the following categories:

Department of Homeland Security
Current Status of Outstanding High-Dollar Overpayments Reported on the Previous Secretary's High-Dollar Overpayments Report for the Quarter Ending December 31, 2011

Debts Sent to the Treasury Offset Program for Collection

A	B	C	D	E	F	G	H	I	J	K	L
Component	**Recipient Type**	**City and State**	**Program(s) Responsible**	**Recovery Actions Taken or Planned**	**Payment Date**	**High $ Overpayment Date Identified**	**Amount Paid**	**Correct Amount**	**Recovered Amount**	**Outstanding Balance**	**Days Outstanding as of December 31, 2011**
FEMA	Individual	Seabrook, TX	Individuals and Households Payments	Recoupment package sent to individual. Debt later sent to the Treasury Offset Program for collection.	November 11, 2008	September 30, 2010	$19,239.54	$0.00	$0.00	$19,239.54	457
USCG	Entity	Miami, FL	Air Station Miami	Contacted vendor who confirmed overpayment. Vendor added to USCG "Do Not Pay List" with automatic offset of overpayment on next invoice. Debt sent to Treasury Offset Program for collection.	September 25, 2010	January 10, 2011	$76,740.37	$38,177.37	$0.00	$38,563.00	355
						Totals	$95,979.91	$38,177.37	$0.00	$57,802.54	

Debts Under Collection by DHS

FEMA	ENTITY	Carson City, NV	Homeland Security Grant Program	Additional supporting documentation received from grantee. FEMA reviewing for sufficiency with resolution expected by January 2012. DHS senior management to elevate this issue to FEMA senior management to ensure timely resolution. State is appealing improper payment.	September 30, 2009	August 5, 2010	$27,609.10	$0.00	$0.00	$27,609.10	513

FIGURE 3.44 High dollar overpayments still in the collection process.

Debts Under Collection by DHS

FEMA	ENTITY	District of Columbia, DC	Homeland Security Grant Program	Program office completed a review of recipient provided documentation and fully discussed results with grant recipient. Proper support was found for an additional $1,348,108.50 of the original payment. A collection bill for the remaining $643,115.65 was sent.	August 19, 2009	July 28, 2010	$3,133,009.25	$2,489,893.60	$0.00	$643,115.65	521
USCG	INDIVIDUAL	Seattle, WA	Coast Guard Pay & Personnel Center/ Direct Access	Notice of Overpayment sent to member and copy to Servicing Personnel Office. Collection by payroll deductions begun.	November 11, 2008	June 15, 2011	$8,903.21	$1,051.71	$1,023.96	$6,827.54	199
						Totals	$3,169,521.56	$2,490,945.31	$1,023.96	$677,552.29	
						Grand Totals	$3,265,501.47	$2,529,122.68	$1,023.96	$735,354.83	

FIGURE 3.44 (continued) High dollar overpayments still in the collection process.

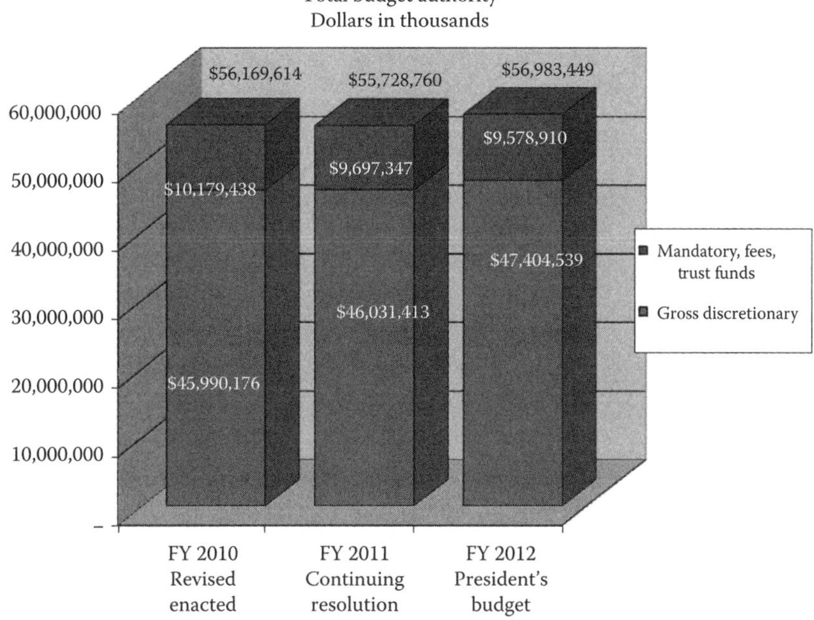

FIGURE 3.45 U.S. Department of Homeland Security total budget authority.

- Citizenship and Immigration Services
- FEMA Grant Programs
- FLETC
- Domestic Nuclear Detection Office

While the reductions are not fantastic, these cuts reflect support for ICE activities in the present administration, as well as the law enforcement sector in its training activities. FEMA is likely just tapped out given the disaster calendar.

All other remaining functions and offices retain their upward trend in budgetary allocation. See Figure 3.46.[35]

For the 2011 Budget Year, there is ample support for technological innovation including but not limited to:

- Advanced Imaging Technology
- Portable Explosive Trace Detection
- Radiological/Nuclear Detection Equipment
- E-Verify Increase
- Cyber Network Funds
- Modernization of Flood Mapping
- Sensor Technology
- Safecon Cargo Scanners

TOTAL BUDGET AUTHORITY BY ORGANIZATION

Gross Discretionary, Mandatory, Fees, and Trust Funds

	FY 2010 Revised Enacted	FY 2011 Continuing Resolution	FY 2012 President's Budget	FY 2012 +/− FY 2011	FY 2012 +/− FY 2011
	$000	$000	$000	$000	%
Departmental Operations	$809,531	$800,931	$947,231	$146,300	18
Analysis and Operations (A&O)	333,030	335,030	355,368	20,338	6
Office of the Inspector General (OIG)	113,874	129,874	144,318	14,444	11
US Customs and Border Protection (CBP)	11,540,501	11,544,660	11,845,678	301,018	3
US Immigration and Customs Enforcement (ICE)	5,741,752	5,748,339	5,822,576	74,237	1
Transportation Security Administration (TSA)	7,656,066	7,649,666	8,115,259	465,593	6
US Coast Guard (USCG)	10,789,076	10,151,543	10,338,545	187,002	2
US Secret Service (USSS)	1,710,344	1,722,644	1,943,531	220,887	13
National Protection and Programs Directorate (NPPD)	2,429,455	2,432,756	2,555,449	122,693	5
Office of Health Affairs (OHA)	136,850	139,250	160,949	21,699	16
Federal Emergency Management Agency (FEMA)	6,200,618	6,181,718	6,218,433	36,715	1
FEMA: Grant Programs	4,165,200	4,165,200	3,844,663	(320,537)	−8
US Citizenship & Immigration Services (USCIS)	2,870,997	3,054,829	2,906,866	(147,963)	−5

Federal Law Enforcement Training Center (FLETC)	282,812	282,812	276,413	(6,399)	−2
Science &Technology Directorate (S&T)	1,006,471	1,006,471	1,176,432	169,961	17
Domestic Nuclear Detection Office (DNDO)	383,037	383,037	331,738	(51,299)	−13
TOTAL BUDGET AUTHORITY:	$56,169,614	$55,728,760	$56,983,449	1,254,689	2.25
Mandatory, Fee, and Trust Funds	(10,179,438)	$(9,697,347)	$(9,578,910)	118,437	−1.22
Discretionary Offsetting Fees	(3,533,561)	(3,442,780)	(4,180,357)	(737,577)	21
NET DISC. BUDGET AUTHORITY:	$42,456,615	$42,588,633	$43,224,182	635,549	—
Less Rescission of Prior-Year Carryover-Regular Appropriations:	(151,582)	(40,474)	(41,942)	—	0
ADJUSTED NET DISC. BUDGET AUTHORITY:	$42,305,033	$42,548,159	$43,182,240	634,081	1
SUPPLEMENTAL:	$5,865,603	—	—	—	—

FIGURE 3.46 US Department of Homeland Security, total budget authority by organization.

FIGURE 3.47 A TSA VIPR member.

In addition to these innovations, DHS allotted a plethora of funds to new positions in Canine, Behavioral Detection Teams, Detachment Units, Federal Air Marshal, and Intelligence Analysts.

The 2012 Budget requests include a host of ambitious projects. True to its general trend, DHS mixes personnel with emerging technologies in hopes of fielding the most efficient practices. On the personnel front, the agency increases the use of Behavior Detection Officers in both airports and other settings. The budget simultaneously seeks funding for 37 Visual Intermodal Prevention and Response Teams (VIPR) whose task is to identify terrorist by behavior, security screening, and other methods of target. See Figure 3.47.

Internet Resource: Find out about VIPR teams at http://www.tsa.gov/press/happenings/vipr_blockisland.shtm.

The 2012 Budget seeks funds to bolster ranks in the historically understaffed Coast Guard, and at the same time increases funding for Marine Safety programs, Environmental Protection and Response as well as Patrol Vigilance in American fishing zones. The Coast Guard will also receive funds for its severely depleted capital fleet and facilities. The Budget requests increases for various technological innovations including:

- Federal Network Protection and the Deployment of Einstein 3-Computer Protection
- BioWatch 2–3 Detection Systems
- Southwest and Northern Border Technology

Finally, the 2012 Budget appears most dedicated to workplace enforcement in the matter of immigration violations. For many years, critics of ICE urged more emphasis on the businesses that employ illegals. DHS officials seem inclined to go in that direction with increased funding requests for:

- Workplace Enforcement
- E-Verify
- VISA Security Program
- Detention Reform
- Funding for Beds
- Secure Communities

Over the last decade, the inevitable march of bureaucratic growth and budgetary increase unfolds. While there may be less funding to go around, DHS has now become a fixture in the budgetary landscape.

3.4 Conclusion

Exactly how DHS was established, shaped, and foundationally organized receives significant attention in this chapter. DHS arises from both political and security influences, though it could not be erected until a legal framework had been established. The various executive orders and legislative enactments that lead to DHS are fully analyzed. In addition, aligned legislation that impacts how DHS conducts its business, such as the USA Patriot Act, is fully covered. Specialized subject matter legislation is given a broad overview, examples being the REAL ID Program, the US-VISIT regulations, the SAFETY Act, and the laws governing registration of select industries.

The chapter also delves into the budget and finance aspects of DHS. In particular, the chapter traces the budgetary history of DHS and correlates budgetary allotments to mission decisions. Hence, budget years 2002–2012 evidence both consistency and adaptability in how budgets are calculated. Basic homeland functions remain a constant in every budget, though the rise of technology funds in the delivery of homeland services surely has seen growth. The budgetary analysis also features new initiatives that require an infusion of funds, such as the SBInet initiative. Budgets can also be reviewed in light of new hardware and software demands that ensure the homeland defense.

Keywords

Allotments
Best practices
Biometrics
Budgeting
Cabinet
CBP targeting systems
Container Security Initiative
Core values

Customs Trade Partnership Against Terrorism
Cyber security
Domestic Nuclear Detection Office
Emergency Alert System
Executive branch
Executive order
Exigent circumstances
Federal Communications Commission
Finance
Jurisdiction
Laws
Legal authority
Legislation
National Biodefense Analysis and Countermeasure Center
National Incident Management System
National Preparedness Integration Program
Office of Management and Budget
Passive radiation detection
Posse Comitatus Act
Private sector justice
Privatization
Project BioShield
Radiation detection monitors
Radiography
REAL ID Program
Regulations
Rescue 21
SAFETY Act
SBInet
Secure Border Initiative
Secure Flight system
Spectroscopic portal
USA Patriot Act
USNORTHCOM or NORTHCOM
US-VISIT

Discussion Questions

1. Explain how the DHS of today differs from the DHS of 2003.
2. Critics of the early acts and executive orders relating to the establishment of DHS often say these promulgations suffered from a lack of vision and thinking. Can you make this argument in any meaningful way?
3. The USA Patriot Act is often on the receiving end of blistering critiques from civil libertarians. Why? Do you concur?
4. Why do early executive orders and legislation so firmly emphasize the role of infrastructure?
5. In the assessment of budget histories, point out two trends over the 11-year life of DHS.
6. In the assessment of the DHS budget, are there any shortcomings or oversights? Lay out precise examples.

7. Discuss two recent initiatives involving global trade and DHS.
8. If you had to predict, will future budgets of DHS be increased or decreased in the next decade?

Practical Exercises

1. Visit www.whitehouse.gov. Find and summarize three recent executive orders relating to homeland security.
2. Assess and evaluate recent amendments to the Homeland Security Act of 2002. List four major categories of adaptation and adjustment in the act since 2002.
3. Compare and contrast the original USA Patriot Act with the provisions enacted in 2008. Some have argued that the later act lacks teeth and rigor. Any truth to this assertion? Provide proof by the language of the acts.
4. Prepare a form file for the US-VISIT program.
5. Review the budgetary cycle of DHS over the period 2003–2012. Identify four major trends in the allotment of funds. Evaluate whether budgetary cycles are influenced by trends and pressures to target specialized activities.

Notes

1. Federal Register, Friday, December 3, 2010, 75(232), Proclamation 8607, 75613.
2. Federal Register, Tuesday, January 27, 2009, Executive Order 13493, 74 FR 4901, available at: https://federalregister.gov/a/E9-1895.
3. Federal Register, Thursday, March 10, 2011, Executive Order 13567, 76 FR 13277, available at http://www.gpo.gov/fdsys/pkg/FR-2011-03-10/pdf/2011-5728.pdf.
4. American Civil Liberties Union, President Obama Issues Executive Order Institutionalizing Indefinite Detention, March 7, 2011, available at: http://www.aclu.org/national-security/president-obama-issues-executive-order-institutionalizing-indefinite-detention.
5. Homeland Security Act of 2002. Public Law 107-296, November 25, 2002, available at: http://www.dhs.gov/xlibrary/assets/hr_5005_enr.pdf.
6. President's Remarks at Homeland Security Bill Signing. Department of Homeland Security Official Home Page. November 25, 2002. Available at: http://www.dhs.gov/xnews/speeches/speech_0073.shtm.
7. See K. L. Hermann, Reviewing Bush-Era Counter-terrorism Policy after 9/11: Reconciling ethical and practical considerations, *Homeland Security Review*, 4(2010): 139; See also C. L. Richardson, The creation of judicial compromise: Prosecuting

detainees in a National Security Court System in Guantanamo Bay, Cuba, *Homeland Security Review*, 4 (2010): 119.

8. U.S. Department of Homeland Security, *Fact Sheet: The USA Patriot Act—A Proven Homeland Security Tool* (12/14/050).
9. C. Savage, Deal reached on extension of Patriot Act, *New York Times*, May 19, 2011.
10. Republican Study Committee, *Legislative Bulletin*, May 26, 2011.
11. See U.S. Patriot Act, section 215 (2011).
12. REAL ID Act of 2005, P.L. 109-13, *U.S. Statutes at Large*, 119 (2005): 231, http://www.govtrack.us/congress/bill.xpd?tab=summary&bill=h109-418.
13. Department of Homeland Security, Office of Inspector General, *Potentially High Costs and Insufficient Grant Funds Pose a Challenge to REAL ID Implementation*, 1 (OIG-09-36) (March 2009).
14. Center for Immigration Studies, *REAL ID Implementation: Less Expensive, Doable, and Helpful in Reducing Fraud* (Jan. 2011), available at http://cis.org/real-id.
15. Center for Immigration Studies, *REAL ID Implementation: Less Expensive, Doable, and Helpful in Reducing Fraud* (Jan. 2011), available at http://cis.org/real-id.
16. Department of Homeland Security, Office of Inspector General, *Potentially High Costs and Insufficient Grant Funds Pose a Challenge to REAL ID Implementation*, 6 (OIG-09-36) (March 2009).
17. J. Harper, *Florida's Implementation of the Federal Real ID Act of 2005* (February 24, 2011) available at http://www.cato.org/pub_display.php?pub_id=12818.
18. Homeland Security Appropriations Act of 2007, P.L. 109-295, Section 550, *U.S. Statutes at Large*, 120 (2006): 1355.
19. For a complete list of chemicals subject to the administrative regulations, see Code of Federal Regulations, title 6, part 27 (2007), http://www.dhs.gov/xlibrary/assets/chemsec_appendixa-chemicalofinterestlist.pdf.
20. Code of Federal Regulations, title 6, sec. 25.7(j) (2004).
21. M. Paddock, Homeland Security funding since 9/11, *Homeland Security Today*, (September 2011): 9.
22. Congressional Budget Office, *Economic and Issue Brief: Federal Funding for Homeland Security* (April 30, 2004), 5, http://www.cbo.gov/ftpdocs/54xx/doc5414/homeland_security.pdf.
23. U.S. Dept. of Homeland Security, *Sample National Terrorism Advisory System Alert*, available at http://www.dhs.gov/xlibrary/assets/ntas/ntas-sample-alert.pdf.
24. Department of Homeland Security, *Budget in Brief: Fiscal Year 2005* (Washington, DC: U.S. Government Printing Office, 2005), 12, http://www.dhs.gov/xlibrary/assets/FY_2005_BIB_4.pdf.
25. Department of Homeland Security, *Performance Budget Overview FY 2005* (Washington, DC: U.S. Government Printing Office, 2005), 8, http://www.dhs.gov/xlibrary/assets/2004PBO_FINAL_29_JAN_04.pdf.
26. Department of Homeland Security, *Budget-in-Brief: Fiscal Year 2006* (Washington, DC: U.S. Government Printing Office, 2006), 16, http://www.dhs.gov/xlibrary/assets/Budget_BIB-FY2006.pdf.
27. General Dynamics, *Rescue 21: Saving Lives for the 21st Century*, C4 Systems, http://www.gdc4s.com/content/detail.cfm?item=816a4a1c-1316-4879-adff-430e9f7972fa.
28. J. Edwards, *U.S. Coast Guard Taking a Coast Guard Mission to New Heights*, Military.com, February 23, 2007, http://www.military.com/features/0,15240,126499,00.html.

29. For a full analysis of various detection systems, see A. Glaser, *Detection of Special Nuclear Materials* (Princeton University, April 16, 2007), http://www.princeton.edu/~aglaser/lecture2007_detection.pdf.
30. Department of Homeland Security, *Budget-in-Brief: FY 2008* (Washington, DC: U.S. Government Printing Office, 2008), 15, http://www.dhs.gov/xlibrary/assets/budget_bib-fy2008.pdf.
31. M. Paddock, Cuts affect more than just the bottom line, *Homeland Security Today*, June (2011): 9.
32. See Executive Order: Reducing Improper Payments and Eliminating Waste in Federal Programs, November 23, 2009.
33. Memorandum from DHS Secretary Janet Napolitano to C. K. Edwards Acting Inspector General, Council of Inspectors General on Integrity and Efficiency, *Quarterly High-Dollar Overpayments Report for the period October to December 2011*, February 22, 2012, available at http://www.dhs.gov/xlibrary/assets/mgmt/cfo-high-dollar-overpayments-october-december-2011.pdf.
34. U.S. Department of Homeland Security, *Budget-in-Brief, Fiscal Year 2012*, 17 (2011).
35. U.S. Department of Homeland Security, *Budget-in-Brief, Fiscal Year 2012*, 21 (2011).

Chapter 4

Risk Management, Threats, and Hazards

Objectives

1. To define standard and best practices used in risk management in the world of homeland security.
2. To describe the process of basic risk assessment and the CARVER+Shock assessment tool.
3. To distinguish between threats and hazards and describe how they are analyzed and rated in risk assessment.
4. To define the various categories of weapons of mass destruction (WMD), including nuclear, chemical, biological, and nerve agents.
5. To differentiate between specific nuclear and radiological WMD and biological and chemical agents, such as anthrax, sarin, and ricin, their delivery methods and effects.
6. To comprehend the importance of the country's information infrastructure and its vulnerability to an attack and identify the steps taken to secure it.
7. To recognize the various government agencies involved in the cyber security of the United States and outline their mission and responsibilities.
8. To illustrate the various public–private partnerships in homeland security and analyze their effectiveness.

4.1 Introduction

The fundamental thrust of homeland security, dealing with risk, threats, and hazards, and how to prepare, respond, and recover from its effects, encompasses this chapter. In other words, how does government operate in the world of risk and threat and simultaneously provide for a secure homeland? What means and methods for prediction, mitigation, and recovery in the matter of risk are the most suitable? What types of plans and planning seem to work best in the world of homeland security? How does the governmental entity prepare and train for such events? This chapter delves into standard as well as best practices in the defense of a nation. First, it will consider the idea of threat, its scope and definition, its types and categories, and the distinction between the natural and man-made varieties. Second, the coverage will include an analysis of risk theory—that body of thought that teaches operatives how to identify risk, how to assess its impact, and how to track its influence. In addition to risk and threat, the chapter will evaluate the most efficacious means of planning and preparedness. It could be no truer than an ounce of prevention is worth a pound of cure in the world of homeland security. How one prepares for tragedy has much to do with its success or failure in response and recovery. How one trains and educates the homeland professional can be just as telling. Finally, this section will evaluate how agencies and their operatives need to communicate in order that homeland protocol achieves its ultimate end—that of safety and security for the community.

4.2 Risk Management

The work of homeland security delves into the nature of risk, whether at airports or busways, public courthouses, or national monuments. Risk constitutes what might happen or what is likely to happen given a certain set of circumstances. Risk is what can go wrong. Risk is what the stay-behind homeowner takes when he or she fails to get out of the path of a hurricane. Risk is what air travelers are willing to tolerate in an air system that lacks security checkpoints. Risk is what the country will tolerate when no mechanisms exist to check visitors at the border. In a word, risk is something each person lives with each day, from driving in a car to cycling across the hinterlands. Yet some risks are more preventable and less serious than others. In evaluating risk one must look to not only the nature of any risk, but its consequences in both an individual and collective sense. Some refer to this formula in an equational sense[1]—as a series of risk constituents. The risk is calculated relative to the harm the hazard causes and the level and magnitude of exposure to the said harm. The formula might look like this:

$$\text{Risk} = \text{Hazard} \times \text{Exposure}$$

Hazard is the mechanism that causes the harm, and exposure the extent, depth, and breadth of the risk as influenced by the nature of the hazard. Thus, if anthrax is plugged into the risk equation, it is a small chore to conclude that anthrax constitutes the type of risk the individual and the collective should avoid. In a policy context, therefore, it makes perfect sense for governments to marshal resources to attack this risk—more so than an avalanche of candy bars from an upended truck. Herein lays the rub—to weigh and factor the risk in light of harm and its scope. Some risks are high, others lower, and some "risks" pose no risk at all. To be sure, terrorism is high up on the list of potential harms that homeland specialist must prepare for. "Terrorism has many faces and countless are the possibilities of implementing an attack against American interests under the umbrella of terrorism."[2] The risk manager must anticipate every imaginable version of terrorist act to properly prepare for it.

Looked at from a different perch, risk relies upon probability analysis.

4.2.1 The Nature of Risk

Risk is not an easy concept to fully define for it has both actual and anticipatory qualities.[3] On the one hand, all one can do is predict or anticipate what might happen yet on the other, experience dictates the reality of risk. For example, will the risk injure a human? Is it likely that this risk will be in the form of a weapon? Is there a correlation between some religious practice and an act of terror? Is there a particular day, holiday, or anniversary—such as the September 11, 2012, Benghazi consulate attack—where terrorist events are more apt to occur? If a chemical industry fails to secure a certain substance, what are the health ramifications? One could endlessly go on about the nature of risk and its various types. To be sure, the concept is forever evolving. FEMA makes a valiant effort to quantify the process. FEMA employs probability theory when making judgments about risk. In short, risk is the probability that something will occur with an evaluation of consequence.[4] See Figure 4.1.

The Department of Homeland Security (DHS) defines the nature of risk by three principal variables: *threat*, or the likelihood of a type of attack that might be attempted; *vulnerability*, or the likelihood that an attacker would

Definition of risk
Risk is a combination of:

- The probability that an event will occur
- The consequences of its occurrence

	Low risk	Medium risk	High risk
Risk factors total	1–60	61–175	≥176

Risk = Asset value × threat rating × vulnerability rating

FIGURE 4.1 Definition of risk table.

Quantifying risk
Risk assessment
Determine asset value
Determine threat rating value
Determine vulnerability rating value
Determine relative risk for each threat against each asset

FIGURE 4.2 Quantifying risk.

succeed with a particular attack method; and *consequence*, or the potential impact, individually or collectively, of a particular attack. In this context, one deals in generalities rather than specifics. Sound risk reasoning demands that a measure or modality of quantification be employed when making policy about risk. In other words, can risk be quantified in some way? FEMA thinks so by evaluating some specific variable relative to the nature of the risk.[5] See Figure 4.2.

Here, the evaluator of risk moves beyond the definition seeking to formalize the precise nature and attributes of risk. What is this risk worth? How much, in terms of assets will it destroy? What level, in a global sense, of seriousness does this risk pose? How much is at stake? When, compared to other assets, is it worth our dedication to thwart all risks? For homeland security the thrust will be toward quantification—using distinct variables with assigned point values to type the risk. The DHS risk formula would look something like this:

$$\text{Risk} = \text{Asset value} \times \text{threat rating} \times \text{vulnerability rating}$$

The severity of a risk will be assessed in light of its value, the nature of the threat itself, and the potential for harm and injury. So, as evident in Table 4.1, infrastructure damage is heavily weighted yet variably dependent upon the method employed to inflict the damage and harm.[6]

TABLE 4.1 Critical Infrastructure

Infrastructure	Cyber Attack	Armed Attack (Single Gunman)	Vehicle Bomb	CBR Attack
Site	48	80	108	72
Asset value	4	4	4	4
Threat rating	4	4	3	2
Vulnerability	3	5	9	9
Structural Systems	48	128	192	144
Asset value	8	8	8	8
Threat rating	3	4	3	2
Vulnerability rating	2	4	8	9

So this leads to the matter of risk assessment in particular terms. How do our homeland professionals and policymakers decide that this risk is worth more than another? Can they devise a meaningful system of quantification that reliably measures the effect and consequence of a risk gone wrong?

4.2.2 Risk Assessment

There are diverse ways in which risk can be measured. The Rand Organization suggests three methodologies of risk assessment:[7]

- *Analytic*: An analytic process must address all three factors that determine terrorism risk—threat, vulnerability, and consequences.
- *Deliberative*: A deliberative process is necessary because the notion of a cold, actuarial terrorism risk assessment is unrealistic. Values and judgment are part and parcel of the process and require transparency and a comprehensive public discussion of outcomes.
- *Practical*: Finally, risk assessment must be practical, which means that data collection and management requirements must be technically and economically feasible.

If DHS has any preference it would be the analytic, though it would be shortsighted to avoid the other modalities. DHS posits new interesting variables into its risk assessment formula primarily in two ways: the value of asset and the impact on geography. In both instances, the more value, the more coverage, and the greater the impact on the populace, the higher the event will place in tabulations. At first glance it may seem arbitrary, although nothing in the soft sciences can ever lay claim to the certitude of the hard sciences. What is so strikingly evident is that DHS is willing to place a value on these two things. In a sense, it is about as good as it can be in the imperfect world of risk assessment.

As for value, the DHS risk assessment model highlights the most notable of the targets a terrorist might choose—chemical plants, stadiums, and commercial airports. DHS then analyzes the vulnerability of each asset type relative to each attack method and plausibility of the chosen attack method.

Additionally, DHS computes the consequential costs of a successful attack and its impact on the value of assets, the health of the collective, our economic system, military, and overall psychological impact on the national psyche. This analysis yields a relative risk estimate for each asset type, applied to a given geographic area, and based on the number of each asset type present within that area. DHS lists those assets that carry higher values in its equation in Figure 4.3.[8]

The risk assessment formula is then tested geographically. The geographic-based approach weighs the value of assets in that particular

- Chemical manufacturing facilities
- City road bridges
- Colleges and universities
- Commercial airports
- Commercial overnight shipping facilities
- Convention centers
- Dams
- Electricity generation facilities
- Electricity substations
- Enclosed shopping malls
- Ferry terminals–buildings
- Financial facilities
- Hospitals
- Hotel casinos
- Levees
- Liquefied natural gas (LNG) terminals
- Maritime port facilities
- Mass transit commuter rail and subway stations
- National health stockpile sites
- National monuments and icons
- Natural gas compressor stations
- Non-power nuclear reactors
- Nuclear power plants
- Nuclear research labs
- Petroleum pumping stations
- Petroleum refineries
- Petroleum storage tanks
- Potable water treatment facilities
- Primary and secondary schools
- Railroad bridges
- Railroad passenger stations
- Railroad tunnels
- Road commuter tunnels
- Road interstate bridges
- Road interstate tunnels
- Stadiums
- Tall commercial buildings
- Telcomm-telephone hotels
- Theme parks
- Trans-oceanic cable landings

FIGURE 4.3 High-value assets as determined by DHS.

region. Geographic regions are weighted in accordance with their area listings.[9] See Figure 4.4.

In light of this valuation, DHS computes the threat level, police and law enforcement activity relative to threats, as well as intelligence from Customs and Immigration, and other suspicious incident data. Then, DHS considers vulnerability factors for each geographic area, such as the area's proximity to international borders and the potential for international incident. Lastly, DHS estimates the potential consequences of an attack on that area, including human health, size of population, economic conditions, military complex, and overall business and industry. DHS charts its methodology in Figure 4.5.[10]

On a narrower front, the task of risk assessment can be departmentally and programmatically driven. For example, risk for FEMA may be distinctively different than the risks of concern to immigration and citizenship.

- Defense industrial base facilities
- Federal bureau of investigation (FBI) basic and special cases
- Gross domestic product (GDP)
- I–94 visitors from countries of interest
- Intelligence community credible and less credible threat reports
- Immigration and customs enforcement (ICE) basic and special cases
- Miles of international border
- Military bases
- Nuclear waste isolation pilot plan (WIPP) transportation routes
- Population
- Population density
- Port of entry/border crossings (people from countries of interest and annual throughput)
- Ratio of law enforcement to population
- Special events
- State international export trade
- State total agriculture sales
- Sum of population density of urban areas in state
- Sum of population of urban areas in state
- Suspicious incidents (credible and less credible)

FIGURE 4.4 High-value geographic target regions.

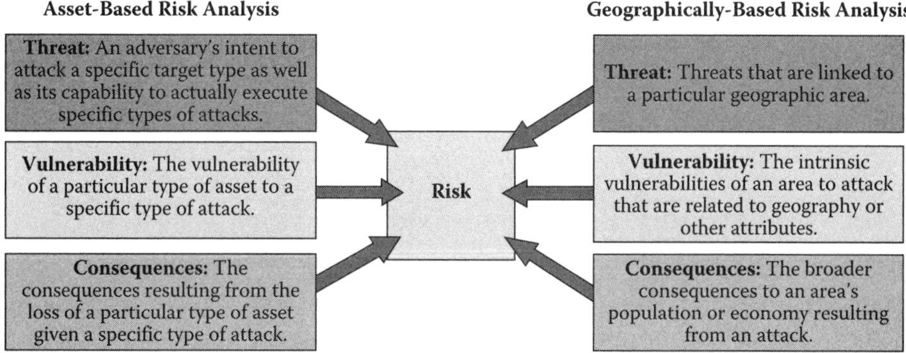

Asset-Based Risk Analysis
Geographically-Based Risk Analysis
Threat: An adversary's intent to attack a specific target type as well as its capability to actually execute specific types of attacks.
Vulnerability: The vulnerability of a particular type of asset to a specific type of attack.
Consequences: The consequences resulting from the loss of a particular type of asset given a specific type of attack.
Risk
Threat: Threats that are linked to a particular geographic area.
Vulnerability: The intrinsic vulnerabilities of an area to attack that are related to geography or other attributes.
Consequences: The broader consequences to an area's population or economy resulting from an attack.

FIGURE 4.5 Asset-based risk analysis versus geographically-based risk analysis methodology comparison.

Each agency and department needs to perceive risk in light of its overall mission. One of the more telling illustrations can be discovered in the workings of the Federal Protective Service (FPS) which is entrusted with the protection of nearly 9000 federal facilities. Risk assessment is central to its overall task and mission. Therefore, the FPS has developed a Risk Assessment and Management Program (RAMP) which aid FPS officers carrying out facility assessment plans.

RAMP is a risk assessment too that is multitasked and multivariate in approach. RAMP's intent is to:

- Assess and analyze risk posed to federal facilities from terrorism, crime, natural hazards, and other serious incidents
- Centrally store, access, and report risk assessment findings, including historical information from previous assessments and other documentation
- Manage all aspects of the FSA process
- Manage security post inspections, contracts, and individual guard certification compliance
- Recommend and track the implementation of countermeasures throughout their life cycle
- Perform inventory-wide analysis of the risks posed to federal facilities and the means of reducing them
- Automate and track countermeasure recommendations, implementation status, and life cycle replacement schedules
- Track financial information for countermeasures throughout their life cycle
- Provide Occupancy Emergency Plan information, call-back lists, and so on
- Provide security access to tools and information, including a comprehensive help file

- Generate and route letters, reports, presentations, statistical analyses, and perform other administrative functions
- Provide a comprehensive comparison across the entire GSA inventory that FPS protects.

Whatever approach is taken with risk assessment, it is critical to gather information, anticipate events and incidents, understand the value of assets and potential harm, and weigh and contrast the functionality and importance of geographic territory. FEMA lists the potential incidents, and plugging into the formula is what is required in Table 4.2.

Internet Exercise: Become familiar with HITRAC—a risk-informed analytic tool that deals with infrastructure at http://www.dhs.gov/xabout/structure/gc_1257526699957.shtm#1.

TABLE 4.2 Possible Hazards and Emergencies Risk Abatement

	Hazards	
Possible Hazards and Emergencies	**Risk Level (None, Low, Moderate, or High)**	**How Can I Reduce My Risk?**
Natural Hazards		
1. Floods		
2. Hurricanes		
3. Thunderstorms and lightning		
4. Tornadoes		
5. Winter storms and extreme cold		
6. Extreme heat		
7. Earthquakes		
8. Volcanoes		
9. Landslides and debris flow		
10. Tsunamis		
11. Fires		
12. Wildfires		
Technological Hazards		
1. Hazardous materials incidents		
2. Nuclear power plants		
Terrorism		
1. Explosions		
2. Biological threats		
3. Chemical threats		
4. Nuclear blasts		
5. Radiological dispersion device (RDD)		

Do not forget to mitigate potential harm. Every event can be influenced in some way, whether it is the movement of people or the protection of property. Every risk can be addressed in some fashion. Government has choices in the matter to some extent. Hazard mitigation planning is the process of determining how to reduce or eliminate the loss of life and property damage resulting from natural and human-caused hazards. See Figure 4.6, which charts the four-step process of mitigation.[11]

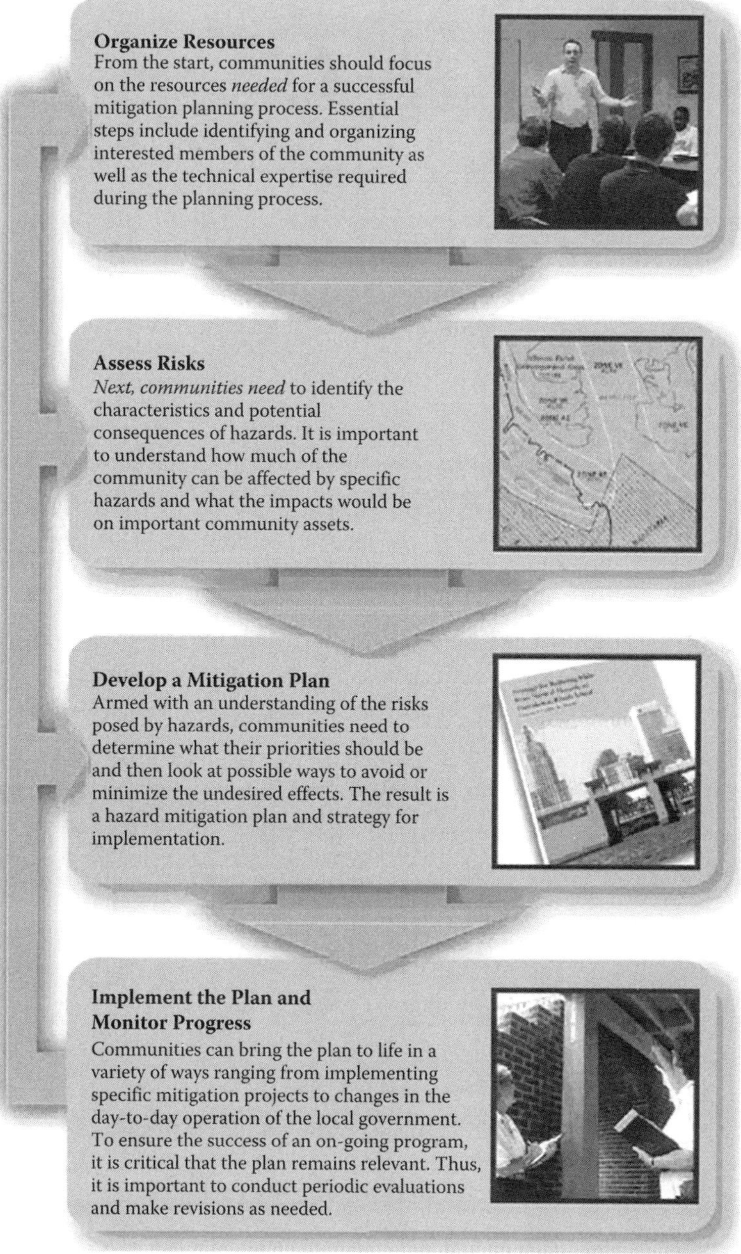

Organize Resources
From the start, communities should focus on the resources *needed* for a successful mitigation planning process. Essential steps include identifying and organizing interested members of the community as well as the technical expertise required during the planning process.
Assess Risks
Next, communities need to identify the characteristics and potential consequences of hazards. It is important to understand how much of the community can be affected by specific hazards and what the impacts would be on important community assets.
Develop a Mitigation Plan
Armed with an understanding of the risks posed by hazards, communities need to determine what their priorities should be and then look at possible ways to avoid or minimize the undesired effects. The result is a hazard mitigation plan and strategy for implementation.
Implement the Plan and Monitor Progress
Communities can bring the plan to life in a variety of ways ranging from implementing specific mitigation projects to changes in the day-to-day operation of the local government. To ensure the success of an on-going program, it is critical that the plan remains relevant. Thus, it is important to conduct periodic evaluations and make revisions as needed.

FIGURE 4.6 Four-step mitigation process.

4.2.3 CARVER+Shock Assessment Tool

How assessments are carried out inexorably depends upon the subject matter. In the area of food supply, water, and consumables, risk evaluators have come to depend upon the CARVER+Shock assessment methodology. The CARVER system employs various criteria labeled as CARVER; CARVER is an acronym for the following six attributes used to evaluate the attractiveness of a target for attack:

- Criticality—Measure of public health and economic impacts of an attack.
- Accessibility—Ability to physically access and egress from target.
- Recuperability—Ability of system to recover from an attack.
- Vulnerability—Ease of accomplishing attack.
- Effect—Amount of direct loss from an attack as measured by loss in production.
- Recognizability—Ease of identifying target.

In addition, the modified CARVER tool evaluates a seventh attribute, the combined health, economic and psychological impacts of an attack, or the shock attributes of a target.

The CARVER system attempts to quantify risk by the assignment of specific numbers for specific conditions. It looks to products and food, facilities, and manufacturing processes. So valued is its methodology that the U.S. Food and Drug Administration (FDA) has developed and disseminated software that is downloadable on the web. CARVER+Shock software requires the user to build a process flow diagram for the system to be evaluated and answer a series of questions for each of the seven CARVER+Shock attributes for each process flow diagram node. Flow processes can be shaped and designed in a host of applications. The CARVER program employs an icon system that correlates to a particular industry or business application. Table 4.3 is a sample listing of the flow process possibilities.[12]

Each question has an associated score. Based on the answers given, the software calculates a score for each CARVER+Shock attribute and sums them to produce a total score for each node. Analogous to a face-to-face session, total scores range from 1 to 10 for each CARVER+Shock attribute, and therefore 7 to 70 for each node.

The interview questions seek to corroborate the flow process, as to the variables under the CARVER acronym. Then, once the results are tabulated, a scoring system is linked to each of these variables. Table 4.4 displays the scoring criteria for accessibility.

This process relies upon a comprehensive interview schema in order that calculations have reliability. In Figure 4.7, a sample interview page, published by the software, is provided.

TABLE 4.3 CARVER+Shock Flow Process Possibilities

Icon	Category	Sub-Category	Description
Acid	Materials	Processed ingredients	A water-soluble chemical compound with a pH less than 7 when dissolved. Has a sour taste.
Air dryer	Processing	Drying	Device that dries product by direct contact with heated air.
Aircraft	Transportation/ Distribution		Using an aircraft for the transportation of materials from one location to another.
Aseptic packager	Packaging		Equipment that places and seals product in a sterile container/ package.
Auger tank	Processing	Processing tanks	Enclosure for a large mechanical screw that mixes and moves material/product.
Bags	Packaging	Packaging materials	A container of flexible material (paper, plastic, etc.) used for packaging.
Bakery	Retail food service		Location where products like bread, cake, and pastries are baked.
Balance tank	Processing	Processing tanks	Used to balance the pH of a discharge so it is within certain parameters.
Barge	Transportation/ Distribution		Transportation of materials along a body of water from one location to another.
Batch tank	Storage	Storage tanks	A mixing/storage tank large enough for a single batch of product.
Batterer	Processing	Other processing	A machine used to mix or beat a material.
Bin/tub	Storage	Other storage	A large open storage vessel.
Blancher	Processing	Cooking	Equipment that uses water or steam to parboil or scald material/product to remove skin or stop enzymatic action.
Blast freezer	Processing	Chilling	Device that quickly freezes materials or products as they move along a conveyor using a controlled stream of cold air. Generally used when small pieces need to be kept separate as they freeze, such as cut-up vegetables.
Blend tank	Processing	Processing tanks	A tank used to blend/mix materials.
Blender	Processing	Mixing	Mechanical mixer for chopping, mixing, or liquefying materials.

continued

TABLE 4.3 (continued) CARVER+Shock Flow Process Possibilities

Icon	Category	Sub-Category	Description
Blower	Conveyance		A machine, such as a fan, that produces an air current to move materials.
Bottle cleaner	Cleaning/ washing		A process to clean, wash, and sterilize bottles.
Bottle hopper	Packaging		Provides continuous flow of containers to be loaded on a conveyor.
Bottler	Packaging		Automated equipment for filling bottles.
Bottles	Packaging	Packaging materials	Containers with a narrow neck and no handles that can be plugged, corked, or capped.
Boxes	Packaging	Packaging materials	Container with four sides and a lid or cover used for storage or transport.
Breader	Processing	Other processing	Equipment used to coat meat/fish/ poultry with a crumb coating.
Briner	Processing	Other processing	Process to preserve food using a concentrated salt solution.
Browner	Processing	Cooking	Equipment used to sear the outside surface of meats.
Bulk storage	Storage	Other storage	Storage for a large amount of ingredient/product in a single container.
Butcher	Processing	Meat processing	To cut up meat or poultry.
Cans	Packaging	Packaging materials	Cylindrical metal container.
Capper	Packaging		Applies caps to containers.
Car	Storage	Other storage	Storage for a material waiting to be shipped.
Caser	Packaging		Sorts and places product into cases.
Centrifuge	Processing	Separation/ Extraction	Machine that uses centrifugal force to separate substances with different densities.
Check weigher	Control checks		A scale to check the weight of product.
Chemicals	Materials	Processing materials	Cleaning chemicals.
Chilled distribution	Transportation/ Distribution		Refrigerated transport of product.

Source: United States Food and Drug Administration, *CARVER+Shock Users' Manual*, Version 1.0, 2007, Appendix B: Alphabetical Icons with Descriptions.

TABLE 4.4 CARVER+Shock Scoring Criteria

Accessibility Criteria	Scale
Easily accessible (e.g., target is outside building and no perimeter fence). Limited physical or human barriers or observation. Attacker has relatively unlimited access to the target. Attack can be carried out using medium or large volumes of contaminant without undue concern of detection. Multiple sources of information concerning the facility and the target are easily available.	9–10
Accessible (e.g., target is inside building, but in unsecured part of facility). Human observation and physical barriers limited. Attacker has access to the target for an hour or less. Attack can be carried out with moderate to large volumes of contaminant, but requires the use of stealth. Only limited specific information is available on the facility and the target.	7–8
Partially accessible (e.g., inside building, but in a relatively unsecured, but busy, part of facility). Under constant possible human observation. Some physical barriers may be present. Contaminant must be disguised, and time limitations are significant. Only general, nonspecific information is available on the facility and the target.	5–6
Hardly accessible (e.g., inside building in a secured part of facility). Human observation and physical barriers with an established means of detection. Access generally restricted to operators or authorized persons. Contaminant must be disguised and time limitations are extreme. Limited general information available on the facility and the target.	3–4
Not accessible. Physical barriers, alarms, and human observation. Defined means of intervention in place. Attacker can access target for less than 5 min with all equipment carried in pockets. No useful publicly available information concerning the target.	1–2

Internet Resource: Visit, download, and survey the CARVER software at http://www.cfsan.fda.gov/~dms/carver.html.

4.3 Threats and Hazards

4.3.1 The Concept of Threat and Hazard

Threats come in many forms, and if anything is true about the last decade, it would be the evolution in the definition of threat. Some might argue that threats are those things emanating from military sources alone—in the form of armies or weaponry. Of even more compelling recent interest has been the emergence of the homegrown, domestic terrorist threat where our enemies reside amongst the populace, waiting to carry out the deed. This is part of what Secretary Janet Napolitano calls the "New Threat Picture."[13] Others might claim that a threat is driven by natural disaster or events that

ABC
Criticality Category Interview Report

What is the serving size for the product? (If the product is used as an ingredient, how much of the product is used in each serving?)

What is the distribution unit (package size sold to the consumer)?

How many retail outlets typically receive units from one batch?

- O 1
- O 2–3
- O 3–20
- O >10

What percentage of each batch is sold…

–	Within one day of purchase?
–	Within first three days after purchase?
–	Within first two weeks after purchase?
–	Within first month after purchase?
–	During the first two months?

What percentage of the product is typically consumed…

–	Within one day of purchase?
–	Within the first three days after purchase?
–	Within the first week after purchase?
–	Within two weeks after purchase?
–	Within first month after purchase?
–	Within first two months after purchase?

On average, how many individuals eat from the same distribution unit?

Does the company have a published support line for end consumers with concerns or questions?

- O Yes
- O No

Is there a formal company procedure for communicating information on a contamination incident to the public?

- O Yes
- O No

Does your company or facility have a mechanism in place to effectively implement a recall and withdraw product from the marketplace?

- O Yes
- O No

Does your company conduct mock product recalls?

- O Yes
- O No

How well can you trace your product to the distribution centers (D.C.s) and retail outlets?

- O Cannot trace at all.
- O Can identify independent D.C.s and entire distribution chains to major distributors that may have received units from one batch.
- O Can trace specific pallets to independent D.C.s and entire distribution chains to major distributors such as Wal-Mart.
- O Can identify all retail outlets that received units from a batch.
- O Can trace specific pallets to each retail outlet that received it.

Is this product an uncoded product or uncoded raw ingredient?

- O Yes
- O No

Are you aware of large-scale counterfeiting or diversion for this product?

- O Yes
- O No

FIGURE 4.7 CARVER+Shock sample interview page.

CARVER+SHOCK DEFINITIONS

Criticality—A target is critical when the introduction of threat agents into food at this location would cause significant sickness, death, or economic impact.

Accessibility—A target is accessible when an attacker can reach the target, conduct the attack, and leave the target undetected.

Recognizability—A target's recognizability is the degree to which it can be identified by an attacker without confusion.

Vulnerability—Given a successful attack, vulnerability is the likelihood that the contaminant will achieve the attacker's purpose. It considers both processing steps and analytical steps at and downstream of the point of attack.

Effect—Effect is a measure of the percentage of system productivity damaged by an attack at a single facility. Thus, effect is inversely related to the total number of facilities producing the same product.

Recuperability—A target's recuperability is measured in the time it will take for the specific system to recover productivity.

Shock—Shock is the combined measure of the psychological and collateral national economic impacts of a successful attack on the target system. Shock is considered on a national level. The psychological impact will be increased if the target has historical, cultural, religious, or other symbolic significance. Mass casualties are not required to achieve widespread economic loss or psychological damage. Collateral economic damage includes such items as decreased national economic activity, increased unemployment in collateral industries, and so on. Psychological impact will be increased if victims are members of sensitive subpopulations, such as children or the elderly.

are unpredictable, such as a typhoon or hurricane. And still another conception deals with the threats of nuclear, chemical, and biological incidents. Threats and hazards are often distinguished by their motive and purpose. Hazards are generally construed as acts of nature, unintentional events without political motive or purpose. Threats, on the other hand, are usually bound to some improper aim or end, such as the political destruction of a government or the radical altering of leadership. Hurricanes and floods are events lacking any animus and, as such, are relegated to the hazard category.

What can be agreed upon is that the United States daily remains subject to a host of threats and hazards from every imaginable direction. Professor Daniel Dunai, of Hungary's National Defence University, graphically charts the onslaught in Figure 4.8.[14]

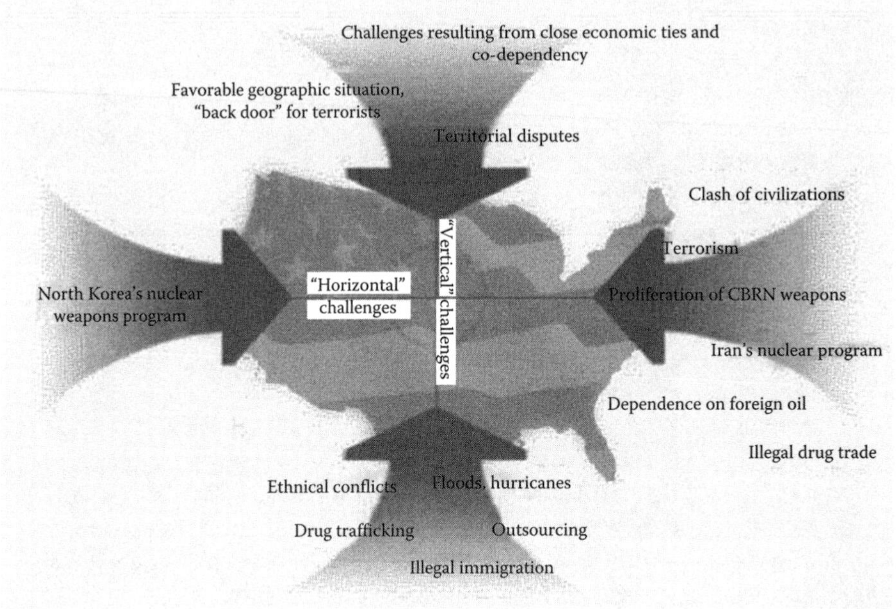

FIGURE 4.8 A convenient scheme for categorizing different threats and challenges.

Natural hazards fall into these categories:

- Hurricanes
- Tornadoes
- Floods
- Winter storms
- Heat-related emergencies
- Droughts
- Wildfires
- Thunderstorms
- Geologic events

Government agencies and policy makers frequently underestimate the full impact of these natural disasters, at least as to the homeland defense mindset. These events wreak extraordinary havoc. The death toll alone is a distressingly impressive count. See Figure 4.9.[15]

More than 26 million people have been negatively impacted by natural disasters in the last century—a statistic that lays out a permanent obligation for homeland personnel. See Figure 4.10.[16]

Threats fall into these typologies:

- Crimes
- Terrorism
- Unintentional events
- Blackouts

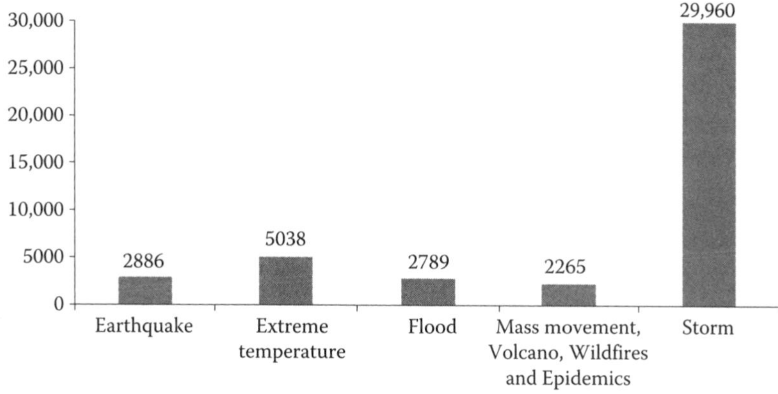

FIGURE 4.9 Deaths from natural disasters in the United States from September 1900 to March 2012.

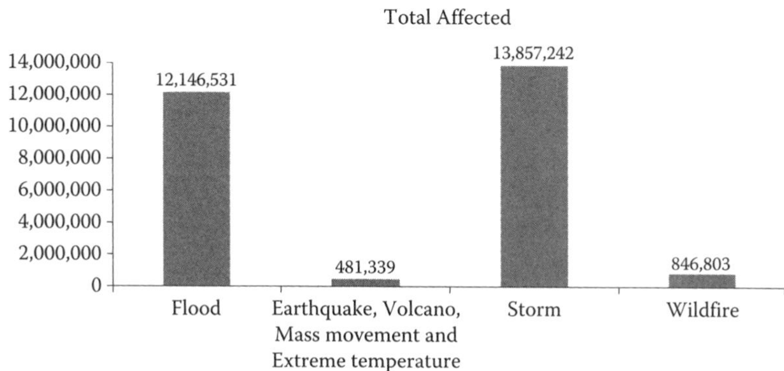

FIGURE 4.10 People affected by natural disasters in the United States from September 1900 to March 2012.

- Radiological events
- Hazmat incidents
- Fires

Threats arising from terrorism signify a malicious intent to cause widespread harm. Terrorism and civil hazards include actions that people intentionally do to threaten lives and property. These acts may range from a single person on a shooting rampage, to a cyber-attack that harms computer systems, to the organized use of WMD. WMD events could involve chemical, biological, explosive, or radioactive weapons. Acts of terrorism include threats of terrorism, assassinations, kidnappings, hijackings, bomb scares, and bombings. High-risk targets for acts of terrorism include military and civilian government facilities, international airports, large cities, and high-profile landmarks. Terrorists might also target large public gatherings, water and food supplies, utilities, and corporate centers. Infrastructure of every variety needs constant vigilance in the matter of threat, from its original construction phase to its maintenance. Building design must anticipate threat even in the materials side so that the structure might withstand natural disasters, blast, projectiles, and fire.[17]

Identifying, anticipating, and defending against such a broad band of threats can only be described as daunting. For if homeland policymakers have learned anything over the last decade, it is that these concepts, like threat and disaster, have an evolutionary quality. In short, both the ideas and the means of execution change whether we admit it or not. Those entrusted must stay "in the box" as well as be capable of jumping "out of the box." In other words, past history tells us much about these events, although these same events may not evolve in just the way predicted. Alain Bauer's insights on this dilemma are most helpful for he urges the policy maker to find the commonality in all the forms of terror. No matter what the group, he argues, what the religious sect, what the purpose or aim, all terrorists

- Have common harmonies
- Frequent common lands and territories
- Have a common (submerged) economy
- Offer real opportunities for symbiosis[18]

Agencies and communities can chart potential threats by use of the checklist in Table 4.5.

Of course, hazards can arise by human negligence and carelessness, which gives rise to a man-made catastrophe.

4.3.2 Weapons of Mass Destruction

No ambition is more glorifying for the terrorist than the successful delivery of a WMD. The terror associated with WMD is well founded and not to be addressed cavalierly. The stuff of WMD can only be described as frightful and has the capacity to inflict global injury. There are four generally accepted categories of WMD, covered in the following subsections.

4.3.2.1 Nuclear

Some terrorist organizations, such as Al Qaeda, openly declare their desire to acquire and use nuclear weapons. Even the complexities of devising a nuclear delivery mechanism are amply documented. The complete production of a nuclear weapon largely depends on the terrorist group's access to nuclear material and a high level of scientific expertise. Black market materials can be utilized, though the crudeness of the enterprise is dangerous in and of itself (Figure 4.11).

TABLE 4.5 Local Threats and Hazards

Type of Hazard	Likelihood of Occurrence	Potentially Devastating Impact on People	Potentially Devastating Impact on Structures
Natural Hazards			
Floods			
Winter storms			
Tornadoes			
Thunderstorm			
Hurricanes			
Extreme heat/cold			
Viral epidemics			
Human-Induced Hazards			
Hazardous materials incidents			
Transportation accidents			
Infrastructure disruptions			
Workplace violence			
Civil disorder/disobedience			
Terrorist Hazards			
Conventional weapons			
Incendiary devices			
Biological and chemical agents			
Radiological			
Cyber-terrorism			
Weapons of mass destruction			

Source: Hazard Analysis and Vulnerability Study, done under contract to DC Emergency Management Agency, May 2002.

DHS, by and through its office of Domestic Nuclear Detection, is entrusted with the detection and prevention of nuclear terrorist threats. The basic objectives of the office are:

- Develop the global nuclear detection and reporting architecture.
- Develop, acquire, and support the Domestic Nuclear Detection and Reporting System.
- Fully characterize detector system performance before deployment.
- Establish situational awareness through information sharing and analysis.

FIGURE 4.11 Nuclear power plant.

- Establish operation protocols to ensure detection leads to effective response.
- Conduct a transformational research and development program.
- Establish the National Technical Nuclear Forensics Center to provide planning, integration, and improvements to USG nuclear forensics capabilities.

The demands and complexities of nuclear threat call for constant and continuous assessment. Aside from perimeter concerns and access issues, the typical nuclear power facility not only utilizes physical materials capable of mass destruction but also must find ways to store and treat the by-products of nuclear power and production. Hence, DHS has recently tried to regularize practices in the nuclear industry regarding data storage and collection, physical security plans, and disposal.[19] The Domestic Nuclear Detection Office is constructed in Figure 4.12.

Physical security at nuclear power plants is provided by well-armed and well-trained security personnel who remain ready to respond to an attack 24 hours a day, 7 days a week. The sites are protected by sensitive intrusion detection equipment, fences, and barriers and are monitored by cameras and security patrols (Figure 4.13).

DHS has realized that the department cannot function in an isolated fashion when it comes to nuclear threat; they have realized that interagency cooperation is central to its mission. "Federal, state, local and private sector partners regularly and actively assess the risk environment in the Nuclear Sector in light of changes or potential changes to threats, vulnerabilities and consequences."[20] In 2002, the Nuclear Regulatory Commission (NRC)

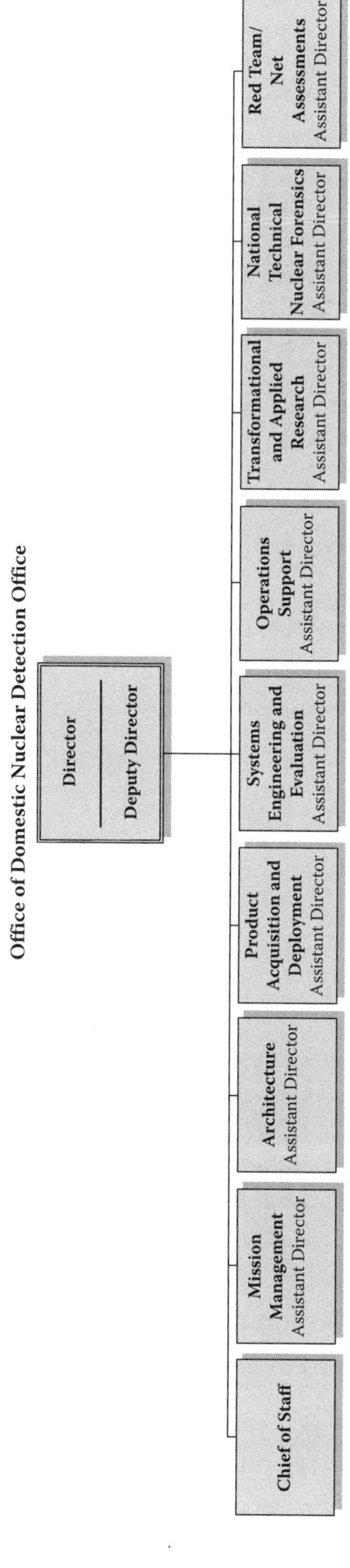

FIGURE 4.12 Organization chart of Domestic Nuclear Detection Office.

FIGURE 4.13 Protection officer at a nuclear facility.

announced the creation of the Office of Nuclear Security and Incident Response (NSIR) to improve NRC effectiveness in ensuring protection of the public health and safety from security threats at licensed facilities. On January 20, 2004, the commission announced the creation of the Emergency Preparedness Project Office (EPPO) to improve NRC's effectiveness. On June 13, 2004, EPPO was integrated within NSIR, creating the Emergency Preparedness Directorate (EPD), and aligned the NRC's preparedness, security, and incident response missions.

Nuclear terrorism can also be carried out at nuclear facilities. Each nuclear facility has high-level security responsibilities and must take seriously its charge to thwart any attempts on the facility. Nuclear facilities are required to have layers of security systems in place to prevent intrusion, contamination, or release of materials, or loss or theft of radioactive and plutonium materials. In the most general terms, a security program for nuclear facilities minimally includes:

- A well-trained security force
- Robust physical barriers
- Intrusion detection systems

- Surveillance systems
- Plant access controls

In addition, nuclear facilities are required to conduct threat assessments regularly and are subject to regular and continuous security visitations by the Nuclear Regulatory Commission.

Internet Resource: Visit the NRC web location for the results of security visits and requirements at plants throughout the United States at http://www.nrc.gov/reading-rm/doc-collections/insp-manual/manual-chapter/mc0320.pdf.

Training is rigorous and continuous. So concerned are the operators of nuclear reactors that extensive training, labeled Force on Force (FOF) training, anticipates an assault on the facility itself. Two sets of security officers—the first for maintenance of the actual facility, and the other the attack force—will engage one another in mock battle. The FOF exercise is highly realistic and essential to a preventive security program. See Figure 4.14.

The NRC requires nuclear power plant operators to defend the plant against attackers seeking to cause damage to the reactor core or spent fuel to prevent the release of radiation. Post-assessment highlights any deficiencies

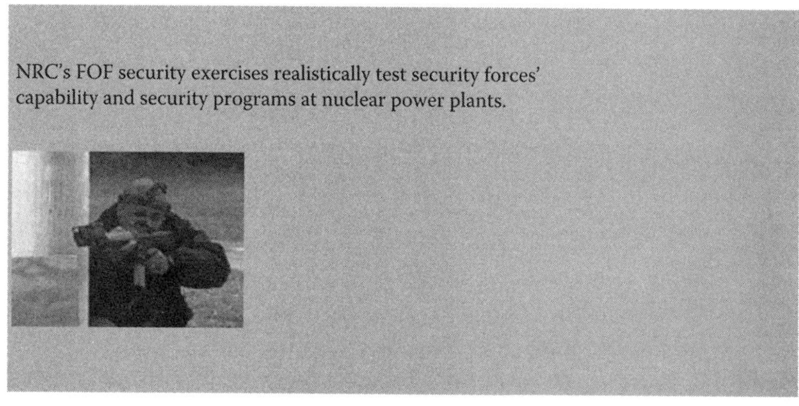

NRC's FOF security exercises realistically test security forces' capability and security programs at nuclear power plants.

The NRC requires nuclear power plant operators to defend the plant against attackers seeking to cause damage to the reactor core or spent fuel, resulting in a release of radiation.
During FOF exercises, a number of commando-style attacks are carried out against a plant's security forces, looking for deficiencies in the plant operator's defensive strategy.
Any significant problems are promptly identified, reviewed, and fixed.
Each nuclear power plant site will have at least one FOF exercise every three years.
The NRC and plant operator ensure the safety of plant employees and the security of the plant during FOF exercises.

FIGURE 4.14 NRC Force on Force training.

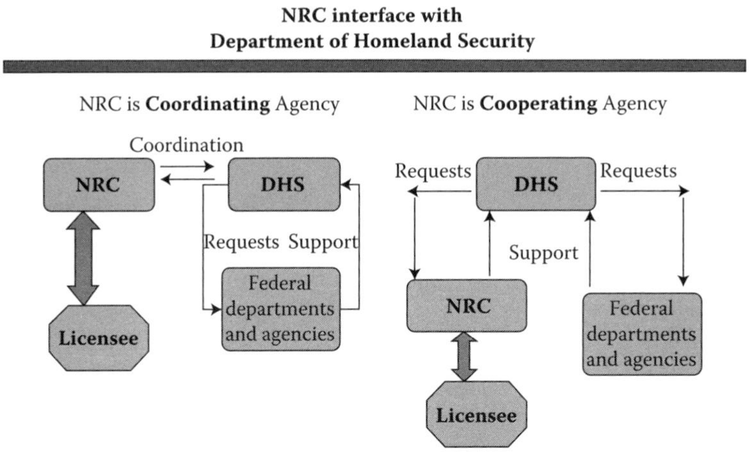

FIGURE 4.15 NRC interface with DHS.

in training and security protocol and is an important part of the day-to-day security plan at the facility.

As in all aspects of nuclear security, there must be clear lines of authority and agency cooperation at every level of government. In the event of a nuclear breach, the line between the Nuclear Regulatory Commission and DHS is precisely drawn, as shown in Figure 4.15.[21]

Finally, in terms of response and advance mitigation, FEMA is entrusted with dealing with the effects and after-effects of a nuclear blast. The extent of that participation will depend on a host of variables including the size of the nuclear device, its detonation height, the nature of the ground surface and existing meteorological conditions. Not only will FEMA encounter the damage resulting from blast and explosion, but also the long-term influences of fall-out.

Practitioners are now lucky enough to conduct measurements for present and future harm regarding nuclear and radiological threats and consequences by modeling and software programs. The Radiological Assessment System for Consequence Analysis (RASCAL) is considered the industry's best example of this sort of measuring tool.

Internet Exercise: To gain an overview of how RASCAL works, visit pbadupws nrc.gov/docs/ML1008/ML100810144.pdf.

4.3.2.2 Radiological

Some terrorists seek to acquire radioactive materials for use in a radiological dispersal device (RDD) or "dirty bomb." In conjunction with the Nuclear Regulatory Commission, the Domestic Nuclear Detection Office is always on the hunt for individuals or groups intent on delivering nuclear WMD (Figure 4.16).

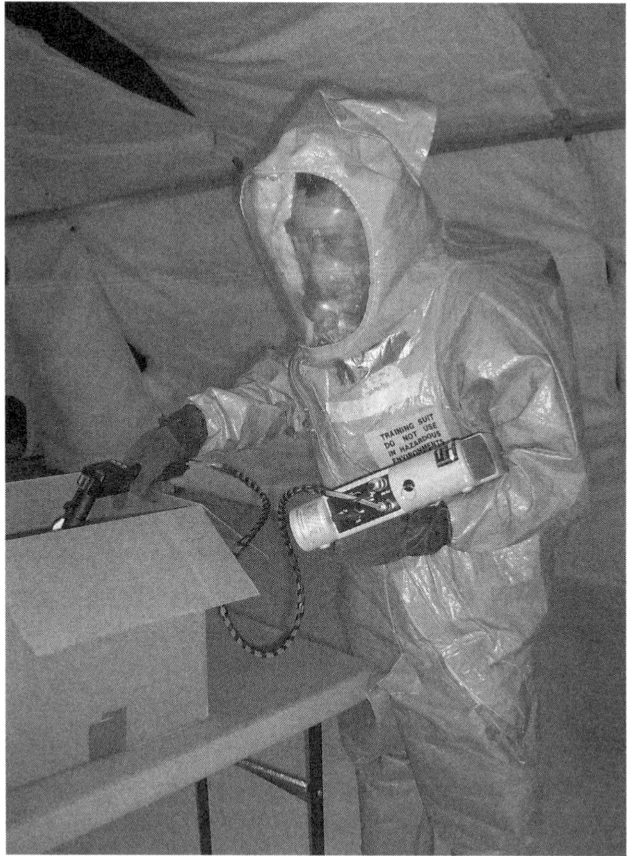

FIGURE 4.16 Nuclear specialist at Nellis Air Force Base.

The most referenced threat in this sector is the use of a dirty bomb. The dirty bomb combines a conventional explosive, such as dynamite, with radioactive material. Upon detonation, aside from the immediate injuries inflicted, there will be severe collateral damage from the nuclear material itself.

The extent of local contamination will depend on a number of factors, including the size of the explosive, the amount and type of radioactive material used, means of dispersal, and weather conditions. The effects of radiation exposure would be determined by:

- Amount of radiation absorbed by the body
- Type of radiation (gamma, beta, or alpha)
- Distance from the radiation to an individual
- Means of exposure—external or internal (absorbed by the skin, inhaled, or ingested)
- Length of time exposed

See the graphic from the Nuclear Regulatory Commission at Figure 4.17 representing the various modes of exposure.

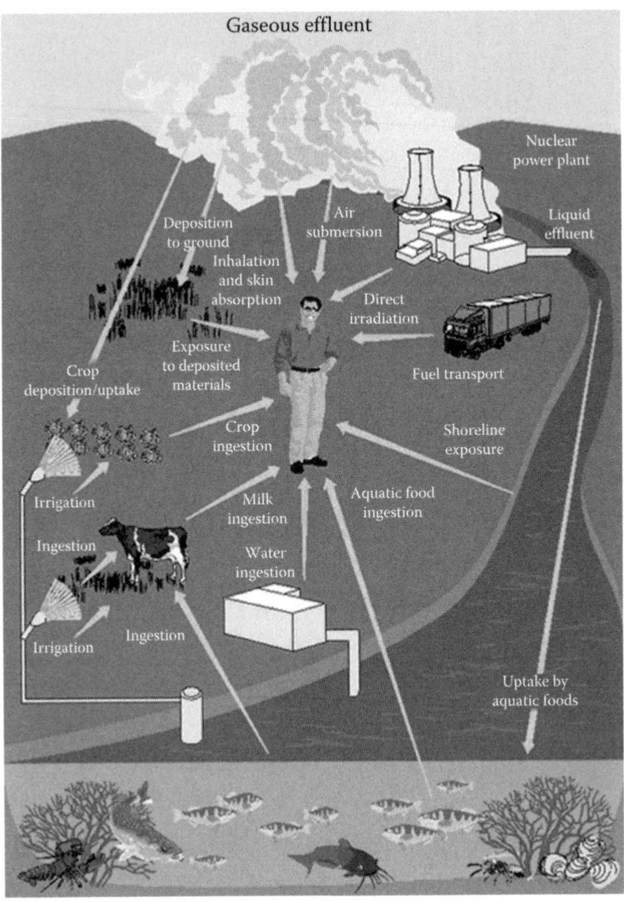

FIGURE 4.17 Radiation released in the environment will result in the exposure of general members of the public. The diagram above shows some of the pathways that may lead to exposure.

Most radioactive materials lack sufficient strength to present a significant public health risk once dispersed, and the materials posing the greatest hazard would likely infect the terrorists themselves. The secondary and cultural effects of a dirty bomb would be quite acute since fear and panic would naturally be expected. The availability of radiological source material is more extensive than most known since this product is used widely in industrial, medical, and research applications, cancer therapy, food and blood irradiation techniques, and radiography.

Internet Resource: To learn about survival steps in the event of a nuclear attack by dirty bomb or other method, read the CDC's instructions at http://www.bt.cdc.gov/radiation/dirtybombs.asp.

Law enforcement takes the dirty bomb seriously, and agencies throughout the country regularly engage in tabletop or field exercises anticipating the

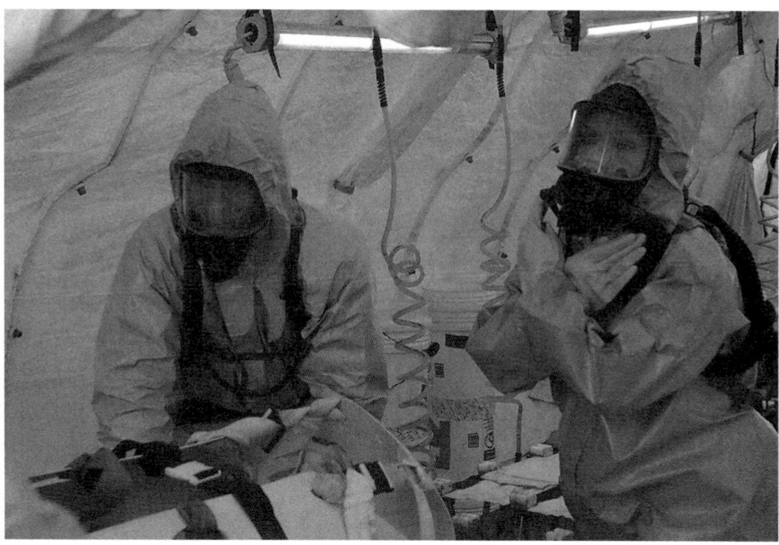

FIGURE 4.18 KINGSTON,N.Y.—Soldiers from the 222nd Chemical Company in full Hazardous Material gear assist civilian participants during the decontamination phase of a joint force first responders exercise in reaction to a radioactive attack. New York National Army and Airmen Guardsmen collaborate with local authorities to help train for the response to a radioactive terrorist attack, Nov. 6, 2011. (Photo Credit: Spc. Brian Godette, New York Army National Guard, 138th PAD.)

dynamics of the event. In May 2003, DHS hosted a large, multiagency, and international exercise dealing with a dirty bomb in Seattle and a covert biological attack in Chicago. In all, 25 federal agencies, as well as the American Red Cross, were involved in the 5-day exercise, as well as partner agencies from the Canadian Government. The trend continues with regularly scheduled dirty bomb and disaster drills on the federal, state, and local levels (Figure 4.18).

Internet Resource: For an NRC fact sheet on dirty bombs, see http://www.nrc.gov/reading-rm/doc-collections/fact-sheets/dirty-bombs.pdf.

4.3.2.3 Biological

Bioterrorism, another deadly threat, and discussed widely throughout this chapter, is the deliberate dispersal of pathogens through food, air, water, or living organisms in order to launch disease and other harms to the public. Biological agents can kill on a massive scale and have the potential to move quickly through large populations, leaving high rates of mortality.[22] Biological agents are, for the most part, tasteless, odorless, and invisible. The havoc occurs quickly and without much warning. Biological agents can be introduced by air, water, or in the food supply. FEMA categorizes agents by application, duration, extent of effects, and mitigation in Figure 4.19.

Agent Type	Disease/Condition *Causative Agent/ Pathogen*	Description of Agent	Transmissible Person to Person	Infectivity/ Lethality	Incubation Period	Duration of Illness	Persistence/ Stability	Vaccination/ Toxoids	Rate of Action	Symptoms	Treatment	Possible Means of Delivery
BACTERIA	Anthrax (inhalation) *Bacillus anthracis*	Rod-shaped, gram-positive, aerobic sporulating micro-organism, individual spores ~(1–1.2)x(3–5)μ	No	Moderate/ High	1–7 days	3–5 days	Spores are highly stable	Yes	Symptoms in 2–3 days; Shock and death occurs with 24–36 hrs after symptoms	Fever, malaise, fatigue, cough and mild chest discomfort, followed by severe respiratory distress with dyspnea, diaphoresis, stridor, and cyanosis	Usually not effective after symptoms are present, high dose antibiotic treatment with penicillin, ciprofloxacin, or doxycycline should be undertaken. Supportive therapy may be necessary.	Aerosol.
	Brucellosis *Brucella suis, melitensis & abortus*	All non-motile, non-sporulating, gram negative, aerobic bacterium; ~(0.5-1)x(1-2)μ	No	High/Low	Days to months	Weeks to months	Organisms are stable for several weeks in wet soil and food.	Yes	Highly variable, usually 8-60 days.	Chills, sweats, headache, fatigue, myalgias, arthralgias, and anorexia. Cough may occur. Complications include sacroiliitis, arthritis, vertebral osteomyelitis, epididymoorchitis, and rarely endocarditis.	Recommended treatment is doxycycline (200 mg/day) plus rifampin (900 mg/day) for 6 weeks.	Aerosol. Expected to mimic a natural disease.
	Cholera *Vibrio cholerae*	Short, curved, motile, gram-negative, non-sporulating rod. Strongly anaerobic, these organisms prefer alkaline and high salt environments.	Negl.	Low/Moderate-High	1-5 days	1 or more weeks	Unstable in aerosols and pure water, more so in polluted water.	Yes	Sudden onset after 1-5 day incubation period.	Initial vomiting and abdominal distension with little or no fever or abdominal pain. Followed rapidly by diarrhea, which may be either mild or profuse and watery, with fluid losses exceeding 5 to 10 liters or more per day. Without treatment, death may result from severe dehydration, hypovolemia, and shock.	Therapy consists of fluid and electrolyte replacement. Antibiotics will shorten the duration of diarrhea and thereby reduce fluid losses. Tetracycline, ampicillin, or trimethoprim-sulfamethoxazole are most commonly used.	1. Sabotage (food/water supply) 2. Aerosol
	Glanders *Burkholderia mallei*	Gram-negative bacillus primarily noted for producing disease in horses, mules, and donkeys	Negl.	/Moderate-High	10-14 days	N/A	N/A	No	N/A	Inhalational exposure produces fever, rigors, sweats, myalgia, headache, pleuritic chest pain, cervical adenopathy, splenomegaly, and generalized papular/pustular eruptions. Almost always fatal without treatment.	Few antibiotics have been evaluated *in vivo*. Sulfadiazine may be effective in some cases. Ciprofloxacin, doxycycline, and rifampin have *in vitro* efficacy. Extrapolating from melioidosis guidelines, a combination of TMP-SMX + ceftazidime ± gentamicin might be considered.	Aerosol.
	Plague (pneumonic, bubonic) *Yersinia pestis*	Rod-shaped, non-motile, non-sporulating, gram-negative, aerobic bacterium; ~(0.5-1)x(1-2)μ	High	High/Very High in untreated personnel, the mortality is 100%	2 to 6 days for bubonic and 3 to 4 days for pneumonic	1-2 days	Less important because of high transmissibility.	Yes	Two to three days	High fever, chills, headache, hemoptysis, and toxemia, progressing rapidly to dyspnea, sturdier, and cyanosis. Death results from respiratory failure, circulatory collapse, and a bleeding diathesis.	Early administration of antibiotics is very effective. Supportive therapy for pneumonic and septicemic forms is required.	May be delivered via contaminated vectors (fleas) causing bubonic type, or, more likely, via aerosol causing pneumonic type.
	Shigellosis *Shigella Dysenteriae*	Rod-shaped, gram-negative, non-motile, non-sporulating bacterium	Negl.	High/Low	1-7 days (usually 2-3)	N/A	Unstable in aerosols and pure water, more so in polluted water.	No	Symptoms usually within 2-3 days, however, known to demonstrate in as little as 12 hours or as long as 7 days.	Fever, nausea, vomiting, abdominal cramps, watery diarrhea, and occasionally, traces of blood in the feces. Symptoms range from mild to severe with some infected individuals not experiencing any symptoms.	The antibiotics commonly used for treatment are ampicillin, trimethoprim/sulfamethoxazole (also known as Bactrim* or Septra*), nalidixic acid, or ciprofloxacin. Persons with mild infections will usually recover quickly without antibiotic treatment. Antidiarrheal agents such as loperamide (Imodium*) or diphenoxylate with atropine (Lomotil*) are likely to make the illness worse and should be avoided.	Contaminated food or water
	Tularemia *Francisella tularensis*	Small, aerobic, non-sporulating, non-motile, gram-negative cocco-*bacillus* ~0.2x(0.2-0.7)μ	No	High/ Moderate if untreated	1-10 days	2 or more weeks	Not very stable	Yes	Three to five days	Ulceroglandular tularemia with local ulcer and regional lymphadenopathy, fever, chills, headache, and malaise. Typhoidal or septicemic tularemia presents with fever, headache, malaise, substernal discomfort, prostration, weight loss, and non-productive cough.	Administration of anitbiotics with early treatment is very effective. Streptomycin – 1 gm I. M. q. 12 hrs x 10 10-14 d. Gentamicin – 3-5 mg/kg/day x 10-14 d.	Aerosol.
	Typhoid *Salmonella typhi*	Rod-shaped, motile, non-sporulating gram-negative bacterium	Negl.	Moderate/ Moderate if untreated	6-21 days	Several weeks	Stable	Yes	One to three days	Sustained fever, severe headache, malaise, anorexia, a relative bradycardia, splenomegaly, nonproductive cough in the early stage of the illness, and constipation more commonly than diarrhea.	Chloramphenicol amoxicillin or TMP-SMX. Quilone derivatives and third generation cephalusporins and supportive therapy.	Sabotage of food and water supplies.
RICKETTSIAE	Q-Fever *Coxiella burnetii*	Bacterium-like, gram-negative organism, pleomorphic 300-700 nm	No	High/Very low	10-20	2 days to 2 weeks	Stable	Yes	Onset may be sudden	Chills, retrobulbar headache, weakness, malaise and severe sweats.	Tetracycline or doxycycline are the treatment of choice and are given orally for 5 to 7 days.	May be a dust cloud either from a line source or a point source (downwind one-half mile or more).
	Typhus (classic) *Rickettsia prowazeki*	Non-motile, minute, coccoid or rod shaped rickettsiae, in pairs or chains, 300 nm	No	High/High	6-15 days	Weeks to months	Not very stable	No	Variable onset, often sudden. Terminates by rapid lysis after about 2 weeks of fever	Headache, chills, prostration, fever, and general pain. A macular eruption appears on the fifth to sixth day, initially on the upper trunk, followed by spread to the entire body, but usually not the face, palms, or soles.	Tetracyclines or chlormphenical orally in a loading dose of 2-3 g, followed by daily doses of 1-2 g/day in 4 divided doses until Ind. becomes afelorite (usually 2 days) plus 1 day.	May be delivered via contaminated vectors (lice or fleas).
VIRUSES	Encephalitis	Lipid-enveloped virions of 50-60 nm dia., icosohedral nucleocapsid w. 2 glycoproteins										
	-Eastern/Western Equine Encephalitis (EEE, WEE)		Negl.	High/High	5-15 days	1-3 weeks	Relatively unstable	Yes		Inflammation of the mengies of the brain, headache, fever, dizziness, drowsiness or stupor, tremors or convulsions, muscular incoordination.	No specific treatment; supportive treatment is essential	Airborne spread possible.
	-Venezuelan Equine Encephalitis		Low	High/Low	1-5 days	Days to weeks	Relatively unstable	Yes	Sudden	Inflammation of the mengies of the brain, headache, fever, dizziness, drowsiness or stupor, tremors or convulsions, muscular incoordination.	No specific treatment; supportive treatment is essential	Airborne spread possible.
	Hemorrhagic Fever									Malaise, myalgias, headache, vomiting, and diarrhea may occur with any of the hemorrhagic fevers	No specific treatment; intensive supportive treatment is essential	Airborne spread possible.
	-Ebola Fever	Filovirus	Moderate	High/High	7-9 days	5-16 days	Relatively unstable	No		May also include a macular dermatologic eruption.		
	-Marburg	Filovirus	Moderate					No		May also include a macular dermatologic eruption.		
	-Yellow Fever	Flavivirus. Isosahedral nucleocapsid 37-50 nm diam., lipoprotein env. w/ short surface spikes	Negl.	High/High	3-6 days	1-2 weeks	Relatively unstable	Yes	Sudden			
	Variola Virus (Smallpox)	Asymmetric, brick-shaped, rounded corners; DNA virus	High	High/High	7-17 days	1-2 weeks	Stable	Yes	2-4 days	Malaise, fever, rigors, vomiting, headache, and backache. 2-3 days later lesions appear which quickly progress from macules to papules, and eventually to pustular vesicles. They are more abundant on the extremities and face, and develop synchronously.	No specific treatment; supportive treatment is essential	Airborne spread possible.
TOXIN	Botulinum Toxin	any of the seven distinct neurotoxins produced by the bacillus, *Clostridium botulinum*	No	NA/High	Variable (hours to days)	24-72 hours/Months if lethal	Stable	Yes	12-72 hours	Initial signs and symptoms include ptosis, generalized weakness, lassitude, and dizziness. Diminished salivation with extreme dryness of the mouth and throat may cause complaints of a sore throat. Urinary retention or ileus may also occur. Motor symptoms usually are present early in the disease; cranial nerves are affected first with blurred vision, diplopia, ptosis, and photophobia. Bulbar nerve dysfunction causes dysarthria, dysphonia, and dysphagia. This is followed by a symmetrical, descending, progressive weakness of the extremities along with weakness of the respiratory muscles. Development of respiratory failure may be abrupt.	(1) Respiratory failure—tracheostomy and ventilatory assistance, fatalities should be <5%. Intensive and prolonged nursing care may be required for recovery (which may take several weeks or even months). (2) Food-borne botulism and aerosol exposure—equine antitoxin is probably helpful, sometimes even after onset of signs of intoxication. Administration of antitoxin is reasonable if disease has not progressed to a stable state. Use requires pretesting for sensitivity to horse serum (and desensitization for those allergic). Disadvantages include rapid clearance by immune elimination, as well as a theoretical risk of serum sickness.	1. Sabotage (food/water supply) 2. Aerosol
	Ricin	Glycoprotein toxin (66,000 daltons) from the seed of the castor plant	No	NA/High	Hours	Days	Stable	Not effective	6-72 hours	Rapid onset of nausea, vomiting, abdominal cramps and severe diarrhea with vascular collapse; death has occurred on the third day or later. Following inhalation, one might expect nonspecific symptoms of weakness, fever, cough, and hypothermia followed by hypotension and cardiovascular collapse.	Management is supportive and should include maintenance of intravascular volume. Standard management for poison ingestion should be employed if intoxication is by the oral route.	Aerosol
	Staphylococcal enterotoxin B	One of several exotoxins produced by *Staphylococcus aureus*	No	NA/Low	Days to weeks	Days to weeks	Stable	Not effective	30 min-6 hours	Fever, chills, headache, myalgia, and nonproductive cough. In more severe cases, dyspnea and retrosternal chest pain may also be present. In many patients nausea, vomiting, and diarrhea will also occur.	Treatment is limited to supportive care. No specific antitoxin for human use is available.	1. Sabotage (food/water supply) 2. Aerosol
	Trichothecene (T-2) Mycotoxins	A diverse group of more than 40 compounds produced by fungi.	No	NA/High	Hours	Hours	Stable	Not effective	Sudden	Victims are reported to have suffered painful skin lesions, lightheadedness, dyspnea, and a rapid onset of hemorrhage, incapacitation and death. Survivors developed a radiation-like sickness including fever, nausea, vomiting, diarrhea, leukopenia, bleeding, and sepsis.	General supportive measures are used to alleviate acute T-2 toxicoses. Prompt (within 5-60 min of exposure) soap and water wash significantly reduces the development of the localized destructive, cutaneous effects of the toxin. After oral exposure management should include standard therapy for poison ingestion.	1. Sabotage 2. Aerosol

FIGURE 4.19 Selected biological agent characteristics.

DHS has played an increasing role in this sort of detection. Through its Science and Technology Directorate, a series of programs which identify and detect biological agents have been implemented. Of recent interest is BioWatch—a program which measures air samples in 30 urban areas across the United States. Using BioWatch sensors, the technology monitors specific locations as well as events of national significance such as the Olympics or Superbowl.[23] Figure 4.20 illustrates the latest generation in BioWatch technology.

When compared to nuclear, it is a much easier scientific row to hoe, and anyone with some level of biological training and access to common laboratory equipment can develop terror tools that emerge from biological products. Biological agents, as the Anthrax cases of the last decade demonstrate, foment high rates of fear in the general public (Figure 4.21).

The Centers for Disease Control and Prevention (CDC) assumes the preeminent position when it comes to the identification, mitigation, response, and recovery from a biological attack. It classifies biological agents into three major categories

Category A diseases/agents: The U.S. public health system and primary healthcare providers must be prepared to address various biological agents, including pathogens that are rarely seen in the United States. High-priority agents include organisms that pose a risk to national security because they:

- Can be easily disseminated or transmitted from person to person
- Result in high mortality rates and have the potential for major public health impact

FIGURE 4.20 BioWatch: Generation 3 monitoring station. DHS.

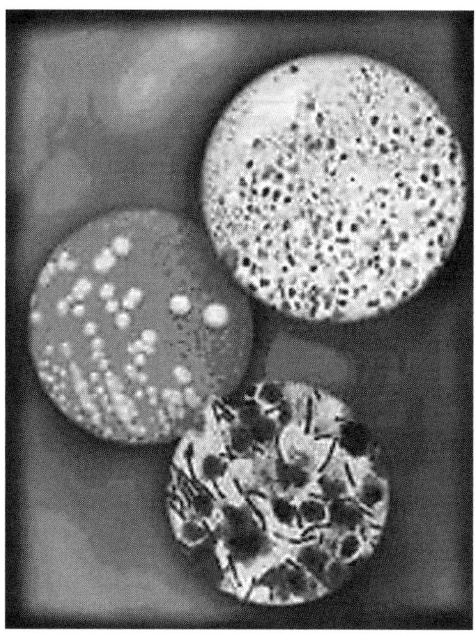

FIGURE 4.21 Biological agents under a high-powered microscope.

- Might cause public panic and social disruption
- Require special action for public health preparedness

Category B diseases/agents: Second highest-priority agents include those that:

- Are moderately easy to disseminate
- Result in moderate morbidity rates and low mortality rates
- Require specific enhancements of the CDC's diagnostic capacity and enhanced disease surveillance

Category C diseases/agents: Third highest-priority agents include emerging pathogens that could be engineered for mass dissemination in the future because of:

- Availability
- Ease of production and dissemination
- Potential for high morbidity and mortality rates and major health issues

The CDC types of all known biological agents are listed into these three categories. As of 2008 the list of biological agents were comprised of:

Category A

- Anthrax (*Bacillus anthracis*)
- Botulism (*Clostridium botulinum* toxin)
- Plague (*Yersinia pestis*)
- Smallpox (*Variola major*)

- Tularemia (*Francisella tularensis*)
- Viral hemorrhagic fevers (filoviruses [e.g., Ebola, Marburg] and arenaviruses [e.g., Lassa, Machupo])

Category B

- Brucellosis (*Brucella* species)
- Epsilon toxin of *Clostridium perfringens*
- Food safety threats (e.g., *Salmonella* species, *Escherichia coli* O157:H7, *Shigella*)
- Glanders (*Burkholderia mallei*)
- Melioidosis (*Burkholderia pseudomallei*)
- Psittacosis (*Chlamydia psittaci*)
- Q fever (*Coxiella burnetii*)
- Ricin toxin from *Ricinus communis* (castor beans)
- Staphylococcal enterotoxin B
- Typhus fever (*Rickettsia prowazekii*)
- Viral encephalitis (alphaviruses [e.g., Venezuelan equine encephalitis, eastern equine encephalitis, western equine encephalitis])
- Water safety threats (e.g., *Vibrio cholerae*, *Cryptosporidium parvum*)

Category C

- Emerging infectious diseases, such as Nipah virus and hantavirus

For the present, the bulk of attention has been on four to five biological agents with the potential for severe harm. A summary analysis of these follows.

4.3.2.3.1 Anthrax Few words evoke the terror that anthrax does. Anthrax has a long history of infecting nations and individuals and even today does not respond readily to medical intervention. Anthrax is caused by *Bacillus anthracis*, a disease-causing bacterium that forms spores. A spore is a cell that is dormant (asleep) but over time may arise from its slumber.

Anthrax can be broken down anatomically:

- Skin (cutaneous)
- Lungs (inhalation)
- Digestive (gastrointestinal)

The diagnosis of anthrax will be evidenced by certain warning signs in the infected party and where the disease has found a home:

Cutaneous: Initial symptoms are blisters that eventually turn black.
Gastrointestinal: Symptoms are nausea, loss of appetite, bloody diarrhea, fever, and significant stomach pain.

Inhalation: Cold or flu symptoms, including a sore throat, mild fever, and muscle aches. Later symptoms include cough, chest discomfort, shortness of breath, tiredness, and muscle aches.

The effects of anthrax on the human body are both painful and extreme (Figure 4.22). Without care, death is the ultimate end of the infected party.

Remediation of anthrax will be dependent on its stage and the party's resistance to antibiotics. The sooner medical attention is sought, the better the cure.

Emergency providers include anthrax in their planning and preparedness model. In general, the emergency plan should include:

- Response plans and procedures for anthrax
- Training and equipping emergency response teams
- Collaborative arrangements with health departments, veterinarians, and laboratories to watch for suspected cases of anthrax
- Sufficient laboratories for quick testing of suspected anthrax cases
- Sufficient medical supplies

The Coast Guard and the four branches of the U.S. military are so concerned that anthrax may be used in conflict against them that all military branches launched the Anthrax Vaccine Immunization Program (AVIP).

See the general order implementing the AVIP program for all personnel in Figure 4.23.

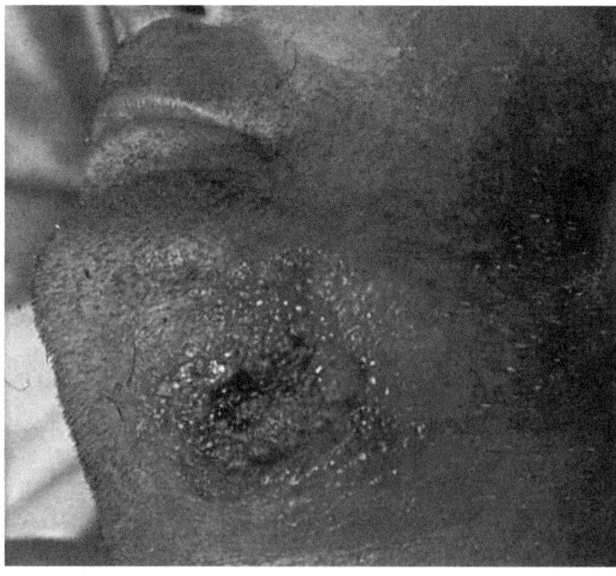

FIGURE 4.22 Anthrax infection. (Anthrax Vaccine Immunization Program for Combined Services.)

DEPUTY SECRETARY OF DEFENSE
1010 DEFENSE PENTAGON
WASHINGTON, DC 20301-1010

OCT 12 2006

MEMORANDUM FOR SECRETARIES OF THE MILITARY DEPARTMENTS
CHAIRMAN OF THE JOINT CHIEFS OF STAFF
UNDER SECRETARIES OF DEFENSE
ASSISTANT SECRETARIES OF DEFENSE
GENERAL COUNSEL, DEPARTMENT OF DEFENSE
INSPECTOR GENERAL, DEPARTMENT OF DEFENSE
DIRECTORS OF DEFENSE AGENCIES
COMMANDANT OF THE US COAST GUARD

SUBJECT: Anthrax Vaccine Immunization Program

Based on the continuing heightened threat to some U.S. personnel of attack with anthrax spores, the Department of Defense will resume a mandatory Anthrax Vaccine Immunization Program, consistent with Food and Drug Administration guidelines and the best practice of medicine, for designated military personnel, emergency-essential and comparable Department of Defense civilian employees, and certain contractor personnel performing essential services. Vaccination is mandatory for these personnel based on geographic area of assignment or special mission roles, except as provided under applicable medical and administrative exemption policies.

As it was under the Deputy Secretary of Defense Memorandum of June 28, 2004, "Expansion of Force Health Protection Anthrax and Smallpox Immunization Programs for DoD Personnel," the scope of the mandatory Anthrax Vaccine Immunization Program shall encompass personnel assigned to or deployed for 15 or more consecutive days in higher-threat areas and certain other personnel with special mission roles. Other personnel determined by the Assistant Secretary of Defense for Health Affairs, in consultation with the Chairman of the Joint Chiefs of Staff, to be at higher risk of exposure to anthrax may also be included in the program. Vaccinations shall begin, to the extent feasible, up to 60 days prior to deployment or arrival in higher-threat areas.

Consistent with the FDA-approved guidelines for use of anthrax vaccine, all personnel who begin the six-dose vaccine series (unless excluded for medical reasons) will be offered all six doses and the annual booster as long as they remain members of the armed forces or maintain a civilian employee or contractor status covered by the program. For those no longer deployed to a higher threat area or no longer assigned designated special mission roles, these later vaccine doses will be on a voluntary basis. Individuals whose vaccine series was interrupted are not required to restart the vaccine series, but will proceed in accordance with appropriate medical practice.

FIGURE 4.23 General Order from the Deputy Secretary of Defense implementing the Anthrax Vaccine Immunization Program (AVIP) for all personnel.

4.3.2.3.2 Plague The term plague conjures up images of the Dark Ages, where disease ravaged the countryside killing millions over short periods of time. Yet plague is a very real phenomenon that those concerned about biological attacks should never forget. Just as in centuries past, plague is an infectious bacteria carried by rats, flies, and fleas. Plague is an infectious airborne disease that affects others who come into contact with its strain of bacteria. Plague is normally transmitted from an infected rodent to man by infected fleas. Bioterrorism-related outbreaks are likely to be transmitted through dispersion of an aerosol. Person-to-person transmission of pneumonic plague is possible by a large dose of aerosol droplets. There are three kinds of plague:

- Pneumonic plague can spread from person to person through the air. Transmission can take place if someone breathes in aerosolized bacteria, which could happen in a bioterrorist attack.
- Bubonic plague is the most common form of plague. This occurs when an infected flea bites a person or when materials contaminated with *Y. pestis* enter through a break in a person's skin.
- Septicemic plague occurs when plague bacteria multiply in the blood. It can be a complication of pneumonic or bubonic plague, or it can occur by itself.

Several terrorist groups and some nations are experimenting with biological weapons programs. Plague could be used in an aerosol that would cause the pneumonic version. Once the disease is contracted, the bacteria can spread to others by close contact. Bubonic plague could be generated by releasing plague-infected fleas or animals. The *Y. pestis* bacterium occurs in nature and also is widely available in microbiology laboratories around the world. Thousands of scientists are working with plague organisms on a daily basis.

If detected early enough, antibiotics can be effective. A vaccine has yet to be developed.

Internet Resource: Watch the CDC video on the history and impact of plague at http://emergency.cdc.gov/training/historyofbt/03plague.asp.

4.3.2.3.3 Smallpox Smallpox has been referred to as the king of bioterrorism due to its ease of transmission and simplicity of delivery. It was the scourge of many a nation until its almost complete eradication in the 1970s. Unfortunately, the world has seen a return of this virulent disease and, just as distressingly, heard of its potential to be a weapon of mass destruction. Smallpox is a serious, contagious, and sometimes fatal infectious disease. Smallpox comes in two varieties: *Variola major*, the most severe and most common form of smallpox, and *Variola minor*, a less common presentation of smallpox with medical effects.

There is no specific treatment for smallpox, and the only prevention is vaccination. Generally, direct and fairly prolonged face-to-face contact is required to spread smallpox, usually by saliva, from one person to another. Smallpox can also be spread through direct contact with infected bodily fluids or contaminated objects (Figure 4.24).

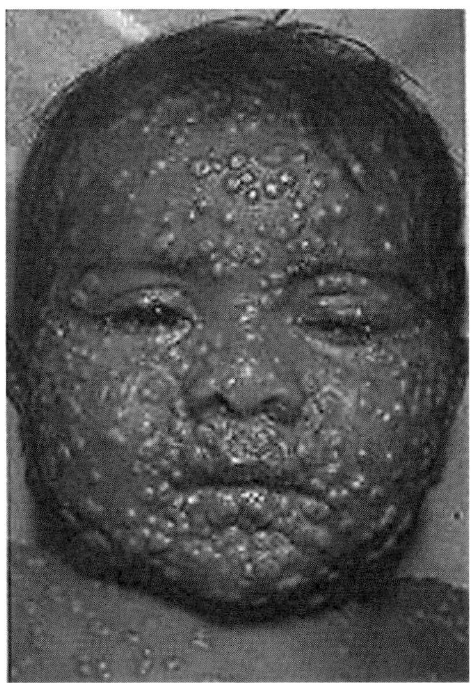

FIGURE 4.24 The rash and body lesions that result from smallpox are intense and unrivaled in epidemiology. Less than a week after an infection, the results are plain enough.

Smallpox has the capacity to inflict horrid damage and is considered part of the arsenal for the terrorist. Containment and isolation are urgent requirements. Calming the public, the victims' families, and loved ones is another essential task. The CDC publishes protocols on how to handle the smallpox case—from the initial communications chain, to isolation, to vaccination, to subsequent media demands. Use the checklist in Table 4.6 to organize that sort of operation.[24]

Internet Resource: The United Nations has dedicated a good portion of its resources to the eradication of biological weapons. The UN library in Geneva is an excellent source center for data and literature on these efforts. Visit the library at http://librarycat.unog.ch.

4.3.2.4 Chemical

Chemical weapons represent another form of WMD for terrorists. Chemical weapons have seen usage in both accidental and intentional terms. For example, the release of chemical toxins in an industrial accident can wreak havoc on the public health. More maliciously, the intentional infliction of chemical toxins by a terrorist manifests the mindset and a complete and utter disregard for human life. In World War I, soldiers on the trench fronts experienced the ferocity and terminal quality of

TABLE 4.6 General List of Actions and Decisions to Be Considered—Team Leaders (Medical and PHA)

Action or Decision	Lead Person – State or Local HD	Lead Person – CDC Team
Identify key decision-makers and infrastructure at state and local HD		
Identify with above officials the counterparts for CDC team members		
Identify and review existing state/local emergency or BT plans		
Identify state/local chains of command for action and decisions and communications and agree on access points		
Negotiate roles of CDC team in collaboration with state/local officials		
Identify office space, transport, and facilities for team members		
Identify and clarify roles of press spokespersons		
Review smallpox response plan and priority task lists and establish plan for implementation		
Identify other state/local/federal agencies involve and their roles		
Identify serious issues (isolation policy, quality of medical care versus isolation) for which immediate, high-level discussions and decisions are needed—note 8 areas below		
• Immediate need to determine number, composition and identify personnel for state/local 1st response team and facilities such as vaccination clinics and isolation hospitals, assure training, vaccination, transport, and other support needs		
• Surveillance/reporting—provider and public health alert system; laboratory alert system; active/passive rash illness reporting networks; ER alert; case response plan in place; source of exposure; data compiling support		
• Contact and contacts of contact identification, tracing, vaccination, and surveillance for fever/rash, vaccine site and severe adverse events; risk prioritization for contact tracing		
• Vaccination policy(s): who, where, when and by whom; containment or containment and mass; fixed vaccination clinics, household/neighborhood vaccination, mobile teams; separate vaccination sites for contacts, response teams, and essential services (police, water, power, fireman, other security groups, child health services, etc. Smallpox vaccine storage, distribution and security		

TABLE 4.6 (continued) General List of Actions and Decisions to Be Considered—Team Leaders (Medical and PHA)

Action or Decision	Lead Person–State or Local HD	Lead Person–CDC Team
• Decide on isolation policy(s): home, hospital, smallpox isolation facility; transport of cases; security, enforcement and maintenance issues; level of medical care to be provided; status of state quarantine rules/laws and who and how would they be implemented		
• Training and educational plans: supplies of educational and training materials; facilities, trainers, schedules needed; various curricula; identifying personnel to be trained; web-based and other alternatives for training and education		
• Security arrangements for all team members; plans for controlling the population and enforcement of vaccination and isolation		
• Supplies on hand/needed such as: bifurcated needles, forms of many types. Spox disease identification cards, vaccine take cards, VIS (languages), etc.		
Delegate assignments reflecting above needs and begin implementation with written notes of persons responsible and deadlines		
Identify political officials needed (e.g., Governor, Mayor, etc.) to reach decision quickly		
Reach consensus and schedule daily (or more frequent) meetings with key officials		
Schedule phone briefings and meetings with team members daily		
Arrange conference calls with CDC "Smallpox central" in Atlanta		

various chemical gases. Chemical weapons can cause high levels of mortality. Often referred to as the chemist's war, the range, depth, and breadth of usage shocks even today's hardened soldier. These agents could cause mass casualties, as demonstrated by the use of chemical weapons during World War I. See Table 4.7.

Today's terrorist threat is just as real and dangerous. As recently as 1995 the Tokyo subway was flooded with sarin gas, delivered via plastic bottles; it is miraculous that more injuries and deaths did not occur (Figure 4.25).

More recently, terrorists have concentrated on acquiring and employing chemical materials with dual uses, such as pesticides, poisons, and industrial chemicals. Chemical threats come in a variety of forms and delivery

TABLE 4.7 Types of Chemical Weapons Utilized in World War I

Name	First Use	Type
Chlorine	1915	Irritant/lung
Phosgene	1915	Irritant/skin and mucous membranes, corrosive, toxic
Chloromethyl chloroformate	1915	Irritant/eyes, skin, lungs
Trichloromethyl chloroformate	1916	Severe irritant, causes burns
Chloropicrin	1916	Irritant, lachrymatory, toxic
Stannic chloride	1916	Severe irritant, causes burns
a-Chlorotoluene (benzyl chloride)	1917	Irritant, lachrymatory
Bis(chloromethyl) ether (dichloromethyl ether)	1918	Irritant, can blur vision
Diphenylchloroarsine (diphenyl chlorasine)	1917	Irritant/sternutatory
Ethyldichloroarsine	1918	Vesicant
N-Ethylcarbazole	1918	Irritant
Benzyl bromide	1915	Lachrymatory
Ethyl iodoacetate	1916	Lachrymatory
Bromoacetone	1916	Lachrymatory, irritant
Bromomethyl ethyl ketone	1916	Irritant/skin, eyes
Acrolein	1916	Lachrymatory, toxic
Hydrocyanic acid	1916	Paralyzing
Hydrogen sulfide	1916	Irritant, toxic
Mustard gas	1917	Vescant (blisters)

FIGURE 4.25 Shoko Ashara, cult leader who carried out Tokyo terrorism.

systems. These agents are far more common and much easier to develop and distribute than the biological and nuclear counterparts. Many household products, farm fertilizers, and other agricultural and industrial products contain the elements necessary to shape the chemical terror.

The general typology of chemical agents includes:

- Biotoxins—Poisons that come from plants or animals.
- Blister agents/vesicants—Chemicals that severely blister the eyes, respiratory tract, and skin on contact.
- Blood agents—Poisons that affect the body by being absorbed into the blood.
- Caustics (acids)—Chemicals that burn or corrode people's skin, eyes, and mucus membranes.
- Choking/lung/pulmonary agents—Chemicals that cause severe irritation or swelling of the respiratory tract.
- Incapacitating agents—Agents that can affect consciousness.
- Long-acting anticoagulants—Poisons that prevent blood from clotting properly.
- Metals—Agents that consist of metallic poisons.
- Nerve agents—Highly poisonous chemicals that work by preventing the nervous system from working properly.
- Organic solvents—Agents that damage the tissues of living things by dissolving fats and oils.
- Riot control agents/tear gas—Highly irritating agents normally used by law enforcement for crowd control.
- Toxic alcohols—Poisonous alcohols that can damage the heart, kidneys, and nervous system.
- Vomiting agents—Chemicals that cause nausea and vomiting.

Internet Resource: Find out more about chemical threats by visiting the National Institute of Occupational Safety and Health pocket guide on chemical threats at http://www.cdc.gov/niosh/npg.

The sheer volume of chemical agents makes full coverage impossible. Those agents most likely to be encountered in the world of homeland security will be part of this overview. See Figure 4.26.

4.3.2.4.1 Ricin Ricin is a poison found naturally in castor beans. Ricin can be made from the waste material left over from processing castor beans (Figure 4.27).

Ricin may be produced in various forms, including powder, mist, or pellet. It can also be dissolved in water or weak acid. Castor beans are processed throughout the world to make castor oil, and its by-product, the "mash," provides the source material for the dangerous chemical.

Be Informed

Chemical Threat

1. A chemical attack is the deliberate release of a toxic gas, liquid, or solid that can poison people and the environment.

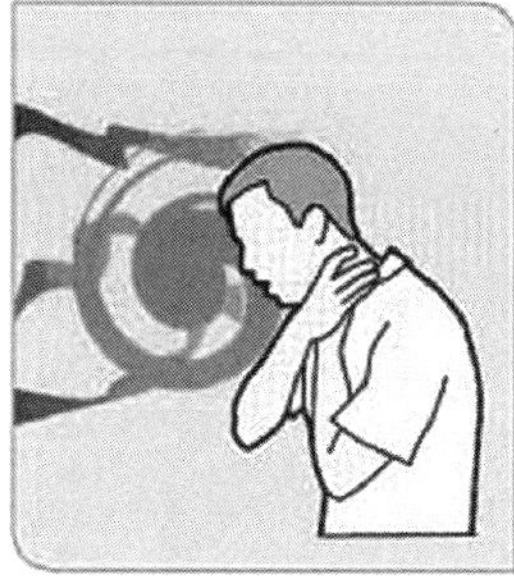

2. Watch for signs such as many people suffering from watery eyes, twitching, choking, having trouble breathing, or losing coordination.

3. Many sick or dead birds, fish, or small animals are also cause for suspicion.

4. If you see signs of a chemical attack, quickly try to define the impacted area or where the chemical is coming from, if possible.

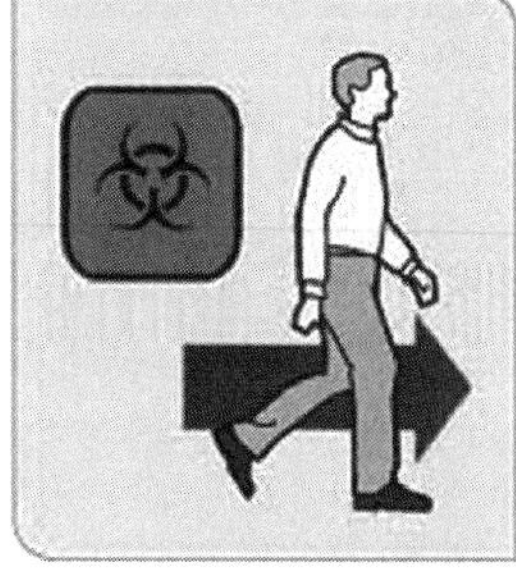

5. Take immediate action to get away from any sign of a chemical attack.

6. If the chemical is inside a building where you are, try to get out of the building without passing through the contaminated area, if possible.

FIGURE 4.26 Chemical threat response actions.

FIGURE 4.27 Castor beans. (Minnesota Department of Health.)

The production is not a natural by-product but an intentional manufacture, which indicates malevolence on the part of the maker of the ricin. Ricin can be delivered in various ways, including:

- *Indoor air*: Ricin can be released into indoor air as fine particles (aerosol).
- *Water*: Ricin can be used to contaminate water.
- *Food*: Ricin can be used to contaminate food.
- *Outdoor air*: Ricin can be released into outdoor air as fine particles.
- *Agricultural*: If ricin is released into the air as fine particles, it can damage and contaminate agricultural products.

Ricin can be absorbed into the body through ingestion, inhalation, or eye contact. Ricin can be absorbed through open skin or wounds, but most likely not through intact skin, unless aided by a solvent. Ricin causes acute respiratory problems, impacts central organs in the human body, and can negatively affect eyes and ears. It can cause death in less than 24 hours (Figure 4.28).

Clues that indicate the presence or release of ricin include but are not limited to:

- An unusual increase in the number of patients seeking care for potential chemical-release-related illness
- Unexplained deaths among young or healthy persons
- Emission of unexplained odors by patients
- Clusters of illness in persons who have common characteristics, such as drinking water from the same source
- Rapid onset of symptoms after an exposure to a potentially contaminated medium

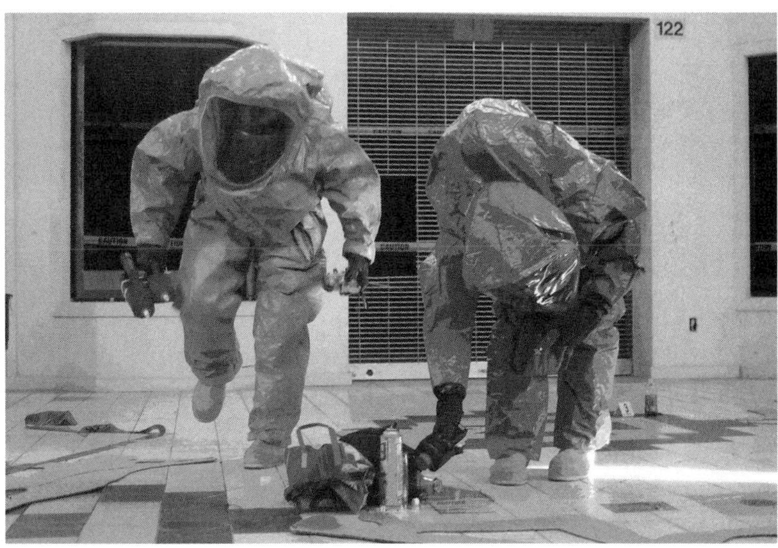

FIGURE 4.28 A ricin exercise conducted by the U.S. Army.

- Unexplained death of plants, fish, or animals (domestic or wild)
- A syndrome suggesting a disease associated commonly with a known chemical exposure (e.g., neurologic signs or pinpoint pupils in eyes of patients with a gastroenteritis-like syndrome or acidosis in patients with altered mental status)[25]

Internet Resource: For a recent case of ricin contamination at a South Carolina postal facility, see http://www.cdc.gov/nceh/hsb/chemicals/pdfs/mmwr5246p1129.pdf.

4.3.2.4.2 Nerve Agents Chemicals can also influence, in an extremely negative way, the central nervous system of the human body. Chemical nerve agents and gases have been around for more than a century. There are four main nerve agents: nerve agents GA (Tabun), GB (Sarin), GD (Soman), and VX are manufactured compounds. The G-type agents are clear, colorless, tasteless liquids miscible in water and most organic solvents. Sarin is odorless and is the most volatile nerve agent. Tabun has a slightly fruity odor, and Soman has a slight camphor-like odor. VX is a clear, amber-colored, odorless, oily liquid. It is miscible with water and dissolves in all solvents. VX is the least volatile nerve agent.

Most of the nerve agents were originally produced in a search for insecticides, but because of their toxicity, they were evaluated for military use.

Sarin was produced before the commencement of World War II and was primarily used as a pesticide. However, the gas was quickly valued for its capacity for chemical weaponry and was tested, though not used, during World War II. It has been alleged that Saddam Hussein used sarin against the Iranians in the long and very costly war between Iraq and Iran in the 1980s and early 1990s.[26] As noted above, it was delivered into a Tokyo subway by the radical terrorist cult Aum Shinrikyo, a cell that intended to install Shoko Asahara as its new savior. Asahara, who strove "to take over Japan and then the world," according to the State Department, was arrested in May 1995 for his role in the subway attack. His trial took 8 years, from 1996 until 2004, when he was sentenced to death.

Sarin gas is a preferred method for the terrorist due to its ease of delivery. Aerosol or vapor forms are the most effective for dissemination, which can be carried by sprayers or an explosive device.

Internet Resource: Chemical facilities, due to their stockpiles and ready availability of chemical substances, need to conduct vulnerability assessments of their facilities. DHS has published a vulnerability assessment guide at http://www.dhs.gov/xlibrary/assets/chemsec_csattopscreenquestions.pdf.

Tabun is a man-made chemical warfare agent classified as a nerve agent. Nerve agents are the most toxic and rapidly acting of the known chemical warfare agents. Tabun was originally developed as a pesticide in Germany in 1936. In a plot to kill Hitler in early 1945, Reich Minister of Armaments Albert Speer made inquiries about a certain quantity to be introduced into an airshaft in Hitler's final bunker. The deed was never carried out.

As in all other forms of nerve agents and other threats, the CDC disseminates educational literature to the professional community. Known as cards, these informational pieces lay out symptoms and response regarding a particular agent. See the complete description of Tabun in Table 4.8.

VX is another recent nerve agent originally developed for industrial purposes but then construed to be an effective tool in chemical warfare. VX was originally developed in the United Kingdom in the early 1950s. VX is tasteless and slow to evaporate. Following release of VX into the air, people can be exposed through skin or eye contact or inhalation. It can also be ingested through contaminated water or food (Figure 4.29).

VX, like other nerve gases, generally causes death by asphyxiation. The symptoms include:

- Blurred vision
- Runny nose
- Slurred speech
- Tightness in the chest and constriction of the pupils
- Breathing difficulties, along with vomiting, drooling, urinating, and defecating
- Areflexia (loss of reflexes)
- Ataxia (lack of muscle control)—twitching and jerking

After the victim has lost control of his or her bodily functions, suffocation and convulsive spasms cause death. Atropine is an effective antidote if given in time.

Soman also qualifies under the definition of nerve agent. Soman was originally developed as an insecticide in Germany in 1944. Soman is commonly referred to as GD. It will become a vapor if heated. Soman is not found naturally in the environment. Soman, like other nerve agents, can be exposed by air, touch, or contaminated food or water. The most likely method of transmission is for people to breathe air containing Soman gas or droplets, or when the liquid form of Soman comes into contact with the skin or eyes. Because Soman mixes easily with water, it has the potential to be used as a poison for food and water supplies. Clothing from a contaminated person can release vapors for about 30 min after exposure, thus endangering people who were not in an original area of release.

Exposure to Soman can be treated with specific antidotes—Atropine and pralidoxime chloride (2-PAM)—along with supportive medical care in a hospital. These nerve agent antidotes are most effective when given within minutes of exposure.

TABLE 4.8 Tabun Card

Nerve Agent CAS #77-81-6 RTECS# Counter Terrorism Card 0002	TABUN (GA) Dimethylphosphoramidocyanidic Acid, Ethyl Ester Ethyl *N,N*-Dimethylphosphoramidocyanidate Chemical Formula C5H11N2O2P Molecular mass: 162.12		
Types of Hazard/ Exposure	**Acute Hazards/Symptoms**	**Prevention**	**First Aid/Fire Fighting**
Fire	React with steam or water to produce toxic and corrosive vapors.	Contain to prevent contamination to uncontrolled areas.	Water mist, fog, and foam, CO_2. Avoid methods that will cause splashing or spreading.
Explosion	May result in the formation of hydrogen cyanide.		
Exposure	Liquid or vapors can be fatal. Clothing releases agent for about 30 min after contact with vapor. Contaminated surfaces present long-term contact hazard.	Do not breathe fumes. Skin contact must be avoided at all times.	Seek medical attention immediately.
Inhalation	Inhalation can cause symptoms in 2–5 min. Same sequence of symptoms despite the route of exposure: MILD • Runny nose • Tightness of the chest and breathing difficulty • Eye pain, dimness of vision and pin pointing of pupils (miosis) • Difficulty in breathing and cough	Hold breath until respiratory protective mask is donned. Fire-fighting personnel should wear full protective clothing and respiratory protection during fire-fighting and rescue.	If severe signs, immediately administer, in rapid succession, all three Nerve Agent Antidote Kit(s), Mark I injectors (or atropine if directed by a physician). If signs and symptoms are progressing, use injectors at 5–20 min intervals. (No more than 3 injections unless directed by medical personnel.) Maintain record of all injections given.

	MODERATE • Increased eye symptoms with blurred vision • Drooling and excessive sweating • Severe nasal congestion • Increased tightness of the chest and breathing difficulty • Nausea, vomiting, diarrhea, and cramps • Generalized weakness, twitching of large muscle groups • Headache, confusion, and drowsiness SEVERE • Involuntary defecation and urination • Very copious secretions • Twitching, jerking, staggering and convulsions • Cessation of breathing, loss of consciousness, coma and death.	Positive pressure, full face piece, NIOSH-approved self-contained breathing apparatus (SCBA) will be worn.	Give artificial respiration if breathing has stopped. Use mouth-to-mouth when mask-bag or oxygen delivery systems not available. Do not use mouth-to-mouth if face is contaminated. Administer oxygen if breathing is difficult.
Skin	See Inhalation Lethal doses can kill in 1–2 hours. Pupil size may range from normal to moderately reduced.	Protective Gloves: Butyl Rubber Glove M3 and M4 Norton, Chemical Protective Glove Set	The primary mode for decontamination of chemical agents is soap and water. A 0.5% hypochlorite solution can be used. There are differing guidelines for decontamination and more research is needed to identify the optimal decontamination method. See "Personal Decontamination" and "Appendix D" in Treatment of Chemical Agent Casualties and Conventional Military Chemical Injuries (from the U.S. Navy Counterproliferation Office).

continued

TABLE 4.8 (continued) Tabun Card

Nerve Agent CAS #77-81-6 RTECS# Counter Terrorism Card 0002	TABUN (GA) Dimethylphosphoramidocyanidic Acid, Ethyl Ester Ethyl *N,N*-Dimethylphosphoramidocyanidate Chemical Formula C5H11N2O2P Molecular mass: 162.12		
Types of Hazard/ Exposure	**Acute Hazards/Symptoms**	**Prevention**	**First Aid/Fire Fighting**
			See also the Medical Management of Chemical Casualties Handbook (from the U.S. Army Medical Research Institute of Chemical Defense [USAMRICD]) for a general review of the issues and more on the military decontamination powder approach.
Eyes	See Inhalation Very rapid onset of symptoms (<2–3 min).	Chemical goggles and face shield.	Immediately flush eyes with water for 10–15 min, then don respiratory protective mask.
Ingestion	See Inhalation Pupil size may range from normal to moderately reduced.		Do not induce vomiting. First symptoms are likely to be gastrointestinal. Immediately administer Nerve Agent Antidote Kit, Mark I.

FIGURE 4.29 VX palate. (Courtesy of the U.S. Army.)

4.3.2.5 Improvised Explosive Devices

In addition to WMD and potential weapons of mass effect, there is the threat of terrorist attack by means of improvised explosive device (IED). IED weapons are explosive devices fashioned and deployed by means other than through conventional military operations, thus the term "improvised." They can be created from traditional explosive devices such as bombs, warheads, grenades, land mines, or otherwise fashioned from explosive raw materials. Ball bearings, nails, metal filings, and other materials can be utilized as damage-causing projectiles.[27] Detonation can be accomplished by wired means or remotely through a rigged cell phone, handheld device, or other wireless technology. The fuel to ignite the IED can be common products such as "drain openers, sulfuric acid, and car batteries."[28] The FBI disseminates an IED Threat Card which categorizes the various products, compounds and chemicals common to IEDs. See Figure 4.30.[29]

The methods of IED delivery will vary depending on the target as well as the IED design. The Consortium of National Academies including Science, Engineering, Medicine and the National Research Council, charts the variety in Figure 4.31.

An inordinately high number of incidents of IED attack globally over the last several years have occurred in Iraq and Afghanistan, in addition to attacks in a number of other countries that have begun to experience increased terrorist attacks first hand. Unfortunately, there exist numerous online terrorist organization websites and sources that provide detailed instructions, including videos, on how to construct and deploy bombs. Often new sites crop up as quickly as sites can be discovered and deactivated by authorities.

IED attacks have given rise to other means and related classifications of attack. Multiple IEDs can be strung together to create a "daisy chain" whereupon multiple devices can be discharged, either at once or concurrently,

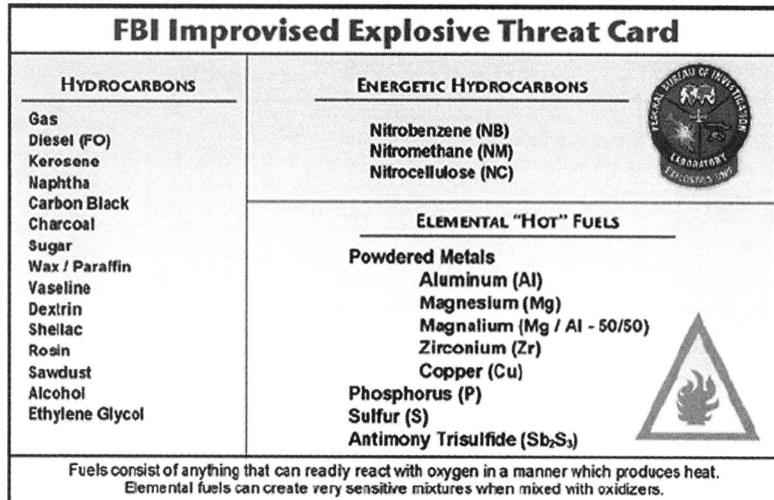

FIGURE 4.30 IE fuels.

Threat	Threat Description	Explosive Capacity	Building Evacuation Distance	Outdoor Evacuation Distance
	Small package/letter	1 lb	40 ft	900 ft
	Pipe bomb	5 lb	70 ft	1200 ft
	FedEx package	10 lb	90 ft	1080 ft
	Vest/container bombs	20 lb	110 ft	1700 ft
	Parcel package	50 lb	150 ft	1850 ft
	Compact car	500 lb	320 ft	1900 ft
	Full size car/minivan	1000 lb	400 ft	2400 ft
	Van/SUV/pickup truck	4000 lb	640 ft	3800 ft
	Delivery truck	10,000 lb	860 ft	5100 ft

FIGURE 4.31 Methods of IED delivery. (Courtesy U.S. Technical Support Working Group (TSWG).)

with a single signal. Other means of attack include VBIED (Vehicle-Borne Improvised Explosive Device), SVBIED (Suicide Vehicle-Borne Improvised Explosive Device), and SPBIED (Suicide Pedestrian-Borne Improvised Explosive Device).

Internet Resource: Complete the WMD class offered by the Office of Domestic Preparedness at http://www.ojp.usdoj.gov/odp/docs/coursecatalog.pdf.

Either way, the results are often physically devastating. Health impacts are immediate when in proximity to and IED and include:

- Overpressure damage to the lungs, ears, abdomen, and other pressure-sensitive organs. Blast lung injury, a condition caused by the extreme pressure of an explosion, is the leading cause of illness and death for initial survivors of an explosion.
- Fragmentation injuries caused by projectiles thrown by the blast—material from the bomb, shrapnel, or flying debris that penetrates the body and causes damage.
- Impact injuries caused when the blast throws a victim into another object, that is, fractures, amputation, and trauma to the head and neck.
- Thermal injuries caused by burns to the skin, mouth, sinus, and lungs.
- Other injuries including exposure to toxic substances, crush injuries, and aggravation of preexisting conditions (asthma, congestive heart failure, etc.).

Timothy McVeigh carried out a VBIED attack in the case of the Oklahoma City bombing in 1995. A waterborne SVBIED attack method was utilized in the Bombing of the USS *Cole* in 2000. It can be argued that the 9/11 attacks were the largest ever SVBIED attack carried out, with the jet fuel on board the planes serving as the explosive material. A series of SBIED attacks were carried out in perpetrating the July 7, 2005 London bombings.

While generally smaller in scale than WMD attacks, the various IED attack methods pose an increasingly real and challenging threat in the United States and particularly to interests globally. In addition, the acquisition of bomb-making materials and delivery and discharge of the weapon is generally far easier than with WMD weapons, and the effects are certainly just as deadly.

The level of harm caused by IED attacks will also depend on its delivery location. A deserted road is a very different setting than a mass transit station. Terrorists are always looking for the maximum effect possible.

Internet Exercise: See how cameras might capture the explosive attack on a transit authority setting at http://www.dhs.gov/files/programs/gc_1236624692490.shtm.

4.4 Computer Security and Information Infrastructure

The cyber world presents its own array of security challenges, and not to be forgotten is that the terrorists know that damage to the national cyber system can be devastating. Cyberspace has been defined as "the independent network of information technology infrastructures, and includes the Internet, telecommunications networks, computer systems, and embedded processors and controllers in critical Industries."[30]

From a terrorist perspective, the virtual world provides a host of avenues of attack. From their vantage point, terrorists see a world of opportunity—the disruption of essential systems, the ruination of data and protection systems, the destruction of finance and banking, and the chance to destroy and disrupt on a major scale. Security in the virtual world should not be taken lightly. In essence, the computer system is nothing less than information infrastructure—as legitimate and likely a target for the terrorist as a bridge or water treatment center. The information infrastructure, including government, educational institutions, and research centers, as well as business and industry, is rich in potential damage. Terrorists will target U.S. corporations, facilities, personnel, information, or computer, cable, satellite, or telecommunications systems—all of which are part of the information infrastructure. The possibilities are limitless and can include:

- Denial or disruption of computer, cable, satellite, or telecommunications services
- Unauthorized monitoring of computer, cable, satellite, or telecommunications systems
- Unauthorized disclosure of proprietary or classified information stored within or communicated through computer, cable, satellite, or telecommunications systems
- Unauthorized modification or destruction of computer programming codes, computer network databases, stored information, or computer capabilities
- Manipulation of computer, cable, satellite, or telecommunications services resulting in fraud, financial loss, or other federal criminal violations[31]

Internet Resource: For a full listing of potential avenues of harm in the virtual world, visit the US-CERT reading room at http://www.us-cert.gov/reading_room.

So serious and continuous are the threats to our cyber security structure that in the early days of DHS's formation, there was a keen recognition that a unit dedicated to this protection would be necessary. US-CERT—the United State Computer Emergency Readiness Team was designated as that unit. US-CERT is responsible for the management, defense, and mitigation of cyber-attacks for the federal government. To get some sense of just how extensive and continuous these threats to the cyber world are, review the reportable, high-level threats, for one week, as catalogued by the U.S. Computer Emergency Readiness Team in Figure 4.32. Threats can be categorized as shown in Table 4.9.[32]

National Cyber Alert System
Cyber Security Bulletin SB07-344

Vulnerability Summary for the Week of December 3, 2007
The US-CERT Cyber Security Bulletin provides a summary of new vulnerabilities that have been recorded by the National Institute of Standards and Technology (NIST) and National Vulnerability Database (NVD) in the past week. The NVD is sponsored by the Department of Homeland Security (DHS), National Cyber Security Division (NCSD)/ United States Computer Emergency Readiness Team (US-CERT). For modified or updated entries, please visit the NVD, which contains historical vulnerability information. The vulnerabilities are based on the CVE vulnerability naming standard and are organized according to severity, determined by the Common Vulnerability Scoring System (CVSS) standard. The division of high, medium, and low severities correspond to the following scores:

- High—Vulnerabilities will be labeled High severity if they have a CVSS base score of 7.0–10.0
- Medium—Vulnerabilities will be labeled Medium severity if they have a CVSS base score of 4.0–6.9
- Low—Vulnerabilities will be labeled Low severity if they have a CVSS base score of 0.0–3.9

Entries may include additional information provided by organizations and efforts sponsored by US-CERT. This information may include identifying information, values, definitions, and related links. Patch information is provided when available. Please note that some of the information in the bulletins is compiled from external, open source reports and is not a direct result of US-CERT analysis.

High Vulnerabilities

Primary Vendor—Product	Description	Discovered Published	CVSS Score	Source and Patch Info
APC—Rack Power Distribution Unit APC—OAS	The American Power Conversion (APC) AP7932 0u 30amp Switched Rack Power Distribution Unit (PDU), with rpdu 3.5.5 and aos 3.5.6, allows remote attackers to bypass authentication and obtain login access by making a login attempt while a different client is logged in, and then resubmitting the login attempt once the other client exits.	Unknown 2007-12-04	7.1	CVE-2007-6226 BUGTRAQ BID SECTRACK XF
Beehive Forum—Beehive Forum	Multiple unspecified vulnerabilities in Beehive Forum 0.7.1 have unknown "critical" impact and attack vectors, different issues than CVE-2007-6014.	Unknown 2007-12-05	7.5	CVE-2007-6241 OTHER-REF SECUNIA

FIGURE 4.32 National Cyber Alert System. Cyber Security bulletin.

TABLE 4.9 Cyber Security Threats

Threat	Description
Bot-network operators	Bot-network operators are hackers; however, instead of breaking into systems for the challenge or bragging rights, they take over multiple systems in order to coordinate attacks and to distribute phishing schemes, spam, and malware attacks. The services of these networks are sometimes made available in underground markets (e.g., purchasing a denial-of-service attack, servers to relay spam, or phishing attacks, etc.).
Criminal groups	Criminal groups seek to attack systems for monetary gain. Specifically, organized crime groups are using spam, phishing, and spyware/malware to commit identity theft and online fraud. International corporate spies and organized crime organizations also pose a threat to the United States through their ability to conduct industrial espionage and large-scale monetary theft and to hire or develop hacker talent.
Foreign intelligence services	Foreign intelligence services use cyber tools as part of their information-gathering and espionage activities. In addition, several nations are aggressively working to develop information warfare doctrine, programs, and capabilities. Such capabilities enable a single entity to have a significant and serious impact by disrupting the supply, communications, and economic infrastructures that support military power—impacts that could affect the daily lives of U.S. citizens across the country.
Hackers	Hackers break into networks for the thrill of the challenge or for bragging rights in the hacker community. While remote cracking once required a fair amount of skill or computer knowledge, hackers can now download attack scripts and protocols from the Internet and launch them against victim sites. Thus while attack tools have become more sophisticated, they have also become easier to use. According to the Central Intelligence Agency, the large majority of hackers do not have the requisite expertise to threaten difficult targets such as critical U.S. networks. Nevertheless, the worldwide population of hackers poses a relatively high threat of an isolated or brief disruption causing serious damage.
Insiders	The disgruntled organization insider is a principal source of computer crime. Insiders may not need a great deal of knowledge about computer intrusions because their knowledge of a target system often allows them to gain unrestricted access to cause damage to the system or to steal system data. The insider threat also includes outsourcing vendors as well as employees who accidentally introduce malware into systems.
Phishers	Individuals, or small groups, who execute phishing schemes in an attempt to steal identities or information for monetary gain. Phishers may also use spam and spyware/malware to accomplish their objectives.
Spammers	Individuals or organizations who distribute unsolicited e-mail with hidden or false information in order to sell products, conduct phishing schemes, distribute spyware/malware, or attack organizations (i.e., denial of service).

TABLE 4.9 (continued) Cyber Security Threats

Threat	Description
Spyware/ malware authors	Individuals or organizations with malicious intent carry out attacks against users by producing and distributing spyware and malware. Several destructive computer viruses and worms have harmed files and hard drives, including the Melissa Macro Virus, the Explore.Zip worm, the CIH (Chernobyl) Virus, Nimda, Code Red, Slammer, and Blaster.
Terrorists	Terrorists seek to destroy, incapacitate, or exploit critical infrastructures in order to threaten national security, cause mass casualties, weaken the U.S. economy, and damage public morale and confidence. Terrorists may use phishing schemes or spyware/malware in order to generate funds or gather sensitive information.

The US-CERT program is expected to advance information sharing amongst all agencies dedicated to the defense of the homeland. Its overall mission can be summarized as:

- Support to national and international public and private sectors
- Event monitoring, predictive analysis, and aligned reporting tools
- Advance warnings regarding emerging threats
- Incident response for national agencies, malware analysis and recovery support
- Involvement in national and international exercises

Threats of every sort and variety are vulnerabilities to both software and hardware. US-CERT defines cyber threats by using six distinct categories.

Category 1 (CAT 1)—Unauthorized Access

In this category an individual gains logical or physical access without permission to a federal agency network, system, application, data or other resource.

Category 2 (CAT 2)—Denial of Service (DoS)

An attack that successfully prevents or impairs the normal authorized functionality of networks, systems or applications by exhausting resources. This activity includes being the victim or participating in the DoS.

Category 3 (CAT 3)—Malicious Code

Successful installation of malicious software (e.g., virus, worm, spyware, bot, Trojan horse, or other code-based malicious entity that infects or affects an operating system or application). Agencies are not required to report malicious logic that has been successfully quarantined by antivirus (AV) software.

Category 4 (CAT 4)—Improper usage

A person violates acceptable computing use policies.

Category 5 (CAT 5)—Scans, Probes, or Attempted Access

Any activity that seeks to access or identify a federal agency computer, open ports, protocols, service, or any combination for later exploit. This activity does not directly result in a compromise or denial of service.

Category 6 (CAT 6)—Investigation

Unconfirmed incidents of potentially malicious or anomalous activity deemed by the reporting entity to warrant further review.

Internet Exercise: Find out about one of the worst cyber threats in the last decade—the Torpig Trojan at: http://cyberinsecure.com/category/cybercrime/page/14/.

The National Strategy to Secure Cyberspace delineates the challenges of the cyber world in the world of terrorism. Security will depend on mastery of the following tasks:

- Establish a public–private architecture for responding to national-level cyber incidents
- Provide for the development of tactical and strategic analysis of cyber-attacks and vulnerability assessments
- Encourage the development of a private sector capability to share a synoptic view of the health of cyberspace
- Expand the Cyber Warning and Information Network to support the role of DHS in coordinating crisis management for cyberspace security
- Improve National Incident Management Systems (NIMS)
- Coordinate processes for voluntary participation in the development of national public–private continuity and contingency plans
- Exercise cyber security continuity plans for federal systems
- Improve and enhance public–private information sharing involving cyber-attacks, threats, and vulnerabilities[33]

The author of these threats is not always discernible. What is clear has been the dramatic increase in every type of vulnerability that attacks systems and software. Carnegie Mellon University operates a Computer Emergency Readiness Team (CERT), and its statistics tracking vulnerabilities show a steady and dramatic rise of these intrusions. From 1995 to 2002, the increase has been quite marked, from 1090 to over 4100.[34] See Figure 4.33.

4.4.1 National Cyber Security Division

DHS erected the National Cyber Security Division (NCSD) to be the chief DHS entity setting policy for cyber threats and the protection of cyber assets.

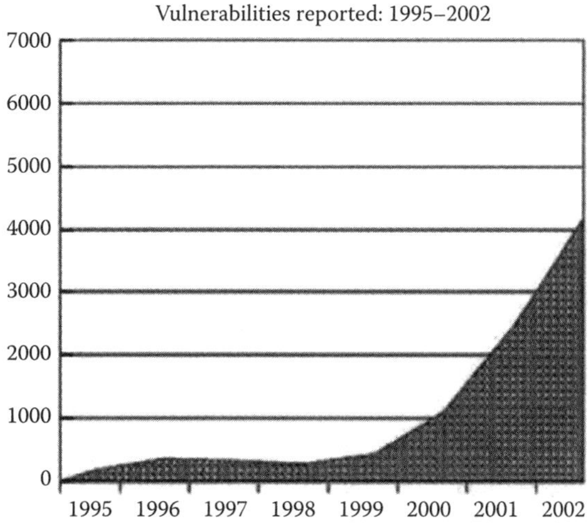

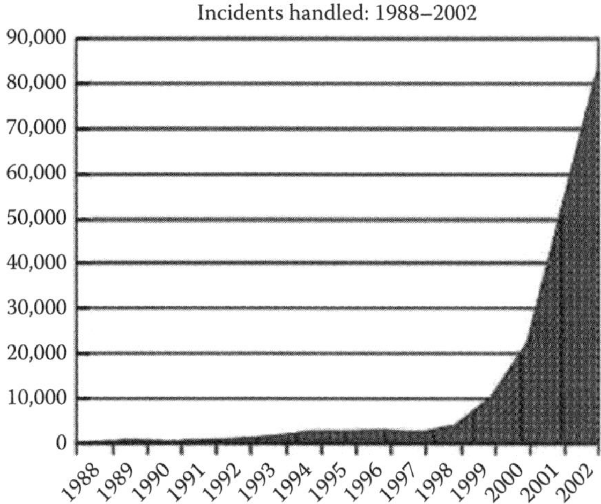

FIGURE 4.33 CERT vulnerabilities reported and incidents handled.

The NCSD seeks to protect the critical cyber infrastructure 24 hours a day, 7 days a week. NCSD has identified these fundamental objectives:

- To build and maintain an effective national cyberspace response system
- To implement a cyber-risk management program for protection of critical infrastructure

NCSD, in order to give operational meaning to the National Strategy to Secure Cyberspace, established the National Cyberspace Response System. The National Cyberspace Response System coordinates the cyber leadership, processes, and protocols that will determine when and what actions need to be taken as cyber incidents arise. The Cyberspace Response System tackles other projects as well, such as:

- Cyber security preparedness and the National Cyber Alert System—Information and alert system that warns of vulnerabilities.
- US-CERT operations—US-CERT is responsible for analyzing and reducing cyber threats and vulnerabilities, disseminating cyber threat warning information, and coordinating incident response activities.
- National Cyber Response Coordination Group—Made up of 13 federal agencies—principal federal agency mechanism for cyber incident response.
- Cyber cop portal—Coordination with law enforcement helps capture and convict those responsible for cyber-attacks.
- Cyber risk management—Assesses risk, prioritizes resources, and executes protective measures critical to securing our cyber infrastructure.
- Cyber exercises: Cyber Storm—Cyber Storm is a nationwide cyber security exercise series that takes place every 2 years. Cyber Storm was DHS's first cyber exercise testing response across the private sector and public agencies.

4.4.2 US-CERT: Computer Emergency Response Team

That virtual security poses similar challenges as physical threats have not been lost on our nation's leaders in homeland security. Even in 2003, Homeland Security Presidential Directive 7 proclaimed that critical infrastructure includes much more than highways and transportation systems—that it just as rightfully includes the physical, virtual, and technological. America's open and technologically complex society includes a wide array of critical infrastructure and key resources that are potential terrorist targets. The majority of these are owned and operated by the private sector and state or local governments. These critical infrastructures and key resources are both physically and virtually based and span all sectors of the economy.[35]

In the National Strategy to Secure Cyberspace, the designation of infrastructure relating to cyberspace could not have been clearer:

> Our Nation's critical infrastructures are composed of public and private institutions in the sectors of agriculture, food, water, public health, emergency services, government, defense industrial base, information and telecommunications energy, transportation, banking and finance, chemicals and hazardous materials, and postal and shipping. Cyberspace is their nervous

> system—the control system of our country. Cyberspace is composed of hundreds of thousands of interconnected computers, servers, routers, switches, and fiber optic cables that allow our critical infrastructures to work. Thus, the healthy functioning of cyberspace is essential to our economy and our national security.[36]

At DHS, the recognition that the virtual world was a critical component of our infrastructure was adopted head on. With the implementation of the US-CERT department, the agency made plain its prioritization in the virtual world. The US-CERT is a partnership between DHS and the public and private sectors. US-CERT is the operational arm of the NCSD at DHS (Figure 4.34).

The NCSD was established by DHS to serve as the federal government's cornerstone for cyber security coordination and preparedness. Established in 2003, it is charged with protecting the U.S.'s Internet infrastructure by coordinating defense against and response to cyber-attacks. US-CERT is responsible for:

- Analyzing and reducing cyber threats and vulnerabilities
- Disseminating cyber threat warning information
- Coordinating incident response activities

US-CERT depends upon the cooperative endeavors of other federal agencies, industry, the research community, state and local governments, and premier companies such as Apple and Microsoft and regular contributors to their protection program.

US-CERT provides a reporting mechanism in the event of threat or assault on computer infrastructure. The reporting should not be for technical

FIGURE 4.34 Cyber security should not be forgotten in terrorist incident control.

malfunction, nor should the error or problem in hardware and software be construed as unfounded or illegal. US-CERT lays out some general parameters for what types of events may qualify for reporting:

- Attempts (either failed or successful) to gain unauthorized access to a system or its data, including PII-related incidents
- Unwanted disruption or denial of service
- The unauthorized use of a system for processing or storing data
- Changes to system hardware, firmware, or software characteristics without the owner's knowledge, instruction, or consent

If the violation fits this schema, the intrusion should be reported. See Figure 4.35.

Internet Resource: Visit the National Vulnerability Center at http://nvd.nist.gov/.

US-CERT was expected to be the facilitator of communication between the diverse agencies of homeland security. Part of the 9/11 critique was the lack of communication between police and fire, state and local, federal, state and local, to list just a few disconnects. US-CERT has to deal with "the various network architectures" of competing and even incompatible systems.[37] In addition, intelligence agencies do not naturally and easily share sensitive data and some agencies "lack access to classified networks."[38] US-CERT is required to compile and analyze information on cyber security incidents and to share it with diverse constituencies. US-CERT "disseminates reasoned and actionable cyber security information to the public; and facilitates information sharing with state and local government, industry and international partners."[39]

In a recent Office of the Inspector General (OIG) assessment, US-CERT is clearly struggling to reach this mandate. The OIG is quite cognizant of the compatibility problems and other issues but makes plain that the department is really faltering on this responsibility, despite earnest efforts at a sophisticated program called "Einstein." Einstein collects network flow information and observes and identifies malicious activity in the computer network traffic. Newer versions of Einstein automatically detect intrusions and then automatically alert US-CERT to the presence of these threats. See Figure 4.36[40] for a schematic of the Einstein process and method.

The OIG notes that while on paper these software approaches seem sensible, their operational reliability is less than a sterling.

It is clear that the task of full integration in the world of cyber systems will be a generational undertaking.[41]

Section: Reporter's Contact Information	
First Name *(Required)*	
Last Name *(Required)*	
Email Address *(Required)*	
Telephone number *(Required)*	
Are you reporting as part of an Information Sharing and Analysis Center (ISAC)?	No, this is not an ISAC report
What type of organization is reporting this incident? *(Required)*	Please select
What is the impact to the reporting organization? *(Required)*	Please select
What type of followup action are you requesting at this time? *(Required)*	Please select
Describe the current status or resolution of this incident. *(Required)*	Please select
From what time zone are you making this report? *(Required)*	Please select a time zone
What is the approx time the incident started? (localtime)	August 21, 2008 : 22 : 20
When was this incident detected? (localtime)	August 21, 2008 : 22 : 20

Section: Incident Details

Please provide a short description of the incident and impact *(Required)*	
How many systems are impacted by this incident? (Leave blank if Unknown)	
How many sites are impacted by this incident? (Leave blank if Unknown)	
Was the data involved in this incident encrypted?	N/A
Was critical infrastructure impacted by this incident?	N/A
What was the primary method used to identify the incident	Unknown
If available, please include 5-10 lines of time-stamped logs in plain ASCII text. (e.g.,CSV).	

FIGURE 4.35 Cyber security intrusion report form.

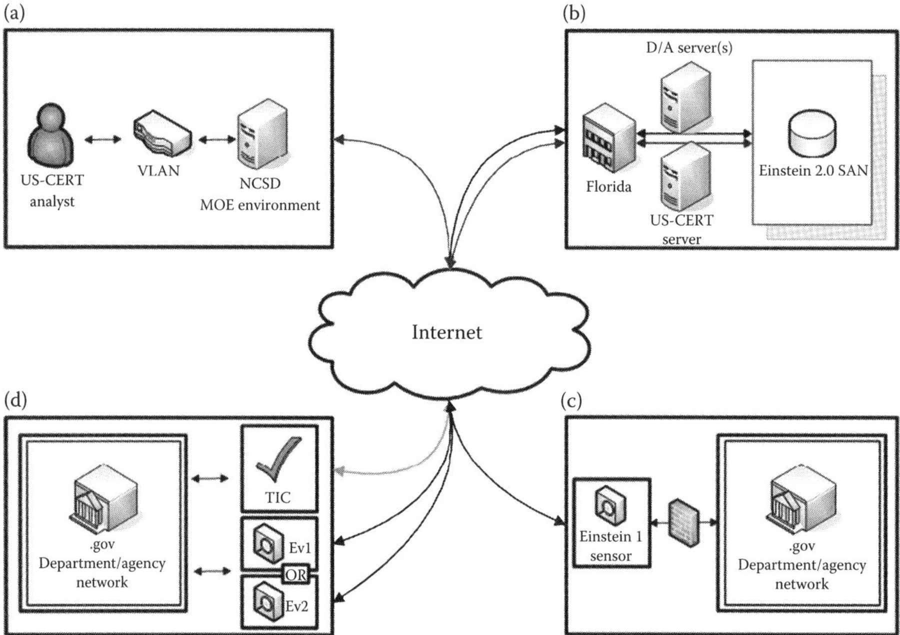

FIGURE 4.36 Einstein data collection infrastructure and process. (a) US-CERT coordination center and MOE in Virginia. (b) Einstein and MOE operations in Florida. (c) No TIC in place at department or agency. (d) TIC in place at department or agency. *Acronyms*: D/A, Department or agency; Ev1, Einstein version 1.0 sensor; Ev2, Einstein version 2.0 sensor; SAN, Storage area network; VLAN, Virtual local area network; VPN, Virtual private network. *Data flow connection colors*: dark line, Encrypted Einstein data; gray line, MOE VPN connection: light gray line, TIC connection.

4.5 The Private Sector and Homeland Security

How the private sector contributes to the fight against terrorism is a story worth telling. Since 9/11, governmental agencies have urged the participation of not only state and local governments, but also the active input and involvement of the general citizenry.[42] On top of this, there has been a continuous push for private business and commercial entities to be involved and an expectation that much of the American economy would need to be active players in the fight against terrorism. For example, America's chemical, water, utility, and nuclear sectors would have to be aggressively involved in the defense of their facilities, and thus the country itself.[43] Commercial interests could not simply wait for the government to do it all but instead had to jump into the mix of deterrence and prevention of terror. Infrastructure is largely owned by private enterprise and in need of a homeland defense plan. "Industries must plan to respond … and undertake recovery under severe conditions where much of the infrastructure of the surrounding area is unavailable and site access is limited."[44] Preparedness is an industrial and commercial concern. And it is also the private citizen that encompasses the private sector as well. The question of how much more prepared private homes and families are has yet to be fully measured.[45]

Each facet of the private sector needs to understand:

- How communities are impacted by terrorism
- How to create a plan of response consistent with state and federal standards
- How to mitigate loss in the event of catastrophe and disaster
- How to be active partners in the development of homeland policy
- How to work closely with public agencies
- How to add new programs in traditional Neighborhood Watch programs that focus on terrorism[46]

The National Infrastructure Advisory Council, in its report on public–private sector intelligence coordination, identified 17 business and commercial sectors that need to be step up in the fight against terrorism:

- Communications
- Chemical and hazardous materials
- Commercial facilities
- Dams
- Defense industrial base
- Energy
- Emergency services
- Financial services
- Food and agriculture
- Government facilities
- Information technology
- National monuments and icons
- Nuclear power plants
- Postal and shipping
- Public health and healthcare
- Transportation
- Water[47]

On a second front, the role of private sector security firms and personnel can only be described as significant. The private sector portion of criminal justice operations grows at an almost immeasurable clip.[48] According to the Homeland Security Research Corporation, by 2011 the private sector "will trail only DHS in HLS industry procurement volume. This stems from the forecasted 50% private sector procurement growth from 2007–2011, totaling an accumulated $28.5B."[49] The face of private sector justice can be discovered across the DHS spectrum; from privatized forces seeking out terrorists in Iraq and Afghanistan to the protection of federal installations across the

FIGURE 4.37 Private sector security personnel with Iraqi citizens.

mainland, private sector justice makes extraordinary contributions in the defense of the country (Figure 4.37).[50]

From Iraq to the local water facility, private sector justice operatives are engaged in a host of activities once exclusively reserved for the public sector. This trend, often labeled "privatization," assumes that the private sector, with its usual efficiencies and profit motivations, will carry out its task with greater effectiveness. Unions and entrenched government bureaucracies tend to be on the defensive with those promoting privatization. Those seeking greater accountability and freedom of operation tend to the privatized.[51] On paper, the concept is attractive, and in many cases, it is clear that the private sector can do a better job than the government in ensuring safety and security. It will all depend on the subject matter of that security and the corresponding costs. To illustrate, there are some who have argued that the Transportation Security Agency (TSA) should never have been invented, but these same services should be subcontracted to private business. Of course, this is the model pre-9/11. Since 9/11 there has been a continuous debate over the preferability of public or private in the delivery of security services. What can be agreed upon is that both domains have essential responsibilities in combating terrorism—some exclusive, though most shared.

Internet Resource: To see how private security's premier professional association, the American Society for Industrial Security (ASIS), gets involved in the standards and practices of homeland security, see http://www.asisonline.org/guidelines/guidelines.htm#standards.

In this sense, private sector justice is driven by bottom-line considerations more than its governmental counterpart. It is motivated by efficiencies never weighed or evaluated in the public sector. And given this general motivation to the profit mentality, there are those who critique it as being willing to cut corners so that the bottom line will be brighter. Quality allegedly suffers. Indeed, many are suspicious of the qualifications of those entrusted with security responsibilities from the private sector. Do recent attempts to increase qualification and conduct legitimate background investigations on security officer applicants calm frayed nerves?[52] Ian Patrick McGinley, when critiquing federal legislation to ensure suitable licensure and background requirements for security officers, found that the industry is in a state of market failure.

> Nevertheless, significant problems with leaving regulation to the market make this option unfeasible. For one, despite laudable attempts, the industry's self-regulation track record has been poor. Second, profit margins in the security industry are tight because many companies view security as a necessary evil. As a result, there is a race to the bottom—in terms of pricing and salaries—in order to gain a competitive advantage relative to other firms, resulting in less qualified officers.[53]

However, this argument does not pan out in so many governmentally operated entities. What of the public school system nationally? Are these systems not in crisis? What of public transportation systems? What of roads and bridges in near collapse? It is not difficult to discern where government fails to meet its mission. Privatization is evident everywhere—prisons, policing, and courts, to name just three, are examples of fields seeing these trends.[54] As the Bureau of Justice Assistance notes in its *Engaging Private Security to Promote Homeland Security*, private sector justice can jump in with feet first.

Private security can:

- Coordinate plans with the public sector regarding evacuation, transportation, and food services during emergencies.
- Gain information from law enforcement regarding threats and crime trends.
- Develop relationships so that private practitioners know whom to contact when they need help or want to report information.
- Build law enforcement understanding of corporate needs (e.g., confidentiality).
- Boost law enforcement's respect for the security field.

Working together, private security and law enforcement can realize impressive benefits:

- Creative problem solving
- Increased training opportunities
- Information, data, and intelligence sharing
- Force multiplier opportunities

- Access to the community through private sector communications technology
- Reduced recovery time following disasters[55]

The National Defense Industrial Association (NDIA), another premier professional group for the private sector, argues as if the task of homeland is integral to any private security firm. Its mission unequivocally declares:

- To provide legal and ethical forums for the exchange of information, ideas and recommendations between industry and government on homeland security issues.
- To promote a vigorous, robust and collaborative government-industry homeland security team.
- To advocate for best-in-class, high-technology equipment, systems, training and support for America's first responder community.[56]

And not only is it capable of carrying out its own mission in the world of homeland security, but it should do so with collaboration and collegiality in regards to its public partners. The world of public–private is not distinct or radically different; rather, these are compatible and complementary domains where a shared mission is obvious. Partnerships are what each should be looking for since the public and the private share 12 essential components:

- Common goals
- Common tasks
- Knowledge of participating agencies' capabilities and missions
- Well-defined projected outcomes
- A timetable
- Education for all involved
- A tangible purpose
- Clearly identified leaders
- Operational planning
- Agreement by all partners as to how the partnership will proceed
- Mutual commitment to providing necessary resources
- Assessment and reporting[57]

DHS formally encourages the interplay and cooperation between private sector justice entities and the public law enforcement function. Throughout DHS policy making is the perpetual recognition that it cannot go alone and that it needs the daily cooperation of the private sector. Within its Office of Policy, DHS has erected a Private Sector Office, its chief aims being:

- To engage individual businesses, trade associations, and other non-governmental organizations to foster dialogue with the department

- To advise the secretary on prospective policies and regulations and in many cases on their economic impact
- To promote public–private partnerships and best practices to improve the nation's homeland security
- To promote department policies to the private sector

The Private Sector Office focuses on two major functions: the Business Outreach Group and Economics Group. In the first instance, DHS affirmatively connects with the business and commercial sector fully realizing that cooperation and joint endeavors fare better than isolation or turf protection. The Outreach Group seeks input and advice from the business sector before the institution or implementation of policy. The Outreach Group:

- Meets with private sector organizations and department components to promote public–private partnerships
- Promotes departmental policies
- Gathers private sector perspectives for use by the department

The Economics Group weighs policy in cost–benefit terms. Here DHS displays a deaf ear regarding the costs of policy implementation since each new regulation or requirement does have a corresponding price tag. As a result, the group looks at the impact of policy from various directions, including:

- Policy analysis—Evaluates the economic impacts of departmental policies on the private sector.
- Process analysis—Evaluates departmental processes that will allow the private sector to operate efficiently while meeting national security needs.
- Regulatory analysis—Provides a resource to the department on regulatory/economic analyses.
- Metrics—Promotes the use of metrics to identify successes and areas needing improvement.
- Benefits methodology—Actively works on the development of methodologies to quantify the benefits of homeland security investments.

The Economics Group coordinates economic roundtables and publishes white papers and other studies that highlight cost–benefit.

Finally, DHS, not long after 9/11, instituted an advisory committee on private sector cooperation and collaboration. Members of the committee represent the full panoply of industry, corporate interests, and security firms with shared interests. From the outset of DHS, it was clear that policy making would not occur without the input of industry and commerce. It was equally evident that the skilled practitioners of private sector justice would be crucial contributors.

The current constitution of the committee is

Private Sector Senior Advisory Committee Members,
Homeland Security Advisory Council

- Richard D. Stephens (chair), senior vice president, Human Resources and Administration, The Boeing Company
- Herbert Kelleher (vice chair), founder and chairman emeritus, Southwest Airlines Co.
- Stephen M. Gross, president, BiNational Logistics, LLC
- Monica Luechtefeld, executive vice president, Business Development and IT, Office Depot, Inc.
- Maurice Sonnenberg, senior international advisor and director, JP Morgan Chase
- Jean E. Spence, executive vice president, Global Technology and Quality, Kraft Foods Inc.
- George A. Vradenburg III, president, Vradenburg Foundation
- Emily Walker, international consultant/former 9/11 commission staff
- William C. Whitmore, Jr., chief executive officer, AlliedBarton Security Services
- Houston L. Williams, principal owner, Raven Oaks Vineyards and Winery
- Jack L. Williams, former president and chief executive officer, Eos Airlines

Internet Resource: For a collaboration and partnerships course through the operational philosophy of DHS, see http://www.adcouncil.org/files/seminar_series/JoiningForces06/ReadyPPT.pdf.

4.6 Conclusion

Any operational notion of what homeland security is must include a look at traditional aspects of security, such as risk and threat, as well as new and emerging hazards. This chapter surveys the likely and even unlikely events that will challenge those laboring in the field of homeland security. First, how does the professional define and measure risk? What criteria and variables need to be considered when assessing risk? Are some risks worth taking and others never tolerable? Are some locations more vulnerable to risk than others? Are the costs of the risk, relative to its potential harm, worth the investment? In short, risk cannot be assessed in a vacuum but must be weighed in light of likelihood of occurrence, costs of prevention, and the nature of the harm to be inflicted. Various systems of measurement relative to risk are also provided, including CARVER+Shock methodology.

Next, the chapter's coverage turns to the typology of threat and hazard. From natural to terrorist in design, threats and hazards must be evaluated in light of the perpetrator's motivation. In the natural world, there is no malice. In the world of terrorism, the homeland professional must anticipate to what extent the actor will go to achieve a particular end. Hijackings, bombs, and WMD manifest a direct intentionality, while the hurricane and flood does not.

As for threats that impact the homeland dimension, nothing is more pressing or compelling than the world of WMD. WMD are unique in many senses, especially when one considers the nature of the harm inflicted and the potentiality for widespread destruction.[58]

The fear and dread of a nuclear event is probably the most pronounced of any form of WMD. In particular, the chapter looks at the relative ease of delivery of various WMD by a dirty bomb mechanism. In addition, particular agencies such as the Nuclear Regulatory Commission (NRC) are highlighted regarding radiological security programs. The world of bioterrorism is just as frightening, and the accessibility and general availability of bioagents should give any homeland professional cause for concern. The chapter expends considerable energy discussing anthrax, plague, and smallpox—three biological invasions that would cause both terror and widespread injury. Also covered are the diverse means to deliver and infect by chemical substance. The use of sarin gas, used as recently as 1995, indicates the extraordinary potential for harm that these agents can inflict. Biotoxins, blister agents, blood agents, acids, and other caustics, as well as respiratory agents, are all evaluated. Special coverage of ricin, Tabun, and other specific nerve agents is included.

The next portion of this chapter deals with the need to protect computer data and secured information and the equal imperative placed on information sharing between the full array of agencies involved in the homeland response. DHS fosters this approach by erecting a National Cyber Alert System, where threats to computer infrastructure are catalogued and publicly announced. DHS posts a National Strategy to Secure Cyberspace, which urges both the public and private sectors to take the necessary steps to ensure continued operation of computer functions and maintenance of data integrity. Cyber threats are just as real as any other threat. The NCSD is DHS's chief arm to ensure integrity in the system. US-CERT plays a deterrence and prevention role in cyber threats and also serves as an analysis reaction team to cyber threats.

The final section reviews the collaboration of private sector interests with the public functionality of homeland practice. Exactly how does the private sector aid in the fight against terrorism? To illustrate, the American industrial complex of utilities, chemical facilities, and manufacturing centers that produce defense products are all relevant to homeland defense. These private entities are construed as critical infrastructure in need of both plan and protection. The National Infrastructure Advisory Council highlights the need for private interests to aggressively participate in the defense of the country. Just as significant will be the rise of private sector justice operatives fighting terrorism. In Iraq, the growth of private security firms, the recognition that private soldiers now engage or protect, and that private companies and firms are better suited to the reconstruction of Iraq than governmental entities are now indisputable conclusions. DHS encourages the partnership of public with the private by and through its Private Sector Office and its Advisory Committee on the Private Sector.

Keywords

Accessibility
Analytic risk assessment
Anthrax
Asset value
Biological WMD
Bioterrorism
Biotoxin
Blister agent
Blood agent
CARVER+Shock assessment
Chemical WMD
Civil hazard
Consequence
Criticality
Cyber Warning and Information Network
Cyberspace
Daisy chain
Deliberative risk assessment
Dirty bomb
Effect
Flow process
Force on Force training
Harm
Hazard
IED (Improvised Explosive Device)
Information infrastructure
National Cyber Security Division National Cyberspace Response Team
National Vulnerability Center
Natural hazard
Nerve agent
Nuclear Regulatory Commission
Nuclear WMD
Pathogen
Plague
Practical risk assessment
Private sector
Privatization
Public health risk
Public–private partnership
Radiological dispersion device
Radiological WMD
Recognizability
Recuperability
Ricin
Risk
Risk assessment
Risk management
Sarin
Shock
Smallpox
Soman
SPBIED (Suicide Pedestrian-Borne Improvised Explosive Device)
SVBIED (Suicide Vehicle-Borne Improvised Explosive Device)
Tabun
Threat

Threat rating
US-CERT
VBIED (Vehicle-Borne Improvised Explosive Device)
Vulnerability
Vulnerability rating
VX
WMD

Discussion Questions

1. In the area of risk analysis, the question of exposure is heavily emphasized. Can you envision a circumstance when a risk that lacks significant exposure would still be considered more serious than a risk with a higher exposure?
2. Can another formula for the measure of risk be formulated?
3. Relay your view of the CARVER+Shock system of risk assessment. What are its strengths and shortcomings?
4. Some have argued that DHS should not concern itself with the world of natural hazards and threats. Comment on this school of thought.
5. It has been said that the world of WMD is highly exaggerated. How so? Can you provide an example of this hyperbole?
6. Biological terrorism is probably the easiest form of WMD to construct and deliver. Explain.
7. Chemical weaponry can be produced with easy access to products and components. Discuss.
8. Chemical weapons are not always the invention of the chemist but instead natural in design and makeup. Discuss.
9. Discuss the role and functions of a US-CERT team.
10. Discuss how computer networks can be designated critical infrastructure.
11. Relate three common threats to a cyber-system.
12. The role of the private sector in homeland defense continues unabated. Why do you think privatization of homeland services will march forward with very little resistance?
13. What types of industries need the highest level of concern regarding homeland security?

Practical Exercises

1. Conduct a threat and risk assessment regarding chemical facilities in your region. Respond to the following:
   What type of products?
   What potential injuries can arise from these products?
   What is the potential for mass destruction?
   What safety and security information on the company's web location address risk in the community?

2. Create a flowchart assessment mechanism, under the CARVER+Shock method, to measure a manufacturing threat in your area.

3. Identify nuclear facilities within 100 miles of your residence. Respond to the following:
   Describe the facility.
   How many people and communities does the facility serve?
   In the event of a nuclear event, explain how surrounding environs would be impacted.
   In what way would injury touch the largest base of people?
   Discuss the facility's evacuation policy relative to the community.

4. Contact your local office dedicated to homeland security. Gather information on your area's Anthrax program. Explain in two paragraphs what that plan or program is.

5. Identify and chart transportation infrastructure in your area. Respond to the following:
   Which infrastructure has the capacity to inflict the most damage?
   What steps are being taken to secure that infrastructure?
   Despite these steps, how can a terrorist bypass the protections?
   Point out specific vulnerabilities that you can identify.

6. The Emergency Management Institute publishes a bevy of very useful assessment tools. Complete the community and geography survey at http://training.fema.gov/EMIWeb/edu/docs/hram/Session%2013%20-%20Identifying%20the%20Risks%20-%20Community%20and%20Environme.doc.

7. Find out about FEMA's HAZUS program—a risk assessment tool for natural disasters (http://www.fema.gov/hazus/hazus-tools).

8. Visit the Cyber Storm web location and evaluate how your department or community might have responded. Provide a two- to three-page response and assessment.

9. Make a list and database for at least 10 private companies that design and manufacture explosive detection equipment, scanning devices, cargo and container scanners, and other novelties in the screening of commercial goods and trade.
10. List six applications of biometrics and the companies that produce the technology.

Notes

1. J. C. Chicken and T. Posner, *The Philosophy of Risk* (London: Thomas Telford, 1998).
2. D. Dunai, A framework of cardinal directions: Threats and challenges to the United States, *AARMS Security*, 10, 2011: 327–357, at 331.
3. See Appendix B for the full range of definitions and terms relevant to risk analysis.
4. Federal Emergency Management Agency, *Building Design for Homeland Security* (Washington, DC: U.S. Government Printing Office, 2004), V-5.
5. FEMA, *Building Design*, V-6.
6. FEMA, *Building Design*, V-9.
7. H. R. Willis, *Risk Informed Resource Allocation at the Department of Homeland Security* (Santa Monica: Rand Corporation, 2007), 3.
8. U.S. Department of Homeland Security, *Risk Analysis: Fact Sheet Series*, 2006.
9. USDHS, *Risk Analysis Sheet.*
10. USDHS, *Risk Analysis Sheet.*
11. Federal Emergency Management Agency, *Mitigation Planning How-To Guide #3: Developing the Mitigation Plan* (Washington, DC: U.S. Government Printing Office, April 2003), 1.
12. See U.S. Food and Drug Administration, *CARVER+Shock Users' Manual*, Version 1.0, 2007, Appendix B.
13. Prepared Remarks by Secretary Napolitano at *Harvard University's John F. Kennedy Jr. Forum*, April 15, 2010, at www.dhs.gov/ynews/speeches/sp_1271366935471.shtm.
14. D. Dunai, *A Framework*, at 330.
15. *EM-DAT: The OFDA/CRED International Disaster Database*, www.emdat.be—Université catholique de Louvain—Brussels—Belgium Events recorded in the CRED EM-DAT. First Event: Sep/1900, Last Entry: Mar/2012. Epidemics include: Viral Infectious Diseases (Encephalitis), Parasitic Infectious Diseases (Cryptosporidiosis), Viral Infectious Diseases (West Nile Fever),—, Viral Infectious Diseases (Acute respiratory syndrome (SARS)).
16. *EM-DAT: The OFDA/CRED International Disaster Database*, www.emdat.be—Université catholique de Louvain—Brussels—Belgium Events recorded in the CRED EM-DAT. First Event: Sep/1900, Last Entry: Mar/2012. Epidemics include: Viral Infectious Diseases (Encephalitis), Parasitic Infectious Diseases (Cryptosporidiosis), Viral Infectious Diseases (West Nile Fever),—, Viral Infectious Diseases (Acute respiratory syndrome (SARS)).
17. See Department of Homeland Security, Science and Technology Directorate Office of Research Infrastructure and Geophysical Division Focus Areas at http://www.dhs.gov/xabout/structure/gc_1242418528241.shtm.
18. A. Bauer, War on terror or policing terrorism? *Radicalization and Expansion of the Threats, Police Chief*, January, 2011: 46–52, 52.

19. See Department of Homeland Security, *Nuclear Reactors, Materials, and Waste Sector-Specific Plan: An Annex to the National Infrastructure Protection Plan*, 2010.
20. Department of Homeland Security, *Nuclear Sector—Specific Plan* 47, 2010.
21. U.S. Nuclear Regulatory Commission, *Office of Nuclear, Security and Incident Response* (Washington, DC: U.S. Government Printing Office, April 2005), 44.
22. House introduces new biological weapons legislation, *Homeland Security News Wire*, June 27, 2011, available at http://homelandsecuritynewswire.net/.
23. *Testimony of Tara O'Toole before the House Subcommittee on Homeland Security Appropriations, on Biosurveillance*, April 16, 2010, Washington, DC.
24. Centers for Disease Control, *Smallpox Response Plan and Guidelines* (Washington, DC: U.S. Government Printing Office, November 2002), Annex 8.
25. M Patel, MD et al., Recognition of illness associated with exposure to chemical agents—United States, 2003, *Morbidity and Mortality Weekly Report*, 52 (October 3, 2003): 938–40, http://www.cdc.gov/mmwr/preview/mmwrhtml/mm5239a3.htm#tab.
26. The Arms Control Association makes this claim at M. Nguyen, Report confirms Iraq used Sarin in 1991, *Arms Control Today*, 36 (January/February 2006), http://www.armscontrol.org/act/2006_01-02/JANFEB-IraqSarin.
27. H. Hogan, Identifying explosives, after the fact, *Homeland Security Today Magazine*, September, 2011: 18–19.
28. K. Yeager, What law enforcement needs to know about improvised explosives, *Police Chief*, September, 2011: 52–55.
29. National Academies & Department of Homeland Security, *Fact Sheet: IED Attack Improvised Explosive Devices, News & Terrorism, Communicating in a Crisis*.
30. National Security Presidential Directive 54, *Cyber Security and Monitoring*, January 8, 2008.
31. The National Threat Center, *Counterintelligence Guide: The National Security Threat List*, http://www.ntc.doe.gov/cita/ci_awareness_guide/T1threat/Nstl.htm.
32. Government Accountability Office (GAO), *Department of Homeland Security's (DHS's) Role in Critical Infrastructure Protection (CIP) Cybersecurity, GAO-05-434* (Washington, DC: May 2005), http://www.gao.gov/htext/d05434.html.
33. Office of the President, *The National Strategy to Secure Cyberspace* (February 2003), x, http://www.whitehouse.gov/pcipb/cyberspace_strategy.pdf.
34. See Carnegie Mellon University, *Computer Emergency Readiness Team: Vulnerability Statistics*, http://www.cert.org/stats/vulnerability_remediation.html. See also President, Strategy to Secure Cyberspace, 10.
35. Office of the President, *Homeland Security Presidential Directive 7*, December 2003, 3.
36. President, *Strategy to Secure Cyberspace*, viii.
37. R. Skinner, Einstein presents big challenge to US-CERT. IG: US-CERT fails to adequately share critical data with agencies. *GovInfo Security*, June 22, 2010, available at www.govinfosecurity.com/p_print.php?t=a&id=2677.
38. R. Skinner, Einstein presents big challenge to US-CERT. IG: US-CERT fails to adequately share critical data with agencies. *GovInfo Security*, June 22, 2010, available at www.govinfosecurity.com/p_print.php?t=a&id=2677, at 2.
39. Office of the Inspector General, Department of Homeland Security, *DHS Needs to Improve the Security Posture of its Cybersecurity Program Systems* 2, July 30, 2010.
40. Office of the Inspector General, Department of Homeland Security, *DHS Needs to Improve the Security Posture of its Cybersecurity Program Systems 5*, July 30, 2010.
41. See J. G. Schwitz, Risk-based cybersecurity policy, *American Intel Journal*, 29, 2011.

42. This approach has been repeatedly advanced by those arguing for private policing systems working side by side with public policing systems. See J. F. Pastor, Public–private policing arrangements & recommendations, *The Homeland Security Review*, 4, 2010: 71; See also C. P. Nemeth and K. C Poulin, The Prevention Agency, 2006; C. P. Nemeth and K. C. Poulin, *Private Security and Public Safety: A Community Based Approach,* 2005; J. F. Pastor, *Terrorism and Public Safety Policing: Implications for the Obama Presidency,* 2010.
43. N. Santella and L. J. Steinberg, Accidental releases of hazardous materials and relevance, *Journal of Homeland Security & Emergency Management*, 8, 2011.
44. Santella & Steinberg, at 11.
45. M. Kano et al., Terrorism preparedness and exposure reduction since 9/11: The status of public readiness in the United States, *Journal of Homeland Security & Emergency Management*, 8, 2011.
46. J. Fleischman, Engaging the private sector in local homeland defense: The Orange County private sector terrorism response group, *Sheriff*, September/October, 2004: 33.
47. National Infrastructure Advisory Council, Public–private sector intelligence coordination: Final report and recommendations by the council, July 2006, 67.
48. C. P. Nemeth, *Private Security and the Law* (London: Elsevier, 2008), 12.
49. Homeland Security Research Corporation, Private Sector to Become 2nd Largest Homeland Security Industry Customer by 2011, news release, April 9, 2008.
50. For an examination of how these privatized practices prompt ethical concerns, see K. Carmola, *Private Security Contractors in the Age of New Wars: Risk, Law & Ethics* (New York: Routledge Press, 2008).
51. P. Starr, The meaning of privatization, *Yale Law and Policy Review*, 6, 1988: 6–41. This article also appears in Alfred K. and S. Kamerman, eds., *Privatization and the Welfare State* (Princeton, NJ: Princeton University Press, 1989).
52. Private Security Officer Employment Authorization Act of 2004, U.S. Code 28, 2004, § 534.
53. I. P. McGinley, Regulating 'Rent-A-Cops' Post 9/11: Why the private security officer employment act fails to address homeland security concerns, *Cardozo Public Law, Policy and Ethics*, 6, 2007: 145.
54. C. P. Nemeth, *Private Security and the Investigative Process*, 2nd ed. (Boston: Butterworth Heinemann, 2000), 1–4.
55. Bureau of Justice Assistance, *Engaging the Private Sector to Promote Homeland Security: Law Enforcement-Private Security Partnerships*, 2003, 11.
56. National Defense Industrial Association, www.ndia.org/Aboutus/pages/default.aspx.
57. Bureau of Justice Assistance, Engaging the Private Sector, 13.
58. This is why efforts at Threat Reduction as to nuclear arsenals are a sensible part of the homeland plan. See A. F. Woolf, Department of Defense Cooperative Threat Reduction Program, Nonproliferation and Threat Reduction Assistance: U.S. Programs in the Former Soviet Union (Congressional Research Service, March 6, 2012).

Chapter 5

Training and Exercises in Homeland Security

Objectives

1. To appraise the mission of the Department of Homeland Security's Office of Grants and Training (G&T), and its opportunities for training and funding.
2. To describe TOPOFF exercises and simulation programs, to whom they are offered, as well as the goals of the training program.
3. To explain the mission and objectives of the Center for Domestic Preparedness (CDP) and their training programs.
4. To summarize the activities of the Emergency Management Institute, including their course offerings and the constituencies they serve.
5. To evaluate the usefulness and effectiveness of the Homeland Security Exercise and Evaluation Program (HSEEP) and LLIS.gov.
6. To compare the seven types of exercises defined by the HSEEP and identify the difference between discussion-based and operations-based exercises.
7. To evaluate the usefulness and effectiveness of Community Emergency Response Teams (CERTs) across the country, and explain their mission and goals.
8. To outline the organization, purpose, and processes of the National Incident Management System (NIMS) and its various components.

5.1 Introduction

The breadth, depth, scope, and coverage of training programs in homeland security are simply mind-boggling. Not only do agencies of government at the state, local, and federal levels devise, design, and deliver training in all the affairs of homeland, but so too a plethora of private companies and businesses. In a nutshell, training is a fast-growing business for both the public and the private sector. In the public sense, government agencies, in seeking to carry out their mission, educate the public and the professionals who must labor each day in the justice and emergency model. The Department of Homeland Security is the preeminent figure in the training modality and delivers programs to every imaginable sector. A partial list of the agency's more prominent programs is charted in Figure 5.1.

This section will scan some of these training systems with a full recognition that it can only touch the surface of most. DHS not only delivers a wide array of educational programs but also seeds the entire country with grants and other support so that localities and nonfederal jurisdictions can educate their constituencies with a local flavor. Billions of dollars in grants flow to every state, with most major urban areas receiving additional funding—so

FEMA Training and National Domestic Preparedness Consortium—Direct training for state and local jurisdictions to enhance capacity and preparedness

The Federal Law Enforcement Training Center—Up-to-date, low or no cost training opportunities for state and local law enforcement officers

National Preparedness Network (PREPnet)—First responder information programming schedule, all open and available to the public

The National Fire Academy—Training and educational opportunities for members of the fire, emergency services and allied professionals

Noble Training Center—Hospital-based medical training in disaster preparedness and response

The Emergency Management Institute—Training to ensure the effectiveness of organizations and individuals working together in disasters and emergencies

National Integration Center (NIC)—Incident Management Systems Division Information, guidance and resources to assist state, local, tribal, and federal agencies in adopting and implementing the National Incident Management System

National Incident Management System (NIMS) Online Training—Introduction to the purpose, principles, key components, and benefits of NIMS

Comprehensive Haz-Mat Emergency Response Capability Assessment Program (CHER-CAP)—Resource to prepare for hazardous materials incidents

National Exercise Program—Training, exercising, and collaboration among partners at all levels

Homeland Security Exercise and Evaluation Program—Threat- and performance-based exercise activities of varying degrees of complexity and interaction

Lessons Learned Information Sharing—Best practices and lessons learned from actual terrorist events and training exercises

U.S. Fire Administration Publications—Free publications for emergency responders including manuals, reports and incident reports

FIGURE 5.1 Department of Homeland Security programs.

too with various special agencies at the federal level. As this chapter makes plain, while DHS leads the overall effort in homeland, other agencies of government have their fingers in the homeland pie. Witnessed in Chapter 11 is the oversight role of the Centers for Disease Control and Prevention (CDC) in matters of bioterrorism, chemical attacks, and other weapons of mass destruction (WMD). Other agencies, such as Agriculture, the Nuclear Regulatory Commission, the FDA, and the military, play integral roles as well. Both funding and training spill out to the practitioners from these agencies in the same way as DHS does.

5.2 Office of Grants and Training

DHS, in its quest for centralization and improved efficiency, recently blended a host of diverse offices into the Office of Grants and Training (G&T). The *Post-Katrina Emergency Reform Act of 2006* amended the Homeland Security Act and mandates some mergers and realignments. As part of this reorganization, major national preparedness components and functions, which include the Office of G&T, the United States Fire Administration, National Capital Region Coordination, Chemical Stockpile Emergency Preparedness, and the Radiological Emergency Preparedness Program, while still operational under the DHS heading, were transferred to FEMA, effective April 1, 2007.

The new organization reflects the expanded scope of FEMA's departmental responsibilities. It strengthens FEMA's coordination with other DHS components, as well as agencies and departments outside of DHS. It also enhances FEMA's ability to partner with emergency management, law enforcement, preparedness organizations, and the private sector. Aside from this bureaucratic realignment, the Office of G&T makes possible a bevy of training opportunities for homeland specialists. Its mission is multifaceted but directed primarily to those in the first responder category, such as fire and EMT, police and paramedic. The agency posts a well-defined mission:

> The mission of G&T is to prepare America for acts of domestic terrorism by developing and implementing a national program to enhance the capacity of state and local agencies to respond to incidents of terrorism, particularly those involving chemical, biological, radiological, nuclear and explosive (CBRNE) incidents, through coordinated training, equipment acquisition, technical assistance, and support for Federal, state, and local exercises.[1]

Soon after these mergers, FEMA set out specific strategic goals that advance its grand vision to be the "Nation's Preeminent Emergency Management and Preparedness Agency."[2] The extensive grant programs had to be aligned with FEMA's overall Strategic Goals and Mission. Review Figure 5.2[3] to see how it envisions the compatibility of these goals as it carries out the mission.

GPD strategic goals \ FEMA strategic goals	Goal 1: Lead an integrated approach that strengthens the nation's ability to address disasters, emergencies, and terrorist events	Goal 2: Deliver easily accessible and coordinated assistance for all programs	Goal 3: Provide reliable information at the right time for all users	Goal 4: FEMA invests in people and people invest in FEMA to insure mission success	Goal 5: Build public trust and confidence through performance and stewardship
Goal 1: Emphasize employee development and human capital planning				✓	
Goal 2: Team with internal and external stakeholders	✓		✓		
Goal 3: Provide accurate and timely information and services		✓	✓		
Goal 4: Build a robust and standardized data analysis capability	✓		✓		✓
Goal 5: Streamline, standardize and document key processes		✓			✓

FIGURE 5.2 GPDs alignment to FEMA's strategic goals.

FEMA sees the entire picture of G&T in an agency–individual employee horizon making a noble effort to connect the larger purposes of the Agency's purpose with the roles, tasks, and functions of its employees downstream. It labels this a "cascade up" or a "cascade down." Hence, the agency authors grant and training policies that compliment individual performance and the efficacy of the agency itself. See Figure 5.3.[4]

G&T fulfills this mission through a series of program efforts responsive to the specific requirements of state and local agencies. G&T works directly with emergency responders and conducts assessments of state and local needs and capabilities to guide the development and execution of these programs.

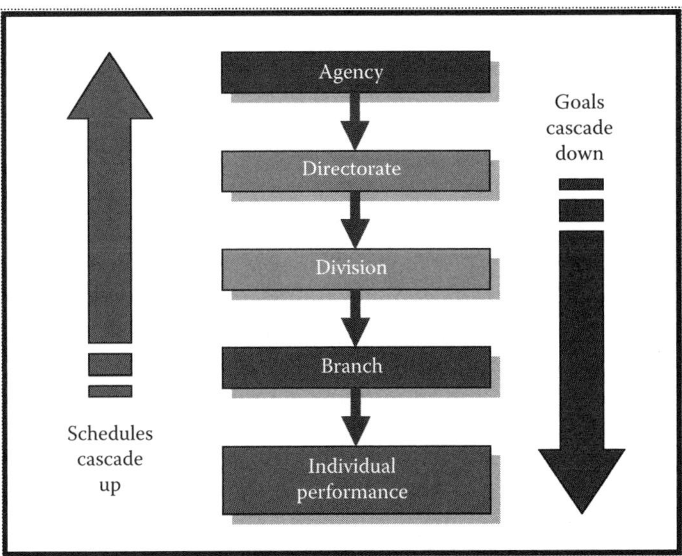

FIGURE 5.3 Strategy implementation chart.

Assistance provided by G&T is directed at a broad spectrum of state and local emergency responders, including firefighters, emergency medical services, emergency management agencies, law enforcement, and public officials.

G&T attends to this mission in a variety of ways by providing grants to states and local jurisdictions, providing hands-on training through a number of residential training facilities and in-service training at the local level, funding and working with state and local jurisdictions to plan and execute exercises, and providing technical assistance on-site to state and local jurisdictions. In many respects, the office fervently addresses Homeland Security Presidential Directive 8, which encourages all agencies of government to be prepared, train their personnel, and establish a national program and a multiyear planning system to conduct homeland security preparedness-related exercises that reinforce identified training standards, provide for evaluation of readiness, and support the national preparedness goal. The establishment and maintenance of the program will be conducted in maximum collaboration with state and local governments and appropriate private sector entities.[5] For the 2011 grant cycle, the Office of G&T sets its priority on the funding of these programs:

- State Homeland Security Program (SHSP)
- Urban Areas Security Initiative (UASI)
- Tribal Homeland Security Grant Program (THSGP)
- Nonprofit Security Grant Program (NSGP)
- Regional Catastrophic Preparedness Grant Program (RCPSP)
- Emergency Operations Center Grant Program (EOC)
- Driver's License Security Grant Program (DLSGP)
- Transit Security Grant Program (TSGP)

- Freight Rail Security Grant Program (FRSGP)
- Intercity Passenger Rail (IPR-Amtrack) Program
- Intercity Bus Security Grant Program (IBSGP)
- Port Security Grant Program (PSGP)
- Emergency Management Performance Grants (EMPG)

The Office of G&T supports cooperative partnerships among all relevant homeland constituencies. By and through the National Domestic Preparedness Consortium, the Office of G&T identifies, develops, tests, and delivers training to state and local emergency responders (see Figure 5.4).

Internet Resource: To get an inkling of how much training has been supported by the Office of G&T, visit the agency course catalog at https://www.firstrespondertraining.gov/content.do?page=training.

The Office of G&T also funds equipment purchases for justice and emergency agencies. An approved equipment list is published by the department. As of 2008, the office had supported the following equipment acquisitions:

- Personal protective equipment
- Equipment—explosive device mitigation and remediation
- CBRNE operational and search and rescue equipment
- Information technology equipment
- Cyber security enhancement equipment
- Interoperable communications equipment
- Detection equipment
- Decontamination equipment
- Medical equipment
- Power equipment

FIGURE 5.4 National Domestic Preparedness Consortium logo.

- CBRNE reference materials
- CBRNE incident response vehicles
- Terrorism incident prevention equipment
- Physical security enhancement equipment
- Inspection and screening systems
- Agricultural terrorism prevention, response, and mitigation equipment
- CBRNE prevention and response watercraft
- CBRNE aviation equipment
- CBRNE logistical support equipment
- Intervention equipment
- Other authorized equipment

The Office of G&T coordinates TOPOFF exercises and simulation programs. TOPOFF signifies "top officials" or higher-ups in the homeland supervisory chain. Officials from state, local, and federal agencies work collaboratively on a homeland problem, assess and evaluate the homeland dilemma, and publish best practices in dealing with the security question. As of 2011, the Office of G&T had conducted four major TOPOFF exercises, as portrayed in Figure 5.5.

The TOPOFF program has been replaced by what is now designated the "National Exercise Program (NEP)." The NEP allows federal, state, and local agencies to work collaboratively on all sorts of risks and hazards. Thus far, there have been three NEP programs whose coverage included:

National Level Exercise 2011 (NLE 11) National Level Exercise NLE 2011 was an operations-based exercise centered on the scenario of a catastrophic earthquake in the New Madrid Seismic Zone, encompassing four FEMA Regions (IV, V, VI, and VII) and eight Central U.S. Earthquake States: Alabama, Arkansas, Kentucky, Illinois, Indiana, Mississippi, Missouri, and Tennessee. NLE 2011 exercised initial incident response and recovery capabilities, tested and validated existing plans, policies and procedures to include the New Madrid Catastrophic Plan. NLE 2011 was conducted in May 2011.

National Level Exercise 2010 (NLE 10) The Federal Emergency Management Agency conducted National Level Exercise (NLE) 2010 on May 17–18. NLE 2010 engaged federal, state, and local partners in a series of events and opportunities to demonstrate and assess federal emergency preparedness capabilities pertaining to a simulated terrorist attack scenario involving an improvised nuclear device.

National Level Exercise 2009 (NLE 09) NLE 09 was designated as a Tier I National Level Exercise. Tier I exercises (formerly known as the Top Officials exercise series or TOPOFF) are conducted annually in accordance with the National Exercise Program (NEP), which serves as the nation's overarching exercise program for planning, organizing, conducting, and evaluating national level exercises. The NEP

TOPOFF 4: Increasing Coordination through Collaboration

Conducted in October 2007, TOPOFF 4 took place in Portland, Ore.; Phoenix, Ariz.; and for the first time, the U.S. territory of Guam as well as in Washington, DC for federal partners.

The exercise built on past lessons learned while adding new goals, including: an increased level of coordination with U.S. Department of Defense exercises to combat global terrorism, closer cooperation with the private sector, an expanded emphasis on prevention, a deeper focus on mass decontamination and long-term recovery and remediation issues, and strengthened coordination and communications with international allies.

More than 15,000 participants representing federal, state, territorial, and local entities, as well as the governments of Australia, Canada, and the United Kingdom, participated in the exercise.

All venues responded to a radiological RDD attack.

TOPOFF 3: Exercising National Preparedness

Conducted in April 2005, TOPOFF 3 was the first test of the National Response Plan (NRP) and National Incident Management System (NIMS).

TOPOFF 3 continued to evolve and included an increased focus on bolstering international and private sector participation, terrorism prevention activities, risk communication and public information functions, and long-term recovery and remediation issues.

Over 10,000 participants, including responders and officials from Canada and the United Kingdom, responded to a simulated chemical attack in New London, Conn., and a biological attack in the state of New Jersey.

The exercise marked the launch of a new simulated media tool—the interactive website VNN.com.

TOPOFF 2: Assessing Homeland Security Planning

Conducted in May 2003, TOPOFF 2 was the first national exercise following the September 11, 2001 attacks and was led by the newly formed Department of Homeland Security (DHS).

TOPOFF 2 provided the first opportunity for DHS to exercise its organizational functions and assets, including tests of the Homeland Security Advisory System (HSAS).

Participants in Seattle faced a simulated radiological dispersal device (RDD) attack, while those in the Chicago faced a biological attack.

The exercise engaged 8500 responders and top officials from the United States and Canada—the first international partner to participate.

TOPOFF 2000: Coordinated, Strategic National Response

In May 2000, the Department of Justice, the Department of State, and the Federal Emergency Management Agency (FEMA) led the first exercise in the TOPOFF series.

The primary goal of the exercise was to improve the capability of government officials and agencies, both within the United States and abroad to provide an effective, coordinated, and strategic response to a terrorist attack.

More than 6500 federal, state, and local personnel—including top officials—responded to a simulated biological attack in Denver, Colorado and a simulated chemical attack in Portsmouth, N.H.

The exercise introduced a new element in preparedness exercises: a simulated media outlet known as the Virtual News Network (VNN). VNN kept players up-to-date on unfolding events and forced decision makers to face the challenge of communicating with real-world media in a crisis.

FIGURE 5.5 TOPOFF exercises through 2011.

was established to provide the U.S. government, at all levels, exercise opportunities to prepare for catastrophic crises ranging from terrorism to natural disasters.

The office reserves a portion of its grant funding exclusively for fire fighters and fire administration. DHS is well aware of this pressing need since

FIGURE 5.6 Assistance to Firefighters Grant Program logo.

so much of what fire personnel undertake often relates to hazardous activities. Three types of grants are available: Assistance to Firefighters Grant (AFG), Fire Prevention and Safety (FP&S), and Staffing for Adequate Fire and Emergency Response (SAFER) (Figure 5.6).

Eligible applicants for AFG are limited to fire departments and nonaffiliated EMS organizations operating in any of the 50 states plus the District of Columbia, the Commonwealth of the Northern Mariana Islands, the Virgin Islands, Guam, American Samoa, and Puerto Rico.[6]

Internet Resource: Take the tutorial on how to apply for AFG grants at http://www.firegrantsupport.com/prog/grantsmgt/.

5.3 Center for Domestic Preparedness

The Center for Domestic Preparedness (CDP) operates within the FEMA construct and delivers key training and education in specialized fields. Located in Aniston, Alabama, the CDP is fully accredited and a comprehensive facility that provides both resident and commuter training in highly technical areas. Its specialty training relates to WMD. At the Chemical, Ordnance, Biological, and Radiological Training Facility (COBRATF), the CDP offers the only program in the nation featuring civilian training exercises in a true toxic environment, using chemical agents. The advanced, hands-on training enables responders to effectively respond to real-world incidents involving chemical, biological, explosive, radiological, or other hazardous materials.

The CDP educates homeland professionals with graduated levels of sophistication and recognizes the most highly proficient practitioners. FEMA's CDP has trained more than 93,500 local, state, and tribal responders from across the United States in preventing and responding to disasters and other terrorist threats involving chemical, biological, radiological, nuclear, and explosive materials.

5.4 Emergency Management Institute

The Emergency Management Institute (EMI), located in Emmittsburg, Maryland, is the lead national emergency management training, exercising, and education institution. EMI is located on a pristine campus near Mt. St. Mary's College and shares its facilities with the U.S. Fire Administration's training center. EMI offers a plethora of course offerings covering all aspects of emergency preparedness in conjunction with its agency partners. The scope and influence of EMI has been significant since it has served an impressive number of customers including:

- Nearly 22 million student course completions since the beginning of 1951.
- Nearly 73,000 classroom-based training opportunities since 1981.
- Over 5 million individual active student accounts on the EMI database.
- 15 million Independent Study online course completions—nearly 2 million during FY 2010 alone.

A partial listing of course offerings includes:

Integrated Emergency Management
E900 IEMC: All Hazards Preparation and Response
E901 IEMC: All Hazards Recovery and Mitigation
E905 IEMC: Hurricane Preparedness and Response
E910 IEMC: Earthquake Preparedness and Response
E915 IEMC: Homeland Security Preparedness and Response
E920 IEMC: Hazardous Materials Preparedness and Response
E930 IEMC: Community-Specific
E945 State National Response Framework (NRF) IEMC
E947 IEMC: Emergency Operations Center-Incident Management Team Interface

Master Exercise Practitioner Program (MEPP)
E132 Discussion-based Exercise Design and Evaluation
E133 Operations-based Exercise Design and Evaluation
E136 Operations-based Exercise Development

Professional Development
E388 Advanced Public Information Officer

Master Trainer Program
E601 Management and Supervision of Training
E602 Performance & Needs Assessment

E603 Instructional Design
E604 Course Development
E605 Instructional Delivery
E607 Master Trainer Practicum
E609 Master Trainer Practicum Workshop
K606 Evaluation of Training

Mitigation Branch
E155 Building Design for Homeland Security
E170 HAZUS Multi-Hazards for Hurricanes
E172 HAZUS Multi-Hazards for Flood
E174 HAZUS-Multi-Hazard for Earthquake
E179 Application of HAZUS-MH for Disaster Operations
E190 Intro to ArcGIS for Emergency Managers
E194 Advanced Floodplain Management Concepts
E273 Managing Floodplain Development through the National Flood Insurance Program
E276 Benefit–Cost Analysis: Entry-Level Training
E278 National Flood Insurance Plan/Community Rating System
E279 Retrofitting Flood-Prone Residential Buildings
E282 Advanced Floodplain Management Concepts II
E284 Advanced NFIP
E296 HAZUS Multi-Hazard/DMA 2000 Risk Assessment
E313 Basic HAZUS Multi-Hazards
E317 Comprehensive Data Management for HAZUS Multi-Hazards
E344 Mitigation Planning for Tribal Officials
E361 Multi-Hazard Emergency Planning for Schools (formerly E362 Multi-Hazard Emergency Planning for Schools Train-the-Trainer)
E386 Residential Coastal Construction
E436 Earthquakes: A Teacher's Package for K-6
E439 Seismic Sleuths: A Teacher's Package on Earthquakes for Grades 7–12

Readiness
E340 Radiological Emergency Preparedness Planning Course
E407 Homeland Security Planning for Local Governments (TTT)
E449 Incident Command System Curricula TTT
E580 Emergency Management Framework for Tribal Governments
E581 Emergency Management Operations for Tribal Governments

Disaster Operations and Recovery
E202 Debris Management
E208 State Coordinating Officer
E210 Recovery from Disaster: The Local Government Role
E430 EMAC TTT

Internet Exercise: For a complete listing of courses in 2012, visit http://training.fema.gov/EMICourses/docs/FY2012%20EMI%20Course%20Catalog.pdf.

EMI supports national and international emergency management with more than 50 countries participating in EMI's training and educational activities. EMI also enjoys close relations with several nationally recognized professional emergency management and related organizations, such as the International Association of Emergency Managers (IAEM), National Emergency Management Association (NEMA), Association of State Flood Plain Managers (ASFPM), American Public Works Association (APWA), American Society of Civil Engineers (ASCE), and American Society of Engineering Management (ASEM). EMI is fully accredited by the International Association for Continuing Education and Training (IACET) and the American Council on Education (ACE). In 2007, EMI delivered 514 resident courses at the National Emergency Training Center (NETC) campus, training 14,565 individual students. The EMI Independent Study (IS) Program, a web-based distance learning program open to the public, which has delivered extensive online training from 62 courses and trained more than 2.8 million individuals. The EMI IS website receives from 2.5 to 3 million visitors a day.

The EMI operates the Disaster Field Training Organization (DFTO). The mission of the DFTO is to:

- Provide a professional training resource to ensure that all training requirements in the field are identified and met
- Ensure that disaster staff has the skills and knowledge needed to provide effective and efficient services
- Enhance the professional expertise of disaster staff to ensure preparedness for future deployments

DFTO trained 24,950 disaster response employees and volunteers directly at disaster sites throughout the United States (Figure 5.7).

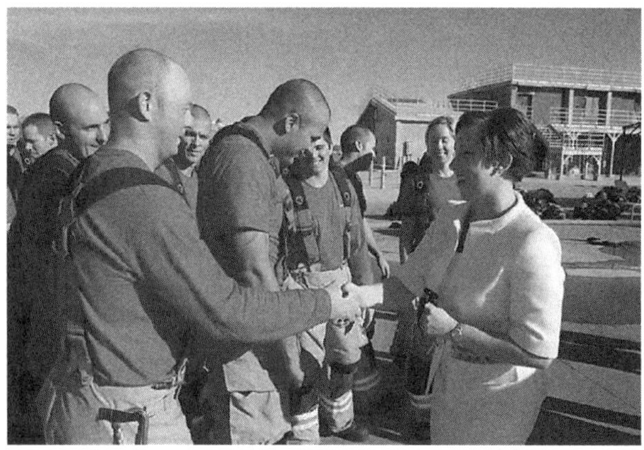

FIGURE 5.7 Firefighters in training at EMI 2011.

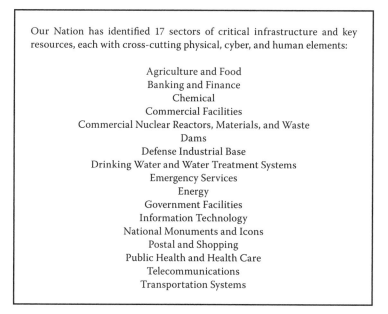

Our Nation has identified 17 sectors of critical infrastructure and key resources, each with cross-cutting physical, cyber, and human elements:

Agriculture and Food
Banking and Finance
Chemical
Commercial Facilities
Commercial Nuclear Reactors, Materials, and Waste
Dams
Defense Industrial Base
Drinking Water and Water Treatment Systems
Emergency Services
Energy
Government Facilities
Information Technology
National Monuments and Icons
Postal and Shopping
Public Health and Health Care
Telecommunications
Transportation Systems

FIGURE 5.8 Critical infrastructure and key resources.

EMI conducts national-level conferences that are well received, including the National Preparedness Annual Training and Exercise Conference and the EMI Higher Education Conference. The conference collects and catalogs institutions, course materials such as syllabi and university texts, and programmatic directions in emergency management. EMI has just implemented a "School Program" which prepares elementary and secondary administrators for risk and threat.

Internet Resource: See the EMI compilation of college and university syllabi at http://www.training.fema.gov/EMIWeb/edu/syllabi.asp. See Figure 5.8.[7]

5.5 Homeland Security Exercise and Evaluation Program

The Homeland Security Exercise and Evaluation Program (HSEEP), a unit of DHS, provides a standardized methodology and terminology for exercise design, development, conduct, evaluation, and improvement planning. HSEEP develops national standards for training exercises and promulgates means and modalities of assessments and evaluation to ensure agency efficiency.[8] The key component of HSEEP is the design and implementation of exercises—simulations and reenactments of events and circumstances likely to be encountered in the world of homeland security. Exercises allow homeland security and emergency management personnel, from first responders

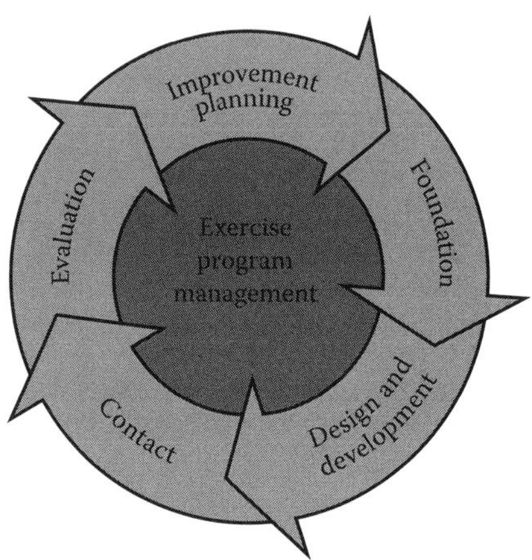

FIGURE 5.9 Program management cycle.

to senior officials, to train and practice prevention, protection, response, and recovery capabilities in a realistic but risk-free environment.

The intent of HSEEP is to provide common exercise policy and program guidance capable of constituting a national standard for all exercises. HSEEP employs consistent terminology and protocols that can be used by agencies and individuals universally (Figure 5.9).

HSEEP publishes its recommendations in a series of volumes, the content of which comprises:

- *HSEEP Volume I*: HSEEP Overview and Exercise Program Management provides guidance for building and maintaining an effective exercise program and summarizes the planning and evaluation process described in further detail in Volumes II through V.
- *HSEEP Volume II*: Exercise Planning and Conduct helps planners outline a standardized foundation, design, development, and conduct process adaptable to any type of exercise.
- *HSEEP Volume III*: Exercise Evaluation and Improvement Planning offers proven methodology for evaluating and documenting exercises and implementing an improvement plan.
- *HSEEP Volume IV*: Sample Exercise Documents and Formats provide sample exercise materials referenced in HSEEP Volumes I through V.
- *HSEEP Volume V*: Prevention Exercises contain guidance consistent with the HSEEP model to assist jurisdictions in designing and evaluating exercises that test pre-incident capabilities such as intelligence analysis and information sharing.

HSEEP advises agencies on best practices and lessons learned in given scenarios. There are seven types of exercises defined within HSEEP, each of which is either discussion based or operations based.

Discussion-based exercises include:

- *Seminar.* A seminar is an informal discussion, designed to orient participants to new or updated plans, policies, or procedures.
- *Workshop.* A workshop resembles a seminar, but is employed to build specific products, such as a draft plan or policy.
- *Tabletop exercise (TTX).* A tabletop exercise involves key personnel discussing simulated scenarios in an informal setting.
- *Games.* A game is a simulation of operations that often involves two or more teams, usually in a competitive environment, using rules, data, and procedures designed to depict an actual or assumed real-life situation.

Operations-based exercises include:

- *Drill.* A drill is a coordinated, supervised activity usually employed to test a single, specific operation or function within a single operation.
- *Functional exercise (FE).* A functional exercise examines or validates the coordination, command, and control between various multi-agency coordination centers.
- *Full-scale exercise (FSE).* A full-scale exercise is a multiagency, multi-jurisdictional, multidiscipline exercise involving functional response.

For operations-based exercises, HSEEP recommends broad-based participation and the widest array of agency inclusion feasible. HSEEP publishes a recommended list of participants for the planning phase of the exercise:

Emergency management
- Emergency manager
- Homeland security
- Public health
- Public works
- Transportation/transit authority
- Public affairs
- Exercise venue/site management (e.g., stadium security)

Fire
- Fire department
- Communications/dispatch
- Special operations (e.g., hazmat, Metropolitan Medical Response System [MMRS])
- Mutual aid fire

Law enforcement
- Police
- Special operations (e.g., bomb squad, Special Weapons and Tactics [SWAT])

- Sheriff's department
- Local Federal Bureau of Investigation (FBI)
- Mutual aid law enforcement

Medical

- Hospital representatives (primary trauma center or hospital association)
- Emergency medical services (i.e., public and private)
- Mutual aid
- Medical examiner/coroner

In discussion-based exercises, the participants consider the threat and security dilemma involved and then determine the necessary players. In other words, not all homeland security threats will need medical personnel, nor will law enforcement necessarily be the preeminent actor in a homeland dilemma. HSEEP has authored a discussion-based exercise that gets the relevant constituencies thinking long and hard about what planning team members should be involved. See Figure 5.10.[9]

HSEEP urges agency trainers and instructional personnel to target the purpose and end of any selected training exercise. Professional participation makes far more sense when those enrolled understand the nature of the training, its ultimate purpose, and how the training achieves a homeland security purpose.

5.6 Lessons Learned: Best Practices (LLIS.gov)

Training, in order to be effective, must correlate to best practices and success in the field. Training that lacks the cohesion of theory and application, training that appears disconnected from a stated goal or end, lacks relevance to those laboring in homeland security. With so much at stake, and so many opportunities for intellectual and practical advancement in the field, those entrusted with training must be mindful of its effectiveness. Lessons Learned Information Sharing (LLIS.gov) (Figure 5.11) is a national network of lessons learned and best practices for emergency response providers and homeland security officials. The web page and various requirements have just undergone a major overhaul. On January 18, 2010, LLIS.gov was redesigned to rely more heavily on member and participant input.

The redesign also allows its visitors to tailor their interests by their individual responsibilities and to navigate to new features such as:

- Member collaboration
- Document Library
- Message Boards
- Exercise Support[10]

HSEEP Exercise Guidance
Recommended Planning Team Members for Discussion-Based Exercises

Exercise Planning Team members should be determined based on the scope and type of exercise as well as the scenario and/or subject. For example, a tabletop exercise (TTX) with a scenario involving a biological agent should include planners and subject matter experts (SMEs) from the medical and public health communities.

The following sample list of Exercise Planning Team members should be modified to meet the jurisdiction's requirements.

Emergency Management

- Emergency management
- Homeland security

Public Safety

- Fire
- Hazardous materials (HazMat)
- Law enforcement
- Emergency medical services (EMS)
- Special operations
- Bomb squad
- Federal Bureau of Investigation (FBI)

Public Health

- Public health department
- Communicable disease
- Epidemiologists
- Infectious disease
- Pathology
- Poison control

Medical

- Hospital administrators
- Coroner/medical examiner
- Hospital infection control
- Hospital lab managers
- Hospital emergency room
- Medical society
- Private practitioners
- Veterinary

Other

- Public works
- Public Information Officer (PIO)
- Volunteer organizations (e.g., American Red Cross)
- Communications/dispatch
- Government officials
- Environmental quality

1

FIGURE 5.10 Recommended planning team members for discussion-based exercises.

LLIS.gov delivers the practices that work, not the initiatives that simply get played and replayed due to some mindless funding or programmatic fad. LLIS.gov is an encrypted system that is not readily available to the general public. Terrorists, hoping to discern our security practices, would be regular visitors without the encryption. Learned and best practices are peer validated by homeland security professionals. After Action Reports and an information clearinghouse are catalogued and monitored and include the bulk of serious and significant documents for homeland security.

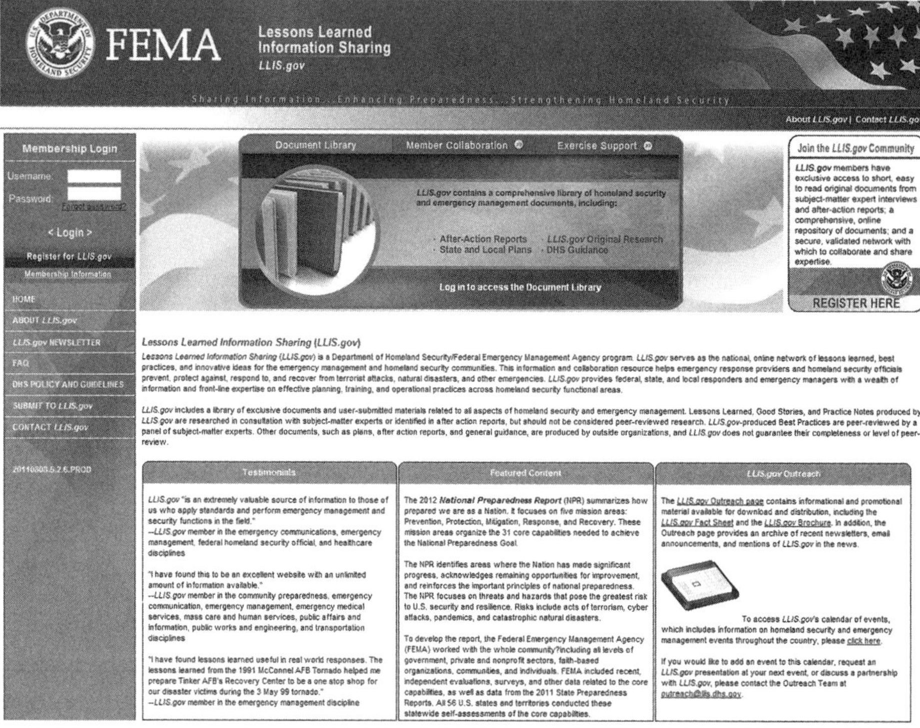

FIGURE 5.11 LLIS.gov homepage. (https://www.llis.dhs.gov/index.do.)

There are four types of LLIS.gov original research:

Lessons learned are positive or negative experiences derived from actual incidents, operations, training, or exercises.

Best practices are peer-validated techniques, procedures, and solutions that have demonstrated their effectiveness in operations, training, and exercises across multiple jurisdictions or organizations.

Practice notes describe procedures, techniques, or methods that have been adopted by a single jurisdiction or organization.

Good stories describe successful, innovative programs and initiatives developed by a jurisdiction that others may wish to emulate.

The most significant contribution of the LLIS has to be its documentary repository of After Action Reports (AARs). LLIS houses an extensive catalog of AARs as well as an updated list of homeland security documents from DHS and other federal, state, and local organizations, validated by subject matter experts, to capture expertise and innovation at the state and local levels.[11] See Figure 5.12 for some basic information on LLIS.gov.

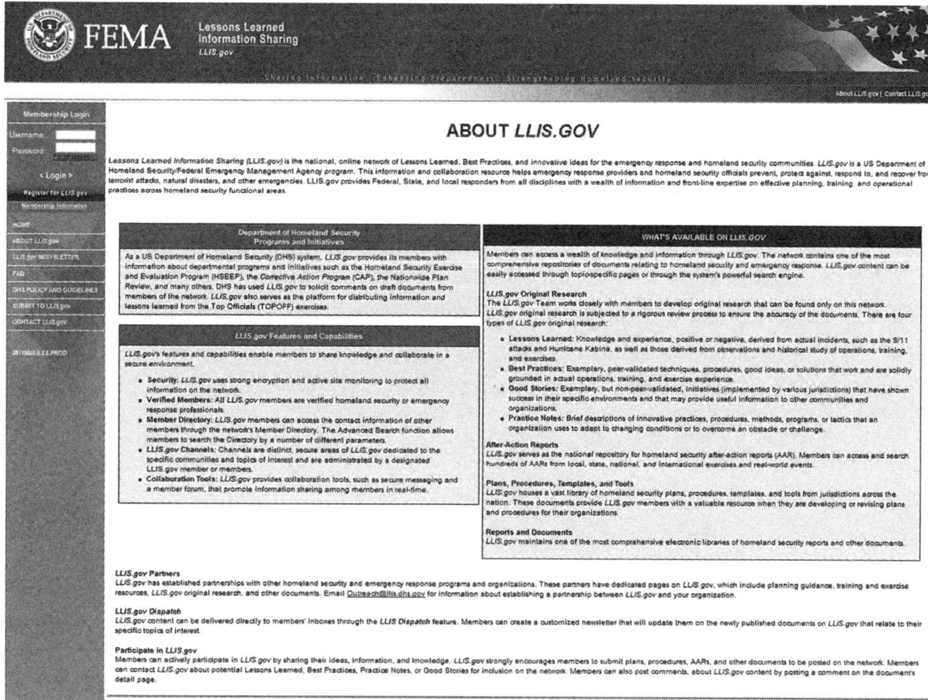

FIGURE 5.12 About LLIS.gov webpage.

5.7 Community Emergency Response Teams

Another avenue of education and training rests with Community Emergency Response Teams (CERT) training and CERT teams. The CERT Program educates people about disaster preparedness, the nature of hazards, and basic disaster response skills, such as fire safety, light search and rescue, team organization, and disaster medical operations. CERT teams dot the entire American landscape and serve a crucial educational function. CERT personnel train to prepare for a disaster or overwhelming events by:

- Identifying and mitigating potential hazards in the home and workplace
- Initiating plans to prepare themselves and their loved ones for the hazards that they face
- Learning skills to help themselves, loved ones, and neighbors or fellow employees until professional response resources arrive
- Working cooperatively as a team within their neighborhoods or workplaces
- Maintaining a relationship with the agency that sponsors the CERT Program

- Participating in continuing education and training
- Volunteering for projects to enhance the public safety of their communities
- Understanding their capabilities and limitations when deployed

Internet Resource: See the CERT tutorial on search and rescue at http://www.citizencorps.gov/cert/training_mat.shtm.

There is much more that can be said about the critical role that training and education play in the world of homeland security. Throughout this text there will be other references to the training mentality that is now so heavily engrained in the task of homeland security. In other portions of this text, you have already analyzed the role of FLETC—the Federal Law Enforcement and Training Center—a place where the training goes on day and night. And there are other forums in the mix, such as the U.S. Fire Administration, the National Fire Academy, and the Community Hazards Emergency Response-Capability Assurance Process (CHER-CAP). You can visit these and many locations as you discover the world of homeland security.

Internet Resource: Visit Community Hazards Emergency Response-Capability Assurance Process (CHER-CAP) at http://www.fema.gov/plan/prepare/cher_capfs.shtm. Visit the National Fire Academy at http://www.usfa.dhs.gov/nfa. Visit the U.S. Fire Administration at http://www.usfa.dhs.gov/about.

5.8 National Incident Management System

Another approach relevant to preparedness and readiness is the National Incident Management System (NIMS). NIMS is a by-product of Homeland Security Presidential Directive 5, which held:

> To prevent, prepare for, respond to, and recover from terrorist attacks, major disasters, and other emergencies, the United States Government shall establish a single, comprehensive approach to domestic incident management. The objective of the United States Government is to ensure that all levels of government across the Nation have the capability to work efficiently and effectively together, using a national approach to domestic incident management. In these efforts, with regard to domestic incidents, the United States Government treats crisis management and consequence management as a single, integrated function, rather than as two separate functions.[12]

FEMA takes the lead in the administration of the NIMS program. FEMA's National Integration Center (NIC) Incident Management Systems Integration Division was established by the secretary of Homeland Security to oversee NIMS and provide a research and evaluation arm regarding its standards and procedures. See Figure 5.13.

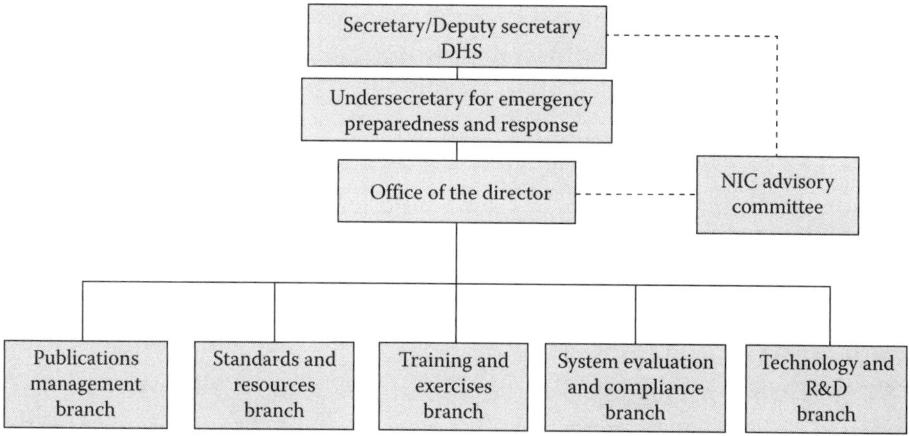

FIGURE 5.13 NIMS integration center (NIC) organization chart.

The NIMS mandate extends to every sector of government. Each and every agency of government has to plan and prepare for disaster—and do so internally as well as externally by working efficiently and effectively with all other departments of government. NIMS reflects the clear and unbridled need for less turf protection by departments and more cooperation along federal, state, and local lines. NIMS expects that these parties and entities will work to a common purpose regarding terror and disaster:

- Federal government
- States
- Territories
- Cities, counties, and townships
- Tribal officials
- First responders

NIMS extends to the private sector as well as to facilities of import, such as hospitals, power plants, and chemical and other related industrial centers, and all are expected to be on the same page. NIMS provides a systematic, proactive approach guiding departments and agencies at all levels of government, the private sector, and nongovernmental organizations to work seamlessly to prepare for, prevent, respond to, recover from, and mitigate the effects of incidents, regardless of cause, size, location, or complexity, in order to reduce the loss of life, property, and harm to the environment. This consistency mirrors the need for uniform practices in the world of homeland security and ensures predictable and dependable protocols when dealing with terror or disaster.

Internet Resource: For a suggested NIMS plan for business and industry, published by FEMA, see http://www.fema.gov/emergency/nims/ImplementationGuidanceStakeholders.shtm#item5.

The NIMS program is broken down into various components. First, compliance as to standards and practices in incident command and response is required. To accomplish this, the NIMS Compliance and Technical Assistance Branch relies on input from federal, state, local, tribal, multidiscipline, and private sector stakeholders to ensure continuity and accuracy of ongoing implementation efforts. Compliance ensures that best practices are adopted and that ineffective programs and stratagems are abandoned. Each year, DHS issues compliance standards for both the public and the private sector. In 2008, by way of illustration, the NIMS compliance standards on preparedness were published. See Table 5.1.

NIMS tracks compliance progress over its life cycle. When an agency fails to meet the NIMS goal or standard, the expectation for compliance carries over into the next cycle. For a more historical view of NIMS compliance mandates, see Figure 5.14.

Next, the NIMS program depends upon a common command and managerial structure to identify, respond to, and mitigate risk and harm. The NIMS command and management construct finds a home in the Incident Command System (ICS). ICS is a standardized on-scene incident management concept designed specifically to allow responders to adopt an integrated organizational structure equal to the complexity and demands of any single incident or multiple incidents without being hindered by jurisdictional boundaries. Before the ICS, the handling of disaster, catastrophe, or terror could only be described as nonuniform. Each incident would be tackled differently depending upon jurisdiction. The differences were starkly apparent with personnel and chain of command. Unpredictable communications systems, incompatible and not interoperable, caused a lack of interagency communication, and even language, often confusing and contradictory, were all challenges. The Incident Command System promotes uniformity of practice, multiagency coordination, and a public information system that all constituencies can comprehend. The ICS, instead of a fractured hodgepodge of differing practices, brings to the table a common language, a common set of operating principles, and standardization to terror and disaster sorely needed.

The ICS usually takes the form illustrated in Figure 5.15.[13]

The Incident Command System stresses preparedness in every context of homeland protection. Preparedness involves an integrated combination of planning, training, exercises, personnel qualification and certification standards, equipment acquisition and certification standards, and publication management processes and activities.

Planning also takes center stage in the ICS model. Plans describe how personnel, equipment, and other resources are used to support incident management and emergency response activities. Plans provide mechanisms and systems for setting priorities, integrating multiple entities and

TABLE 5.1 NIMS Compliance Standards of 2008

	FY 2008 NIMS Compliance Objectives	State/ Territory	Tribal Nation	Local Govts.
Preparedness: Planning				
7.	Revise and update emergency operations plans (EOPs), standard operating procedures (SOPs), and standard operating guidelines (SOGs) to incorporate NIMS and NRF components, principles, and policies, to include planning, training, response, exercises, equipment, evaluation, and corrective actions.	✓	✓	✓
8.	Promote and/or develop intrastate and interagency mutual aid agreements and assistance agreements (to include agreements with the private sector and NGOs).	✓	✓	✓
Total Preparedness: Planning Objectives		2	2	2
Preparedness: Training				
9.	Use existing resources such as programs, personnel, and training facilities to coordinate and deliver NIMS training requirements.	✓	✓	✓
10.	Complete *IS-700 NIMS:* An Introduction or equivalent by appropriate personnel (as identified in the Five-Year NIMS Training Plan, February 2008).	✓	✓	✓
11.	Complete *IS-800 National Response Framework:* An Introduction or equivalent by appropriate personnel (as identified in the Five-Year NIMS Training Plan, February 2008).	✓	✓	✓
12.	Complete *ICS-200 Introduction to ICS* training or equivalent by appropriate personnel (as identified in the Five-Year NIMS Training Plan, February 2008).	✓	✓	✓
13.	Complete *ICS-200 ICS* for Single Resources and Initial Action Incidents training of equivalent by appropriate personnel (as identified in the Five-Year NIMS Training Plan, February 2008).	✓	✓	✓
14.	Complete *ICS-300 Intermediate ICS* training or equivalent by appropriate personnel (as identified in the Five-Year NIMS Training Plan, February 2008).	✓	✓	✓
Total Preparedness: Training Objectives		**6**	**6**	**6**

continued

TABLE 5.1 (continued) NIMS Compliance Standards of 2008

FY 2008 NIMS Compliance Objectives		State/ Territory	Tribal Nation	Local Govts.
Preparedness: Exercise				
15.	Incorporate NIMS concepts and principles into all appropriate State/Territorial training and exercises.	✓	✓	✓
16.	Plan for and/or participate in an all-hazards exercise program (e.g., HSEEP) that involves emergency management/response personnel from multiple disciplines and/or multiple jurisdictions.	✓	✓	✓
17.	Incorporate corrective actions into preparedness and response plans and procedures.	✓	✓	✓
Total Preparedness: Exercises Objectives		3	3	3

functions, and ensuring that communications and other systems are available and integrated in support of a full spectrum of incident management requirements.

Other characteristics of the Incident Command System emphasize the importance of training for personnel—not only for internal agency preparation but also multiagency coordination. NIMS training modules are professionally developed and widely available to the professional community. For a survey of NIMS classes, see Table 5.2.

NIMS command staff author realistic training exercises that organizations and personnel participate in. Interoperability and other multiagency interactions are the key thrusts in these exercises. Drills and exercises are used often to test disaster and emergency response plans and to provide qualitative and quantitative measurements as to the effectiveness of the plan. Exercises that involve responders from multiple disciplines and multiple jurisdictions are the best way to measure incorporation of NIMS principles and practices and provide a measurement criterion for NIMS compliance.

The Incident Command System provides mechanisms for personnel, institutions, and equipment to be certified or officially endorsed. NIMS provides a checklist for compliance with its standards. NIMS is presently developing a credentialing program for particular occupations in homeland security. Called the National Emergency Responder Credentialing System it will document minimum professional qualifications, certifications, training, and education requirements that define the standards required for specific emergency response functional positions.

Job titles under consideration for the credential program are:

- Incident management
- Emergency medical services
- Fire/hazardous materials

FY 2008 NIMS Compliance Objectives

NIMS Compliance Objectives (requirements) from previous federal fiscal years remain on-going commitments in the present fiscal year. Therefore, state territorial, tribal, and local jurisdictions must continue to support all NIMS objectives required or underway in order to achieve full NIMS compliance.

The chart below depicts the 27 NIMS Compliance Objectives prescribed by National Integration Center's Incident Management Systems Integration (IMSI) Division in FY 2008 [note: many of these activities were originally prescribed in FYs 2005–2007]. To be compliant in FY 2008, jurisdictions must affirmatively answer Compliance Metrics relating to those specific NIMS Compliance Objectives listed below.

NIMS Component	NIMS Compliance Objective	Original FY Prescribed to:		
		State/ Territory	Tribal Nations	Local
ADOPTION	1. Adopt NIMS for all Departments/Agencies; as well as promote and encourage NIMS adoption by associations, utilities, nongovernmental organizations (NGOs) and private sector emergency management and incident response organizations.	2005		
	2. Establish and maintain a planning process to communicate, monitor, and implement all NIMS compliance objectives across the state/territory/tribal nation (including Departments/Agencies), to include local governments. This process must provide a means for measuring progress and facilities reporting.	2006	2008	N/A
	3. Designate and maintain a single point of contact within government to serve as principal coordinator for NIMS implementation jurisdiction-wide (to include a principal coordinator for NIMS implementation within each Department/ Agency)	2006	2007	
	4. Ensure that Federal Preparedness Awards [to include, but not limited to, DHS Homeland Security Grant Program and Urban Area Security Initiative Funds] to state/territorial/tribal departments/ agencies, as well as local governments, support all required NIMS Compliance Objectives (requirements).	2005	2008	
	5. Audit agencies and review organizations should routinely include NIMS Compliance Objectives (requirements) in all audits associated with Federal Preparedness Awards.	2006	2008	
	6. Assist Tribal Nations with formal adoption and implementation of NIMS.	2007	N/A	

FIGURE 5.14 Detailed NIMS compliance mandates.

NIMS Component		NIMS Compliance Objective	Original FY Prescribed to:		
			State/ Territory	Tribal Nations	Local
PREPAREDNESS	Planning	7. Revise and update emergency operations plans (EOPs), standard operating procedures (SOPs), and standard operating guidelines (SOGs) to incorporate NIMS and National Response Framework (NRF) components, principles, and policies, to include planning, training, response, exercises, equipment, evaluation, and corrective actions.		2005	
		8. Promote and/or develop intrastate and interagency mutual aid agreements and assistance agreements (to include agreements with the private sector and NGOs).		2005	
		9. Use existing resources such as programs, personnel, and training facilities to coordinate and deliver NIMS training requirements.	2006		2008
		10. Complete IS-700 NIMS: An introduction or equivalent by appropriate personnel (as identified in the *Five-Year NIMS Training Plan*, February 2008)		2006	
	Training	11. Complete IS-800 *National Response Framework (NRF):* An introduction or equivalent by appropriate personnel (as identified in the *Five-Year NIMS Training Plan*, February 2008)		2006	
		12. Complete ICS-100 *Introduction to ICS* training or equivalent by appropriate personnel (as identified in the *Five-Year NIMS Training Plan*, February 2008)		2006	
		13. Complete ICS-200 *for Single Resources and Initial Action Incidents* training or equivalent by appropriate personnel (as identified in the *Five-Year NIMS Training Plan*, February 2005)		2006	
	Exercises	14. Complete ICS-300 *Intermediate ICS* training or equivalent by appropriate personnel (as identified in the *Five-Year NIMS Training Plan*, February 2005)		2007	
		15. Incorporate NIMS concepts and principles into all appropriate state/territorial/tribal training and exercises.		2005	
		16. Plan for and/or participate in an all-hazards exercise program [for example, Homeland Security Exercise and Evaluation Program] that involves emergency management response personnel from multiple disciplines and/or multiple jurisdictions.		2006	
		17. Incorporate corrective actions into preparedness and response plans and procedures.		2006	
COMMUNICATION AND INFORMATION MANAGEMENT		18. Apply common and consistent terminology as used in NIMS, including the establishment of plain language (clear text) communications standards.		2006	

FIGURE 5.14 (continued) Detailed NIMS compliance mandates.

NIMS Component		NIMS Compliance Objective	Original FY Prescribed to: State/ Territory	Tribal Nations	Local
COMMUNICATION AND INFORMATION MANAGEMENT		19. Utilize systems, tools, and processes to present consistent and accurate information (e.g., common operating picture) during an incident/planned event.		2007	
RESOURCE MANAGEMENT		20. Inventory response assets to conform to NIMS National Resource Typing Definitions, as defined by FEMA Incident Management Systems Integration Division.		2006	
		21. Ensure that equipment, communications, and data systems acquired through state/ territorial and local acquisition programs are interoperable.		2006	
		22. Utilize response asset inventory for intrastate/interstate mutual aid requests [such as Emergency Management Assistance Compact (EMAC)], training, exercises, and incidents/planned events.		2007	
		23. Initiate development of a state/territory/ tribal-wide system (that incorporate local jurisdictions) to credential emergency management/response personnel to ensure proper authorization and access to an incident including those involving mutual aid agreements and/or assistance agreements.		2008	
COMMAND AND MANAGEMENT	Incident Command System	24. Manage at incidents/planned events in accordance with ICS organizational structures, doctrine, and procedures. ICS implementation must include the consistent application of incident Action Planning (IAP), common communications plans, implementation of Area Command to oversee multiple incidents that are handled by separate ICS organizations or to oversee the management of a very large or evolving incident that has multiple incident management teams engaged, and implementation of united command (UC) in multijurisdictional or multiagency incident management, as appropriate.		2006	
	Multiagency Coordination System (MACS)	25. Coordinate and support emergency management and incident response objectives through the development and use of integrated MACS [i.e., develop/ maintain connectivity capacity between local incident Command Posts (ICPs), local 911 Centers, local/regional/state/territorial/ tribal/federal Emergency Operations Centers (EOCs), as well as NRF organizational elements].		2006	
	Public Information	26. Institutionalize, within the framework of ICS, Public Information [e.g., Joint Information System (JIS) and a Joint Information Center (JIC)] during an incident/planned event.		2006	
		27. Ensure that Public Information procedures and processes can gather, verify, coordinate, and disseminate information during an incident/planned event.		2007	

FIGURE 5.14 (continued) Detailed NIMS compliance mandates.

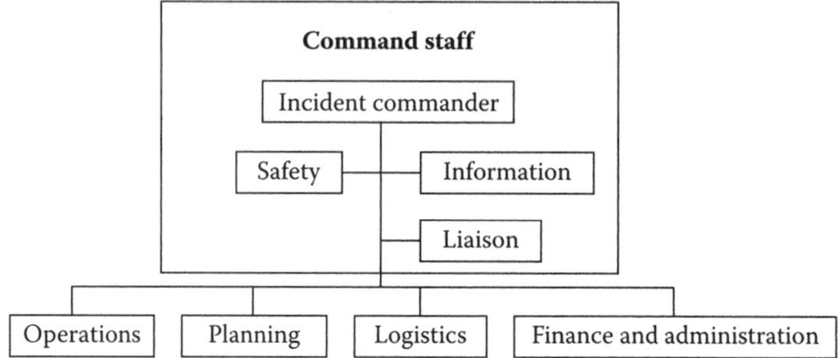

FIGURE 5.15 Incident command system organization chart.

TABLE 5.2 NIMS Class List

Course Grouping	Course ID	Course Title
Overview	IS-700	NIMS, an Introduction
	IS-800	NRF, an Introduction
ICS courses	ICS-100	Introduction to the Incident Command System
	ICS-200	ICS for Single Resources and Initial Action Incidents
	ICS-300	Intermediate ICS
	ICS-400	Advanced ICS
NIMS components and subcomponents	IS-701	NIMS Multiagency Coordination System
	IS-702	NIMS Public Information Systems
	IS-703	NIMS Resource Management
	IS-704	NIMS Communication and Information Management
	IS-705	NIMS Preparedness
	IS-706	NIMS Intrastate Mutual Aid, an Introduction
	IS-707	NIMS Resource Typing
ICS position-specific courses	P-400	All-Hazards Incident Commander
	P-430	All-Hazards Operations Section Chief
	P-440	All-Hazards Planning Section Chief
	P-450	All-Hazards Logistics Section Chief
	P-460	All-Hazards Finance Section Chief
	P-480	All-Hazards Intelligence/Investigations Function
	P-402	All-Hazards Liaison Officer
	P-403	All-Hazards Public Information Officer
	P-404	All-Hazards Safety Officer

- Law enforcement
- Medical and public health, public works
- Search and rescue

Institutions can be certified as compliant with NIMS standards and requirements. See Figure 5.16.

NIMS fosters interagency cooperation by recognizing the need for mutual aid and cooperation rather than insular turf protection. NIMS encourages governmental entities to enter into formal agreements to assist one another in the event of disaster or a terrorist event. See the sample mutual aid agreement, courtesy of the Minnesota Municipalities Utilities Association, in Figure 5.17.

The ICS plays a central role in the publication of NIMS forms and publications and educational materials. NIMS, as part of its mission, seeks out its constituencies with an educational aim.

The ICS is charged with the management of resources relating to a given incident. NIMS establishes requirements for inventory and the mobilization, dispatch, tracking, and recovery of resources over the life cycle of an incident. In addition, NIMS provides a standardized protocol for all communications and media at every level of incident management, including the sharing of information among all interested agencies, the implementation of interoperable communication systems, and the storage and management of information relating to the incident. See Figure 5.18.

Internet Resource: To access the entire NIMS guide, published by FEMA, see http://www.fema.gov/emergency/nims/rm/guide.shtm.

NIMS is an ongoing process with improvements, refinements, and adjustments occurring on a regular basis. From another perspective, NIMS builds on its infrastructure year by year. NIMS, being of relatively young design, learns from both its successes and failures. In directing agencies to implement the program, it looks not only to the present requirements, but also to past demands and future expectations. NIMS expects the agency to track its history and trace its evolution in the process. See Figure 5.19 for this historical approach.

5.9 Conclusion

Identifying risk, threats, and hazards is the first piece in the homeland puzzle. Homeland security professionals must prepare, plan for, and respond to these potential risks. Hence, the role of training and exercises that anticipate these harms is crucial in any homeland plan. DHS stresses training for all eventualities, as evidenced through its organizational structure, budgets and grants, and core competencies. The DHS Office of G&T is the funding

NIMS CERTIFICATION

Please sign and return this form with your Homeland Security Grant Program

I certify that ______________________ (Jurisdiction/Tribe/Agency Name) has successfully complied with the following 23 NIMS compliance requirements ("taken as a whole") as directed by the NIMS Integration Center and the U.S. Department of Homeland Security for the Homeland Security Grant Programs.

Jurisdiction Adoption and Infrastructure

- Adopted NIMS at the jurisdictional/tribal/agency level as well as promoted and encouraged jurisdiction-wide adoption.
- Established a planning process to ensure the communication and implementation of NIMS requirements across the jurisdiction. This process must provide a means for measuring progress and facilitate reporting.
- Designated a single point of contact within the jurisdictional government to serve as the principal coordinator for NIMS implementation jurisdiction-wide.
- To the extent permissible by law, ensured that federal preparedness funding to the jurisdiction/tribe/agency is linked to satisfactory progress in meeting the requirements related to FY06 NIMS implementation requirements.
- To the extent permissible by jurisdictional/tribal/agency law, audit agencies, and review organizations routinely included NIMS implementation requirements in all audits associated with federal preparedness grant funds. This process will validate the self-certification process for NIMS compliance.

Command and Management

- Incident Command System (ICS): Managed all emergency incidents and preplanned (recurring/special) events in accordance with ICS organizational structure, doctrine, and procedures, as defined in NIMS. ICS implementation must have included the consistent application of Incident Action Planning and Common Communication Plans.
- Multi-agency Coordination System: Coordinated and supported emergency incident and event management through the development and use of integrated multi-agency coordination systems.
- Public Information System: Institutionalized, within the framework of ICS, the Public Information System, comprising of the Joint Information System (JIS) and a Joint Information Center (JIC). The Public Information System ensures an organized, integrated, and coordinated mechanism to perform critical emergency information, crisis communications and public affairs functions which is timely, accurate, and consistent. This includes training for designated participants from the jurisdiction/tribe/agency management and key agencies.

Preparedness: Planning

- Established the jurisdiction's NIMS baseline against the FY05 and FY06 implementation requirements.
- Coordinated and leveraged all federal preparedness funding to implement the NIMS.
- Revised and updated plans and SOPs to incorporate NIMS and National Response Plan (NRP) components, principles and policies, to include planning, training, response, exercises, equipment, evaluation, and corrective actions.
- Promoted intrastate and interagency mutual aid agreements, to include agreements with the private sector and non-governmental organizations.

Preparedness: Training

- Leveraged training facilities to coordinate and deliver NIMS training requirements in conformance with the NIMS National Standard Curriculum.
- Completed IS-700 NIMS: An Introduction

FIGURE 5.16 NIMS certification.

- Completed IS-800 NRP: An Introduction
- Completed ICS 100 and ICS 200 Training

Preparedness: Exercises

- Incorporated NIMS/ICS into all regional and jurisdictional training and exercises.
- Participated in an all-hazard exercise program based on NIMS that involves responders from multiple disciplines and multiple jurisdictions.
- Incorporated corrective actions into preparedness and response plans and procedures.

Resource Management

- Inventoried jurisdictional response assets to conform to Homeland Security resource typing standards.
- Developed state plans for the receipt and distribution of resources as outlined in the National Response Plan (NRP) Catastrophic Incident Annex and Catastrophic Incident Supplement.
- To the extent permissible by state and local law, ensured that relevant national standards and guidance to achieve equipment, communication and data interoperability are incorporated into state and local acquisition programs.

Communication and Information Management

- Applied standardized and consistent terminology, including the establishment of plain English communication standards across public safety sector.

(Name & Title of Jurisdictional Official): ______________________

(Name of Jurisdiction/Tribe/Agency): ______________________

Signature: ______________ Date: ______________________

Exceptions to the above (please list): ______________________

FIGURE 5.16 (continued) NIMS certification.

mechanism for training. DHS coordinates major training events, at a national scale, by its TOPOFF program. The emergency side of homeland training is centered at the Emergency Management Institute, which delivers a bevy of programs for first responders. In the world of WMD, the CDP is considered the key trainer. All training for homeland security is evaluated by the HSEEP, which delivers standardized methodology and terminology for exercise design, development, and planning. HSEEP regularly promulgates best practices for the homeland security industry. Specialized training for critical infrastructure holds a prominent place in the training portion of the homeland mission. Other training modalities include Lessons Learned Information Sharing (LLIS), CERTs, and the NIMS—a planning process for institutions, in both the private and the public sectors, that anticipates threat and hazard.

How homeland security professionals respond to and recover from threats and hazards is keenly dealt with in this chapter. Response is how government

MUTUAL AID AGREEMENT

In consideration of the mutual commitments given herein each of the Signatories to this Mutual Aid Agreement agrees to render aid to any of the other Signatories as follows:

1. Request for aid. The Requesting Signatory agrees to make its request in writing to the Aiding Signatory within a reasonable time after aid is needed and with reasonable specificity. The Requesting Signatory agrees to compensate the Aiding Signatory as specified in this Agreement and in other agreements that may be in effect between the Requesting and Aiding Signatories.
2. Discretionary rendering of aid. Rendering of aid is entirely at the discretion of the Aiding Signatory. The agreement to render aid is expressly not contingent upon a declaration of a major disaster or emergency by the federal government or upon receiving federal funds.
3. Invoice to the Requesting Signatory. Within 90 days of the return to the home work station of all labor and equipment of the Aiding Signatory, the Aiding Signatory shall submit to the Requesting Signatory an invoice of all charges related to the aid provided pursuant to this Agreement. The invoice shall contain only charges related to the aid provided pursuant to this Agreement.
4. Charges to the Requesting Signatory. Charges to the Requesting Signatory from the Aiding Signatory shall be as follows:
    a. Labor force. Charges for labor force shall be in accordance with the Aiding Signatory's standard practices.
    b. Equipment. Charges for equipment, such as bucket trucks, digger derricks, and other special equipment used by the Aiding Signatory, shall be at the reasonable and customary rates for such equipment in the Aiding Signatory's location.
    c. Transportation. The Aiding Signatory shall transport needed personnel and equipment by reasonable and customary means and shall charge reasonable and customary rates for such transportation.
    d. Meals, lodging, and other related expenses. Charges for meals, lodging, and other expenses related to the provision of aid pursuant to this Agreement shall be the reasonable and actual costs incurred by the Aiding Signatory.
5. Counterparts. The Signatories may execute this Mutual Aid Agreement in one or more counterparts, with each counterpart being deemed an original Agreement, but with all counterparts being considered one Agreement.
6. Execution. Each party hereto has read, agreed to, and executed this Mutual Aid Agreement on the date indicated.

Date ____________________ Entity

____________________ By

Title ____________________

FIGURE 5.17 Mutual aid agreement.

Incident Radio Communications Plan			1. INCIDENT NAME	2. DATE/TIME PREPARED	3. OPERATIONAL PERIOD DATE/TIME
4. BASE RADIO CHANNEL UTILIZATION					
SYSTEM/CACHE	CHANNEL	FUNCTION	FREQUENCY/TONE	ASSIGNMENT	REMARKS
5. PREPARED BY (COMMUNICATIONS UNIT)					

FIGURE 5.18 Incident radio communications plan.

attends to the event in an immediate sense. The lessons learned from both Hurricane Katrina and Hurricane Sandy say much about the importance of response. DHS publishes an NRF to guide homeland and governmental agencies. The framework stresses the need to partner and work collaboratively, the necessity that layers of government work in unity, the recognition that one command will corral these various constituencies, and that flexibility and readiness in response are central to the mission.

Keywords

After Action Reports
Assistance to Firefighters Grant
Best practices
Center for Domestic Preparedness
Chemical, Ordnance, Biological, and Radiological Training Facility
Community Emergency Response Teams
Compliance standards
Continuing education
Credentialing
Disaster Field Training Organization
Disaster preparedness
Discussion-based exercises
Emergency Management Institute
EMI Independent Study Program
Fire Prevention and Safety Grant

FEMA NIMS IMPLEMENTATION ACTIVITY SCHEDULE

The matrix below summarizes by Federal Fiscal Year (FY) all ongoing NIMS implementation activities that have been prescribed by the NIMS Integration Center in FYs 2005 and 2006, as well as the seven new activities for states and territories and six new activities for tribes and local jurisdictions required in FY 2007. State territorial, tribal, and local jurisdictions should in mind that implementation activities from previous fiscal years remain on-going commitments in the present fiscal year. Jurisdictions must continue to support *all* implementation activities, required or underway in order to achieve NIMS bear compliance.

Future refinement of the NIMS will evolve as policy and technical issues are further developed and clarified. As a result, the NIMS Integration Center may issue additional requirements to delineate what constitutes NIMS compliance in FY 2008 and beyond. With the completion of the FY 2007 activities, state, territorial, tribal, and local jurisdictions will have the foundational support for future NIMS implementation and compliance. The effective and consistent implementation of the NIMS nationwide will result in a strengthened national capability to prevent, prepare for, respond to and recover from any type of incident.

	NIMS IMPLEMENTATION ACTIVITY	FY 2007		FY 2006		FY2005	
		STATE/ TERRITORY	TRIBAL/ LOCAL	STATE/ TERRITORY	TRIBAL/ LOCAL	STATE/ TERRITORY	TRIBAL/ LOCAL
ADOPTION	1. Support the successful adoption and implementation of the NIMS.					✓	✓
	2. Adopted NIMS for all government departments and agencies; as well as promote and encourage NIMS adoption by associations, utilities, non-governmental organizations (NGOs), and private sector incident management and response organizations.			✓	✓		
	3. Monitor formal adoption of NIMS by all tribal and local jurisdictions.			✓			
	4. Establish a planning process to ensure the communication and implementation of NIMS requirements. thereby providing a means for measuring progress and facilitate reporting.			✓			
	5. Designate a single point of contact to serve as the principal coordinator for NIMS implementation.		✓	✓			
	6. Designate a single point of contact within each of the jurisdiction's Departments and Agencies.	✓					
	7. To the extent permissible by law. ensure that Federal preparedness funding. including DHS Homeland Security General Program and the Urban Areas Security Initiative (UASI) support NIMS implementation at the state and local levels and incorporate NIMS into existing training programs and exercises.					✓	
	8. To the extent permissible by law, ensure that federal preparedness funding to state and territorial agencies and tribal and local jurisdictions is linked to satisfactory process in meeting FY2006 NIMS implementation requirements.			✓			
	9. To the extent permissible by state and territorial law and regulations, audit agencies and review organizations routinely include NIMS implementation requirements in all audits associated with federal preparedness grant funds validating the self-certification process for NIMS compliance.			✓			
	10. Monitor and assess outreach and implementation of NIMS Requirements.	✓					
COMMAND & MANAGEMENT	11. Coordinate and provide technical assistance to local entities regarding NIMS institutionalized use of ICS.					✓	
	12. Manage all emergency incident and pre-planned (recurring/special) events in accordance with ICS organizational structures, doctrine and procedures, as defined in NIMS. ICS implementation must include the consistent application of Incident Action Planning and Common Communications Plans.			✓	✓		
	13. Coordinate and support emergency incident and event management through the development and use of integrated multi-agency coordination systems, i.e. develop and maintain connectively capability between local Incident Command Posts (ICP) local 911Centers, local Emergency Operations Centers (EOCs), the state EOC and regional and federal EOCs and NRP organizational elements.			✓	✓		
	14. Institutionalize, within the transmission of ICS the Public Information System (PIS), comprising the Joint Information Systems (JIS) and a Joint Information Center (JIC).			✓	✓		
	15. Establish public information system to gather, verify, coordinate, and disseminate information during an incident.	✓	✓				
	16. Establish NIMS baseline against the FY2005 and FY2006 implementation requirements.			✓	✓		
	17. Develop and implement a system to coordinate and leverage all federal preparedness funding to implement the NIMS.			✓	✓		

FIGURE 5.19 NIMS implementation activity schedule.

PREPAREDNESS PLANNING	18. Incorporate NIMS into Emergency Operation Plans (EOP).					✓	
	19. Revise and update plans and SOPs to incorporate NIMS and National Response Plan (NRP) components, principles and polices, to include planning, training, response, exercises, equipment, evaluation, and corrective actions.			✓	✓		
	20. Promote intrastate mutual aid agreements, to include agreements with private sector and non-governmental organizations.					✓	✓
	21. Participate in and promote intrastate and interagency mutual aid agreements, to include agreements with the private sector and non-governmental organizations.			✓	✓		
PREPAREDNESS TRAINING	22. Leverage training facilities to coordinate and deliver NIMS training requirements in conformance with the NIMS National Standard Curriculum.			✓			
	23. Complete-training--IS-700 *NIMS; An introduction, IS-800 NRP. An introduction* , ICS-100 and ICS-200.			✓	✓		
	24. Complete training--ICS-300, ICS-400.	✓	✓				
PREPAREDNESS EXERCISES	25. Incorporate NIMS/ICS into training and exercises.					✓	✓
	26. Participate in an all-hazard exercise program based on NIMS that involves responders from multiple disciplines and multiple jurisdictions.			✓	✓		
	27. Incorporate corrective actions into preparedness and response plans and procedures.			✓	✓		
RESOURCE MANAGEMENT	28. Inventory response assets to conform to FEMA Resource Typing standards.			✓	✓		
	29. Develop state plans for the receipt and distribution of responses as outlined in the National Response Plan (NRP) Catastrophic incident Annex and Catastrophic incident Supplement.			✓			
	30. To the extent Permissible by state and local law, ensure that relevant national standards and guidance to achieve equipment, communication and data interoperability are incorporated into state and local acquisition programs.			✓	✓		
	31. Validate that inventory of response assets conform to FEMA Resource Typing Standards.	✓	✓				
	32. Utilize response assets inventory for mutual aid requests, exercises, and actual events.	✓	✓				
COMMUNICATION & INFORMATION MANAGEMENT	33. Apply standardized and consistent terminology, including the establishment of plain language communications standards across public safety sector.			✓	✓		
	34. Develop systems and processes to ensure that incident managers at all levels share a common operating picture of an incident.	✓	✓				

FIGURE 5.19 (continued) NIMS implementation activity schedule.

Fire safety
Homeland Security Exercise and Evaluation Program
HSEEP exercises
Incident Command System
In-service training
Lessons Learned Information Sharing
National Domestic Preparedness Consortium
National Emergency Responder Credentialing System
National Incident Management System
National Integration Center
NIMS certification
Office of Grants and Training
Operations-based exercises
Residential training facility
Search and rescue
TOPOFF exercise
U.S. Fire Administration

Discussion Questions

1. Discuss the importance of training in the world of homeland security.
2. Critics of DHS frequently cite the agency's tendency to bite off more than it can chew. In the area of training, is this legitimate?
3. Explain the critical function of the EMI.
4. Why did DHS design and implement the HSEEP?
5. Discuss how homeland professionals train for the protection of critical infrastructure.
6. Of what import is the LLIS program? How does such a program benefit homeland leaders?
7. What are the general goals of NIMS?
8. Why is it essential that an Incident Command System be implemented?
9. What is the value of a NIMS certification program?
10. Explain the philosophy of the NRF. In particular, comment on why shared responsibility is so important in the NRF.

Practical Exercises

1. Collect and collate a NIMS file. Prepare an index of these documents.
2. Draft a NIMS implementation plan for your place of work. Use the FEMA template for the implementation at http://www.fema.gov/doc/emergency/nims/nims_implementation_plan_template.doc.

3. Contact your statewide DHS office. Determine whether a TOPOFF exercise will occur in your region.
4. Contact a local police department. Find out if that office has applied for DHS training funds.
5. Write to EMI for a course catalog.
6. Find out where CERTs exist in your area.

Notes

1. Department of Homeland Security, *Federal Emergency Management Agency, Office of Grants and Training, G&T Mission*, www.ojp.usdoj.gov/odp/about/mission.htm.
2. FEMA, *Grant Programs Directorate Strategic Plan, FY 2009–2010*, on October 9, 2008.
3. FEMA, *Grant Programs Directorate Strategic Plan, FY 2009–2010*, on October 9, 2008.
4. FEMA, *Grant Programs Directorate Strategic Plan, FY 2009–2010*, on October 10, 2008.
5. Office of the President, *Homeland Security Presidential Directive 8*, December 17, 2003.
6. See M. Paddock, Get your fire grants while they last, *Homeland Security Today*, August 2011: 8.
7. Homeland Security Council, *National Strategy for Homeland Security* October 2007: 20, http://www.whitehouse.gov/infocus/homeland/nshs/2007/sectionII.html or http://www.whitehouse.gov/infocus/homeland/nshs/NSHS.pdf.
8. Practitioners are generally favorable to the reality-based exercise. HSEEP stress that sort of training as well as scenario based learning. See D. R. Hales and P. Race, Applying a framework of defining emergency management scenarios, *Journal of Emergency Management*, 9 2011: 15.
9. FEMA, *HSEEP Vol. IV, Planning Team Members Recommendation*, available at https://hseep.dhs.gov/HSEEP_Vols.
10. FEMA, *Navigating the New LLIS.gov*, available at https://www.llis.dhs.gov/index.do.
11. R. Kelly, 10 Years after 9/11: Lessons learned by the New York City Police Department, *Police Chief*, September 2011: 20–25.
12. Office of the President, *Homeland Security Presidential Directive 5*, February (2003): 3.
13. National Response Team, Incident Command System/Unified Command (ICS/UC) Technical Assistance Document, 9.

Chapter 6

DHS Challenges

National vs. State and Local, National Security vs. Homeland Security

Objectives

1. To evaluate the various national, state, and local relationships relating to homeland security that exist in U.S. government agencies.
2. To compare and contrast homeland security agencies at the state level, including their organization, policies, and operating parameters.
3. To analyze the many types of homeland security task forces and commissions that exist at the state level.
4. To describe the homeland security structures that are in place at the local level and analyze the differences that arise in major metropolitan, urban, suburban, and rural areas.
5. To describe fusion centers, their purpose, staffing, and locations.
6. To explain the various funding programs available from the federal government for state and local homeland security initiatives.
7. To describe current military initiatives specifically relating to homeland security intelligence gathering.
8. To describe current military initiatives specifically relating to specialized units dedicated to homeland security and the identification and tracking of weapons of mass destruction.

6.1 Introduction

From its earliest conception, authors of a national Department of Homeland Security envisioned the widespread participation of states and localities as the programs and policies of Homeland Security were implemented. As early as 2004, the shift away from centralized authority had taken root in the culture of homeland security. The department's own *Report from the Task Force on State and Local Homeland Security Funding* unequivocally endorses not only local involvement but local control. In addition, it urges policymakers to author policy from the ground level up rather than descendant from DHS itself.

> Those at the municipal, state, tribal and federal level responsible for using these funds have a better understanding of what each needs to do to achieve success. Recommendations for major changes would have only added confusion where clarity is emerging. It is our belief that these recommended actions coupled with expected maturity of the program will result in measurable progress towards making the nation safer, stronger, and better.[1]

The federal government, despite its agency status, cannot carry out the local and regional field requirements of DHS, nor would it be wise to overcentralize these diverse functions. At the outset of DHS, there was an unequivocal understanding concerning shared responsibilities in these matters. Early on in the life of DHS, there was full recognition of the necessity of federal, state, and local interaction. Under the DHS Office of Intelligence and Analysis, there is a structure for such reporting under the "State and Local Program Office" slot. See Figure 6.1.

Intelligence, in order to have any significant meaning in homeland defense, must be naturally and continuously shared rather than protected or hidden due to bureaucratic layers of multiple agencies. Intelligence is the best and most telling example of how important the interaction between state, federal, and local authorities is and must be.[2] President Bush, when recommending the establishment of DHS, wanted to set a tone and mission for the new federal agency. He did, however, allow for states to maintain autonomy as well as have a mechanism for input. By his presidential directive, it was clear that a collaborative and integrative approach in the application of homeland security was the intended goal. Bush noted:

> The Federal Government recognizes the roles and responsibilities of State and local authorities in domestic incident management. Initial responsibility for managing domestic incidents generally falls on State and local authorities.

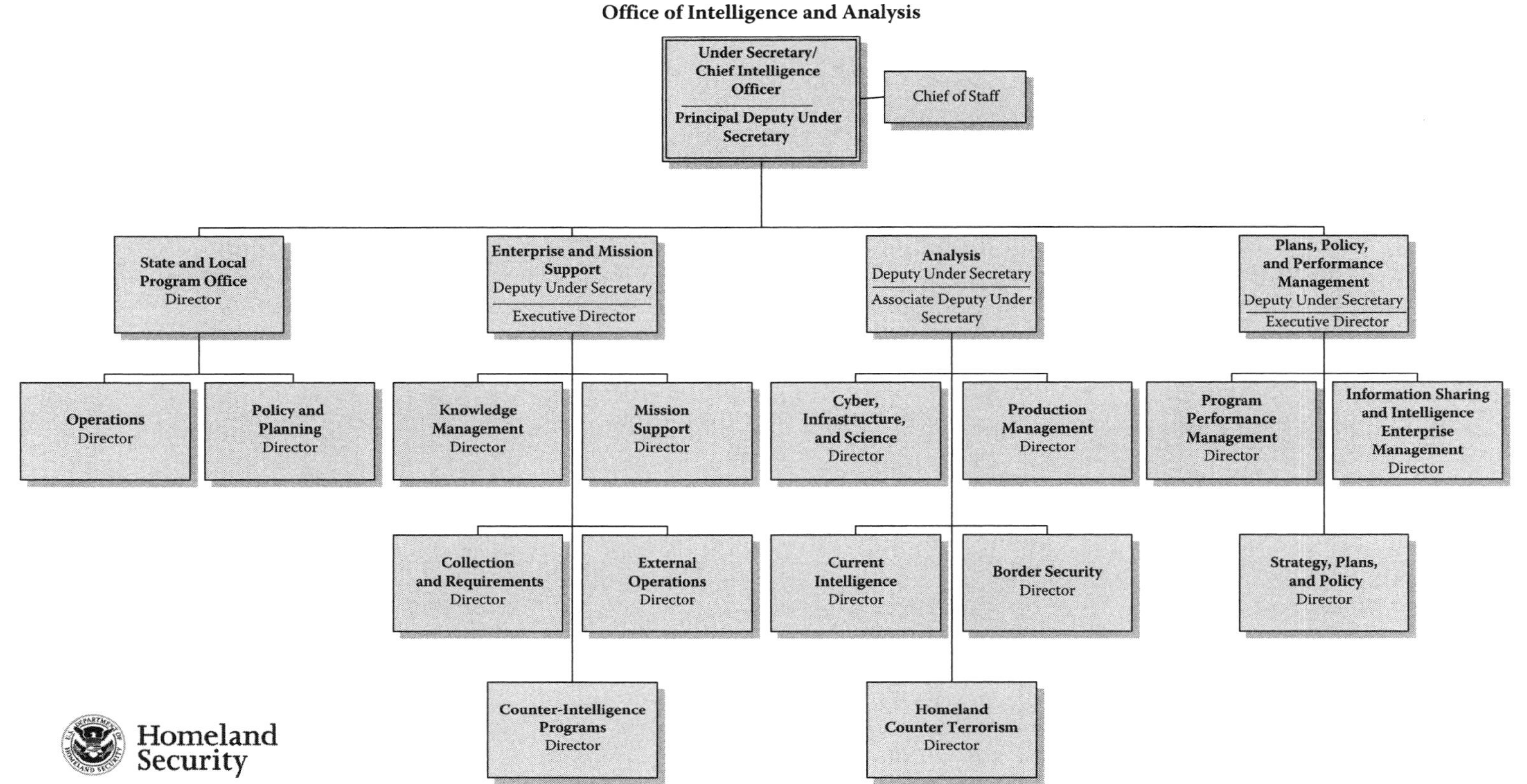

FIGURE 6.1 Department of Homeland Security, Office of Intelligence and Analysis organizational chart.

> The Federal Government will assist State and local authorities when their resources are overwhelmed, or when Federal interests are involved. The Secretary will coordinate with State and local governments to ensure adequate planning, equipment, training, and exercise activities. The Secretary will also provide assistance to State and local governments to develop all-hazards plans and capabilities, including those of greatest importance to the security of the United States, and will ensure that State, local, and Federal plans are compatible.[3]

Internet Resource: Become familiar with the nature and structure of our 50 state centers for homeland security by visiting http://www.nga.org/cda/files/homesecstructures.pdf.

6.2 Challenge of National Policy at the State and Local Levels

The department itself fully understood the necessity for fruitful and productive relationships with state and local authorities. By setting up the State, Local, Tribal, and Territorial Government Coordinating Council (SLTTGCC), DHS sought the membership of those in the state and local trenches. Membership criteria included:

- A state, local, tribal, or territorial homeland security director or equivalent with relevant programmatic planning and operational responsibilities
- Accountable for the development, improvement, and maintenance of critical infrastructure protection policies or programs at the state, local, or tribal level
- Recognized among his or her peers as a leader
- Committed to acting as national representative regarding homeland practices relevant to states and localities

The council conducts much of its business through working groups, charted in Figure 6.2.

Hence, while policy making emanates from the federal system, management inevitably falls on the states and localities. How these policies are carried out, and whether they can be carried out, is a question more appropriate for the local level.

6.2.1 Structure at the State Level

Relevant departments and agencies of the federal government must take the lead in implementing this system, while state and local governments must

Policy and Planning Working Group

Reviews Department of Homeland Security Critical Infrastructure/Key Resources protection plans, such as the National Infrastructure Protection Plan Sector Specific Plans (SSPs) and the National Response Framework;
Provides feedback from a State, Local, Tribal, and Territorial (SLTT) perspective to the Department; and
Particularly well positioned to provide SLTT insight into Federal planning efforts which gives a strong voice to the concerns of these levels of government.

Communication and Coordination Working Group

Facilitates the release of coordinated SLTTGCC-related information to the SLTT community, or other critical communities;
Develops clearer and more direct channel of communication with and among SLTT CI/KR leadership and with the Department on CI/KR issues and plans; and
Helps to identify and support platforms that enable members of the SLTT community to share best practices in CI/KR protection, issues of interest, and more.

Chemical-Terrorism Vulnerability Information Working Group

Design an implementation process for the controlled dissemination of CVI to appropriate state and local officials;
Provide feedback on the CVI outreach program; and
Develop and Sustain on-going feedback process during CVI implementation

Information Sharing Working Group

Helps the SLTTGCC better understand CI/KR information sharing at the SLTT levels of government, determine what practices are effective, and identify opportunities for integration with each other and Federal government resources;
Construct an analysis of the CI/KR information-sharing landscape in the SLTT environment in order to appraise best practices and identify gaps, opportunities for leverage, or areas requiring enhancement.

FIGURE 6.2 State, Local, Tribal, and Territorial Government Coordinating Council working groups.

implement and adopt homeland policies consistent with DHS policy. State Homeland Security entities were created to ensure states were prepared at the front lines for terrorist attacks. State entities provide a structural entity for a mission of state protections by coordinating the various needs of the governor's office, the Homeland Security director, the state emergency management office, other state agencies, local governments, the private sector, volunteer organizations, and the federal government. Every state erected an Office of Homeland Security soon after 9/11. The current compendium includes those offices shown in Figure 6.3.

How states choose to construct their Offices of Homeland Security is unique to the given jurisdiction. Most states relied upon the governor to designate a person to be a homeland security director. The position is advisory panel and agency driven, as well as the office where related functions of homeland security are coordinated, such as emergency

Alabama	Spencer Collier Director	Alabama Department of Homeland Security	P.O. Box 304115	Montgomery, Ala. 36130-4115	334-353-3050	http://www.dhs.alabama.gov
Alaska	John Madden Director	Alaska Division of Homeland Security & Emergency Services Department of Military and Veteran Affairs	P.O. Box 5750 Bldg. 4900, Suite B-214	Ft. Richardson, Alaska 99505	907-428-7062	www.ak-prepared.com/
Arizona	Gilbert M. Orrantia Director	Arizona Department of Homeland Security	1700 West Washington Street, #210	Phoenix, Ariz. 85007	602-542-7013	http://www.azdohs.gov/
Arkansas	Dave Maxwell Director	Arkansas Department of Emergency Management	Building 9501 Camp Joseph	North Little Rock, Ark. 72119-9600	501-683-6700	www.adem.arkansas.gov
California	Mike Dayton Acting Secretary	California Emergency Management Agency	3650 Schriever Avenue	Mather, Calif. 95655	916-324-9809	http://www.oes.ca.gov/
Colorado	James Davis Executive Director	Colorado Department of Public Safety	700 Kipling Street	Denver, Colo. 80215	303-239-4400	http://cdpsweb.state.co.us/
Connecticut	Bill Hackett Interim State Director of Emergency Management	Division of Emergency Management and Homeland Security	25 Sigourney Street	Hartford, Conn. 06106-5042	860-256-0800	http://www.ct.gov/demhs/

FIGURE 6.3 List of State Homeland Security Office contacts.

Delaware	Kurt Reuther Delaware Homeland Security Advisor	Department of Safety and Homeland Security	303 Transportation Circle P.O. Box 818	Dover, Del. 19903	302-744-2680	http://dshs.delaware.gov/
District of Columbia	Millicent Williams Director	Homeland Security & Emergency Management Agency	2720 Martin Luther King Jr. Avenue, SE	Washington, D.C. 20032	202-727-6161	http://www.dcema.dc.gov/dcema/site/default.asp
Florida	Mark Perez Homeland Security Advisor	Florida Department of Law Enforcement	P.O. Box 1489	Tallahassee, Fla. 32302-1489	850-410-7060	www.fdle.state.fl.us/osi/DomesticSecurity/
Georgia	Charley English Director	Georgia Emergency Management Agency/Homeland Security	P.O. Box 18055	Atlanta, Ga. 30316-0055	404-635-7000	www.gema.state.ga.us
Hawaii	MG Darryl Wong Adjutant General		3949 Diamond Head Rd.	Honolulu, Hawaii 96816-4495	808-733-4246	www.scd.state.hi.us
Idaho	BG Bill Shawver Director	Bureau of Homeland Security	4040 West Guard Street, Bldg 600	Boise, Idaho 83705-5004	208-422-3040	www.bhs.idaho.gov
Illinois	Jonathon Monken Director	Illinois Emergency Management Agency	2200 South Dirksen Parkway	Springfield, Ill. 62703	217-557-6225	http://iema.illinois.gov/iema/index.asp

FIGURE 6.3 (continued) List of State Homeland Security Office contacts.

Iowa	BG Derek Hill Administrator	Iowa Homeland Security and Emergency Management Division	7105 NW 70th Avenue Camp Dodge Building W-4	Johnston, Iowa 50131		www.iowahomelandsecurity.org
Kansas	Major General Lee Tafanelli Homeland Security Advisor		2800 SW Topeka	Topeka, Kan. 66611-1287	785-274-1001	http://kansastag.ks.gov/kshls_default.asp
Kentucky	Gene Kiser Executive Director	Kentucky Office of Homeland Security	200 Mero Street	Frankfort, Ky. 40622	502-564-2081	http://homelandsecurity.ky.gov/
Louisiana	Kevin Davis Director	Governor's Office of Homeland Security and Emergency Preparedness	7667 Independence Blvd	Baton Rouge, La. 70806	225-925-7500	www.gohsep.la.gov
Maine	MG John Libby	Department of Defense, Veterans, & Emergency Management	33 State House Station, Camp Keyes	Augusta, Maine 04333-0001	207-430-6000	http://www.maine.gov/mema/homeland/
Maryland	Andrew Lauland Homeland Security Advisor	State of Maryland Executive Department Governor's Homeland Security Office	The Jeffrey Building 16 Francis Street	Annapolis, Md. 21401	(800) 492-8477	www.gov.state.md.us/homelandsecurity.html
Massachusetts	Kurt Schwartz Undersecretary of Homeland Security	Executive Office of Public Safety and Security	1 Ashburton Place, Rm. 2133	Boston, Mass. 02108	617-727-7775	http://www.mass.gov/?pageID=eopshomepage&L=1&L0=Home&sid=Eeops

FIGURE 6.3 (continued) List of State Homeland Security Office contacts.

Michigan	Kriste Etue Homeland Security Advisor		333 S. Grand Avenue P.O. 30634	Lansing, Mich. 48909	517-241-0401	www.michigan.gov/homeland/
Minnesota	Kris Eide Director	Homeland Security & Emergency Management	444 Cedar Street	St. Paul, Minn. 55101	651-201-7400	https://dps.mn.gov/divisions/hsem/Pages/default.aspx
Mississippi	Jay Ledbetter Director	Mississippi Office of Homeland Security	P.O. Box 958	Jackson, Miss. 39296-4501	601-346-1500	www.homelandsecurity.ms.gov
Missouri	Jerry Lee Director	Missouri Department of Public Safety	P.O. Box 749	Jefferson City, Mo. 65102	573-522-3007	www.dps.mo.gov/homelandsecurity/
Montana	Ed Tinsley Division Administrator	MT Disaster & Emergency Services Division Department of Military Affairs	P.O. Box 4789-1956 Mt Majo Street	Fort Harrison, Mont. 59636	406-324-4777	http://dma.mt.gov/DES/default.asp
Nebraska	Rick Sheehy Lt. Governor		P.O. Box 94848	Lincoln, Neb. 68509-4848	402-471-2256	http://www.nema.ne.gov/preparedness/homeland-security-home.html
Nevada	Christopher Smith Chief of Emergency Management		2478 Fairview Drive	Carson City, Nev. 89711	775-684-5678	http://homelandsecurity.nv.gov/
New Hampshire	Christopher Pope Director	Division of Homeland Security and Emergency Management	33 Hazen Drive	Concord, N.H. 03305	603-271-2231	http://www.nh.gov/safety/divisions/hsem/index.html
New Jersey	Charlie McKenna Director	New Jersey Office of Homeland Security and Preparedness	P.O. Box 091	Trenton, N.J. 08625	609-584-4000	www.njhomelandsecurity.gov

FIGURE 6.3 (continued) List of State Homeland Security Office contacts.

New Mexico	Michael Duvall Secretary	New Mexico Deptartment of Homeland Security & Emergency Management	13 Bataan Blvd.	Santa Fe, N.M. 87504	505-476-1051	http://nmdhsem.org
New York	James Sherry Acting Commissioner & Director	Office of Counter Terrorism Division of Homeland Security and Emergency Services	1220 Washington Avenue State Office Campus- Building 7A Suite 710	Albany, N.Y. 12242	518-242-5000	http://www.dhses.ny.gov/oct/
North Carolina	Reuben Young Secretary	NC Department of Crime Control and Public Safety	4701 Mail Service Center	Raleigh, N.C. 27699	919-733-2126	www.nccrimecontrol.org
North Dakota	Greg Wilz Director	Homeland Security Division Department of Emergency Services	P.O. Box 5511	Bismarck, N.D. 58506	701-328-8100	www.nd.gov/des/
Ohio	Richard Baron Executive Director	Ohio Homeland Security	1970 W. Broad Street	Columbus, Ohio 43223-1102	614-387-6171	www.homelandsecurity.ohio.gov
Oklahoma	Kim Edd Carter Director	Oklahoma Office of Homeland Security	P.O. Box 11415	Oklahoma City, Okla. 73136-0415	405-425-7296	www.homelandsecurity.ok.gov/
Oregon	MG Raymond F. Rees Homeland Security Advisor	Oregon Military Department	P.O. Box 14350	Salem, Ore. 97309-5047	503-584-3991	http://www.oregon.gov/OMD/

FIGURE 6.3 (continued) List of State Homeland Security Office contacts.

Pennsylvania	Frank Noonan Commissioner	Pennsylvania State Police	1800 Elmerton Avenue	Harrisburg, Penn. 17110		http://www.psp.state.pa.us
Puerto Rico	Ramón Rosario Cortes Homeland Security Advisor		P.O. Box 9066597	San Juan, P.R. 00906-6597	787-721-0435	
Rhode Island	MG Kevin McBride Homeland Security Advisor	Joint Force Headquarters	645 New London Ave.	Cranston, R.I. 02920	401-275-4102	http://www.or.ng.mil/sites/RI/TAG/default.aspx
South Carolina	Mark Keel Chief	South Carolina Law Enforcement Division	4400 Broad River Run Road.	Columbia, S.C. 29210	803-896-7001	http://www.sled.sc.gov/HSOfficeHome.aspx?MenuID=HSOffice
South Dakota	James Carpenter Director	Office of Homeland Security	118 West Capitol Avenue	Pierre, S.D. 57501	605-773-3450	http://dps.sd.gov/homeland_security/default.aspx
Tennessee	David W. Purkey Assistant Commissioner	Tennessee Department of Safety and Homeland Security	312 Rosa L. Parks Avenue, 25th Floor TN Tower	Nashville, Tenn. 37243	615-532-7825	http://www.tn.gov/homelandsecurity
Texas	Steve McCraw Director	Texas Department of Public Safety	P.O. Box 4087	Austin, Texas 78773-0001	512-424-2000	http://www.txdps.state.tx.us/index.htm
Utah	Keith D. Squires Deputy Commissioner	Department of Public Safety	4501 South 2700 West P.O. Box 1411775	Salt Lake City, Utah 84114-1775	801-965-4461	http://publicsafety.utah.gov/
Vermont	Captain Christopher Reinfurt Director	Department of Public Safety	103 South Main Street	Waterbury, Vt. 05671-2101	802-241-5357	http://www.dps.state.vt.us/homeland/home_main.html

FIGURE 6.3 (continued) List of State Homeland Security Office contacts.

Virginia	Terri Suit	Secretary of Veterans Affairs & Homeland Security	Patrick Henry Building 1111 East Broad Street	Richmond, Va. 23219	804-225-3826	http://www.commonwealthpreparedness.virginia.gov/
Washington	MG Timothy J. Lowenberg Adjutant General and Director	State Military Department	Washington Military Dept., Bldg 1	Camp Murray, Wash. 98430-5000	253-512-8201	http://mil.wa.gov/index.shtml
West Virginia	Jimmy Gianato Secretary	Department of Military Affairs and Public Safety	State Capitol Complex, Bldg 6, Rm B-122	Charleston, W.V. 25305	304-558-3795	http://www.wvdhsem.gov/
Wisconsin	BG Donald Dunbar Homeland Security Advisor		P.O. Box 8111	Madison, Wisc. 53708-8111	608-242-3000	http://homelandsecurity.wi.gov/
Wyoming	Guy Cameron Director	Wyoming Office of Homeland Security	122 W. 25th Street Herschler Bldg 1st Floor East	Cheyenne, Wyo. 82002-0001	307-777-4663	http://wyohomelandsecurity.state.wy.us/main.aspx
Guam	James McDonald, Homeland Security Advisor		221-B Chalan Palasyo	Hagatna, Guam 96910	671-475-9600	http://www.guamhs.org/main/
Northern Mariana Islands	Marvin Seman	Special Advisor for Homeland Security	Caller Box 10007	Saipan, Northern Mariana Islands 96950	670-322-8004	
Virgin Islands	Elton Lewis Director	USVI Territorial Emergency Management Agency	8221 Estate Nisky	St. Thomas, V.I. 00803	340-774-2244	http://www.vitema.gov/index.html
American Samoa	Mike Sala Director	Department of Homeland Security	American Samoa Government	Pago, Pago, American Samoa 96799	684-633-2827	

FIGURE 6.3 (continued) List of State Homeland Security Office contacts.

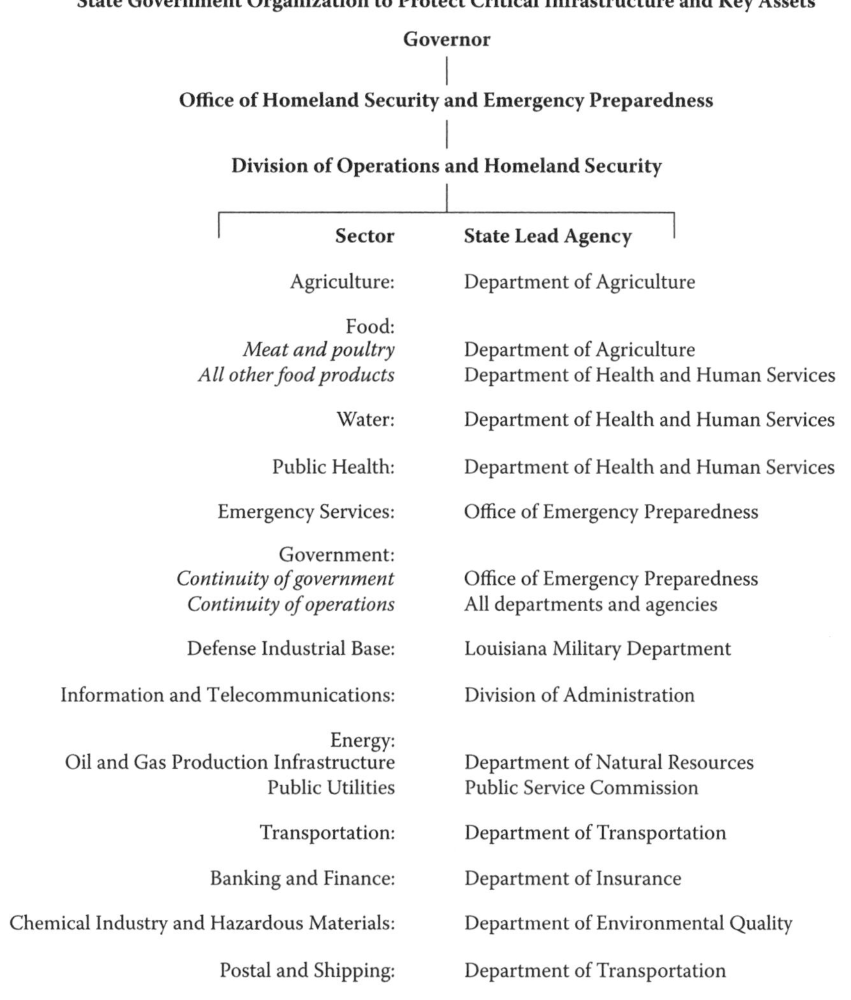

Louisiana Homeland Security Strategy
State Government Organization to Protect Critical Infrastructure and Key Assets
Governor
Office of Homeland Security and Emergency Preparedness
Division of Operations and Homeland Security
Sector
State Lead Agency
Agriculture:
Department of Agriculture
Food:
Meat and poultry
Department of Agriculture
All other food products
Department of Health and Human Services
Water:
Department of Health and Human Services
Public Health:
Department of Health and Human Services
Emergency Services:
Office of Emergency Preparedness
Government:
Continuity of government
Office of Emergency Preparedness
Continuity of operations
All departments and agencies
Defense Industrial Base:
Louisiana Military Department
Information and Telecommunications:
Division of Administration
Energy:
Oil and Gas Production Infrastructure
Department of Natural Resources
Public Utilities
Public Service Commission
Transportation:
Department of Transportation
Banking and Finance:
Department of Insurance
Chemical Industry and Hazardous Materials:
Department of Environmental Quality
Postal and Shipping:
Department of Transportation

FIGURE 6.4 Louisiana state Homeland Security strategy.

management, law enforcement, health, and related public safety functions. To see a common design, review the example from Louisiana in Figure 6.4.

Other designs incorporate existing offices at the state level, such as the adjutant general, the National Guard, or specialized task forces that are composed of executive office staff and agency heads from law enforcement, fire and rescue, public health, and public works. See the example in Figure 6.5.

States are increasingly being asked to assume more under homeland security protocols. For some, the farther away from federal control the process is, the more effective. DHS itself realizes the necessity of state and local

Illinois Terrorism Task Force

The Illinois Terrorism Task Force (ITTF) is charged with the task of assuring that Illinois is ready to respond to an act of terrorism. Due to the commitment of the members of the Task Force and the ability of the associated agencies to come together in a spirit of cooperation and teamwork, Illinois has plans in place to deal with a terrorist attack in our state.

Pat Quinn, Governor

Jonathon E.Monken
Director, Illinois Emergency Management

FIGURE 6.5 Illinois Terrorism Task Force members.

influence and allots a sizable portion of government funding to advance this ambition. For the fiscal year 2009, the budgetary allotment increases in terms of both size and scope of operations.[4] See Table 6.1.

Tennessee, for example, has a sophisticated network of homeland programs and personnel carrying out the homeland mission. Its overall purpose is:

> The Tennessee Office of Homeland Security has the primary responsibility and authority for directing statewide activities pertaining to the prevention of, and protection from, terrorist related events. This responsibility includes the development and implementation of a comprehensive and coordinated strategy to secure the state from terrorist threats and attacks. Further, the office of Homeland Security serves as a liaison between federal, state, and local agencies, and private sector on matters relating to the security of our state and citizens.
>
> - AWARENESS—Identify and understand terrorist threats within Tennessee.
> - PREVENTION—Detect, deter, and mitigate terrorist threats to Tennessee.
> - PROTECTION—Safeguard our citizens, their freedoms, property, and the economy of Tennessee from acts of terrorism.
> - RESPONSE—Assist in coordinating the response to terrorist-related events.
> - ORGANIZATIONAL EXCELLENCE—Putting the safety of our citizens first.[5]

As in other jurisdictions, Tennessee sets out to educate its citizens and to play an instrumental role in the prevention of and protection of its citizens from terror and its threats. It also publishes and adopts protocols for the more typical threats likely to be encountered. An example, in Figure 6.6, deals with the Anthrax threat.

Task forces and commissions play a central role in state homeland policy since the composition of these bodies tends to include major players in law enforcement and emergency preparedness.

TABLE 6.1 FY2010 Enacted and FY2011 Budget Request for State and Local Programs (All Amounts in Millions of Dollars)

Programs	FY2010 Enacted	FY2011 Budget Request
State and Regional Preparedness Programs		
State Homeland Security Grant Program	950	1050
Emergency Management Performance Grant Program	340	345
Regional Catastrophic Preparedness Program	35	35
Assistance to Firefighters	810	610
Metropolitan Statistical Area Preparedness Programs		
Urban Area Security Initiative	887	1100
Port Security Grant Program	300	300
Public Transportation Security Grant Program	300	300
Over-The-Road Bus Security	12	0
Buffer Zone Protection Program	50	50
Training, Measurement, and Exercise Programs		
Continuing Training Grants	29	22
National Domestic Preparedness Consortium	102	52
Center for Domestic Preparedness/ Noble Training Center	63	63
National Exercise Program	40	42
Technical Assistance Programs	13	15
Evaluations and Assessments	16	18
Programs Proposed for Elimination by the Administration		
Driver's License Security Program	50	0
Metropolitan Medical Response System	41	0
Citizen Corps Programs	13	0
Interoperable Emergency Communications Program	50	0
Emergency Operations Centers	60	0
Cybercrime Counterterrrorism Training	2	0
Rural Domestic Preparedness Consortium	3	0
Total	**4166**	**4002**

Source: CRS analysis of the FY2011 DHS Congressional Budget Justifications, and the FY2011 DHS Budget in Brief.

SUSPICIOUS LETTER AND PACKAGE RISK ASSESSMENT AND LABORATORY SAMPLE SUBMISSION GUIDELINES

Emergency responders are critical frontline providers and are urged to exercise sensible risk assessment skills in determining the appropriateness of an item for submission, taking into consideration the overall risk of a particular situation. Federal, state, and local response agencies should be mindful of the potential for exposure to potentially harmful substances from suspicious or threatening packages or letters. To optimize the use of law enforcement and laboratory resources, the following guidelines for risk assessment should be used for determining whether to submit a sample of a suspicious item for testing.

Measures can be taken that are the same for suspicious letters and packages and should take into account whether the item is opened, whether it contains a threat, and whether persons in contact with or nearby the package are ill.

Part I: Assess the Risk and Collect the Sample

1) HIGH RISK, consider submission to state public health laboratory for testing:

A. Item is associated with suspicious packages or items that are clearly not a mass mailing or "junk" mail **AND** has a powder or other substance on, leaking from, or in it. "Suspicious" mail can be defined as associated with a terrorist group or with a threatening message or phone call. It might be sent to a high-profile recipient (i.e., government office, political candidate, news reporter, etc.);

OR

B. Powder or other substance not associated with the mail, but associated with a verbal or written threat;

OR

C. Persons in contact with or nearby the package are exhibiting signs of illness (i.e., burning eyes, vomiting, difficulty breathing, etc.).

Under no circumstances should unprotected or untrained responders attempt to collect specimens from or otherwise disturb the item. The State Emergency Operation Center (SEOC), local FBI Joint Terrorism Task Force (JTTF) fileld office, and HAZMAT unit must be notified immediately. Under the direction of a law enforcement representative, a HAZMAT technician, in a minimum of level–B equipment, will perform field screening and collect and turn the sample over to law enforcement for delivery to the closest Tennessee Department of Health Laboratory for testing. There are laboratories that service the western, middle, and eastern divisions of the state. The field safety screening process shall be clearly documented and include but not be limited to screening for pH, explosives, radioactivity, and if possible, volatile organic compounds, flammable materials, and oxidizing agents. If qualified HAZMAT technicians are not available in your vicinity, the SEOC must be called to coordinate external support.

FIGURE 6.6 Tennessee Department of Health Suspicious Letter and Package Risk Assessment and Laboratory Sample Submission Guidelines.

It is **required** that samples submitted be collected with the Biological Sampling Kit provided by the Tennessee Department of Health Laboratory. Items not submitted according these guidelines will NOT be accepted for testing.

The State defines samples as a small portion of the suspicious material. **Do not send all the evidence to the laboratory** for testing, just a sample. The Tennessee Department of Health Laboratory does not investigate crimes, it only tests samples and provides results to law enforcement and public health officials. Therefore, local, state or federal law enforcement must retain control of any potential evidence.

2) UNCERTAIN RISK, requires further risk assessment:

A. Item associated with suspicious mail without an articulated threat and in the absence of a powder or other substance.

OR

B. Item with unknown powder or substance, no articulated threat and no illness.

Responders should consult with law enforcement to evaluate the context in which the substance or letter was discovered or received and make a determination as to whether that item poses a credible threat. Examples might include hate mail, protest letters sent to an abortion clinic, etc.

3) LOW RISK, does not need laboratory testing but requires disposal: Items not in categories 1 or 2 as described above. Responders are asked to decline accepting items for submission and provide advice on proper disposal in regular trash. Law enforcement or regional or metropolitan health departments can be consulted for questions. Examples include items that might be expected to have powder already associated with them (i.e., bubble gum, potato chips, donuts, pills, magazines, etc.), powders found in an area where the public is not in immediate danger (i.e., by the roadside), and other isolated powders or items found in the absence of an overt threat or other suspicious circumstances.

Part II: Submit the Sample

All samples submitted for testing at the Tennessee Department of Health Laboratory must be submitted by law enforcement and **must fit into the Biological Sampling Kit provided by the Tennessee Department of Health Laboratory.** Larger items will not be accepted by the Laboratory because they cannot be safely handled in their Biological Safety Cabinets. Agencies will be furnished with a new Biological Sampling Kit as used or when contents are expired. Standard FBI notification and chain-of-custody procedures shall continue to be followed as prescribed. **The State Emergency Operations Center (SEOC) must be notified upon the decision to submit a specimen for testing.**

Contact Information

State Emergency Operations Center (SEOC)		(615) 741-0001 or (800) 262-3400
FBI Joint Terrorism Task Force:	– Knoxville	(865) 544-0751
	– Nashville	(615) 292-5159
	– Memphis	(901) 747-4300
Governor's Office of Homeland Security		(615) 532-7825
Tennessee Department of Health - Laboratory		(615) 262-6300
Tennessee Department of Health - Central Office		(615) 741-7247

Department of Health, Authorization No. 343710 2,000 copies. This public document was promulgated at a cost of $.90 per copy. 5/05

FIGURE 6.6 (continued) Tennessee Department of Health Suspicious Letter and Package Risk Assessment and Laboratory Sample Submission Guidelines.

All 50 states have some version of an agency dedicated to the task of homeland security. As the states soon discovered, participation at even lower levels, that of the locality, is just as necessary as the federal–state nexus.

6.2.2 Structure at the Local Level

States as large as Texas or Pennsylvania came to realize that local input, local direction, and assessment are crucial to any plan of homeland security. And in major metropolitan areas, such as New York and Los Angeles, cooperation at the state level is mandatory. What is inevitable is sweeping change in how things have been carried out in traditional law enforcement. Structures changed simply due to the new and corresponding demands. Some argue that the "organizational boundaries" have been changed in ways never envisioned by traditional law enforcement.[6] States such as Pennsylvania divide up the geography into distinct regions. See the map in Figure 6.7.

In each region, the pertinent agencies, for example, Federal Bureau of Investigation, Bureau of Alcohol, Tobacco, and Firearms, Pennsylvania State Police, National Guard, Environmental Protection Agency, and health and medical entities, compose its membership. The objectives of the regional program are to:

- Develop county task forces
- Develop regional counterterrorism task forces
- Integrate federal/state/county response
- Institutionalize mutual aid in the region
- Establish standing regional response groups
- Encourage regional networking

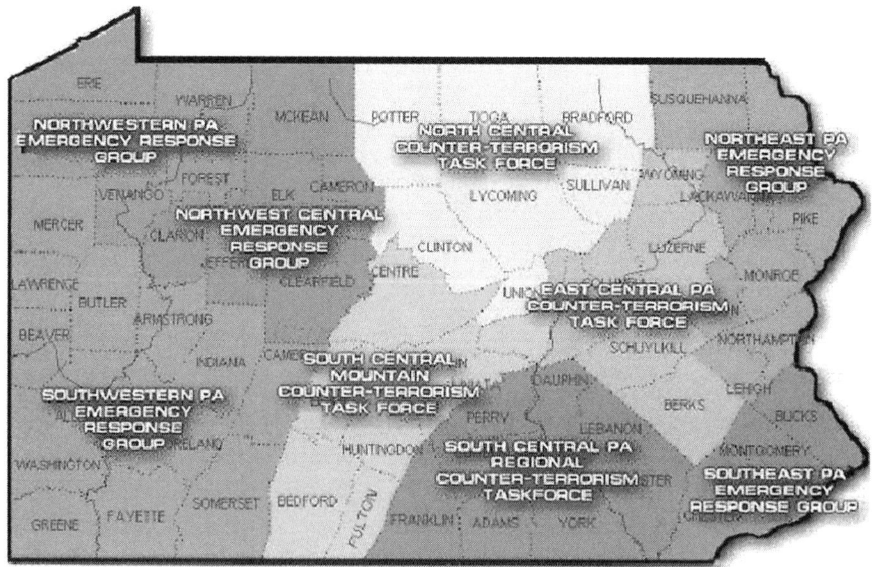

FIGURE 6.7 Map of Pennsylvania Homeland Security regions.

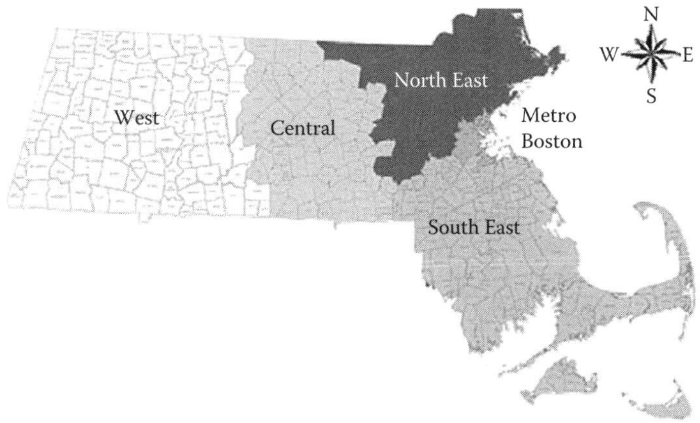

FIGURE 6.8 Map of Massachusetts Homeland Security regions.

Another example of state to regional design resides in the Commonwealth of Massachusetts. Reporting directly to the statewide Homeland Security Office are five geographically designed regions—the Northeast, Southeast, Central, Western, and Metro Boston—created to support strategic planning and operational coordination at the local level. Regional planning councils are responsible for developing and guiding the implementation of regional homeland security plans. The councils oversee all grant program expenditures. In addition, five regional homeland security advisory councils implement the strategic vision of the state Office of Homeland Security. Collaboration between the regions and the state is now commonplace. See Figure 6.8.

6.2.2.1 Fusion Centers

DHS has provided liberal funding sources for the creation of data fusion centers in a host of states and increasingly in major metropolitan areas. Fusion centers are sharing centers for information and intelligence within their jurisdictions, as well as with the federal government.[7] The crucial dynamic for the fusion center is its potentiality for sharing and dissemination. The fundamental, baseline capacities for the fusion center must be and are:

- Ability to receive classified/unclassified information from federal partners
- Ability to assess local implications of threat information through formal risk assessment process
- Ability to further disseminate threat information to other SLTT and private sector entities
- Ability to gather locally generated information, aggregate it, analyze it, and share it with federal partners, as appropriate[8]

Internet Exercise: Discover much more about the baseline capabilities that every fusion center should advance at http://www.dhs.gov/files/programs/gc_1296491960442.shtm.

At its center, the fusion center must become the locale for a "unified process for reporting, tracking, and accessing"[9] intelligence and information of every variety. Every state now has a fusion center. In addition, major urban or regional areas such as Orange County, CA, and Boston Regional, to name two, have erected centers.[10]

DHS's Office of Intelligence and Analysis provides personnel with operational and intelligence skills to staff the fusion centers. The centers:

- Help the classified and unclassified information flow
- Provide expertise
- Coordinate with local law enforcement and other agencies
- Provide local awareness and access (see Figure 6.9)

As of 2012, there were 72 fusion centers around the country, like the Commonwealth of Massachusetts, for example, shown in Figure 6.10.[11]

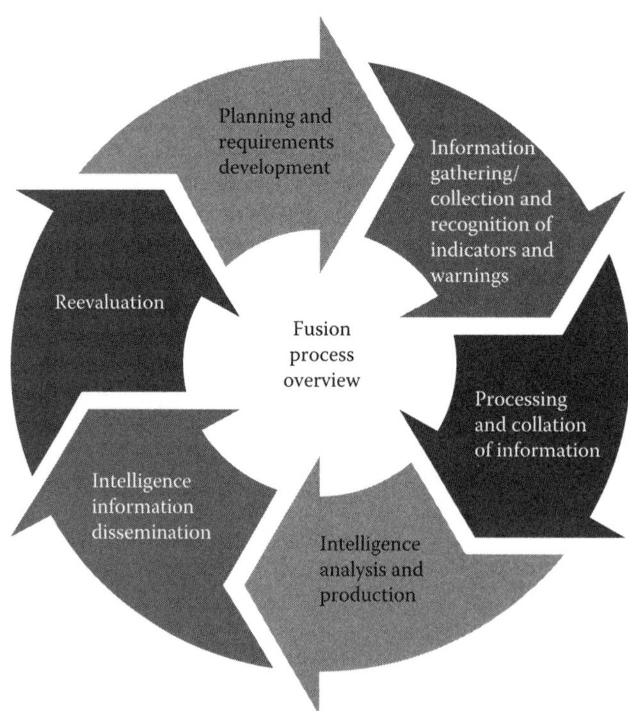

FIGURE 6.9 Figure from the U.S. Government's Information Sharing Environment depicting the fusion process as a continuous cycle in which inputs from various sources are brought together to provide state and local context to help enhance the national threat picture. Available at: http://ise.gov/national-network-state-and-major-urban-area-fusion-centers.

FIGURE 6.10 Massachusetts Fusion Center logo.

The department has deployed intelligence officers to state fusion centers in:

- Arizona
- California
- Colorado
- Connecticut
- Georgia
- Florida
- Illinois
- Indiana
- Louisiana
- Maryland
- Massachusetts
- New Jersey
- New York
- Ohio
- South Carolina
- Virginia
- Washington

The department has also deployed support to fusion centers in New York City, Los Angeles, and the Dallas region.

Internet Exercise: Find out about the many facets of the fusion center at http://www.dhs.gov/files/programs/gc_1296484657738.shtm.

6.2.3 Funding and Local Initiatives

The funding and grant systems for DHS recognize the fundamental decentralization of local and state homeland security efforts. The Homeland Security Grant Program funds planning, organization, equipment, training, and exercise activities in support of the National Preparedness Guidelines, as well as the National Incident Management System (NIMS), National Response

Framework (NRF), and National Infrastructure Protection Plan (NIPP). The funds are sent directly to states for specific programs and purposes, including planning, equipment, training, and exercise activities, as well as dollars for implementation of new programs and initiatives. DHS additionally earmarks funds for four other sectors essential to homeland security

Urban Area Security Initiative (UASI) Grant Program funds address the unique multidisciplinary planning, operations, equipment, training, and exercise needs of high-threat, high-density urban areas.

Law Enforcement Terrorism Prevention Program (LETPP) focuses upon the prevention of terrorist attacks and provides law enforcement and public safety communities with funds to support the following activities: intelligence gathering and information sharing through enhancing/establishing fusion centers, hardening high-value targets, planning strategically, continuing to build interoperable communications, and collaborating with nonlaw enforcement partners, other government agencies, and the private sector.

Public Safety Interoperable Communications (PSIC) Grant Program assists public safety agencies in the acquisition of, deployment of, or training for the use of interoperable communications systems that can utilize a reallocated public safety spectrum in the 700 MHz band for radio communication.

Infrastructure Protection Program supports specific activities to protect critical infrastructure, such as ports, mass transit, highways, rail, and transportation. IPP grants fund a range of preparedness activities, including strengthening infrastructure against explosive attacks, preparedness planning, equipment purchase, training, exercises, and security management and administration costs. IPP comprises five separate grant programs: Transit Security, Port Security, Buffer Zone Protection, Trucking Security, and Intercity Bus Security.

On top of all of this, DHS, by and through FEMA, erects Citizen Corps Councils in nearly 2500 communities across the United States. Citizen Corps, coordinated by the Department of Homeland Security, focuses on opportunities for people across the country to participate in a range of measures to make their families, homes, and communities safer from the threats of terrorism, crime, and disasters of all kinds. Citizen Corps also brings together a community's first responders, firefighters, emergency healthcare providers, law enforcement, and emergency managers with its volunteer resources. Citizen Corps will help people across America take a more active role in crime prevention, support the emergency medical community, and be better trained in a wide range of emergency preparedness and disaster response activities. See Figure 6.11.

The focus of Citizen Corps work is at the local level. The scope of the Citizen Corps covers a wide range of activities. Citizen Corps Councils help

FIGURE 6.11 Citizen Corps logo.

drive local citizen participation by coordinating Citizen Corps programs, developing community action plans, assessing possible threats, and identifying local resources. Examples of corps programs are shown in Figure 6.12.

Internet Resource: Review the many organizations and associations involved in Citizen Corps at http://www.citizencorps.gov/pdf/council.pdf.

6.3 Fine Line of National and Homeland Security

It is unlikely that any firm line can be drawn between the worlds of national and homeland security. At one time this may have been possible. Given the events of 9/11, the interconnectedness and integration of military/defense function with that of law enforcement and security became grotesquely obvious. Indeed, the terrorists seemed to have deduced this by their mixture of targets, from the attempted White House attack, to the Towers, and the distressing crash into the Pentagon (Figure 6.13).

In a way, it is absurd to think that these dual lines of defense do not merge in many sectors. Some might even argue that the Iraq and Afghanistan campaigns are extensions of a security and police effort to track down the perpetrators of terror. The argument has both appeal and merit. That there must be some sort of collaboration between the military complex and the arm of homeland security is now standard operating procedure.

When speaking of the military we reference the historic four major branches of the service. The Coast Guard has long been out of the DoD province, initially being located in the U.S. Treasury Department while today it is housed in DHS. Hence, the mindset of the Coast Guard has always been in hazard and human tragedy. So too the continuous contribution of the

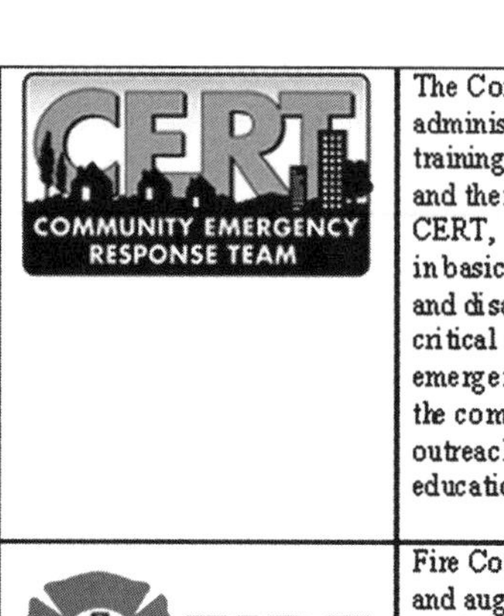	The Community Emergency Response Team (CERT) Program program is administered by FEMA's Community Preparedness Division. CERT is a training program that prepares people to help themselves, their families and their neighbors in the event of a disaster in their community. Through CERT, citizens can learn about disaster preparedness and receive training in basic disaster response skills such as fire safety, light search and rescue, and disaster medical operations. With this training, volunteers can provide critical support by giving immediate assistance to victims before emergency first responders arrive on scene. CERT volunteers also support the community year-round by participating in community preparedness outreach activities and distributing materials on disaster preparedness and education. http://www.citizencorps.gov/cert/index.shtm
	Fire Corps promotes the use of citizen advocates (volunteers) to support and augment the capacity of resource-constrained fire and emergency service departments at all levels: volunteer, combination, and career. Fire Corps is funded through the Department of Homeland Security and is managed and implemented through a partnership between the National Volunteer Fire Council and the International Association of Fire Chiefs, and with direction from the National Advisory Committee, a group of 15 national organizations representing the fire and emergency services, to provide the program with strategic direction and important feedback from the field. http://www.firecorps.org/
	The Office of the Civilian Volunteer Medical Reserve Corps (MRC) Program reports directly to the Surgeon General of the U.S. in the Department of Health and Human Services. MRC strives to improve the health and safety of communities across the country by organizing and utilizing public health, medical and other volunteers who want to donate their time and expertise to prepare for and respond to emergencies. Volunteer MRC units accomplish this mission by supplementing existing emergency and public health resources during local emergencies and other times of community need. http://www.medicalreservecorps.gov
	USAonWatch is the face of the National Neighborhood Watch Program. The program is managed nationally by the National Sheriffs' Association in partnership with the Bureau of Justice Assistance, Office of Justice Programs, US Department of Justice. Time-tested practices such as "eyes-and-ears" training and target-hardening techniques continue to be at the core of the program. As groups continue to grow, the roles of citizens have become more multifaceted and tailored to local needs. USAonWatch empowers citizens to become active in homeland security efforts through community participation. USAonWatch provides information, training, technical support and resources to local law enforcement agencies and citizens. http://www.usaonwatch.org/
	The Volunteers in Police Service (VIPS) Program serves as a gateway to information for law enforcement agencies and citizens interested in law enforcement volunteer programs. The program's ultimate goal is to enhance the capacity of state and local law enforcement agencies by incorporating the time and skills that volunteers can contribute to a community law enforcement agency. The International Association of Chiefs of Police (IACP) manages the VIPS Program in partnership with and on behalf of the Bureau of Justice Assistance, Office of Justice Programs, U.S. Department of Justice. http://www.policevolunteers.org/

FIGURE 6.12 An assortment of Citizen Corps programs.

National Guard—an agency that attends to human suffering with professionalism and skill. Shortly after the attack of 9/11, the remaining arms of the military swung into action. The entire structure of the military was reorganized into a unified command as outlined in Figure 6.14.

FIGURE 6.13 The Pentagon on 9/11.

These five combatant zones apportioned the responsibility for defense against terror based on the designated geography:

- U.S. Northern Command (USNORTHCOM)
- U.S. Southern Command (USSOUTHCOM)
- U.S. Pacific Command (USPACOM)
- U.S. European Command (USEUCOM)
- U.S. Central Command (USCENTCOM)

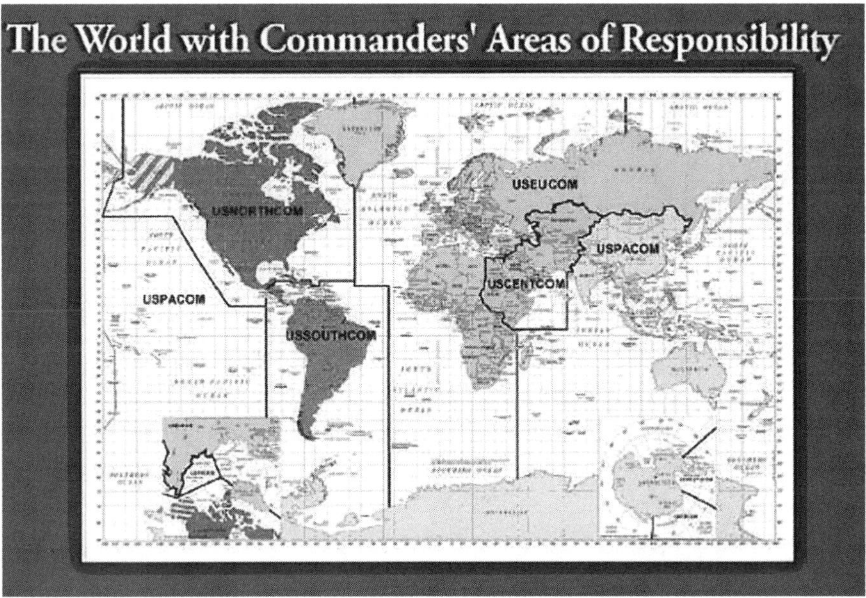

FIGURE 6.14 A world map with military commanders' areas of responsibility.

The reorientation of the military into a terror mentality has been nothing short of dramatic, but the events of 9/11 prompted the reexamination. To be sure, Americans are generally reticent about military authority, and only in cases of extreme national emergency are the armed forces called in to assist. It could be argued that part of Katrina's problem related to this hesitancy. As we gazed at the television sets, how many of us wondered aloud: Where is the military assistance? By any measure it was slow in coming (Figure 6.15).

Exactly how the military assists in the homeland arena is both complicated and innovative when compared to past practices. Aside from the defense of soil from foreign armies and attackers, the military is being asked to be partners in the fight against terrorism—tackling nontraditional enemies. Common examples of civil cooperation are:

- Immediate response (any form of immediate action taken to save lives, prevent human suffering, or mitigate property damage under imminently serious conditions)
- Military support to civilian law enforcement agencies (loans of equipment, facilities, or personnel to law enforcement)
- Military assistance for civil disturbances
- Support for domestic counterterrorism operations
- Sensitive support operations
- Counterdrug operational support

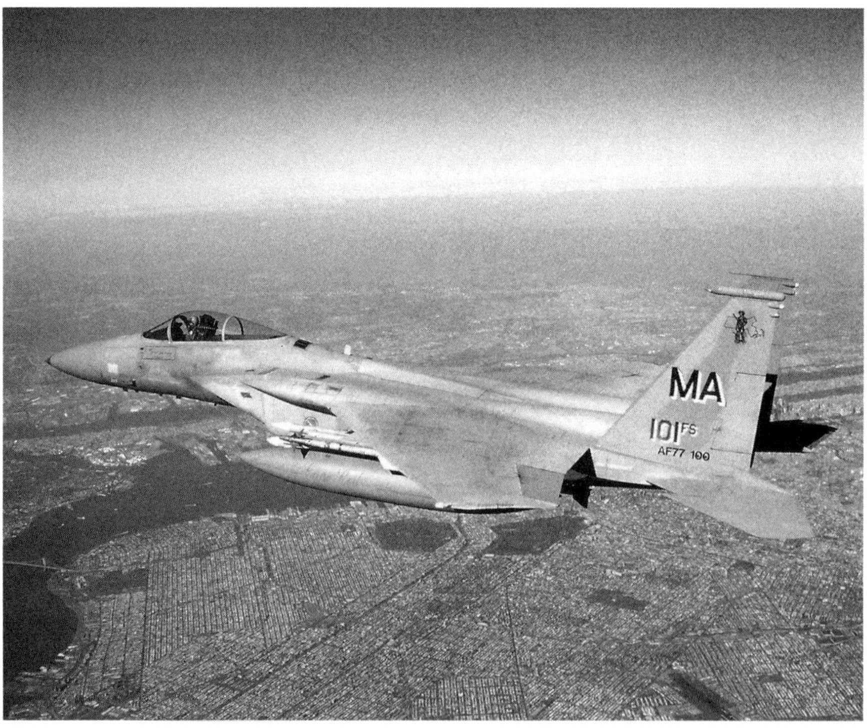

FIGURE 6.15 Air National Guard over New York City area.

- Terrorism consequence management (to include chemical, biological, radiological, nuclear, and high-yield explosive consequence management)
- Military support to civil authorities
- Support for civil disasters—natural or man made (other than terrorism)
- Military cooperation with civil agencies
- Response under other authorities
- Oil or hazardous material spills
- Radiological emergencies/incidents
- Emergency water requirements
- Response to flooding
- Forest fire emergencies
- Mass immigration
- Transportation support[12]

While this section cannot possibly cover each and every aspect of military cooperation, it will seek to address the most notable.

6.3.1 Department of Defense and Homeland Security

The defense of a nation fundamentally relies upon its military infrastructure. Yet in the affairs of homeland security, especially in a free society, the military sector cannot tackle the internal affairs of law enforcement and safety. That is not the military's integral mission. Nor is it the province of the military to meddle in the duties of state, local, or federal law enforcement—these being distinct and, for the most part, civilian counterparts and colleagues of the military. It is a delicate balance with the DoD assuming primary control of the military confrontation that arises from foreign enemies and DHS and its aligned agencies and departments handling the internal. The Joint Chiefs of Staff for the military lay out the respective obligations.

> DoD is the lead, supported by other agencies, in defending against traditional external threats/aggression (e.g., air and missile attack). However, against internal asymmetric, nontraditional threats (e.g., terrorism), DoD may be in support of DHS. When ordered to conduct Homeland Defense (HD) operations within U.S. territory, DoD will coordinate closely with other federal agencies or departments. Consistent with laws and policy, the services will provide capabilities to support combatant command requirements against a variety of air, land, maritime, space, and cyber incursions that can threaten national security. These include invasion, computer network attack, and air and missile attacks.
>
> The purpose of HD is to protect against and mitigate the impact of incursions or attacks on sovereign territory, the domestic population, and defense critical infrastructure.[13]

A graphic portrayal of this series of interrelationships is shown in Figure 6.16.[14]

These are distinct though very complementary missions. Since 9/11, those entrusted with military affairs have had to reconsider these traditional lines. Places like the Department of Defense (DoD) are by nature bureaucratically entrenched and slow to change. Moving away from the historic mission will not occur readily, although in administrative agency time, the DoD has sprinted to this new vision—that view that the military plays a central role in the fight against terrorism. It is now safe to say that DoD has blended the homeland function into the military model. In a recent study by the Joint Chiefs of Staff, the merger is blatantly apparent.[15] See Figure 6.17.

In Iraq and Afghanistan, the military has assumed a major role in the pro-vision of safety and security for these populations. It is not just the military tactic at play here but something dramatically larger—that of the safety and security of nation-states. At no place is this more obvious than in the reporting of deaths in Iraq, where the task of minimizing human harm and tragedy weighs heavily on military commanders and boots on the ground. At some stages of the Iraq campaign, the casualty rates were absolutely distressing and public outcry raged over these losses. In recent months, the military adjustments, in both size and strategy, seemed to have halted the unceasing and unmitigated levels of violence.[16] See Figure 6.18.

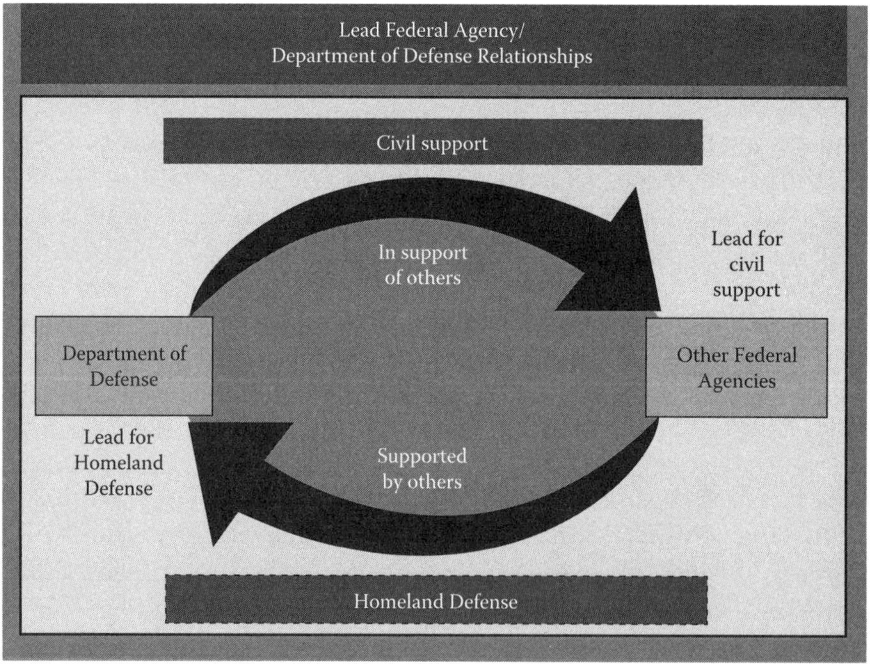

FIGURE 6.16 Lead federal agency and DoD relationships.

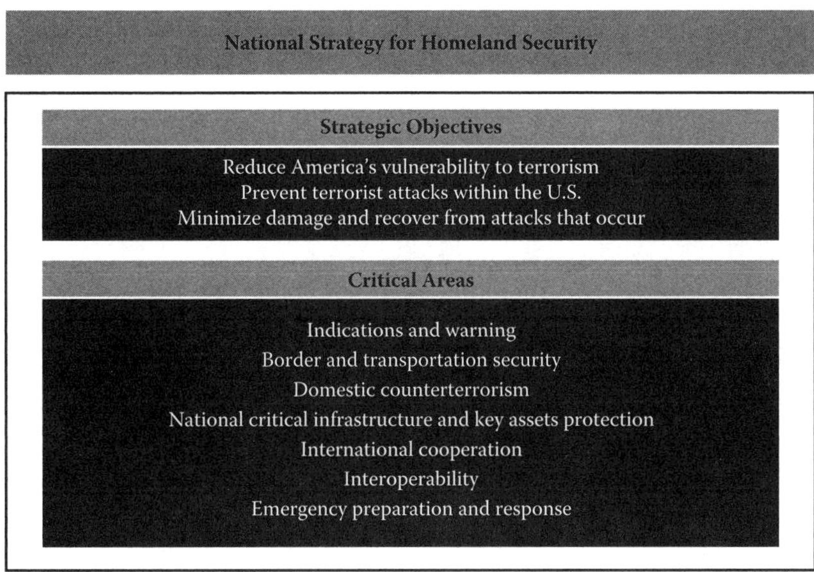

FIGURE 6.17 National strategy for homeland security strategic objectives and critical areas of concern.

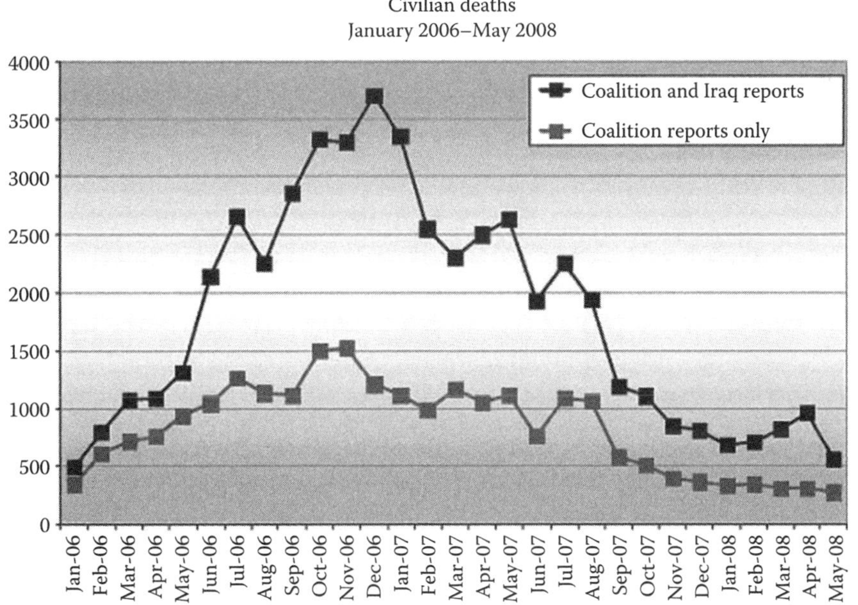

FIGURE 6.18 Rates of civilian deaths, 2006–2008. (MNF-I SPA assessments SIGACTS III database (coalition reports only) and (coalition and Iraq reports) as of June 1, 2008. Does not include civilian deaths due to accidents unrelated to friendly or enemy actions.)

FIGURE 6.19 Army personnel providing security in Afghanistan.

Internet Exercise: To update the figures on civilian deaths, visit: http://www.iraqbodycount.org/analysis/numbers/2011/.

In general, the Defense Department now thinks in terms of terror and a new war on nontraditional combatants. The DoD reported its numerous activities in the fight against terrorism in its Defend America program. Defend America has since been merged into the DoD general operations. However, DoD policy and pronouncement never strays far from the analysis of terror as it covers the Iraq and Afghanistan campaigns (Figure 6.19).

The integration of the DoD into the affairs of terror and global threat can be gleaned from its own organizational changes. The DoD has erected a wide array of offices dedicated to this new war, designated and delineated its responsibility in specific instances of attack, and erected a new bureaucratic structure under the auspices of an assistant secretary of defense for homeland defense—all of which targets terror and threat.[17] See Figure 6.20.

6.3.2 Intelligence Gathering and Sharing

All sectors of the military are now gathering, as well as sharing, intelligence information. Each of the four major branches has an intelligence arm that focuses its attention on threat and attack.

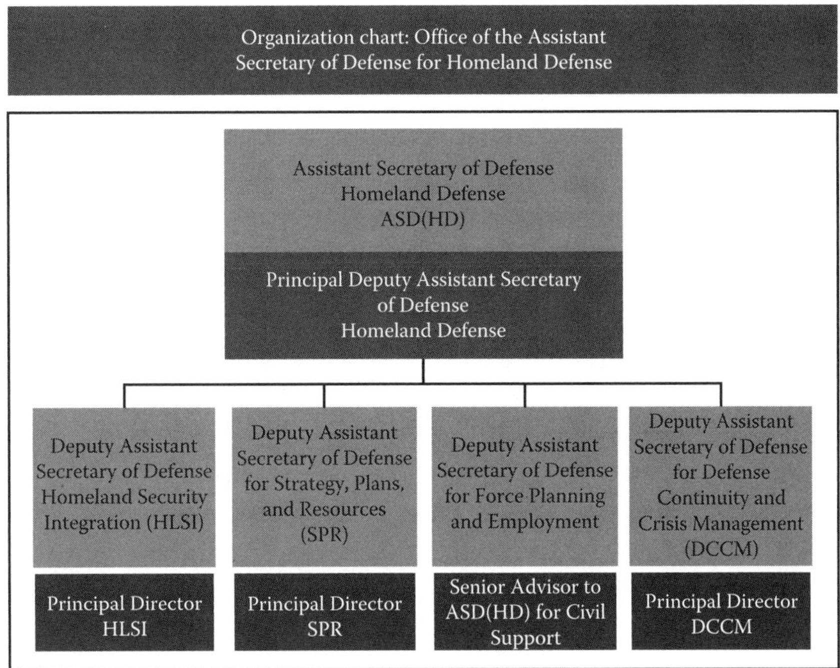

FIGURE 6.20 Organization chart of the Office of the Assistant Secretary of Defense for Homeland Defense.

Internet Resource: For an excellent overview of how the military commands train for and anticipate global terrorism, see http://hsdec.org/coursematerial/DCSINT%20Hdbk%20No1%20x5%2012oct04%20.pdf.

Since 9/11 each sector has redirected part of its approach to the prevention of terrorism. A short sketch of each follows.

6.3.2.1 Office of Naval Intelligence

The Office of Naval Intelligence (ONI) deals with both historic and new challenges. Today, ONI's mission includes providing intelligence on the capabilities of foreign naval powers, providing Global Maritime Intelligence Integration supporting the global fight against terrorism, and enabling maritime domain awareness for homeland defense. ONI's Civil Maritime Intelligence Division supports the disruption of maritime smuggling operations and enforcement of international trade sanctions to deny terrorists the use of the sea as a means of attack. Naval Intelligence—with Marine Corps Intelligence, the Coast Guard, the Drug Enforcement Agency, and U.S. Customs—has also devoted an increased effort to nontraditional maritime intelligence missions.

6.3.2.2 Air Force Intelligence

While there has been some heated debate over the role of the Air Force in matters of homeland defense, it appears that this branch of the service is crucial to success. Terrorism is now part of the Air Force mission. Dealing with this threat rests on many fronts, though none more essential than the work of the North American Aerospace Defense Command (NORAD), a binational U.S. and Canadian organization charged with providing aerospace warning and control for North America (Figures 6.21 and 6.22).

To accomplish this mission, NORAD uses a network of ground-based radars and fighters to detect, intercept, and if necessary, engage any probable threat to the continent. See Figure 6.23.

The Air Force also operates a newly restructured intelligence center—the Air Force Intelligence, Surveillance, and Reconnaissance Agency. The Air Force Intelligence, Surveillance, and Reconnaissance Agency's headquarters is at Lackland Air Force Base, Texas, although the agency's 12,000 people serve at approximately 72 locations around the world. The agency's mission is to organize, train, equip, and present assigned forces and capabilities to conduct intelligence, surveillance, and reconnaissance for combatant commanders and the country.

One tool of intelligence gathering has been the Predator Drone, used by the Navy in great quantity. The Air Force has been recently prompted to increase its production and capability in this area (Figure 6.24).

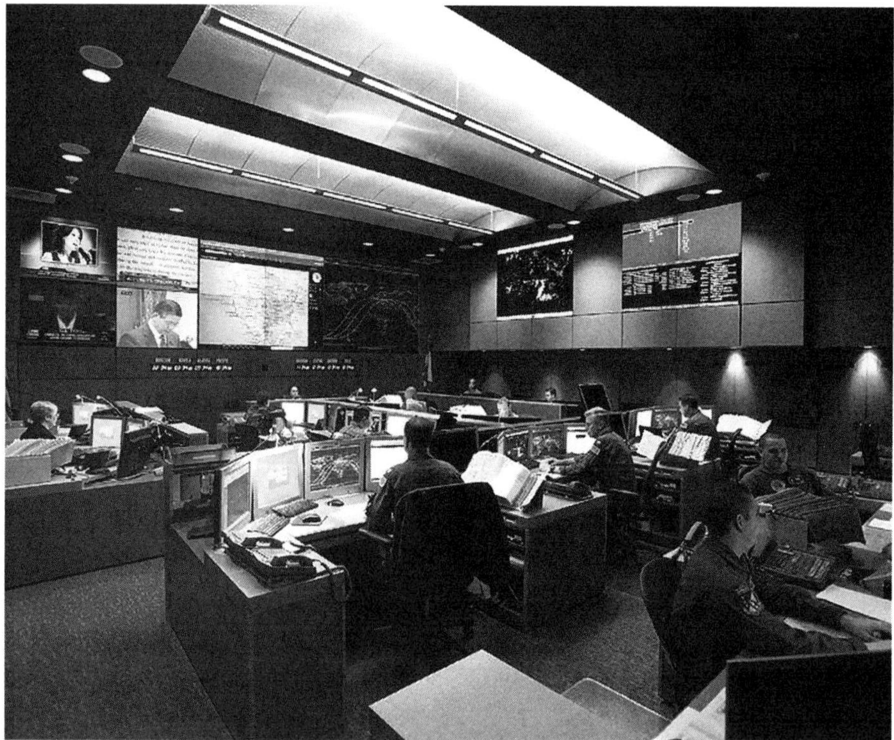

FIGURE 6.21 NORAD command center.

FIGURE 6.22 NORAD mission.

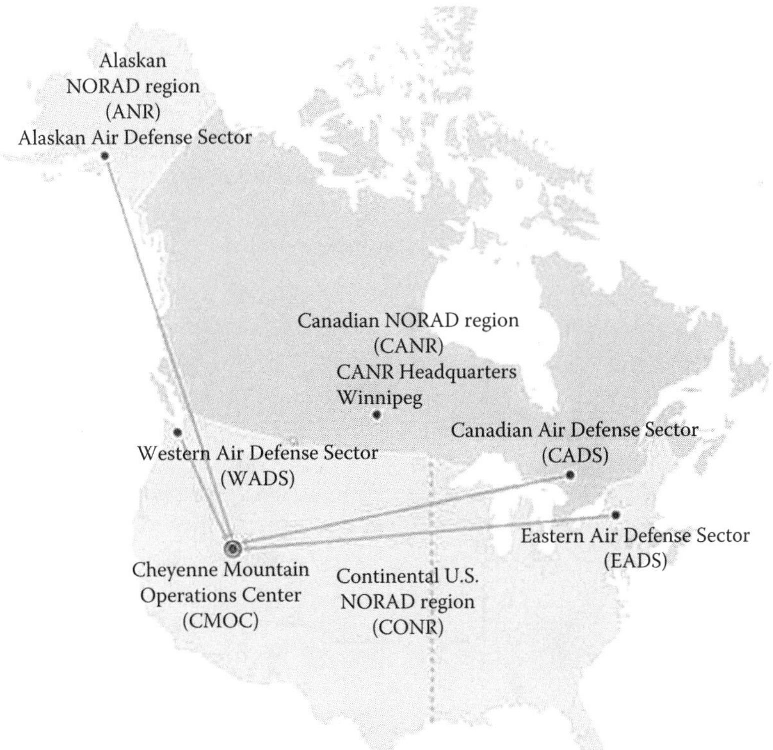

FIGURE 6.23 Map of NORAD geographic regions.

FIGURE 6.24 The Air Force MQ-1 Predator.

6.3.2.3 U.S. Marine Corps

While the U.S. Marine Corps (USMC) is under the operational control of the Navy, it has constructed a plethora of intelligence organizations and operational programs relevant to the fight against terrorism. At its marine base in Quantico resides its intelligence headquarters, with its primary functions being:

- Discharge Marine Corps responsibilities for intelligence estimates, plans, reports, and studies
- Review, analyze, and coordinate joint papers that pertain to Marine Corps intelligence matters
- Recommend positions for approval and use by the Commandant of the Marine Corps (CMC) and the Headquarters of the Marine Corps (HQMC) staff
- Develop plans, policies, operational concepts, doctrine, and techniques in the fields of intelligence, counterintelligence, and cryptologic/signals intelligence in coordination with staff agencies
- Coordinate with the HQMC staff to develop plans and policies

The Marine Corps developed a cultural studies program for its professional and enlisted class as it seeks to understand and converse with both friendly citizens and the combatant enemy. The Commandant of the Marine Corps, in his Vision and Strategy for 2025 states that the Corps "will go to great lengths to understand enemies and the range of cultural, societal and political factors affecting all people Marines interact with."[18]

FIGURE 6.25 USMC Center for Advanced Operational Culture Learning (CAOCL).

The USMC Center for Advanced Operational Culture Learning (CAOCL) promotes a grasp of culture and language as regular, mainstream components of the operating environment—the human terrain—throughout the full spectrum of military operations, and is the Corps one-stop clearinghouse for operational culture and language training. See Figure 6.25.

The Marine Corps Culture and Language Center of Excellence, CAOCL, ensures Marines are equipped with operationally relevant regional, cultural, and language knowledge to allow them to plan and operate successfully in the joint and combined expeditionary environment:

- In any region of the world
- In current and potential operating conditions
- Targeting persistent and emerging threats and opportunities

The Marine Corps employs distance education techniques in its portal, Marine.net. A recent sampling of courses pertinent to homeland security include:

- Terrorism Awareness for Marines
- Expeditionary Warfare School Leadership and Ethics Program
- Global War on Terror Mod 4: Total Recall: Situational Awareness and Attention
- Global War on Terror Mod 5: Tapping into Technology: An Introduction to Automation Airmanship
- HQMC Security Division Curriculum[19]

6.3.2.4 U.S. Army

The U.S. Army established its own security command—the U.S. Army Intelligence and Security Command (INSCOM). The U.S. Army Intelligence and Security Command conducts intelligence, security, and information operations for military commanders and national decision makers.

Headquartered at Fort Belvoir, Virginia, INSCOM is a global command with 10 major subordinate commands and a variety of smaller units with personnel dispersed over 180 locations worldwide. The subordinate commands are:

66th Military Intelligence Brigade conducts theater level multidiscipline intelligence and security operations and, when directed, deploys prepared forces to conduct joint/combined expeditionary and contingency operations in support of U.S. Army Europe and U.S. European Command.

116th Military Intelligence Group, located at Fort Gordon, Georgia, provides personnel, intelligence assets, and technical support to conduct signals intelligence operations within the National Security Agency/Central Security Service Georgia (NSA/CSS Georgia) and worldwide.

300th Military Intelligence Brigade (Linguist) provides trained and ready linguist and military intelligence soldiers to commanders from brigade through Army level.

470th Military Intelligence Brigade provides timely and fused multidiscipline intelligence in support of U.S. Army South, U.S. Southern Command, and other national intelligence agencies.

500th Military Intelligence Brigade, located at Schofield Barracks, Hawaii, provides multidisciplined intelligence support for joint and coalition warfighters in the U.S. Army Pacific area of responsibility.

501st Military Intelligence Brigade is dedicated to supporting combined forces operations upholding the armistice agreement that ended hostile action on the Korean Peninsula in 1953.

513th Military Intelligence Brigade deploys in strength or in tailored elements to conduct multidiscipline intelligence and security operations in support of Army components of U.S. Central Command, U.S. Southern Command, and other theater Army commanders.

704th Military Intelligence Brigade conducts synchronized full-spectrum signals intelligence, computer network, and information assurance operations directly and through the National Security Agency to satisfy national, joint, combined, and Army information superiority requirements.

902nd Military Intelligence Group provides direct and general counterintelligence support to Army activities and major commands.

1st Information Operations Command (land) is the only Army full-spectrum IO organization engaged, from information operations theory development and training to operational application, across the range of military operations.

Army Operations Activity conducts human intelligence operations and provides expertise in support of ground component priority intelligence requirements using a full spectrum of human intelligence collection methods.

Central Clearance Facility serves as the U.S. Army's executive agency for personnel security determinations in support of Army worldwide missions.

Army Joint Surveillance Target Attack Radar System Company (JSTARS) provides Army aircrew members aboard JSTARS aircraft to support surveillance and targeting operations of Army land components.

National Ground Intelligence Center is the Defense Department's primary producer of ground forces intelligence.

Internet Resource: Visit the INSCOM web location for a full view of the Army Intelligence Service.

6.3.3 Specialized Military/Defense Units Dedicated to Homeland Security

There are simply too many military entities and groups to enumerate that relate to the world of homeland security. Each branch of the service dedicates some portion of its resources to the fight against terrorism, and each lends its expertise to particular tasks and challenges. This section will cover representative examples of these military contributions.

6.3.3.1 National Maritime Intelligence Center

Primarily a center for Naval intelligence, its resources and information are available to all branches of the military and the Coast Guard. The National Maritime Intelligence Center (NMIC) is home of the Office of Naval Intelligence and is the central location for maritime intelligence (Figure 6.26).

FIGURE 6.26 National Maritime Intelligence Center.

NMIC displays a narrow intelligence interest though it has a global vision and approach. Threats are assessed and evaluated in the maritime environment rather than the whole framework in which threats occurs. Hence NMIC targets threats in these basic categories:

- *Asymmetric*: Terrorism, weapons of mass destruction (WMD) proliferation, cyber-attack, global supply chain disruption, and so on.
- *Conventional*: Antiship ballistic missiles, cruise missiles, torpedoes, mines, and so on.
- *Criminal/Illicit Activities*: Maritime piracy, narcotics and contraband smuggling, human trafficking, illegal exploitation of marine resources, and so on.
- *Environmental Destruction*: Toxic waste, illegal dumping, overfishing, and so on.[20]

Located at the Suitland Federal Center in Suitland, Maryland, NMIC supports joint operational commanders with a worldwide organization and an integrated workforce of active duty, reserve, and civilian personnel. NMIC supports the Navy's acquisition activities by providing scientific and technical analysis of naval weapons systems.

6.3.3.2 National Reconnaissance Office

Coordinating reconnaissance activities is the DoD's National Reconnaissance Office (NRO). The NRO designs, builds, and operates the country's reconnaissance satellites. NRO products, provided to an expanding list of customers like the Central Intelligence Agency (CIA) and the DoD, can warn of potential trouble spots around the world, help plan military operations, and monitor the environment. A DoD agency, the NRO is staffed by DoD and CIA personnel. It is funded through the National Reconnaissance Program, part of the National Foreign Intelligence Program. See Figure 6.27.

6.3.3.3 Weapons of Mass Destruction Civil Support Teams

The U.S. Army and the National Guard play a central role in the WMD protocol. Civil Support Teams (CSTs) will aid civilian authorities with military expertise regarding chemical, biological, radiological, and nuclear materials (Figure 6.28).

The CST was designed to augment local and regional terrorism response capabilities in events known or suspected to involve use of chemical, biological, or radiological agents. The team can be en route within 3 hours to support civil authorities in the event or suspicion of a WMD attack. Specifically, the CST deploys to an area of operations to:

- Support civil authorities to identify chemical, biological, radiological, and nuclear agents/substances
- Assess current and projected consequences

FIGURE 6.27 National Reconnaissance Program, part of the National Foreign Intelligence Program.

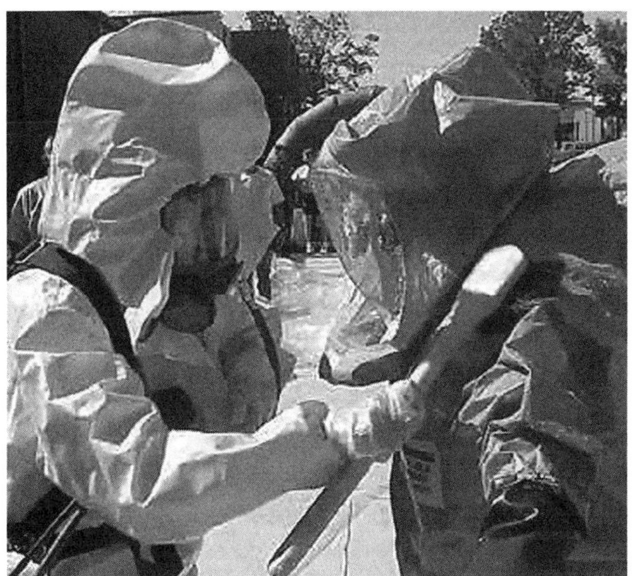

FIGURE 6.28 Civil support team.

- Advise on response measures
- Assist with mitigation and additional support

The role of the U.S. military in the matter of WMD has been essential. The sharing and collaboration between civil authorities seems almost natural and without equivocation. Given the seriousness of the subject matter, both the Army and public authorities share a similar vision regarding WMD. The U.S. Army lays out its operational approach, which is clearly collaborative.[21] See Figure 6.29.

1. U.S. Armed Forces, in conceit with other elements of U.S. national power, deter WMD use.
2. U.S. Armed Forces are prepared to defeat an adversary threatening to use WMD and prepare to deter follow-on use.
3. Existing worldwide WMD is secure and the U.S. Armed Forces contribute as appropriate to secure, reduce, reverse or eliminate it.
4. Current or potential adversaries are dissuaded from producing WMD.
5. Current or potential adversaries' WMD is detected and characterized and elimination sought.
6. Proliferation of WMD and related materials to current and/or potential adversaries is dissuaded, prevented, defeated, or reversed.
7. If WMD is used against the United States or its interests, U.S. Armed Forces are capable of minimizing the effects in order to continue operations in a WMD environment and assist United States civil authorities, allies, and partners.
8. U.S. Armed Forces assist in attributing the source of attack, respond decisively, and/or deter future attacks.
9. Allies and U.S. civilian agencies are capable partners in combating WMD.

FIGURE 6.29 U.S. Armed Forces WMD strategy.

6.3.3.4 Center for Combating Weapons of Mass Destruction and the Defense Threat Reduction Agency

Initially located in the U.S. Strategic Command, the center has been aligned with the Defense Threat Reduction Agency (DTRA). The center provides recommendations to dissuade, deter, and prevent the acquisition, development, or use of WMD and associated technology. Through collaboration with the United States and allied organizations, the center provides situational awareness of worldwide WMD and related activities, as well as provides day-to-day and operational crisis support via the operations center. Among its responsibilities are:

- Provide manning, facilities, technical support, funding, and expertise to the U.S. Strategic Command
- Provide assessments support, advocacy, planning, training teams, and support teams to U.S. Strategic Command and other combatant command customers to combat WMD
- Provide command, control communications, information, and technical support and design exercises and daily operations
- Provide near-real-time combating WMD support by providing subject matters experts, modeling and simulation support, and 24-hour support service

The Defense Threat Reduction Agency (DTRA) is a combat support agency of the U.S. DoD (Figure 6.30).

Founded in 1998, the agency headquarters is located in Fort Belvoir, Virginia. DTRA employs 2,000 men and women, both military and civilian, at more than 14 locations around the world.

FIGURE 6.30 DTRA symbol at headquarters entrance.

Internet Exercise: Discover where DTRA is located globally. Do you see logic in these locations? Visit: http://www.dtra.mil/Info/Locations.aspx.

The DTRA safeguards America and its allies from weapons of mass destruction (chemical, biological, radiological, nuclear, and high explosives) by providing capabilities to reduce, eliminate, and counter the threat, and mitigate its effects. It is sometimes designated as the Strategic Command of WMD.

The DTRA expends a considerable portion of its time and energy on conducting basic scientific research regarding WMD. It uses "science to secure WMD." DTRA's research seeks:

- To improve scientific knowledge that supports verification of treaties, safeguards, and nonproliferation
- To safely handle, transport, secure, or eliminates WMD components and weapons; and novel means that lead to physical or other methods to monitor compliance and reduce illegal proliferation pathways
- To advance capabilities for safe and verifiable control of materials, systems, and facilities that underpin greater confidence for entering, exiting, or sustaining multi-national WMD-related agreements[22]

Internet Resource: Read about the DRTA's campaign regarding WMD at http://www.dtra.mil/campaigns/campaign1.cfm.

6.4 Conclusion

The chapter scrutinizes how homeland functions need governmental collaboration. DHS alone cannot carry out the multitude of homeland functions. The chapter urges practitioners to see wisdom in the mutual support of local, state, and federal agencies in the fight against terrorism. On top of this, from its earliest days of inception, DHS fostered an environment of decentralization over centralization—concluding that local officials understood the demands and dynamics of their constituencies better than removed bureaucrats. The political and structural intermix and interdependency of homeland security is the chief stress of this chapter. Not exclusively a federal obligation, the content lays out the mandatory and absolute need for state and local cooperation. The various state departments are highlighted, with some of the better examples of state homeland offices fully covered. How states and localities structure the homeland mission and carry out the aligned tasks of homeland is a crucial topic. Special emphasis on the use of task forces and coordinating committees is provided in the chapter, as well as the novel innovation known as the fusion center. In addition, the reader will encounter the growing local role in homeland security. In a continuous move to decentralization, the locality, whether county or city, is increasingly called upon to deliver services to the homeland quarter. Fusion centers are covered too, where intelligence is disseminated at regional levels throughout the United States. Presently there are 58 fusions centers in the United States. Other programs that foster the collaboration of governmental entities include Citizen Corps, CERT, Fire Corps, and Volunteers in Public Service.

The chapter distinguishes the differing yet complementary roles of our national security mission, the military intelligence complex, and DHS. How the branches of our military complex serve the country is narrowly covered in light of the terrorist threat. Since military commands throughout the world deal with a host of homeland issues, the line between the two forces tends to merge rather than remain separate. The military itself divides up its responsibility to now include combatant zones with homeland defense considerations. Homeland personnel rely upon Air Force equipment and mission activity to secure the borders. FEMA regularly depends upon military capacity to serve those victimized by natural disaster. The entire DoD has integrated homeland functions into its mission and purpose. Some even argue that the present campaigns in Iraq and Afghanistan are merely extensions of the homeland defense strategy. Surely the missions are complementary though not identical. Both DHS and the military are concerned with intelligence and information gathering. The chapter highlights the more prominent programs of the major military branches dedicated to homeland questions. Coverage also includes a quick look at emergent departments and entities dedicated to the mix of the military and the homeland, such as the National Maritime Intelligence Center, the NRO, and the Center for Combating Weapons of Mass Destruction.

Keywords

Adjutant general
Center for Advanced Operational Culture Learning
Citizen Corps Council
Civil Support Teams
Combatant zone
Cultural Studies Program
Decentralization
Defend America
Defense Threat Reduction Agency
Fusion center
Ground-based radar
Infrastructure Protection Program
Intelligence and Security Command
Intelligence officer
Intelligence Surveillance and Reconnaissance Agency
Joint Chiefs of Staff
Law Enforcement Terrorism Prevention Program
Metropolitan area
Military incursion
Military tactic
National Foreign Intelligence Program
National Guard
National Infrastructure Protection Plan
National Maritime Intelligence Center
National Preparedness Guidelines
National Reconnaissance Office
North American Aerospace Defense Command
Office of Intelligence and Analysis
Office of Naval Intelligence
Predator drone
Public Safety Interoperable Communications Grant Program
Public works
Regional planning council
Sovereign territory
State homeland security director
State, Local, Tribal, and Territorial Government Coordinating Council
Task force
U.S. Strategic Command
Unified command
Urban Area Security Initiative Grant Program
Working group

Discussion Questions

1. What is the purpose and aim of the fusion center?
2. How do DHS funding and grants manifest the department's preference for local input and implementation?
3. Describe three DHS program initiatives that signify the importance of local control and involvement.

4. When does the line between military command and services become muddled with the services of DHS?
5. Discuss the diverse ways in which the military commands make contributions to the fight against terrorism.
6. Explain how the typical state might garner funding for homeland security and deliver its services.
7. Relay two major challenges to the idea of state, local, and federal cooperation in the world of homeland security.
8. Is it a fair conclusion to hold that DHS prefers decentralization over centralization of services?
9. What is the best argument for local initiative in the delivery of homeland services?
10. Give three examples of DHS programs or policies that encourage intergovernmental cooperation.

Practical Exercises

1. Contact your regional or state Office of Homeland Security. List five initiatives of this office.
2. Discover whether Citizen Corps works in your community. If so, explain its current endeavors.
3. Interview a state DHS official. Try to discern how positive this office's relation to and with DHS is.
4. Discover at least two differing funding sources for local implementation of homeland security activities.

Notes

1. Department of Homeland Security, Homeland Security Advisory Council, *Report from the Task Force on State and Local Homeland Security Funding 15*, June 2004.
2. R. E. Brooks, *Improving Criminal Intelligence Sharing: How the Criminal Intelligence Coordinating Council Support Law Enforcement and Homeland Security* 34, February 2011.
3. Office of the President, *Homeland Security Presidential Directive 5*, February 2003, 6.
4. CRS Report to Congress, *FY 2009 Appropriations for State and Local Homeland Security*, February 7, 2008, http://fpc.state.gov/documents/organization/101807.pdf (accessed February 29, 2009). See also CRS Report for Congress, *Fiscal Year 2011 Department of Homeland Security Assistance to States and Localities*, April 26, 2010, http://www.fas.org/sgp/crs/homesec/R41105.pdf (accessed April 12, 2012).

5. State of Tennessee, *Office of Homeland Security*, http://state.tn.us/homelandsecurity/index.htm (accessed February 27, 2009).
6. D. E. Marks and I. Y. Sun, The impact of 9/11 on organizational development among state and local law enforcement agencies, *Journal of Contemporary Criminal Justice*, 23, May 2007: 159–173.
7. B. R. Johnson, Fusion centers: Strengthening the nation's homeland security enterprise, *Police Chief*, February 2011: 62.
8. Johnson, Fusion Centers.
9. D. Keyer, Nationwide SAR initiative delivers value to fusion centers, *Police Chief*, February 2011: 40.
10. See Fusion Center Locations and Contact Information at: http://www.dhs.gov/files/programs/gc_1301685827335/shtm.
11. Commonwealth of Massachusetts, *State Homeland Security Strategy*, September 2007, 10.
12. S. J. Tomisek, Homeland security: New role for defense, *Strategic Forum (Institute for National Strategic Studies)*, 189, February 2002.
13. Department of Defense: Joint Chiefs of Staff, *Joint Publication 3-26: Homeland Security*, August 2005, viii, http://www.fas.org/irp/doddir/dod/jp3_26.pdf.
14. Joint Chiefs, *Homeland Security*, II-17.
15. Joint Chiefs, *Homeland Security*, I-2.
16. Department of Defense, *Measuring Stability and Security in Iraq: Report to Congress in Accordance with the Department of Defense Appropriations Act 2008*, June 28, 21.
17. Joint Chiefs, *Homeland Security*, II-6.
18. Cpl. G. Gonzalez, *CAOCL Helps Marines Navigate through 'Cultural Terrain,'* go to: http://www.marines.mil/unit/basecamppendleton/Pages/home.aspx and search "caocl helps marines" (last accessed April 12, 2012).
19. For more information on CAOCL, visit: www.tecom.usmc.mil/caocl.
20. National Maritime Intelligence Center, *About NMIC*, http://www.nmic.gov/aboutnmic.htm (accessed October 3, 2011).
21. Chairman of the Joint Chiefs of Staff, *National Military Strategy to Combat Weapons of Mass Destruction*, February 4, 2006.
22. DTRA, *Basic Research for Countering Weapons of Mass Destruction*, 2010.

Chapter 7

FEMA, Response, and Recovery

Objectives

1. To describe the early twentieth-century history of the Federal Emergency Management Agency (FEMA).
2. To outline the changes that FEMA underwent, both structural and policy oriented, between 1980 and 2000.
3. To define the structural and policy changes that FEMA initiated as a result of the events of 9/11.
4. To recognize the concept of preparedness and describe FEMA's philosophy, programs, and policies that relate to it.
5. To distinguish the various types of emergencies that exist, that is, natural disasters vs. terrorist incidents, routine events vs. catastrophic events, and their relative response differences.
6. To comprehend the principle of mitigation in preparedness and outline the various FEMA programs that address mitigation.
7. To understand the importance of post-assessment reports in preparedness, mitigation, response, and recovery planning.
8. To distinguish the concepts of response and recovery and list the various initiatives undertaken by FEMA to make response more timely and effective.

7.1 Historical Foundation for FEMA

The pre-9/11 world was quite comfortable with the language of the protocol for disaster and its mitigation. From the 1930s onward, there were structural mechanisms to deal with disaster in the American landscape. The Reconstruction Finance Corporation provided loans for repair and reconstruction of certain public facilities following disasters. The Bureau of Public Roads had the authority to fund the repairs of highways and bridges damaged by flood, earthquake, and other disaster. In addition, the U.S. Army Corps of Engineers played an increasingly active role in the design of floodplains, levees, dams, and other edifices. Aside from the predictability of terror, as well as its use for pressing social and political change, the citizenry had come to expect that the federal government would respond in times of emergency and disaster. It is a reasonable expectation that was sorely lacking in the Katrina debacle.

By the 1960s it was evident that historic agencies were incapable of handling the larger natural disasters that plagued the country. It was clear that a major federal response and recovery agency was essential to serve those victimized by natural disaster. The Federal Disaster Assistance Administration, housed in Housing and Urban Development, was established. The National Flood Insurance program was erected in 1968, and executive orders and other presidential authority now became a normative part of the disaster environment.

7.1.1 Federal Emergency Management Agency: Pre-9/11

In 1979, President Jimmy Carter, by executive order, merged a multitude of disaster agencies into FEMA. FEMA was to author an integrated emergency management system that covered "small isolated events to the ultimate emergency—war." FEMA struggled to corral in competing agency and bureaucratic interests and readily discovered the complexities of managing large- and small-scale disasters. Early in its operation FEMA had to contend with:

- Love Canal chemical disaster in Niagara Falls, New York
- Cuban boat refugee crisis
- Three Mile Island, Pennsylvania, nuclear plant crisis
- Hurricane Andrew
- Loma Prieta, California, earthquake

That FEMA adjusted mission based on natural disaster and other environmental pressures is undeniable. FEMA also was continually reorganized in hopes that centralized service would be a better brand of government response. For example, Reorganization Plan #3, adopted in 1978, integrated the National Fire Prevention Control Office, the Federal Broadcast System, the Defense Civil Preparedness Agency, the Federal Disaster Assistance Administration, and the Federal Preparedness Agency. Other inclusions in the latter twentieth century were agencies that monitored earthquakes, dam safety, nuclear warning systems, and severe weather policy. In general, FEMA sought to implement an Integrated Emergency Management System (IEMS). In the early 1990s, FEMA's capacity to respond to hurricane and other natural disaster was severely tested, and "FEMA seemed incapable of carrying out the essential government function of emergency management."[1]

In its early life, FEMA's philosophy of operation was narrower—in that it stressed the disaster side of emergency. That traditional definition, which includes flood, wind, earthquake, fire, and other natural disaster, tends to be distinctly different than the notion of terror. FEMA would eventually have to encompass terror—that intentionally inflicted disaster driven by an assortment of motivations. The Oklahoma City Bombing of 1995 catapulted FEMA into the world of terrorist activity. Yet the culture of FEMA, bound to the natural disaster mentality, struggled to fit into the world of terror. At first, FEMA expended considerable energy urging communities to become disaster resistant and to erect mitigation policies that would prevent disaster of all sorts. Implementing *Project Impact: Building Disaster Resistant Communities* was the chief programmatic aim of FEMA in the late 1990s. In Project Impact, communities were to examine their communities in light of risk and adopt corresponding measures to mitigate the harm. FEMA's central contribution during this period was to refocus communities, leaders, and the citizenry into the world of risk—natural or otherwise.

7.1.2 Federal Emergency Management Agency: Post-9/11

After the horrid events of 9/11, the mission of FEMA, its operational philosophy, and its ability to carry out its command were put to the test.[2] After 9/11, FEMA had to reorganize in two ways: first, it had to continue its historic mission to deal with and respond to disaster, and second, it had to integrate a threat mentality as part of its obligation in serving the Department of Homeland Security. While natural disasters continue to be a crucial responsibility for FEMA, the world of terrorism increasingly dominates its outlook and mission. Hence, FEMA's mission is more encompassing than its historic expectation.

> FEMA's mission is to support our citizens and first responders to ensure that as a nation we work together to build, sustain, and improve our capability to prepare for, protect against, respond to, recover from, and mitigate all hazards. (FEMA, About FEMA, www.fema.gov/about/index.shtm)

FEMA's merger has policy implications that it must adapt to. Figure 7.1 charts the current structure of FEMA.

FEMA is led by an administrator and a whole host of deputy directors and administrators. FEMA also depends upon the input and advice of its National Advisory Council, whose membership includes experts from both

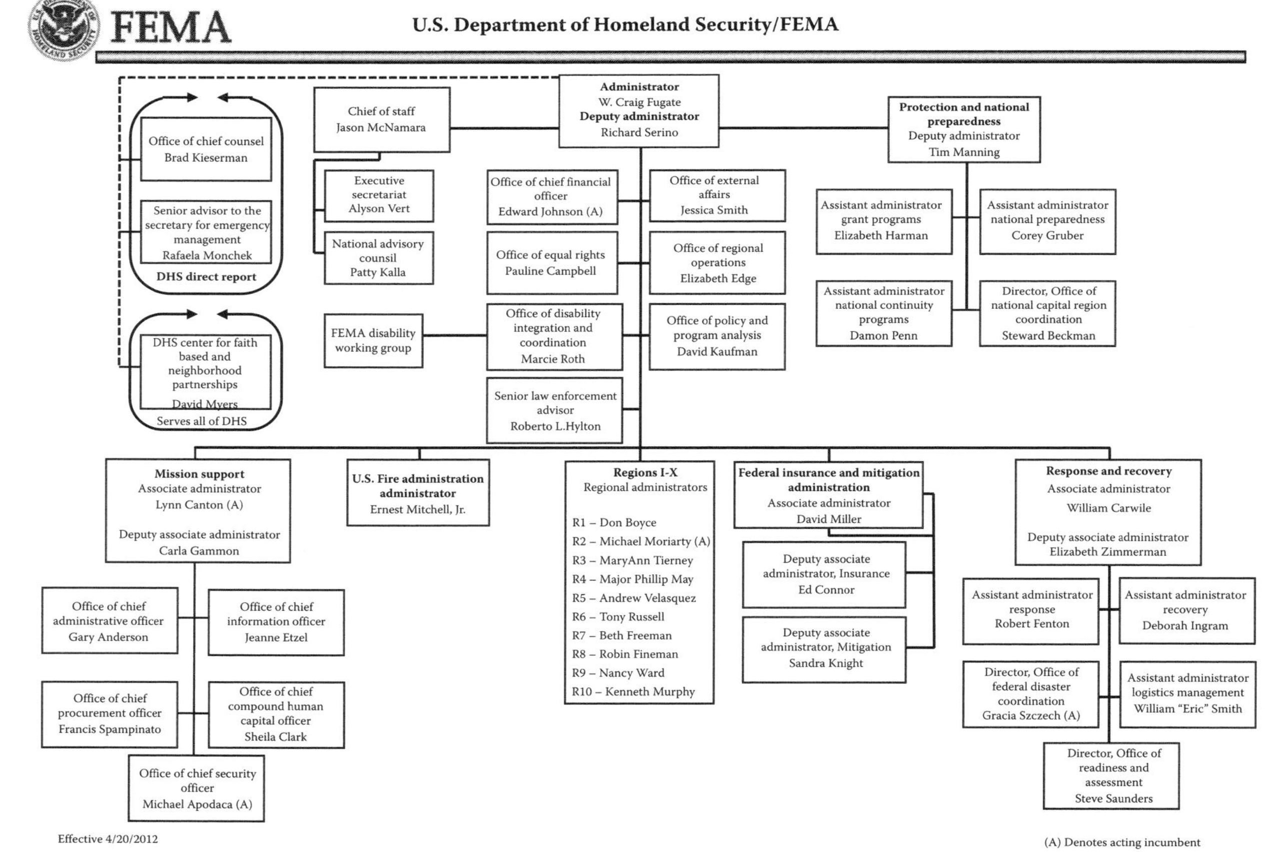

FIGURE 7.1 FEMA organization chart.

the public and the private sector. The National Advisory Council's input has been quite laudatory and more than pro forma comment. Since 2007, the Advisory Council has directly dealt with many challenges but with many success stories. The major accomplishments include:

- Supplied key input on the development, implementation, and revision of the National Response Framework, the National Incident Management System (NIMS), and the National Disaster Housing Strategy
- Provided valuable feedback on the revised National Exercise Program, including recommendations on how to successfully implement the revised program
- Maintained open lines of communication to help engage the private sector in emergency management
- Recommended the creation of a Regional Disability Coordinator position within each of the 10 FEMA regions
- Reviewed and provided input on regulatory and policy Robert T. Stafford Disaster Relief and Emergency Assistance Act issues that might help ease administrative burdens on jurisdictions

Internet Exercise: Check out the biographies of the current NAC at http://www.fema.gov/pdf/about/nac/nac_member_bio_book.pdf.

Geographically, FEMA is further broken down into 10 distinct regions to allow for greater local input and participation. See Figure 7.2.

Finally, FEMA targets its subject matter by decentralizing into various *Directorates*. These divisions provide the core, coordinated federal operational, and logistical capability needed to save and sustain lives, minimize suffering, and protect property in a timely and effective manner in communities that become overwhelmed by natural disasters, acts of terrorism, or other emergencies. From assistance to mitigations, from logistics to the continuity programs, FEMA depends upon its subject matter specialists to deliver these services. The current directorates are:

- Disaster Assistance
- Disaster Operations
- Logistics
- Mitigation
- National Continuity Programs
- National Preparedness
- Response
- Recovery

Internet Exercise: Read FEMA's strategic plan for the years 2008–2013 at http://www.fema.gov/about/strategicplan2011–2014.

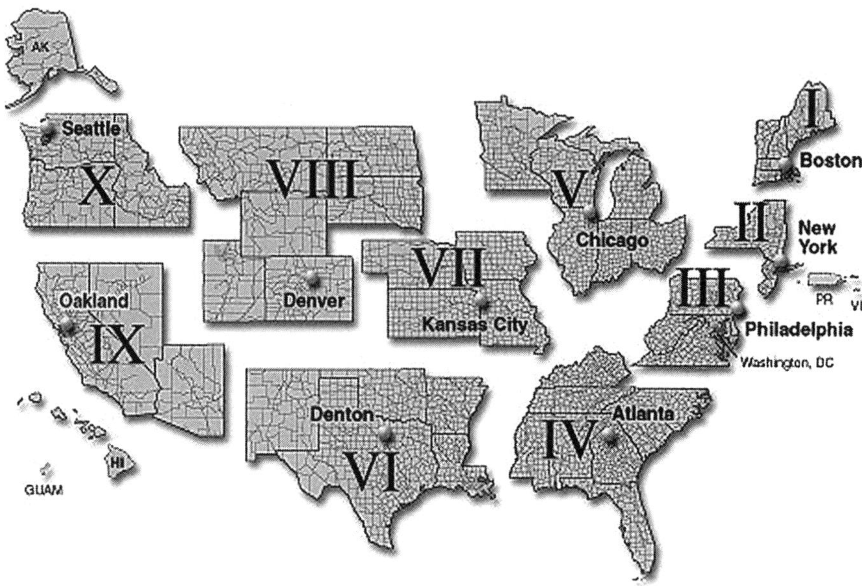

FIGURE 7.2 FEMA regions.

There has been some debate recently as to what FEMA's role is during and in the wake of man-made and natural disasters, particularly in the area of recovery spending. Disasters present unique challenges according to the Center for Disaster Philanthropy:

> The challenge … is that regardless of the size of the disaster, some affected individuals do not meet eligibility requirements for government disaster aid—and still others will have unmet needs even after receiving federal and/or state assistance. As FEMA Administrator Craig Fugate has said, "There's no way government can solve the challenges of a disaster with a government-centric approach. It takes the whole team. And the private sector provides the bulk of the services every day in the community."[3]

So the questions become, where should the money for response and recovery come from? What criteria do disaster victims need to meet to be eligible for funds? Should taxpayers bear the cost of such funding? Is this a federal obligation or should it be a state and local issue? What role should the private sector play? Should those who pay for flood or hazard insurance be somehow rewarded for their advance planning while others penalized?

Professor William Shughart II of the University of Mississipi sees those who have taken proper precautions—those who purchased insurance prior to the disaster event and understood the risks—as the party worthy of our protection and admiration. His argument is that this is good public policy that leads to a better, independent citizenry rather than individuals who are waiting for, and dependent solely on, government assistance. According to Schugart:

> People who voluntarily put themselves in harm's way, taking on the additional risks of living and working in disaster-prone areas, adequately insuring their lives and property against wind and flood—and paying actuarially fair premiums that reflect the greater risk—have every right to expect prompt reimbursement for the damages they sustained and every right to rebuild if they wish.[4]

As major disasters increase in scope, frequency, and damage costs—as has been the trend the last few decades—this debate as to who bears the cost of rebuilding and when to rebuild or not will certainly continue.

7.2 FEMA and Preparedness

Any effective response, recovery, or other answer to a threat or catastrophe heavily depends upon preparedness. By preparedness, one means that the agency, community, and constituency affected, and public and private partners, stand ready to deal with the threat in an effective manner.

Questions regarding the country's preparedness rose to the front and center after Katrina. Various amendments to the *Homeland Security Act of 2002* established the National Preparedness Directorate (NPD). The directorate tackles many tasks in the area of preparedness, including:

- Strategy, policy, and planning guidance to build prevention, protection, response, and recovery capabilities
- Training courses, exercises, and technical assistance to ensure capabilities are standardized
- Coordination of FEMA regions as well as emergency management personnel at the federal, state, and local levels
- Coordination with other FEMA offices and directorates to produce a unified approach to emergency management

Running things at a national level is never an easy undertaking and this challenge always adds to the difficulties. For example, there is not even consensus of "colors" when it comes to the warning system. Is it orange or red that drives the level of concern most accurately? Does the national Emergency Alert System really work?[5]

Preparedness encompasses a whole range of operational and policy concerns for the homeland professional. Preparedness models envelop the capacity to plan, organize, train, equip, exercise, evaluate, and improve. FEMA charts the cycle of preparedness in Figure 7.3.[6]

The catalogue of FEMA resources regarding preparedness is quite extensive. Already discussed in the text has been the citizen portal titled "Ready.gov" as well as the many functions and activities of the "Citizen Corps." In addition to these resources, FEMA publishes a Digital Library—a searchable web-based collection of all publicly accessible FEMA information resources, including: CDs, DVDs, VHS tapes, audio tapes, disability resources, posters

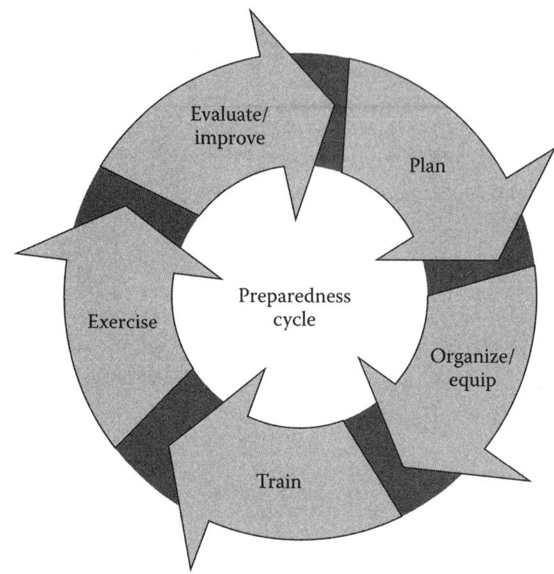

FIGURE 7.3 Cycle of preparedness.

and display items, brochures, publications, guidance and policy papers, then program regulations and guidelines, forms, slide presentations, and other documents. The Library is catalogued and organized in accordance with the hazard forms in Figure 7.4.

FEMA orchestrates a narrower portal dedicated to natural disasters aptly titled DisasterAssistance.gov. The portal's primary aim is to assist those already harmed by natural disasters. See Figure 7.5.

Being prepared for radiological fallout from nuclear contamination is another FEMA responsibility. FEMA's Radiological Emergency Preparedness Program prepares for harms that may emerge in nuclear accidents and educates the public about these unique harms.[7] Just as critically, FEMA plays a central preparedness role in the care, protection, and mitigation of chemical stockpiles across the continental United States. FEMA works in partnership with the United States Army to not only protect the stockpile but to assure the integrity of the same for the public at large. While stockpiles are slowly but assuredly being eliminated in the United States, there are nine locales for the storage of the same in the United States. See Figure 7.6 for current locations.

Internet Exercise: Even individuals and families must be prepared for all eventualities. See the preparedness guide prepared by the State of Alabama at http://ema.alabama.gov/FileLibrary/files/HomePage/PreparednessChecklist.pdf.

Preparing the citizenry for hazard, disaster, and threat is a core mission of FEMA. Being ready—understanding the risk and taking preventive and mitigatory steps to minimize the damage—are the essential FEMA principles.[8] How one goes about these functions largely depends on the type of threat or

Hazard Type Associations

Use this guide if you are unable to find what you are looking for in the list of hazard type selections provided.

If you are looking for:	Consider using:
Aftershock	Earthquake
Ash Fall	Volcano
Avalanche	Mudslide/Landslide, Winter Storm
Blizzard	Severe Storm, Winter Storm
Brush Fire	Wildfire
Cold	Extreme Temperatures, Winter Storm
Cyclone	Hurricane/Tropical Storm, Typhoon
Dust Storm	Drought, Extreme Temperatures, Severe Storm
Erosion	Coastal Storm, Hurricane/Tropical Storm, Typhoon
Explosion	Chemical/Biological, Fire, Nuclear, Technological, Terrorism
Flood, Flash Flood	Dam/Levee Break, Flooding
Forest Fire	Wildfire
Freeze	Extreme Temperatures, Winter Storm
Freezing Rain	Severe Storm, Winter Storm
Funnel Cloud	Tornado
Ground Saturation	Flooding
Hail	Severe Storm, Winter Storm
Heat	Extreme Temperatures
High Surf	Coastal Storm, Hurricane/Tropical Storm, Tsunami, Typhoon
Ice	Extreme Temperatures, Winter Storm
Ice Jam	Flooding
Lava/Debris Flow	Volcano
Mold	Flooding
Power Outage	Technological, Terrorism
Radiological	Chemical/Biological, Nuclear, Terrorism
Rain Storm	Flooding, Hurricane/Tropical Storm, Severe Storm, Typhoon, Winter
Rock Slide	Mudslide/Landslide
Seismic Wave	Earthquake
Snow	Winter Storm
Snow Melt	Flooding
Storm Surge	Hurricane/Tropical Storm, Typhoon
Thunderstorm	Severe Storm
Tropical Depression	Hurricane/Tropical Storm, Severe Storm
Tidal Wave	Tsunami
Virus	Chemical/Biological, Terrorism
Wind	Coastal Storm, Hurricane/Tropical Storm, Severe Storm, Typhoon, Winter Storm
Waterspout	Tornado

FIGURE 7.4 FEMA hazard forms cross-references.

FIGURE 7.5 After the storm cleanup.

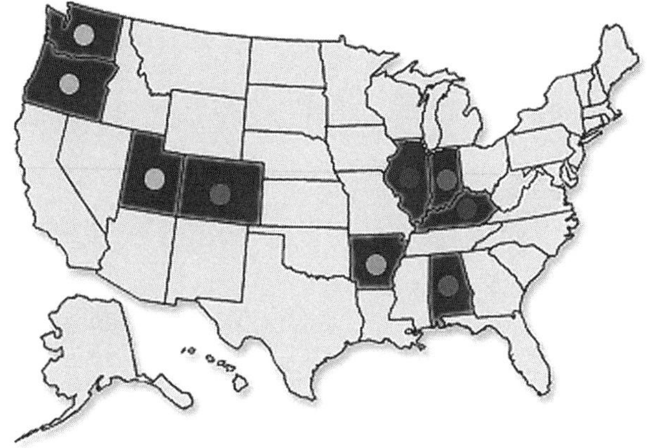

FIGURE 7.6 National chemical stockpile.

hazard under review.[9] Floods and hurricanes are very different animals than nuclear leaks or sarin gas inhalation. The types of emergencies that occur on a daily basis, such as car accidents, road spills, or house fires, are routine events. Catastrophic events, such as tornadoes, terrorist attacks, superstorms like Hurricane Sandy or floods, tend to cover a larger area, impact a greater number of citizens, cost more to recover from, and occur less frequently.[10] See the table in Figure 7.7[11] for event duration estimates.

The homeland specialist must first identify the risk and then take the necessary steps compatible with that risk. Some of the usual events are:

Dam failure	Fire or wildfire	Wildfire
Hurricane	Nuclear explosion	Hazardous material
Tornado	Volcano	Thunderstorm
Earthquake	Flood	Winter storm
Landslide	Terrorism	Heat
Tsunami		

	Routine		Catastrophic	
Classification	**Local**	**Regional**	**State**	**National**
Examples	• Minor traffic incidents • Minor load spills • Vehicle fires • Minor train/bus accidents • Accidents with injuries but no fatalities	• Train derailment • Major bus/rail transit accidents • Major truck accidents • Multi-vehicle crashes • HazMat spills • Accidents with injuries and fatalities	• Train crashes • Airplane crashes • HazMat incidents • Multi-vehicle accidents • Tunnel fires • Multiple injuries and fatalities • Port/airport incidents • Large building fire or explosion • Industrial incidents • Major tunnel/bridge closure	• Terrorist attack/ WMD • Floods, blizzards, tornadoes • Transportation infrastructure collapse • Extended power/ water outages • Riots • Mass casualties
Expected event duration	**0–2 Hours**	**2–24 Hours**	**Day**	**Weeks**

FIGURE 7.7 Duration estimates for catastrophic and routine emergency events.

FEMA uses high-level technology to estimate and predict damage and potential harm. It has developed comprehensive software programs that are crucial to predicting the outcomes of particular events (Figure 7.8).

HAZUS is a product that uses current scientific and engineering knowledge, coupled with the latest geographic information systems (GIS) technology, to produce estimates of hazard-related damage before, or after, a disaster occurs. Depending on the threat or harm, HAZUS will evaluate and estimate losses after inputting criteria. The HAZUS software program assesses risk in a five-step process, as outlined in Figure 7.9.[12]

FIGURE 7.8 The HAZUS-MH data extractor is a tool for extracting data from HAZUS-MH data sources.

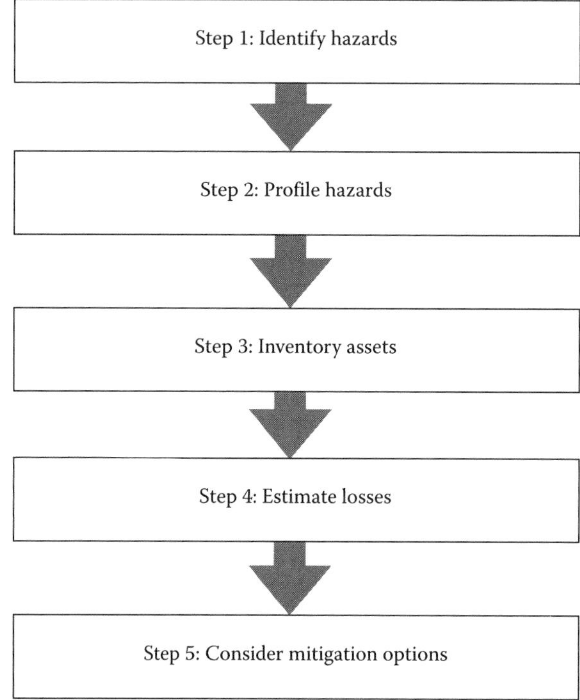

FIGURE 7.9 HAZUS process flowchart.

Hence, preparedness steps will largely depend upon the threat. While HAZUS works in natural disasters, its effectiveness in terror is less predictable and useful.[13]

To close the knowledge gap on the national level, FEMA sponsors Annual HAZUS Conferences which have included specialized training in flood mitigation, cost–benefit analysis, storm surge, and other coastal threats.

Internet Exercise: Discover the most cutting-edge practices discussed at the annual conference at www.HAZUS.net.

Be mindful that software updates are going to be regular occurrences in the HAZUS market. FEMA just released HAZUS 2.0 and one can expect another edition in another year or so.

Since Katrina, FEMA has evolved in mostly beneficial ways for many of its responses. Katrina was a wakeup call about the concept of preparedness—being able to respond with professionalism and efficacy. Since Katrina, the agency has been bombarded with a legion of natural disasters and can mostly hold its head high in its handling of these many events. "FEMA gets high marks from disaster experts for inserting field staff into the disaster zone quickly and opening up communication with local and state officials."[14] Some have even argued that the last 5 years displays an agency that is now in the "groove."[15] The advance warning notification and response, in large part, to Hurricane Sandy is a direct reflection of some of the positive change, particularly since Administrator Craig Fugate has headed up FEMA.

7.2.1 Role of Mitigation in the Preparedness Model

Once the threat has been identified and the inventory or potential costs calculated, the homeland professional seeks ways to mitigate these harms. The term *mitigation* implies an intervention before the threat or catastrophe takes place. Mitigation is the effort to reduce loss of life and property by lessening the impact of disasters. Effective mitigation measures can break the cycle of disaster damage, reconstruction, and repeated damage. While it cannot work in all homeland threats, the idea of mitigation works particularly well in the case of natural disasters, fire, and other catastrophes. For example, in the event of a hurricane or flood, or even a nuclear attack, there are mitigation steps that may prevent the level of expected destruction. Building design, for instance, goes a long way in mitigating the impact of either the earthquake or the flood. Hence, FEMA encourages a variety of mitigation programs to minimize and limit damage and threat. Particular attention is provided for the mitigation of buildings against terrorist threat, and the security and safety of schools, hospitals, and government installations. See Figure 7.10.[16]

Congress has repeatedly increased the funding for mitigation programs since it is now self-evident that mitigation is quantifiably demonstrable. Mitigation programs have "demonstrated cost reductions following disasters due earlier mitigation investments."[17] What is just as deducible is that mitigation plans lack a universality and national design with states and localities treating some portion of the total variable relevant in a mitigation program. For example, the pre-mitigation analysis must consider evacuation as a legitimate part of the mitigation program. If one does not account for the means, the method, or the alternatives in evacuation, aside from being caught flat-footed, the expense of failing to plan will surely be higher than the expense of being organized. Drs. Olornilua and Ibitaya surprisingly conclude that this lack of uniformity directly undermines our planned efficiencies and that every mitigation plan must prepare for "multihazard" situations. The lack of uniformity is portrayed a "dismal."[18]

In the area of earthquakes, FEMA sponsors the National Earthquake Hazards Reduction Plan (NEHRP) (Figure 7.11).

Its primary goals are:

- Develop effective practices and policies for earthquake loss reduction and accelerate implementation
- Improve techniques to reduce seismic vulnerability of facilities and systems

What is the Risk Management Series?

The Risk Management Series (RMS) is a new FEMA series directed at providing design guidance for mitigating multihazard events. The objective of the series is to reduce physical damage to structural and nonstructural components of buildings and related infrastructure, and to reduce resultant casualties during natural and manmade disasters.

The RMS is intended to minimize conflicts that may arise from a multihazard design approach. A multihazard approach requires a complex series of tradeoffs. Security concerns need to be balanced with requirements in terms of earthquakes, floods, high speed winds, accessibility, fire protection, and aesthetics, among others. Designing to mitigate natural hazards should avoid considering manmade hazards as an afterthought, but rather as a critical concern to be studied early during the project cycle. Natural hazards are the largest single contributor to catastrophic or repetitive damage to communities nationwide. Manmade hazards can be categorized as rare events with a potential high impact and very difficult to predict.

Risk Management Series

Minimizing the Effects of Natural Disasters and Potential Terrorist Attacks on Large Buildings

FIGURE 7.10 FEMA's risk management series.

FIGURE 7.11 National earthquake hazards reduction plan.

- Improve seismic hazards identification and risk assessment methods
- Improve the understanding of earthquakes

In earthquake design, the building must be capable of withstanding the move and sway caused by the earthquake. The recent completion of the Paramount, a high-rise office complex in San Francisco, an earthquake-prone area, manifests the role of engineering design in building plans. In the Paramount, precast concrete is utilized as well as the Precast Hybrid Movement Resistant Frame (PHMRF) system (Figure 7.12).

These same mitigation principles apply to a host of other settings, including dams and waterways. FEMA's National Dam Safety Program (NDSP) identifies, develops, and enhances technology to track the condition of the dam infrastructure. FEMA hosts the following initiatives:

- National Inventory of Dams—A computerized database of U.S. dams.
- Dam Safety Program Management Tools—An information collection and management system used by federal and state dam safety program managers.
- National Performance of Dams Program—A national effort headquartered at Stanford University that tracks dam performance.

Internet Exercise: Read the biennial report of the National Dam Safety Program at http://www.fema.gov/library/viewRecord.do?id=2139.

FIGURE 7.12 The Paramount in San Francisco. (Courtesy of FEMA.)

The preparedness and mitigation stress continues into the world of hurricanes. FEMA, in collaboration with a host of other agencies, such as the National Oceanic and Atmospheric Association, National Weather Service, U.S. Department of Transportation, and U.S. Army Corps of Engineers, is deeply involved in the preparation, planning, and mitigation of hurricanes. Some activities include:

- Planning for safe and effective evacuations
- National Hurricane Program training
- Response and recovery
- Post storm assessments
- Mitigation as to hurricane losses

Established in 1985, the National Hurricane Program (NHP) conducts assessments and provides tools and technical assistance to assist state and local agencies in developing hurricane evacuation plans. Aside from planning, preparedness, and mitigation, FEMA, by and through the NHP, relies upon a Hurricane Liaison Team (HLT) that coordinates the various levels of government response, as well as private sector players. HLT members provide critical storm information to government agency decision makers at all levels to help them prepare for their response operations, which may include evacuations, sheltering, and mobilizing equipment. The HLT works closely with states and localities.[19]

FEMA also relies upon Mitigation Assessment Teams (MATs) that it assigns to vulnerable areas. MATs see the real and meaningful impact of natural disaster and the steps that could have eliminated some of the losses. The MAT will:

- Assess the vulnerability of buildings
- Increase building resistance to damage caused by hazard events

MATs look closely at building codes and standards, designs, methods, and materials used for new construction and postdisaster repair and recovery.

Internet Exercise: Find out about new careers on MATs and the current recruitment efforts by FEMA at http://www.fema.gov/rebuild/mat/mat_join.shtm.

Flood threats are a continual concern to the FEMA mission and its operational personnel. The last decade has witnessed a wave of flood events caused by anything from heavy rains to hurricanes. This includes areas that are regularly prone to reoccurrences of disaster-level flooding. Critics, and even the independent government Congressional Research Service, have questioned the efficacy of the National Flood Insurance Program (NFIP), originally established in 1968 as a measure to "address the nation's flood exposure and challenges inherent in financing and managing flood risks in the private sector."[20]

DHS even publishes a list of repeat and very expensive performers in the world of floods. See Table 7.1.

Homebuilders are now required to anticipate the reality of flood when designing residential and commercial buildings. Gone are the days when design could disregard the elements.

TABLE 7.1 Top Events Covered by the National Flood Insurance Program Since Its Inception

Top 15 Significant Flood Events Covered by the National Flood Insurance Program (1978–2012; $ nominal)					
Rank	**Event**	**Date**	**Number of Paid Losses**	**Amount Paid**	**Average Paid Loss**
1	Hurricane Katrina	August 2005	167,216	$16,172,136,626	$96,714
2	Hurricane Ike	September 2008	46,219	2,629,409,589	56,890
3	Hurricane Ivan	September 2004	27,637	1,582,348,735	57,255
4	Hurricane Irene	August 2011	43,844	1,301,682,155	29,689
5	Tropical Storm Allison	June 2001	30,632	1,103,877,235	36,000
6	Louisiana Flood	May 1995	31,343	585,071,593	18,667
7	Hurricane Isabel	September 2003	19,860	492,830,017	24,815
8	Hurricane Rita	September 2005	9504	470,413,959	49,496
9	Hurricane Floyd	September 1999	20,438	462,268,248	22,618
10	Tropical Storm Lee	September 2011	9731	440,127,933	45,229
11	Hurricane Opal	October 1995	10,343	405,527,543	39,208
12	Hurricane Hugo	September 1989	12,840	376,433,739	29,317
13	Hurricane Wilma	October 2005	9609	363,798,528	37,860
14	Nor'Easter	December 1992	25,142	346,150,356	13,768
15	Tropical Storm Isaac	August 2012	8259	291,832,958	35,335

Source: U.S. Department of Homeland Security, Federal Emergency Management Agency.

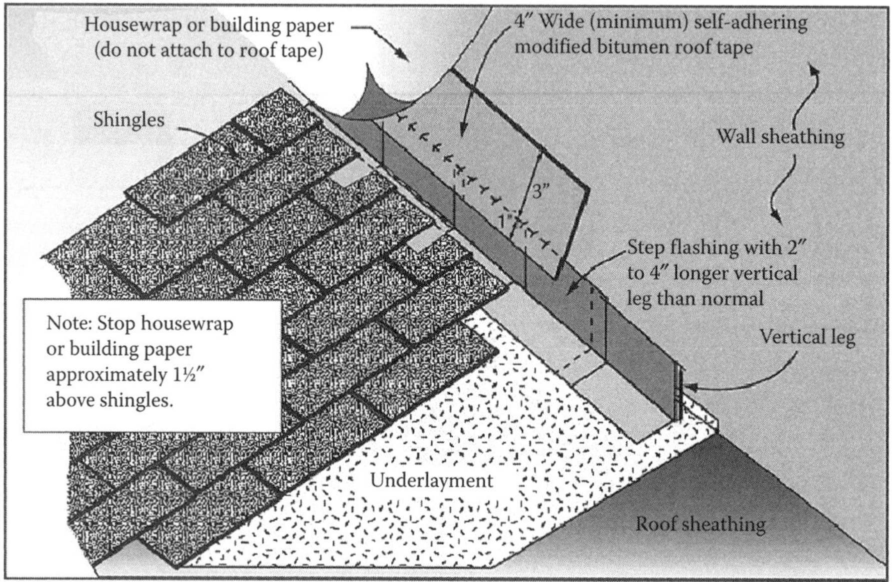

FIGURE 7.13 FEMA construction guidelines to help mitigate roof damage.

FEMA publishes how-to guides for construction companies so that damage may be mitigated. Figure 7.13[21] portrays the need for a stainless-steel house wrap that minimizes water damage.

Internet Exercise: Read the FEMA construction advice on building in flood-prone areas at http://www.fema.gov/library/viewRecord.do?id=1645.

So important is the minimization of flood damage before the flood occurs that FEMA has erected a directorate solely dedicated to its mitigation (Figure 7.14).

The directorate deals with three main areas:

- *Analyzing risk*: Determining the impact of natural hazards that lead to effective strategies for reducing risk.
- *Reducing risk*: Reducing or eliminating long-term risk from hazards on the existing built environment and future construction.
- *Insuring for flood risk*: Reducing the impact of floods on the nation by providing affordable flood insurance.

In the area of risk assessment, the directorate has instituted a wide array of programs, including:

Flood hazard mapping
HAZUS-MH—the software program for disasters
Mitigation planning—the full body of steps to minimize damage

FIGURE 7.14 Kelso, Washington, February 17, 2009. As a result of the heavy rainfall in January in Washington, earth broke loose from a hill and rammed into this home. The owner applied for assistance from FEMA and received a grant to cover reconstruction costs. (Courtesy of Savannah Brehmer/FEMA.)

In mapping, the directorate has made its greatest contribution. In the FEMA Map Center, professionals can scan and assess just about every geographic area prone to flooding. FEMA's new MAP MOD program is an ambitious attempt to draw the flood-prone areas. Using the latest mapping technology, including but not limited to geographic information system (GIS)-based format, flood maps are now digitally produced. New flood maps have been drawn for the bulk of flood-prone areas as of 2008.

Internet Exercise: Find out your neighborhood's flood potential by visiting the FEMA's Map Center at http://msc.fema.gov/webapp/wcs/stores/servlet/CategoryDisplay?catalogId=10001&storeId=10001&categoryId=12001&langId=1&userType=G&type=1.

Risk reduction weighs on FEMA policymakers daily, for if there is any truism about floods and other natural disasters, these events will reoccur. FEMA expends significant energy educating the public about floods and how to prepare.[22] For example, FEMA's FloodSmart program delineates some excellent suggestions on how to minimize the damage in an upcoming flood event.[23] See Figure 7.15.[24]

Aside from its educational role, FEMA promotes a host of other risk reductions, including its National Flood Insurance Program, its Flood Map Center, and its software programs for both individual and commercial interests. Additionally, FEMA has devised a repetitive loss program where flood-prone areas must implement mitigation steps to thwart the ensuing damages. See Figure 7.16 for the cover page relating to repetitive loss.

FEMA provides grants and other financial support to implement mitigation plans. To spend money now to avoid future catastrophic costs evidences

After getting flood insurance, there are several things you can do to minimize losses in your home and ensure your family's safety.

1. Safeguard your possessions.
   Create a personal "flood file" containing information about all your possessions and keep it in a secure place, such as a safe deposit box or waterproof container. This file should have:
   - A copy of your insurance policies with your agent's contact information.
   - A room-by-room inventory of your possessions, including receipts, photos, and videos.
   - Copies of all other critical documents, including finance records or receipts of major purchases.
2. Prepare your house.
   - Make sure your sump pump is working.
   - Clear debris from gutters and downspouts.
   - Anchor any fuel tanks.
   - Raise your electrical components (switches, sockets, circuit breakers, and wiring) at least 12 inches above your home's projected flood elevation.
   - Place the furnace, water heater, washer, and dryer on cement blocks at least 12 inches above the projected flood elevation.
   - Move furniture, valuables, and important documents to a safe place.
3. Develop a family emergency plan.
   - Create a safety kit with drinking water, canned food, first aid, blankets, a radio, and a flashlight.
   - Post emergency telephone numbers by the phone and teach your children how to dial 911.
   - Plan and practice a flood evacuation route with your family. Know safe routes from home, work, and school that are on higher ground.
   - Ask an out-of-state relative or friend to be your emergency family contact.
   - Have a plan to protect your pets.

FIGURE 7.15 FEMA's FloodSmart Program–Educate yourself.

sound policy. Just as compellingly, FEMA serves as a depository for best practices in the world of catastrophic mitigation. By best practices, we mean a collection of what in fact works in the event of flood or other hazard or threat. FEMA labels the most effective mitigation practices as either superior or commendable. FEMA publishes a compendium of exemplary or best practices in the area of mitigation and preparedness. It asks practitioners in the homeland field to submit programs that they consider not only workable but on the cutting edge of innovation in mitigation. FEMA defines an exemplary program as:

> an exemplary practice in emergency management is any practice, project, program, technique, or method that works in one place and is worthy of copying and can be copied elsewhere. It includes initiatives such as inventive coordination among organizations, volunteer projects and resource sharing, and other innovative and highly effective emergency management activities.[25]

Federal Emergency Management Agency OMB 1660-0022 EXPIRES August 31, 2010
National Flood Insurance Program

NFIP REPETITIVE LOSS (RL) UPDATE WORKSHEET (AW-501)

NOTE: SEE REVERSE SIDE FOR MITIGATION ACTION CODES AND PAPERWORK BURDEN STATEMENT

Printed On: **THE INFORMATION ON THIS FORM IS BASED ON CLAIMS ON OR BEFORE:**

REPETITIVE LOSS NUMBER:

Internal use only ☐ **A** ☐ **N/A** ☐ **FRR**

CURRENT NFIP COMMUNITY NAME:

COMMUNITY ID # :

CURRENT PROPERTY ADDRESS	PREVIOUS PROPERTY ADDRESS/COMMUNITY ID #
LAST CLAIMANT:	

INSURED: **NAMED INSURED:**

DATES OF LOSSES **TOTAL NUMBER OF LOSSES FOR PROPERTY:**

REQUESTED UPDATES

MARK ALL UPDATES BELOW THAT APPLY **(IMPORTANT – READ THE INSTRUCTIONS)**

1.☐ INFORMATION PROVIDED NOT SUFFICIENT TO IDENTIFY PROPERTY.
Choose this update if all attempts to locate the property fail. Please describe the steps you took to locate the property in the comments section below.

2.☐ COSMETIC CHANGES REQUIRED TO THE ADDRESS:
Use this update to correct or update the property address shown above.
Only change the address not the name.

3.☐ PROPERTY NOT IN OUR COMMUNITY OR JURISDICTION:
Choose this update if you have positively determined that the property shown is not located in your community. Please provide the correct community name and if known the NFIP Community ID Number. If available, please attach a map showing the property location.

ASSIGN TO COMMUNITY NAME: ____________ NFIP COMMUNITY ID # ________

4.☐ FLOOD PROTECTION PROVIDED.
Choose this update only if some type of structural intervention has occurred to the building, property or the source of flooding that protects the building from future events similar to those that occurred in the past. The correction must be supported by documentation such as an Elevation Certificate and the Mitigation information below must be provided.

Mitigation Action 1.) ☐ **Source of Mitigation Funding 3.)** ☐ **See the back of this form for the appropriate codes.**

5.☐ NO BUILDING ON PROPERTY.
Choose this update only if the property in question can be positively identified as the site of the previously flooded building and documentation is available to support that an insurable building no longer exists at this site. The correction must be supported by documentation such as a Demolition or Relocation Permit and the Mitigation information below must be provided.

Mitigation Action 2.) ☐ **Source of Mitigation Funding 3.)** ☐ **See the back of this form for the appropriate codes.**

6.☐ DUPLICATE LISTING WITH RL NUMBER: ____________ COMBINE AS ONE LISTING.
Choose this update to identify two or more separate listings that are for the same building. List all other RL numbers that are duplicates to this property. Please indicate which address shown is the correct address to use.

7.☐ HISTORIC BUILDING: Check this box if you know the building is listed on a State or National Historic Registry.

ADDITIONAL COMMENTS: ____________

A SIGNED RL TRANSMITTAL SHEET MUST ACCOMPANY THIS FORM FOR APPOVAL OF THE UPDATE!

SEE PRIVACY ACT STATEMENT ON THE BACK

FIGURE 7.16 Repetitive loss update worksheet.

Finally, FEMA relies on agencies to conduct post-assessment reports after the hurricane has passed. Post-assessment reports are essential for FEMA's future operations since these documents provide lessons learned from past storms; measures of hurricane and coastal flooding preparedness; the need for reform in public policy, building performance, and hurricane mitigation; the assessment of growth and the efficacy of evacuation shelter selection guidelines; and other contingency planning. FEMA also needs to determine where it can be more efficient and cost conscious. With

FIGURE 7.17 NASA/NOAA's Suomi NPP captures a nighttime view of Hurricane Sandy, October 2012.

rising economic challenges, the agency must carry out its functions with fewer funds and fewer people. In age of Blackberry's and iPads, the agency must incorporate more innovative technology when communicating with its constituencies.[26]

Mitigation teams play a crucial role in this stage of the natural or catastrophic event (Figure 7.17).

At post assessment, the team can determine the efficacy of risk reduction methods and simultaneously recommend protocols for improvement. Post assessment is central to homeland policy making since it looks to:

- Assess factors that contributed to disaster effects
- Identify risk reduction opportunities
- Educate the public and local government officials in methods to reduce future risks
- Promote hazard mitigation community planning and project development that will result in sustainable community development
- Provide grants to fund hazard mitigation projects
- Assist communities in marketing the National Flood Insurance Program (NFIP)
- Provide technical assistance to state, tribal, and local governments to utilize rebuilding as an opportunity for enhanced local codes and ordinances

7.3 FEMA Response and Recovery

How a nation responds to terror and disaster says much about its makeup and capacity to protect its citizens. The term *response* connotes many things, including immediate actions to save lives, protect property and the environment, and meet basic human needs.[27] Response also includes the execution of emergency plans and actions to support short-term recovery. The level of response will depend upon the circumstances and conditions at specific locations.[28]

The turmoil and anguish caused by the event is burdensome enough. When government fails to respond or does so in an unprofessional way, it simply adds to the pain and suffering of the general public. Nothing could have seared the national psyche more than the glaring ineptitude of state, local, and federal officials in the matter of Katrina.[29] The level of incompetence roused up even the most jaded of bureaucrats, and the toll from Katrina mounted and rose like the waters swirling about the New Orleans region.[30]

When one looks back on these events, it is almost incomprehensible that government could function so miserably. In this sense, response and recovery are just as critical to the homeland professional as planning and preparation. In many ways, response and recovery need to be embedded in any concept of planning and preparedness. These actions are not divisible but united in purpose and practice. If there is any lesson from Katrina, it is that these two worlds cannot remain disjointed but must be intimately interconnected (Figure 7.18).

It is not enough to say that Katrina was a gargantuan storm—for that was self-evident. What is equally telling is the collapse of basic services while in a disaster. Things as simple as transportation assets, such as buses, which

FIGURE 7.18 Thousands of people sought refuge in the New Orleans Convention Center, which was lacking in basic necessities and security as nightmarish stories of crime were told and retold.

could have been utilized to ferry people away, were left to wallow in the water by the hundreds. Mayor Ray Nagin has been rightfully faulted for his malfeasance in this matter (Figures 7.19 and 7.20).[31]

FIGURE 7.19 Buses in New Orleans during Hurricane Katrina.

FIGURE 7.20 Cameron, Louisiana, May 20, 2006. Before (left) and after photographs of FEMA-funded debris removal. Five years later in Louisiana demonstrates the slow pace (right). (Courtesy of FEMA.)

It was painfully obvious that a response and recovery protocol had completely escaped those entrusted with the disaster. As a result, DHS and FEMA authored this essential component of the homeland security model—the National Response Framework.[32]

7.3.1 National Response Framework

The framework is a guide for a national, all-hazards response—from the smallest incident to the largest catastrophe.[33] The framework identifies the key response principles, as well as the roles and structures that organize national response. How communities, states, the federal government, the private sector, and nongovernmental partners apply these principles for a coordinated, effective national response is the chief aim of the national response.[34]

Internet Exercise: Familiarize yourself with the many resources relevant to a response plan by visiting the national response framework resource center at http://www.fema.gov/emergency/nrf/.

The framework systematically incorporates public sector agencies at all levels, the private sector, and nongovernmental organizations. The framework also emphasizes the importance of personal preparedness by individuals and households. FEMA lays out the key principles of a functional and effective response plan in Figure 7.21.

Response Doctrine: Key Principles

- **Engaged Partnership.** Leaders at all levels must communicate and actively support engaged partnerships by developing shared goals and aligning capabilities so that no one is overwhelmed in times of crisis.
- **Tiered Response.** Incidents must be managed at the lowest possible jurisdictional level and supported by additional capabilities when needed.
- **Scalable, Flexible, and Adaptable Operational Capabilities.** As incidents change in size, scope, and complexity, the response must adapt to meet requirements.
- **Unity of Effort through Unified Command.** Effective unified command is indispensable to response activities and requires a clear understanding of the roles and responsibilities of each participating organization.
- **Readiness to Act.** Effective response requires readiness to act balanced with an understanding of risk. From individuals, households, and communities to local, tribal, State, and Federal governments, national response depends on the instinct and ability to act.

FIGURE 7.21 Response doctrine key principles.

The framework operates from very distinct and enlightened premises. Its ideology is primarily one of decentralization. Both FEMA and DHS appear to agree that the best understanding of any problem resides in those experiencing it. Local, decentralized response is usually more responsive than waiting in line for the federals to show up. Here again, we saw clearly how New Orleans acted without decisiveness since it had been, at least in some ways, trained to await the federal invasion before taking action itself. On top of this, the federal bureaucracy of FEMA and aligned agencies is simply a lumbering giant that must accept its limitations. The response must be first and foremost a local one. As FEMA points out:

> Incidents begin and end locally, and most are wholly managed at the local level. Many incidents require unified response from local agencies, NGOs, and the private sector, and some require additional support from neighboring jurisdictions or the State. A small number require Federal support.[35]

In a comparative sense, the Twin Towers experience edified that preeminence of local control. Few would argue that the City of New York, its police and fire, as well as its agencies from port authorities and neighboring states, did a superlative job (Figure 7.22).

Mayor Giuliani became the stuff of legend in how he aggressively tackled the dilemma, while Mayor Ray Nagin and Governor Kathleen Blanco

FIGURE 7.22 New York City Police Department at Ground Zero. (Courtesy of the NYPD Police Benevolent Association.)

became targets of constant derision in their handling of Katrina. In a nutshell, it is all about response. As a result, the framework advanced the partner, tiered model—fully recognizing that the locality can and will do a better job in response. Incidents must be managed at the lowest possible jurisdictional level and supported by additional capabilities when needed.

On the other hand, it is crucial that a chain of command and leadership be part of any response and recovery program. While DHS and FEMA both exhort local and state authorities to be major players in every form of threat and disaster, the scope and magnitude of these events sometimes make the federal authorities the dominant force. Congress has tried to lay out standard protocols in the matter of jurisdiction and leadership.

Another feature of the response framework is its inherent flexibility. Instead of a one-size-fits-all mentality, the framework urges emergency professionals to apply a response that fits the event. Incidents come in many shapes and sizes, and their complexity or simplicity will affect the nature of the response. As the framework recommends:

> As incidents change in size, scope, and complexity, the response must adapt to meet requirements. The number, type, and sources of resources must be able to expand rapidly to meet needs associated with a given incident. The Framework's disciplined and coordinated process can provide for a rapid surge of resources from all levels of government, appropriately scaled to need. Execution must be flexible and adapted to fit each individual incident. For the duration of a response, and as needs grow and change, responders must remain nimble and adaptable. Equally, the overall response should be flexible as it transitions from the response effort to recovery.[36]

The response framework recommends a unified command structure in the mold and type as advanced in NIMS. Calling upon responders to image the Incident Command System (ICS), the framework steadily encourages competing agencies to work in a unified way—without battles over territory or responsibility. The framework rightfully advances unity in command as:

> indispensable to response activities and requires a clear understanding of the roles and responsibilities of each participating organization. Success requires unity of effort, which respects the chain of command of each participating organization while harnessing seamless coordination across jurisdictions in support of common objectives. Use of the Incident Command System (ICS) is an important element across multi-jurisdictional or multi-agency incident management activities. It provides a structure to enable agencies with different legal, jurisdictional, and functional responsibilities to coordinate, plan, and interact effectively on scene. As a team

> effort, unified command allows all agencies with jurisdictional authority and/or functional responsibility for the incident to provide joint support through mutually developed incident objectives and strategies established at the command level. Each participating agency maintains its own authority, responsibility, and accountability.[37]

Finally, the framework advances the perpetual concept of readiness in the design of any response plan. Agencies must be prepared and ready to carry out the response mission. Agencies must understand the dilemma, have mastered the problem, and present themselves as being capable of a prepared and ready response.[38]

Agencies must not victimize those harmed by delay in their operations or responsibilities. Agencies must move quickly in response and avoid the cumbersome delays that always emerge from a lack of preparation and readiness.[39]

Not only must emergency and justice professionals know the risk is to be dealt with, but just as compellingly, they need to place a high priority on the timeliness of response:

> Acting swiftly and effectively requires clear, focused communication and the processes to support it. Without effective communication, a bias toward action will be ineffectual at best, likely perilous. An effective national response relies on disciplined processes, procedures, and systems to communicate timely, accurate, and accessible information on the incident's cause, size, and current situation to the public, responders, and others. Well-developed public information, education strategies, and communication plans help to ensure that lifesaving measures, evacuation routes, threat and alert systems, and other public safety information are coordinated and communicated to numerous diverse audiences in a consistent, accessible, and timely manner.[40]

Internet Exercise: Visit the National Response Framework web location at http://www.fema.gov/emergency/nrf/index.htm.

Depending upon the subject matter, the critical infrastructure in question, and the event itself, any response will need to be tailored to it. For example, the National Framework Resource location provides response protocols for industries and business, critical infrastructure, and other likely targets in need of response. An excellent illustration of this response plan can be seen in transportation. Figure 7.23 is a sample page from the response plan.

For a complete look at a response plan for a biological attack, review the annex published by the National Response Framework.

Emergency Support Function #I –Transportation Annex

ESF Coordinator:

Department of Transportation

Primary Agency:

Department of Transportation

Support Agencies:

Department of Agriculture
Department of Commerce
Department of Defense
Department of Energy
Department of Homeland Security
Department of the Interior
Department of Justice
Department of State
General Services Administration
U.S. Postal Service

INTRODUCTION

Purpose

Emergency Support Function (ESF) #1 - Transportation provides support to the Department of Homeland Security (DHS) by assisting Federal, State, tribal, and local governmental entities, voluntary organizations, nongovernmental organizations, and the private sector in the management of transportation systems and infrastructure during domestic threats or in response to incidents. ESF # 1 also participates in prevention, preparedness, response, recovery, and mitigation activities. ESF #1 carries out the Department of Transportation (DOT)'s statutory responsibilities, including regulation of transportation, management of the Nation's airspace, and ensuring the safety and security of the national transportation system.

Scope

ESF #1 embodies considerable intermodal expertise and public and private sector transportation stakeholder relationships. DOT, with the assistance of the ESF #1 support agencies, provides transportation assistance in domestic incident management, including the following activities:

- Monitor and report status of and damage to the transportation system and infrastructure as a result of the incident.
- Identify temporary alternative transportation solutions that can be implemented by others when systems or infrastructure are damaged, unavailable, or overwhelmed.
- Perform activities conducted under the direct authority of DOT elements as these relate to aviation, maritime, surface, railroad, and pipeline transportation.
- Coordinate the restoration and recovery of the transportation systems and infrastructure.
- Coordinate and support prevention, preparedness, response, recovery, and mitigation activities among transportation stakeholders within the authorities and resource limitations of ESF #1 agencies.

FIGURE 7.23 Response plan sample page.

7.4 Conclusion

The chapter delivers essential information on the role of FEMA. FEMA, once independent of DHS, was the country's agency of natural disaster. Floods, hurricanes, fires, and earthquakes consumed its planning and response mentality. Slowly but surely, and with extraordinary reservation, the FEMA model came to expect that the regimens and protocols for natural as well as man-made disasters in the form of terrorism are really the same. While this may be conceptually true, the fit of FEMA into DHS has been tougher than anticipated. Every imaginable type of threat and hazard receives some scrutiny in this chapter, though the emphasis is on the planning and preparation—rather than response and recovery.

This chapter covers the historic role of FEMA as well as its contemporary structure and organizational design under DHS. In addition, the chapter emphasizes the role of preparedness in the FEMA mission, the importance of mitigation in the control and containment of disasters, and techniques of response and recovery.

Keywords

All-hazards response
Army corps of engineers
Catastrophic event
Decentralization
Disaster
Exemplary practice
Federal broadcast system
Federal disaster assistance administration
Flood hazard mapping
FloodSmart
Geographic information system
HAZUS-MH
Hurricane liaison team
Integrated emergency management system
MAP MOD
Mitigation
Mitigation assessment team
Mitigation planning
National dam safety program
National earthquake hazards reduction plan
National fire prevention control office
National flood insurance program
National hurricane program
National preparedness directorate
Post-assessment report
Preparedness
Project impact
Protocol
Reconstruction finance corporation
Response and recovery
Routine emergency

Discussion Questions

1. Discuss the mission of FEMA prior to 9/11. Since 9/11 how has that mission been modified?
2. Why have there been growing pains for the new FEMA since incorporation into the Department of Homeland Security?
3. Why is planning so critical to effective homeland policy?
4. Why does mitigation have a pre- and post-role in homeland defense?
5. Discuss areas where hazards are likely events in your community.
6. What type of mitigation plan would work well once a hazard has been identified?
7. Why do response and recovery have important public relations issues?
8. What is the general thrust of agency cooperation between federal, state, and local entities?
9. In what region of FEMA does your jurisdiction lie?
10. If a hazard or disaster took place in your region, what agency would likely be the lead player in response and recovery?
11. Compare the preparedness and response exhibited in Hurricane Katrina versus Hurricane Sandy.

Practical Exercises

1. Enroll and take the training of FEMA regarding the reading and interpretation of flood maps at http://www.fema.gov/plan/prevent/fhm/ot_firmr.shtm/.
2. Visit FEMA's software tool for mitigation at http://www.fema.gov/plan/prevent/floodplain/data_tool.shtm.
3. Discover best practices of interest to your community. Visit the FEMA database of best practices at http://www.fema.gov/mitigationbp/briefRotate.do.
4. Take a tour of the National Response Framework at http://www.fema.gov/emergency/nrf/training.htm.

Notes

1. J. A. Bullock et al., *Introduction to Homeland Security* (New York: Elsevier, 2005), 6.

2. R. T. Stafford, *Disaster Relief and Emergency Assistance Act, P.L. 100-707*, signed into law November 23, 1988; amended the Disaster Relief Act of 1974, P.L. 93-288. This act constitutes the statutory authority for most federal disaster response activities, especially as they pertain to FEMA and FEMA programs.
3. "The Role of FEMA in Disasters," Center for Disaster Philanthropy, http://disasterphilanthropy.org/where/issue-insights/the-role-of-fema-in-disasters (accessed January 3, 2013).
4. W. F. Shughart II, Disaster relief as bad public policy, *The Independent Review*, 15(4) (Spring 2011): 530.
5. R. Wimberly, *First-Ever National EAS Test Will Come from the White House, Emergency Management*, at http://www.emergencymgmt.com/safety/National-Test-EAS-032111.html, March 21, 2011.
6. Department of Homeland Security, *National Response Framework*, January, 2008: 27.
7. Department of Homeland Security, *FEMA: Radiological Emergency Preparedness Program Manual and Supplement*, 2011.
8. For an overview of *Preparedness for the Citizen and the Community*, see http://www.fema.gov/pdf/areyouready/basic_preparedness.pdf.
9. For a general series of considerations on planning and preparation, see R. W. Perry and M. K. Lindell, Preparedness for emergency response: Guideline for the emergency planning process, *Disasters*, 27, 2003: 336–350.
10. Department of Homeland Security, *Safe Rooms and Shelters—Protecting People against Terrorist Attacks National Geospatial Preparedness Needs Assessment*, May 2006, Figure 4.3.
11. Department of Homeland Security, *Safe Rooms and Shelters*, Figure 4.1.
12. Department of Homeland Security, *Using HAZUS-MH for Risk Assessment: How-to Guide*, August 2004.
13. For a look at disaster preparedness, see *National Fire Protection Association, Implementing NFPA 1600: National Preparedness Standards*, ed. D. Schmidt (Quincy, MA: National Fire Protection Association, 2008).
14. K. Vlahos, A season of wild wind, *Wind & Water, Homeland Security Today*, August, 2011: 34.
15. K. Vlahos, A season of wild wind, *Wind & Water, Homeland Security Today*, August, 2011: 34.
16. FEMA, Risk Management Series at www.fema.gov/plan/prevent/RMS/ (accessed August 30 2009).
17. Congressional Research Service, FEMA's Pre-Disaster Mitigation 21.
18. O. O. Olonilua and O. Ibitayo, Toward multihazard mitigation: An evaluation of FEMA-approved hazard mitigation plans under the Disaster Mitigation Act of 2000, *Journal of Emergency Management*, 9 (January/February 2011): 37–49, 48.
19. FEMA, Guide for All-Hazard Emergency Operations Planning, Chapter 4, 1996 at www.fema.gov/pdf/plan/4-ch.pdf.
20. Congressional Research Service, *National Flood Insurance Program: Background, Challenges, and Financial Status*, 2011.
21. FEMA, *The Homebuilder's Guide to Coastal Construction*, August 2005.
22. For an excellent resource on flood and wind damage, see *Catalog of FEMA Flood and Wind Publications, and Training Courses*, http://www.fema.gov/library/viewRecord.do?id=3184 (accessed March 9, 2009).
23. FEMA, FloodSmart.Gov, http://www.floodsmart.gov/floodsmart/pages/preparation_recovery/before_a_flood.jsp (accessed March 7, 2009).

24. FEMA, FloodSmart.Gov, http://www.floodsmart.gov/floodsmart/pages/preparation_recovery/before_a_flood.jsp (accessed March 7, 2009).
25. FEMA, *An Invitation to Nominations of Exemplary Practices*, http://www.fema.gov/emergency/managers/partnr13.shtm (accessed March 8, 2009).
26. Congressional Research Service, *Social Media and Disasters: Current Uses, Future Options, and Policy Considerations*, 2011.
27. R. McCreight, Establishing a national emergency response and disaster assistance corps, *Homeland Defense Journal*, 10, September 2007; C. Hines, Disaster management, *Law & Order*, 58, August 2006: 54.
28. For an example of distinctly and very differently FEMA would act in the case of a Dirty Bomb, see *Congressional Research Service, "Dirty Bombs": Technical Background, Attack Prevention and Response, Issues for Congress*, 2011, http://www.fas.org/sgp/crs/nuke/R41890.pdf.
29. See J. Flynn, Review of disasters and the law: Katrina and beyond, *Journal of Homeland Security and Emergency Management*, 1, 2007: 4.
30. There is little question that FEMA was rightfully criticized. One benefit from the criticism was an avalanche of new research in the area, such as R. McCreight, Aspects of emergency management, *Homeland Defense Journal*, 5, May 2007: 22–28; J. Dowle, Prepare for homeland security, *Law & Order*, 5, May 2007: 55; H. Stone, Emergencies and action plans, *Security*, 62, October 2006: 43; R. Elliott, State of readiness, *Security Management*, 50, December 2006: 51–57; C. Perrow, *The Next Catastrophe: Reducing Our Vulnerabilities to Natural, Industrial and Terrorist Disasters* (Princeton, NJ: Princeton University Press, 2007).
31. If we did this poorly at Katrina, how would we handle a tsunami? See A. Kimery, Next tsunami, *Homeland Security Today*, July, 2011: 34.
32. For a list of authorities that permit federal, state, and local authorities to engage in homeland defense and intervention, see http://www.fema.gov/pdf/emergency/nrf/nrf-authorities.pdf.
33. See Department of Homeland Security, *National Response Framework Fact Sheet*, at http://www.fema.gov/pdf/emergency/nrf/NRFOnePageFactSheet.pdf.
34. A. Bitto, Say what? Who? Me? Right here in the trenches? Collaborate or what? Seeking common ground in regional All-Hazards preparedness training, *Journal of Environmental Health*, 69, January/February 2007: 28–33.
35. Department of Homeland Security, *National Response Framework*, January 2008, 9. Despite this preference, national exercises are still in vogue at FEMA. DHS still sponsors National Level Exercise programs. See E. Pitman, National response, *Emergency Management*, March/April, 2011: 30.
36. Department of Homeland Security, *The National Response Framework* (Washington, DC: U.S. Government Printing Office, January 2008), 10, http://www.fema.gov/pdf/emergency/nrf/nrf-core.pdf.
37. Department of Homeland Security, *National Response Framework*, 10.
38. Department of Homeland Security, *National Response Framework*, 27.
39. See R. Humphress, Building an emergency response competency system: Optimizing emergency personnel mobilization, *Journal of Homeland Security and Emergency Management*, 1 (2007): 4; D. Barbee, Disaster response and recovery: Strategies and tactics for resilience, *Journal of Homeland Security and Emergency Management*, 1, 2007: 4; D. Philpott, Emergency preparedness communications, *Homeland Defense Journal*, 44, June 2007.
40. Department of Homeland Security, *National Response Framework*, 10–11.

Chapter 8

Intelligence

Objectives

1. To comprehend the nature of the intelligence cycle.
2. To outline the Department of Homeland Security's (DHS) intelligence gathering approach in the aftermath of 9/11.
3. To define the mission of the Federal Bureau of Investigation (FBI) as it relates to intelligence gathering and sharing.
4. To list the various new policies, programs, and initiatives of the FBI since 9/11.
5. To define the mission of the Central Intelligence Agency (CIA) as it relates to intelligence gathering and sharing.
6. To list the various new policies, programs, and initiatives of the CIA since 9/11.
7. To list the mission, policies, programs, and initiatives of the new Office of the Director of National Intelligence.
8. To list the mission, policies, programs, and initiatives of the Defense Intelligence Agency (DIA) since 9/11.

8.1 Introduction

Much is expected of those entrusted with homeland protection. At a minimum, there is the expectation of basic security and safety—the notion that the homeland will be safe from attack from both domestic and foreign enemies. As already noted, exactly what the functionaries of homeland security should tackle is an evolutionary project. Today's threat may be tomorrow's less worrisome problem. However, there are certain core competencies that the professional class of employees in Homeland Security need to master. These are the nonnegotiable skill sets that the homeland system must demonstrate competence in. These are the essential underpinnings of what makes the homeland system work in any context. These competencies include:

- Intelligence
- Border security
- Immigration
- Transportation security
- Public health

8.2 Intelligence

The task of intelligence gathering and analysis could be considered an overreaching competence, for just about everything in Homeland Security is guided by what we do, or should, or must know. Intelligence, in a sense, is the lifeblood of operations. Sometimes practitioners witness the mindlessness, the almost unintelligence that policymakers impose. In other words, the bureaucratic mindset, in some cases, simply acts without intelligence because it acts or has been acting in a particular way for so long. Intelligence is more than mindless motion.[1] The idea of intelligence can be discerned in a host of contexts—domestic and international, military and covert, criminal and civil—as well as the intelligence of homeland security. Intelligence is, at its base, nothing more than information assessment. One way of describing it might be:

> The intelligence cycle is an iterative process in which collection requirements based on national security threats are developed, and intelligence is collected, analyzed, and disseminated to a broad range of consumers. Consumers sometimes provide feedback on the finished intelligence products, which can be used to refine any part of the intelligence cycle to ensure that consumers are getting the intelligence they need to make informed decisions and/or take appropriate actions.[2]

Intelligence activities largely reflect the agency mission and overall purpose of the task at hand. In some circles, intelligence is broken down into

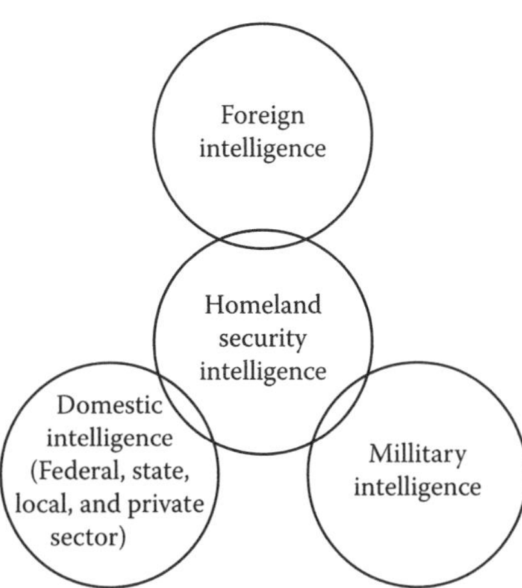

FIGURE 8.1 Intelligence gathering matrix.

various disciplines. "Three major intelligence disciplines or 'INTs'—signals intelligence (*sigint*), imagery intelligence (*imint*), and human intelligence (*humint*)—provide the most important information for analysts and absorb the bulk of the intelligence budget."[3]

Some might argue that homeland intelligence is a unique animal invented in the last ten plus years. Others claim that intelligence is an interconnected dynamic—that homeland information can only come about in a holistic context, that homeland security is impossible without the larger intelligence community inputting information. Homeland security is no better or worse than its aligned agencies of intelligence gathering. Figure 8.1[4] portrays this interdependence.

DHS tends to favor this integrative approach and for good reason. If there was any persistent critique of government in the aftermath of 9/11, it was the failure of intelligence. But even more compellingly, the critics and commissions repeatedly castigated the intelligence community for its failure to share, to disseminate, and to work collaboratively with sister and brother agencies. Intelligence was boxed in prior to 9/11; it was departmentalized and compartmentalized rather than scrutinized in the national, integrative framework. Former secretary of DHS Michael Chertoff eloquently described this dilemma:

> Intelligence, as you know, is not only about spies and satellites. Intelligence is about the thousands and thousands of routine, everyday observations and activities. Surveillance, interactions—each of which may be taken in isolation as not a particularly meaningful piece of information, but when fused together, gives us a sense of the patterns and the flow that really is at the core of what intelligence analysis is all about .... We [DHS] actually generate a lot of intelligence ... we have many interactions every day, every hour at the border, on airplanes, and with the Coast Guard.[5]

In this sense, intelligence is merely information shared that it might give meaning. It is the patterns and connections that analysts are looking for. It is the overall fit of the information into particular facts and circumstances that the intelligence analyst seeks. Just as crucially, the idea of intelligence has become fixated on things beyond basic knowledge, and in a sense, tending toward technology and gadgets over the basic acquisition of information. Many professionals in the intelligence community remind us that intelligence is first and foremost knowledge—something gathered and then disseminated. Mark M. Lowenthal, president of the Security and Intelligence Academy, has long been a critic of our tendency to forget about the "basics" in intelligence gathering and he urges us to "get back to the 'knowledge building' business."[6]

From the outset of the agency, DHS looked squarely and keenly into the world of intelligence and saw the necessity for integration and cohesion among all governmental agencies. Indeed in early 2002, so did Congress by enacting the Homeland Security Act of 2002, which not only contained the administrative underpinnings of DHS, but set the professional parameters of intelligence.[7] The act precisely mandates and lays out expectations regarding the gathering of information and intelligence. It forces government as a whole to collaborate rather than insulate. The act contained provisions for information analysis and intelligence within DHS. The act did not transfer to DHS existing government intelligence and law enforcement agencies but envisioned an analytical office utilizing the products of other agencies—both unevaluated information and finished reports—to provide warning of terrorist attacks, assessments of vulnerability, and recommendations for remedial actions at federal, state, and local levels, and by the private sector. In 2003, DHS set up the Terrorist Threat Integration Center (TTIC)—an entity directed to assess threats, but then just as commandingly ordered the sharing and collaborative interchange of said intelligence (Figure 8.2).

FIGURE 8.2 Terrorist Threat Integration Center logo.

The TTIC was established to:

- Optimize use of terrorist threat-related information, expertise, and capabilities to conduct threat analysis and inform collection strategies
- Create a structure that ensures information sharing across agency lines
- Integrate terrorist-related information collected domestically and abroad in order to form the most comprehensive possible threat picture
- Be responsible and accountable for providing terrorist threat assessments for our national leadership

The TTIC was subsequently merged and renamed The National Counterterrorism Center, under the control and supervision of the United States Director of National Intelligence.[8]

8.3 Terror, Threats, Disaster, and Intelligence Agencies

The array of federal agencies dedicated to the task of intelligence is simply mind-boggling. Long before 9/11, the governmental and military complex was incessantly in need of intelligence. Governments cannot be run without intelligence, nor can wars be fought or borders secured. Intelligence has been part of our national fabric since the days of the American Revolution. In another portion of this chapter, we examine intelligence and defense of the homeland from the post-Civil War period, to the Cold War, to the riots of the 1960s, and end in the present. In each time frame, those who labor to protect the country need intelligence. After 9/11, these agencies had to adjust and redefine traditional definitions and outlooks on exactly what intelligence is effective. Added to the agency demands was the world of terror—an evolving terror erected by the jihadist and those who hate the American experience. It changed the way the intelligence business is carried out. To be sure, even DHS sees intelligence as a core function of its purpose and operational philosophy. DHS's Office of Intelligence and Analysis has four strategic goals:

- Promote understanding of threats through intelligence analysis
- Collect information and intelligence pertinent to homeland security
- Share information necessary for action
- Manage intelligence for the homeland security enterprise

Its structure reflects the multivariate nature of intelligence with special sections dedicated to Counterintelligence (CI) and Counterterrorism as well as Border, and Intelligence Management. See Figure 8.3.

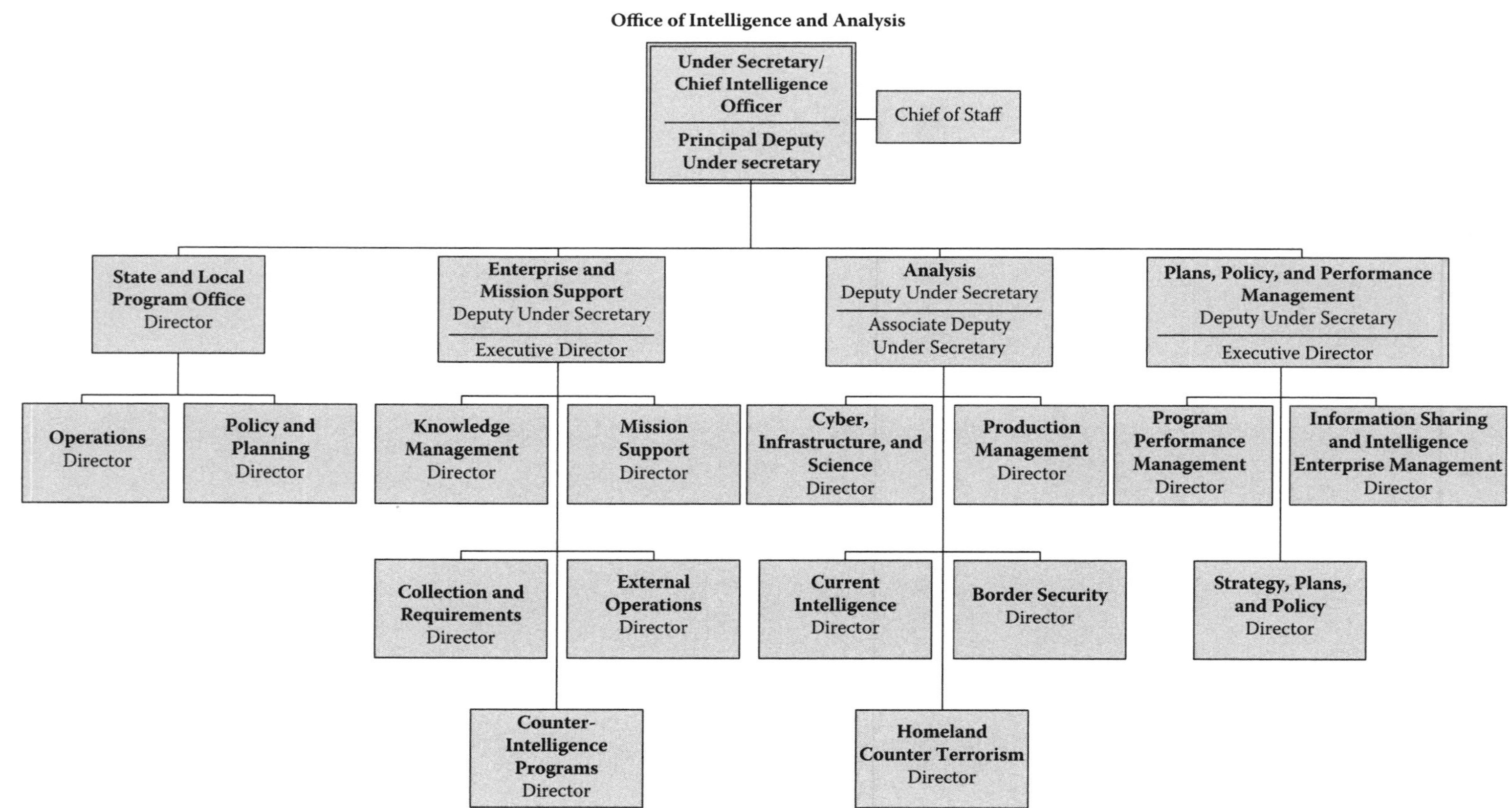

FIGURE 8.3 Office of Intelligence and Analysis organization chart.

Terror is not a new reality since 9/11 for federal and state justice agencies. While the attacks of 9/11 surely enhanced the nature of global terrorism in the domestic sphere, law enforcement leadership could not have been surprised by the possibility or actuality of any attack on American soil. The American intelligence community generally comprises these agencies:

- Office of the Director of National Intelligence
- Office of the National Counterintelligence Executive
- Information-Sharing Environment
- National Counterterrorism Center
- National Intelligence Council
- Central Intelligence Agency
- Defense Intelligence Agency
- Federal Bureau of Investigations
- Marine Corps Intelligence
- National Geospatial Intelligence Agency
- National Reconnaissance Office
- National Security Agency
- Office of Naval Intelligence
- U.S. Air Force Office of Special Investigations
- U.S. Army Intelligence and Security Command
- U.S. Coast Guard
- U.S. Department of Energy
- U.S. Department of Homeland Security
- U.S. Department of State
- U.S. Treasury Department

Throughout this chapter, the reader has been exposed to a good many members of this community. It is impossible to cover it all due to its sheer size and scope. What follows is a cursory look at the historic and emerging agencies entrusted with diverse intelligence responsibilities.

8.3.1 Federal Bureau of Investigation

The FBI has held jurisdictional authority in matters involving terrorism since 1986. Indeed, the FBI had been busy with all sorts of terrorist activity since the early 1980s. In its long and distinguished history, the FBI has been called upon in a wide array of law enforcement initiatives, from rackets and organized crime to public corruption, from attacks on U.S. embassies to terror plots against the United States.

The FBI has long been an agency capable of adaptation and mission adjustment—a characteristic referred to as "change of mandate." This is one of its greatest strengths—that it is capable of addressing new and emerging threats to the country (Figures 8.4 and 8.5).

FIGURE 8.4 FBI seal.

FIGURE 8.5 FBI investigators at work.

WHAT WE INVESTIGATE[9]

The very heart of FBI operations lies in our investigations—which serve, as our mission states, "to protect and defend the United States against terrorist and foreign intelligence threats and to enforce the criminal laws of the United States." We currently have jurisdiction over violations of more than 200 categories of federal law, and you can find the major ones below, grouped within our three national security priorities and our five criminal priorities. Also visit our Intelligence program site, which underpins and informs all our investigative programs.

National Security Priorities	Criminal Priorities	
1. Counterterrorism • International terrorism • Domestic terrorism • Weapons of mass destruction 2. Counterintelligence • Counterespionage • Counterproliferation • Economic espionage 3. Cyber crime • Computer intrusions • Online predators • Piracy/intellectual property theft • Internet fraud	4. Public corruption • Government fraud • Election fraud • Foreign corrupt practices 5. Civil rights • Hate crime • Human trafficking • Color of law • Freedom of access to clinics 6. White-collar crime • Antitrust • Bankruptcy fraud • Corporate/ securities fraud • Health care fraud • Identity theft • Insurance fraud • Money laundering • Mortgage fraud • Telemarketing fraud • More white-collar frauds	7. Organized crime • Italian Mafia/LCN • Eurasian • Balkan • Middle eastern • Asian • African • Sports bribery 8. Major thefts/violent crime • Art theft • Bank robberies • Cargo theft • Crimes against children • Cruise ship crime • Indian country crime • Jewelry and gems theft • Murder for hire • Retail theft • Vehicle theft • Violent gangs

Internet Resource: For the history of the FBI, see http://www.fbi.gov/libref/historic/history/text.htm.

The FBI has extensive experience in the world of intelligence and espionage, but these skills were largely shaped after World War II and the emergence of the Cold War. For nearly 40 years, the FBI's main thrust in the world of international activity coalesced around Cold War enemies rather than modern-day jihadists wishing the end of America and its allies. While the skill set may be complementary in both worlds, there is little question that the FBI realized that its world and the world around was changing. In the late 1980s, throughout the 1990s, the soil of the United States was stained with domestic terrorism. Both the Oklahoma City Bombing and the World Trade Center attacks triggered a new approach at the FBI. The shift largely dwelled upon the impact of terrorism, both domestically and internationally. After 9/11, the FBI was increasingly asked to adjust and adapt its mission to contend with terror threats. At this time, Director Robert S. Mueller III called for a reengineering of FBI structure and operations to closely focus the bureau on prevention of terrorist attacks, on countering

FIGURE 8.6 Robert S. Mueller III.

foreign intelligence operations against the United States, and on addressing cybercrime-based attacks and other high-technology crimes (Figure 8.6).

From 2001 forward, the FBI will commence new programs and policies that reflect the new mandate of terrorism.

8.3.1.1 Joint Terrorism Task Forces

The FBI reinforced the importance and operational role of the Joint Terrorism Task Forces (JTTFs), an amalgam of state, federal, and local law enforcement in major American cities like New York. There are more than 100 JTTF's presently operating—56 of which are housed in local FBI headquarters. At the federal level, full-time membership in the JTTF is granted automatically to the following entities:

- FBI
- U.S. Marshals Service
- Bureau of Alcohol, Tobacco, and Firearms
- U.S. Secret Service
- U.S. State Department/Diplomatic Security Service
- Immigration and Customs Enforcement
- U.S. Border Patrol
- Postal Inspection Service
- Treasury Inspector General for Tax Administration
- Internal Revenue Service
- U.S. Park Police
- Federal Protective Service
- Department of Interior's Bureau of Land Management
- Defense Criminal Investigative Service
- Air Force Office of Special Investigations
- U.S. Army

- Naval Criminal Investigative Service
- Central Intelligence Agency
- State and Local Law Enforcement

PROTECTING AMERICA AGAINST TERRORIST ATTACK

A Closer Look at the FBI's Joint Terrorism Task Forces

12/01/04

They are our nation's front line on terrorism: small cells of highly trained, locally based, passionately committed investigators, analysts, linguists, SWAT experts, and other specialists from dozens of U.S. law enforcement and intelligence agencies.

When it comes to investigating terrorism, they do it all: chase down leads, gather evidence, make arrests, provide security for special events, conduct training, collect and share intelligence, and respond to threats and incidents at a moment's notice.

They are the FBI's Joint Terrorism Task Forces, or JTTFs.

Where are they based? In 100 cities nationwide, including at least one in each of our 56 field offices. Sixty-five of these JTTFs were created after 9/11/01.

How many members? 3723 nationwide—more than four times the pre-9/11 total—including 2196 Special Agents, 838 state/local law enforcement officers, and 689 professionals from other government agencies (the DHS, the CIA, and the Transportation Security Administration, to name a few).

The first JTTF? New York City, established way back in 1980.

The newest? Actually, there are 16 of them: in Montgomery, Alabama; Fayetteville, Arkansas; Fresno, California; Colorado Springs, Colorado; West Palm Beach, Florida; Bloomington, Indiana; Covington, Kentucky; Portland, Maine; Grand Rapids, Michigan; Helena, Montana; Erie, Pennsylvania; Providence, Rhode Island; Midland, Lubbock, and Plano, Texas; and Everett, Washington.

Their contributions? More than we could possibly capture here, but JTTFs have been instrumental in breaking up cells like the "Portland Seven," the "Lackawanna Six," and the Northern Virginia jihad. They've traced sources of terrorist funding, responded to anthrax threats, halted the use of fake IDs, and quickly arrested suspicious characters with all kinds of deadly weapons and explosives. Chances are if you hear about a counterterrorism investigation, JTTFs are playing an active and often decisive role.

How do these JTTFs coordinate their efforts? Largely through the interagency National Joint Terrorism Task Force, working out of FBI Headquarters, which makes sure that information and intelligence flows freely among the local JTTFs.

And here's the final—and most important—thing you should know about these JTTFs: They are working 24/7/365 to protect you, your families, and your communities from terrorist attack.

Source: Federal Bureau of Investigation, *"Headline Archives," Protecting America against Terrorist Attack: A Closer Look at the FBI's Joint Terrorism Task Forces*, http://www.fbi.gov/page2/dec04/jttf120114.htm.

In nearly 60 major American centers, JTTFs were operating before the Twin Towers or the Pentagon were ever struck. After the attack, increased emphasis on the intelligence contribution was quite evident. For a representative example of a JTTF, review the organization and structure of Albany, New York. The Albany JTTF combines federal, state, and local police forces, the U.S. Postal Service, as well as geographically aligned agencies that would work in close proximity to the task force. See Figure 8.7.

Of recent interest has been the nationwide collaboration and cooperation between JTTF's and Fusion Centers. No two entities could better prove the advantages of information sharing than these entities. "While JTTF's get their information from a variety of sources, fusion centers also aid in the sharing of intelligence and assist ... by providing information gathered through combining the knowledge, expertise, and information resident within law enforcement and homeland security agencies operating throughout the nation."[10]

In the recent attempt of a car bomber in Times Square, New York, the cooperation of the JTTF and the Fusion Center model was obvious to those investigating the case. See Figure 8.8.

Albany, NY Joint Terrorism Task Force (JTTF)

The JTTF is responsible for all domestic and international terrorism matters in the two-state territory. The JTTF mission is to prevent acts of terrorism before they occur, and to effectively and swiftly respond to any actual criminal terrorist act by identifying and prosecuting those responsible. The following agencies participate in the JTTF on a full-time or part-time basis:

- Central Intelligence Agency
- U.S. Bureau of Alcohol, Tobacco and Firearms
- U.S. Immigration and Customs Enforcement
- U.S. Internal Revenue Service
- U.S. Department of State (Bureau of Diplomatic Security)
- U.S. Marshals Service
- U.S. Postal Inspection Service
- New York State Office of Inspector General
- New York State Police and Vermont State Police
- Albany, New York, Police Department
- Schenectady, New York, Police Department
- Troy, New York, Police Department

FIGURE 8.7 Duration estimates for catastrophic and routine emergency events.

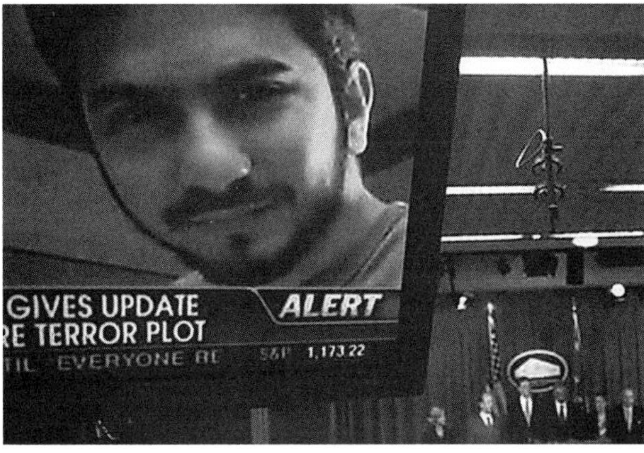

FIGURE 8.8 Faisal Shazhad—homegrown terrorist attempt in Times Square.

8.3.1.2 National Security Branch

The National Security Branch (NSB), established on September 12, 2005, combines the missions, capabilities, and resources of the counterterrorism, CI, and intelligence elements of the FBI under the leadership of a senior FBI official. The NSB reflects the new focus of the FBI by assigning a significant portion of its manpower and resources to the detection, elimination, and prevention of terrorist activity. The mission and vision of the NSB are:

> ***NSB Mission Statement***
>
> To optimally position the FBI to protect the U.S. against weapons of mass destruction, terrorist attacks, foreign intelligence operations, and espionage by:
>
> - Integrating investigative and intelligence activities against current and emerging national security threats.
> - Providing useful and timely information and analysis to the intelligence and law enforcement communities.
> - Effectively developing enabling capabilities, processes, and infrastructure, consistent with applicable laws, attorney general and director of National Intelligence guidance, and civil liberties.
>
> ***NSB Vision Statement***
>
> To the extent authorized under the law, build a national awareness that permits recognition of a national security threat, sufficiently early to permit its disruption. This will be a discerning process that promotes the collection of relevant information and minimizes the accumulation of extraneous data that unnecessarily distracts from the analytical process.

The NSB focuses on four major initiatives within the bureau: counterterrorism, CI, intelligence, and weapons of mass destruction. An organizational chart is shown in Figure 8.9.

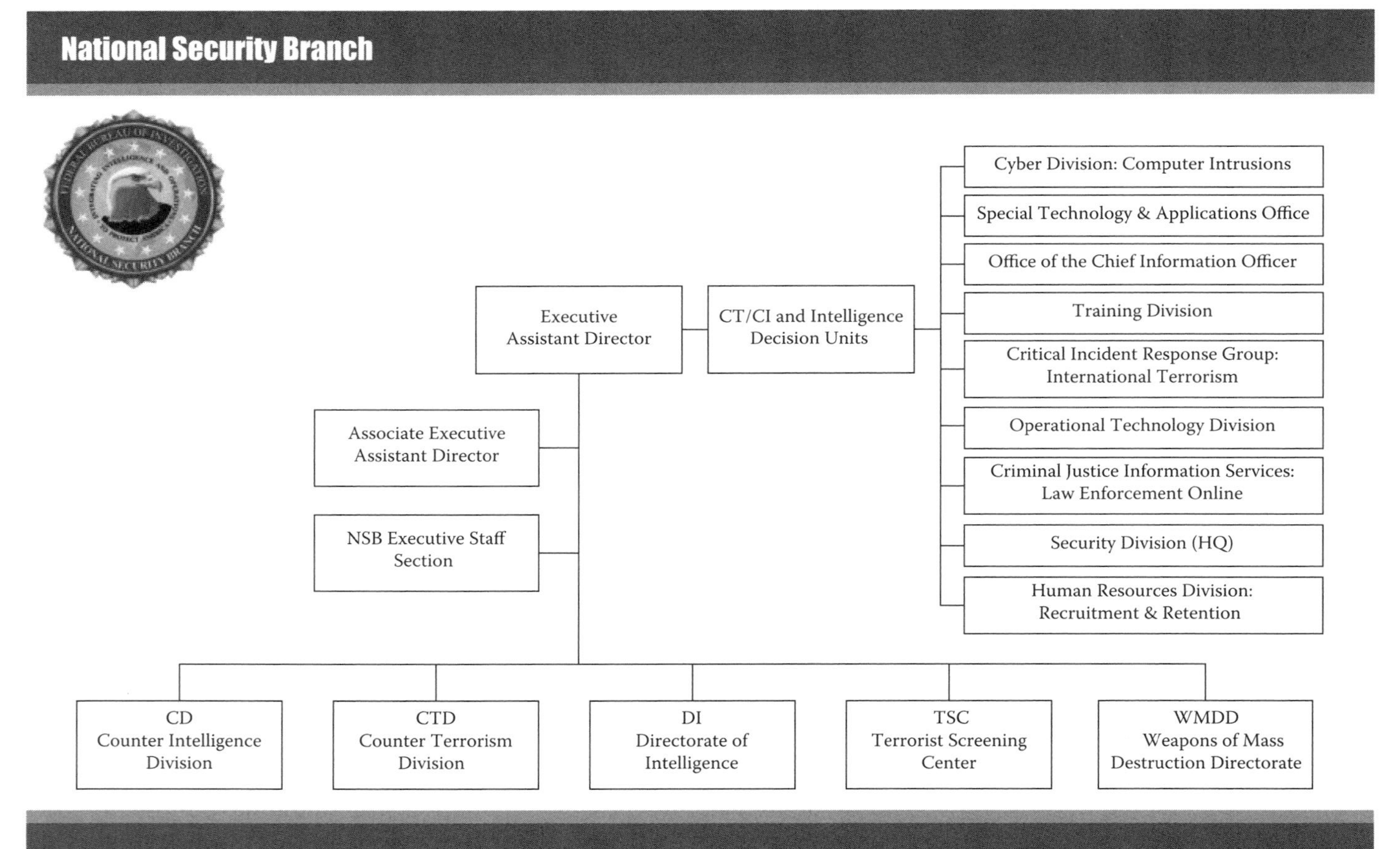

FIGURE 8.9 FBI National Security Branch organizational chart.

FIGURE 8.10 Seal of the Terrorist Screening Center.

The counterterrorism unit tracks known and suspected terrorists in its Terrorist Screening Center (TSC). The TSC now provides "one-stop shopping" so that every government screener is using the same terrorist watch list—whether it is an airport screener, an embassy official issuing visas overseas, or a state or local law enforcement officer on the street. The TSC allows government agencies to run name checks against the same comprehensive list with the most accurate, up-to-date information about known and suspected terrorists (Figure 8.10).

In the area of intelligence gathering, the FBI extends its efforts across the world by using diverse approaches in the gathering of pertinent information. The general approaches are:

- Human intelligence (HUMINT) is the collection of information from human sources. The collection may be done openly, as when FBI agents interview witnesses or suspects, or it may be done through clandestine or covert means (espionage).
- Signals intelligence (SIGINT) refers to electronic transmissions that can be collected by ships, planes, ground sites, or satellites.
- Imagery intelligence (IMINT) is sometimes also referred to as photo intelligence (PHOTINT).
- Measurement and signatures intelligence (MASINT) is a relatively little-known collection discipline that concerns weapons capabilities and industrial activities. MASINT includes the advanced processing and use of data gathered from overhead and airborne IMINT and SIGINT collection systems.
- The DIA's Central MASINT Office (CMO) is the principal user of MASINT data. Measurement and signatures intelligence has become

increasingly important due to growing concern about the existence and spread of weapons of mass destruction.

- Open-source intelligence (OSINT) refers to a broad array of information and sources that are generally available, including information obtained from the media.

8.3.1.3 Analysis of Intelligence

In July 2006, the Weapons of Mass Destruction Directorate (WMD Directorate) was created within the NSB to integrate WMD components previously spread throughout the FBI (Figure 8.11).

A WMD is defined as:

- Any explosive or incendiary device, as defined in Title 18 USC, Section 921: bomb, grenade, rocket, missile, mine, or other device with a charge of more than four ounces
- Any weapon designed or intended to cause death or serious bodily injury through the release, dissemination, or impact of toxic or poisonous chemicals or their precursors
- Any weapon involving a disease organism
- Any weapon designed to release radiation or radioactivity at a level dangerous to human life

The FBI provides support nationally to agencies of government at the state, local, and federal levels in the prevention, containment, and detection of WMDs. The mission of the WMD Directorate is essentially fourfold: (1) setting national policies regarding WMD, (2) providing local assistance

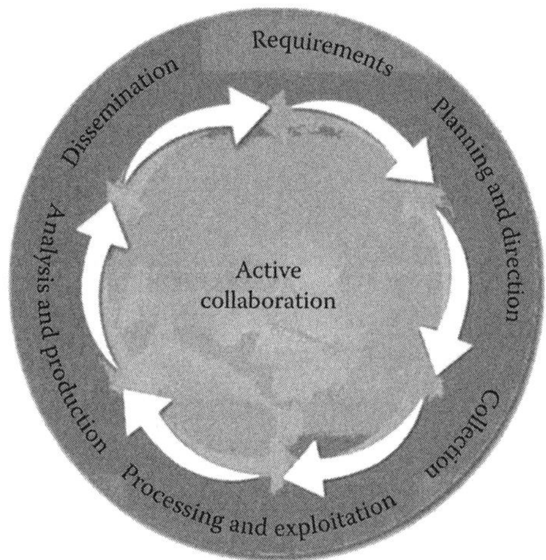

FIGURE 8.11 A graphic representation of the benefits of active collaboration between departments and agencies.

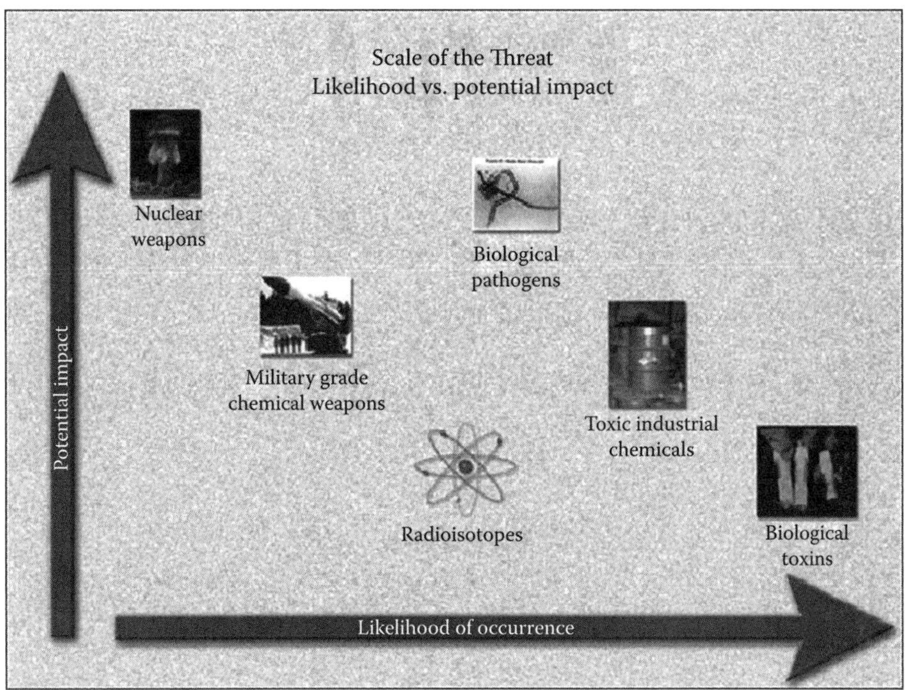

FIGURE 8.12 Scale of the threat: likelihood versus potential attack.

from the FBI's 56 field offices relative to WMD, (3) outreach to communities in need of assistance as well as educating and sharing relevant information, and (4) creating preparedness exercises that deal with actual or potential harm from WMDs. See Figure 8.12.

Education is an increasingly important function of the FBI in all matters relating to homeland security. In the area of WMD, the FBI takes a special interest. See the mock exercise on a dirty bomb in Figure 8.13.

Internet Resource: Watch the training video produced by the NSB for local and state law enforcement at http://www.fbi.gov/hq/nsb/nsb_video.htm.

8.3.2 Central Intelligence Agency

Since 1947, the CIA has been a central figure in the collection and assessment of data and intelligence (Figure 8.14).

Spawned during the era of the Cold War, the agency, like so many of its fellow agencies, has had to apply its skill and knowledge in the intelligence sector, but carrying out its mission in light of terror and threats to the homeland. In 2004, President George W. Bush restructured the CIA by including a new office of the director of CIA and a director of National Intelligence—an office that oversees intelligence nationally and coordinates the activities

A. PREPARING FOR DISASTER

How to Respond to a Dirty Bomb

An FBI SWAT team member is checked for possible radiological contamination. The event was part of a staged drill at the Orange Bowl in Miami to show the basics of how we'd respond to a threat involving a weapon of mass destruction. See more images below.

An FBI SWAT team prepares to assault the warehouse.

FBI and Miami Police SWAT teams use paintball weapons to clear the warehouse and capture the terrorist suspects. In the process, they find a mock "dirty bomb" or radiological dispersal device.

If terrorists ever do try to attack our country with a nuke or dirty bomb, the FBI and its partners must be ready.

And we are. On Wednesday, we staged a mock drill at the Orange Bowl in Miami to show the basics of how we'd respond to a threat involving a weapon of mass destruction.

In the scenario, a terrorist cell was in the process of constructing a dirty bomb in a mock warehouse set up on the field at the Orange Bowl. Two Special Weapons and Tactics (SWAT) teams—one from the FBI and one from the Miami Police—descended on the scene, cleared the warehouse, and discovered an improvised explosive device in one room and radiological material in another room. A Department of Energy Radiological Assistance Program Team used sensors to help determine the presence of radiation, and, with the help of the Miami Fire Department, a robot later destroyed the device. Then, an FBI Hazmat team in full protective gear collected radiological evidence at the scene.

The drill came on day three of the FBI's week-long event, the "Global Initiative to Combat Nuclear Terrorism Law Enforcement Conference." Delegates from 28 countries observed the demonstration from the press boxes and later saw equipment and displays showing the WMD capabilities of 15 local, state, and federal agencies.

A member of the FBI Hazardous Materials Response Team uses a long pole to safely collect evidence related to the dirty bomb.

A Miami police robot like this one destroyed an improvised explosive device with streams of water during the exercise.

FIGURE 8.13 How to respond to a dirty bomb.

of the National Counterintelligence Office.[11] The mission and core values of the agency are:

Mission

We are the nation's first line of defense. We accomplish what others cannot accomplish and go where others cannot go. We carry out our mission by:

FIGURE 8.14 Seal of the CIA.

- Collecting information that reveals the plans, intentions, and capabilities of our adversaries and provides the basis for decision and action.
- Producing timely analysis that provides insight, warning, and opportunity to the president and decision makers charged with protecting and advancing America's interests.
- Conducting covert action at the direction of the president to preempt threats or achieve U.S. policy objectives.

Core Values

Service. We put Country first and Agency before self. Quiet patriotism is our hallmark. We are dedicated to the mission, and we pride ourselves on our extraordinary responsiveness to the needs of our customers.

Integrity. We uphold the highest standards of conduct. We seek and speak the truth—to our colleagues and to our customers. We honor those Agency officers who have come before us and we honor the colleagues with whom we work today.

Excellence. We hold ourselves—and each other—to the highest standards. We embrace personal accountability. We reflect on our performance and learn from that reflection.

The CIA is primarily a covert intelligence community. Its methods and means are distinct from traditional law enforcement, yet despite these differences, the need for collaboration and meaningful lines of communication became quite clear on September 11, 2001. The 9/11 Commission Report caustically critiqued the lack of communication lines between the CIA and FBI.

The CIA is organizationally arranged into four parts:

- Directorate of Intelligence
- National Clandestine Service
- Directorate of Science and Technology
- Directorate of Support

8.3.2.1 Directorate of Intelligence

In the intelligence section, the bulk of what the CIA has refined and honed in matters of data collection and interpretation finds a home. Officers in the CIA's Directorate of Intelligence anticipate and quickly assess rapidly evolving international developments and their impact, both positive and negative, on U.S. policy concerns. The intelligence support and findings are disseminated to a specific audience in need of those findings. The President's Daily Brief and the World Intelligence Review (WIRe) are examples of this intelligence reporting.

The Directorate of Intelligence contains myriad officers and offices dedicated to the collection, assessment, and dissemination of intelligence. Some of the more prominent sections are:

- The CIA Crime and Narcotics Center collects and analyzes information on international narcotics trafficking and organized crime for policymakers and the law enforcement community.
- The CIA Weapons, Intelligence, Nonproliferation, and Arms Control Center provides intelligence support aimed at doing all it can to protect America from the strategic threat of foreign weapons.
- The Counterintelligence Center Analysis Group identifies, monitors, and analyzes the efforts of foreign intelligence entities against U.S. persons, activities, and interests.
- The Information Operations Center Analysis Group evaluates foreign threats to U.S. computer systems, particularly those that support critical infrastructures.
- The Office of Asian Pacific, Latin American, and African Analysis studies the political, economic, leadership, societal, and military developments in Asia, Latin America, and sub-Saharan Africa.
- The Office of Collection Strategies and Analysis provides comprehensive intelligence collection expertise to the DI, a wide range of senior agency and intelligence community officials, and key national policymakers.
- The Office of Iraq Analysis provides multidisciplinary intelligence analysis on Iraq to the president and his top advisors.
- The Office of Near Eastern and South Asian Analysis provides policymakers with comprehensive analytic support on Middle Eastern and

North African countries, as well as on the South Asian nations of India, Pakistan, and Afghanistan.

- The Office of Policy Support customizes DI analysis and presents it to a wide variety of policy, law enforcement, military, and foreign liaison recipients.
- The Office of Russian and European Analysis provides intelligence support on a large number of countries that have long been of crucial importance to the United States as allies or as adversaries and are likely to continue to occupy a key place in U.S. national security policy.
- The Office of Terrorism Analysis is the analytic component of the CIA Counterterrorism Center.
- The Office of Transnational Issues applies unique functional expertise to assess existing and emerging threats to U.S. national security and provides the most senior U.S. policymakers, military planners, and law enforcement with analysis, warning, and crisis support.

8.3.2.2 Office of Clandestine Services

Clandestine operations connote many images—some forbidden, others unapproved or denied upon discovery. That is a fair assessment since to be clandestine is, minimally, to be secretive. That the United States has engaged in clandestine operations is really no secret at all. From the failed Bay of Pigs invasion to operating secret prisons for terrorists, the CIA has been a prime player in these covert activities. The agency and its supporters make no apologies for it either. Secret operations are not only essential in the protection of a country, but mandatory. Complex targets such as terrorism prompt complicated responses. Operating within the CIA is the National Clandestine Service (NCS), which conducts specialized operations for the purpose of gathering intelligence and ensuring U.S. security. The CIA references the NCS as a body that collects "information not obtainable through other means."

Internet Resource: For once classified operations now unclassified regarding covert, clandestine operations of the CIA, see https://www.cia.gov/library/center-for-the-study-of-intelligence/csi-publications/csi-studies/index.html.

8.3.2.3 Directorate of Science and Technology

The Directorate of Science and Technology supports the CIA's mission by its expertise in technological and scientific applications. Intelligence requires the highest levels of equipment and protocol. Clandestine operations require cutting-edge equipment and technology. The mission of the Directorate is to fashion and invent tradecraft that aids the operatives of the CIA and to create and develop technical collection systems, and to apply enabling technologies to the collection, processing, and analysis of information. The

FIGURE 8.15 CIA's Directorate of Science and Technology.

Directorate of Science and Technology includes the men and women of the CIA who apply their expertise and training in pure science—applied engineering, master craftsmanship, operational tradecraft, and linguistics—to provide U.S. decision makers with critically important intelligence on the world (Figure 8.15).

8.3.2.4 Office of Support

The support to mission team provides mission-focused support to the CIA through a full range of support services. The office is responsible for building and operating facilities; providing robust, secure communications over multiple networks, connecting officers sitting in dispersed locations; and acquiring and shipping a full range of critical equipment. The Office of Support also helps hire, train, and assign CIA officers for every directorate, as well as manage the "businesses" within the CIA—contracts and acquisitions, financial services, administrative support, and even the CIA's own phone company. The Office of Support does everything it can to ensure that CIA officers serving around the world are safe, secure, and healthy.

8.3.3 Office of the Director of National Intelligence

What was painfully obvious to intelligence specialists was the lack of coordination among so many distinct bureaucracies of intelligence.[12] By 2006, it was clear that there were too many cooks in the intelligence kitchen. As a result,

President Bush created an Office of the Director of National Intelligence (ODNI), or in some circles this position is labeled "executive" or "czar."

When Congress authorized the creation of the ODNI, it charged the department with diverse authorities and duties including:

- Ensure that timely and objective national intelligence is provided to the president, the heads of departments and agencies of the executive branch; the chairman of the Joint Chiefs of Staff and senior military commanders; and the Congress;
- Establish objectives and priorities for collection, analysis, production, and dissemination of national intelligence;
- Ensure maximum availability of and access to intelligence information within the Intelligence Community;
- Develop and ensure the execution of an annual budget for the National Intelligence program (NIP) based on budget proposals provided by IC component organizations;
- Oversee coordination of relationships with the intelligence or security services of foreign governments and international organizations;
- Ensure the most accurate analysis of intelligence is derived from all sources to support national security needs;
- Develop personnel policies and programs to enhance the capacity for joint operations and to facilitate staffing of community management functions;
- Oversee the development and implementation of a program management plan for acquisition of major systems, doing so jointly with the Secretary of Defense for DoD programs, that includes cost, schedule, and performance goals and program milestone criteria.

The idea was to pool all the intelligence resources, or to funnel these myriad sources through a central office with a central director. This way, one agency could not fail, either inadvertently or intentionally, to withhold intelligence from sister agencies. John Negroponte, a seasoned diplomat and security guru, was the first appointee to this position. Negroponte, by all accounts, skillfully coordinated these diverse constituencies and left the office in high esteem. After President Obama assumed office, Dennis Blair, a former Navy Commander of the Pacific Fleet, whose background includes impeccable experiential and educational preparation, was appointed to the role and served for 2 years. Blair set clear goals for the position, which include:

- To serve as the principal intelligence advisor to the president and his national security team. We will continue to enhance the quality of our analysis and the depth and range of collection that supports it. We will integrate contributions from all IC partners, call it as we see it and lay out the alternatives with clear statements of our level of confidence in our judgments.

- To make the whole of the Intelligence Community greater than the sum of its parts. All 17 intelligence organizations can expect clear mission direction. Common areas such as personnel, intra-IC communications, clearances, and classification deserve special emphasis, as do missions that require the capabilities of more than one agency for success. All of us are then accountable for mission success.
- To assess mission and resources and then provide resources adequate to meet assigned responsibilities and build future capabilities.[13]

His recent replacement is James R. Clapper, a retired military officer with significant Intelligence experience (Figure 8.16).

The mission of the ODNI is multifaceted, but its central aim is the coordination of intelligence information across a host of agencies and operatives (Figure 8.17).

In its strategic statement, the ODNI lists the constituencies that it serves. Turf battles give way to collective cooperation and sound homeland policy. ODNI holds that intelligence will integrate foreign, military, and domestic intelligence capabilities through policy, personnel, and technology actions to provide decision advantage to policymakers, warfighters, homeland security officials, and law enforcement personnel.

This ambition can only be termed a lofty one, for it properly hopes for the type of sharing and intelligence cooperation that government historically resists. The ODNI has many tools at its disposal. A summary look follows.

Internet Exercise: Visit the ODNI's Electronic Reading Room for a sample of its many findings and reports at http://www.dni.gov/electronic_reading_room/electronic_reading_room.htm.

FIGURE 8.16 James R. Clapper, Director of National Intelligence.

FIGURE 8.17 Seal of the Office of the Director of National Intelligence.

8.3.3.1 National Counterterrorism Center

The National Counterterrorism Center (NCTC) was created to be a central clearinghouse for integrating and analyzing terrorism information. NCTC comprises people from its many partner agencies and is a center based on cooperation, collaboration, and partnership. The NCTC seal symbolizes this and, like the design of the great seal of the United States, represents a united center engaged in the global fight against terrorism (Figure 8.18).

A special emphasis of the NCTC is the detection and prediction of domestic activities that threaten the homeland. The NCTC has come under some withering criticism for its failure to share intelligence on Major Hassan—the mass murderer at Fort Hood (Figure 8.19).[14]

FIGURE 8.18 National Counterterrorism Center seal.

FIGURE 8.19 Major Nidal Malik Hassan: the shooter at Fort Hood.

Congressional hearings confirm that the structural difficulties of intelligence sharing still existed nearly a decade later and the "wall" between "law enforcement and intelligence"[15] still exists. And this persistent shortfall may be "inevitable"[16] given the complexities of the intelligence function. However, it seems a necessary ambition to improve the methods and means by which NCTC shares its information, as well as how all other intelligence agencies share their knowledge base.

8.3.3.2 Office of the National Counterintelligence Executive

The Office of the National Counterintelligence Executive (ONCIX) is part of the Office of the Director of National Intelligence and staffed by counterintelligence (CI) and other specialists. The ONCIX develops, coordinates, and produces:

- Foreign intelligence threat assessments and other analytic CI products
- CI strategy for the U.S. government
- CI policy on collection, investigations, and operations
- CI program budgets and evaluations
- Espionage damage assessments (Figure 8.20)
- CI awareness, outreach, and training standards policies

See Figure 8.21 for the organizational breakdown of ONCIX.

This office develops the National Intelligence Strategy,[17] which lays out broad policies on intelligence and produces recommendations on how to undermine terrorists and terrorism and protect intelligence capabilities.[18] The Office has merged two previous sectors, namely the Special Security Center and the Center for Security Evaluation, effective 2010. The Executive has announced four major areas of CI concern in the short term which

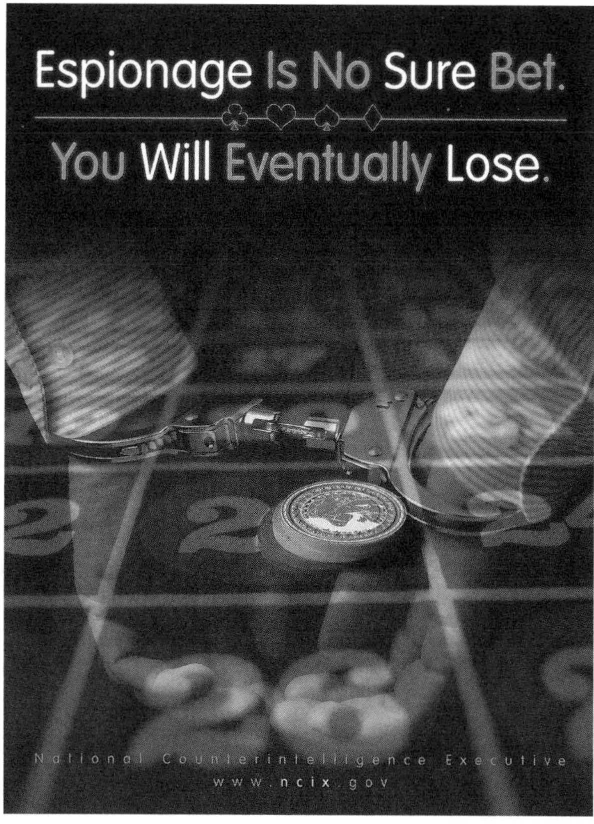

FIGURE 8.20 The ONCIX poster "Espionage Is No Sure Bet" serves as a reminder that there are no winners in the espionage game.

include: insider threat, supply chain threats, economic espionage, and cyber security.[19]

The Office of the Executive engages the intelligence community in the following ways:

- Builds an integrated intelligence capability to address threats to the homeland, consistent with U.S. laws and the protection of privacy and civil liberties.
- Strengthens analytic expertise, methods, and practices; taps expertise wherever it resides; and explores alternative analytic views.
- Rebalances, integrates, and optimizes collection capabilities to meet current and future customer and analytic priorities.
- Attracts, engages, and unifies an innovative and results-focused intelligence community workforce.
- Ensures that intelligence community members and customers can access the intelligence they need when they need it.

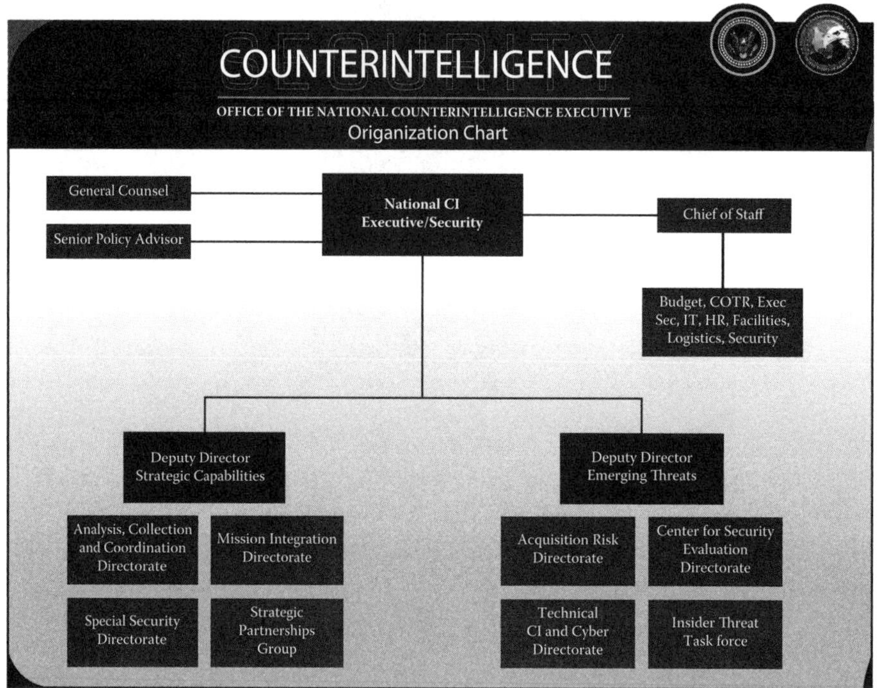

FIGURE 8.21 Organizational chart of the Office of the National Counterintelligence Executive.

- Establishes new and strengthens existing foreign intelligence relationships to help us meet global security challenges.
- Creates clear, uniform security practices and rules that allow us to work together, protect U.S. secrets, and enable aggressive CI activities.
- Exploits path-breaking scientific and research advances that will enable us to maintain and extend our intelligence advantages against emerging threats.
- Learns from our successes and mistakes to anticipate and be ready for new challenges.
- Eliminates redundancy and programs that add little or no value and redirects savings to existing and emerging national security priorities.[20]

8.3.3.3 National Intelligence Council

The National Intelligence Council (NIC) provides an intellectual and policy-making center for the director of national intelligence. Its key responsibilities are:

- To support the director of national intelligence as head of the intelligence community

- To provide a focal point for policymakers to task the intelligence community
- To reach out to nongovernment experts in academia and the private sector
- To contribute to the intelligence community's effort to allocate
- To lead the intelligence community's effort to produce national intelligence estimates (NIEs) and other NIC products

The National Intelligence Council expends a good portion of its energy and time on projections—that is, what it expects the future holds. For terror prevention, the policy maker and homeland professional need to always stay a step or two ahead to succeed. The NIC's projections are short term and long term in design. Its projections to the year 2025 paint a world with the types of problems presently witnessed and a bold projection of emergent issues likely to be encountered.[21] A sample of these projections is reproduced in Figure 8.22.

The National Intelligence Council authors influential NIEs that comprise the coordinated judgments of the intelligence community regarding the likely course of future events. The NIC makes every attempt to stay apolitical in its advice to politicians and policymakers, although the content of the estimate is often used for political reasons The NIC estimates have been fodder for those opposing the war in Iraq and Afghanistan since the pictures drawn in the estimates have not always been complementary to decisions relating to these campaigns. The estimates can ruffle feathers, but at their foundation is the desire of the NIC to deliver objective information on tough security problems.

The NIC depends upon a cadre of national intelligence officers (NIOs) who engage the security questions in an applied sense and gather intelligence both nationally and internationally. Some of the common functions for the NIO are:

- Advise the DNI
- Interact regularly with senior intelligence consumers
- Produce top-quality estimates
- Engage with the outside
- Help assess the capabilities and needs of IC analytic producers
- Promote collaboration among IC analytic producers on strategic warning, advanced analytic tools, and methodologies
- Articulate substantive priorities to guide intelligence collection, evaluation, and procurement

NIOs are among the more lucrative career posts in federal service. Figure 8.23 contains a recent recruitment announcement for a senior position.

The 2025 Global Landscape

Relative Certainties	Likely Impact
A global multipolar system is emerging with the rise of China, India, and others. The relative power of nonstate actors—businesses, tribes, religious organizations, and even criminal networks—also will increase.	By 2025 a single "international community" composed of nation-states will no longer exist. Power will be more dispersed with the newer players bringing new rules of the game while risks will increase that the traditional Western alliances will weaken. Rather than emulating Western models of political and economic development, more countries may be attracted to China's alternative development model.
The unprecedented shift in relative wealth and economic power roughly from West to East now under way will continue.	As some countries become more invested in their economic well-being, incentives toward geopolitical stability could increase. However, the transfer is strengthening states like Russia that want to challenge the Western order.
The United States will remain the single most powerful country but will be less dominant.	Shrinking economic and military capabilities may force the U.S. into a difficult set of trade-offs between domestic versus foreign policy priorities.
Continued economic growth—coupled with 1.2 billion more people by 2025—will put pressure on energy, food, and water resources.	The pace of technological innovation will be key to outcomes during this period. All current technologies are inadequate for replacing traditional energy architecture on the scale needed.
The number of countries with youthful populations in the "arc of instability"[1] will decrease, but the populations of several youth-bulge states are projected to remain on rapid growth trajectories.	Unless employment conditions change dramatically in parlous youth-bulge states such as Afghanistan, Nigeria, Pakistan, and Yemen, these countries will remain ripe for continued instability and state failure.
The potential for conflict will increase owing to rapid changes in parts of the greater Middle East and the spread of lethal capabilities.	The need for the U.S. to act as regional balancer in the Middle East will increase, although other outside powers—Russia, China, and India—will play greater roles than today.
Terrorism is unlikely to disappear by 2025, but its appeal could lessen if economic growth continues in the Middle East and youth unemployment is reduced. For those terrorists that are active the diffusion of technologies will put dangerous capabilities within their reach.	Opportunities for mass-casualty terrorist attacks using chemical, biological, or less likely, nuclear weapons will increase as technology diffuses and nuclear power (and possibly weapons) programs expand. The practical and psychological consequences of such attacks will intensify in an increasingly globalized world.

FIGURE 8.22 The 2025 projected global landscape.

Internet Exercise: Find out about the many careers in this arm of the intelligence community at http://diajobs.dia.mil/.

8.3.4 Defense Intelligence Agency

The DIA, founded on October 1, 1961, was, for a large part of its history, a combat support agency. DIA collects and produces foreign military intelligence for the Department of Defense and aligned intelligence agencies. DIA reports to the defense agencies as well as the national security staff of the president, members of Congress, and military commanders. DIA directs

Agency: Office of the Director of National Intelligence

Job Announcement Number: 22438

Team lead/Senior Intelligence Officer

Salary Range: 120,830.00–153,200.00 USD per year

Open Period:

Series & Grade: GS-0132-15/15

Position Information: Full-Time Permanent

Duty Locations: 1 vacancy-Washington, DC Metro Area, DC

Who May Be Considered:

Applications will be accepted from United States citizens and nationals.

Job Summary:

The National Counterintelligence Executive (NCIX) serves as the head of national counterintelligence (CI) for the United States Government and is directly responsible to the Director of National Intelligence. NCIX facilitates and enhances US counterintelligence efforts and awareness by enabling the CI community to better identify, assess, prioritize, and counter intelligence threats from foreign powers, terrorist groups, and other non-state entities. NCIX operates the Community Acquisition Risk Section (CARS) to address the threat from foreign subversions of Intelligence Community (IC) acquisitions. As international companies and foreign individuals play a greater role in information technology and other critical industries, the risk of persistent, stealthy subversion is raised, particularly by foreign intelligence and military services, as well as international terrorists and criminal elements.

CARS evaluates the risk to the IC posed by commercial entities conducting business with the individual components of the IC.

FIGURE 8.23 National intelligence officer recruitment announcement.

itself to six main areas: "all-source analysis, human intelligence, CI, a worldwide secure information technology backbone measurements and signatures intelligence."[22] The DIA also operates a fully accredited university, the Defense Intelligence University, which offers undergraduate and graduate programs.

DIA serves as lead agency for the intelligence needs of the Department of Defense.

Internet Exercise: To find out more about the DIA college, visit http://www.dia.mil/college/mission.htm.

The DIA summarizes its mission and vision as follows:

Mission

Provide timely, objective, and cogent military intelligence to warfighters, defense planners, and defense and national security policymakers.

Vision

Integration of highly skilled intelligence professionals with leading edge technology to discover information and create knowledge that provides warning,

> identifies opportunities, and delivers overwhelming advantage to our warfighters, defense planners, and defense and national security policymakers.

With nearly 17,000 employees, DIA is a major player in the world of intelligence. DIA intelligence covers a broad spectrum of topical coverage and includes but is not limited to:

- Foreign military and paramilitary forces
- Proliferation of weapons of mass destruction
- International terrorism
- International narcotics trafficking
- Information operations
- Defense-related foreign political, economic, industrial, geographic, and medical and health issues

DIA is headquartered at the Pentagon in Washington, DC, with major operational activities at the Defense Intelligence Analysis Center, the National Center for Medical Intelligence in Frederick, Maryland, and the Missile and Space Intelligence Center in Huntsville, Alabama.

A major component of the agency, the Defense HUMINT Service, meaning human intelligence, gathers information by traditional face-to-face interaction rather than technical services. DIA also manages the Defense Attaché System, which has military attachés assigned to more than 135 embassies overseas. In addition to these functions, DIA operates and coordinates the functions of the Joint Intelligence Task Force for Combating Terrorism (JITF-CT) (Figure 8.24).

Internet Exercise: For a timeline and historical perspective on the DIA, see http://www.dia.mil/history/time/index.html.

FIGURE 8.24 Seal of the Defense Intelligence Agency.

8.4 Conclusion

The idea and concept known as intelligence is the chapter's chief aim, and how intelligence becomes part of the homeland security mission is a secondary purpose. In intelligence, the homeland professional recognizes that information is the lifeblood of any meaningful operation or policy. Without information, and shared distribution of the same, the homeland operative works in the dark in a literal and figurative sense. Intelligence takes the guesswork out of homeland task and function. DHS promotes the integrative approach to intelligence, whereby information is gathered by the various arms of government, namely, the military, federal, state, local, and private sector justice agencies, foreign and friendly information from foreign allies is weighed and evaluated. DHS encourages cooperation among historic competitors in the bureaucratic sense. It calls upon agencies of government to shun traditional turf systems and parochial protection mechanisms that hardly promoted a policy of sharing. There are a host of structural obstacles to the sharing of intelligence. DHS devises the Terrorist Threat Integration Center to serve as a central repository for relevant terrorist intelligence.

Additionally, the chapter paints the picture of intelligence agencies that have been part of the historic and contemporary landscape. Predictably, the CIA and its various branches dedicated to intelligence are featured. Special attention is given to the FBI, whose international thrust and historic responsibility for crimes of terror and espionage provide early expertise in the fight against terrorism. Terrorism would eventually sweep up the agency and consume it in ways it had never originally envisioned. The FBI developed advanced CI systems, the capacity to trace, detect, and prevent attacks by WMD, and devised and erected the Terrorist Screening Center. The FBI is on the forefront of information sharing. The educational role of the FBI in matters of terrorism is also being evaluated. With the FBI working closely with the CIA, the traditional turf protection systems that thwarted the sharing of information will end. Eventually all agencies will contribute to the National Counterintelligence Center—a clearinghouse of information on threats.

Special attention is given to new agencies that have arisen since the tragedy of 9/11 as well as the reorientation of existing agencies that have had to revise operational missions to contend with the terrorist threat. In particular, the chapter scrutinized efforts to centralize and coordinate the massive volume of intelligence across a plethora of federal agencies. Here the Office of the Director of National Intelligence (ODNI) will play a central role. Known as the Office of Intelligence Czar, ODNI has become a focal point for intelligence systems. The director oversees a host of intelligence operations and functions, including the National Counterterrorism Center, the Office of National Counterintelligence Executive, and the National Intelligence Council. Each of these entities carries out critical work in the world of intelligence. Finally, the chapter ends its coverage of the intelligence sector by reviewing the work of the DIA—that crucial collaboration of military and civilian intelligence gathering and sharing. The DIA's more essential contributions to the intelligence theater were highlighted.

Keywords

Change of mandate
Clandestine operations
Counterintelligence
Counterterrorism
Covert intelligence community
Defense Attaché System
Defense Intelligence Agency
Director of National Intelligence
Directorate of Intelligence
Directorate of Science and Technology
Espionage
Federal Bureau of Investigation
Global terrorism
HUMINT
Intelligence community
Intelligence
Joint Terrorism Task Force
National Clandestine Service
National Counterintelligence Executive
National Counterterrorism Center
National Espionage Estimates
National Intelligence Council
National intelligence officers
National Intelligence Strategy
National Security Branch
Office of Science and Technology
Office of Support
President's Daily Brief
Terrorist Screening Center
Terrorist Threat Integration Center
World Intelligence Review

Discussion Questions

1. Explain how the FBI had to change its outlook and mission after 9/11. How significant was this reorientation?
2. Previous to 9/11, the FBI stressed what when compared to terrorism?
3. JTTFs assimilate many agencies into the mix. How does this assist in their outlook and work?
4. Evaluate and comment on the CIA's Office of Science and Technology. What is its purpose and aim?

5. Discuss the ramifications of an intelligence practice based upon a non-shared environment. Why do some argue that 9/11 would never have occurred if information sharing had been commonplace?
6. Explain why cooperation between the military complex and federal intelligence agencies is so important in the fight against terrorism.
7. What types of projections make sense in the intelligence arena? What is a projection worth making?
8. Does it make sense to create an Office of the Director of National Intelligence? Are there alternatives to this design?
9. What do you envision is the greatest challenge for the director of national intelligence?
10. How has the mission of the DIA changed in the last 50 years?

Practical Exercises

1. Find and locate a Joint Terrorism Task Force in your area. Respond to the following:

   What geographic area does the task force cover?

   Whom or what is eligible to join?
2. Describe at least three initiatives the JTTF is presently undertaking.
3. Watch any training video prepared by the FBI relating to terrorism. State four major findings agreed to after reviewing the media.
4. Search DIA for career opportunities. Create a form file for these career tracks.
5. Find out about career opportunities for intelligence officers in today's military branches.
6. Visit any of the centers mentioned in this chapter.
7. Visit the CIA's Office of Clandestine Services. Analyze, assess, and critique a current operation relating to homeland security.
8. Prove whether the FBI is correct in concluding that eco-terrorists are a mighty dangerous lot.
9. Identify and create a job file for the following occupations in homeland security:
   - Federal Protective Service
   - Secret Service

- Border Patrol
- Customs officer
- FBI agent
- CIA officer

10. Determine where the closest intelligence center is relative to your residence. Check to determine whether any of the following apply:

- Military base
- Fusion center
- JTTF
- Regional Office of State Homeland
- Special Operations Unit

Notes

1. See D. Khan, An historical theory of intelligence, *Intelligence and National Security 16* (Autumn 2001): 87–88; P. Gorman, *Hearings before Select Committee on Intelligence of the United States Senate, S. 2198 and S. 421, 102nd Congress* (Washington, DC: Library of Congress, 1992), 262.
2. Congressional Research Service (CRS), T. Masse, ed., *Homeland Security Intelligence: Perceptions, Statutory Definitions, and Approaches* (Washington, DC: Library of Congress, 2006), 2, http://www.fas.org/sgp/crs/intel/RL33616.pdf.
3. Congressional Research Service (CRS), R. A. Best, Jr. ed., *Intelligence Issues for Congress* (Washington, DC: Library of Congress, 2011), 5, http://www.fas.org/sgp/crs/intel/RL33539.pdf.
4. CRS, Homeland Security Intelligence, 5; See also C. G. Pernin, L. R. Moore, and K. Comanor, *The Knowledge Matrix Approach to Intelligence Fusion* (Rand Corporation, 2007).
5. See M. Chertoff, "Current and Planned Information Sharing Initiatives," Keynote presentation, *SEARCH Symposium on Justice and Public Safety Information Sharing*, Washington, DC, March 14, 2006.
6. M. Lowenthal, Transforming intelligence, *American Intelligence Journal*, 29, 2011: 10.
7. Homeland Security Act of 2002, P.L. 107–296, *U.S. Statutes at Large*, 116, 2002: 2135.
8. The Intelligence Reform and Terrorism Prevention Act of 2004 (IRTPA), P.L. 108–458, *U.S. Statutes at Large*, 118, 2004: 3638.
9. Federal Bureau of Investigation, "*What We Investigate*," http://www.fbi.gov/hq.htm.
10. U.S. Dept. of Homeland Security, *Fusion Centers and Joint Terrorism Task Forces*, at www.dhs.gov/files/programs/gc_1298911926746.shtm.
11. Congressional Research Service (CRS), R. A. Best, Jr. ed., *Intelligence Issues for Congress* (Washington, DC: Library of Congress, 2011), 20, http://www.fas.org/sgp/crs/intel/RL33539.pdf.
12. See Office of the Director of National Intelligence, *ODNI Fact Sheet*, October 2011, http://www.dni.gov/content/ODNI%20Fact%20Sheet_2011.pdf.
13. ODNI, Letter of Dennis C. Blair to employees, January 30, 2009, http://www.dni.gov/20090130_letter.pdf; accessed March 11, 2009.

14. Congressional Research Service (CRS), R. A. Best, Jr. ed., *The National Counterterrorism Center (NCTC)-Responsibilities and Potential Congressional Concerns* (Washington, DC: Library of Congress, 2011), 8–9, http://www.fas.org/sgp/crs/intel/R41022.pdf.
15. Congressional Research Service (CRS), R. A. Best, Jr. ed., *The National Counterterrorism Center (NCTC)—Responsibilities and Potential Congressional Concerns* (Washington, DC: Library of Congress, 2011), 9, http://www.fas.org/sgp/crs/intel/R41022.pdf.
16. Congressional Research Service (CRS), R. A. Best, Jr. ed., *The National Counterterrorism Center (NCTC)-Responsibilities and Potential Congressional Concerns* (Washington, DC: Library of Congress, 2011), 10, http://www.fas.org/sgp/crs/intel/R41022.pdf.
17. See Office of the National Counterintelligence Executive, The National Counterintelligence Strategy of the United States, 2009.
18. Finding out exactly who the enemy may be, is always a challenge, even in the case of Al Qaeda. See M. L. Hummel, Who is running Al Qaeda, *The Homeland Security Review*, 5, 2011: 1
19. Office of the National Counterintelligence Executive, *Top Counterintelligence Issues*, at www.ncix.gov/issues/ithreat/index.html.
20. See Office of Director of National Intelligence, *The National Intelligence Strategy*, October 2005, http://www.dni.gov/publications/NISOctober2005.pdf; accessed March 12, 2009.
21. The National Intelligence Council, *Global Trends 2025: A Transformed World*, November 2008, iv, www.dni.gov/nic/NIC_2025_project.html; accessed March 12, 2009.
22. R. C. Ackerman, Honing defense intelligence, *Signal*, October 2011: 47.

Chapter 9

Border Security, U.S. Citizenship, and Immigration Services

Objectives

1. To identify the various government agencies and their offices that are responsible for securing America's borders.
2. To outline the history of what is now Customs and Border Protection (CBP).
3. To explain the various programs of CBP for securing our borders from the illegal entry of immigrants.
4. To summarize the programs that CBP has initiated to facilitate the efficient processing and securing of cargo in ports across the globe.
5. To outline the history of what is now Citizenship and Immigration Service.
6. To summarize the various policies and law that has been enacted relative to immigration since the 1920s.
7. To explain the mission, policies, and procedures of Citizenship and Immigration Services as they relate to illegal immigration and terrorism.
8. To summarize the programs that Citizenship and Immigration Service has developed in response to the threat of terrorism.

FIGURE 9.1 A portal observation tower that is gaining popularity on the border.

9.1 Introduction

The task of protecting the nation's borders constitutes a major core competency for those involved in homeland security. It is an astounding responsibility with coverage areas that are almost impossible to compute. The sheer size of American geography makes the task overwhelming, though with increasing usage of technology and aircraft tools, our borders are dramatically improving (Figure 9.1).

9.2 U.S. Customs and Border Protection

Since 1924, a Border Patrol office has been responsible for making our territorial lines secure, but much has changed since the early days of border protection. In the 1980s, Americans became very familiar with the wave after wave of illegal immigrants coming across the porous lines of defense. Millions of Mexican and Third World immigrants trekked across without much resistance.

In recent years, the Border Patrol has become correctly occupied with another type of immigrant, one of the terrorist sort. The Border Patrol, as a result of the events of 9/11, was merged into the Department of Homeland Security and then further aligned with its historic partner—Customs. Customs has an even longer history than the Border Patrol. Originally established as a revenue collector source with the founding of the United States in

1776, Customs evolved into much more than the revenue machine it continues to be today. Customs has primary oversight on questions of cargo, duties, and revenue enforcement; trade and environmental law questions; imports and exports; and cargo and port issues. The range and breadth of responsibilities simply impresses. In 2007, by way of example, CBP encountered:

- 1.13 million passengers and pedestrians, including 653,000 aliens
- 70,200 truck, rail, and sea containers
- 251,000 incoming international air passengers
- 74,100 passengers/crew arriving by ship
- 304,000 incoming privately owned vehicles
- 82,800 shipments of goods approved for entry
- $88.3 million in fees, duties, and tariffs

Today, DHS delegates the integrity of our land border to a newly formed entity within DHS—the U.S. CBP program. CBP is responsible for guarding 7,000 miles of land border the United States shares with Canada and Mexico and 2,000 miles of coastal waters surrounding the Florida peninsula and the coast of Southern California. The agency also protects 95,000 miles of maritime border in partnership with the U.S. Coast Guard (Figure 9.2).

The structure of the CBP can be seen in Figure 9.3.

The various departments of the CBP manifest the overall mission of the agency—to approach homeland security from two distinct directions. In

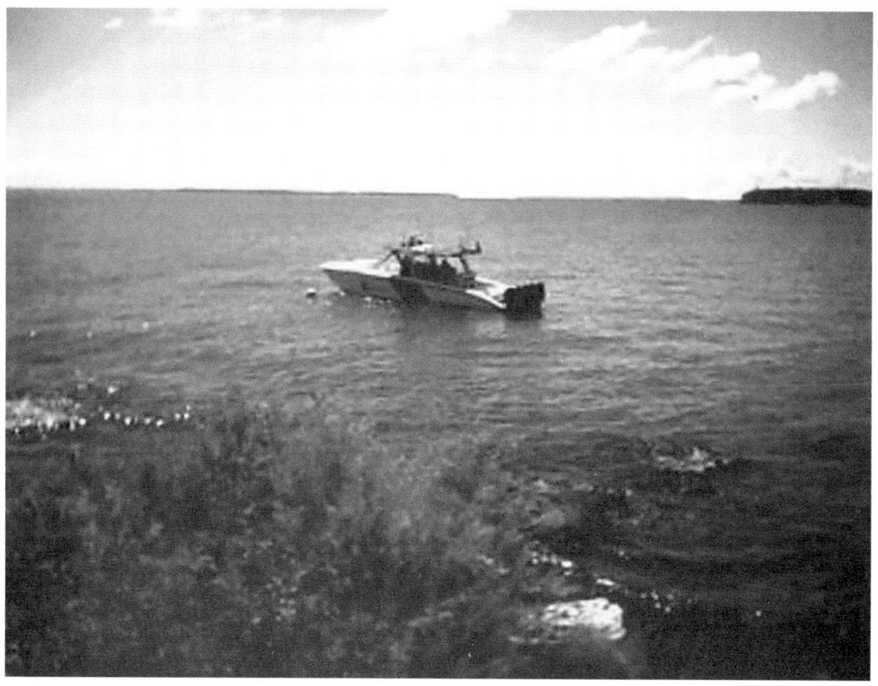

FIGURE 9.2 The U.S. Coast Guard on border patrol.

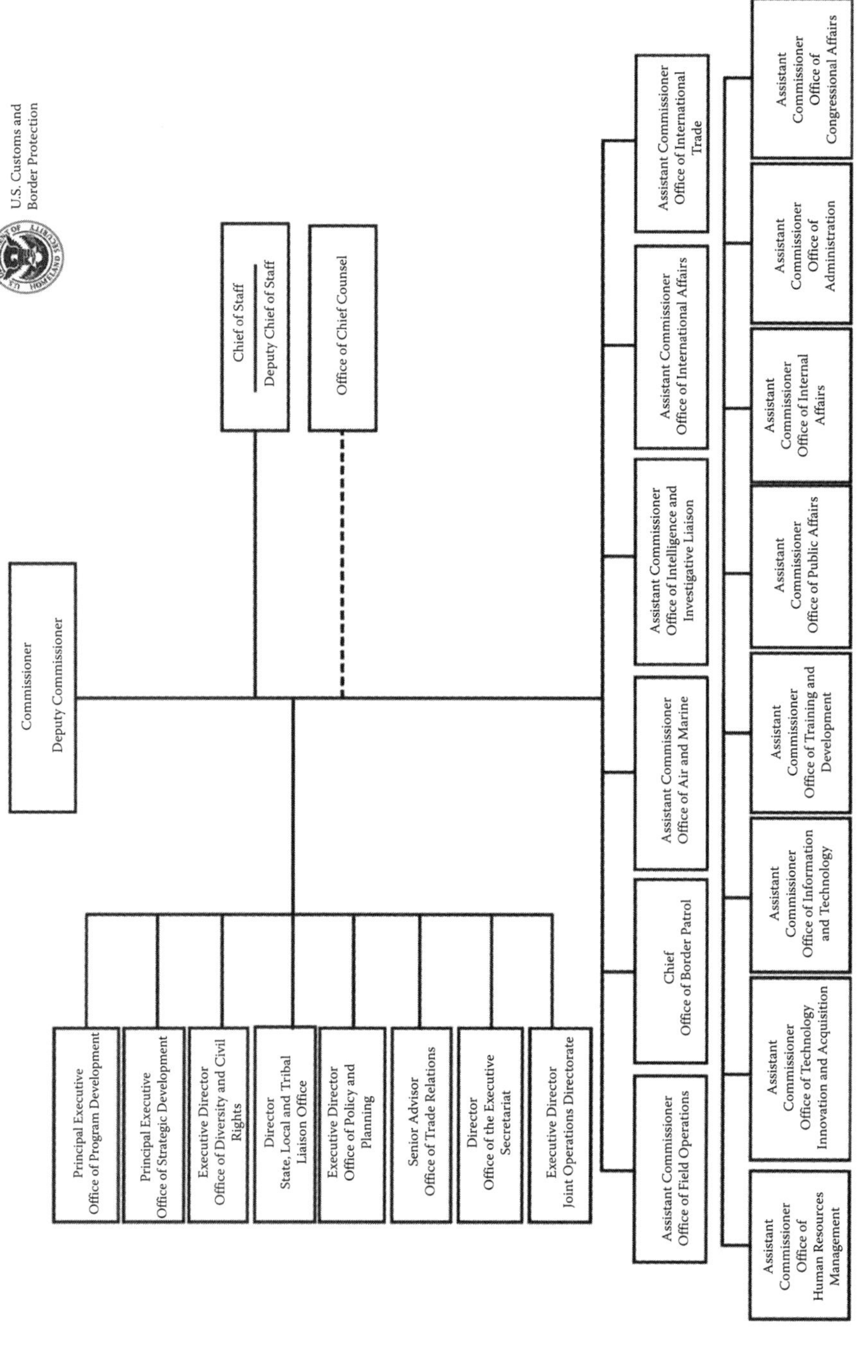

FIGURE 9.3 U.S. CBP organization chart.

the first instance, the CBP concerns itself with the threat of terrorism and the paths of entry the terrorist may follow into the American landscape, as well as the influx of illegal immigration. In the second instance, the CBP, due to its responsibility for cargo and port, commerce and revenue collection, constantly concerns itself with the intricacies of travel and trade. The agency knows its police role keenly and, at the same time, realizes that it plays a critical role in the movement of goods and services. A closer look at these two missions of the CBP follows.

9.2.1 Border Protection

With nearly 7,000 miles of American border the CBP has a serious problem when it comes to ensuring the integrity of our borders. Few issues rile up public debate more than the growing issue of illegal aliens crossing into American territory, even though the illegals seeking work and a better life are not the stuff of Al Qaeda. Terrorism cannot be held to be a primary motivation for the illegal, yet one fully comprehends that illegal border crossing is a more likely means of entry for the terrorist. Terrorists are now less likely to use commercial aircraft as was done during 9/11. Hence, it is a fact that CBP must concern itself with border protection more than it has historically done. Indeed, since 2004, the CBP has reoriented its mission in radical ways, and produced some very radical results. For 2010 alone, the CBP list of activities and results filled a large catalog:

Fiscal Year 2010 Statistical Highlights

- Ports of entry: 331
- Border Patrol sectors: 20 (with 139 Border Patrol stations nationwide and 35 permanent checkpoints)
- Air units: 46 (1 training location and 3 radar/communications locations)
- Marine units: 71 (2 training locations and 1 maintenance location)
- Trade entries processed: 28 million
- Total revenue collected: $32 billion (includes custodial and entity revenue)
- Illegal narcotics seized: 2.7 million pounds (represents narcotics held by CBP until disposal or destruction) (CBP's Financial Statements Note 8 reports all seized illegal drugs, including steroids, and in kilograms instead of pounds.)
- Illegal alien apprehensions between the ports of entry: 463,382
- Inadmissible aliens interdicted at the ports of entry: 227,061
- Pedestrians and passengers processed: 352 million
- Conveyances processed: over 105 million
- Aircraft passengers processed: over 90 million

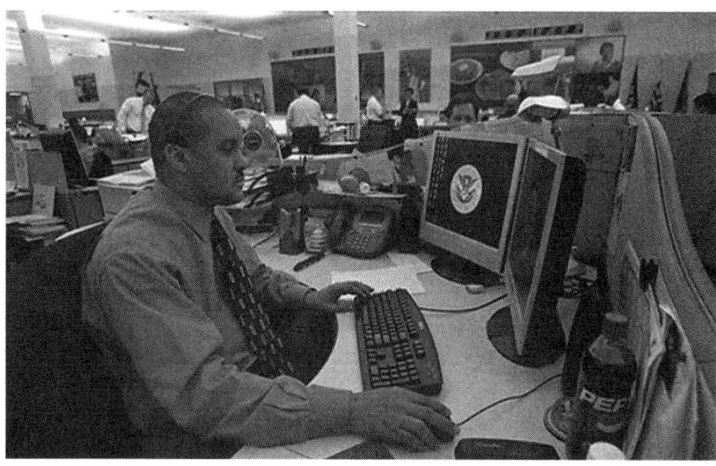

FIGURE 9.4 CBP's National Targeting Center.

- Prohibited plant and animal materials seized at the ports of entry: 1,707,876
- Agricultural plant and pest intercepted at the ports of entry: 196,815[1]

The CBP represents the best in adaptation and operational flexibility in government service. At every level of its operation the CBP has targeted its attention on the border while simultaneously honing in on the terrorist. The CBP established the National Targeting Center (NTC) as the centralized coordination point for all of CBP's antiterrorism efforts (Figure 9.4).

NTC also coordinates with other federal agencies, such as the U.S. Coast Guard, Federal Air Marshals, Federal Bureau of Investigation, Transportation Security Administration, and Departments of Energy and Agriculture.

Despite all these advances, the CBP cannot forget its fundamental mission of securing the border—in both a physical and an intelligence sense.[2] At other sections within this chapter, programs of border protection are featured. The more prominent initiatives of the CBP will be briefly covered.

9.2.1.1 Secure Border Initiative

The Secure Border Initiative (SBI) is a comprehensive multiyear plan to secure America's borders and reduce illegal migration. When first announced in 2005, SBI was thought to be only a few years away from full implementation.[3] The goals of SBI include, but are not limited to:

- More agents to patrol our borders, secure our ports of entry, and enforce immigration laws
- Expanded detention and removal capabilities to eliminate "catch and release"
- A comprehensive and systemic upgrading of the technology used in controlling the border, including increased manned aerial assets,

FIGURE 9.5 Predator B unmanned aerial vehicle (UAV).

expanded use of unmanned aerial vehicles (UAVs) (Figure 9.5), and next-generation detection technology

- Increased investment in infrastructure improvements at the border—providing additional physical security to sharply reduce illegal border crossings
- Increased interior enforcement of our immigration laws—including more robust worksite enforcement

As the last few years have shown, these dynamic ambitions were at best naive, especially when the overall issue of immigration itself has yet to be fully tackled for "SBI was mean to be the enforcement component to some sort of substantive immigration reform, which has yet to take place."[4] The SBI is driven by various interests: first, the very real danger of illegal entry by terrorists, and second, the increase in illegal immigrants, the latter of which results in significant social impacts, including strains on health, education, and other systems.

Illegal immigration represents a significant challenge for law enforcement too. To put the issue into perspective, the Pew Hispanic Center estimated that the number of illegal immigrants in the United States in 2011 was 11.5 million individuals. According to DHS, the illegal immigration population grew by 27% from 2000 to 2009. SBI seeks to minimize illegal immigration by new initiatives and technology.[5] The use of surveillance and remote equipment has been greatly enhanced over the last 5 years (Figure 9.6).

The entire border infrastructure is under upgrade, with existing facilities being renovated and fence and border barriers constantly under construction or repair across the continental United States. But the results, the General Accounting Office reports, are only partially successful.[6] The Southwest

FIGURE 9.6 Border security surveillance cameras.

region of the United States has long been in dire need of perimeter and barrier protection. More than 670 miles of new fence has been installed and a wide array of natural barriers employed to halt the onslaught of illegal immigrants entering the country. While physical fencing is still heavily relied upon, the nature of barriers continues to evolve. Aside from fence, the CBP uses:

- Vehicle bollards similar to those found around federal buildings
- "Post on rail" steel set in concrete with a mesh option
- Steel picket-style fence set in concrete
- Concrete jersey walls with steel mesh
- Normandy vehicle fence consisting of steel beams to thwart vehicular attacks (Figure 9.7)

Internet Resource: To find out more on the Southwest Border Fence, visit http://www.dhs.gov/xprevprot/programs/gc_1207842692831.shtm.

Border protection also employs natural barriers such as rivers, streams, ravines, mountains, cliffs, and other natural artifices to deliver security. Rivers make exceptional barriers, though illegal aliens have long mastered the art of crossing them.

Aside from physical fencing, border protection now relies upon the virtual world of fence and barrier. With the rise of technology and the sophistication of surveillance equipment, it is now possible to detect a border crossing and then detach border units within seconds even in the absence of physical fencing. The use of canines has significantly increased as well and with particular success in matters of drug interdiction.[7] The rise in personnel at the border has been astronomical in the last decade (Figures 9.8 and 9.9).

FIGURE 9.7 Higher Normandy fencing keeps out intruders.

Since 2004, the amount of Border Patrol officers has risen 85% with nearly 20,000 officers on the ground. See Figure 9.10 for a graphical representation.

Despite this dramatic investment, any plan of securing our border must consider practices and policies above and beyond traditional law enforcement. It has been the historic mission of the Border Patrol to identify, detect, and detain illegal immigrants. Accepting this as a continuing responsibility of any plan of homeland security is not debatable. However, change and innovation need to take the forefront in the homeland defense, and law enforcement alone will not be able to carry out this basic task. Congress and DHS fully understood that law enforcement, in an exclusive sense, would

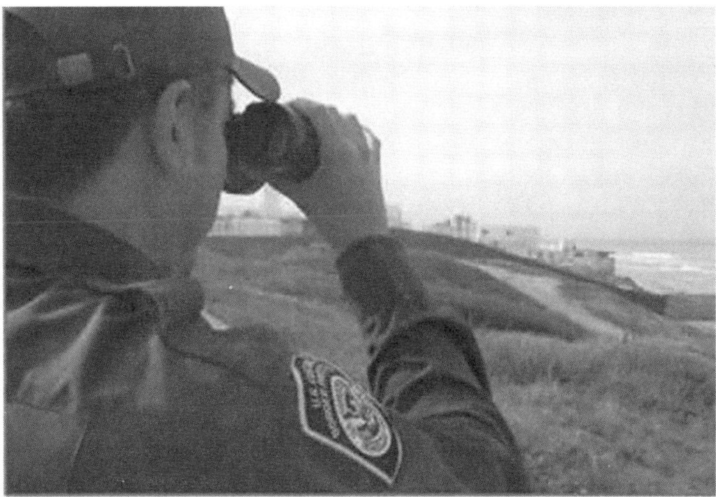

FIGURE 9.8 Customs and border protection agent searching shore near San Diego.

FIGURE 9.9 CBP officer monitoring surveillance cameras.

be incapable of securing our borders. Hence, with the merger of Customs and Border, and with the decision to integrate these functions into the Department of Homeland Security, CBP looks at the border in an eclectic way—far beyond a traditional policing function.

CBP developed the SBInet program, which pulls in and melds all aspects of the border function and incorporates the best of what each agency has to offer in border protection and integrates technology into the mix of service. SBInet integrates multiple state-of-the-art systems and traditional security infrastructure into a single division of CBP. The SBInet unified border control strategy encompasses both the northern and southern land borders, including the Great Lakes, and the interdiction of cross-border violations between the ports and at the official Ports of Entry (POEs). This strategy will

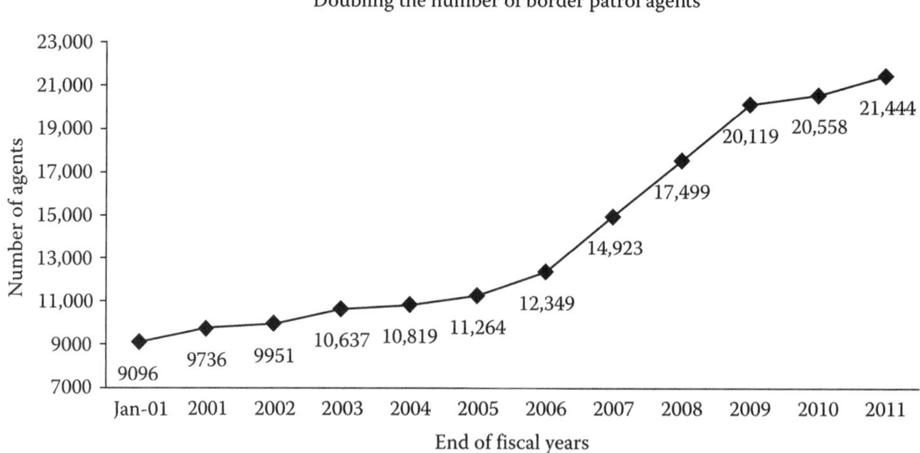

FIGURE 9.10 Doubling the number of Border Patrol agents was accomplished by the end of FY 2009.

funnel traffic to the United States through POEs where DHS has a greater level of control. The underlying goals of SBInet are:

- Detect entries when they occur
- Identify what the entry is
- Classify its level of threat (who they are, what they are doing, how many, etc.)
- Effectively and efficiently respond to the entry and bring the situation to the appropriate law enforcement resolution

The SBInet program correctly relies on private industry and the entrepreneur for its necessary equipment, and thus awards competitively based contracts to providers of relevant hardware and software. For example, the Boeing Company was awarded a $64 million contract to develop software capable of unified and regular use at all CBP stations and locations. This same mentality will be expected in all aspects of border protection—that of universal usage over singular locale. Therefore, border protection expects that its remote towers will be wired identically for use across the entire system, including communication systems and field transmitters. SBInet delivers uniformity in practice, procedure, and hardware for those entrusted with border protection. This penchant for sameness is sometimes referred to as the Common Operating Picture (COP). In sum, SBInet's overall goals seek uniform practices in border security and utilize the private sector in a competitive sense for the development of equipment and tactics. Despite these novel and most noble ambitions, the results of SBInet have been mixed and labeled by the Immigration Policy Council as "Poor Results at a High Cost."[8] Todd Steinmetz concludes that SBInet suffers from "critical deficiencies."[9]

Internet Resource: For a PowerPoint presentation on how borders are secured, see http://www.cbp.gov/xp/cgov/about/mission/.

Mission confusion further lends its heavy hand to the SBI for it is one thing to plan for the illegal alien and quite another to devise policy for the terrorist. Yet border protection must constantly and carefully weigh the threat of the terrorist before issuing any policy. "Terrorists also know that large segments of both the northern and southern border remain relatively unsecured."[10] Hence every CBP policy need anticipate these dual threats when issuing policy.

9.2.1.2 CBP Air and Marine

While the CBP expends most of its energies on illegal immigrants coming into America, its mission now rightfully includes the identification, detection, and apprehension of the terrorist, as well as the interdiction of contraband. With the merger of Customs into DHS, its historic mission has shifted to other protection efforts. Realizing this, the CBP developed an Air and Marine (A&M)-based program. The mission of Air and Marine is to:

- Provide support to CBP's antiterrorism mission at U.S. borders, including air-to-ground interception of people and contraband illegally crossing land borders, air-to-air interception of aircraft, and air-to-water interception of transportation vessels
- Provide support for CBP's traditional work, such as border interceptions unrelated to terrorism and other DHS missions as well
- Conduct air operations in support of other federal, state, and local needs, such as disaster relief

With nearly 200 boat and support vessels, the CBP is now a major player relative to marine security seeking out illegals and potential terrorists at sea[11] (Figure 9.11).

The CBP has developed a law enforcement position, the marine interdiction agent, who is on the front line in the fight against terrorism.

Internet Resource: To see a job announcement for the marine interdiction agent, visit http://www.usajobs.org/jobs/72914194/CBP%20Marine%20Interdiction%20Agent.htm.

In the air, the CBP is just as impressive. To accomplish this mission, CBP A&M utilizes more than 700 pilots and 267 aircraft, including the use of unmanned aircraft systems (UASs). The use of unmanned drones is a critical tool in the fight against terrorism, the interception of drugs, and other illegal activity. The range and breadth of aircraft indicates the seriousness

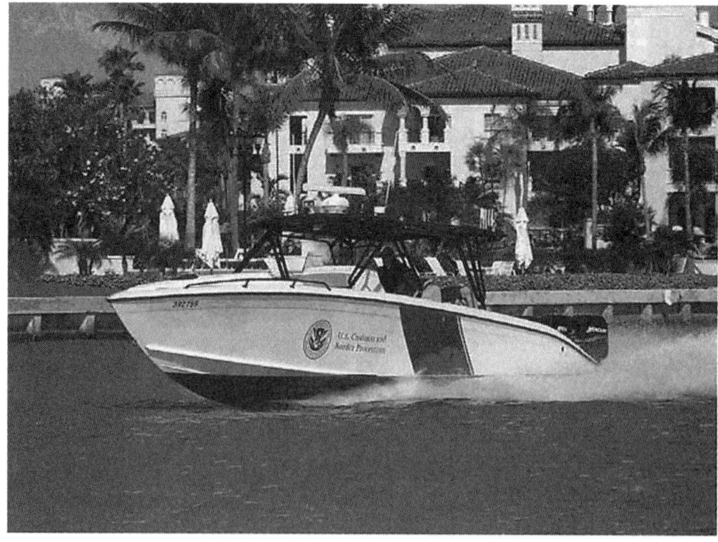

FIGURE 9.11 U.S. Customs and Border Protection patrol boat.

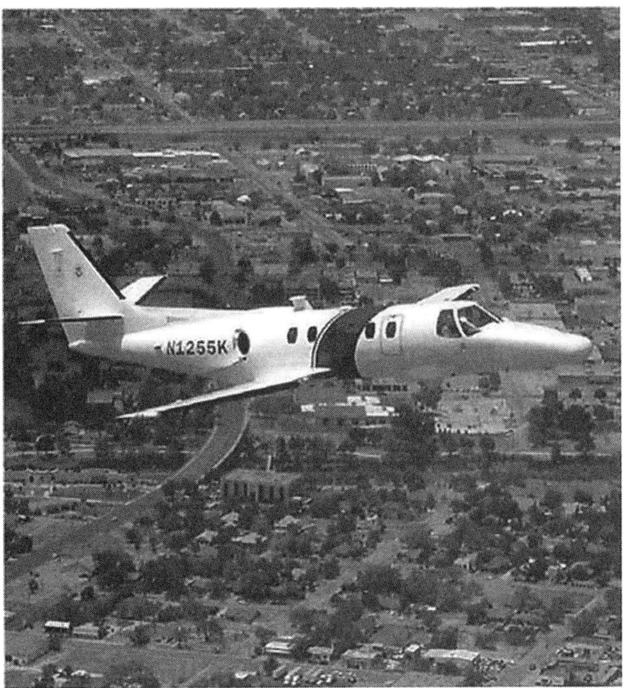

FIGURE 9.12 U.S. Customs and Border Protection patrol plane.

of the CBP purpose in the air. From small-propeller to Sikorsky helicopters, the CBP marshals extraordinary hardware to carry out its mission.

Internet Resource: For an exceptional presentation on the UAS and other drones, see http://nemo.cbp.gov/opa/videos/2010/uas_texas.wmv.

The CBP Air and Marine (A&M) program greatly increases the productivity and coverage area involved in its mission (Figure 9.12).

The A&M program delivers many services, including:

- Aids and implements CBP antiterrorism programs
- Utilizes both manned and unmanned aircraft
- Delivers advanced technology by detection systems
- Provides unrivaled capacity to interdict aircraft, boats, vehicles and personnel
- Fosters collaborative relationships with law enforcement and the military
- Provides secure airspace

9.2.2 CBP and the Facilitation of Trade and Commerce

Along with its partners in the Coast Guard, other military arms, and state and federal law enforcement, the CBP assumes essential control and

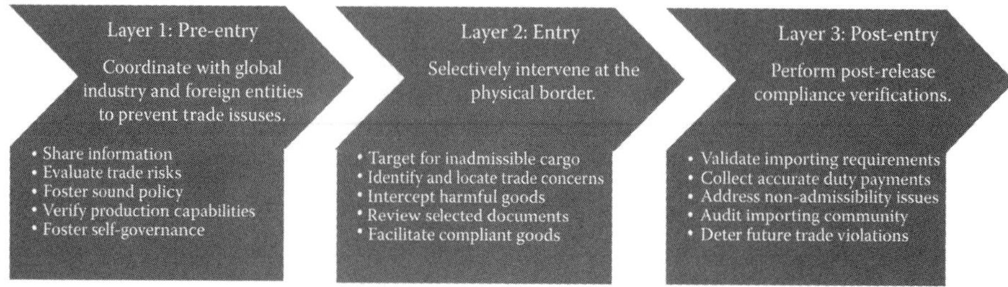

FIGURE 9.13 CBP trade strategy.

oversight of trade into the American economy—across land, sea, and air. It is not always an easy task for the policymaker must balance safety and security with the swift and efficient movement of goods. "This becomes a growing challenge in a global economy where consumers, just-in-time processes, and integrated supply chains demand reliability, accuracy and speed."[12]

The goals of the CBP in matters of Trade Policy are essential to the lifeblood of the American economy.

- Goal 1: Facilitate legitimate trade into the United States and ensure compliance
- Goal 2: Enforce U.S. Trade laws and collect accurate revenue
- Goal 3: Advance national and economic security
- Goal 4: Intensify modernization of CBP's trade processes

The CBP methodology on trade and commerce weighs impacts at three stages or layers: pre-entry, entry, and post-entry. The layered ideal hopes and seeks to mitigate and, more importantly, to have sufficient time to communicate and work cooperatively with aligned defenders of the homeland. See Figure 9.13.[13]

9.2.2.1 Cargo

CBP tracks cargo at various points of entry in the United States. The rules and protocols are quite legalistic, and the agency realizes that the layers of bureaucratic requirements do impact the flow of goods and services on the world market. In a global economy, it is critical that goods and services move expeditiously while at the same time safely and securely. The CBP, in conjunction with DHS and other agencies, has implemented some innovative programs relative to cargo. A sketch of the more notable programs follows.

9.2.2.1.1 Secure Freight Initiative The Secure Freight Initiative (SFI) evaluates capabilities for large-scale radiation scanning of cargo before it ever reaches the United States. Presently, the SFI program is operating at less than a dozen foreign ports with a goal to fully scan all inbound cargo. The stress

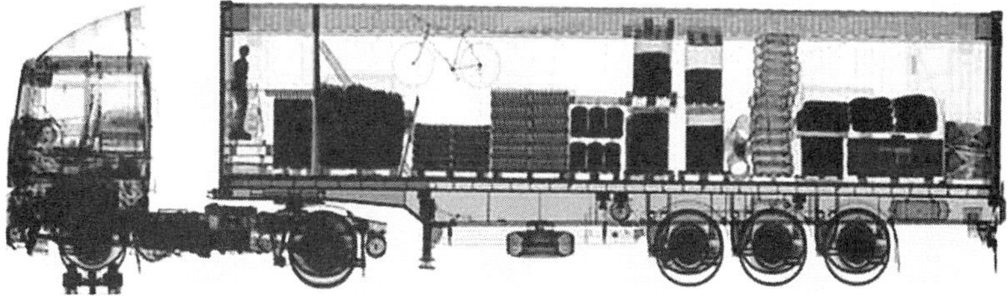

FIGURE 9.14 X-ray image at SFI location.

of SFI is the nuclear and radiological material that might be employed as WMD. Using both active and passive detection systems, SFI scans cargo in large quantities. Passive radiation detection technology used includes radiation portal monitors. As the cargo and its hold pass through the system, the equipment generates various images by spectrograph, bar graph, infrared or thermograph reading, as well as traditional x-ray imagery. Radiography uses x-rays or gamma rays to penetrate a container (Figure 9.14).

SFI tends to favor what are known as megaports, that is, locations with huge volumes of cargo. This first phase of the Secure Freight Initiative partners with Pakistan, Honduras, the United Kingdom, Oman, Singapore, and Korea, and it will provide these governments with a greater window into potentially dangerous shipments moving across their territory. In Port Qasim, Puerto Cortes, and Southampton, the deployed scanning equipment will capture data on all containers bound to the United States, fulfilling the pilot requirements set out by Congress in the SAFE Ports Act[14] (Figure 9.15).

The SFI program operates in selected foreign ports to scan outgoing cargo before leaving port. At the same time, Secure Freight integrates new data into U.S. government screening and targeting systems, including the proposed new U.S. CBP security filing, as well as the creation of a proposed private sector operated Global Trade Exchange (GTX). The Secure Freight Initiative is testing the feasibility of scanning 100% of U.S.-bound cargo.

FIGURE 9.15 SFI scan.

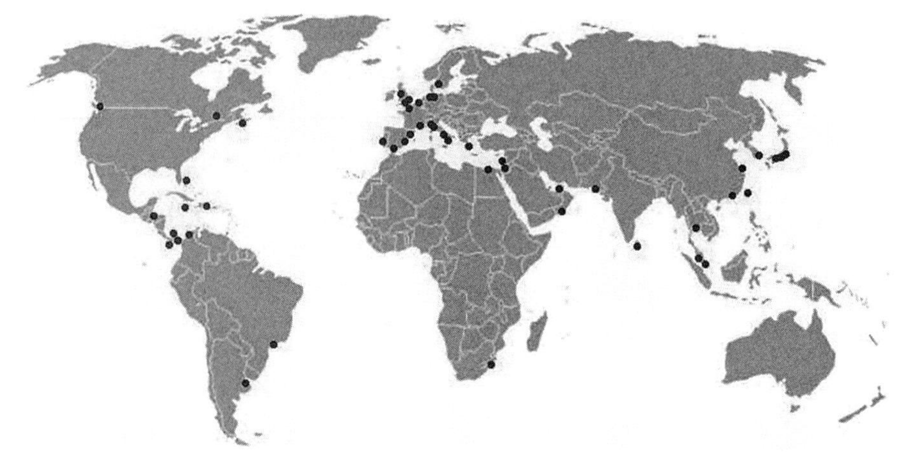

FIGURE 9.16 CSI partner ports.

9.2.2.1.2 Container Security Initiative Beginning in January 2002, CBP proposed the Container Security Initiative (CSI). CSI inspects cargo units rather than the entire freight load and pushes U.S. port security back into the supply chain at its port of origin. CSI pre-screens and evaluates containers before they are shipped. Under the CSI program, high-risk containers receive security inspections by both x-ray and radiation scan. Containers, before being loaded on board vessels destined for the United States, are inspected at CSI ports. Upon arrival, these same containers are exempt from further inspection, and as a result, goods move through our port system with greater efficiency. CSI is operational in 58 foreign ports, as shown in Figure 9.16.

A total of 35 customs administrations from other jurisdictions have committed to join the CSI program.

CSI now covers 86% of all maritime containerized cargo destined to the United States. CSI ports now include:

In the Americas:
Montreal, Vancouver, and Halifax, Canada
Santos, Brazil
Buenos Aires, Argentina
Puerto Cortes, Honduras
Caucedo, Dominican Republic
Kingston, Jamaica
Freeport, The Bahamas
Balboa, Colon, and Manzanillo, Panama
Cartagena, Colombia

In Europe:
Rotterdam, The Netherlands

Bremerhaven and Hamburg, Germany
Antwerp and Zeebrugge, Belgium
Le Havre and Marseille, France
Gothenburg, Sweden
La Spezia, Genoa, Naples, Gioia Tauro, and Livorno, Italy
Felixstowe, Liverpool, Thamesport, Tilbury, and Southampton, United Kingdom
Piraeus, Greece
Algeciras, Barcelona, and Valencia, Spain
Lisbon, Portugal

In Asia and the Middle East:
Singapore
Yokohama, Tokyo, Nagoya, and Kobe, Japan
Hong Kong
Busan (Pusan), South Korea
Port Klang and Tanjung Pelepas, Malaysia
Laem Chabang, Thailand
Dubai, United Arab Emirates (UAE)
Shenzhen and Shanghai, China
Kaohsiung and Chi-Lung, Taiwan
Colombo, Sri Lanka
Port Salalah, Oman
Port Qasim, Pakistan
Ashdod and Haifa, Israel
Alexandria, Egypt

In Africa:
Durban, South Africa

9.2.2.1.3 Customs Trade Partnership against Terrorism (C-TPAT) CBP realizes the essential role that private cargo carriers play in the safety and security of goods flowing through ports and harbors. C-TPAT is a voluntary government-business initiative that works closely with the prime players in international cargo, namely, importers, carriers, consolidators, licensed customs brokers, and manufacturers. C-TPAT asks business to ensure the integrity of their security practices and communicate and verify the security guidelines of their business partners within the supply chain. The goals of C-TPAT are to:

- Ensure that C-TPAT partners improve the security of their supply chains pursuant to C-TPAT security criteria
- Provide incentives and benefits to include expedited processing of C-TPAT shipments to C-TPAT partners

- Internationalize the core principles of C-TPAT through cooperation and coordination with the international community
- Support other CBP security and facilitation initiatives
- Improve administration of the C-TPAT program

The general theme of C-TPAT is to promote efficiency in the cargo processes and to provide a forum for private—public cooperation in matters of cargo movement. The benefits of C-TPAT are numerous and streamline various inspection processes for cargo and container carriers:

- A reduced number of inspections and reduced border wait times.
- A C-TPAT supply chain specialist to serve as the CBP liaison for validations, security issues, procedural updates, communication, and training.
- Access to the C-TPAT members through the Status Verification Interface.
- Self-policing and self-monitoring of security activities.
- In the Automated Commercial System (ACS), C-TPAT-certified importers receive a reduced selection rate for compliance measurement examinations and exclusion from certain trade-related local and national criteria.
- C-TPAT-certified importers receive targeting benefits by receiving a credit via the CBP targeting system.
- Certified C-TPAT importers are eligible for access to the FAST lanes on the Canadian and Mexican borders.
- Certified C-TPAT importers are eligible for the Office of Strategic Trade's (OST) Importer Self-Assessment Program (ISA) and have been given priority access to participate in the Automated Commercial Environment (ACE).
- C-TPAT-certified highway carriers, on the Canadian and Mexican borders, benefit from their access to the expedited cargo processing at designated FAST lanes. These carriers are eligible to receive more favorable mitigation relief from monetary penalties.
- C-TPAT-certified Mexican manufacturers benefit from their access to the expedited cargo processing at the designated FAST lanes.
- All certified C-TPAT companies are eligible to attend CBP-sponsored C-TPAT supply chain security training seminars.

Internet Resource: For an application regarding C-TPAT membership, see https://ctpat.cbp.dhs.gov/CompanyProfile.aspx.

9.2.2.1.4 Automated Commercial Environment Modernizing the free flow of goods takes much more than mere personnel and novel policies. The sheer

FIGURE 9.17 Automated Commercial Environment program logo.

volume of material flowing in and out of the global marketplace demands the highest systems of technology. The CBP is upgrading and electronically manifesting the flow of goods through its Automated Commercial Environment (ACE) program. ACE is part of a multiyear CBP modernization effort that is not yet fully operational and is being deployed in phases (Figure 9.17).

The Automated Commercial Environment seeks to:

- Allow trade participants access to and management of their trade information via reports
- Expedite legitimate trade by providing CBP with tools to efficiently process imports/exports and move goods quickly across the border
- Improve communication, collaboration, and compliance efforts between CBP and the trade community
- Facilitate efficient collection, processing, and analysis of commercial import and export data
- Provide an information-sharing platform for trade data throughout government agencies

For example, in trucking, relative to cargo and container, the Automated Commercial Environment electronic truck manifest capabilities are now available at all 99 U.S. land border ports of entry. Truckers electronically author E-manifests, which provide CBP with cargo information, such as crew, conveyance, equipment as applicable, and shipment details. In ports of entry, there are now mechanisms to file reports and paperwork electronically. As of late 2007, the ACE program was making significant inroads into the cargo and container fabric of America with mandatory e-manifests, the processing of 200,000 trucks per week, faster processing times for e-manifests, the establishment of 14,000 ACE secure data portal accounts, and the collection of nearly 38% of dues and fees computed through electronic periodic reports.

The benefits to the ACE program are well documented and include:

- Financial savings with the periodic monthly payment capability
- Reduced processing time at the border with features like electronic truck manifest
- Ability to view shipment status and store data via the ACE secure data portal
- Capabilities to develop over 100 customized reports

Internet Exercise: The ACE program has many features and initiatives. Visit http://www.cbp.gov/xp/cgov/trade/automated/modernization/ace and click to the ACE Resource Center.

9.3 U.S. Citizenship and Immigration Services

Immigration has played an important role in the American experience. Immigrants have a natural home in the newly developed country pre- and post-Revolutionary War. To encourage economic development, immigration was widely supported. In its earliest days, the question of immigration was left to the states. Major ports such as New York and Philadelphia became entry points long before the federal involvement. In time, by 1875, the Supreme Court would rule that immigration is a federal responsibility. By 1891, Congress had created the Immigration Service, which foretold and dealt with waves of immigrants during the Industrial Revolution.

From 1900 to 1920, nearly 24 million immigrants arrived during what is known as the "Great Wave" (Figure 9.18).

At first, immigration numbers were not limited, but eventually a quota system based on past U.S. Census figures was implemented. In 1924, Congress established the U.S. Border Patrol. For the next three to four decades, the waves of immigrants subsided, but by the 1960s Congress would have to deal with two new constituencies: refugees and transient agricultural workers. Congress passed the Refugee Act of 1980, which delineated U.S. policy on refugees.

Internet Resource: To see where and when the waves took place, see http://flowingdata.com/wp-content/uploads/2008/12/21.pdf.

In 1986, Congress passed the *Immigration Reform and Control Act (IRCA)*. This legislation had two major eligibility standards: amnesty and enforcement. IRCA provided amnesty to aliens who had completed one of two stipulations; they had resided continually in the United States since January 1982, or they had completed 90 days of agricultural work between May 1985 and May 1986. In 1996, Congress passed the *Illegal*

FIGURE 9.18 Ellis Island, New Jersey.

Immigrant Reform and Immigrant Responsibility Act (IIRIRA). During this same period various amnesties for illegal immigrants were promulgated. During this same period various amnesties for illegal immigrants were promulgated. In 1994, Section 245(i) amnesty was enacted, which pardoned 578,000 illegal aliens, who were each fined $1,000. This amnesty was later renewed in 1997 and again in 2000. The *Nicaraguan Adjustment and Central American Relief Act (NACARA)* was passed in 1997 and gave legal status to approximately 1 million illegal aliens, mostly from Central America, who had lived in the United States since 1995. In 1998, the *Haitian Refugee Immigration and Fairness Act (HRIFA)* passed after it was argued that excluding Haitians from NACARA was discriminatory. The most recent amnesty, passed in 2000, was the *Legal Immigration Family Equity Act (LIFE).*

The terrorist attacks on September 11, 2001, provoked a profound reexamination of immigration practices since the terrorists themselves were here as illegal parties. The attack exposed longstanding holes in our immigration system that included failures at visa processing, internal enforcement, and information sharing. Various commissions and other groups have issued reports and recommendations on how improvements might be forthcoming.

In December 2005, the House passed the *Border Protection, Anti-terrorism, and Illegal Immigration Control Act of 2005*, which focused on enforcement and on both the border and the interior. Attempts to pass recent legislation granting amnesty to illegals have been widely condemned by public opinion. Various efforts from 2006 to the present regarding immigration reform faltered.

Internet Exercise: Find out about the history of immigration in the PowerPoint program developed by the Library of Congress at http://memory.loc.gov/learn/features/immig/introduction.html.

While issues of immigration frequently touch the agencies such as Border Patrol and the Coast Guard, from the prism of law enforcement, there are other issues within the province of U.S. Citizenship and Immigration Services (USCIS). Once referred to as the Immigration and Naturalization Service (INS), the department was merged into DHS in 2002. The USCIS is the primary entity responsible for the administration of immigration status and claims, the adjudication of findings and appeals, and the promulgation of policies and practices concerning the agency. Functions of the agency include, but are not limited to:

- Adjudication of immigrant visa petitions
- Adjudication of naturalization petitions
- Adjudication of asylum and refugee applications
- Adjudications performed at the service centers
- All other adjudications performed by the INS

See Figure 9.19.

The agency is involved in a wide assortment of aligned activities relating to terrorism and potential harm to the United States and its citizens. By its very nature, USCIS has the capacity to be a barrier of entry or a point of forced departure for those intent on doing harm to the United States.

9.3.1 Project Shield America Initiative

Project Shield America seeks to prevent foreign adversaries, terrorists, and criminal networks from obtaining and trafficking in WMD (Figure 9.20).

The program seeks to thwart terrorist groups from obtaining sensitive information about American technologies, commodities, munitions, and firearms. Furthermore, Project Shield America traces financial transactions that violate U.S. sanctions or embargos. It also checks the propriety of exports to determine whether the goods shipped are legal and consistent with the laws of the United States. Most importantly, the Shield program focuses in on high-level technology that can be used against the United States in negative ways. The types of exported technology that would be subject to Project Shield's scrutiny would encompass:

- Modern manufacturing technology for the production of microelectronics, computers, digital electronic components, and signal processing systems.
- Technology necessary for the development of aircraft, missile, and other tactical weapon delivery systems.

Naturalization Self Test

To get the next set of 4 questions, click the Generate Questions button. When you are ready to review your answers, click the Review Answers button.

1. What are some of the basic beliefs of the Declaration of Independence?

○ Freedom of speech, freedom of religion, freedom of the press

○ That all men are created equal and have the right to life, liberty, and the pursuit of happiness

○ That there are three branches of government

○ That there should be checks and balances within the government

2. Who is Commander-in-Chief of the United States military?

○ The Secretary of State

○ The Secretary of Defense

○ The Vice President

○ The President

3. Where is the White House located?

○ Camp David

○ New York City

○ Virginia

○ Washington, DC

4. In what month is the new president inaugurated?

○ July

○ January

○ November

○ June

FIGURE 9.19 Naturalization self-test.

- All types of advanced signal and weapons detection, tracking, and monitoring systems.
- Technology and equipment used in the construction of nuclear weapons and materials.
- Biological, chemical warfare agents and precursors, and associated manufacturing equipment.

FIGURE 9.20 Project Shield America logo.

Project Shield America tackles its job in three fundamental ways:

- Inspection and interdiction—Working at ports especially, both USCIS and CBP monitor potential harms.
- Investigations and outreach—UCIS conducted wide-ranging criminal investigations dealing with illegal munitions. In addition, the program educates exporters and importers on legal compliance.
- International cooperation—The agency helps support investigations by foreign law enforcement into illegal weapons and technology trafficking.

Internet Exercise: Read about legal cases and prosecutions of violators caught because of Project Shield at http://www.ice.gov/news/library/fact-sheets/counter-proliferations.htm.

9.3.2 Fugitive Operations Program

On February 25, 2002, the National Fugitive Operations Program (NFOP) was officially established under the banner department of Immigration and Customs Enforcement (ICE). The primary mission of NFOP is to identify, locate, apprehend, process, and remove fugitive aliens from the United States, with the highest priority placed on those fugitives who have been convicted of crimes. Furthermore, NFOP's goal is to eliminate the

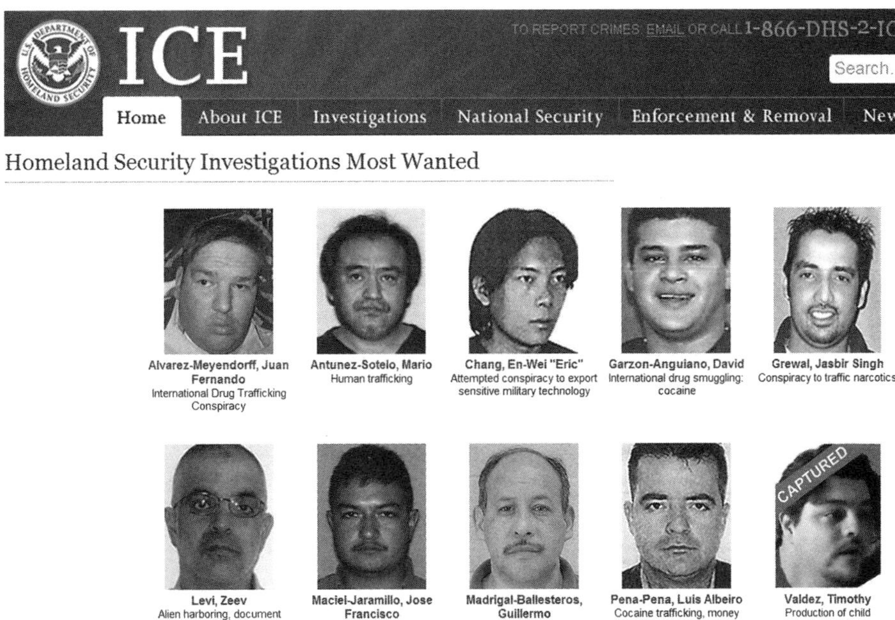

FIGURE 9.21 ICE most wanted Homeland Security fugitives.

backlog of fugitives and ensure that the number of aliens deported equals the number of final orders of removal issued by the immigration courts in any given year.

The NFOP fugitive operations teams strategically deployed around the country work solely on those cases identified as fugitives, and attempt to locate and apprehend those persons, who will ultimately be removed from the United States. The NFOP publishes a "most wanted" list of criminals, terrorists, and other unsavory characters. A current collection includes the individuals shown in Figure 9.21.

Internet Resource: For a current look at the ICE's list of foreign criminal aliens, see http://www.ice.gov/doclib/pi/investigations/wanted/mostwanted.pdf.

The NFOP training course is conducted at the ICE Academy located at the Federal Law Enforcement Training Center (FLETC). The training stresses utilization of the Internet, databases, and other sources of information to locate where a fugitive lives, visits, and works. NFOP teams are frequent participants in joint task forces at the state and local levels.

9.3.3 Cornerstone Initiative

Terrorist and other criminal organizations need cash and finance to support illegal operations. The Cornerstone Initiative detects and closes those means to exploit the financial sector. Some of the more common targets of enforcement are:

- Bulk cash smuggling
- Alternative financing mechanisms used to launder illicit proceeds
- Money service businesses, financial institutions, and international trade and transportation sectors
- Common highly profitable cross-border crimes such as commercial fraud, intellectual property rights (IPR) violations, immigration violations, identity and benefits fraud, contraband and alien smuggling, and human trafficking
- Trade-based money laundering (TBML) using the international trade system to disguise illicit proceed by altering customs and banking paperwork

The Cornerstone team looks for patterns and select indicators of behavior in the transfer of money and funds.[15] There are a host of red flags that indicate the money trail is out of mainstream financial practice. See Figure 9.22 for an example of some of the more common red flags.

Within the Cornerstone Initiative rests the National Bulk Cash Smuggling Center which works with diverse law enforcement agencies nationally and internationally in seeking to end the smuggle of large cash sums. Such sums are usually associated with drugs and other nefarious acts.

Internet Exercise: To learn about the complexities of this form of law enforcement visit the Center's FAQ at http://www.ice.gov/bulk-cash-smuggling-center/faq/.

9.3.4 Cyber Crimes Center

Created in 1997, the Cyber Crimes Center, known as the C3, brings a full range of ICE computer and forensic assets together in a single location to combat such Internet-related crimes as possession, manufacture, and distribution of child pornography; money laundering and illegal cyber banking; arms trafficking and illegal export of strategic/controlled commodities; drug trafficking; trafficking in stolen art and antiquities; and intellectual property rights violations. Cyber-crimes units are not exclusively the province of CBP but exist side by side in many federal and state agencies including the FBI and large metropolitan police departments.[16]

There are serious critics of the type of oversight and intervention evident in forensic computing and software. Civil libertarians constantly wail about privacy considerations and policymakers need always keep their practices in check in light of these considerations.[17]

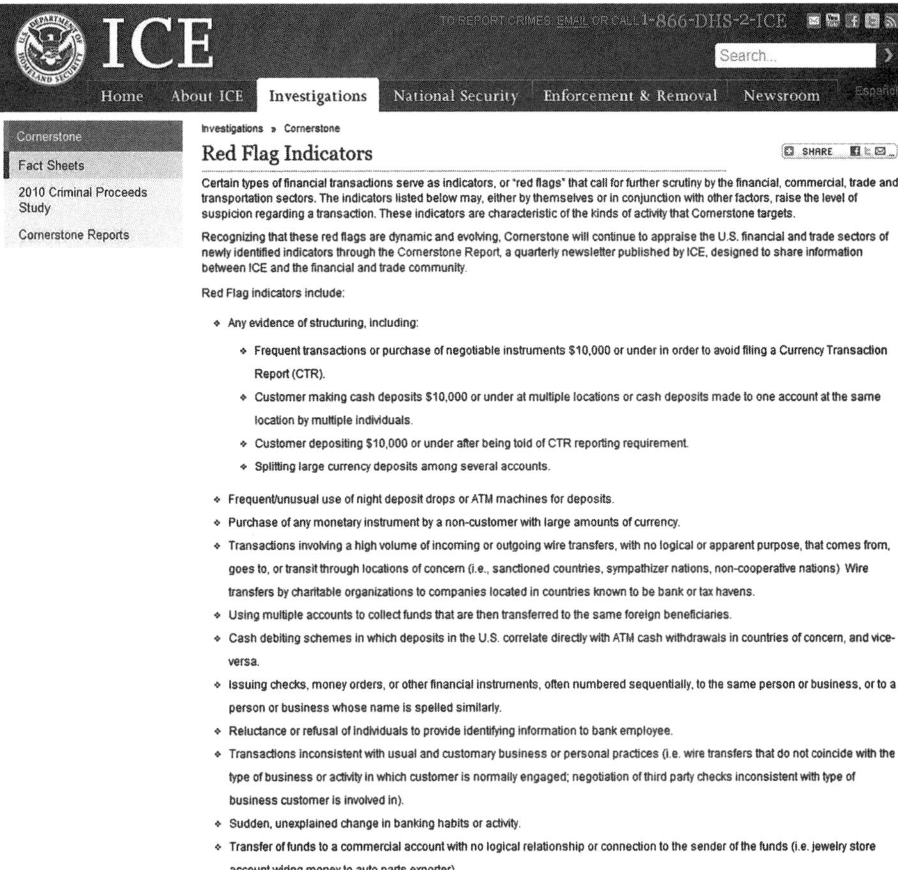
ICE

TO REPORT CRIMES: EMAIL OR CALL 1-866-DHS-2-ICE

Search...

Home | About ICE | Investigations | National Security | Enforcement & Removal | Newsroom | Español

Cornerstone
- Fact Sheets
- 2010 Criminal Proceeds Study
- Cornerstone Reports

Investigations » Cornerstone

Red Flag Indicators

SHARE

Certain types of financial transactions serve as indicators, or "red flags" that call for further scrutiny by the financial, commercial, trade and transportation sectors. The indicators listed below may, either by themselves or in conjunction with other factors, raise the level of suspicion regarding a transaction. These indicators are characteristic of the kinds of activity that Cornerstone targets.

Recognizing that these red flags are dynamic and evolving, Cornerstone will continue to appraise the U.S. financial and trade sectors of newly identified indicators through the Cornerstone Report, a quarterly newsletter published by ICE, designed to share information between ICE and the financial and trade community.

Red Flag indicators include:

- Any evidence of structuring, including:
  - Frequent transactions or purchase of negotiable instruments $10,000 or under in order to avoid filing a Currency Transaction Report (CTR).
  - Customer making cash deposits $10,000 or under at multiple locations or cash deposits made to one account at the same location by multiple individuals.
  - Customer depositing $10,000 or under after being told of CTR reporting requirement.
  - Splitting large currency deposits among several accounts.
- Frequent/unusual use of night deposit drops or ATM machines for deposits.
- Purchase of any monetary instrument by a non-customer with large amounts of currency.
- Transactions involving a high volume of incoming or outgoing wire transfers, with no logical or apparent purpose, that comes from, goes to, or transit through locations of concern (i.e., sanctioned countries, sympathizer nations, non-cooperative nations) Wire transfers by charitable organizations to companies located in countries known to be bank or tax havens.
- Using multiple accounts to collect funds that are then transferred to the same foreign beneficiaries.
- Cash debiting schemes in which deposits in the U.S. correlate directly with ATM cash withdrawals in countries of concern, and vice-versa.
- Issuing checks, money orders, or other financial instruments, often numbered sequentially, to the same person or business, or to a person or business whose name is spelled similarly.
- Reluctance or refusal of individuals to provide identifying information to bank employee.
- Transactions inconsistent with usual and customary business or personal practices (i.e. wire transfers that do not coincide with the type of business or activity in which customer is normally engaged; negotiation of third party checks inconsistent with type of business customer is involved in).
- Sudden, unexplained change in banking habits or activity.
- Transfer of funds to a commercial account with no logical relationship or connection to the sender of the funds (i.e. jewelry store account wiring money to auto parts exporter).

FIGURE 9.22 ICE red flag indicators.

Much of what the Cyber Crimes Center undertakes relates to child pornography. The scourge of predators and their tie to cyber pornography is amply documented. ICE'S Child Exploitation Unit tackles this difficult and emotionally wrenching job (Figure 9.22).

The Virtual Global Taskforce (VGT) is made up of law enforcement agencies from around the world working together to fight child abuse online. VGT aims to build an effective, international partnership of law enforcement agencies that helps to protect children from online child abuse. VGT strives to make the Internet a safer place, identify, locate, and help children at risk and hold perpetrators accountable.

The VGT comprises the Australian High Tech Crime Centre, the Child Exploitation and Online Protection Centre in the United Kingdom, the Royal Canadian Mounted Police, the U.S. Department of Homeland Security, Italian Postal and Communication Police Service, and Interpol.

ICE'S Operation Predator program, in collaboration with national and international partners, targets the worst of the worst in the dark world of child victimization. In addition, ICE maintains a National Child Victim Identification System.

Internet Exercise: ICE relies heavily on the information relayed by the general public. The agency has created a Tipline system. See its contents at http://www.ice.gov/exec/forms/hsi-tips/tips.asp.

Since 9/11, the USCIS, through its enforcement unit, the ICE division, has used these pertinent skills in the hunt for the terrorist as well. The mission of the Cyber Crimes Center is to investigate domestic and international criminal activities occurring on or facilitated by the Internet. The Cyber Crimes Center is blessed with a state-of-the-art center that offers cyber-crime training to federal, state, local, and international law enforcement agencies.

Terrorists use the Internet and find the means and methods to conduct business, transfer funds, share information, and issue instructions. ICE distinguishes itself in the area of illegal arms and money laundering. ICE's Arms and Strategic Technology division looks to prevent the proliferation of weapons, as well as the movement of terrorists and other criminals from entering the United States (Figure 9.23).

The Cyber Crimes Center has an additional competence regarding documents and related fraud. If 9/11 made plain any conclusion, it was the ease with which terrorists could fabricate documents to gain access. The threat posed by document fraud is evidenced by the ease with which seven of the 9/11 hijackers obtained identity documents in the State of Virginia.

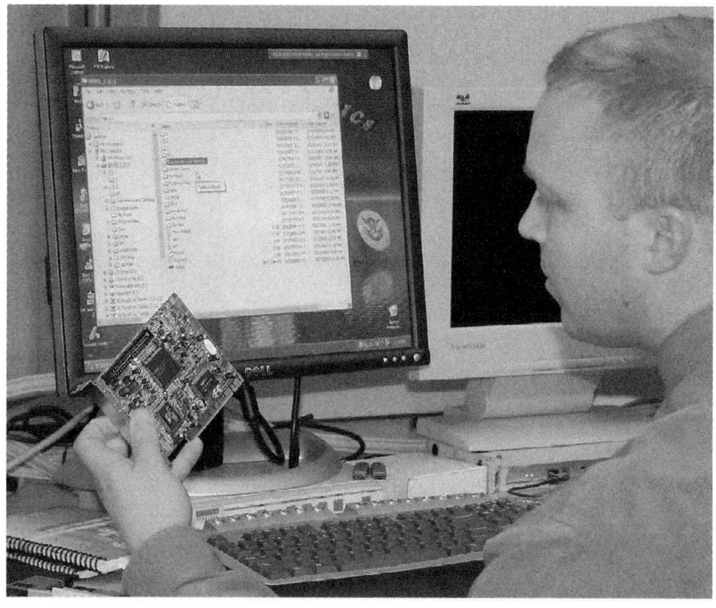

FIGURE 9.23 A member of ICE's Arms and Strategic Technology division at work.

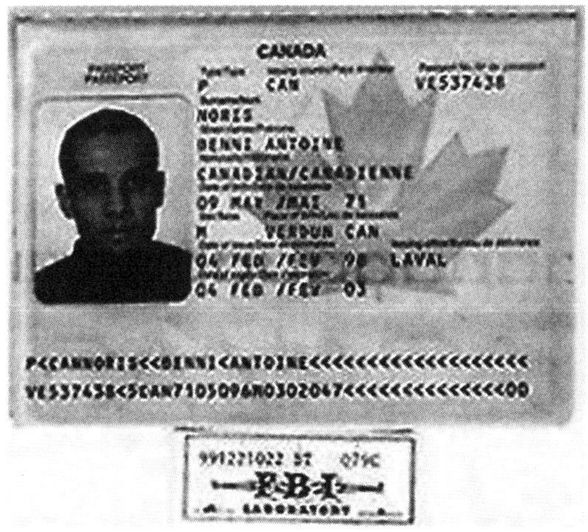

FIGURE 9.24 Counterfeit passport.

Passports are a particular problem for USCIS since the range and design will depend on country of issue. Figure 9.24 shows an example of a terrorist who was caught before his attempted act of terror at the Los Angeles airport in 1999. He is presently serving a 22-year term in a federal penitentiary.

Documents give telltale signs of fraud, and Customs and Immigration personnel have been trained to detect it. The more common fraud indicators are:

- Physically altered passports
- Passports with serial numbers that are watch-listed as lost or stolen
- Handwritten documents that are easily forged or altered
- Multiple passports used by the same person with variations in the spelling/structure of the name and date of birth
- Ambiguous or contradictory information submitted to consular or border control officials
- Absence of supporting documents to corroborate passport information
- Passports with glued-in photographs
- Large gaps in travel history as reflected in stamps and visas

Internet Resource: The U.S. Department of State has authored a quick course in passport fraud at http://www.state.gov/m/ds/investigat/c10714.htm.

9.3.5 US-VISIT Program

The U.S. Department of Homeland Security's US-VISIT program provides visa-issuing posts and ports of entry with the biometric technology that enables the U.S. government to establish and verify the identities of those who visit the United States (Figure 9.25).

FIGURE 9.25 US-VISIT logo.

Internet Exercise: See the DHS fact sheet that outlines parties covered under the US-VISIT program at http://www.dhs.gov/xtrvlsec/programs/gc_1231972592442.shtm.

The goals of US-VISIT are to:

1. Enhance the security of our citizens and visitors
2. Expedite legitimate travel and trade
3. Ensure the integrity of the immigration system
4. Safeguard the personal privacy of our visitors

This process begins overseas at a U.S. visa-issuing post, where a traveler's biometrics—digital fingerprints and a photograph—are collected and checked. Upon arrival in the United States, these same biometrics verify the identity of that person at the port of entry.

Internet Exercise: Watch the video on what to expect under the US-VISIT program at http://www.dhs.gov/xtrvlsec/programs/editorial_0525.shtm.

Even though US-VISIT is an additional layer of security, most travelers will not notice the difference. At an airport or seaport, travel documents such as a passport and a visa will be reviewed and a U.S. CBP officer will ask specific questions regarding the visitor's stay in the United States.

Visitors traveling on visas will have two fingerprints scanned by an inkless device and a digital photograph taken. Data and information are then used to assist the border inspector in determining whether to admit the traveler. All data obtained from the visitor are securely stored as part of the visitor's travel record. This information is made available only to authorized officials and selected law enforcement agencies on a need-to-know basis in their efforts to help protect the country against those who intend to harm American citizens or visitors to the United States.

9.4 Conclusion

Protection of the border rightfully consumes the energy of the homeland community. The idea of border extends far beyond any notions of continental geography, but includes the diverse ways in which visitors to the United States can find entry. Soon after 9/11, DHS recognized the need to subsume the functions of Border with those of Customs—erecting a new department,

Customs and Border Patrol (CBP). The work of the CBP is extensive and includes encounters with millions of passengers and pedestrians, thousands of truck, rail, and sea containers and air travelers, shipments, and the computation of tariffs, duties, and other fees. More than a million illegal aliens have been apprehended since 2004. The CBP has also erected targeted operations such as the SBI, which increases manpower and resources across the entire national border. SBI upgrades all facets of border hardware and infrastructure, employs new technology to discover breaches in the border, and erects and maintains natural and artificial barrier systems to stem illegal entry. The rise in Border Patrol agents—some 50,000 additional needed in the next decade—proves the seriousness of the task.

CBP continually adds sophisticated equipment and technology to carry out its mission. The use of drones and other unmanned air devices is now part and parcel of the delivery system. CBP now has an Air and Marine division that zeroes in on breach locations or unsafe entry points. Seven hundred pilots now man 267 differing types of aircraft in this challenge.

CBP assumes an integral role in the world of trade and commerce. With its cargo responsibilities, CBP scans and screens incoming cargo throughout the nation and even in foreign ports before its departure to the United States. In its Secure Freight Initiative, radiation scanners inspect large-scale shipping holds before ever leaving worldwide ports. Usually at megaports like England's Southampton or Singapore, the Secure Freight Initiative not only scans vessels but registers and tracks them over the life of their journey. In the area of cargo containers, the CSI inspects by both radiation and x-ray incoming goods. CSI is operational in foreign ports as well, covering 86% of the world's cargo destined to the United States. CBP partners with private companies in shipping and cargo through its Customs Trade Partnership Against Terrorism (C-TPAT) program. C-TPAT promotes efficiency in cargo processes and serves as a liaison for business and industry security practices and the requirements of the CBP. Electronic modernization of cargo manifests and other practices are made possible by the protocols of the Automated Commercial Environment program.

In the area of immigration and citizenship, the DHS department of USCIS, once referred to as the INS, administers the status of immigrants, their claims, and adjudication processes, as well as promulgates protocols on naturalization, asylum, and refugee petitions and the granting or denial of visas. The Project Shield America Initiative is a USCIS function that tracks illegal financial transactions, illegal munitions, and trafficking in contraband and WMD. The USCIS runs the Fugitive Operations Program, which targets a most wanted list of illegal aliens and criminals. The USCIS administers a host of other programs relating to cyber-crime and fraud, financial support for terrorists transfers, and passport forgery.

Keywords

Air and marine
Amnesty
Automated Commercial Environment
Automated Commercial System
Biometrics
Border Patrol
Citizenship and Immigration Service
Common operating procedure
Container Security Initiative
Contraband
Cornerstone Initiative
Customs
Customs and Border Protection
Customs Trade Partnership Against Terrorism
Cyber Crimes Center
Fugitive operations team
Global Trade Exchange
The Great Wave
Illegal immigration
Immigrant
Immigration and Naturalization Service
Immigration reform
Marine interdict officer
Megaport
National Fugitive Operations Program
National Targeting Center
Natural barriers
Naturalization
Partner ports
Ports of entry
Project Shield America
Radiation portal monitor
Refugees
Secure Border Initiative
Secure data portal account
Secure Freight Initiative
SFI scan
Transient workers
US-VISIT
Visa

Discussion Questions

1. Given the resource and expenditure investment in border security, is it fair to expect safe and secure borders? Is there a correlation between the dollars invested and success at the border?
2. Evaluate how the merger of Border, Customs, and Immigration into DHS has affected the operational outlook of these former agencies. Has it been a healthy merger?
3. Discuss how armed law enforcement aides plane and travel security. Highlight specific programs.
4. Critics of the border fencing hold that it cannot work. Why not?
5. Lay out three perennial problems in the protection of the U.S.'s borders.
6. In what ways does the CBP aid or interfere with commerce?

Practical Exercises

1. Review your geography. Where does the influx of illegal immigrants occur in your region? If not a border state, explain the social, cultural, and economic implications of a border unguarded. What is the public sentiment concerning illegal aliens?
2. Visit usajobs.com. Create a job database of present opportunities for Border, Customs, and Immigration officers. Provide examples of each career opportunity.
3. Prepare a form file for the Automated Commercial Environment (ACE) program.
4. Customs deals with trade in diverse ways. Give four examples of how technology aids or even eliminates manpower in the moves of trade.
5. Take the Naturalization Test for Citizenship administered by Immigration and Citizenship. Evaluate the level of ease or difficulty.

Notes

1. CBP Summary of Performance and Financial Information–Fiscal Year 2010, 04/15/2011.
2. And this is not a uniquely American experience either. See R. Nicholson, Swedish open immigration policies—Correlation with terrorism, *The Homeland Security Review*, 4, 2010: 193.
3. American Immigration Center, *Looking for a Quick Fix: The Rise and Fall of the Secure Border Initiative's High-Tech Solution to Unauthorized Immigration,* April 15, 2010, www.immigrationpolicy.org.
4. Immigration Policy Center, at 1.
5. C. Bolkcom, *Homeland Security: Unmanned Aerial Vehicles and Border Surveillance* (Washington, DC: Library of Congress, 2005), http://www.fas.org/sgp/crs/homesec/RS21698.pdf; Border Security: Preliminary Observations on the Status of Key Southwest Border Technology Programs. (2011); Moving Illegal Proceeds: Opportunities Exist for Strengthening the Federal Government's Efforts to Stem Cross-Border Currency Smuggling. (2011); Border Security: Preliminary Observations on Border Control Measures for the Southwest Border. (2011); Border Security: Enhanced DHS Oversight and Assessment of Interagency Coordination Is Needed for the Northern Border. (2010); Border Security: Additional Actions Needed to Better Ensure a Coordinated Federal Response to Illegal Activity on Federal Lands. (2010); Moving Illegal Proceeds: Challenges Exist in the Federal Government's Effort to Stem Cross-Border Currency Smuggling. (2010).
6. U.S. Government Accountability Office, *Border security: DHS Progress and Challenges in Securing the U.S. Southwest and Northern Borders* (Washington, DC: U.S. Government Printing Office, 2011).
7. H. Hogan, CBP's best- and newest-friends, *Homeland Security Today*, 17, July 2011.

8. American Immigration Center, at 6.
9. T. Steinmetz, Mitigating the exploitation of U.S. borders by jihadists and criminal organizations, *Journal of Strategic Security*, 4, 2011: 36.
10. Steinmetz, at 35.
11. C. Collins, Border enforcement: Migrant interdiction at sea, *Year in Homeland Security,* 2010/2011: 76.
12. U.S. Customs and Border Protection, *CBP Trade Strategy 2009–2013*, 24, 2009.
13. CBP Trade Strategy, 2009–2013, at 5.
14. Security and Accountability for Every Port Act of 2006, P.L. 109-347, *U.S. Statutes at Large*, 120, 2006: 1884.
15. The Cornerstone Report, Homeland Security Investigations: Trade Transparency Unit, Winter 2011.
16. A. P. Gerglas, The New York FBI and the Cyberthreat, 6 *Homeland Security Today,* July 2011; See also J. R. Wilson, *IT & Cyber Security, Year in Homeland Security,* 2010/2011: 83.
17. M. McCarter, ID Management, *Homeland Security Today,* August 2011: 48.

Chapter 10

Transportation Security

Objectives

1. To describe the mission and scope of operation of the Transportation Security Administration (TSA).
2. To explain the programs and policies created by TSA to ensure secure air transportation in the United States.
3. To outline the technological advances in transportation security in use at airport screening points.
4. To describe the mission and scope of operation of the U.S. Coast Guard.
5. To explain the programs and policies created by the U.S. Coast Guard to ensure secure maritime transportation in the United States.
6. To outline the technological advances in security in use at maritime and cargo screening points.
7. To explain the programs and policies in place to ensure secure passenger rail transportation in the United States.
8. To explain the programs and policies in place to ensure secure cargo rail transportation in the United States.

10.1 Introduction

In the broadest context, transportation security encompasses air, rail, bus, shipping and ports, and mass transit safety. Most of these centers of movement can properly be characterized as critical infrastructure. Many agencies of government deal with transportation safety and security questions. Department of Homeland Security (DHS) and Federal Aviation Administration (FAA) first come to mind since each regulates and promulgates administrative practices regarding these industries. The Department of Commerce involves itself in a host of travel questions as does the Federal Highway Administration. Because of the multiagency involvement in the world of travel and transportation, it would be impossible to cover each and every aspect of the homeland question relative to the diversity of government agencies and missions. What we will try to do is highlight the most relevant for homeland security purposes, starting with the Transportation Security Administration.

10.2 Transportation Security Administration

If any portion of the homeland front touches the general public it is the work of the Transportation Security Agency (TSA). Most American citizens come face-to-face with TSA—the visible arm of airport safety in our terminals. Passenger and baggage screening are the prime tasks of TSA. Despite these responsibilities, TSA engages in a broad range of other activities. TSA is a component of DHS and not only is responsible for the security of the country's airline transportation systems, but also, with state, local, and regional partners, oversees security for the highways, railroads, buses, mass transit systems, ports, and the 450 U.S. airports. TSA employs approximately 50,000 people. TSA is a large bureaucracy that is still finding its way in many respects. By any reasonable measure, TSA scores low in public opinion. There have been many national news articles and stories written on controversial practices as well as scandals. Controversial practices include an enhanced physical pat-down search of young children and the elderly as well as scanners that have provided near naked pictures of passengers.[1] Scandals include naked body imagery shared on the Internet, undetected contraband making it through screenings at various airports, and TSA agents indicted for corruption and drug trafficking.

TSA is well aware of how public aggravation at the screening process, increasing public distrust, and the agency's high attrition rate undercut its efforts to become a professional body. In 2010, TSA began a program with Global Corporate College—provided through regional community colleges around the country—to further educate and train TSA employees. In addition,

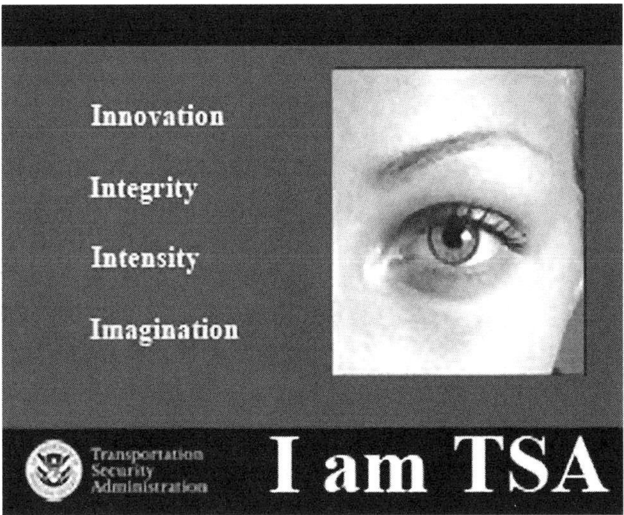

FIGURE 10.1 TSA public relations campaign.

it has recently engaged in a series of public relations campaigns to bolster its image. See Figure 10.1 for an example from a public relations campaign.

The Agency designates a Public Affairs officer line in its organizational structure. See Figure 10.2.

TSA recently adopted a series of Core Values that stress the professionalism and integrity it so sorely needs. The Agency indicates the need for a positive "culture" to carry out its stated mission. The Core Values include:

- Integrity:
  - We are a people of integrity who respect and care for others and protect the information we handle.
  - We are a people who conduct ourselves in an honest, trustworthy, and ethical manner at all times.
  - We are a people who gain strength from the diversity in our cultures.
- Innovation:
  - We are a people who embrace and stand ready for change.
  - We are a people who are courageous and willing to take on new challenges.
  - We are a people with an enterprising spirit, striving for innovations who accept the risk taking that comes with it.
- Team Spirit:
  - We are a people who are open, respectful, and dedicated to making others better.
  - We are a people who have a passion for challenge, success, and being on a winning team.
  - We are a people who will build teams around our strengths.

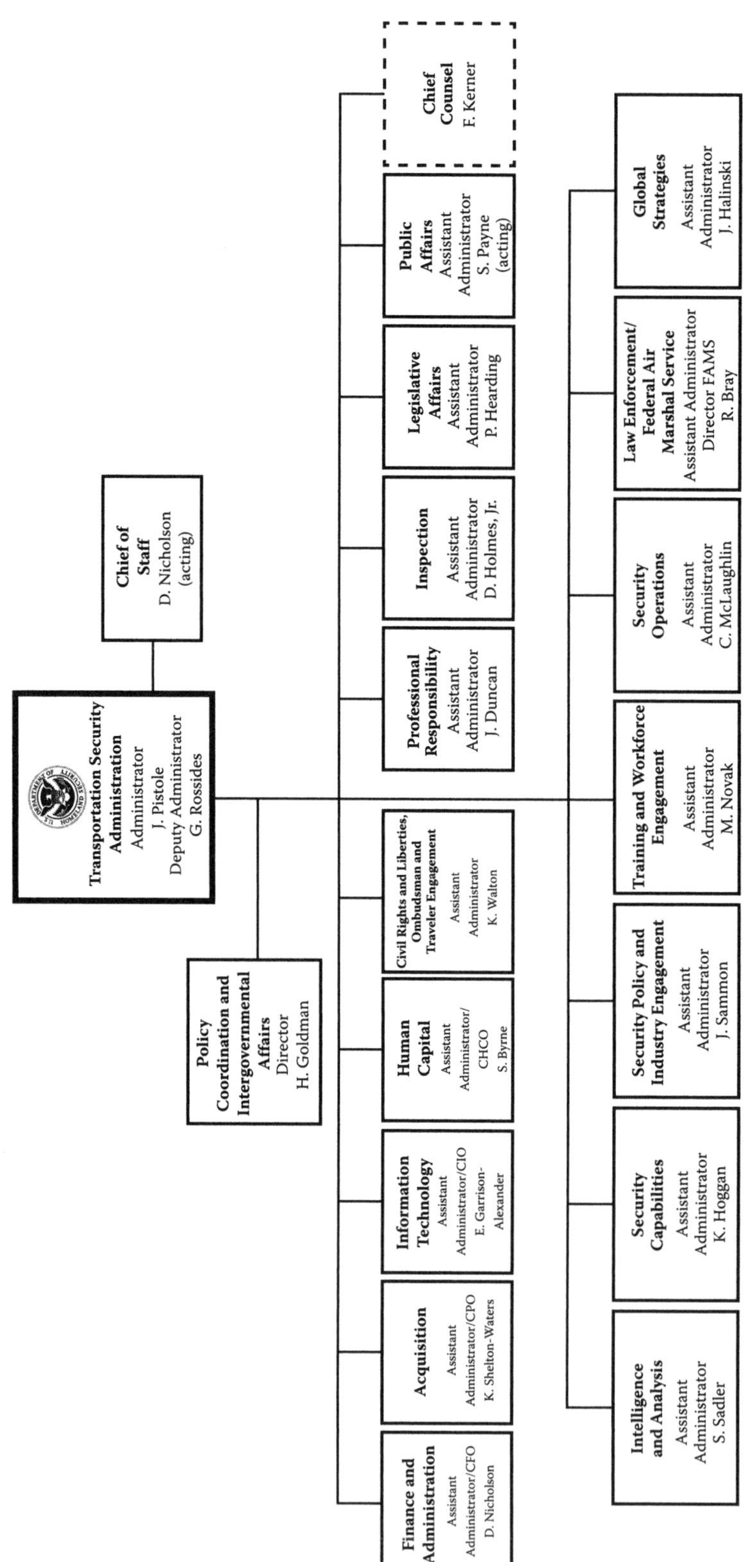

FIGURE 10.2 TSA organization chart.

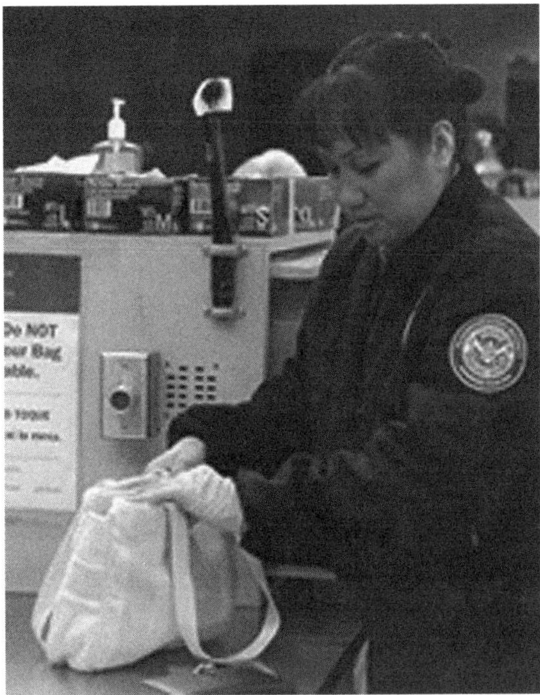

FIGURE 10.3 TSA officer at a security checkpoint.

The bulk of what TSA does relates to airline safety. Indeed, if the terrorist attacks of 9/11 had occurred on a boat, the likely location for our front line of defense would be in the harbor. Location has much to do with policy and practice. Then again, the nature of the 9/11 attacks also prompted this emphasis. It may be misguided, but it surely adds a layer of safety to the culture (Figure 10.3).

TSA's primary mission is transportation—all forms and all locales. It is a gargantuan responsibility. Consider the scope of the jurisdiction:

- 3.9 million miles of public roads
- 100,000 miles of rail
- 600,000 bridges
- 300 tunnels and numerous seaports
- 2 million miles of pipeline
- 500,000 train stations
- 500 public use airports
- 1.2 million trucking companies operating 15.5 million trucks including 42,000 hazmat trucks
- 10 million licensed commercial vehicle drivers including 2.7 million hazmat drivers
- 2.2 million miles of hazardous liquid and natural gas pipeline
- 120,000 miles of major railroads

- Nearly 15 million daily riders on mass transit and passenger rail systems nationwide
- 25,000 miles of commercial waterways
- 361 ports
- 9.0 million containers through 51,000 port calls
- 11.2 million containers via Canada and Mexico
- 19,576 general aviation airports, heliports, and landing strips
- 459 federalized commercial airports
- 211,450 general aviation aircraft
- General aviation flights represents approximately 77% of all flights in the United States

From airports to bus stations, rail terminals to pipelines, TSA is entrusted with extraordinary responsibilities. In each of these sectors TSA must be mindful of the:

- Completion of industry threat, vulnerability, and consequence assessment
- Development of baseline security standards
- Assessment of operator security status vs. existing standards
- Development of plan to close gaps in security standards
- Enhancement of systems of security

TSA has shown little hesitation in expanding its reach into all forms of transportation. For example, recent implementation of the VIPR program (Visible Intermodal Prevention and Response)—including teams of local and federal law enforcement officers, along with TSA specialists combing the subways, the ferries, and all forms of public transportation—signifies TSA's reach over the entire national transportation system (Figure 10.4).

Whatever system is reviewed, TSA's mission includes the development of various layers of security protection at the facilities it is entrusted with. By layers, we mean barriers or checkpoints for protection. The more checkpoints that exist, the greater the likelihood is that a threat is detected. In the aviation sector, the layers of security are both sophisticated and largely effective. TSA works to identify questionable passengers long before the security checkpoint including intelligence analysis, watch lists and passenger manifests, random canine searches, insertion of federal air marshals and flight deck officers and crew. TSA charts these layers in Figure 10.5.

At any given point along this detection continuum, the terrorist is vulnerable. Whether at the airport screening machine or vetted by random checks, in order to succeed, the terrorist will have to pass through a multi-tiered checkpoint system. The sheer volume of detection points reduces the chance for terrorist activity.

Aside from staffing airport screening lines, TSA involves itself in a diversity of programs (Figure 10.6).

FIGURE 10.4 VIPR team at subway in New York City.

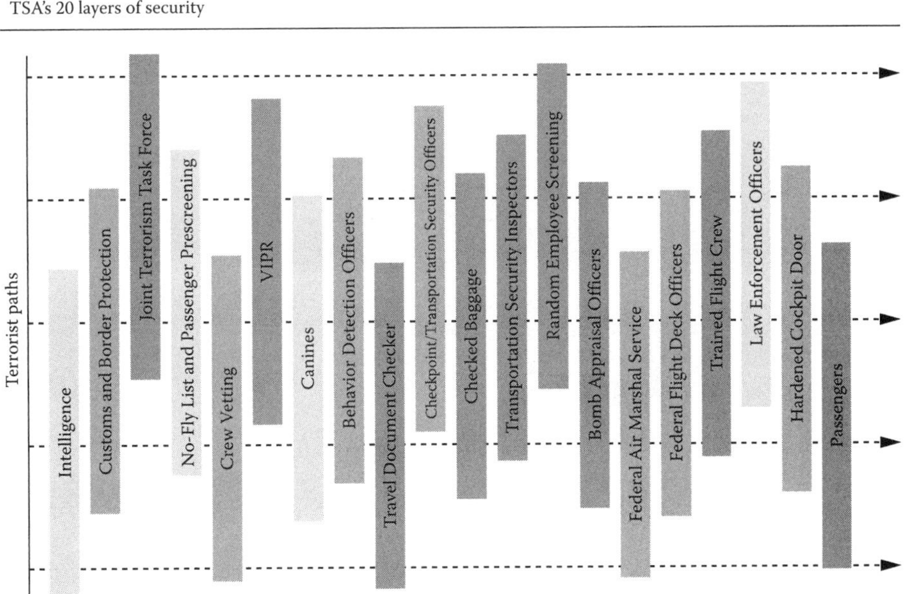

FIGURE 10.5 Layers of U.S. aviation security.

FIGURE 10.6 Seal of TSA.

10.2.1 Federal Air Marshals

The Federal Air Marshal program plants undercover law enforcement on airline flights. The program operates with specific intelligence or through random flight assignment. Federal air marshals are skilled in the use of weaponry and defense/offense tactics that involve restraint. Marshals must blend in with passengers, keeping any unsuspecting terrorist unaware of his or her presence on that plane. Marshals employ investigative techniques, criminal terrorist behavior recognition, firearms proficiency, aircraft-specific tactics, and close-quarters self-defense measures to protect the flying public (Figure 10.7).

Internet Exercise: Learn more about a career in the Federal Air Marshal Service at www.tsa.gove/lawenforcement/mission/index.shtm.

FIGURE 10.7 Federal Air Marshal patch.

10.2.2 Federal Flight Deck Officers

The Federal Flight Deck Officer (FFDO) program permits aviation pilots to be fully armed in the cockpit. TSA identifies and trains qualified officers for this position. Under this program, eligible flight crew members are authorized by the TSA Office of Law Enforcement/Federal Air Marshal Service to use firearms to defend against an act of criminal violence or air piracy that attempts to gain control of an aircraft. A flight crew member may be a pilot, flight engineer, or navigator assigned to the flight. The program is required to maintain strict confidentiality of its participants. The FFDOs are further characterized and empowered by these criteria:

- FFDOs are considered federal law enforcement officers only for the limited purposes of carrying firearms and using force, including lethal force, to defend the flight deck of an aircraft from air piracy or criminal violence.
- FFDOs are not granted or authorized to exercise other law enforcement powers, such as the power to make arrests, or seek or execute warrants for arrest, or seizure of evidence, or to otherwise act as federal law enforcement outside the jurisdiction of aircraft flight decks.
- FFDOs are issued credentials and badges to appropriately identify themselves to law enforcement and security personnel, as required in the furtherance of their mission.
- FFDOs are issued firearms and other necessary equipment by the Federal Air Marshal Service.
- FFDOs are responsible for the readiness and daily security of their firearms, credentials, and equipment.
- FFDOs are authorized to transport secured firearms in any state for a flight on which they are flying to or from as approved by the Federal Air Marshal Service as necessary for their participation and activities in the program.

10.2.3 Law Enforcement Officers Flying Armed

TSA always oversees a program on instruction and general guidance for law enforcement officers wishing to fly while armed. The program recognizes the critical role a legitimately armed law enforcement officer might play in the event of a terrorist incident. Just as critical is the program's desire to promulgate standards for any law enforcement officer flying yet on official business. Transporting prisoners, tailing a suspect, or other investigative practice demands an official protocol for the use and storage of firearms. Any officer desiring to fly armed must complete a course of instruction and file the required paperwork giving notice of this intention.

Internet Resource: For a policy directive from Ohio on flying armed, see http://www.cincinnati-oh.gov/police/downloads/police_pdf15847.pdf.

10.2.4 TSA's Canine Explosive Detection Unit

Given the broadening responsibilities of TSA, moving beyond the airports and venturing into seaports and harbors, train and municipal transit facilities, TSA has had to get creative in how it carries out its task. The use of canines has long been a beneficial and very economical police practice. TSA uses canines to detect explosives in various quarters (Figure 10.8).

Canines are particularly effective in ports and harbor areas where the sheer volume of coverage area can be daunting for law enforcement. TSA has developed certification standards for canine units for purposes of uniformity and quality in practice. TSA is aggressively developing units and teams throughout the United States. The agency will train and certify more than 400 explosives detection canine teams, composed of one dog and one handler, during the next 2 years. Eighty-five of these teams will be TSA employee led and will primarily search cargo bound for passenger-carrying aircraft. TSA handlers will be nonlaw enforcement employees and will complement the 496 TSA-certified state and local law enforcement teams currently deployed to 70 airports and 14 mass transit systems (Figure 10.9).

TSA operates a puppy breeding program to fill the ranks of the future. Volunteers staff the operation and raise the puppies who will work in TSA functions. During this time, volunteers provide a well-rounded, socialized,

FIGURE 10.8 TSA canine officer performing a luggage search.

FIGURE 10.9 TSA canine searching for contraband in a shipment.

FIGURE 10.10 TSA puppy breeding program recruits.

and nurturing environment. TSA delivers an orientation program for volunteers and makes technical staff available during this period of upbringing (Figure 10.10).

10.2.5 Risk Management Programs

TSA has played an integral role in the development of risk assessment protocols and tools for the transportation system, though not without regular criticism.[2] Opponents of TSA argue that there is not much thinking going on when it comes to new and innovative protocols. Some have said that the Agency agrees too quickly to adopting new technology. Even the General Accounting Office found that TSA "does not routinely consider costs and benefits when acquiring new technologies."[3]

Despite this, TSA completely appreciates the interrelationship between a risk or series of risks and the critical infrastructure and assets it protects. To understand the risk is to comprehend the landscape to be protected. To comprehend the landscape to be protected surely leads to the identification and mitigation of risk. TSA also recognizes that transportation assets, such as airplanes and tunnels, are part of larger systems, such as the national aviation system or a mass transit system. Taken together, all the individual transportation systems form the national transportation system. Essentially, TSA discerns systems within systems. The behavior of transportation systems cannot be fully explained by confining observations to individual cars, vessels, and aircraft or fixed infrastructure. As a result, TSA has developed self-assessment tools for maritime, transportation, and mass transit systems.

Internet Resource: Visit TSA for instructions on how to access these risk tools at http://www.tsa.gov/approach/risk/editorial_1733.shtm.

10.2.6 TSA Technology and Innovation

Cutting-edge technology is a desired end for TSA. The costs of human intelligence versus mechanical versions are always higher, and realizing the volume of TSA activities, the need for high-level technology has never been greater. The world is a very large place to screen, and the human eye is simply incapable of seeing it all. To stay ahead of the terrorist, TSA has developed and employed some incredible technology, again not without some controversy. In air, cargo holds, ports, and harbor shipping, the use of technology will permit TSA to extend its reach.[4] A thumbnail review of a few of the more exciting advances is covered below.

10.2.6.1 Trace Portals

The use of the trace portal is now a reality in various airports. When compared to the baggage screen, the trace portal is capable of identifying minute quantities of dangerous items, from explosives to Anthrax. As passengers enter the trace portal, standing still for a few seconds, several puffs of air are released, dislodging microscopic particles from passengers that are then collected and analyzed for traces of explosives. TSA has already installed trace portals in Baltimore; Boston; Gulfport, Mississippi; Jacksonville, Florida; Las Vegas; Los Angeles; Miami; Newark; New York (JFK); Phoenix; Providence, Rhode Island; Rochester, New York; San Francisco; San Diego; and Tampa, Florida. See Figure 10.11 for a trace portal.

FIGURE 10.11 Trace portal.

10.2.6.2 Millimeter Wave/Advanced Imaging Technology

A new means for discerning explosives, improvised explosive devices (IEDs), and other concealed materials is the millimeter wave device and advanced imaging technology. TSA currently uses both types at 78 airports. 500 AIT and 300 millimeter wave machines are presently in use (Figure 10.12).

FIGURE 10.12 Advanced imaging technology machine—the millimeter wave unit.

Millimeter wave imaging technology uses harmless electromagnetic waves to detect potential threats. Beams of radio frequency (RF) energy in the millimeter wave spectrum are projected over the body's surface at high speed from two antennas simultaneously rotating around the body. The RF energy reflected back from the body or other objects on the body constructs a three-dimensional image. The three-dimensional image of the body, with facial features blurred for privacy, is displayed on a remote monitor for analysis. The machine itself is innocuous. Earlier imagery lacked specificity relative to identity and hence could not be used for illicit purposes.

However, more modern AIT machines provide exquisite detail as to the physical features and as a result, been the subject of some passenger abuse. The results imaged are labeled "backscatter." Backscatter technology projects an ionizing x-ray beam over the body surface at high speed. The reflection, or "backscatter," of the beam is detected, digitized, and displayed on a monitor.

Both systems have generated a stir of comment and criticism. For some, the safety of the imagery and its mechanics, trump the safety of the general public. If the technology utilizes waves, in whatever form, critics indicate there may be health risks. TSA has taken these critiques seriously and tried to calm the public by making comparisons. For example, the exposure to waves during a backscatter scan is like flying a plane for 2 min while those experienced during a millimeter wave scan similar to using a cell phone (Figure 10.13).

Internet Exercise: Read about the various health assessments that have been done on AIT at: http://www.tsa.gov/research/reading/index.shtm.

Even more common has been the privacy challenge to intrusive machinery.[5] AIT and millimeter wave machines peer deep into the private range of human operations. Balancing the rationale of safe travel with minimal intrusiveness may be less compelling than the searched bag comparison. Surely, every traveler realizes that privacy concerns are not idyllic and untouchable. In a post-9/11 world, most people accept the burdens and inconveniences of

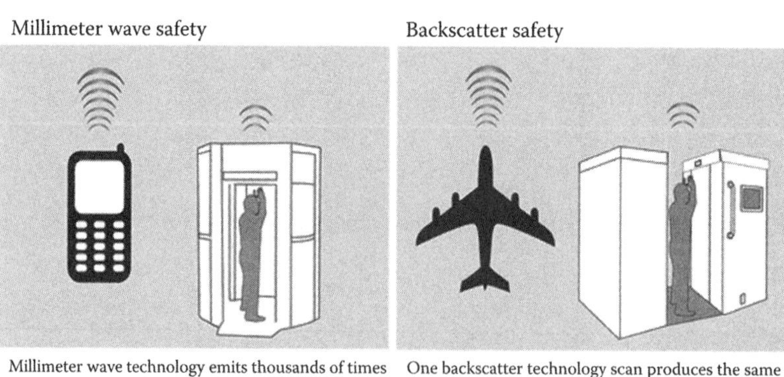

Millimeter wave safety
Backscatter safety
Millimeter wave technology emits thousands of times less energy than a cell phone transmission.
One backscatter technology scan produces the same exposure as two minutes of flying on an airplane.

FIGURE 10.13 AIT safety information from TSA.

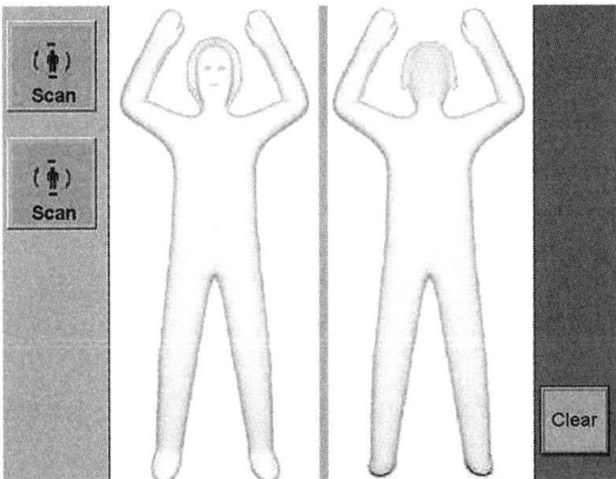

FIGURE 10.14 TSA is using software that enhances privacy by highlighting any potential threats on the same generic outline of a person for every passenger.

security checkpoints. Even so, the intrusiveness has limits and this machinery may have reached the threshold to the point where the public's patience runs out. TSA has some sensitivity to the privacy concerns. It has altered the imagery to a generic format which cannot personally be identified; it has the screener in a distinct position than the officer assisting the customer, and it has assured that imagery cannot be stored, printed, transmitted, or saved.[6]

The agency has modified its software packages to show a generic figure that lacks specificity. Known as Automated Target Recognition, ATR eliminates the image of the individual body while still recognized anomalies. See Figure 10.14 for an ATR image.

10.2.6.3 Biometrics

The world of biometrics has clearly invaded the day-to-day life of TSA. Biometrics can be defined as follows:

- Biometrics is a general term used alternatively to describe a characteristic or a process.
- As a characteristic, a biometric is a measurable biological (anatomical and physiological) and behavioral characteristic that can be used for automated recognition.
- As a process, a biometric is an automated method of recognizing an individual based on measurable biological (anatomical and physiological) and behavioral characteristics.[7]

Biometrics is a means of identification using both machine and man.[8] Presently, biometrics can target various bodily components for identification, including:

- Palm
- Fingerprint
- Face

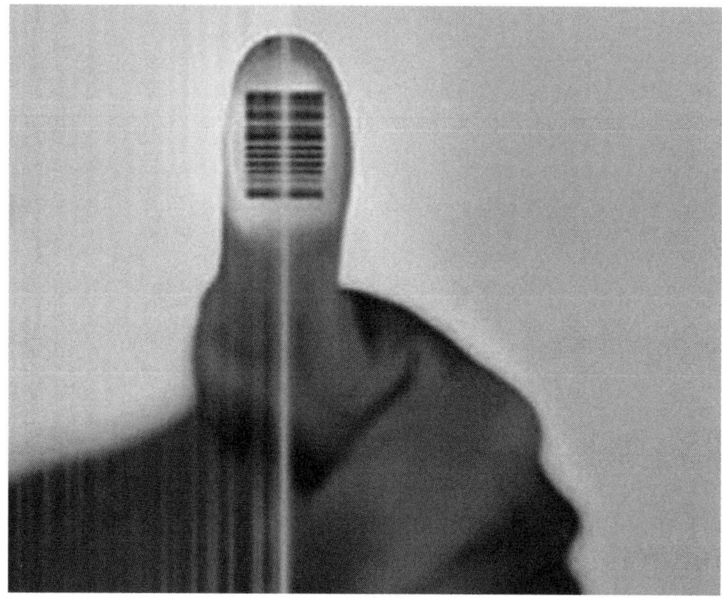

FIGURE 10.15 Biometric fingerprint scanner.

- Vascular
- Speech
- Eye

Both retinal scans and fingerprint analysis by digital means are available to the agency. Biometric fingerprint machines are becoming a common experience for both residential and international travelers (Figure 10.15).

Machines that trace and match retinal patterns are sure to grow just as quickly.

10.2.6.3.1 Biometric Application: The Registered Traveler Program Biometric applications are becoming very common in the travel and transportation industries. The Registered Traveler (RT) program is growing and highly dependent on biometric technology.

TSA and private industry, in an effort to speed up the traveling process for business and repeat travelers, have developed the RT program. In order to participate, passengers undergo a TSA-conducted security threat assessment (STA). It is a voluntary program with both corporate entities and individuals participating. Biometrics plays a key role in this program. To enroll, applicants voluntarily provide RT sponsoring entities (participating airports/air carriers) and service providers with biographic and biometric data needed for TSA to conduct the STA and determine eligibility. To date, the following agencies participate in the RT program:

- Air France (operating out of Terminal 1 at JFK)

- AirTran Airways (operating out of the Central Terminal at LGA)
- Albany International Airport (ALB)
- British Airways (operating out of Terminal 7 at JFK)
- Cincinnati/Northern Kentucky International Airport (CVG)
- Denver International Airport (DEN)
- Gulfport-Biloxi International Airport (GPT)
- Indianapolis International Airport (IND)
- Jacksonville International Airport (JAX)
- Little Rock National Airport (LIT)
- Norman Mineta San Jose International Airport (SJC)
- Oakland International Airport (OAK)
- Orlando International Airport (MCO)
- Reno/Tahoe International Airport (RNO)
- Ronald Reagan Washington National Airport (DCA)
- Salt Lake City International Airport (SLC)
- San Francisco International Airport (SFO)
- Virgin Atlantic (operating out of Terminal B at EWR)
- Virgin Atlantic (operating out of Terminal 4 at JFK)
- Washington Dulles International Airport (IAD)
- Westchester County Airport (HPN)

The RT program has largely been turned over to outside, private contractors to run as negotiated at select airports. The results have been mixed and are hardly national in design.

Internet Resource: The Department of the Army has produced an excellent overview of biometric applications at http://www.biometrics.dod.mil/Bio101/1.aspx.

10.2.6.3.2 TSA: Paperless Boarding Pass In an effort to streamline the security processes and to assure a free flow of traffic in congested airports, TSA has implemented the "Paperless Boarding Pass" program. Here, the passenger downloads the boarding pass to the cell phone or other device and scans it at a designated station. Currently, 69 airports have adopted the program. Using a scan code, the TSA agent verifies the pass by a mere swipe (Figure 10.16).

The program has been favorably received by the general public though there are the usual caveats about privacy issues and the sharing of this personal information. TSA has issued strict guidelines on privacy requirements and reigned in the technology to prevent unauthorized disclosure.[9]

There is much more that could be written concerning the activities of TSA. Throughout the remainder of this chapter, the role of TSA in other aspects involving the transportation industry will be highlighted. In fact, our coverage turns to two key areas in the transportation arena: maritime and rail.

FIGURE 10.16 An example of a paperless boarding pass as it appears on a smartphone.

10.3 Maritime Security

Maritime security is an interagency operation at the federal level with the prime players being the Coast Guard, Customs and Immigration Service, and DHS. In 2011, DHS announced a more formal association of the major players in maritime security titled the "Marine Operations Coordination Plan" (MOC). MOC will coordinate and plan for the integration of maritime operations of the U.S. Coast Guard, Customs and Border Protection, and Immigration and Customs Enforcement. The MOC plan focuses on improved collaboration across five key sectors

- Coordination
- Planning
- Information sharing
- Intelligence integration
- Response activities

DHS has also fostered interagency cooperation in maritime threat affairs by the creation of the Global Maritime Operational Threat Response program. The primary aim of the program is to coordinate all relevant agencies of government that might encounter maritime threats and to assure the free flow of information to all interested agencies. A schematic of how all agencies report to Maritime Operational Threat Response (MOTR) is in Figure 10.17.

Previous to 9/11, conceptions of maritime security largely dealt with smuggling, theft, and drug trafficking.[10] Since that time, maritime security has been evaluated in more global terms. Maritime enforcement can only be described as a major undertaking that draws in all sectors of defense, including the traditional branches of the armed services.[11]

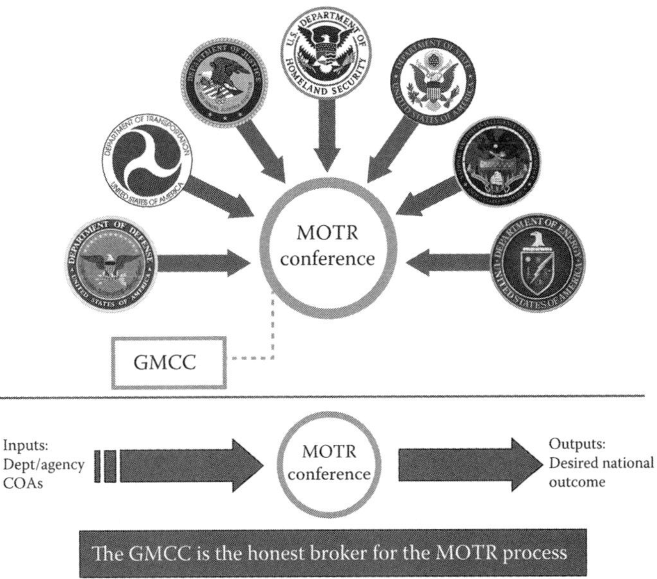

FIGURE 10.17 Maritime operational threat response process.

The maritime domain is defined as all areas and things of, on, under, relating to, adjacent to, or bordering on a sea, ocean, or other navigable waterway, including all maritime-related activities, infrastructure, people, cargo, and vessels, and other conveyances. The maritime domain for the United States includes the Great Lakes and all navigable inland waterways, such as the Mississippi River and the Intracoastal Waterway.

In the most general terms, maritime security seeks to accomplish the following ends:

- Prevent terrorist attacks and criminal or hostile acts
- Protect maritime-related population centers and critical infrastructures
- Minimize damage and expedite recovery
- Safeguard the ocean and its resources

The *Maritime Security Transportation Act of 2002*[12] was the initial legislative response after the attack of 9/11. The act requires vessels and port facilities to conduct vulnerability assessments and develop security plans that may include passenger, vehicle, and baggage screening procedures, security patrols, establishing restricted areas, personnel identification procedures, access control measures, and installation of surveillance equipment. Developed using risk-based methodology, the security regulations focus on those sectors of maritime industry that have a higher risk of involvement in a transportation security incident, including various tank vessels, barges, large passenger vessels, cargo vessels, towing vessels, offshore oil and gas platforms, and port facilities that handle certain kinds of dangerous cargo or service the vessels listed above.

Internet Resource: For the entire language of the act, see http://www.tsa.gov/assets/pdf/MTSA.pdf.

10.3.1 National Strategy for Maritime Security

The complexities of maritime security arise from both geography, legal issues, and a host of competing agencies and departments who have some portion of the pie—for example, defense, energy, interior, state, and DHS. Matters of territorial waters can be daunting and any effort to secure the homeland must weigh these competing interests.

In 2005, DHS published its *National Strategy for Maritime Security*.[13] The national strategy hones in on these fundamental objectives:

- Detect, deter, interdict, and defeat terrorist attacks, criminal acts, or hostile acts in the maritime domain, and prevent its unlawful exploitation for those purposes.
- Protect maritime-related population centers, critical infrastructure, key resources, transportation systems, borders, harbors, ports, and coastal approaches in the maritime domain.
- Define and set out the maritime domain.
- Minimize damage and expedite recovery from attacks within the maritime domain.
- Safeguard the ocean and its resources from unlawful exploitation and intentional critical damage.
- Enhance international cooperation to ensure lawful and timely enforcement actions against maritime threats.
- Embed security into commercial practices to reduce vulnerabilities and facilitate commerce.
- Deploy layered security to unify public and private security measures.
- Ensure continuity of the marine transportation system to maintain vital commerce and defense readiness.

The national strategy fully accepts that the world's waterways depend upon extraordinary cooperation at both the national and international levels. Any strategy must balance commerce with defense considerations, international rights with sovereignty of the coastline, and with the full recognition that certain bodies of water are internationally accessible while others protected. Figure 10.18 portrays all these dynamics.

Both government and commercial interests need to work together. Nations and states must coordinate response and action and adopt common definitions and parameters for what constitutes the maritime domain. The National Strategy on Maritime Security realizes the complexity of protecting the world's seas and waterways. It realizes that governmental entities and bodies need coordination. As a result, the strategy erects the Interagency

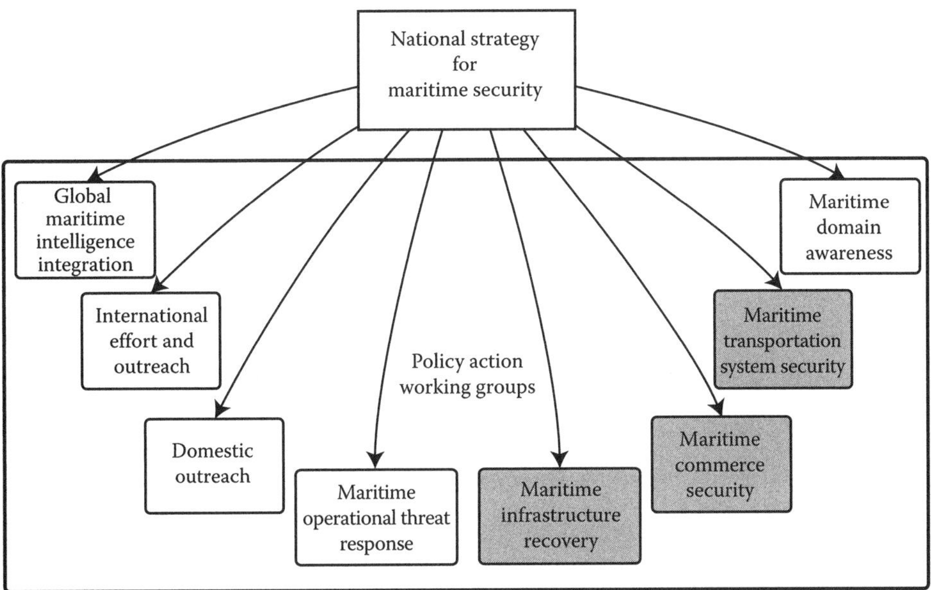

FIGURE 10.18 National strategy for maritime security.

Maritime Security Policy Coordinating Committee—established to serve as the primary forum for coordinating U.S. government maritime security policies. The committee reviews existing interagency practices, and coordination and execution of U.S. policies and strategies relating to maritime security, and recommends improvements, as necessary.

10.3.2 Other Maritime Plans

At the national level there are eight other plans or programs dedicated to the protection of the maritime domain, namely:

- *The National Plan to Achieve Maritime Domain Awareness* lays the foundation for an effective understanding of anything associated with the maritime domain that could impact the security, safety, economy, or environment of the United States.
- *Maritime Transportation System Security Plan* responds to the president's call for recommendations to improve the national and international regulatory framework regarding the maritime domain.
- *Maritime Commerce Security Plan* establishes a comprehensive plan to secure the maritime supply chain.
- *Maritime Infrastructure Recovery Plan* recommends procedures and standards for the recovery of the maritime infrastructure following attack or similar disruption.
- *International Outreach and Coordination Strategy* provides a framework to coordinate all maritime security initiatives undertaken with foreign governments and international organizations.

- *Global Maritime Intelligence Integration Plan* uses existing capabilities to integrate all available intelligence regarding potential threats to U.S. interests in the maritime domain.
- *Maritime Operational Threat Response Plan* aims for coordinated United States Government response to threats against the United States and its interests in the maritime domain by establishing roles and responsibilities.
- *Domestic Outreach Plan* engages non-Federal input to assist with the development and implementation of maritime security policies.

Space limitations prevent full coverage of each of the Plans but it shall be sufficient to cover the more prominent ideas in maritime security.

10.3.2.1 National Plan to Achieve Maritime Domain Awareness

The National Plan to Achieve Maritime Domain Awareness educates the public about the nature of a maritime domain in order that threats may be identified. Maritime domain awareness involves anything associated with the global maritime domain that could impact the United States' security, safety, economy, or environment. A range of federal departments and agencies will need to coordinate closely to identify threats as early and as distant from our shores as possible. By unifying U.S. government efforts and supporting international efforts, this plan will help achieve maritime domain awareness across the federal government, with the private sector and civil authorities within the United States, and with our allies and partners around the world.[14]

10.3.2.2 Maritime Transportation System Security Plan

The Maritime Transportation System (MTS) Security Plan seeks to improve the national and international regulatory framework regarding the maritime domain. The MTS evaluates maritime security in light of its various systems. MTS is a network of maritime operations that interface with shoreside operations at intermodal connections as part of overall global supply chains or domestic commercial operations. The various maritime operations within the MTS operating network have components that include vessels, port facilities, waterways and waterway infrastructure, intermodal connections, and users. DHS will issue a series of continuing recommendations regarding the safety of the network and its various components.

What is undeniable is that terrorists have attempted to use terrorism in the maritime domain. Professionals from all branches of defense and law enforcement constantly watch the horizon for new means and methods of attacks.

10.3.3 DHS: Borders and Marine Division

The long-held view that cargo and port inspections were the exclusive province of the U.S. Coast Guard has been set aright since 9/11. Multiple agencies of government are now taking on active roles to assure the safety and security of what comes in and what goes out. Discussed throughout this chapter is the role of the Border Division and its many dedicated employees. DHS, by and through its Borders and Marine Division takes these activities to a higher plane. Marine security does not end when the boat or ship docks but is simply at another layer of scrutiny. Cargo, containers, cartons, supplies stowed on these vessels are part of that secure continuum. While the Coast Guard interdicts and inspects, it cannot be stretched much thinner than its present state. Hence, the work of DHS in this critical area fills a crucial void in the assuring the flow of goods and the safe environment the public expects. A thumbnail sketch of the more relevant projects follows:

- The *Advanced Container Security Device (ACSD)* project involves developing an advanced sensor system for monitoring a container's integrity from the point of consolidation to the point of deconsolidation in the maritime supply chain. The ACSD is a small unit that attaches to the inside of a container to monitor all six sides to report any intrusion or door opening, including the presence of human cargo in the container. If the ACSD detects an intrusion, it would transmit this alarm information through the Marine Asset Tag Tracking System (MATTS) to the United States Customs and Border Protection (CBP). The ACSD would also build in a standard plug-and-play interface capability so that users can easily integrate other security or commercial sensors (e.g., radiological/nuclear and chemical/biological) through the standard interface.
- The *CanScan* project is developing a next-generation nonintrusive inspection system (NII) that will be used to detect terrorist materials, contraband items (e.g., drugs, money, illegal firearms), and stowaways at border crossings, maritime ports, and airports. These new systems may provide increases in penetration, resolution, and throughput and will support marine containerized cargo as well as airborne break-bulk, palletized, and containerized cargo, CanScan will provide improved cargo screening.
- The *Container Security Device (CSD)* project is developing a security device with sensors that can detect the opening of container doors from the point-of-consolidation to the point-of-deconsolidation in the maritime supply chain. The CSD will provide an interim capability to monitor the status of container doors until the ACSD is available. The CSD is a small, low-cost device mounted on or within a container that detects the opening or removal of container doors and reports its status to CBP.
- The *Hybrid Composite Container* project is developing a next-generation International Standards Organization (ISO) composite shipping

container with embedded security sensors to detect intrusions from the point-of-consolidation to the point-of-deconsolidation in the maritime supply chain. Composites are stronger than steel, 10–15% lighter than current shipping containers, and are easier to repair. Weight savings can benefit shippers by allowing them to load more goods per container within weight limits.
- The *Marine Asset Tag Tracking System (MATTS)* project is establishing a remote, global communications and tracking network that works with Advance Container Security Device from the point-of-consolidation to the point-of-deconsolidation in the maritime supply chain. MATTS communicates security alert information globally through the use of RF, cellular, and satellite technology. In addition, the commercial shipping industry can track and monitor cargo as it moves through the supply chain.
- The *Secure Carton* project develops technology to detect any shipping carton tamper event and transmit an alert to authorities after it leaves the point-of-manufacture to the point that it is delivered in the supply chains. This project provides improved supply chain visibility, chain of custody, and security. It is scalable and applicable across the various shipping modalities including trucking, rail, maritime, and air cargo.
- The *Secure Wrap* project provides a transparent, flexible, and tamper-indicative wrapping material to secure and monitor palletized cargo after it leaves the point-of-manufacture to the point-of-delivery in the land, maritime, and air-cargo supply chains. The wrap will provide a visible and/or fluorescent tamper indication and is deployable with little or no impact to current supply chain logistics and processes. Subsequent iterations of this wrap will support increasing levels of automated monitoring, thereby reducing manpower required to ensure cargo integrity.

10.3.4 Role of the Coast Guard in Maritime Security

At sea and on the continental shelf, in major lakes and rivers, the U.S. Coast Guard assumes the preeminent role in maritime security. With its fleet of cutters and world-class tugs and rescue vessels, high-level technology, skill in port and harbor investigations, and a professional class of officers and staff, it is difficult to find a better fit (Figure 10.19).

The Coast Guard's central mission relates to maritime activities. The Coast Guard's five-part mission focuses on issues integral to a safe maritime environment.

- *Maritime safety*: Eliminate deaths, injuries, and property damage associated with maritime transportation, fishing, and recreational

FIGURE 10.19 U.S. Coast Guard patrol vehicles.

boating. The Coast Guard's motto is semper paratus (always ready), and the service is always ready to respond to calls for help at sea.

- *Maritime security*: Protect America's maritime borders from all intrusions by (1) halting the flow of illegal drugs, aliens, and contraband into the United States through maritime routes; (2) preventing illegal fishing; and (3) suppressing violations of federal law in the maritime arena.
- *Maritime mobility*: Facilitate maritime commerce and eliminate interruptions and impediments to the efficient and economical movement of goods and people, while maximizing recreational access to and enjoyment of the water.
- *National defense*: Defend the nation as one of the five U.S. armed services. Enhance regional stability in support of the National Security Strategy, utilizing the Coast Guard's unique and relevant maritime capabilities.
- *Protection of natural resources*: Eliminate environmental damage and the degradation of natural resources associated with maritime transportation, fishing, and recreational boating.

With this mission in mind, it is no wonder that the Coast Guard so actively intervenes in the day-to-day grind of the maritime sector. Examples of Coast Guard roles and functions in the maritime world are myriad.

10.3.4.1 Emergency Safety

The effectiveness and professionalism of the Coast Guard can always be gleaned from their role in emergency response. Coast Guard assistance in time of storm, hurricane, and floods, and other natural disasters is the stuff of legend (Figure 10.20).

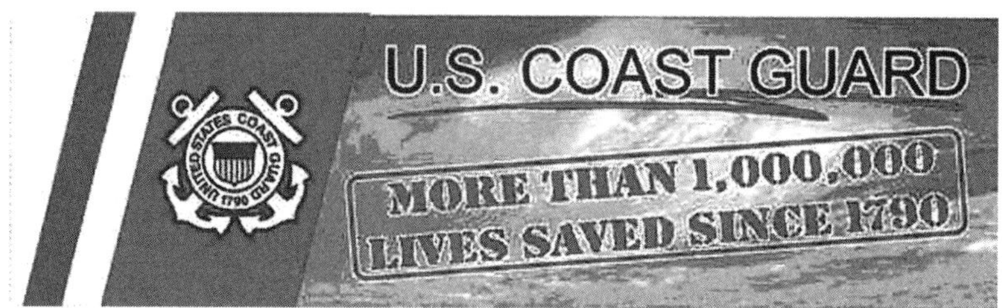

FIGURE 10.20 The U.S. Coast Guard is instrumental in saving lives.

Throughout its distinguished history, the Coast Guard has more than saved lives: it has also rescued whole communities. At no place was this more obvious than during Hurricane Katrina. Referred to as the only shining moment and silver lining in the debacle, Coast Guard personnel swept up person after person in the raging waters of New Orleans. The Coast Guard single-handedly saved more residents of New Orleans than any other governmental authority (Figure 10.21).

Wherever water runs, the Coast Guard is always prepared and ready to serve those in distress. From Hatteras, North Carolina beaches to Lake Superior, maritime safety comes first for this service.

The most prominent safety unit in the Coast Guard is its search and rescue team (SAR) (Figure 10.22).

The primary goal of SAR is to minimize the loss of life to those in distress, and the Guard saves more than 85% of those who call. When one evaluates the locations of these dangerous rescues, it is simply an extraordinary statistic.

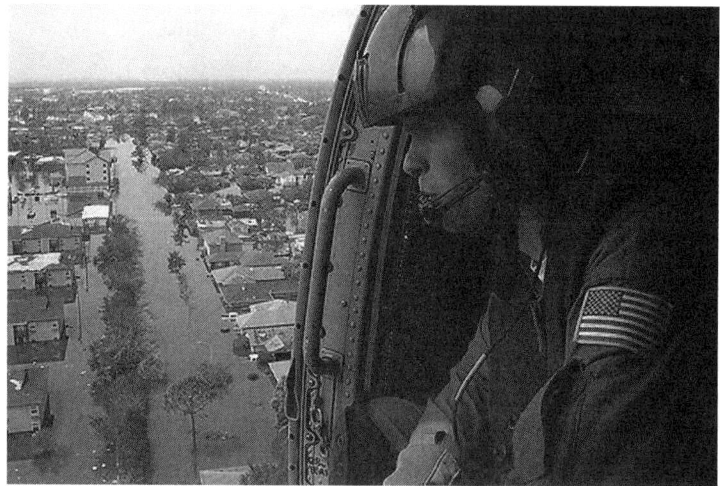

FIGURE 10.21 Coast Guard over New Orleans after Hurricane Katrina.

FIGURE 10.22 Search and rescue patch.

Internet Resource: Read about the SAR program in the *Coast Guard* magazine at http://www.uscg.mil/hq/g-o/g-opr/SAR%20Watch%20newsletter/newsletter.htm.

The SAR program is physically demanding and recruits experience a significant attrition rate of nearly 50%. Check with your local Coast Guard recruiter on eligibility standards (Figure 10.23).

Internet Resource: To learn about the curriculum and the physical demands leading to high attrition rates, see http://www.defenselink.mil/news/newsarticle.aspx?id=25362.

FIGURE 10.23 Coast Guard SAR team member at training.

10.3.4.2 Security and Law Enforcement

Law enforcement functions constitute a major portion of Coast Guard activity. In a way, the Coast Guard polices the waters for a host of things, from smuggling to drugs, from illegal human cargo to WMD. On the water and in the ports, one discovers the critical role of the Coast Guard. The Coast Guard is the law of sea and waterways.

The Coast Guard is the lead federal agency for maritime drug interdiction. In conjunction with the U.S. Customs Service, the Coast Guard combats and interdicts illegal drugs, interferes with and deters the activities of smugglers using the maritime for illegal delivery of drugs, and engages those that seek to pollute our cities and towns with contraband. Over the last decade, Coast Guard activity in the area of drug interdiction has been active. See Table 10.1.[15]

TABLE 10.1 Coast Guard Drug Removal Statistics (in pounds) by Fiscal Year

Fiscal Year	Events	Vessels Seized	Detainees	Marijuana	Cocaine
2012[a]	67	31	176	32,718.0	80,632.1
2011	129	40	191	25,938.8	151,702.0
2010	122	56	229	36,739	202,402.1
2009	123	58	322	71,234.1	352,862.8
2008	85	43	209	22,173.8	367,926.1
2007	65	37	188	12,380.0	355,754.6
2006	64	23	200	9059.3	287,035.4
2005	87	66	364	10,026.0	338,205.6
2004	104	71	326	25,915.0	293,993.0
2003	65	56	283	14,059.0	136,865.0
2002	58	40	207	40,316.0	117,780.0
2001	65	30	114	34,520.0	138,393.0
2000	92	56	204	50,463.0	132,480.0
1999	118	74	304	61,506.0	111,689.0
1998	129	75	297	31,390.0	82,623.0
1997	122	64	233	102,538.0	103,617.0
1996	36	41	112	42,063.0	44,462.0
1995	44	34	56	40,164.0	33,629.0
1994	67	28	73	33,895.0	47,333.0

[a] As of date above.

The Coast Guard has dramatically reoriented its mission to the law enforcement model. The Coast Guard law enforcement mission is statutorily outlined in these general terms:

> The Coast Guard shall enforce or assist in the enforcement of all applicable Federal laws on, under, and over the high seas and waters subject to the jurisdiction of the United States; shall engage in maritime air surveillance or interdiction to enforce or assist in the enforcement of the laws of the United States; shall administer laws and promulgate and enforce regulations for the promotion of safety of life and property on and under the high seas and waters subject to the jurisdiction of the United States covering all matters not specifically delegated by law to some other executive department; shall develop, establish, maintain, and operate, with due regard to the requirements of national defense, aids to maritime navigation, ice-breaking facilities, and rescue facilities for the promotion of safety on, under, and over the high seas and waters subject to the jurisdiction of the United States; shall, pursuant to international agreements, develop, establish, maintain, and operate icebreaking facilities on, under, and over waters other than the high seas and waters subject to the jurisdiction of the United States; shall engage in oceanographic research of the high seas and in waters subject to the jurisdiction of the United States; and shall maintain a state of readiness to function as a specialized service in the Navy in time of war, including the fulfillment of Maritime Defense Zone command responsibilities.[16]

In 2004 the Coast Guard established a Maritime Law Enforcement Academy in Charleston, South Carolina. The academy prepares Coast Guard personnel to perform as boarding officers and boarding team members; develops the maritime law enforcement skills of professionals from federal, state, and local agencies, as well as the international community; and provides assistance to law enforcement agencies (Figure 10.24).

The Coast Guard also operates an investigative service. The office concentrates on drugs and other smuggling, illegal immigration activities, and environmental violations. Charted below are the competencies and skills expected for the professional investigator.[17]

Receipt, analysis, and disposition of allegations(s)

- Obtain data from complainant or source
- Document complaint in writing
- Know prosecutorial or regulatory criteria
- Identify violations (elements of crime) or administrative standards
- Review and identify significant information or potential evidence
- Determine correct disposition of complaint (criminal, civil, or administrative)
- Open investigation, if appropriate, and coordinate with appropriate authorities (internally/externally)

FIGURE 10.24 Maritime Law Enforcement Academy patch.

Assessment, focus, and preparation of investigative plan

- Review available information and evidence
- Review legal decisions and guidelines
- Review agency programs, operational policies, and procedures
- Determine focus and scope of investigation
- Assess and identify required resources
- Identify potential witnesses, suspects, relevant documents, and evidence
- Organize and prioritize investigative activities
- Prepare initial investigative plan

Conduct investigation

- Maintain focus and follow investigative plan (revise as necessary)
- Prepare for anticipated investigative activities (interviews, taking statements)
- Apply knowledge of laws and regulations
- Understand and apply techniques to ensure constitutional rights
- Project a professional image
- Use good oral and written communicative skills
- Know evidentiary rules
- Collect, analyze, and preserve evidence
- Use appropriate specialized techniques (search warrants, forensics, consensual monitoring)
- Conduct reviews and data inquiries and promptly document such activities
- Collect and analyze financial data

- Assess progress and refocus when necessary
- Coordinate progress with supervisor (prosecutors or management, as appropriate)
- Maintain appropriate liaison
- Effectively manage the case and assist personnel and meet planned milestones
- Obtain IG or grand jury subpoenas and testify before grand jury

Review, organize, and evaluate investigative findings

- Review and understand the information gathered
- Organize the information and evidence gathered
- Correlate data, witnesses, and records
- Consider internal/external customer needs

Draft report, validate contents, and submit final report

- Write draft report—ensure accuracy, thoroughness, objectivity, proper format, clarity, and correct grammar
- Review report to ensure information is correct and complete
- Consider issues such as confidentiality, the Privacy Act, the Freedom of Information Act, and security classification
- Include disclosure caveats where appropriate
- Write final report
- Distribute to appropriate entities

Post-investigative tasks

- Know rules of criminal and civil procedures
- Assist with preparation for court/administrative proceedings
- Serve witness subpoenas
- Assist U.S. attorney/district attorney at trial
- Testify at trial
- Document and report results, dispositions, and outcomes
- Obtain disposition of exhibits and evidence after trial/hearing
- Return and document proper disposition of documents and evidence
- Review the organization of investigative files for efficient retrieval
- Archive investigative files
- Ensure information management database reflects accurate and final case information

The Coast Guard tackles law enforcement from the homeland security end too. Here the Coast Guard displays its multitask ability and its capacity to blend safety, emergency, defense, and homeland protection into its mission. "Domestically, the Coast Guard-led Area Maritime Security Committees carry out much of the maritime security regimes effort."[18]

Counterterrorism efforts are an ongoing Coast Guard responsibility as well with a plethora of activities including the Maritime Security Response Team (MSRT)—a first responder to terrorist activities on the seas (Figure 10.25).

In the area of homeland security, the Coast Guard assumes these responsibilities:

- Protect ports, the flow of commerce, and the marine transportation system from terrorism.
- Maintain maritime border security against illegal drugs, illegal aliens, firearms, and weapons of mass destruction.
- Ensure that we can rapidly deploy and resupply our military assets, both by keeping Coast Guard units at a high state of readiness and by keeping marine transportation open for the transit assets and personnel from other branches of the armed forces.
- Protect against illegal fishing and indiscriminate destruction of living marine resources, and prevention and response to oil and hazardous material spills—both accidental and intentional.
- Coordinate efforts and intelligence with federal, state, and local agencies.

The Coast Guard also works closely with the other branches of the military to provide homeland defense and civil support to federal, state, and

FIGURE 10.25 Maritime Security Response Team boat crews maneuver into formation during training on Chesapeake Bay, February 17, 2011. The mission of the MSRT is to provide a short-notice, threat-tailored, maritime response force to deter, protect against, and respond to threats of maritime terrorism and to higher-risk criminal law enforcement threats on the water or in a port. (U.S. Coast Guard photo by Petty Officer 2nd Class Michael Anderson.)

FIGURE 10.26 Operation Noble Eagle patch.

local agencies in the United States, and includes the increased security measures taken after the September 11 terrorist attacks. The Coast Guard joined the other services in making its services available to the larger law enforcement community. This program, dubbed Operation Noble Eagle, seeks to meld the missions of the military into the homeland strategy (Figure 10.26).

Career opportunities abound for those interested in military service with a safety and law enforcement approach. The Coast Guard career track delivers fascinating and challenging paths to professionalism.

10.3.4.3 Cargo and Ports

The responsibility for cargo and port protection resides primarily with the U.S. Coast Guard, though its aligned partners—DHS and Customs and Immigration Service—aid in the endeavor. Bureaucratically, the Coast Guard administers its cargo, container, and facilities program through its Inspection and Compliance Directorate (Figure 10.27).

For the Coast Guard, as part of its overall mission of safety and security on the high seas and waterways, it would be a natural and very complementary function for this service. With billions of tons of cargo, and nearly 52,000 foreign ships visiting the United States, the job can be daunting.[19] Balance this with the entrepreneurial bent of the shipping and cargo industry—that need to move goods and services fast, efficiently, and profitably—and you have a delicate policy problem. On the one hand, the safety and security issue runs front and center, yet on the other hand, the Coast Guard needs to be sensitive to the question of productivity and finance. Some have argued that the costs of maritime security may be too high and not worth the investment.[20] Even afar, the costs associated with ensuring security are staggering and sometimes demonstrate

FIGURE 10.27 Coast Guard Inspection and Compliance Directorate.

the subservience of the maritime industry, which is "at the beck and call of a government whose legal initiatives, understandably, are more in tune with security than economy."[21]In a global economy, with significant trade entering American ports each and every day, the imposition of security measures in a free economy requires keen balancing. Implementing "new security policies with economic and trade objective is a complicated task given the potential risks to human life should the United States under-protect its borders."[22]

Each and every day, the U.S. Coast Guard is responsible for every visitation of a foreign ship, the safety and security of America's ports, and the implementation of sweeping maritime policies. The Coast Guard's Cargo and Facilities Division is responsible for:

- Overseeing onshore and offshore domestic commercial facilities, including deep-water ports, and cargo safety, security, and environmental protection compliance programs, including direction of Coast Guard field activities, and industry partnerships in support of applicable laws and regulations.
- Advising the Office of Investigation and Analysis regarding the notice of violation enforcement program policy as applied to cargo and commercial facilities.
- Maintaining liaison and outreach with key industry, interagency, and international partners on related facility and cargo safety, security, and environmental protection activities.
- Developing policy for facility security plans (FSPs) review and approval, facility alternative security programs (ASPS), and public access/waivers/exemptions.

- Establishing and interpreting standards and regulations, and participating in the rule making and the legislative change process for onshore and offshore domestic commercial facilities.
- Administering the standard safety and security Facility Inspection and Pollution Prevention Compliance programs.
- Administering program activities for military and commercial explosives, radioactive materials, packaged hazardous materials, cargoes of particular hazard, and classified cargoes.
- Maintaining a database of all U.S. waste reception.
- Developing inspection, enforcement, and safety and security policy for the Coast Guard Container Inspection Program and overseeing the operation of the Container Inspection Training and Assist Team (CITAT).
- Developing regulations and policy guidance for the implementation of a biometric credential for port workers and updating access control regulations and security plan requirements to implement requirements for such a credential.
- Establishing policy and policy guidance and overseeing the enforcement of international treaties, conventions, and domestic regulations for domestic onshore and offshore commercial facilities, including deep-water ports, and cargoes.
- Coordinating with interdepartmental agencies and other departments on the application of a coordinated cargo safety and security legislations, regulations, standards, and rules.
- Coordinating U.S. participation in international maritime groups.

10.3.4.3.1 Operation Homeport Homeport is the code name given by the Coast Guard to signify all of its port activities. The activities are extensive and this short section will only highlight a few of them (Figure 10.28).

Internet Resource: To become familiar with the diverse Homeport functions, visit http://homeport.uscg.mil/mycg/portal/ep/home.do.

10.3.4.3.1.1 Port and Harbor Facilities Port facilities are subject to a wide array of safety and security standards. Coast Guard personnel inspect the facilities—some 3,200 facilities in the United States alone. Each facility is required under the Maritime Security Act of 2002 to develop and implement a security plan. By 2005, some 9,500 vessels and 3,500 facilities submitted both a security assessment and a security plan. The Coast Guard was entrusted with assessing these plans and, once determining vulnerabilities, working with these parties to adjust and correct deficiencies. Coast Guard inspectors enter the facility to determine the consistency of the plan with the

FIGURE 10.28 Operation Homeport Inspection.

reality of that facility. Breaches in facilities are noted as well as deficiencies relating to record keeping and access control.

Internet Resource: For the federal regulations regarding the content of the security plan, see http://edocket.access.gpo.gov/cfr_2003/julqtr/pdf/33cfr105.305.pdf.

By 2006, the General Accounting Office, when reviewing the results of Coast Guard inspections, found patterns of deficiencies.[23] See Figure 10.29 for a chart depicting the results.

Upon the completed inspection, the Coast Guard issues a vulnerability report that the carrier will concur with or appeal. See Figure 10.30.

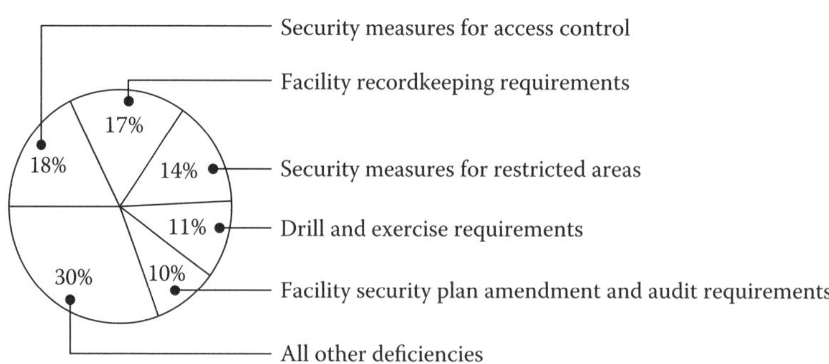

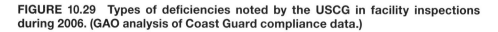

FIGURE 10.29 Types of deficiencies noted by the USCG in facility inspections during 2006. (GAO analysis of Coast Guard compliance data.)

U.S. DEPARTMENT OF HOMELAND SECURITY U.S. COAST GUARD CG-6025 (05/03)	FACILITY VULNERABILITY AND SECURITY MEASURES SUMMARY	OMB APPROVAL NO. 1625-0077

An agency may not conduct or sponsor, and a person is not required to respond to a collection of information unless it displays a valid OMB control number.

The Coast Guard estimates that the average burden for this report is 60 minutes. You may submit any comments concerning the accuracy of this burden estimate or any suggestions for reducing the burden to: Commandant (G-MP), U.S. Coast Guard, 2100 2nd St, SW, Washington D.C. 20593-0001 or Office of Management and Budget, Paperwork Reduction Project (1625-0077), Washington, DC 20503.

FACILITY IDENTIFICATION

1. Name of Facility

2. Address of Facility	3. Latitude
	4. Longitude
	5. Captain of the Port Zone

6. Type of Operation (check all that apply)

☐ Break Bulk	☐ Petroleum	☐ Certain Dangerous Cargo	☐ Passengers (Subchapter H)	☐ If other, explain below:
☐ Dry Bulk	☐ Chemical	☐ Barge Fleeting	☐ Passengers (Ferries)	
☐ Container	☐ LHG/LNG	☐ Offshore Support	☐ Passengers (Subchapter K)	
☐ RO-RO	☐ Explosives and other dangerous cargo		☐ Military Supply	

VULNERABILITY AND SECURITY MEASURES

7a. Vulnerability	7b. Vulnerability Category
	☐ If other, explain
8a. Selected Security Measures (MARSEC Level 1)	8b. Security Measures Category
	☐ If other, explain
9a. Selected Security Measures (MARSEC Level 2)	9b. Security Measures Category
	☐ If other, explain
10a. Selected Security Measures (MARSEC Level 3)	10b. Security Measures Category
	☐ If other, explain

VULNERABILITY AND SECURITY MEASURES

7a. Vulnerability	7b. Vulnerability Category
	☐ If other, explain
8a. Selected Security Measures (MARSEC Level 1)	8b. Security Measures Category
	☐ If other, explain
9a. Selected Security Measures (MARSEC Level 2)	9b. Security Measures Category
	☐ If other, explain
10a. Selected Security Measures (MARSEC Level 3)	10b. Security Measures Category
	☐ If other, explain

FIGURE 10.30 Facility security and vulnerability measures summary form.

10.3.4.3.1.2 Container Inspection The Coast Guard deploys teams to moving and stationary vessels for inspection of cargo and containers. The Coast Guard has developed and deployed Container Inspection Training and Assistance Teams (CITATs) to conduct container inspections at harbors and ports.

10.3.4.3.1.3 Vessel Inspection On the high seas and waterways, the Coast Guard has jurisdictional authority to board vessels for inspection purposes. This practice is one of its most crucial missions. Section 89 of Title 14 of the U.S. Code authorizes the Coast Guard to board vessels subject to the jurisdiction of the United States, anytime upon the high seas and upon waters over which the United States has jurisdiction, to make inquiries, examinations, inspections, searches, seizures, and arrests. Even despite the statutory authority, there are multiple reasons why boarding programs exist.

First, the Coast Guard tracks and issues certificates of operation to vessel owners.

Internet Resource: Download the certification form at http://www.uscg.mil/hq/cg5/nvdc/forms/cg1258.doc.

Second, the Coast Guard maintains a central depository of vessel records at its National Vessel Documentation Center. Records of registered vessels are fully cataloged and documented and serve as an information center in the event of accident or other calamity.

Third, the Coast Guard boards ships to conduct inspections or to carry out interdiction or intervention actions in the event of criminal activities. In the first instance, the Coast Guard may simply board under a voluntary request for ship inspection (Figure 10.31).

To commence the voluntary inspection program, the applicant need only fill out the request as outlined in Figure 10.32.

In the latter instance, the involuntary boarding, the Coast Guard may board if legally justified. Any question regarding safety, any issue of equipment,

FIGURE 10.31 Coast Guard officers conducting inspections.

U.S. DEPARTMENT OF HOMELAND SECURITY U.S. COAST GUARD CG-3752 (Rev. 6-04)	**APPLICATION FOR INSPECTION OF U.S. VESSEL**	FORM APPROVED OMB NO. 1625-0002

An agency may not conduct or sponsor, and a person is not required to respond to, a collection of information unless it displays a valid OMB control number.

The Coast Guard estimates that the average burden for this report is 15 mins. You may submit any comments concerning the accuracy of this burden estimate or any suggestion reducing the burden to: Commandant (G-MOC), U.S. Coast Guard, Washington, DC 20593-0001 or Office of Management and Budget, Paperwork Reduction Project (1625-0002), Washington, DC 20503.

Address to reply to:

TELEPHONE NUMBER:

DATE:

TO: Officer in Charge, Marine Inspection

Marine Inspection Zone ______________________

The undersigned applies to have the ☐ Steam Vessel ☐ Motor Vessel

☐ Motorboat ☐ Barge ☐ Other *(Indicate)* ______________________

named ______________________ Official or Award No. ______________________

inspected under the laws of the United States; to be employed as a ☐ Passenger Vessel *(No. of Passengers* ______ *)*

☐ Cargo Vessel ☐ Tank Vessel ☐ MODU ☐ Other *(Indicate)* ______________________

on the following route: *(Waters, Geographical limits)* ______________________

____

Liquid cargo in bulk ☐ will ☐ will not be carried as follows:

☐ Flammable or Combustible *(Indicate grade)* ______________________

☐ Chemicals *(Indicate)* ______________________

Length of vessel __________ ft.

Hull material: ☐ Steel ☐ Other *(Indicate)* ______________________

Vessel will be at *(Port, Pier, etc.)* ______________________

The current Certificate of Inspection expires on ______________________.

Inspection is desired on ______________________.

Cargo Ship Safety Construction Certificate to be issued by ☐ ABS ☐ USCG.

Vessel ☐ is ☐ is not to be classed.

If classed, indicate Classification Society: ☐ ABS ☐ Other *(Indicate)* ______________________

I CERTIFY that previous application for this inspection ☐ has ☐ has not been made. I further certify that I have instructed the master to present the vessel ready in all respects for the above requested inspection on the date specified. I understand that if this inspection is to be conducted at foreign port or place the vessel owners will be billed for the costs incurred in accordance with 46 USC 385b-1.

(Signature) ______________________

(Title) ______________________

FIGURE 10.32 Application for inspection of a U.S. vessel by the Coast Guard.

and surely any suspicion of illegal activity make boarding, despite a lack of consent, acceptable. When compared to their civilian law enforcement counterparts, whose action generally must be supported by probable cause, the rationale for boarding is much less legally rigorous. The Coast Guard expends considerable energy preparing boarding officers and, just as attentively, refines the boarding process to ensure a professional and legally defensible protocol. The USCG certifies boarding officers in training locales at its network of facilities. The designated curriculum for the boarding officer stresses a legalistic approach to training as evidenced by the subject matter:

- Authority and jurisdiction
- Use of force
- Tactical procedures
- Criminal law
- Constitutional law
- Defensive tactics
- Arrest procedures
- Maritime law enforcement boarding procedures
- PWCS boarding procedures
- Confined spaces
- Boating safety regulations
- Commercial fishing industry regulations
- Boating under the influence enforcement
- Testify in court
- Hostage situations
- Fraudulent document

The Coast Guard lays out a precise protocol for boarding a vessel. A uniformed Coast Guard boarding team gives notification of its intent to board. Generally the team is armed. At first, the team will conduct an initial safety inspection to identify any obvious safety hazards, and to ensure the sea worthiness of the vessel. The boarding officer will then ask to see the vessel registration or documentation, and proceed with the inspection. The scope of the vessel inspection during most boardings is limited to determining the vessel's regulatory status (e.g., commercial, recreational, passenger, cargo, or fishing vessel) and checking for compliance with U.S. civil law applicable to vessels of that status. The Coast Guard may also enforce U.S. criminal law. The boarding officer then completes a Coast Guard boarding form and notes any discrepancies (Figure 10.33).

Space limitations make impossible a full picture of how the U.S. Coast Guard lends its services in the maritime world. In many ways, it is the branch of the service most dedicated to the cause of homeland security. Every minute of its operations are about safety and security, and since 9/11, the Coast Guard has been called upon to do more than it has ever imagined since its inception in 1790. Of all the governmental entities called upon to strike back and detect our enemies, the Coast Guard has been asked to reinvent itself. A recent report about the Coast Guard from the Government Accounting Office warned of this tendency to throw everything at this arm of the service.

> The difficulty of meeting these challenges is compounded because the Coast Guard is not just moving to a new parent agency: it is also substantially

FIGURE 10.33 Coast Guard boarding a vessel for inspection.

> reinventing itself because of its new security role. Basically, the agency faces a fundamental tension in balancing its many missions. It must still do the work it has been doing for years in such areas as fisheries management and search and rescue, but now its resources are deployed as well in homeland security and even in the military buildup in the Middle East. The Coast Guard's expanded role in homeland security, along with its relocation in a new agency, have changed many of its working parameters, and its adjustment to this role remains a work in process. Much work remains.[24]

If history demonstrates anything, it would be the capacity of the Coast Guard to meet any challenge assigned to it. The Coast Guard adapts to meet the mission of homeland protection and makes a mighty contribution in the fight against terrorism.

10.4 Rail and Mass Transit

The task of securing the country's rail and mass transit system is just as critical as the air industry protections. Mass transit systems carry nearly 10 billion passengers per year and the mass transportation fleet is nearly 150,000 vehicles. Amtrak carries nearly 30 million passengers on its national network. The country's rail system, a series of weaving lines for both freight and passenger traffic, constitutes a major part of this country's economic life. In the world of commerce, trains deliver more cargo mile per mile, and more efficiently than any on-land trucking company is capable of doing. "Every

FIGURE 10.34 High-speed passenger train.

day, more than one million shipments of hazardous chemicals are transported throughout the nation's infrastructure; a large percentage of these chemicals are transported by rail and are prone to becoming airborne."[25]

The security of this commercial flow is critical to the U.S.'s economic health, and just the sort of target a terrorist would hope to disrupt. If terrorists seek to inflict widespread harm on the U.S. economy, they have "a number of strategies that pose serious threats to and through the rail system of the country" (Figure 10.34).[26]

The potential for both human and infrastructure destruction is easy to project and anticipate. For the terrorist, the prime aim generally relates to larger, more grandiose impacts. The act may "use the rails as a way of conveying an instrument of mass destruction on its human agents than an attack on any one point in the physical infrastructure."[27]As a result, the target of mass transit and its infrastructure is attractive due to the strength of its destructive message. In London, in the subway and Tube system of 2005, the security professional need worry about the many nightmarish results. A horrid picture of destruction and loss of life occurred in Madrid, Spain in 2004. Two hundred people lost their lives in this terrorist act (Figure 10.35).

It is extremely logical to conclude that either passenger or freight might be the means of transport, and if the human casualties are the end sought, the terrorist act may predictably occur near an urban center. In the final analysis, both rail and mass transit systems are part of the family of critical infrastructure essential to a secure America.

DHS has now rightfully concluded that mass transit systems and rail lines may be the next generation of threat targets.

Internet Exercise: To assess the vulnerabilities of a mass transit system and discover proper steps to prevent, visit http//www.tsa.gov/assets/pdf/mass_transit_action_items.pdf.

FIGURE 10.35 Destroyed railway carriages sit on the tracks after the attack on Atocha railway station in Madrid.

In rail and mass transit, the demands of risk assessment are more global and less contained than the security checkpoint at an airport. TSA, working closely with state, federal, and local law enforcement, must see vulnerability, threat, and risk in a much larger framework. Instead of the targeted emphasis of passenger at a point of entry, the risk analysis in transit and rail must be conducted at various headquarters and stations, as well as in the whole field of operation. The tracks are the path to follow so to speak. In 2010, TSA published a series of recommendations about rail and mass transit, all of which are worthy of our consideration:

1. Designate a lead agency to coordinate periodic modal and cross-modal security risk analyses.
2. Implement an integrated Federal approach that consolidates capabilities in a unified effort for security assessments, audits, and inspections to produce more thorough evaluations and effective follow-up actions to reduce risk, enhance security, and reduce burdens on assessed surface transportation entities.
3. Identify appropriate methodologies to evaluate and rank surface transportation systems and infrastructure that are critical to the nation.
4. Implement a multiyear, multiphase grants program based on a long-term strategy for surface transportation security.
5. Establish a measurable evaluation system to determine the effectiveness of surface transportation security grants.

6. Establish an interagency process to inventory education and training (E&T) requirements and programs; identify gaps and redundancies in surface transportation owner/operator E&T, and ensure that Federal training requirements support counterterrorism and infrastructure protection.
7. Implement a unified environment for sharing transportation security information that provides all relevant threat information and improves the effectiveness of information flow.
8. Reemphasize National Infrastructure Protection Plan (NIPP) framework priorities with the Sector-Specific Agencies (SSA); surface transportation owners/operators; and state, local, tribal, and territorial (SLTT) partners in order to focus development and implementation of a relevant and representative model that enhances security of the Transportation Systems Sector partners.
9. Fully identify Federal roles and responsibilities in surface transportation security, taking steps to efficiently leverage resources and ultimately lead to a budget "cross cut" that extends Federal coordination to include both surface transportation safety and security.
10. Identify an interagency lead to establish a single data repository for all federally obtained security risk-related information on transportation systems and assets.
11. Coordinate data requests with the established single data repository to avoid redundant efforts, take advantage of existing data sets, and establish data access control.
12. Analyze the common features of existing analysis methods and tools, and then perform a gap analysis to identify additional characteristics that would ensure that analyses are more closely comparable and consistent with the risk assessment principles in the NIPP.
13. Define a process to assess and certify extant industry risk assessments for ranking risk remediation projects under the Transit Security Grant Program or other similar Federal programs.
14. Establish a fee-based, centrally managed "clearing house" to validate new privately developed security technologies that meet Federal standards.
15. Encourage the use of SECURE™ (Systems Efficacy through Commercialization, Utilization, Relevance, and Evaluation) and FutureTECH™ programs within appropriate directives.
16. Create a more efficient Federal credentialing system by reducing credentialing redundancy, leveraging existing investments, and implementing the principle of "enroll once, use many" to reuse the information of individuals applying for multiple access privileges.
17. Collaborate with the SCCs to develop a proposal for security threat assessments standards.

18. Incorporate formal and informal methods for surface transportation owners/operators, as well as SCCs that represent them, to provide direct input into setting surface transportation research and development priorities.
19. Develop a formal, recurring surface transportation security grants process for meeting with surface transportation SCCs, owners/operators, and SLTT governments; collecting and adjudicating recommendations; and making final decisions.
20. Review key policy issues and questions identified by the Surface Transportation Security Priority Assessment to address unresolved policy issues and provide solutions for resolving identified security gaps.[28]

With these real threats in mind, DHS has increasingly given higher priority to train and rail over the last few years, strengthened the security of the country's freight and passenger rail systems, and reduced the risk associated with the transportation of security-sensitive materials, such as poisonous by inhalation hazard materials, certain explosive materials, and certain high-level radioactive material shipments. DHS has also formally codified the right of the Transportation Security Agency to inspect rail facilities and equipment for these purposes. DHS works closely with a wide array of other federal agencies to carry out this purpose, including the Department of Transportation, the Federal Railroad Administration, and federal law enforcement agencies concerned about interstate crime and terrorism.[29] DHS also depends upon the cooperation of the country's numerous freight carriers, such as CSX, Union Pacific, and others, to carry out its mission on the rails. DHS created a committee of both public and private entities to consult on rail policy. Its members include:

- Association of American Railroads
- American Short Line and Regional Railroad Association
- Amtrak
- Anacostia and Pacific
- BNSF Railway Company
- Canadian National
- Canadian Pacific Railway
- CSX Transportation
- Genesee & Wyoming
- Iowa Interstate Railroad Ltd.
- Kansas City Southern Railway Company
- Metra
- Norfolk Southern
- RailAmerica
- Union Pacific Railroad Company
- Wheeling & Lake Erie Railway

Both the public and the private sector are stakeholders in ensuring a safe and secure rail and mass transit system. More than 6,000 transit service providers, commuter railroads, and long-distance trains travel daily. Nearly 600 transit systems operate in urban areas, while Amtrak provides passenger service on nearly 22,000 miles of track. The story for freight is equally positive. See Figure 10.36.

With the rise of gasoline prices, the country's commuter lines are showing extraordinary growth in ridership. As a result of this growth, the security dynamics are intensifying. In November 2008, DHS promulgated rules that ensure a safer system, which include:

- *Secure chain of custody*: Shippers will physically inspect security-sensitive materials rail cars prior to shipment. The rule is applicable to 46 key urban areas.
- *Communication*: The rule requires freight and passenger railroad carriers, rail transit systems, and certain rail hazardous materials facilities to designate a rail security coordinator (RSC). The RSC will serve as the liaison to DHS for intelligence information, security-related activities, and ongoing communications with TSA.
- *Reporting security concerns*: The rule requires freight and passenger railroads to immediately report incidents, potential threats, and significant security concerns to TSA.
- *Location tracking*: The rule requires freight railroad carriers and certain rail hazardous materials shippers and receivers, at the request of TSA, to report the location of individual rail cars containing security-sensitive materials within 5 min, and the locations of all cars containing security-sensitive materials within 30 min.

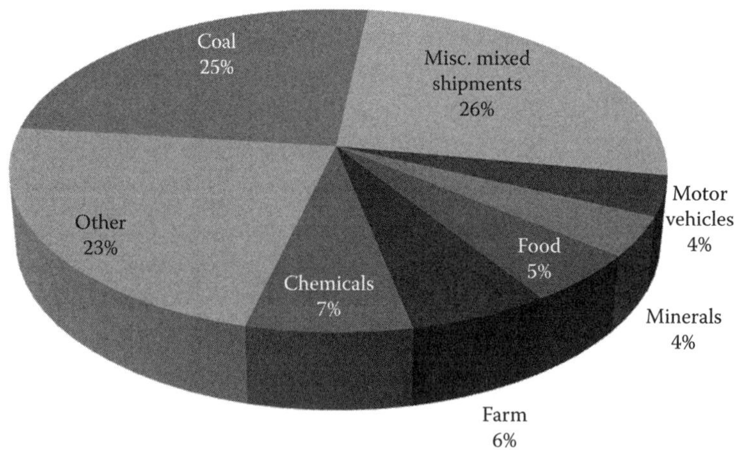

FIGURE 10.36 Types of goods delivered by rail.

- *Inspection authority*: TSA is authorized to inspect freight and passenger railroad carriers, rail transit systems, and certain facilities that ship or receive specified hazardous materials by rail.

TSA, in conjunction with the Federal Transit Administration, has published specific Protective Measures for Mass Transit systems.

Review this comprehensive list of recommendations at Appendix D.

10.4.1 Representative Security Programs for Rail and Transit

To illustrate the emerging homeland security demands for rail, a brief look at some representative programs is in order. Whether for freight or passenger, whether operated by public or private entities, the demand for security protocols has never been greater. Indeed, DHS concluded in 2007 that rail and mass transit operations were woefully inadequate in various areas, including information sharing, research and development, public education, training and exercises, tunnels, and underwater passages (Figure 10.37).[30]

Despite some predictable shortcomings, most rail and transit systems have made enormous strides in the world of homeland security. The General Accounting Office concluded that slow but sure improvements to rail security were being made but further improvements were critical to its future as an industry.[31] The GAO also concluded that the rail industry failed to share information as seamlessly as need be in matters of security and called upon the industry to make improvements in this direction.[32]

The array of new initiatives in rail and mass transit is beginning to make its mark in the world of homeland security. Aside from inculcating a general theory of risk assessment and mitigation, the industry sees itself as a partner with public officials. A cursory outline of these activities follows.

1. *Layers of Security*: The TSA mindset on the various layers of security has now become part of the rail and mass transit approach.
2. *Transit Inspectors through the Surface Transportation Security Program*: 100 officers now inspect the rail infrastructure.

FIGURE 10.37 An engine in the depot awaiting inspection.

3. *VIPR Teams*: Using canines, advanced screening technology, and behavioral detection, the Visible Intermodal Protection Response Team can be dispatched to any rail location.
4. *Grants and Funding*: The rail industry as well as the public transit systems may participate in funding programs which advance security.
5. *Mobile Checkpoints*: An economical way to view containers for security breaches.
6. *Site Assessments*: At any location inspectors and TSA officers can give insight and professional advice on the security and safety of an installation.
7. *Security and Emergency Preparedness Action Items*: The top 20 steps the industry must take to prepare for security risks.
8. *Training for Employees*: Security awareness and skill is essential for all employees.
9. *TSA's Land Transportation Anti-Terrorism Training Program (LTATP)*: Offered at FLETC.
10. *Connecting Communities*: A program which highlights the unique security and emergency issues that arise in transit situations.

10.4.1.1 Amtrak

Amtrak carries out both behind-the-scenes and front-line security measures aimed at improving passenger rail security. Depending upon the locale and other factors, the security practices may be uniform or random in design. Some of the common Amtrak security protocols are:

- Uniformed police officers and mobile security teams
- Random passenger and carry-on baggage screening
- K-9 units
- Checked baggage screening
- On-board security checks
- Identification checks

Amtrak has also received generous funding for the safety and security of its complex infrastructure. In the Northeast corridor, Amtrak operates in diverse environments with dramatic challenges for the security operative. In 2008, DHS awarded $25 million to Amtrak to begin the process of securing bridges, tunnels, overhangs, and other locations with target potential.

Amtrak now deploys specialized mobile tactical units that conduct random baggage searches and other security responsibility. The mobile security team's squads take on many forms, including armed specialized Amtrak police, explosives-detecting K-9 units, and armed counterterrorism special agents in tactical uniforms. The mobile units were developed in conjunction with the federal,

FIGURE 10.38 Amtrak's Mobile Tactical Unit helps secure the railways.

state, and private industry sectors to improve security practices. The mobile security team's procedures will not impact train schedules (Figure 10.38).

The new procedures are an enhancement to strategic security measures already in place, such as:

- Uniformed police and plainclothes officers on trains and in stations
- Security cameras
- Random identification checks
- "See Something, Say Something" passenger education program to promote involvement and raise vigilance
- Investments in state-of-the-art security technology
- Security awareness training for the entire Amtrak workforce
- Behind-the-scenes activities that remain undisclosed

Amtrak is also investing in cutting-edge technologies to improve its security efforts and presently testing intrusion detection technologies, employing explosive detection and vapor K-9 teams, conducting more passenger screenings, and actively participating in the Joint Terrorism Task Force in its various regions. Finally, Amtrak is calling upon its customer base to be active players in the security effort. Through its Partners for Amtrak Safety and Security Program (PASS) customers are asked to be active participants in the who, what, where, when, and how of criminal conduct.

Internet Exercise: Learn about the PASS program at: https://pass.amtrak.com/.

10.4.1.2 CSX: The Freight Line

Just as the public rail entities have core responsibilities, so too do the private rail companies. CSX is an excellent example of a progressive freight shipper with a massive route network in the eastern half of the United States. It, like all other rail concerns, has had to reconsider how it carries out its business since 9/11. As noted above, shipment of hazardous and security-sensitive materials is subject to a host of regulations and other requirements.[33]

Railroads also must:

- Compile security data based on commodity and route type
- Identify security vulnerabilities
- Identify alternative routes
- Develop programs of safety and security
- Revisit route selections
- Communicate with state and federal officials
- Design tracking systems for sensitive material
- Work in unity with the motor carriers whose cargo the rail transports

See Figure 10.39 for a map of CSX's rail system.

CSX, just as its sister carriers, abides by a host of regulations. Of recent interest are the TSA requirements that shipments to designated urban areas be processed according to new protocols, and additionally, that the chain of custody of these shipments be tracked. The materials subject to the rules include explosives, toxic by inhalation materials (TIH), poisonous by inhalation materials (PIH), and bulk amounts of radioactive materials, all of which are now designated rail security-sensitive materials.

TSA now insists that certain rail secure areas be the exclusive points of shipping or receiving facilities in these designated areas. As of February 15, 2009, rail companies, like CSX, are only able to accept shipments of rail security-sensitive materials from rail secure areas. In areas designated high-threat urban areas (HTUA), delivery will only be possible to a rail secure area.

Internet Resource: See the list of HTUAs at http://www.dhs.gov/xlibrary/assets/FY06_UASI_Eligibility_List.pdf.

Another facet of the new rules on rail shipments will involve written certifications of compliance. Shipments of rail security-sensitive materials are subject to TSA chain-of-custody requirements. The rules require (1) all consignors and (2) those consignees located in a HTUA to have personnel physically present for attended handoffs of all railcars containing rail security-sensitive materials. TSA has promulgated that it expects the personnel attending the handoff of railcars with rail security-sensitive materials to document the transfer by recording (1) each railcar's initials and number, (2) the individuals attending the transfer, (3) the location of the transfer, and (4) the date and time of the transfer.

Contending with new rules of the road will be an ongoing demand for the freight industry (Figure 10.40).

Internally, CSX has established a sophisticated and impressive security and safety program. Aside from its materials training, emphasis on

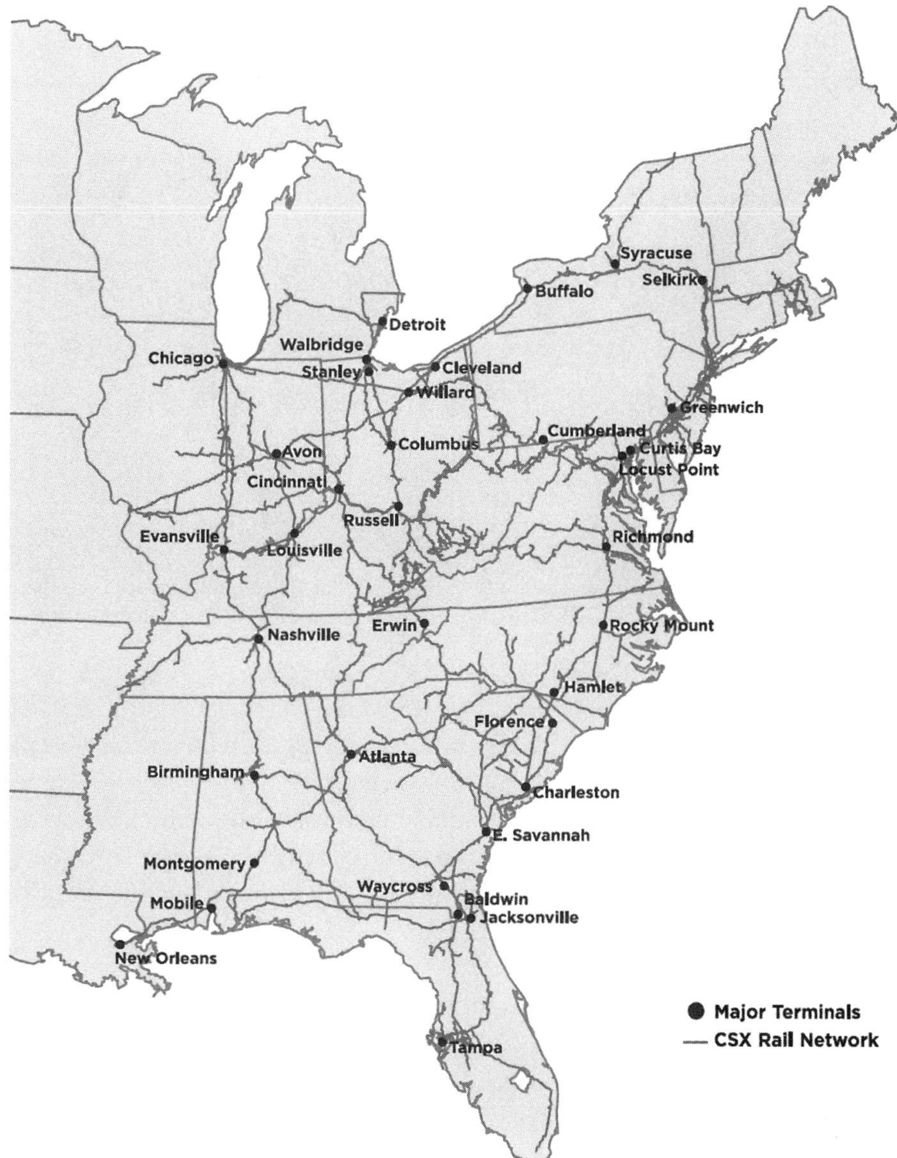

FIGURE 10.39 CSX rail system map.

employee safety, and other industrial applications, CSX fully comprehends the mix of the public and private interests in its rail operation. The line shares information with governmental entities and partners with myriad agencies dedicated to safety and security. Examples of these efforts are:

- CSX Transportation's (CSXT) Network Operations Workstation: A cornerstone of this partnership is CSXT's sharing of its highly

FIGURE 10.40 CSX freight train.

specialized secure Network Operations Workstation (NOW) System. Key highlights of the NOW System include:

- Enhanced monitoring: Provides state homeland security and law enforcement officials with a tool to identify the status of CSXT trains and rail cars in each state. Before, officials needed to call CSXT to access this information.
- Information sharing: Helps security officials prepare for and, if needed, respond to emergency situations.
- Targeted security: With additional information about what is carried on rails, state officials can more efficiently allocate law enforcement resources, coordinate with CSXT security officials, and integrate rail security into ongoing law enforcement operations.

- Joint law enforcement and emergency responder training: Law enforcement officials train with the CSXT Police Rapid Response Team—a group of highly skilled police officers specifically trained to respond to security incidents. Additionally, state and community emergency first responders train alongside CSXT's experts in hazardous materials and emergency response.
- Sharing of hazardous materials density studies: These data help emergency response organizations plan their resources and identify the types of emergency response training applicable to their jurisdiction.

- Closer coordination of law enforcement operations in and around CSXT yards: CSXT can provide its partners with an around-the-clock access to its rail security professionals.
- Developing better rail security policies: States and CSXT continue to work with policymakers to identify important public policy issues that can impact and improve rail security.

CSX, like its counterparts in the industry, sees the world in differing terms than pre-9/11. The industry works closely with local, state, and federal authorities to secure the nation's railroads. Freight railroads remain in constant communication with the U.S. Department of Transportation security personnel, the FBI, the National Security Council, and state and local law enforcement officers.

Internet Resource: Visit a recent DHS grant announcement for freight rail roads at http://www.tsa.dhs.gov/assets/pdf/fy09_frsgp_faqs.pdf.

10.4.1.3 SEPTA: Rail Mass Transit

The Southeastern Pennsylvania Transit Authority (SEPTA) is one of the nation's largest rail commuter systems. It also connects and collaborates with other carriers and is part and parcel of a very large collective of mass transit providers, including New Jersey Transit, Delaware Area Transit, and Amtrak. The system can readily and very easily hook up the rider to New York, Baltimore, and Washington, DC. In this extreme congestion, SEPTA needs always be mindful of the security threat (Figure 10.41).

FIGURE 10.41 SEPTA's Wilmington, Delaware, station.

Prevention of future terrorist attacks is both a national and a local concern. SEPTA takes the threat of terrorism very seriously. Passengers are afforded maximum security and protection. Increased presence of transit police officers on the system's cars and stations have been a high priority for SEPTA management. Also present throughout the transit system, although obviously less visible, is a trained team of undercover, plainclothes SEPTA police officers who are working to ensure the security of our passengers.

SEPTA's police officers have been thoroughly trained in antiterrorism awareness. Specially trained officers have instructed additional SEPTA personnel in an antiterrorism program that includes recognition, response, and prevention techniques.

Internet Resource: Learn about careers in law enforcement on SEPTA at http://autohire.careershop.com/septajobs/default.asp?ContentID=7.

See Figure 10.42 for a route map from SEPTA.

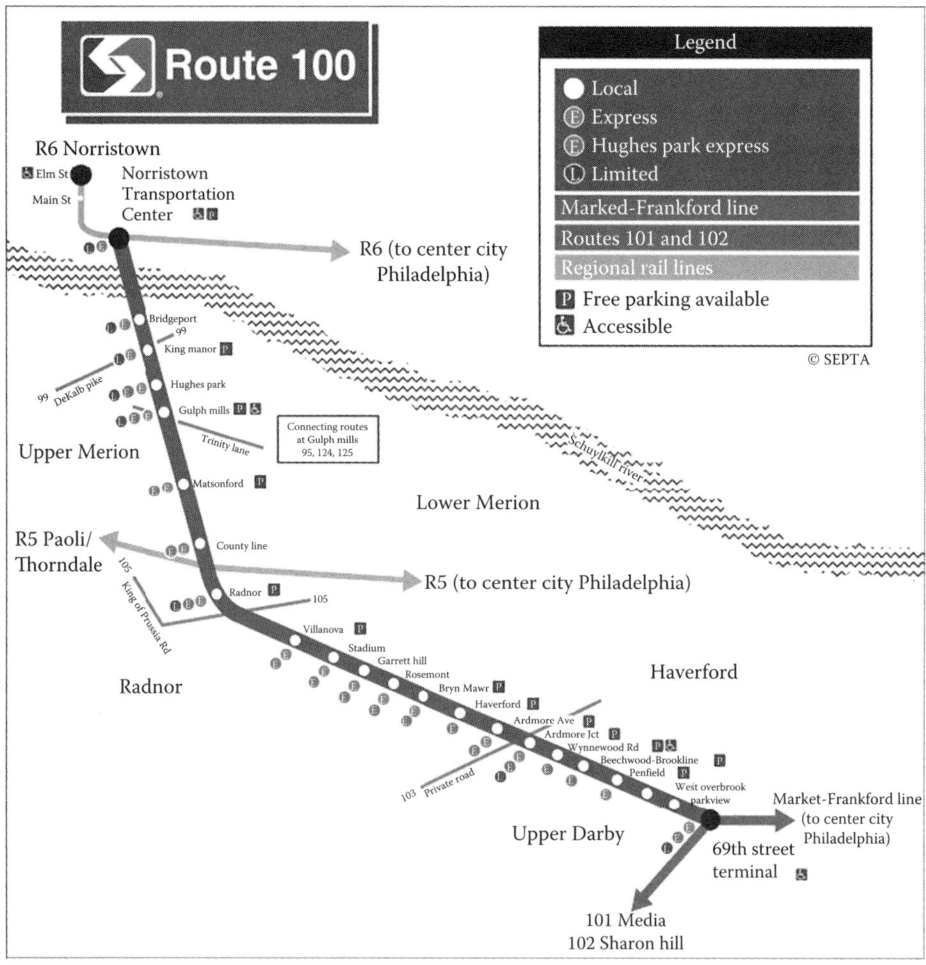

FIGURE 10.42 Railway route map.

Yet when one considers the sheer volume of passengers on this system day to day, are these general recommendations enough? Does a transit police force have the capability to trace and track every imaginable threat? Is the geography alone too much to cover? Most observers of mass transit indicate there are simply too many holes in the dike to be confident about thwarting the terrorist threat—and just as frustratingly, too many players in the overall mix. To be successful, mass transit systems will have to be better organized. Here are some suggestions:

- Make TSA the clear leader for rail and mass transit security.
- Require TSA to complete a national rail and mass transit security strategy.
- Require rail and mass transit owners and operators to submit security plans.
- Conduct vulnerability assessments on all rail and mass transit security systems.
- Develop and enforce a baseline of security.
- Dedicate funding for rail and mass transit security.[34]

While all of the recommendations are poignant, the training side of the security and risk plan cannot be forgotten or neglected. In every facet of mass transit, the risk to passengers and employees is high. Those entrusted with transit operation must be sure to train the employees to the highest level. TSA has devised an excellent matrix of learning to assure that the essential subject matter covered and that costs are contained. See Figure 10.43.

10.5 Conclusion

Transportation runs heavily throughout the pages of this chapter. More specifically, the chapter delves into the full menu of TSA activities. The most visible of homeland departments, TSA is now part of the fabric of travel and travel installations. Usually associated with airports, TSA has additional responsibilities involving public roads, bridges, rail, pipelines, and train stations. At its base, TSA is responsible for transportation threat assessment and vulnerability, the promulgation of standards and practices regarding safety and security, and the entity entrusted with anticipating novel innovations in the homeland dimension. Trace portals, millimeter wave machines, and biometrics are examples of how technology impacts TSA operations. TSA adopts a policy of layered security whereby at various stages of security scrutiny, it is unlikely that a terrorist will escape each and every level of oversight.

Basic Mass Transit Security Training Program											
Training Description	Focus	Categories of Employees to Receive									Total Training Cost
		Front-Line Employees	Station Managers	Administrative and Support Staff	Maintenance Workers	Mid-Level Management	Senior Management	Operations Control Center Staff	Security Guards	Law Enforcement	
Security Awareness	Enhance capability to identify, report, and react to suspicious activity and security incidents										$0
Behavior Recognition	Recognize behaviors associated with terrorists' reconnaissance and planning activities, including the conduct of surveillance. Applies lessons learned from the Israeli security meeting.										$0
Immediate Emergency Response	Prepare passenger rail train operators to deal with explosive detonations, incendiaries, released chemical hazards, and similar threats in the confines of trains and system infrastructure.										$0
National Incident Management System (NIMS)	Ensure transit agency emergency preparedness and response personnel gain and retain the knowledge and skills necessary to operate under NIMS in accordance with the National Response Plan (NRP).										$0

FIGURE 10.43 **Basic mass transit security training program.**

Training Description	Focus	Categories of Employees to Receive									Total Training Cost
		Front-Line Employees	Station Managers	Administrative and Support Staff	Maintenance Workers	Mid-Level Management	Senior Management	Operations Control Center Staff	Security Guards	Law Enforcement	
Operations Control Center Readiness	Identify security vulnerabilities. Understand and exercise role of OCC personnel in preventing terrorist attacks. Distinguish characteristics of improvised explosive devices (IEDs) and weapons of mass destruction. Specify priorities during a terrorist attack and manage incident response. Apply transit agency's operational plans for response to IED and WMD scenarios, directing and coordinating activities in the system.										$0
		Mass Transit Security Follow-on Courses									
Training Description	Focus	Front-Line Employees	Station Managers	Administrative and Support Staff	Maintenance Workers	Mid-Level Management	Senior Management	Operations Control Center Staff	Security Guards	Law Enforcement	Total Training Cost
Management of Transit Emergencies I (4-day course)	Ensure employees throughout the transit agency understand individual roles in emergency response and the transit system's role in emergencies or disasters in the system and the broader community.										$0

FIGURE 10.43 (continued) Basic mass transit security training program.

Management of Transit Emergencies II (1-day course)	Ensure employees throughout the transit agency understand individual roles in emergency response and the transit system's role in emergencies or disasters in the system and the broader community.										$0
Coordinated Interagency Emergency Response	Advance interoperability of the transit agency with multiple responding entities in emergency response.										$0
Managing Counterrorism Programs	Enable transit agency management officials to develop and manage a counterrorism program in a transit system.										$0
Prevention and Mitigation—IEDS and WMD: T4 3-day course	Enhance capabilities to identify threats from improvised explosive devices and weapons of mass destruction (chemical, biological, radiological, nuclear) to identify, report, and react to suspicious activity and security incidents										$0

FIGURE 10.43 (continued) Basic mass transit security training program.

Training Description	Focus	Mass Transit Security Follow-on Courses									Total Training Cost
		Front-Line Employees	Station Managers	Administrative and Support Staff	Maintenance Workers	Mid-Level Management	Senior Management	Operations Control Center Staff	Security Guards	Law Enforcement	
Prevention and Mitigation—IEDS and WMD: CBRNE Incident Management 1-day course	Enhance capabilities to identify threats from improvised explosive devices and weapons of mass destruction (chemical, biological, radiological, nuclear) to identify, report, and react to suspicious activity and security incidents.										$0
Transit Vehicle Hijacking Prevention and Response	Enable employees to develop and implement plans and procedures to respond to transit vehicle hijackings and workplace violence.										$0
Integrated Anti-Terrorism Security Program	Enhance capabilities of transit agency security officials, law enforcement personnel, and others with interaction with passengers to detect, deter, and prevent acts of terrorism.										$0
Transit System Security Design	Expand integration of security considerations into designs of new transit systems and improvements of existing systems.										$0

FIGURE 10.43 **(continued) Basic mass transit security training program.**

Train-the-Trainer Courses											
		Categories of Employees to Receive									
Training Description	Focus	Front-Line Employees	Station Managers	Administrative and Support Staff	Maintenance Workers	Mid-Level Management	Senior Management	Operations Control Center Staff	Security Guards	Law Enforcement	Total Training Cost
Security Awareness Train-the-Trainer	Enhance capability to identify, report, and react to suspicious activity and security incidents.										$0
Behavior Recognition Train-the-Trainer	Recognize behaviors associated with terrorists' reconnaissance and planning activities, including the conduct of surveillance. Applies lessons learned from the Israeli security meeting.										$0
Total Training Costs—All Courses											

FIGURE 10.43 (continued) Basic mass transit security training program.

Other transportation initiatives highlighted in this chapter include the federal air marshal, federal flight deck officers, and law enforcement officers flying armed. Each of these programs provides an added layer of armed protection in the air travel industry. TSA employs canines in various components of its practices, especially regarding explosives.

The chapter looks intently on how homeland functions are pertinent to the world of the maritime. The prevention of terrorist attacks on maritime critical infrastructure, the safeguarding of oceans and corresponding resources, and the minimization of economic losses in the maritime domain are highly relevant homeland functions. In implementing the National Strategy for Maritime Security, DHS operatives accept the broad-based perspective on what constitutes the maritime domain and rely heavily upon the maritime industry to advise as to best practices. In maritime security, government and commerce work collaboratively. Featured with rightful relevancy is the role and function of the U.S. Coast Guard, which naturally operates in the maritime. The Coast Guard, as part of its core mission, provides maritime safety and security in multiple contexts. In addition, the Coast Guard needs to maintain mobility in waterways and other ports of interest, assist in the protection of natural resources, respond to emergencies and catastrophes, and is part of the U.S. national defense. In each of these categories, the Coast Guard's history displays extraordinary success. Saving thousands of lives is simply the mission, a Coastie would argue. Aside from the endless plucking of victims from water peril, the Coast Guard operates the premier search and rescue team (SAR)—legendary in both requirements and results. The Coast Guard wears comfortably the hat of law enforcement as well as by targeting smugglers and drug traffickers, terrorists, and other undesirables. The Coast Guard operates a specialized facility to train its members in law enforcement functions—the Maritime Law Enforcement Academy in Charleston, South Carolina. The sweep of Coast Guard services is difficult to fully catalog since, aside from all these functions, the command deals with port and harbor protections, container and vessel inspection, offshore drilling facilities, cargo safety, and environmental crimes. The Coast Guard's Homeport program encompasses all of these activities.

Finally, the chapter takes a close look at the rail and mass transit industry. While rail is both publicly and privately operated, the types of mass transit make full coverage an impossibility. Hence, the stress here is on rail due to its potential to be a medium of delivery for the terrorist, or the locus with the most potential for human loss of life. As in Spain, a few years ago, the compelling and hideous impact of a terrorist on a train system has unfortunately been displayed. How Amtrak, CSX, and the SEPTA system address the many challenges of homeland security is fully assessed.

Keywords

Baggage screening
Boarding officer
Canine explosive detection unit
Cargo and Facilities Division
Certificate of operation
Container Inspection Training and Assistance Team
Department of Commerce
Federal air marshal
Federal Aviation Administration
Federal flight deck officer
Federal Highway Administration
Inspection and Compliance Directorate
Law enforcement officer flying armed
Maritime security
Mass transit
Millimeter wave
Mobile tactical unit
National Strategy for Maritime Security
National Vessel Documentation Center
Operation Homeport
Operation Noble Eagle
Passenger screening
Poisonous by inhalation
Rail secure area
Rail security sensitive material
Rail transit system
Registered Traveler program
Search and rescue team
Security threat assessment
Toxic by inhalation
Trace portal
Transportation security
Transportation Security Administration

Discussion Questions

1. The Secure Freight and Container Security Initiative assumes much about our trading partners. Comment.
2. In what way has trade and commerce benefited from electronic tracking and computer systems?
3. Some argue that the USCIS is delving into activities best left to other historic agencies. Can you identify an example of where this criticism might be relevant?
4. TSA is often labeled a reactive agency that gives little thought to its practices. Do you think this conclusion is reasonable in any sense?
5. Why does TSA have such turnover problems in personnel?
6. Explain why the layered security practice of TSA works so effectively.

7. How should TSA be a leader in the use of technology and computer innovation in its practices?
8. How do biometric measures replace human function and task?
9. The Coast Guard is often labeled as an entity being asked to do everything and even more. How is this so? And how has this condition led to stresses in the Coast Guard?
10. Discuss some of the more recent plans and programs designed for the maritime world.
11. Discuss three programs of the Coast Guard that deal with vessels and law enforcement function.
12. Why is rail and mass transit rail such a difficult industry in which to apply uniform standards?
13. Of the three types of rail systems, namely, freight, passenger, and public mass transit, which has the greatest demands when it comes to security issues?

Practical Exercises

1. Evaluate TSA's 20 layers of security. Which could readily be eliminated and why?
2. Prepare a career file with representative positions for the following occupations:
   - Federal air marshals
   - Federal flight deck officers
   - TSA
   - TSA canine
3. Review the career options in the Coast Guard. Explain how many of the USCG career paths deal with homeland security. Provide at least three examples.
4. Prepare a mock vessel inspection request for the U.S. Coast Guard.
5. Contact your local mass transit provider. Find out what steps the entity has taken relative to homeland security preparedness.

Notes

1. K. Vlahos, Pat-down dust-up renews screening debate, *Homeland Security Today*, June, 2011: 10–11.
2. U.S. Government Accountability Office, *Aviation Security: TSA Has Made Progress, but Additional Efforts Are Needed to Improve Security*, GAO Highlights, 2011.
3. A. Sternstein, *Experts Chide TSA for Poor Risk Assessment of Security Measures*, NextGov.com, 9/30/11, http://www.nextgov.com/technology-news/2011/09/experts-chide-tsa-for-poor-risk-assessment-of-security-measures/49866; See also U.S. Government Accountability Office, *Aviation Security: A National Strategy and Other Actions would Strengthen TSA's Efforts to Secure Commercial Airport Perimeters and Access Controls,* September 30, 2009.
4. U.S. Transportation Security Administration, Innovation & Technology, http://www.tsa.gov/approach/tech2/index.shtm, July 10, 2011.
5. Privacy problems sprinkle throughout the world of DHS and homeland defense. See B.K. Collins and H. Morrow, Using shared technology in bioterrorism planning and response: Do privacy laws affect administrative judgments? *The Homeland Security Review*, 4 2010: 43.
6. U.S. Dept. of Homeland Security, Privacy Impact Assessment Update for TSA Advanced Imaging Technology, January 25, 2011, http://www.dhs.gov/xlibrary/assets/privacy/privacy-pia-tsa-ait.pdf.
7. Biometric.gov, *Introduction to Biometrics*, 1, http://www.biometrics.gov/Documents/BioOverview.pdf.
8. P. Wolfhope, Mobile biometric devices: What the future holds, *The Police Chief*, September, 2011: 38–40.
9. U.S. Department of Homeland Security, Privacy impact assessment update for the credential authentication technology/boarding pass scanning system, August 11, 2009, http://www.dhs.gov/xlibrary/assets/privacy/privacy_pia_tsa_catbpss.pdf.
10. J. Wade, Maritime security, *Risk Management*, 52, December, 2005: 40.
11. A.G. Grynkewich, Maritime homeland defense, *Air and Space Power Journal*, Winter, 2007: 86.
12. Maritime Transportation Security Act of 2002, P.L. 107-295, U.S. Statutes at Large 116, 2002: 2064.
13. Office of the President, *The National Strategy for Maritime Security,* (Washington, DC: U.S. Government Printing Office, 2005), http://www.whitehouse.gov/homeland/4844-nsms.pdf.
14. At present there is a good bit of discussion as to the future structure and organization of MDA. MDA.gov, *Maritime Domain Awareness: Reconsidering Governance, Structure and Organization,* December 9, 2010, http://www.mda.gov/2010/12/09/maritime-domain-awareness-reconsidering-governance-structure-and-organization.
15. U.S. Coast Guard, Office of Law Enforcement (CG-531), *Coast Guard drug removal statistics*, April 12, 2012, http://www.uscg.mil/hq/cg5/cg531/Drugs/stats.asp.
16. 14 U.S. Code section 2, 2008.
17. President's Council on Integrity and Efficiency, *Quality Standards for Investigations* (Washington, DC: U.S. Government Printing Office, 2003), 17, http://www.ignet.gov/pande/standards/invstds.pdf.
18. U.S. Department of Homeland Security, *U.S. Coast Guard, Office of Counterterrorism and Defense Operations: Ports, Waterways and Coastal Security*, http://www.uscg.mil/hq/cg5/cg532/pwcs.asp, 10/20/2011.

19. D. Philpott, Improving the security of U.S. harbors and seaports, *Homeland Defense Journal*, November, 2007: 31.
20. K.L. Walters III, Industry on alert: Legal and economic ramifications of homeland security act on maritime commerce, *Tulane Maritime Law Journal*, 30, 2006: 311.
21. Walters, *Industry on alert*, 334–35.
22. M. Florestal, Terror on the high seas: The trade and development implications of the U.S. National Security Measures, *Brooklyn Law Review*, 72, 2007: 441.
23. General Accounting Office, *Maritime Security, Coast Guard Inspections Identify and Correct Facility Deficiencies* (Washington, DC: U.S. Government Printing Office, 2008), 1, http://www.gao.gov/new.items/d0812.pdf.
24. General Accounting Office, *Homeland Security, Challenges Facing the Coast Guard as It Transitions to a New Department* (Washington, DC: U.S. Government Printing Office, 2003), 1, http://www.gao.gov/new.items/d03467t.pdf.
25. R.C. Paolino, All aboard: Making the case for a comprehensive rerouting policy to reduce the vulnerability of hazardous rail-cargoes to terrorist attack, *193 Mil. L. Rev.*, 144, 2007.
26. J. Plant, Terrorism and the railroads: Redefining security in the wake of 9/11, *Review of Policy Research*, 293, 2004: 301.
27. J. Plant, Terrorism and the railroads, 301.
28. Surface Transportation Security Priority Assessment, March 2010 http://www.whitehouse.gov/sites/default/files/rss_viewer/STSA.pdf
29. Congressional Research Service, *Transportation Security: Issues for the 112th Congress* 12, February 1, 2011, http://www.fas.org/sgp/crs/homesec/RL33512.pdf.
30. Department of Homeland Security, *Transportation Systems: Critical Infrastructure and Key Resources Sector Specific Plan as Input to the National Infrastructure Protection Plan A81-81,* 2007, http://www.cfr.org/us-strategy-and-politics/transportation-systems-critical-infrastructure-key-resources-sector-specific-plan-input-national-infrastructure-protection-plan/p14638.
31. U.S. Government Accountability Office, *Rail Security: TSA Improved Risk Assessment but Could Further Improve Training and Information Sharing,* June 14, 2011, http://www.gao.gov/assets/130/126419.html.
32. U.S. Government Accountability Office, *Transit Security Information Sharing: DHS could Improve Information Sharing through Streamlining and Increased Outreach*, September 2010, http://www.gao.gov/new.items/d10895.pdf; See also *U.S. Government Accountability Office, Rail Security: TSA Improved Risk Assessment but Could Further Improve Training and Information Sharing,* June 14, 2011, http://www.gao.gov/assets/130/126419.html.
33. J.B. Reed, Securing dangerous rail shipments, *State Legislatures* 38, October/November 2007.
34. U.S. House of Representatives, *Detour Ahead: Critical Vulnerabilities in America's Mass Transit and Rail Programs*, 2006, 40–42, http://homeland.house.gov/SiteDocuments/20060801153711-86476.pdf, accessed February 28, 2009.

Chapter 11

Homeland Security and Public Health

Objectives

1. To define the various public health concerns in the field of homeland security.
2. To outline the various agencies involved in public health risks in homeland security.
3. To comprehend the various methods that may be used in an attack on the public water supply.
4. To describe how vulnerability assessments (VAs) are used in the protection of the country's water and food supplies.
5. To comprehend the various methods that may be used in an attack on the public food supply.
6. To identify the programs in place to protect and test the country's food supply.
7. To explain the various infectious and communicable diseases that can be used as tools of terrorism.
8. To list the various pandemic threats that may be used in a terror attack.

11.1 Introduction

At first glance, it seems that public health and homeland security are unrelated in scope and design. Nothing could be further from the truth, for questions involving public health inexorably wind their way back to issues of safety and security in a host of contexts. By any reasonable intersect, health dilemmas, whether infectious, toxic, metabolic, or otherwise, and regardless of intent or national origin, can cause significant harm to both individuals and the collective. The entire world of biotoxins injures in the health context. For example, anthrax's confrontation is not with the mind, but the body itself. Pathogens, chemical release agents, and biological and chemical substances can wreak havoc on individual chemistry let alone the communal sense of tranquility. As has been witnessed with these types of threats, the fear of the result appears more pronounced than the possible delivery of a dirty bomb.[1] Assaults on the public health can have catastrophic consequences. The destruction of the water supply by the delivery of a toxic substance, the release of a chemical or bacteriological agent into the air, impacts many. Catastrophic health events, such as a terrorist attack with a weapon of mass destruction, or a naturally occurring pandemic, or a calamitous meteorological or geological event, likely would inflict death and destruction in incalculable numbers. These same events would undermine the economic and social fabric, weaken the infrastructure of defense, cause tens or hundreds of thousands of casualties or more, damage public morale and confidence, and threaten our national security. When one considers the draconian potentiality for a public health attack, it no longer seems folly to connect its prevention to the world of homeland defense.

The Department of Homeland Security (DHS) fully connects the dots of health and security in both its mission and operations. In fact, health is one of its 17 critical areas of infrastructure. Hospitals, labs, pharmaceutical companies, water and energy companies, and a host of aligned facilities all play a key role in the event of an attack on the public health.[2] DHS is not the sole agency entrusted with this sort of assessment since others need to be involved, such as Health and Human Services, the Environmental Protection Agency (EPA), the Department of Energy, and the Departments of the Interior and Agriculture. While space cannot allow for coverage of each and every element in the health sector, this section will assess the more commonly known homeland–public health connections.

11.2 Water

It would be difficult to name a more essential component to physical life than water itself. Treatment plants have been a target of the terrorist, and in a perverse way, successful access to a treatment plant would be a dramatic victory for America's enemies. The EPA assumes the lead role in the protection of our water supply from a public health attack. As in all aspects of traditional American life, 9/11 triggered a new way of looking at water facilities. Soon after 9/11, Congress passed the *Public Health Security and Bioterrorism Preparedness and Response Act of 2002*, which zeroed in on the horrid possibility of water contamination as an act of terror. At Section 402 of the act it states:

> VULNERABILITY ASSESSMENTS—(1) Each community water system serving a population of greater than 3,300 persons shall conduct an assessment of the vulnerability of its system to a terrorist attack or other intentional acts intended to substantially disrupt the ability of the system to provide a safe and reliable supply of drinking water. The vulnerability assessment shall include, but not be limited to, a review of pipes and constructed conveyances, physical barriers, water collection, pretreatment, treatment, storage and distribution facilities, electronic, computer or other automated systems which are utilized by the public water system, the use, storage, or handling of various chemicals, and the operation and maintenance of such system. The Administrator, not later than August 1, 2002, after consultation with appropriate departments and agencies of the Federal Government and with State and local governments, shall provide baseline information to community water systems required to conduct vulnerability assessments regarding which kinds of terrorist attacks or other intentional acts are the probable threats to—
>
> A. Substantially disrupt the ability of the system to provide a safe and reliable supply of drinking water; or
> B. Otherwise present significant public health concerns.

As part of our critical infrastructure (CI), they become more than water plants but targets for the terrorist. In response to the September 11, 2001 attacks, the EPA formed the Water Security Division (WSD) in the Office of Ground Water and Drinking Water. WSD oversees all drinking water and wastewater homeland security matters. The Office of Homeland Security (OHS) was created in the EPA Office of the Administrator to oversee all EPA matters related to homeland security. See Figure 11.1.[3]

- There are approximately 160,000 public water systems (PWSs) in the United States.
- 84% of the total U.S. population is served by PWSs. The remainder is served primarily by private wells.
- PWS provide water for domestic (home), commercial, and industrial use.
- PWS produce 51 billion gallons per day (bgd) of drinking water-67% goes to residential customers and 33% to nonresidential customers.
- PWS obtain 63% of their source water from surface sources and 37% from groundwater sources.
- There are about 2.3 million miles of distribution system pipes in the United States.

FIGURE 11.1 Water facts.

The WSD tackled a host of issues relating to security and the water supply, and these tasks can be broken down into:

- Sector profile and goals
- Identifying assets, systems, networks, and functions
- Assessing risks
- Prioritizing infrastructure
- Developing and implementing protective programs
- Measuring progress
- Protection research and development (R&D)
- Managing and coordinating responsibilities

Here one witnesses an agency running full steam regarding the question of security and water. The infection of a water supply would be a major health risk and likely cause more casualties than any aircraft flying into a building. The EPA views threat analysis broadly, encompassing natural events, criminal acts, insider threats, and foreign and domestic terrorism. Natural catastrophic events are typically addressed as part of emergency response and business continuity planning, yet the same skill sets necessary for the planning and mitigation of the terrorist attack on the water supply are needed.

To analyze and prepare for threats and attacks, the agency needs to think of the predictable methods the terrorist would employ. Assessment requires a certain amount of foresight. The oft-cited methodology regarding water facilities usually includes:

- Chemical, biological, or radiological (CBR) contamination attacks on drinking water assets, especially distribution systems
- Vehicle-borne improvised explosive devices and improvised explosive device attacks on infrastructure, especially single points of failure and chemical storage sites
- Cyber-attacks on industrial control systems
- Chemical attacks, which may include introduction of a combustible contaminant into a wastewater collection system, affecting infrastructure or the treatment process

Hence, it is risk assessment in all its glory that water facilities have to engage in. The homeland security professional needs to ask questions that anticipate the risk and corresponding plan. At most water facilities, the threats are encompassed in these queries:

- What are the most plausible threats, contaminants, and threat scenarios facing the drinking water industry?
- How does this information compare with intelligence information on possible threats?

- What types of biological and chemical contaminants could be introduced into water systems, and what are their physical, chemical, and biological properties?
- What are the potential health impacts of these contaminants?
- What are the most effective means to destroy contaminants in water?
- How can this information be combined with reporting, analysis, and decision making to arrive at a reliable system?
- Can effective methods be developed to ensure that a sufficient number of qualified laboratories exist to perform rapid analysis of water contaminants in the event of an attack?
- If contaminants are introduced into a water system, where will they travel?
- How quickly will they travel?
- What will be their concentration at various points along their path?
- Can human exposures and the health impacts of these contaminants be effectively minimized?
- How can water that has been contaminated be effectively treated so that it can be released to wastewater systems or otherwise disposed of?
- Are alternative water supplies available in the event of an attack?
- How would water utilities or governments most effectively select a cost-effective early warning system?

Any meaningful security plan will anticipate these questions and will prompt the security professional to devise a plan that mitigates the damage and redirects the water facility to positive productivity after this event. Most water facilities need to rely upon both internal and external constituencies to fully comprehend the dynamics of their location. The interplay between state and federal regulators alone gives some sense of this necessary interconnection. See Figure 11.2.

Most water facilities engage in a serious self-assessment program that looks to these 14 variables, as published by the EPA:

- Explicit commitment to security
- Promote security awareness
- Defined security roles and employee expectations
- Vulnerability assessment (VA) up-to-date
- Security resources and implementation priorities
- Contamination detection
- Threat-level-based protocols
- Emergency Response Plan (ERP) tested and up-to-date
- Utility-specific measures and self-assessment
- Intrusion detection and access control
- Information protection and continuity

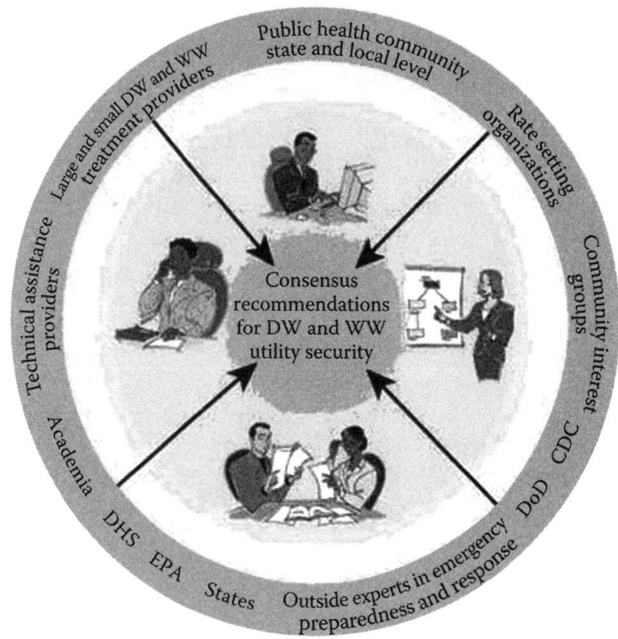

FIGURE 11.2 Recommendation for utility security.

- Design and construction standards
- Communications
- Partnerships

To ensure basic compliance with these criteria, the water facility should conduct its own VA. The EPA, as well as a host of software companies, makes available VA programs. The EPA publishes vulnerability guidelines, which are reproduced in the following section. See Table 11.1.[4]

11.3 Agriculture and Food

Just as water contamination has enormous impacts on the public health of the nation, so too does the integrity of its food supply. Here again, the terrorist envisions a target that has widespread potential for harm to a significant portion of the population.[5] Agriculture and food systems are vulnerable to disease, pests, or poisonous agents that occur naturally, are unintentionally introduced, or are intentionally delivered by acts of terrorism. Food can be attacked on many fronts including:

- Biological and chemical agents
- Naturally occurring, antibiotic-resistant, and genetically engineered substances
- Deadly agents and those tending to cause gastrointestinal discomfort
- Highly infectious agents and those that are not communicable

TABLE 11.1 EPA Vulnerability Guidelines

Basic Element	Points to Consider

1. Characterization of the water system, including its mission and objectives. (Answers to system-specific questions may be helpful in characterizing the water system.)	• What are the important missions of the system to be assessed? Define the highest priority services provided by the utility. Identify the utility's customers
	  • General public
	  • Government
	  • Military
	  • Industrial
	  • Critical care
	  • Retail operations
	  • Firefighting
	• What are the most important facilities, processes, and assets of the system for achieving the mission objectives and avoiding undesired consequences? Describe the
	  • Utility facilities
	  • Operating procedures
	  • Management practices that are necessary to achieve the mission objectives
	  • How the utility operates (e.g., water source including ground and surface water)
	  • Treatment processes
	  • Storage methods and capacity
	  • Chemical use and storage
	  • Distribution system
	In assessing those assets that are critical, consider critical customers, dependence on other infrastructures (e.g., electricity, transportation, other water utilities), contractual obligations, single points of failure (e.g., critical aqueducts, transmission systems, aquifers, etc.), chemical hazards and other aspects of the other utility capabilities that may increase or decrease the criticality of specific facilities, processes, and assets.

2. Identification and prioritization of adverse consequences to avoid.	• Take into account the impacts that could substantially disrupt the ability of the system to provide a safe and reliable supply of drinking water or otherwise could substantially present significant public health concerns to the surrounding community. Water systems should use the VA process to determine how to reduce risks associated with the consequences of significant concern.
	• Ranges of consequences or impacts for each of these events should be identified and defined.
	• Factors to be considered in assessing the consequences may include
	  • Magnitude of service disruption
	  • Economic impact (such as replacement and installation costs for damaged critical assets or loss of revenue due to service outage)
	  • Number of illnesses or deaths resulting from an event

continued

TABLE 11.1 (continued) EPA Vulnerability Guidelines

Basic Element	Points to Consider
	• Impact on public confidence in the water supply • Chronic problems arising from specific events • Other indicators of the impact of each event as determined by the water utility Risk reduction recommendations at the conclusion of the VA should strive to prevent or reduce each of these consequences.
3. Determination of critical assets that might be subject to malevolent acts that could result in undesired consequences.	• What are the malevolent acts that could reasonably cause undesired consequences? Consider the operation of critical facilities, assets and/or processes and assess what an adversary could do to disrupt these operations. Such acts may include physical damage to or destruction of critical assets, contamination of water, intentional release of stored chemicals, interruption of electricity or other infrastructure interdependencies. • The "Public Health Security and Bioterrorism Preparedness and Response Act of 2002" (PL107-188) states that a community water system which serves a population of greater than 3300 people must review the vulnerability of its system to a terrorist attack or other intentional acts intended to substantially disrupt the ability of the system to provide a safe and reliable supply of drinking water. The VA shall include, but not be limited to, a review of • Pipes and constructed conveyances • Physical barriers • Water collection, pretreatment, and treatment facilities • Storage and distribution facilities • Electronic, computer, or other automated systems which are utilized by the public water system (e.g., Supervisory Control and Data Acquisition [SCADA]) • The use, storage, or handling of various chemicals • The operation and maintenance of such systems
4. Assessment of the likelihood (qualitative probability) of such malevolent acts adversaries (e.g., terrorists, vandals).	• Determine the possible modes of attack that might result in consequences of significant concern based on the critical assets of the water system. The objective of this step of a particular attack scenario. This is a very difficult task as there is often insufficient information to determine the likelihood of a particular event with any degree of certainty.

	• The threats (the kind of adversary and the mode of attack) selected for consideration during a VA will dictate, to a great extent, the risk reduction measures that should be designed to counter the threat(s). Some VA methodologies refer to this as a "Design Basis Threat" (DBT) where the threat serves as the basis for the design of countermeasures, as well as the benchmark against which vulnerabilities are assessed. It should be noted that there is no single DBT or threat profile for all water systems in the United States. Differences in geographic location, size of the utility, previous attacks in the local area and many other factors will influence the threat(s) that water systems should consider in their assessments. Water systems should consult with the local FBI and/or other law enforcement agencies, public officials, and others to determine the threats upon which their risk reduction measures should be based. Water systems should also refer to EPA's "Baseline Threat Information for Vulnerability Assessments of Community Water Systems" to help assess the most likely threats to their system. This document is available to community water systems serving populations greater than 3300 people. If your system has not yet received instructions on how to receive a copy of this document, then contact your Regional EPA Office immediately. You will be sent instructions on how to securely access the document via the Water Information Sharing and Analysis Center (ISAC) website or obtain a hardcopy that can be mailed directly to you. Water systems may also want to review their incident reports to better understand past breaches of security.

5. Evaluation of existing countermeasures. (Depending on countermeasures already in place, some critical assets may already be sufficiently protected. This step will aid in identification of the area of greatest concern, and help to focus priorities for risk reduction.)	• What capabilities does the system currently employ for detention, delay, and response?
	  • Identify and evaluate current detection capabilities such as intrusion detection systems, water quality monitoring, operational alarms, guard post orders, and employee security awareness programs.
	  • Identify current delay mechanisms such as locks and key control, fencing, structure integrity of critical assets, and vehicle access checkpoints.
	  • Identify existing policies and procedures for evaluation and response to intrusion and system malfunction alarms, adverse water quality indicators, and cyber system intrusions.
	It is important to determine the performance characteristics. Poorly operated and maintained security technologies provide little or no protection.
	• What cyber protection system features does the utility have in place? Assess what protective measures are in-place for the SCADA and business-related computer information systems such as
	  • Firewalls
	  • Modem
	  • Internet and other external connections, including wireless data and voice communications
	  • Security policies and protocols

continued

TABLE 11.1 (continued) EPA Vulnerability Guidelines

Basic Element	Points to Consider

	It is important to identify whether vendors have access rights and/or “backdoors” to conduct system diagnostics remotely.
	• What security policies and procedures exist, and what is the compliance record for them? Identify existing policies and procedures concerning
	  • Personnel security
	  • Physical security
	  • Key and access badge control
	  • Control of system configuration and operational data
	  • Chemical and other vendor deliveries
	  • Security training and exercise records

6. Analysis of current risk and development of a prioritized plan for risk reduction.	• Information gathered on threat, critical assets, water utility operations. Consequences and existing countermeasures should be analyzed to determine the current level of risk. The utility should then determine whether current risks are acceptable or risk reduction measures should be pursued.
	• Recommended actions should measurably reduce risks by reducing vulnerabilities and/or consequences through improved deterrence, delay, detection, and/or response capabilities or by improving operational policies or procedures. Selection of specific risk reduction actions should be completed prior to considering the cost of the recommended action(s). Utilities should carefully consider both short- and long-term solutions. An analysis of the cost of short- and long-term risk reduction actions may impact which actions the utility chooses to achieve its security goals.
	• Utilities may also want to consider security improvements in light of other planned or needed improvements. Security and general infrastructure may provide significant multiple benefits. For example, improved treatment processes or system redundancies can both reduce vulnerabilities and enhance day-to-day operation.
	• Generally, strategies for reducing vulnerabilities fall into three broad categories
	  • Sound business practices—affect policies, procedures, and training to improve the overall security-related culture at the drinking water facility. For example, it is important to ensure rapid communication capabilities exist between public health authorities and local law enforcement and emergency responders.
	  • System upgrades—include changes in operations, equipment, processes, or infrastructure itself that make the system fundamentally safer.
	  • Security—improve capabilities for detection, delay, or response.

- Substances readily available to any individual and those that are more difficult to acquire
- Agents that must be weaponized and those that are accessible in a useable form[6]

America's agriculture and food system is an extensive, open, interconnected, diverse, and complex structure and, as a result, the perfect forum for the terrorist.

Responsibility for the food supply, from a security perspective, resides in three government agencies: the U.S. Department of Agriculture, the EPA, and DHS. In a recent report, these agencies set out a vision statement on the food supply.[7] See Figure 11.3.[8]

As appropriate, the Department of Agriculture takes the lead role in the protection of our food supply. As it notes, "The protection and integrity of America's agricultural production and food supply are essential to the health and welfare of both the domestic population and the global community"[9] (Figure 11.4).

Internet Exercise: The list of food recalls due to safety and health questions will be surprising. Visit: http://www.fsis.usda.gov/FSIS_Recalls/Recall_Case_Archive/index.asp.

The impact of food and agriculture contamination is not lost on DHS. Its recommendations on the integrity of the food chain are incisive, asking those entrusted with its safety to truly consider the ramifications of contamination. DHS poses seven criteria for consideration when weighing the impact of food contamination:

Vision and Purpose of DHS: Food and Agricultural Section

The FA Sector comprises complex production, processing, and delivery systems. The mission of the FA Sector is to protect against a disruption in the food supply that would pose a serious threat to public health, safety, welfare, or to the national economy. These food and agriculture systems are almost entirely under private ownership, and they operate in highly competitive global markets, strive to operate in harmony with the environment, and provide economic opportunities and an improved quality of life for U.S. citizens and others worldwide.

Differences in commodity type, farm size, operator, and household characteristics complicate prevention and protection efforts for individual operations and, ultimately, the sector as a whole. In recent years, changes in the rules of trade, shifts in domestic policy, and new developments in technology have altered the competitive landscape of global agriculture and challenges facing American farmers.

Securing this sector presents unique challenges because food and agriculture systems in the United States are extensive, open, interconnected, and diverse, and they have complex structures. Food products move rapidly in commerce to consumers, but the time required for detection and identification of attacks and contaminations, such as animal or plant disease introduction or food contamination, can be lengthy and complex. Therefore, attacks and contaminations on the FA Sector could result in severe animal, plant, public health, and economic consequences.

FIGURE 11.3 Vision statement for the food and agriculture sector.

FIGURE 11.4 A midwestern farm.

Criticality: What will be the public health impacts and economic costs associated with the attack?
Accessibility: How easy will it be for a terrorist to gain access and egress from the location of the food and agricultural product?
Recuperability: How readily will the food supply system recover from an attack?
Vulnerability: How easy or difficult will the attack be?
Effect: What calculable losses will there be directly resulting from the attack?
Recognizability: Are targets easy to discover and identify?
Shock: In a cumulative sense, how significant are the health, economic, and psychological impacts that result from the attack?

In each of these categories, the ramifications of a food contamination event are obvious. As in the water supply, the far-reaching impacts of food contamination are almost impossible to measure. Yet those entrusted with production must be mindful of their product's safety and security as well. Whether it is grain or cattle, soybeans or chicken, the agricultural entrepreneur must tend to questions of security on a daily basis.

Determining exactly how to ensure security in the agricultural sphere is no simple undertaking. Aside from the broad range of products and services, there is the added dilemma of multiple agency responsibility. While the USDA may be at the forefront, its policy making on food and its safety is influenced by myriad other agencies, such as the FDA and EPA, and its own internal history has protocols and programs that have historically dealt with food safety. In this area, it is clear that many adjustments and realignments have had to take place—some readily and others with usual bureaucratic resistance. Figure 11.5[10] demonstrates the levels of participation already evident in the USDA prior to and after 9/11.

USDA Mission Area	Agency
Farm and Foreign Agriculture Services	• Farm Service Agency (FSA) • Foreign Agricultural Service (FAS) • Risk Management Agency (RMA)
Food, Nutrition, and Consumer Services	• Center for Nutrition Policy and Promotion (CNPP) • Food and Nutrition Service (FNS)
Food Safety	• Food Safety and Inspection Service (FSIS)
Natural Resources and Environment	• Forest Service (FS) • Natural Resources Conservation Service (NRCS)

FIGURE 11.5 USDA's participation in Homeland Security.

Meshing all of this historic practice into a unified and seamless vision of security in light of 9/11 is a challenging undertaking. What emerges from the USDA is an agency in full recognition of this challenge. It urges its constituency to conduct risk assessments, to realize that security questions are central to farm operation, and to accept some level of personal responsibility for the integrity of facility and product.

In fact, the USDA fully integrates the functions of homeland security into its very makeup, as evidenced by its organizational chart in Figure 11.6.[11]

The USDA calls upon all owners in the agricultural sector to view security in both general and specific product terms. In the more general arena, it recommends the following assessment protocol:

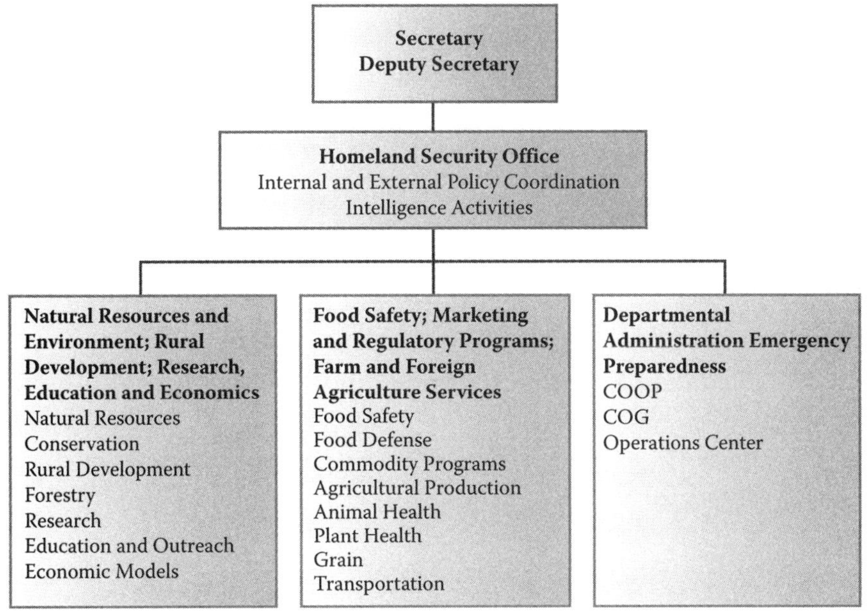

FIGURE 11.6 USDA structure for homeland protection and food safety.

- Procedures are in place for notifying appropriate law enforcement when a security threat is received, or when evidence of actual product tampering is observed.
- Procedures are in place for heightened awareness (especially when the DHS terrorism threat level is elevated) for unusual activities around the farm and increased disease symptoms among animals or crops.
- A current local, state, and federal government Homeland Security contact is maintained.
- All employees are encouraged to report any sign of product tampering.
- Facility boundaries are secured to prevent unauthorized entry.
- "No Trespassing" and "Restricted Entry" signs are posted appropriately.
- Alarms, motion detection lights, cameras, and other appropriate security equipment are used in key areas, as needed.
- Facility perimeter is regularly monitored for signs of suspicious activity or unauthorized entry.
- Doors, windows, gates, roof openings, vent openings, trailer bodies, railcars, and bulk storage tanks are secured at all times.
- Outside lighting is sufficient to allow detection of unusual activities.
- Fire, smoke, and heat detection devices are operable throughout the farm.
- Storage tanks for hazardous materials and potable water supply are protected from, and monitored for, unauthorized access.
- Wells and other water supplies are secured and routine testing is performed.
- Truck deliveries are verified against a roster of scheduled deliveries.
- Unscheduled deliveries are held away from facility premises pending verification of shipper and cargo.
- Records are maintained for all vehicles and equipment: make, model, serial number, service date, and so on.
- Vehicles and equipment are secured or immobilized when not in use; keys are never left in unattended vehicles.
- Machinery is removed from fields and stored appropriately; valuable equipment and tools are locked in a secure building.
- Entry into facility is controlled by requiring positive identification (i.e., picture ID).
- New employees are screened and references are checked.
- Visitors and guests are restricted to nonproduction areas unless accompanied by a facility employee.
- Where required by biosecurity procedures, visitors wear clean boots or coveralls (disposable boots and coveralls are provided for visitors).
- Areas are designated for check-in and check-out for visitors/deliveries (with a sign-in sheet for name, address, phone number, reason for visit).

- An inspection for signs of tampering or unauthorized entry is performed for all storage facilities regularly.
- Hazardous materials are purchased only from licensed dealers.
- A current inventory of hazardous or flammable chemicals (including drugs, chemicals, pesticides, and fertilizers) or other products (including chemical trade names, product type, EPA numbers, quantity, and usage) is maintained, and discrepancies are investigated immediately.
- A current inventory of stored fuel (diesel, gasoline, fuel oil, propane, oxygen, acetylene, kerosene, etc.) is maintained.
- A disease surveillance plan is available.
- Risk management plans have been developed or updated and shared with employees, family, visitors, customers, and local law enforcement.
- Plans include awareness of animal and plant health, as well as signs of tampering with crops, livestock, supplies, vehicles, equipment, and facilities.
- Orientation/training on security procedures is given to all facility employees at least annually.
- Passwords for USDA systems and programs are protected to prevent unauthorized user entry.[12]

11.3.1 Strategic Partnership Program on Agroterrorism

Attacks against the agricultural system would be an effective and frightful way of inflicting a terrorist act and law enforcement needs to anticipate the possibility. "Agroterrorism has been defined as the deliberate introduction of an animal or plant disease with the goal of generating fear, causing economic losses or undermining social stability."[13] Knowledge about food supply resides in a bevy of private and public entities and will require a major collaboration. Blending diverse agencies with distinct approaches to security has been a challenge for those protecting the food supply. Put another way, law enforcement officials, such as the FBI or Customs, will see the food problem through a prism of enforcement, while food safety specialists at the USDA or FDA may see things from a different perspective. The Strategic Partnership Program on Agroterrorism (SPPA) makes a noble effort to meld these various visions and to unify these diverse perspectives into one framework—that of food safety. Just as critically, the SPPA will enlist private industry concerns, from farmers to grain processors, from stockyard owners to fertilizer companies. The objectives of the SPPA are:

- Validate or identify sector-wide vulnerabilities by conducting CI/key resources (CI/KR) assessments.
- Identify indicators and warnings that could signify planning for an attack.

- Develop mitigation strategies to reduce the threat/prevent an attack (strategies may include actions that either industry or government may take to reduce vulnerabilities).
- Validate assessments conducted by the U.S. government (USG) for food and agriculture sectors.
- Gather information to enhance existing tools that both USG and industry employ.
- Provide the USG and industry with comprehensive reports, including warnings and indicators, key vulnerabilities, and potential mitigation strategies.
- Provide subsector reports for the USG that combine assessment results to determine national CI vulnerability points to support the National Infrastructure Protection Plan (NIPP) and national preparedness goals.
- Establish or strengthen relationships between federal, state, and local law enforcement and the food and agriculture industry, along with the critical food/agriculture sites visited.[14]

SPPA relies upon industry visitations to reach its conclusions about safety and security in the agricultural sector. This is why private industry, namely, farmers and food suppliers, is so integral to the SPPA process. SPPA assessments are conducted on a voluntary basis between one or more industry representatives for a particular product or commodity. As recommended by DHS and the USDA, industry production processes are evaluated in light of law enforcement officials. Together, they conduct a VA using the seven criteria noted above: criticality, accessibility, recuperability, vulnerability, effect, recognizability, and shock.

As a result of each assessment, participants identify weaknesses in the production cycle as well as recommendations on protective measures and mitigation steps that may reduce the vulnerability. By 2006, the assessments shown in Table 11.2 had been conducted under the SPPA program.[15]

Proposed future inspections, conducted by the USDA and the FDA, will tackle a host of foodstuffs and agricultural products including those shown in Table 11.3.[16]

Internet Resource: For full instructions on how to devise a food safety program, see http://www.fsis.usda.gov/PDF/Food_Defense_Plan.pdf.

The USDA's Food Safety and Inspection Service (FSIS) has developed a surveillance program to randomly screen and check food facilities as well as be stationed at ports of entry. Food safety officers are a sought-after career track due to the excellent working conditions and challenging work. FSIS has hired 22 import surveillance liaison officers who are responsible for the agency's oversight of food defense issues relating to imported food products

TABLE 11.2 Assessments Conducted or Scheduled

Status	Date	Industry	Sector Specific Agency	State
Completed	11/2005	FDA	Yogurt	TN, MN
Completed	12/2005	FDA/USDA	Grain—export elevators	LA
Completed	01/2006	FDA	Bottled water	NJ
Completed	02/2006	FDA	Baby food—jarred applesauce	MI
Completed	02/2006	FDA	Baby food—jarred applesauce	NC
Completed	03/2006	FDA	Swine production	IA
Completed	03/2006	FDA/USDA	Frozen food—pizza	WI, FL
Completed	04/2006	FDA	Juice industry—apple juice	NH
Completed	04/2006	USDA	Egg products—liquid	PA
Completed	05/2006	FDA	Fresh-cut produce—bagged salads	CA
Completed	06/2006	FDA	Infant formula	AZ
Completed	06/2006	USDA	Poultry processing	AR
Completed	07/2006	FDA	Fluid dairy—processing	NY
Scheduled	07/2006	USDA	Beef cattle feedlot	NE
Scheduled	08/2006	USDA	Ground beef processing	KS
Scheduled	08/2006	USDA	Cattle auction barn	MO, KS
Scheduled	09/2006	USDA	Dairy farm	ID

at ports of entry, border entries, and in-commerce around the country. In particular, they have expanded their liaison activities with DHS's Customs and Border Protection.

Internet Resource: To learn about jobs in food safety, see www.fsis.usda.gov/Factsheets/FSIS_Workforce_Introduction_of_CSO/index.asp.

11.3.2 Infectious Animals

Animals can be efficient carriers of illness, catastrophic pathogens, and other threats to public health. Recent cases of Mad Cow Disease heighten the impact of disease on public health integrity. Avian flu (AI), swine flu, and rabies are other examples of well-publicized cases. "Direct disease threats to livestock have been seen domestically and internationally. They come in the form of foot and mouth disease (FMD), bovine spongiform encephalopathy (BCE), various animal flues and parasites."[17] The USDA has long recognized the meaningful nature of this threat and correlates how these threats can relate to the problem of homeland security. Working hand in hand with DHS, the Department of Agriculture conducts extensive research on animal diseases and their potential for catastrophic consequence at its Plum Island Animal Disease Center (Figure 11.7).

TABLE 11.3 USDA and FDA Site Visits Initially Proposed

USDA Proposed Site Visits	FDA Proposed Site Visits
Production Agriculture	• Animal by-products
• Aquaculture production facility	• Animal foods/feeds
• Beef cattle feedlot	• Baby food
• Cattle stockyard/auction barn	• Breaded food, frozen, raw
• Citrus production facility	• Canned food, low acid
• Corn farm	• Cereal, whole-grain, not heat treated
• Dairy farm	• Deli salads
• Grain elevator and storage facility	• Dietary supplement, botanical, tablets
• Grain export handling facility	• Entrees, fully cooked
• Poultry farm	• Flour
• Rice mill	• Frozen packaged entrees
• Seed production facility	• Fruit juice
• Soybean farm	• Gum Arabic (ingredient)
• Swine production facility	• High fructose corn syrup (ingredient)
• Veterinary biologics firm	• Honey
Food Processing and Distribution	• Ice cream
• Deli meats processing	• Infant formula
• Ground beef processing facility	• Milk, fluid
• Hot dog processing	• Peanut butter
• Import re-inspection facilities	• Produce, fresh-cut and modified atmosphere packaged
• Liquid eggs processing	• Retail setting
• Poultry processing	• Seafood, cooked, refrigerated, ready-to-eat
• Retailers (further processing on-site)	• Soft drink, carbonated
• School food service central kitchens	• Spices
• Transportation companies	• Vitamin/micro-ingredient premixes/flavors
• Warehouses	• Vitamins, capsules
	• Water, bottled
	• Yogurt

The Plum Island Facility conducts high-level animal research under the following mission:

- Development of sensitive and accurate methods of disease agent detection and identification
- Development of new strategies to control disease epidemics, including rDNA vaccines, antiviral drugs, and transgenic, disease-resistant animals
- Assessment of risks involved in importation of animals and animal products from countries where epidemic foreign animal diseases occur
- Diagnostic investigations of suspect cases of FAD outbreaks in U.S. livestock
- Testing of animals and animal products to be imported into the United States to make sure those imports are free of FAD agents

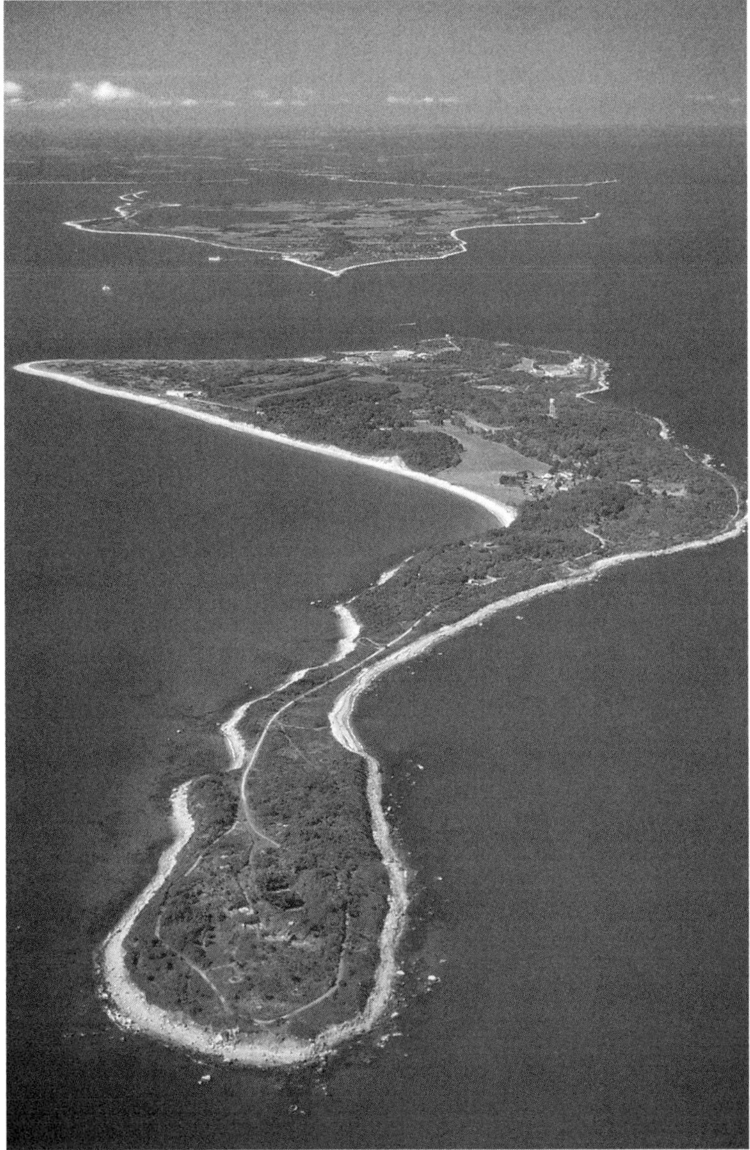

FIGURE 11.7 An aerial view of Plum Island Animal Disease Center.

- Production and maintenance reagents used in diagnostic tests and vaccines
- Training of animal health professionals in the recognition and diagnosis of animal disease

Working in consort with the Plum Island facility is the Animal and Plant Health Inspection Service (APHIS) of the U.S. Department of Agriculture. APHIS performs a host of functions to ensure the safety of animals and the containment of infectious diseases. At airport terminals,

FIGURE 11.8 APHIS logo.

seaports, and border stations, officers inspect international conveyances and the baggage of passengers for plant and animal products that could harbor pests or disease organisms. At international airports, detector dogs in APHIS's Beagle Brigade help find prohibited agricultural materials. Officers also inspect ship and air cargoes, rail and truck freight, and package mail from foreign countries. At animal import centers, APHIS

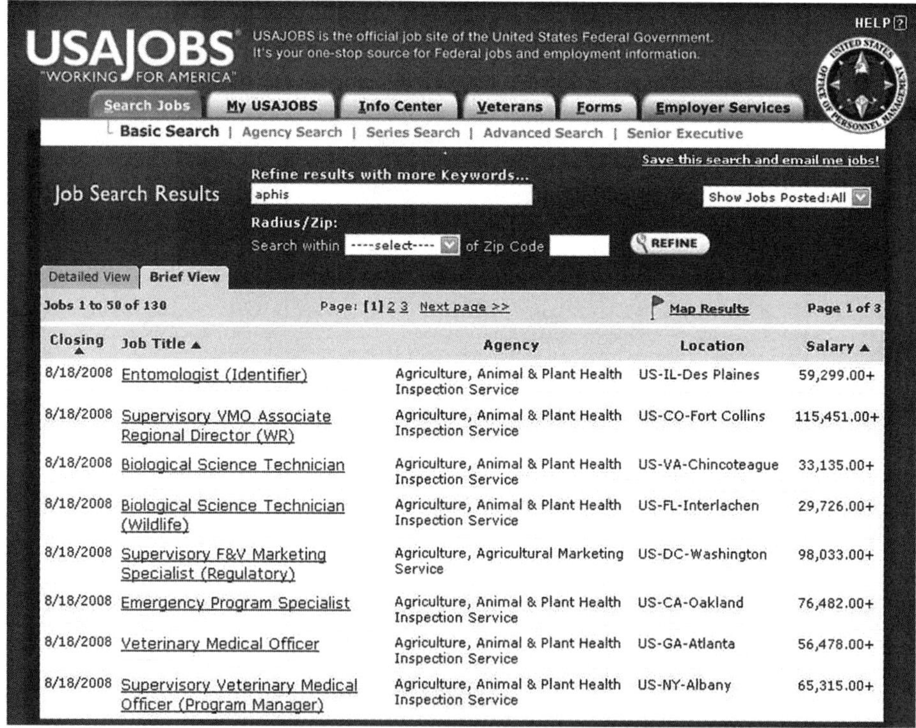

Closing	Job Title ▲	Agency	Location	Salary ▲
8/18/2008	Entomologist (Identifier)	Agriculture, Animal & Plant Health Inspection Service	US-IL-Des Plaines	59,299.00+
8/18/2008	Supervisory VMO Associate Regional Director (WR)	Agriculture, Animal & Plant Health Inspection Service	US-CO-Fort Collins	115,451.00+
8/18/2008	Biological Science Technician	Agriculture, Animal & Plant Health Inspection Service	US-VA-Chincoteague	33,135.00+
8/18/2008	Biological Science Technician (Wildlife)	Agriculture, Animal & Plant Health Inspection Service	US-FL-Interlachen	29,726.00+
8/18/2008	Supervisory F&V Marketing Specialist (Regulatory)	Agriculture, Agricultural Marketing Service	US-DC-Washington	98,033.00+
8/18/2008	Emergency Program Specialist	Agriculture, Animal & Plant Health Inspection Service	US-CA-Oakland	76,482.00+
8/18/2008	Veterinary Medical Officer	Agriculture, Animal & Plant Health Inspection Service	US-GA-Atlanta	56,478.00+
8/18/2008	Supervisory Veterinary Medical Officer (Program Manager)	Agriculture, Animal & Plant Health Inspection Service	US-NY-Albany	65,315.00+

FIGURE 11.9 USAJOBS website listing of APHIS job openings.

veterinarians check animals in quarantine. Overseas, APHIS operates preclearance programs to eliminate pests in some imported products right at the source (Figure 11.8).

For a list of some job opportunities at APHIS, review the USAJOBS list in Figure 11.9.

11.3.3 Infectious Diseases and Bioterrorism

The idea that disease can be an agent of the terrorist is not new.[18] In World War I, mustard gas and other virulent gases were used on the battlefield. In Saddam Hussein's Iraq, he thought so little of the Kurds that he used biological agents on them. Anthrax cases have been in the headlines in the last decade. The release of dangerous pathogens and disease-borne agents has allegedly occurred on the battlefield in certain nations, though we have yet to see a full-scale terrorist attack using these agents.[19] See Figure 11.10.

The list of communicable diseases contains a full range of conditions that need reporting to local, state, and federal health authorities. DHS, HHS, and other agencies mandate the reporting of any case that makes the list of diseases. See Table 11.4.

The list of communicable diseases is regularly updated by both the Centers for Disease Control and Prevention (CDC) and various state health departments.

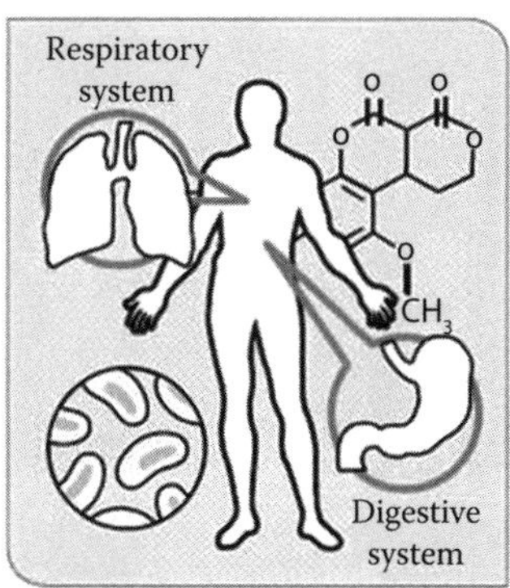

1. A biological attack is the release of germs or other biological substances. Many agents must be inhaled, enter through a cut in the skin or be eaten to make you sick. Some biological agents can cause contagious diseases, others do not.

FIGURE 11.10 Biological attack effects on the major systems of the human body.

TABLE 11.4 List of Reportable Communicable Diseases

AIDS and HIV	Hepatitis B carrier	Preventing infectious diseases
Anthrax	Hepatitis B	Psittacosis
Arboviral encephalitis	Hepatitis C	Rabies
Botulism	Herpes	Rifampin
Campylobacteriosis	Histoplasmosis	Ringworm (Tinea)
Chickenpox	Impetigo	Rocky Mountain spotted fever
Chlamydia	Influenza	Rubella
Conjunctivitis ("pink eye")	Invasive Group A strep	Salmonellosis
Cryptosporidiosis	Kawasaki	Scabies
Cyclosporiasis	Legionellosis (Legionnaire disease)	Scarlet fever
Cytomegalovirus (CMV)	Leprosy	Shigellosis
Diphtheria	Leptospirosis	Smallpox
Ebola	Listeriosis	Strep throat
E. coli O157:H7	Lyme disease	Swimming-related illness
Eastern equine encephalitis	Malaria	Syphilis
Ehrlichiosis	Measles	Tetanus
Fifth disease (*Erythema infectiosum*)	Meningococcal disease	Toxoplasmosis
Food safety	Mononucleosis	Tuberculosis
Genital warts	Mumps	Tularemia
Giardiasis	*Mycobacterium marinum*	Typhoid fever
Gonorrhea	Mycoplasma	*Vibrio vulnificus* illness
Haemophilus influenzae type b (Hib) disease	Permethrin	Viral gastroenteritis
Hand, foot, and mouth disease (Coxsackievirus)	Pertussis (whooping cough)	Viral meningitis
Hantavirus	Pinworm	Warts, genital
Head lice	Plague	West Nile virus
Hepatitis A	Pneumococcal disease	

For those entrusted with security, the problem of disease generally comes in the form of biological agents used in terror attacks. Hence, the term bioterrorism has become part of the security vocabulary.[20] The CDC defines bioterrorism as an attack involving a

> deliberate release of viruses, bacteria, or other germs (agents) used to cause illness or death in people, animals, or plants. These agents are typically found

> in nature, but it is possible that they could be changed to increase their ability to cause disease, make them resistant to current medicines, or to increase their ability to be spread into the environment. Biological agents can be spread through the air, through water, or in food. Terrorists may use biological agents because they can be extremely difficult to detect and do not cause illness for several hours to several days. Some bioterrorism agents, like the smallpox virus, can be spread from person to person and some, like Anthrax, cannot.[21]

The CDC tracks and publishes data on the more pressing agents, such as anthrax[22] (Figure 11.11).

Internet Resource: For the Department of Health and Human Services (HHS) recommended protocol for countermeasures for bioterrorism, see http://www.hhs.gov/aspr/opeo/documents/hhsplncombat.html.

For DHS and HHS, and their collegial partners, both governmental and private, the world of bioterrorism is front and center. At the DHS level, bioterrorism will involve three fronts:

- *Infrastructure*: Strengthen health systems, enhance medical communications, and maximize their contribution to the overall biodefense of the nation.
- *Response*: Improve specialized federal capabilities to respond in coordination with state and local governments.
- *Science*: Meet the medical needs of our bioterrorism response plans by developing specific new vaccines, medicines, and

Fact sheet: Anthrax information for health care providers

Cause	*Bacillus anthracis* • Encapsulated, aerobic, gram-positive, spore-forming, rod-shaped (bacillus) bacterium
Systems affected	• Skin or cutaneous (most common) • Respiratory tract or inhalation (rare) • Gastrointestinal (GI) tract (rare) • Oropharyngeal form (least common)
Transmission	• Skin: Direct skin contact with spores; in nature, contact with infected animals or animal products (usually related to occupational exposure) • Respiratory tract: Inhalation of aerosolized spores • GI: Consumption of undercooked or raw meat products or dairy products from infected animals • NO person-to-person transmission of inhalation or GI anthrax
Reporting	• Report suspected or confirmed anthrax cases immediately to your local or state department of health

FIGURE 11.11 Anthrax information for health providers.

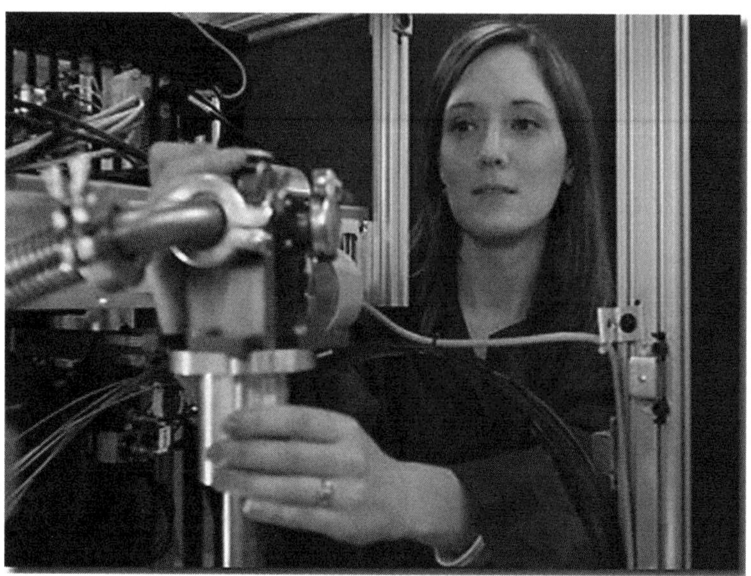

FIGURE 11.12 DHA chemist.

diagnostic tests (Figure 11.12). Develop an early warning system for bioterrorism.

In the area of infrastructure, both DHS and HHS stress the need for hospital facilities to be in a proactive and reactive capacity when bioterrorism strikes. HHS has devised the Hospital Preparedness Program (HPP), which seeks to elevate the capacity of hospitals to handle public health problems and to prepare for and respond to bioterrorism and other public health emergencies. Priority areas include interoperable communication systems, bed tracking, personnel management, fatality management planning, and hospital evacuation planning. During the last 5 years, HPP funds have also improved bed and personnel surge capacity, decontamination capabilities, isolation capacity, pharmaceutical supplies, training, education, and drills and exercises.

Hospitals, outpatient facilities, health centers, poison control centers, EMS, and other healthcare partners work with the appropriate state or local health department to acquire funding and develop healthcare system preparedness through this program. Most hospitals now have designated officers and offices that are responsible for homeland issues and the training of staff and administration in emergency response.

As for response capacity, hospitals and other medical facilities should have interoperable communications systems, task forces and advisory boards, and a steady stream of communication protocols that interconnect state, local, and federal authorities. Response also implies the capacity to react in the event of an attack. In biological and chemical situations, the medical facility needs adequate stockpiles of vaccine. Medical facilities need to be assured that suitable vendors and companies can supply basic medical goods.

Bioterrorism is primarily a study in science, and the countermeasures need to employ the highest and most sophisticated forms of scientific method. Hospitals should be engaged in serious research that relates to bioterrorism. The study of pathogens and corresponding antidotes should be central to that research, as well as analysis of compounds that will counter the effects of biological agents. Finally, scientific investment should include enhanced laboratory facilities. The Biomedical Advanced Research and Development Authority (BARDA) is one of the chief scientific authorities in R&D. BARDA manages Project BioShield, which includes the procurement and advanced development of medical countermeasures for CBR and nuclear agents, as well as the advanced development and procurement of medical countermeasures for pandemic influenza and other emerging infectious diseases.

11.3.3.1 Project BioShield

The Project BioShield Act[23] and a result, Project BioShield, was enacted in 2004.[24] The general aim of the project was to provide suitable vaccines and other medical supplies in the event of bioterrorism. The overall goals of the program were to:

- Expedite the conduct of NIH R&D on medical countermeasures based on the most promising recent scientific discoveries.
- Give the FDA the ability to make promising treatments quickly available in emergency situations.
- Ensure that resources are available to pay for next-generation medical countermeasures (Project BioShield will allow the government to buy improved vaccines or drugs).

Project BioShield's rightful stress is on the pathogens that can cause global damage. Presently, the project has targeted biological threats that either have an antidote or are in need of serious research. In 2007, Project BioShield reported both threats and antidotes in its annual report. See Table 11.5.[25]

Looked at from another vantage point, BioShield spends the bulk of its research allocation on searching out vaccines for anthrax, smallpox, and botulism. The Project BioShield annual report to Congress (Table 11.6) charts this distribution of funds.[26]

TABLE 11.5 Projected Future Top-Priority Medical Countermeasure Programs

				Projected Future Top-Priority Medical Countermeasure Programs		
	Threat	Disease	Current Project Bioshield Acquisition Programs	Threat-Specific Programs	Broad-Spectrum Antibiotic (B) Antiviral (V)	Diagnostic (D) Biodosimetry or Bioassay (B)
Chem	**Volatile nerve agents**	Nerve agent toxicity		Enterprise CHEMPACKs Volatile nerve agent-single antidote		
Biological	***Bacillus anthracis*** (bacteria), including multidrug-resistant strains	Anthrax	Anthrax therapeutics (antitoxins) Anthrax vaccine (AVA, rPA)	Anthrax antitoxin(s) Anthrax vaccine(s) (next-gen)	B	D
	Botulinum toxins (from *Clostridium botuiinum* bacteria)	Botulism	Botulinum antitoxin			D
	Burkholderia mallei ***Burkholderia pseudomallei*** (bacteria)	Glanders Melioidosis			B	D
	Filoviruses Ebola and Marburg	Hemorrhagic fever		Filovirus medical countermeasures	V	D
	Francisella tularensis (bacteria)	Tularemia			B	D
	Junin virus	Argentine hemorrhagic fever			V	D
	Rickettsia prowazekii (bacteria)	Typhus			B	D
	Variola virus	Smallpox	MVA smallpox vaccine	Smallpox antiviral(s) Smallpox vaccine (next-gen)	V	D
	Yersinia pestis (bacteria)	Bubonic plague			B	D
Rad/Nuc	**Radiological/nuclear agents**	ARS, DEARE, various	Pediatric KI DTPA ARS medical countermeasures	Radionuclide-specific agents/ decorporation agents ARS/DEARE medical countermeasures		B

TABLE 11.6 Project BioShield Acquisition Activity

Threat	Product	Doses (Thousands)	Cost ($ Millions)	Company	Award Date
Anthrax	rPA vaccine	75,000	879[a]	VaxGen, Inc	11/4/04 Cancelled 12/19/06
	AVA vaccine	28,750	691[b]	Emergent BioSolutions, Inc. (formerly BioPort Corp.)	5/6/05; 5/5/06; 9/25/07
	Raxibacumab	65	334[c]	Human Genome Sciences, Inc.	6/19/06; 7/29/09
	Anthrax immune globulin	10	144	Cangene Corp.	7/28/06
Smallpox	MVA vaccine	20,000	505	Bavarian Nordic, Inc.	6/4/07
	ST-246	1700	433	SIGA technologies, Inc.	5/13/11
Botulinum toxin	Botulinum antitoxin	200	414[d]	Cangene Corp.	6/1/06
Radiological/ nuclear	Potassium iodide	4800	18	Fleming Pharmaceuticals	3/18/05; 2/8/06
	Ca-DTPA	395	22	Akorn, Inc.	2/13/06
	Zn-DTPA	80			
		Total Announced Awards: 3440			
		Total Current Obligations: 2563[e]			

Source: CRS analysis of HHS, *Project BioShield: Annual Report to Congress July 2004–July 2006*; HHS, *Project BioShield: Annual Report to Congress August 2006–July 2007*; HHS, *Project BioShield Annual Report to Congress August 2007 through December 2008*; HHS, *Project BioShield Annual Report to Congress January 2009–December 2009*; DHS, Office of Health Affairs, *Biodefense Countermeasures Congressional Justification FY2010*; HHS, "BARDA Supports First Project BioShield Contract for Smallpox Drug," press release, May 13, 2011; and personal communications with HHS, June 8, 2009; December 29, 2010; April 20, 2011; and May 18, 2011.

[a] This figure includes approximately $1.5 million that HHS paid to VaxGen, Inc. for mandatory security upgrades. When HHS terminated the vaccine contract, VaxGen, Inc. kept this amount, while approximately $877 million obligated for the vaccine became available for other Project BioShield procurements. Personal communication with HHS, June 8, 2009.

[b] This total does not include a $405 million contract for 14.5 million doses of AVA anthrax vaccine that HHS announced on September 30, 2008. According to HHS, this contract used Centers for Disease Control and Prevention funds rather than the Project BioShield special reserve fund. Personal communication with HHS, June 8, 2009.

[c] This figure includes $8 million in additional payments for studies to support FDA approval. Personal communication with HHS, April 20, 2011.

[d] This figure includes $50 million HHS obligated from the Project BioShield special reserve fund to this company in FY2004 after the DHS Appropriations Act, 2004, funded this account but before passage of the Project BioShield Act. See HHS, *Project BioShield: Annual Report to Congress July 2004–July 2006*, p. 31.

[e] Announced awards minus $877 million for the cancelled rPA contract (see note a).

11.3.3.2 National Pharmaceutical Stockpile

The CDC plays a major role in any bioterrorism event. Their most important task in the event of bioterrorism is the maintenance and oversight of the National Pharmaceutical Stockpile (NPS). The stockpile is a repository for

FIGURE 11.13 CDC stockpiles.

lifesaving pharmaceuticals, antibiotics, chemical interventions, as well as medical, surgical, and patient support supplies, and equipment for prompt delivery to the site of a disaster, including a possible biological or chemical terrorist event anywhere in the United States. The NPS serves in a support role to local and state emergency, medical, and public health personnel.

A primary purpose of the NPS is to provide critical drugs and medical material that would otherwise be unavailable to local communities. The CDC prioritizes the stockpile based on seriousness of the threat and the availability of both the agent and the antidote. The stockpile targets biological agents: smallpox, anthrax, pneumonic plague, tularemia, botulinum toxin, and viral hemorrhagic fevers (Figure 11.13).

Internet Exercise: Find out about the many activities of the Stockpile at http://www.cdc.gov/phpr/stockpile/stockpile.htm#sns1.

11.3.3.3 National Select Agent Registry Program

The CDC net spreads into other territories involving dangerous substances. The National Select Agent Registry Program oversees the use and possession of biological agents and toxins that have the potential to pose a severe threat to public, animal, or plant health. The National Select Agent Registry Program currently requires registration of facilities, including government agencies, universities, research institutions, and commercial entities, that possess, use, or transfer biological agents and toxins that pose a significant threat to the public. Possession, as well as loss or theft of toxins and biological agents, needs to be reported to the CDC. A sample reporting form in the event of loss or theft is provided in Appendix E.

11.4 Pandemic Threats

The term *pandemic* connotes many things and generally conjures up images of fear and trepidation. Some pandemics are more serious than others. A flu outbreak, the nonlethal variety, is a pandemic of sorts. And then there are those outbreaks that are more serious and which cause death on a global scale, such as the Bird Flu—the H1N1 virus where nearly 300 people died worldwide. See Figure 11.14.[27]

At other levels of potential destruction, the fears are well founded, for pandemic instances are global in scope and have the capacity to injure and kill on a widespread basis.[28] Pandemics are not a new phenomenon but have long been tracked globally. Pandemics fall into these basic categories:

- Bird flu is commonly used to refer to AI (see below). Bird flu viruses infect birds, including chickens, other poultry, and wild birds such as ducks.
- AI is caused by influenza viruses that occur naturally among wild birds. Low pathogenic AI is common in birds and causes few problems. Highly pathogenic H5N1 is deadly to domestic fowl, can be transmitted from birds to humans, and is deadly to humans. There is virtually no human immunity and human vaccine availability is very limited.
- Pandemic flu is virulent human flu that causes a global outbreak, or pandemic, of serious illness. Because there is little natural immunity,

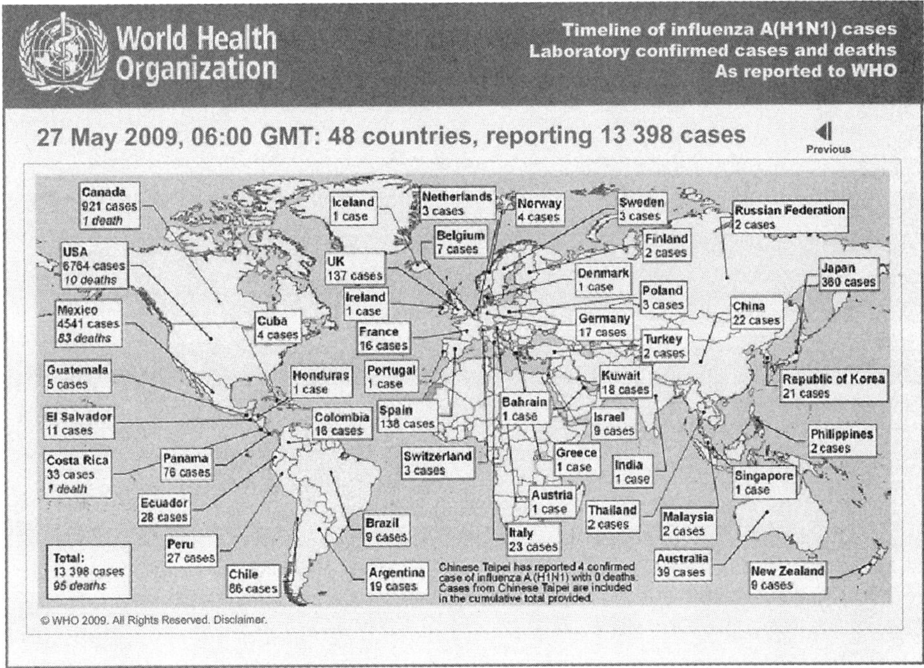

FIGURE 11.14 Timeline of influenza A (H1N1) cases.

the disease can spread easily from person to person. Currently, there is no pandemic flu.
- Seasonal (or common) flu is a respiratory illness that can be transmitted person to person. Most people have some immunity, and a vaccine is available.[29]

To compare and contrast the pandemic form other sorts of flu or influenza, see Figure 11.15.[30]

Pandemics are largely the by-product of influenzas (Figure 11.16).

Influenza viruses have mutated and caused pandemics or global epidemics. In the United States, the most severe outbreaks occurred in 1918 (Figures 11.17 and 11.18).

Internet Resource: For a history of Flu Epidemics visit http://www.flu.gov/pandemic/history/1918/index.html.

The very definition of the pandemic implies a broad impact, a disease or infection with the capacity to cover a large swath of geography. A pandemic is a global disease outbreak. For example, a flu pandemic occurs when a new influenza virus emerges for which people have little or no immunity, and for which there is no vaccine. Or a disease may be spread in an airborne fashion, such as the avain influenza witnessed in China and other Asian locales. The World Health Organization (WHO) gauges the severity of influenza outbreak by phases—with the infection commencing in lower animal forms, professing

Pandemic Flu	Seasonal Flu
Rarely happens (three times in 20th century)	Happens annually and usually peaks in January or February
People have little or no immunity because they have no previous exposure to the virus	Usually some immunity built up from previous exposure
Healthy people may be at increased risk for serious complications	Usually only people at high risk, not healthy adults, are at risk of serious complications
Health care providers and hospitals may be overwhelmed	Health care providers and hospitals can usually meet public and patient needs
Vaccine probably would not be available in the early stages of a pandemic	Vaccine available for annual flu season
Effective antivirals may be in limited supply	Adequate supplies of antivirals are usually available
Number of deaths could be high (The U.S. death toll during the 1918 pandemic was approximately 675,000)	Seasonal flu-associated deaths in the United States over 30 years ending in 2007 have ranged from about 3,000 per season to about 49,000 per season.
Symptoms may be more severe	Symptoms include fever, cough, runny nose, and muscle pain
May cause major impact on the general public, such as widespread travel restrictions and school or business closings	Usually causes minor impact on the general public, some schools may close and sick people are encouraged to stay home
Potential for severe impact on domestic and world economy	Manageable impact on domestic and world economy

FIGURE 11.15 Seasonal flu versus pandemic flu.

FIGURE 11.16 By educating people on how influenza could spread, public health officials hoped to help people avoid it. (Courtesy of the U.S. Department of Health and Human Services, "The Great Pandemic 1918–1919," http://www.flu.gov/pandemic/history/1918/the_pandemic/influenza/careless_spitting.jpg.)

FIGURE 11.17 In July 1918, an American soldier said that while influenza caused a heavy fever, it "usually only confines the patient to bed for a few days." The mutation of the virus changed all that. (http://www.flu.gov/pandemic/history/1918/the_pandemic/influenza/index.html; National Library of Medicine.)

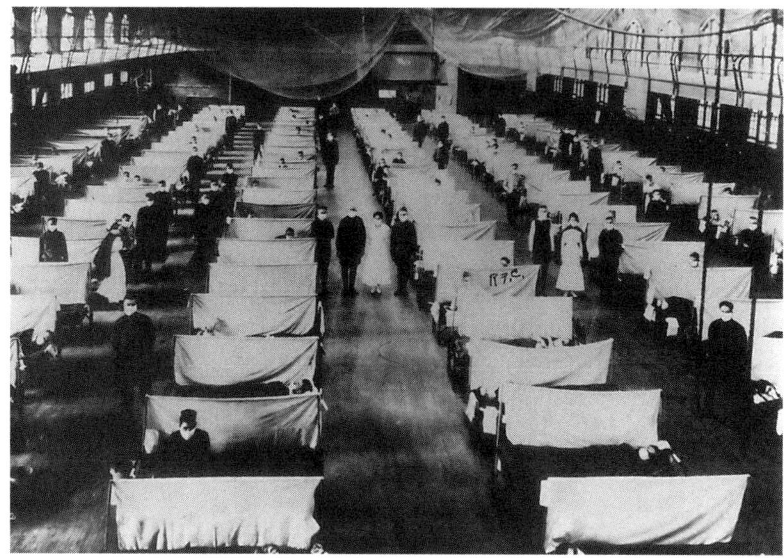

FIGURE 11.18 When it came to treating influenza patients, doctors, nurses, and druggists were at a loss. (http://www.flu.gov/pandemic/history/1918/the_pandemic/iowa_flu2.jpg; Credit: Office of the Public Health Service Historian.)

to various levels of human infection to eventual reductions.[31] It is difficult to predict when the next influenza pandemic will occur or how severe it will be. Wherever and whenever a pandemic starts, everyone around the world is at risk. Countries might, through measures such as border closures and travel restrictions, delay the arrival of the virus, but they cannot stop it.

Health professionals are concerned that the continued spread of a highly pathogenic avian H5N1 virus across eastern Asia and other countries represents a significant threat to human health. The H5N1 virus has raised concerns about a potential human pandemic because:

- It is especially virulent
- It is being spread by migratory birds
- It can be transmitted from birds to mammals and, in some limited circumstances, to humans
- Like other influenza viruses, it continues to evolve

Pandemics have been witnessed throughout human history, with the twentieth century experiencing myriad events. The National Institute of Health tracks the past 100 years (Figure 11.19).[32]

11.4.1 Planning and Response

Recognizing both the epidemiological and terrorist implications of the pandemic, state, federal, and local governments need to prepare and respond for this event.[33] At the federal level, a prevention and response program has been formalized. The National Strategy for Pandemic Influenza guides the country's

Timeline of Human Flu Pandemics*

Including human cases of avian and swine influenza viruses.

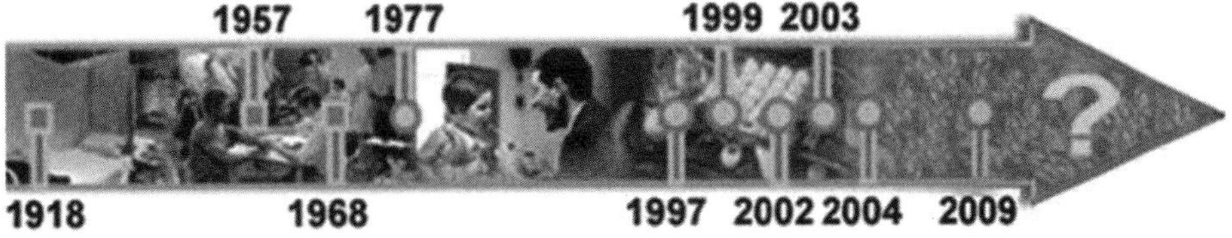

■ **Major pandemic**

● The appearance of a new influenza strain in the human population

1918

■ **Pandemic**

"Spanish flu" H1N1
The most devastating flu pandemic in recent history, killing more than 500,000 people in the United States, and 20 million to 50 million people worldwide.

1957–58

■ **Pandemic**

"Asian flu" H2N2
First identified in China, this virus caused roughly 70,000 deaths in the United States during the 1957–58 season. Because this strain has not circulated in humans since 1968, no one under 30 years old has immunity to this strain.

1968–69

■ **Pandemic**

"Hong Kong flu" H3N2
First detected in Hong Kong, this virus caused roughly 34,000 deaths in the United States during the 1968–69 season. H3N2 viruses still circulate today.

1976

Four soldiers in a US army base in New Jersey are infected with swine influenza, resulting in one death.

1977

● **Appearance of a new influenza strain in humans**

"Russian flu" H1N1
Isolated in northern China, this virus was similar to the virus that spread before 1957. For this reason, individuals born before 1957 were generally protected; however children and young adults born after that year were not because they had no prior immunity.

1997

● **Appearance of a new influenza strain in humans**

H5N1
The first time an influenza virus was found to be transmitted directly from birds to people, with infections linked to exposure to poultry markets. Eighteen people in Hong Kong were hospitalized, six of whom died.

FIGURE 11.19 Timeline of human flu pandemics: including human cases of avian and swine influenza viruses.

preparedness and response to an influenza pandemic, with the intent of (1) stopping, slowing, or otherwise limiting the spread of a pandemic to the United States; (2) limiting the domestic spread of a pandemic, and mitigating disease, suffering, and death; and (3) sustaining infrastructure and mitigating impact to the economy and the functioning of society.[34] The strategy charges the U.S.

1999

Appearance of a new influenza strain in humans

H9N2
Appeared for the first time in humans. It caused illness in two children in Hong Kong, with poultry being the probable source.

2002

Appearance of a new influenza strain in humans

H7N2
Evidence of infection is found in one person in Virginia following a poultry outbreak.

2003

Appearance of a new influenza strain in humans

H5N1
Caused two Hong Kong family members to be hospitalized after a visit to China, killing one of them, a 33-year-old man. (A third family member died while in China of an undiagnosed respiratory illness.)

H7N7
In the first reported cases of this strain in humans, 89 people in the Netherlands, most of whom were poultry workers, became ill with eye infections or flu-like symptoms. A veterinarian who visited one of the affected poultry farms died.

H7N2
Caused a person to be hospitalized in New York.

H9N2
Caused illness in one child in Hong Kong.

2004

Appearance of a new influenza strain in humans

H5N1
Caused illness in 47 people in Thailand and Vietnam, 34 of whom died. Researchers are especially concerned because this flu strain, which is quite deadly, is becoming endemic in Asia.

H7N3
Is reported for the first time in humans. The strain caused illness in two poultry workers in Canada.

H10N7
Is reported for the first time in humans. It caused illness in two infants in Egypt. One child's father is a poultry merchant.

2005

H5N1
The first case of human infection with H5N1 arises in Cambodia in February. By May, WHO reports 4 Cambodian cases, all fatal. Indonesia reports its first case, which is fatal, in July. Over the next three months, 7 cases of laboratory-confirmed H5N1 infection in Indonesia, and 4 deaths, occur.

FIGURE 11.19 (continued) Timeline of human flu pandemics: including human cases of avian and swine influenza viruses.

On December 30, WHO reports a cumulative total of 142 laboratory-confirmed cases of H5N1 infection worldwide, all in Asia, with 74 deaths. Asian countries in which human infection with H5N1 has been detected: Thailand, Vietnam, Cambodia, Indonesia, and China.

2006

H5N1
In early January, two human cases of H5N1 infection, both fatal, are reported in rural areas of Eastern Turkey, while cases in China continues to spread. As of January 25, China reports a total of 10 cases, with 7 deaths. On January 30, Iraq reports its first case of human H5N1 infection, which was fatal, to the WHO.

In March, the WHO confirmed seven cases of human H5N1 infection, and five deaths, in Azerbaijan. In April, WHO confirmed four cases of human H5N1 infection, and two fatalities, in Egypt.

In May, the WHO confirmed a case of human H5N1 infection in the African nation off Djibouti. This was the first confirmed case in sub-Saharan Africa. Throughout 2006, 115 human cases of H5N1 infection occur, with 79 deaths.

2007

H5N1
In early January, two human cases of H5N1 are confirmed in Indonesia. By the end of 2007, 88 confirmed cases occur in Indonesia, Cambodia, China, Lao People's Democratic Republic, Myanmar, Nigeria, Pakistan, and Vietnam, with 59 deaths.

H7N7
In May, four cases of H7N7 avian influenza were confirmed in the United Kingdom among individuals exposed to infected poultry.

2008

H5N1
On May 28, Bangladesh reports its first case of human H5N1 infection to the WHO. By the end of the year, 40 cases are confirmed in Bangladesh, Cambodia, China, Egypt, Indonesia, and Vietnam.

2009

H5N1
On January 7, Indonesia confirmed a new case of human infection with H5N1 influenza. Since that time, new cases have been identified in Egypt, China, Indonesia, and Vietnam.

Appearance of a new influenza strain in humans

H1N1
In April, human infection with a new strain of H1N1 influenza is confirmed in Mexico. Within weeks, human infections spread to the United States and cases begin occurring in other regions around the world.

FIGURE 11.19 (continued) Timeline of human flu pandemics: including human cases of avian and swine influenza viruses.

Department of Health and Human Services with leading the federal pandemic preparedness. Working with the WHO, federal officials seek to mitigate and contain as well as prevent future events from taking place. See Figure 11.20.[35]

SWINE FLU OUTBREAK OF 2009

In the spring of 2009, a new flu virus spread quickly across the United States and the world. The first U.S. case of H1N1 (swine flu) was diagnosed on April 15, 2009. By April 21, the Centers for Disease Control and Prevention (CDC) was working to develop a vaccine for this new virus. On April 26, the U.S. government declared H1N1 a public health emergency.

By June 2009, 18,000 cases of H1N1 had been reported in the United States. A total of 74 countries were affected by the pandemic. H1N1 vaccine supply was limited in the beginning. People at the highest risk of complications received the vaccine first.

By November 2009, 48 states had reported cases of H1N1, mostly involving young people. That same month over 61 million vaccine doses were ready. Reports of flu activity began to decline in parts of the country, which gave the medical community a chance to vaccinate more people. Eighty million people were vaccinated against H1N1, which minimized the impact of the illness.

The CDC estimates that 43 million to 89 million people had H1N1 between April 2009 and April 2010. They estimate there were between 8,870 and 18,300 H1N1-related deaths.

On August 10, 2010, the World Health Organization (WHO) declared an end to the global H1N1 flu pandemic.

Source: Pandemic Flu History, The U.S. Department of Health & Human Services, accessed January 3, 2013, http://www.flu.gov/pandemic/history/index.html#.

The key elements in planning and response include:

1. In advance of an influenza pandemic, HHS will work with federal, state, and local government partners and the private sector to coordinate pandemic influenza preparedness activities and to achieve interoperable response capabilities.
2. In advance of an influenza pandemic, HHS will encourage all Americans to be active partners in preparing their states, local communities, workplaces, and homes for pandemic influenza and will emphasize that a pandemic will require Americans to make difficult choices. An informed and responsive public is essential to minimizing the health effects of a pandemic and the resulting consequences to society.
3. In advance of an influenza pandemic, HHS, in concert with federal partners, will work with the pharmaceutical industry to develop domestic vaccine production capacity sufficient to provide vaccines

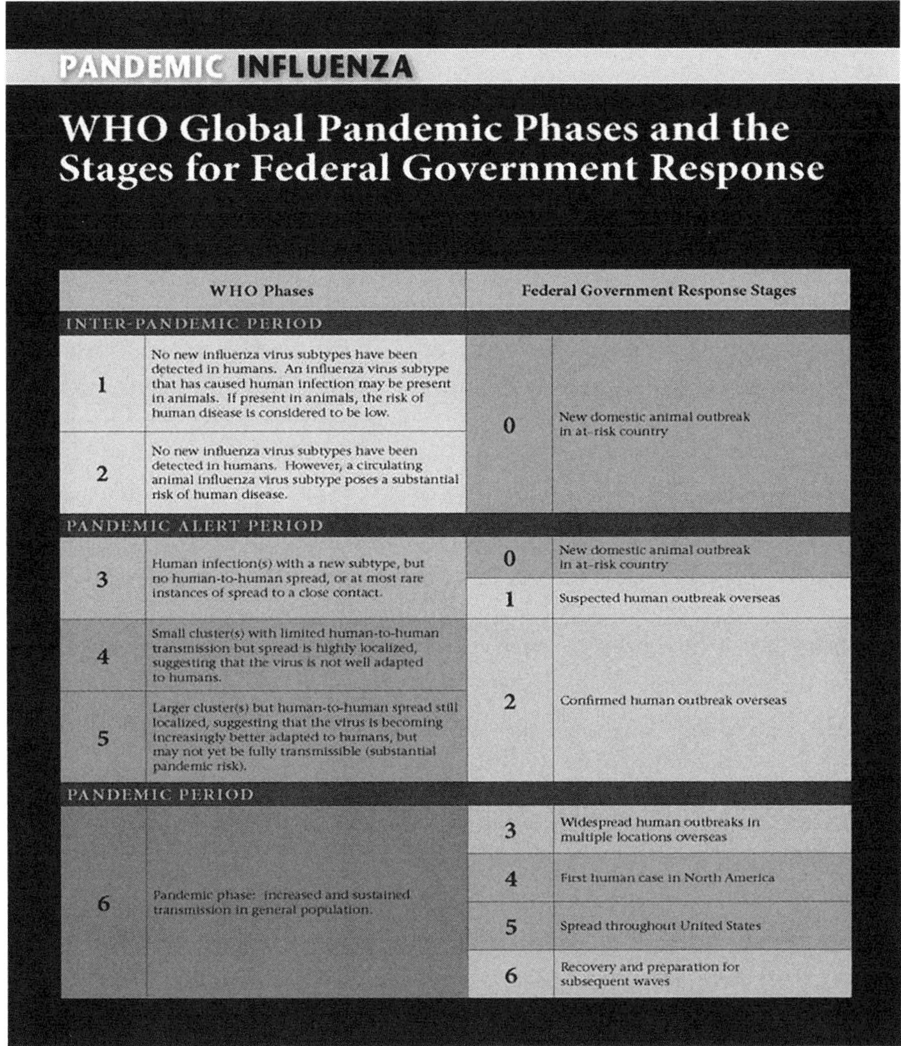

PANDEMIC INFLUENZA

WHO Global Pandemic Phases and the Stages for Federal Government Response

WHO Phases		Federal Government Response Stages	
INTER-PANDEMIC PERIOD			
1	No new influenza virus subtypes have been detected in humans. An influenza virus subtype that has caused human infection may be present in animals. If present in animals, the risk of human disease is considered to be low.	0	New domestic animal outbreak in at-risk country
2	No new influenza virus subtypes have been detected in humans. However, a circulating animal influenza virus subtype poses a substantial risk of human disease.		
PANDEMIC ALERT PERIOD			
3	Human infection(s) with a new subtype, but no human-to-human spread, or at most rare instances of spread to a close contact.	0	New domestic animal outbreak in at-risk country
		1	Suspected human outbreak overseas
4	Small cluster(s) with limited human-to-human transmission but spread is highly localized, suggesting that the virus is not well adapted to humans.	2	Confirmed human outbreak overseas
5	Larger cluster(s) but human-to-human spread still localized, suggesting that the virus is becoming increasingly better adapted to humans, but may not yet be fully transmissible (substantial pandemic risk).		
PANDEMIC PERIOD			
6	Pandemic phase: increased and sustained transmission in general population.	3	Widespread human outbreaks in multiple locations overseas
		4	First human case in North America
		5	Spread throughout United States
		6	Recovery and preparation for subsequent waves

FIGURE 11.20 Global pandemic phases and the stages for federal government response.

for the entire U.S. population as soon as possible after the onset of a pandemic and, during the pre-pandemic period, to produce up to 20 million courses of vaccine against each circulating influenza virus with pandemic potential and to expand seasonal influenza domestic vaccine production to cover all Americans for whom vaccine is recommended through normal commercial transactions.

4. In advance of an influenza pandemic, HHS, in concert with federal partners and in collaboration with the states, will procure sufficient quantities of antiviral drugs to treat 25% of the U.S. population and, in so doing, stimulate development of expanded domestic production capacity sufficient to accommodate subsequent needs through

normal commercial transactions. HHS will stockpile antiviral medications in the Strategic National Stockpile, and states will create and maintain local stockpiles.

5. Sustained human-to-human transmission anywhere in the world will be the triggering event to initiate a pandemic response by the United States. Because we live in a global community, a human outbreak anywhere means risk everywhere.
6. The United States will attempt to prevent an influenza pandemic or delay its emergence by striving to arrest isolated outbreaks of a novel influenza wherever circumstances suggest that such an attempt might be successful, acting in concert with WHO and other nations as appropriate. At the core of this strategy will be basic public health measures to reduce person-to-person transmission.
7. At the onset of an influenza pandemic, HHS, in concert with federal partners, will work with the pharmaceutical industry to procure vaccine directed against the pandemic strain and to distribute vaccine to state and local public health departments for predetermined priority groups based on preapproved state plans.
8. At the onset of an influenza pandemic, HHS, in collaboration with the states, will begin to distribute and deliver antiviral drugs from public stockpiles to healthcare facilities and others with direct patient care responsibility for administration to predetermined priority groups.[36]

Internet Exercise: Review the Essential Planning Elements for Pandemic Influenza outbreak as recommended by FEMA at: http://www.flu.gov/planning-preparedness/federal/operationalplans.html.

Pandemic planning also incorporates the resources of state and local law enforcement—agencies that are on the front lines throughout this public health threat.[37] See Figure 11.21.[38]

Every entity of government and the private sector should anticipate and prepare for the potential pandemic. As in all other areas of homeland security planning, the agency must be predictive yet reasonable in approach and anticipate the needed resource in the event of a pandemic.

Internet Resource: See data from the CDC on how influenza is tracked at www.cdc.gov/flu/weekly/index.htm.

Pandemic planning and preparedness need occur during periods of "calm" when strategic planning is clear and free from the intensity of the moment.[39]

Internet Resource: The U.S. Department of Health and Human Services has produced a bevy of materials that anticipate the prevention as well as impact of the pandemic. See http://www.flu.gov/planning-preparedness/index.html.

LAW ENFORCEMENT PANDEMIC INFLUENZA PLANNING CHECKLIST

In the event of pandemic influenza, law enforcement agencies (e.g., State, local, and tribal Police Departments, Sheriff's Offices, Federal law enforcement officers, special jurisdiction police personnel) will play a critical role in maintaining the rule of law as well as protecting the health and safety of citizens in their respective jurisdictions. Planning for pandemic influenza is critical.

To assist you in your efforts, the Department of Health and Human Services (HHS) has developed the following checklist for law enforcement agencies. This checklist provides a general framework for developing a pandemic influenza plan. Each agency or organization will need to adapt this checklist according to its unique needs and circumstances. The key planning activities in this checklist are meant to complement and enhance your existing all-hazards emergency and operational continuity plans. Many of the activities identified in this checklist will also help you to prepare for other kinds of public health emergencies.

Information specific to public safety organizations and pandemic flu preparedness and response can be found at http://www.ojp.usdoj.gov/BJA/pandemic/resources.html. For further information on general emergency planning and continuity of operations, see www.ready.gov. Further information on pandemic influenza can be found at www.pandemicflu.gov.

Develop a pandemic influenza preparedness and response plan for your agency or organization.

Completed	In Progress	Not Started	
☐	☐	☐	Assign primary responsibility for coordinating law enforcement pandemic influenza preparedness planning to a single person (identify back-ups for that person as well) with appropriate training and authority (insert name, title, and contact information here). ________
☐	☐	☐	Form a multidisciplinary law enforcement/security planning committee to address pandemic influenza preparedness specifically. The planning team should include at a minimum: human resources, health and wellness, computer support personnel, legal system representatives, partner organizations, and local public health resources. Alternatively, pandemic influenza preparedness can be addressed by an existing committee with appropriate skills and knowledge and relevant mission (list committee members and contact information here). This Committee needs to have the plan approved by the Agency Head. ________
☐	☐	☐	Review Federal, State, and local public health and emergency management agencies' pandemic plans in areas where you operate or have jurisdictional responsibilities. Ensure that your plan is NIMS (National Incident Management System) compliant and align your plan with the local Incident Command System (ICS) and local pandemic influenza plans to achieve a unified approach to incident management. See "State and Local Governments," www.pandemicflu.gov/plan/states/index.html and http://www.fema.gov/emergency/nims/index.shtm.
☐	☐	☐	Verify Command and Control areas of responsibility and authority during a pandemic. Identify alternative individuals in case primary official becomes incapacitated.
☐	☐	☐	Set up chain of command and procedures to signal activation of the agency's response plan, altering operations (e.g., shutting down non-critical operations or operations in affected areas or concentrating resources on critical activities), as well as returning to normal operations.
☐	☐	☐	Determine the potential impact of a pandemic on the agency or organization by using multiple possible scenarios of varying severity relative to illness, absenteeism, supplies, availability of resources, access to legal system representatives, etc. Incorporate pandemic influenza into agency emergency management planning and exercise.
☐	☐	☐	Identify current activities (by location and function) that will be critical to maintain during a pandemic. These essential functions might include 911 systems in communities where law enforcement is responsible for this activity, other communications infrastructures, community policing, information systems, vehicle maintenance, etc. Identify critical resources and inputs (e.g., employees, supplies, subcontractor services/products, and logistics) that are necessary to support these crucial activities.

September 4, 2007
Version 1

CDC SAFER·HEALTHIER·PEOPLE™

1

FIGURE 11.21 Law enforcement pandemic influenza planning checklist from the CDC.

11.5 Conclusion

This chapter deals with the public health dimensions of the homeland security problem. Biotoxins and bioterrorism must weigh heavily on the minds of those entrusted with minimizing the effects of these and other threats. DHS fully understands the potential for massive public health risk and

Develop a pandemic influenza preparedness and response plan for your agency or organization *(continued)*

Completed	In Progress	Not Started	
☐	☐	☐	Develop, review, and approve an official law enforcement/security pandemic influenza preparedness and response plan. This plan represents the output of many or all of the activities contained in this checklist. This plan can be an extension of your current emergency or business continuity plans with a special focus on pandemic influenza and should identify the organizational structure to be used to implement the plan. Include procedures to implement the plan in stages based upon appropriate triggering events.
☐	☐	☐	Develop a pandemic-specific emergency communications plan as part of the pandemic influenza preparedness and response plan, and revise it periodically. The communications plan should identify a communication point of contact, key contacts and back-ups, and chain of communications and clearance. Plan may also include potential collaboration with media representatives on the development of scripts based on likely scenarios guided by the public information officer(s). Coordinate with partners in emergency government and public health in advance.
☐	☐	☐	Designate an individual to monitor pandemic status and collect, organize, and integrate related information to update operations as necessary. Develop a plan for back-up if that person becomes ill during a pandemic. Develop a situational awareness capability that leadership can use to monitor the pandemic situation, support agency decisions, and facilitate monitoring of impact.
☐	☐	☐	Distribute pandemic plan throughout the agency or organization and develop means to document employees/staff received and read the plan.
☐	☐	☐	Allocate resources through the budgeting process as needed to support critical components of preparedness and response identified in your plan.
☐	☐	☐	Periodically test both the preparedness and response plan and the communications plan through drills and exercises; incorporate lessons learned into the plans.

Plan for the impact of a pandemic on your employees

Completed	In Progress	Not Started	
☐	☐	☐	Develop contingency plans for 30 – 40% employee absences. Keep in mind that absences may occur due to personal illness, family member illness, community mitigation measures, quarantines, school, childcare, or business closures, public transportation disruptions, or fear of exposure to ill individuals, as well as first responder, National Guard, or military reserve obligations.
☐	☐	☐	As necessary, plan for cross-training employees, use of auxiliary personnel and recent retirees, recruiting temporary personnel during a crisis, or establishing flexible worksite options (e.g., telecommuting) and flexible work hours (e.g. staggered shifts) when appropriate.
☐	☐	☐	Develop a reporting mechanism for employees to immediately report their own possible influenza illness during a pandemic (24/7).
☐	☐	☐	Establish compensation and leave policies that strongly encourage ill workers to stay home until they are no longer contagious. During a pandemic, employees with influenza-like symptoms (such as fever accompanied by sore throat, muscle aches and cough) should not enter the worksite to keep from infecting other workers. Employees who have been exposed to someone with influenza, particularly ill members of their household, may also be asked to stay home and monitor their symptoms.
☐	☐	☐	Employees who develop influenza-like symptoms while at the worksite should leave as soon as possible. Consult with State and local public health authorities regarding appropriate treatment for ill employees. Prepare policies that will address needed actions when an ill employee refuses to stay away from work. Federal agencies can consult guidance provided by the Office of Personnel Management (OPM) at www.opm.gov/pandemic.
☐	☐	☐	Identify employees who may need to stay home if schools dismiss students and childcare programs close for a prolonged period of time (up to 12 weeks) during a severe pandemic. Advise employees not to bring their children to the workplace if childcare cannot be arranged. Plan for alternative staffing or staffing schedules on the basis of your identification of employees who may need to stay home.
☐	☐	☐	Identify critical job functions and plan now for cross-training employees to cover those functions in case of prolonged absenteeism during a pandemic. Develop succession plans for each critical agency position to ensure the continued effective performance of your organization by identifying and training replacements for key people when necessary. These replacements should be integrated into employee development activities, and should include critical contracted services as well.
☐	☐	☐	Develop policies that focus on preventing the spread of respiratory infections in the workplace. This policy might include social distancing practices, the promotion of respiratory hygiene/cough etiquette, the creation of screening mechanisms for use during a pandemic to examine employees for fever or influenza symptoms, using the full range of available leave policies to facilitate staying home when ill or when a household member is ill, and appropriate attention to environmental hygiene and cleaning. (For more information see the www.pandemicflu.gov and http://www.pandemicflu.gov/plan/community/mitigation.html as well as OPM's guidance at www.opm.gov/pandemic.)

2

FIGURE 11.21 (continued) Law enforcement pandemic influenza planning checklist from the CDC.

injury. Working closely with the EPA, Health and Human Services, and the Departments of Agriculture and the Interior, DHS looks for those actions that might cause extensive public harm in a health context. Hence, water, its facilities and corresponding security, and threat assessment plans receive significant attention.

Plan for the impact of a pandemic on your employees *(continued)*

Completed	In Progress	Not Started	
☐	☐	☐	Provide educational programs and materials (language, culture, and reading-level appropriate) to personnel on: • pandemic fundamentals (e.g., signs and symptoms of influenza, modes of transmission, medical care), • personal and family protection and response strategies (e.g., hand hygiene, coughing/sneezing etiquette, etc.). Post instructional signs that illustrate correct infection control procedures in all appropriate locations, including offices, restrooms, waiting rooms, processing rooms, detention facilities, vehicles, etc. and, • community mitigation interventions (e.g., social distancing, etc.). See www.pandemicflu.gov, www.cdc.gov/flu/protect/stopgerms.htm, http://www.cdc.gov/flu/protect/covercough.htm, www.cdc.gov/flu/professionals/infectioncontrol/resphygiene.htm, and http://www.pandemicflu.gov/plan/community/mitigation.html.
☐	☐	☐	Provide training for law enforcement officers, office managers, medical or nursing personnel, and others as needed for performance of assigned emergency response roles. Identify a training coordinator and maintain training records. Ensure all staff are familiar with the local Incident Command System (ICS) and understand the roles and persons assigned within that structure. See http://www.fema.gov/emergency/nims/index.shtm for more information
☐	☐	☐	Stock recommended personal protective equipment (PPE) and environmental infection control supplies and make plans to distribute to employees, contractors, and others (including detainees) as needed. These supplies should include tissues, waste receptacles, single-use disinfection wipes, and alcohol-based hand cleaner (containing at least 60% alcohol). EPA registered disinfectants labeled for human influenza A virus may be used for cleaning offices, waiting rooms, bathrooms, examination rooms, and detention facilities. PPE may include gloves, surgical masks and respirators (disposable N95s or higher respirators or reusable respirators), eye protection, pocket masks (for respiratory resuscitation) and protective cover wear (e.g., impervious aprons). The specific uses for the above supplies will be advised by State and local health officials during a pandemic. Further information can be found at www.pandemicflu.gov. and at http://www.osha.gov/Publications/OSHA3327pandemic.pdf.
☐	☐	☐	Provide information to employees to help them and their families prepare and plan for a pandemic. See www.pandemicflu.gov/plan/individual/index.html.
☐	☐	☐	Work with State and/or local public health to develop a plan for distribution of pandemic influenza vaccine and antiviral medications to law enforcement personnel. See current HHS recommendations for pandemic influenza vaccine and antiviral use at http://www.hhs.gov/pandemicflu/plan/sup6.html and http://www.hhs.gov/pandemicflu/plan/sup7.html.
☐	☐	☐	Encourage and track seasonal influenza vaccination for employees every year. See www.cdc.gov/flu/protect/preventing.htm. Encourage all employees and their families to be up-to-date on all adult and child vaccinations recommended by the Advisory Committee on Immunization Practices. See www.cdc.gov/nip/recs/adult-schedule.htm and www.cdc.gov/nip/recs/child-schedule.htm.
☐	☐	☐	Evaluate employee access to and availability of health care, mental health, social services, community, and faith-based resources during a pandemic, and improve services as needed. See www.hhs.gov/pandemicflu/plan/sup11.html.

Plan for providing services to the public during a pandemic

Completed	In Progress	Not Started	
☐	☐	☐	Identify community-based scenarios and needs likely to occur in a pandemic emergency, and plan how to respond. These might include security of health care and/or vaccine distribution sites, sites that store antiviral medications or vaccines, first-responder activities, protection of critical infrastructure, management of panic and/or public fear, crowd/riot control, enforcement of public health orders, etc.
☐	☐	☐	Develop traffic flow plans to deal with standard traffic management and traffic flow around health-care delivery sites, including vaccine and antiviral distribution sites
☐	☐	☐	Anticipate community vulnerabilities (vulnerable populations, crimes of opportunity, fraudulent schemes, etc.) and specifically train employees to respond.
☐	☐	☐	Develop guidance for managing/assisting special populations (e.g., persons who are homeless, substance abusers, elderly, and individuals with disabilities, etc.) during a pandemic. This will require coordination with public health agencies, social services, correctional facilities, legal system representatives, and community-based organizations serving these populations.
☐	☐	☐	Work with local and/or State health departments or other relevant resources to ensure health protection and care for detainees or other individuals for whom the agency has responsibility.
☐	☐	☐	Establish policies on post-arrest management of an ill or exposed individual, including what to do should a care facility, precinct, and/or other law enforcement facility refuse entry to an ill or exposed individual.

3

FIGURE 11.21 (continued) Law enforcement pandemic influenza planning checklist from the CDC.

Equally important will be potential threats against our agricultural and food supplies. That contamination of the food chain would be an extraordinary public health dilemma cannot be overemphasized. Farm installations must also dwell on secured practices to ensure integrity in the food chain. Diseased animals represent a threat too. Featured within the chapter is the

Plan for coordination with external organizations and help your community

Completed	In Progress	Not Started	
☐	☐	☐	Review your pandemic influenza preparedness and response plan with key stakeholders inside and outside the agency, including employee representatives, and determine opportunities for collaboration, modification of the plan, and the development of complementary responsibilities.
☐	☐	☐	Share preparedness and response plans with other law enforcement agencies and law enforcement support agencies in your region or State (to include the National Guard) in order to share resources, identify collaboration strategies, and improve community response efforts. Develop, review, and modify local and State mutual aid agreements, if necessary. Mutual aid during an influenza pandemic can not be counted on as multiple jurisdictions in a given region may be affected simultaneously and have limited aid to offer. Availability of one State's National Guard to support another States plans under an existing compact (e.g., Emergency Management Assistance Compact) may be limited due to competing demands in their home State.
☐	☐	☐	Coordinate all requests for assistance with the next higher level governmental entity (e.g., local officials coordinate with State officials, State officials coordinate with Federal officials). Coordination is essential to ensure the assets: (1) can be provided in accordance with existing laws, (2) the requested resources are available. During a pandemic influenza, assistance from the next higher level of government may be limited due to competing higher priority demands and the effects of the influenza pandemic on these assets.
☐	☐	☐	Integrate planning with emergency service and criminal justice organizations such as courts, corrections, probation and parole, social services, multi-jurisdictional entities, public works, and other emergency management providers (fire, EMS, mutual aid, etc.).
☐	☐	☐	States should plan on utilizing their National Guard to perform law enforcement and security functions during a pandemic influenza. The National Guard under the command and control of the respective State's Governor is not subject to Posse Comitatus Act restrictions as are Federal military forces. Availability of one State's National Guard to support another States plans under an existing compact (e.g., Emergency Management Assistance Compact) may be limited due to competing demands in their home State.
☐	☐	☐	Security functions are essential during a pandemic influenza. Through your city or county attorney, corporation counsel or other appropriate authority, collaborate with the Office of the State Attorney General to clarify and review the authorities granted to law enforcement to include the National Guard. Suggest clarifications and work arounds as needed, and integrate into agency policy, training, and communications activities.
☐	☐	☐	Identify local or regional entities, such as health-care agencies, community organizations, businesses, or critical infrastructure sites, to determine potential collaboration opportunities. This collaboration might involve situational awareness, exercises or drills, or public safety training.
☐	☐	☐	Collaborate with local and/or State public health agencies to assist with the possible investigation of contacts within a suspected outbreak, the enforcement of public health orders, as well as the provision of security, protection, and possibly, critical supplies to quarantined persons. Each law enforcement agency will need to interact with local, State, county, and tribal public health officials to define the extent of the authorities provided from State legislation, develop procedures for the local initiation, implementation, and use of those authorities, as well as define protections from liability for law enforcement that may arise from quarantine and isolation enforcement. Operational planning must be flexible enough to address all scenarios in an all hazards environment, and in light of emerging infectious diseases.

4 CS113326

FIGURE 11.21 (continued) Law enforcement pandemic influenza planning checklist from the CDC.

infectious animal disease facility at Plum Island in the waters near Rhode Island and New York. The Strategic Partnership on Agroterrorism (SPPA) highlights and targets the most common threats to the agricultural marketplace and its providers. Just as crucial in the homeland defense of our agricultural infrastructure is the inspection plan of facilities by the USDA.

Finally, the chapter introduces the health dimensions of biological agents as threat to public health, the role of medical facilities in terms of response, and the particular strategies for agents.

Keywords

Agroterrorism
Animal and Plant Health Inspection Service
Assessment protocol
Avian flu
Bioterrorism
Bird flu
Chemical agent
Communicable disease
Contamination
Department of Agriculture
Environmental Protection Agency
Epidemic
Food Safety and Inspection Service
Food safety officer
H5N1
Hospital Preparedness Program
Import surveillance liaison officer
Infectious disease
Influenza
Mad Cow Disease
National Pharmaceutical Stockpile
National Select Agency Registry Program
Pandemic
Pandemic flu
Pathogen
Project BioShield
Seasonal flu
Strategic Partnership on Agroterrorism
Swine flu
Virus
Water Security Division
World Health Organization

Discussion Questions

1. In what way do federal and state agencies deal with water and its protection?
2. What role do hospitals play in questions of homeland defense and public health?
3. Explain how the food chain can be compromised.
4. Explain how biotoxins can cause massive damage to the public health. Give specific examples.
5. Why does DHS rely so heavily on the USDA in public health planning?

6. Relate the purpose and aim of Project BioShield.
7. With the rise of medicine and clinical intervention, will the pandemic be more or less likely?

Practical Exercises

1. Visit the EPA's water security home at http://water.epa.gov/infrastructure/watersecurity/index.cfm. Click on and research their various water security tools.
2. Envision how the food production cycle affords the terrorist opportunity. How could this be so? Author a hypothetical fact pattern that shows how food production may oddly be a forum for the terrorist.
3. Animals and plants may also afford the terrorist threat and terror opportunities. Relate four potential scenarios where this might occur.
4. Contact your state Homeland Security agency. Find out about pandemic preparedness and recovery.

Notes

1. All of these activities conjure up devastation and fear in the populace. It will be crucial for government to address the magnitude of the potential harm while respecting the rule of law. See B. K. Collins and H. Morrow, Using shared technology in bioterrorism planning and response: Do privacy laws affect administrative judgments? *The Homeland Security Review*, 4, 2010: 43.
2. D. K. Stocker, P. Griffin, and C. Kocher, A functionalist's perspective on bioterrorism and global adversity, *The Homeland Security Review*, 4, 2010: 2.
3. Department of Homeland Security and Environmental Protection Agency, *Water: Critical Infrastructure and Key Resources Sector Specific Plan as Input to National Infrastructure Protection Plan* (Washington, DC: U.S. Government Printing Office, 2007), 14, http://www.dhs.gov/xlibrary/assets/nipp-ssp-water.pdf.
4. Environmental Protection Agency, *Office of Water, Vulnerability Assessment Fact Sheet* (Washington, DC: U.S. Government Printing Office, 2002), http://www.epa.gov/safewater/watersecurity/pubs/va_fact_sheet_12–19.pdf.
5. See Congressional Research Service, *The Federal Food Safety System: A Primer,* (January 11, 2011), http://www.fas.org/sgp/crs/misc/RS22600.pdf.
6. U.S. Food and Drug Administration, "*Risk Assessment for Food Terrorism and Other Food Safety Concerns,*" 2003, http://www.cfsan.fda.gov/ ~ dms/rabtact.html.
7. Department of Agriculture, Department of Homeland Security, and the Food and Drug Administration, *Critical Infrastructure and Key Resources for Sector Specific Plan as Input to the National Infrastructure Protection Plan* (Washington, DC: U.S. Government Printing Office, 2007), 2.

8. Food and Agriculture DHS, *Sector-Specific Plan: An Annex to the National Infrastructure Protection Plan*, 2010.
9. U.S. Department of Agriculture, *Pre-Harvest Security Guidelines and Checklist 2006* (Washington, DC: U.S. Government Printing Office, 2006), p. 3, http://www.usda.gov/documents/PreHarvestSecurity_final.pdf.
10. Agriculture, *Critical Infrastructure*, 13.
11. Agriculture, *Critical Infrastructure*, 36.
12. USDA, *Pre-Harvest Security Guidelines*, 10–11.
13. D. K. Stocker, P. M. Griffin, C.J. Kocher, and T. M. Raquet, Agroterrorism: Risk assessment and proactive responses, *The Homeland Security Review*, 5, 2011: 17; See also K. Govern, Agroterrorism and ecoterrorism: A survey of Indo-American approaches under law and policy to prevent and defend against these potential threats ahead, *Florida Coastal Law Review*, 10, 2009: 223.
14. U.S. Food and Drug Administration, *Strategic Partnership Program Agroterrorism Initiative—Executive Summary*," 2005, http://www.usda.gov/documents/SPPA ExecutiveSummary.pdf.
15. U.S. Food and Drug Administration, *Strategic Partnership Program Agroterrorism (SPPA) Initiative*, 2006, http://www.cfsan.fda.gov/~dms/agroter5.html.
16. U.S. Food & Drug Admin., *U.S. Dept. of Homeland Security, U.S. Dept. of Agriculture, Federal Bureau of Investigation, Strategic Partnership Program Agroterrorism (SPPA) Initiative*—Second Year Status Report July 2006–September 2007, http://www.fda.gov/Food/FoodDefense/FoodDefensePrograms/ucm08992.htm.
17. D. K. Stocker, P. M. Griffin, C. J. Kocher, and T. M. Raquet, Agroterrorism: Risk assessment and proactive responses, *The Homeland Security Review*, 5, 2011: 17, 20.
18. See Congressional Research Service, *Federal Efforts to Address the Threat of Bioterrorism: Selected Issues and Options for Congress*, Feb. 8, 2011, http://www.fas.org/sgp/crs/terror/R41123.pdf; for examples of experts who downplay the threat posed by bioterrorism, see M. Leitenberg, *Assessing the Biological Weapons and Bioterrorism Threat*, Strategic Studies Institute, U.S. Army War College; *Scientists Working Group on Biological and Chemical Weapons, Center for Arms Control and Non-Proliferation, Biological Threats: A Matter of Balance, Jan. 26, 2010*; Scientists Working Group on Biological and Chemical Weapons, Biological Threats: A Matter of Balance, *Bulletin of the Atomic Scientists*, Feb. 2, 2010.
19. See Congressional Research Service, *Federal Efforts to Address the Threat of Bioterrorism: Selected Issues and Options for Congress*, Feb. 8, 2011: 8–9.
20. See J. Tropper, C. Adamski, C. Vionion, and S. Sapkota, Tracking antimicrobials dispensed during an anthrax attack: A case study from the New Hampshire anthrax exercise, *Journal of Emergency Management* 9 (January/February 2011): 65.
21. Centers for Disease Control and Prevention, "*Bioterrorism Overview*," *Emergency Preparedness and Response*, http://www.bt.cdc.gov/bioterrorism/overview.asp.
22. Centers for Disease Control and Prevention, "Anthrax: Surveillance and Investigation," Emergency Preparedness and Response, http://www.bt.cdc.gov/agent/anthrax/surveillance.
23. Project BioShield Act of 2004, P.L.108-276, *U.S. Statutes at Large* 118, 2004: 835.
24. For an update on BioShield's many activities see Congressional Research Service, Project BioShield: Authorities, Appropriations, Acquisitions, and Issues for Congress, May 27, 2011, http://www.fas.org/sgp/crs/terror/R41033.pdf.
25. U.S. Department of Health and Human Services, *Project BioShield: Annual Report to Congress: 2006–2007* (Washington, DC: U.S. Government Printing Office, 2007), 20, http://www.hhs.gov/aspr/barda/documents/bioshieldannualreport2006.pdf.

26. Congressional Research Service, *Project BioShield: Authorities, Appropriations, Acquisitions, and Issues for Congress,* May 27, 2011, 8, http://www.fas.org/sgp/crs/terror/R41033.pdf.
27. World Health Organization, *Timeline of Influenza A (H1 N1) Cases: Laboratory Confirmed Cases and Deaths as Reported to WHO,* http://www.who.int/csr/disease/swineflu/history_map/InfluenzaAH1N1_maps.html.
28. There are even more legal issues and potential liabilities associated with pandemics when compared to other natural disasters. See B. Courtney, Five legal preparedness challenges for responding to future public health emergencies, *Journal of Law, Medicine & Ethics* (Spring 2011): 60.
29. U.S. Department of Health and Human Services, PandemicFlu.gov, http://pandemicflu.gov/general/index.html, accessed February 27, 2009.
30. Flu.gov, *About Pandemics, Seasonal Flu versus Pandemic Flu,* www.pandemicflu.gov/individualfamily/about/pandemic/index.html.
31. The World Health Organization, *Pandemic Influenza Preparedness and Response: A WHO Guidance Document* (Washington, DC: U.S. Government Printing Office, 2009).
32. National Institute of Allergy and Infectious Diseases, National Institute of Health, *Timeline of Human Flu Pandemics,* http://www3.niaid.nih.gov/topics/Flu/Research/Pandemic/TimelineHumanPandemics.htm.
33. For general advice on the preparedness model, see: World Health Organization, Pandemic influenza preparedness: Sharing of influenza viruses and access to vaccines and other benefits, *63rd World Health Assembly* (April 2010), http://apps.who.int/gb/ebwha/pdf_files/WHA63/A63_4-en.pdf; see also World Health Organization, *Regional Pandemic Influenza Preparedness and Response Plan, 2009–2010* (May 2009) http://www.afro.who.int/index.php?option=com_docman&task=doc_download&gid=3762; J. R. Langabeer II and J. L. DelliFraine, Incorporating strategic management into public health emergency preparedness, *Journal of Emergency Management,* 9, Mar./Apr. 2011: 17.
34. U.S. Department of Homeland Security, *Pandemic Influenza: Preparedness, Response and Recovery Guide for Critical Infrastructure and Key Resources,* 2006, http://www.flu.gov/planning-preparedness/business/cikrpandemicinfluenzaguide.pdf.
35. U.S. Department of Transportation, *Preparing for Pandemic Influenza: Recommendations for Protocol Development for 9-1-1 Personnel and Public Safety Answering Points,* 2007, Appendix E, http://icsw.nhtsa.gov/people/injury/ems/pandemicinfluenza/PDFs/AppE.pdf accessed May 28, 2012.
36. U.S. Department of Health and Human Services, *HHS Pandemic Influenza Plan-Part 1: Strategic Plan,* http://www.hhs.gov/pandemicflu/plan/part1.html, accessed May 28, 2012; See also *DHS, FEMA, Continuity of Operations: An Overview of Continuing Planning for Pandemic Influenza,* 2011, http://www.fema.gov/pdf/about/org/ncp/pandemic_influenza.pdf.
37. G. Waight et al., The role of medical students in influenza pandemic response, *Journal of Emergency Management,* 9, March/April 2011, p. 60.
38. U.S. Department of Health and Human Services, *Law Enforcement Pandemic Influenza Planning Checklist,* www.flu.gov/planning-preparedness/business/lawenforcement.pdf.
39. J. R. Langabeer II and J. L. DelliFraine, Incorporating strategic management into public health emergency preparedness, *Journal of Emergency Management,* 9, March/April 2011: 17, 25.

Chapter 12 The Future of Homeland Security

12.1 Introduction

In its very short life span, the Department of Homeland Security (DHS) has evolved in dramatic ways—in both a bureaucratic and a mission sense. The fact that this agency was born with such speed, and that it subsequently metamorphosized into a full-blown department, is testimony to its unique nature in the world of government. Nothing moves all that quickly in the worlds of bureaucracy and government entities. DHS travels at speeds never before charted in the annals of the political process.

However, viewed another way, it is valid to question whether there is consensus on exactly what "homeland security" even is. The fact that there are hundreds, even thousands of initiatives in homeland defense, proves very little about their universal relevance to what might be described as core missions. Shortly after 9/11, it seems improbable that livestock, corn, avian and swine flu, the Internet and telecommunications would be the vernacular and purview of the homeland initiative. Prior to 9/11, the principles and practices of homeland defense were rather narrowly constructed.

Today there is the very real danger of mission creep. Some entities outside and within the government have convinced themselves that areas that seem far afield from homeland security have direct connections to the homeland security universe. Thinking broadly, just about every human activity could fall under the homeland security umbrella. In some cases this would be right; in other cases, this would be wrong and even counterproductive. Some of these "wrong" choices are often to the detriment of citizens' privacies and civil liberties granted in the Constitution. Security is clearly of prime importance, but we must tread lightly.

DHS as currently constructed and operated still has the capacity to jump on any new program initiative that it can invent or that someone can imagine. In short, DHS never met a program it did not like (or could not rationalize). While the administrators and operatives within DHS may not intend this, the operational life form of DHS plays and feeds on fear itself, to the tune of billions of taxpayer's dollars. Strategists and policymakers bandy about every imaginable solution while fear of the unknown event, plot, or disaster hangs like a specter over every decision. DHS cannot protect every citizen in every quarter, in every situation. DHS cannot possibly design and divine policy for every facet of human life.

Turning to the academic sector, even among colleges and universities there is a lack of consensus on what the homeland curriculum should be and what the homeland student should study. As Drs. William Pelfrey Sr. and Jr. cogently argue:

> Unfortunately, there is no clear roadmap to homeland security nor is there a consensus on appropriate curricula for homeland security programs. A review of federal publications on homeland security is dizzying. A myriad of Presidential Directives, Department of Homeland Security Publications, commission reports, and other publications leaves most academics and practitioners with their heads spinning.[1]

That debate is instructive on how so many constituencies in homeland security have acted since the early days after 9/11. As DHS talks about unification, efficiency, and universal mission, there should be concern about the notion of trying to be all things to all people.

DHS has placed itself in the tenuous position of being guarantor in all aspects of human activity and motion. As an example, one of the most difficult of man-made tragedies to thwart are active shooter scenarios. Lone wolf shooting events such as the July 2012 Aurora, Colorado, movie theater shooting that killed 12; the August 2012 shooting at a Sikh temple in Oak Creek, Wisconsin, that killed 6; and the unspeakable shooting of 26 innocent children, teachers, and school administrators at Sandy Hook Elementary School in Newtown, Connecticut, are only increasing in frequency. DHS has promised that food will be safe, that water will always be drinkable, that planes will never be hijacked, that trains will never be derailed by terrorists. And yet, we still hear new reports of plots to smuggle explosives onto planes, the extremely costly expense, delays, and inability to finish the virtual fence initiative on the U.S.–Mexico border, and an aging U.S. power and utilities infrastructure that is subject to SCADA and cyber attacks. It is no wonder that the public is concerned about DHS's direction, mission, and focus.

DHS must recognize and know, on some level, that it cannot do all it seeks to accomplish. FEMA seems to acknowledge this reality when it labels its current effort as "government centric."

> We fully recognize that a government-centric approach to emergency management is not enough to meet the challenges posed by a catastrophic incident. Whole Community is an approach to emergency management that reinforces the fact that FEMA is only one part of our nation's emergency management team; that we must leverage all of the resources of our collective team in preparing for, protecting against, responding to, recovering from and mitigating against all hazards; and that collectively we must meet the needs of the entire community in each of these areas.[2]

As DHS seeks to generate enthusiasm within the public, especially in publishing documents such as "One Team, One Mission, Securing the Homeland 2008–2013,"[3] the contents of the report paint a somewhat disappointing picture of half successes. At Goal 1: Protect Our Nation from Dangerous People, arguably the central reason for the mission of DHS, the results by and large are mixed to poor no matter how you look at it. See Figure 12.1.

Less than half of the air passengers with major violations of customs and immigration laws and regulations are apprehended. Just over one-third of

Select Reported Measures for Goal 1: Protect Our Nation from Dangerous People

Measure	FY 2013 Target
Border miles under effective control (including certain coastal sectors).	*
Air passenger apprehension rate for major violations. [Percent of the total number of individual passengers with major violations of customs and immigration laws and regulations that were apprehended based on statistical estimates of the total number of violations that came through our international airports.]	43.5%
Land border apprehension rate for major violations. [Percent of the total number of vehicles travelers with major violations of customs and immigration laws and regulations that were apprehended based on statistical estimates of the total number of violations that came through the points of entry (POEs).]	37.5%
Percent of at-risk miles under strategic air surveillance.	95%
Percent of undocumented migrants who attempt to enter the U.S. via maritime routes that are interdicted. [As estimated, based upon data obtained from the U.S. Coast Guard and U.S. Customs and Border Protection.]	71.5%
Number of incursions into the U.S. exclusive economic zone (EEZ).	185
Percent of time that coast guard assets included in the combatant commander Operational Plans are ready at a status of resources and training system (SORTS) rating of 2 or better.	100%

* The degree of effective control will be determined by the resources devoted to the task as developed in the Department's FY 2010–2014 budget proposal and by funding provided by congress.

FIGURE 12.1 Goal 1 performance.

FIGURE 12.2 Bering Sea—The Coast Guard cutter *Healy* breaks ice around the Russian-flagged tanker vessel *Renda* 250 miles south of Nome, Alaska, January 6, 2012. (U.S. Coast Guard photo by Petty Officer 1st Class Sara Francis.)

vehicle travelers with major violations of customs and immigration laws and regulations are apprehended. The only true success story among those listed is that of the Coast Guard—an agency that remains mission-oriented and does what it does exceedingly well. As exhibited by its response in the Haiti Earthquake of 2011 and the BP Oil spill, and per the Coast Guard's own Posture Statement for 2011, it is rightfully characterized as an entity "biased for action" with an "ability to meet expanded mission requirements."[4] DHS as a whole could learn much from this key player in both emergency response and homeland defense roles (Figure 12.2).

At present, DHS seemingly continues down a path of agency building by looking for more items to take over responsibility of. With a nation 15 trillion in debt and counting, and a military complex now facing severe and significant cuts, little—including DHS's massive budget—will be spared the budgetary realities of the decade to come.[5]

12.2 Growth without Reason

From its inception, DHS was running on a different clock than its governmental counterparts. Aside from its origination, it could change like a chameleon. Today's threat was tomorrow's agenda item, only lower on the list. DHS could consume, like a ravenous beast, most of its competing agencies, even those with a historically different approach. Nothing is all that surprising about bureaucracies growing, self-perpetuating, and feeding on mission to develop other parts of the bureaucratic puzzle. Yet this journey is neither trek nor run, but a propulsion that simply knows no bounds. FEMA's inclusion in DHS is an excellent illustration of this phenomenon. In FEMA the natural disaster sets the tone—the hurricane, the earthquake, the fire, and so on. That is what FEMA was intended to direct its energies toward. Even so, FEMA would be subsumed into the DHS model. Some have wondered whether this tendency to simply swallow any event resembling a disaster has been good for DHS or FEMA. It is a question worth asking, and in the hubbub of growth and bureaucratic delirium, a pandemic of frenzy if there ever was one, one must stop and smell the roses. To grow and evolve is natural. To grow without much thought is mindless. Maybe FEMA's response to hurricane damage are not really the building blocks of DHS. Maybe earthquakes are flat out different and do not benefit from the DHS mentality. While not perfect, the generally positive signs in the planning in advance of and response in the wake of Hurricane Sandy in the fall of 2012 indicate that FEMA may in fact be able to operate and function successfully within DHS. Only time will tell.

As you read through the pages of this chapter, you have witnessed growth in both form and substance. You have witnessed the absorption of departments at a pace never seen before. You have gleaned that the term infrastructure means more than brick and mortar—that the FDA has a homeland plan just as the National Monuments Agency does. Everyone has a plan. Everyone combats terrorism. Page by page you have read about new plans, new stratagems, new policies, new mergers, and realignments. You can get dizzy reading about these changes. And one other thing—you can be sure that what is here likely will be different in a short time. I contend that more is not always more. Sometimes more is less. Fewer results, less efficiency, less coordination. Is it possible to take on too many agencies, too much responsibility, and thus lose the focus of what is truly important or necessary?

As an example, does the hiring of 60,000 new border agents—throwing sheer numbers at the problem—automatically guarantee a more secure border? Revisiting policy and enforcing current laws on the books would take care of many of the issues. We build fences to keep people out, but illegal immigration is still a consistent problem. While border security is necessary, a more holistic policy solution would include: (1) increased border security in conjunction with encouraging legitimate immigration and naturalization and (2) a more consistent policy on illegal immigrants within the country. Establishing a reliable, efficient process for those individuals and families who are in the country now and want to become U.S. citizens, would help alleviate some of the strain on the system, set the proper tone, and provide a clear and consistent path to obtaining citizenship.

Why do our agencies neglect targeting those that should be targeted and continue to search the 9-year-old child's Sponge Bob bag, or the coat of an 80-year-old grandmother? These are just singular, but simple and reflective examples of a department that does things in ways that belie notions of efficiency and targeted focus. A DHS that operates like the agency at present will not last into the next century. It will not be nimble enough to last. Even DHS knows this reality. In 2010, DHS announced a threefold mission concerning how it will unfold in the decade to come: first, it will need to consolidate duplicitous operations; second, it will need to streamline these bulky and cumbersome systems, and lastly, it will need to be open to the world. The talk of change is in the air and whether the nature and sheer size of DHS can adapt remains unclear. DHS is well-meaning when it relays:

> We have taken significant steps to create a unified and integrated Department that will enhance our performance by focusing on:
>
> - Accountability
> - Efficiency
> - Transparency, and
> - Leadership development

The future of homeland security can be prosperous and highly effective—it can help prevent attacks and thwart the terrorist who haunts our way of life. Ultimately, it can provide levels of security and safety at costs more aligned with reality and the mission of government in general.

12.3 Curbing Expansionism in Mission

To have any chance at a prosperous future, DHS will have to simplify. There is too much under its roof, and much of what sits under its tent does not belong. DHS's mission is to:

- Prevent terrorist attacks within the United States
- Reduce the vulnerability of the United States to terrorism
- Minimize the damage, and assist in the recovery, from terrorist attacks that do occur within the United States
- Carry out all functions of entities transferred to the Department, including by acting as a focal point regarding natural and man-made crises and emergency planning
- Ensure that the function of the agencies and subdivisions within the Department that are not related directly to securing the homeland

are not diminished or neglected except by a specific explicit Act of Congress
- Monitor connection between illegal drug trafficking and terrorism, coordinate efforts to sever such connections, and otherwise contribute to efforts to interdict illegal drug trafficking[6]

The simplicity of the mission—a secure America through deterrence and prevention of terrorism and secure borders—causes one to pause on the expansionist mentality that has occurred with at the growth of DHS. The agencies in Table 12.1 became part of DHS in 2003. The table lays out the first expansionist event in the history of DHS.

Just for the sake of argument, does the merger and consolidation make sense in all cases? Can the Secret Service not carry out its mission without being tethered to DHS? What about the Energy Security and Assurance Program? Does DHS have the expertise to handle the subject matter? And the Plum Island Infectious Disease Center for Animals—would it not make better sense to leave Plum Island with the Department of Agriculture? Does it seem likely that a terrorist event would occur with livestock? Noted already was the suitability of the FEMA merger. Why would hurricane response assist in DHS's mission? It is the author's view that DHS is struggling with its own identity, from its initial manifestation to its subsequent transformations. Instead of being attentive to its basic mission of security and counterterrorism, it has wandered into peripheral territory, only partially touching upon questions of security. The net effect of this expansionism has been the dilution of other services and functions in government. Some departments are underfunded budget-wise and adapting to missions, some of which, are tangential to their overall purpose. For DHS to survive into the future, it may require shedding functions that stand far afield from its ultimate end or purpose. William L. Waugh Jr. notes in "The Future of Homeland Security and Emergency Management":

> Mission problems were expected with the integration of non-terrorism programs into a department focused on the terrorist threat. FEMA, in particular, has responsibilities unrelated to dealing with terrorism, such as the National Flood Insurance Program and the National Earthquake Hazard Reduction Program. Other DHS components also have diverse non-terrorism responsibilities, not least of which are the U.S. Coast Guard's responsibilities related to oil spills, boating safety, and air-sea rescue.[7]

It is a legitimate critique, for why does DHS involve itself in flood insurance, geospatial maps, and computer security breaches? Are these activities consistent with mission or causing stress internally and externally? To be sure, the financial stress alone, the budgetary demands of new obligations, has either drained historic budgets or added to tightness in existing budgets.

TABLE 12.1 Departmental Movements in the History of DHS

Original Agency (Department)	Current Agency/Office
The U.S. Customs Service (Treasury)	U.S. Customs and Border Protection—inspection, border and ports of entry responsibilities U.S. Immigration and Customs Enforcement—customs law enforcement responsibilities
The Immigration and Naturalization Service (Justice)	U.S. Customs and Border Protection—inspection functions and the U.S. Border Patrol U.S. Immigration and Customs Enforcement—immigration law enforcement: detention and removal, intelligence, and investigation U.S. Citizenship and Immigration Services—adjudications and benefits programs
The Federal Protective Service	U.S. Immigration and Customs Enforcement
The Transportation Security Administration (Transportation)	Transportation Security Administration
Federal Law Enforcement Training Center (Treasury)	Federal Law Enforcement Training Center
Animal and Plant Health Inspection Service (part)(Agriculture)	U.S. Customs and Border Protection—agricultural imports and entry inspections
Office for Domestic Preparedness (Justice)	Responsibilities distributed within FEMA
The Federal Emergency Management Agency (FEMA)	Federal Emergency Management Agency
Strategic National Stockpile and the National Disaster Medical System (HHS)	Returned to Health and Human Services, July 2004
Nuclear Incident Response Team (Energy)	Responsibilities distributed within FEMA
Domestic Emergency Support Teams (Justice)	Responsibilities distributed within FEMA
National Domestic Preparedness Office (FBI)	Responsibilities distributed within FEMA
CBRN Countermeasures Programs (Energy)	Science and Technology Directorate
Environmental Measurements Laboratory (Energy)	Science and Technology Directorate
National BW Defense Analysis Center (Defense)	Science and Technology Directorate
Plum Island Animal Disease Center (Agriculture)	Science and Technology Directorate
Federal Computer Incident Response Center (GSA)	US-CERT, Office of Cyber Security and Communications in the National Programs and Preparedness Directorate
National Communications System (Defense)	Office of Cyber Security and Communications in the National Programs and Preparedness Directorate
National Infrastructure Protection Center (FBI)	Dispersed throughout the department, including Office of Operations Coordination and Office of Infrastructure Protection
Energy Security and Assurance Program (Energy)	Integrated into the Office of Infrastructure Protection
U.S. Coast Guard	U.S. Coast Guard
U.S. Secret Service	U.S. Secret Service

By 2005, departmental changes were being referred to as structural adjustments. Change continued its unabated pace with new recommendations for the department. New offices, directors, realignments, and mergers continued without reservation. For example, a new director of operations coordination was implemented. The director's primary function was to improve coordination and efficiency of operations. By this time, DHS was tackling so many functions that it was feeling the pressure and stress of nonaligned functions. Why else would DHS need a director of operations coordination?

In general, DHS continues to realign itself and is trying to serve many masters. For the future health of the Agency, DHS may need to adhere to a different model that sticks to the fundamentals of what the department can and should do. To that end, what the future holds remains to be seen.

12.4 The Merits of Decentralization

While DHS touts the value of the decentralized model in much of its literature, it has erected centralized superstructures of operations. DHS is about as centralized a department as it gets. It is overly large and overly bureaucratic on a number of levels.

In August 2011, the traditionally conservative think tank the Heritage Foundation, urged DHS to engage in the sort of decentralizing self-assessment that would cause culture shock. In short, get smaller by spinning off the responsibilities or return them from the place originally grabbed. Give back to the states and localities that know their populations the task of homeland defense. One must coordinate but not at the expense of state wide and local visions. Their recommendations:

- Establishing a framework for empowering state and local authorities to meet their responsibilities for disaster response and domestic counterterrorism operations, particularly for ensuring state and local input into national policies and promoting intelligence-led policing.
- Adopting a fair, honest, and realistic approach to immigration enforcement that recognizes state and local authorities as responsible partners and abjures an "amnesty first" strategy, which would simply encourage more illegal border crossings and unlawful presence. Sensible and functional border security, immigration, and workplace laws are vital to focusing scarce resources on the pressing security threat posed by transnational criminal cartels based in Mexico.
- Overhauling the process for declaring federal disasters and dispensing homeland security grants. Current policies and programs waste resources and do not promote resiliency or preparedness.

- Maintaining the use of key counterterrorism tools, such as those authorized under the USA PATRIOT Act, and establishing a national domestic counterterrorism and intelligence framework that clearly articulates how intelligence operations at all levels should function to combat terrorism.
- Rethinking the Transportation Security Administration (TSA) and restructuring its mission from providing airport security to making aviation security policy and regulations and devolving screening responsibility to the airport level under supervision of a federal security director.[8]

While any of these points can be, and have been, debated from multiple angles, this list does identify some of the key issues at the heart of homeland security and the future of DHS. Consensus opinion among many in and around government circles confirms that to change tack and move a new direction will require a major cultural shift in how the respective agencies within DHS see and appreciate the responsibilities of homeland security. This will not happen overnight.

Despite this, there are positive signs of regional, state, and local cooperation. Advisory councils and committees exist to foster local influence. Partnerships abound with the federal DHS and states and localities. Although these are steps in the right direction, it is clear that federalism reigns supreme in the affairs of homeland security. In grants, in policy making, in budgetary allotments, in federal appointments to staff positions, the federal system dominates the states and localities. This domination diminishes the role of local input and control in matters of homeland security.

To that end, I propose the following characteristics of collaborative federalism for homeland security:

> Homeland security is a national issue requiring national solutions. As such, the role of Congress and its executive agent DHS is that of facilitation and leadership, providing guidelines, milestones, and enough funding to make a difference.
>
> State and local governments have maximum flexibility in implementing homeland security programs to gain greater efficiency and better situational awareness.[9]

Collaboration signifies meaningful input and participation rather than a sometimes formulaic reaction to posted policy and funding mechanisms. Instead of implementing one-size-fits-all states and localities, DHS might be better served looking to the localities for their needs assessment and turning over more tasks and functions to localities.

12.5 The Rise of Technology

For too long, both prior to joining DHS and in their current structure, the many functions of homeland security have been performed manually by people, often at extraordinary cost. Mentioned already were the more than 100,000 employees in TSA and Border Patrol. To have any future, DHS will have to operate with leaner staffing and financial budgets. It cannot survive long term with high payrolls necessitated by huge staffing, nor should some of the rote functions of TSA employees be reserved for personnel. It appears that machines can do a comparable job, and we may be on our way to seeing more and more of reliability on technologies to help security functions. DHS already knows that science and technology will lead the way in any future for DHS. Just a few examples of current initiatives are shown in Figure 12.3.[10]

DHS's reliance on outside authority and analysis is one of its greatest recent accomplishments. DHS has aggressively developed partnerships with universities and colleges—as well as private associations, non-profits, think-tanks and research centers—including its 12 designated "Centers for Excellence."

- The Center for Risk and Economic Analysis of Terrorism Events (CREATE), led by the University of Southern California, develops advanced tools to evaluate the risks, costs, and consequences of terrorism.
- The Center for Advancing Microbial Risk Assessment (CAMRA), led by Michigan State University and Drexel University established jointly with the U.S. Environmental Protection Agency, fills critical gaps in risk assessments for mitigating microbial hazards.
- The Center of Excellence for Zoonotic and Animal Disease Defense (ZADD), led by Texas A&M University and Kansas State University, protects the nation's agricultural and public health sectors against high-consequence foreign animal, emerging and zoonotic disease threats.
- The National Center for Food Protection and Defense (NCFPD), led by the University of Minnesota, defends the safety and security of the food system by conducting research to protect vulnerabilities in the nation's food supply chain.
- The National Consortium for the Study of Terrorism and Responses to Terrorism (START), led by the University of Maryland, informs decisions on how to disrupt terrorists and terrorist groups through empirically grounded findings on the human element of the terrorist threat.
- The National Center for the Study of Preparedness and Catastrophic Event Response (PACER), led by Johns Hopkins University, opti-

FOR THE TRANSPORTATION SECURITY ADMINISTRATION

- **Home Made Explosives** signature data that informed the decision so allow air travelers, to carry small quantities of liquids
- **Screening Passenger by Observation Techniques** analysis that delivers enhanced capabilities in detecting suspicions behavior through cross-culturally validated observational and interview techniques that can be employed well before a person commits a hostile act
- **Behavior-Based Deception–Detection Training** enables cross-cultural validation of behavioral indicators of deception and suspicious behavior
- **Hand-Held Vapor-Detection** technology to detect and identify persistent but low-vapor pressure chemical threats on surfaces

FOR OTHER U.S. GOVERNMENT AGENCIES

- The **National Bioforensics Analysis Center** that conducts forensic analysis of evidence from biocrime or bioterrorism events
- High-throughput **integrated mobile laboratories** for broad-based tactical chemical analysis
- Material threat determinations to inform Health and Human Service's medical countermeasure requirements generation
- End-to-end **Bio-Terrorism Risk Assessment, Chemical Terrorism Risk Assessment** and integrated **CBRNE Risk Assessment** capabilities to assess cross-threat risks and evaluate risk-mitigation strategies
- The **Biodefense Knowledge Center** that provides tailored, in-depth biodefense analysis and "24/7" operational support
- The **Chemical Security Analysis Center** that analyses current and evolving chemical threats and provides "24/7" technical reach-bank support
- The **Combinatorial Analysis Utilizing Logical Dependencies Residing on Networks** tool that provides automated analysis of possible attack paths through a cyber network for attack correlation, prediction and response
- A **secure USB device that** corrects a significant cyber-security vulnerability

FOR STATE AND LOCAL FIRST-RESPONDERS

- A man-portable **Interoperable Tactical Operations Center**
- The **critical infrastructure inspection** management system that enables officers to locate quickly and inspect critical infrastructure
- Seven **hurricane scenario models** for New York City restoration planning
- Guidance for **critical transportation facilities** following a biological incident
- A networked **chemical detection system** for rail transportation facilities
- A nationwide **validation and testing program for communications equipment** to ensure interoperability

FOR EVERY ONE

- A **Global Terrorism Database** combining more than 85,000 events to analyze and understand factors that influence the likelihood of a terrorist attack

FIGURE 12.3 Current DHS initiatives.

mizes our nation's preparedness in the event of a high-consequence natural or man-made disaster.

- The Center of Excellence for Awareness & Location of Explosives-Related Threats (ALERT), led by Northeastern University and the University of Rhode Island, will develop new means and methods to protect the nation from explosives-related threats.
- The National Center for Border Security and Immigration (NCBSI), led by the University of Arizona in Tucson (research co-lead) and the University of Texas at El Paso (education co-lead), are developing

technologies, tools, and advanced methods to balance immigration and commerce with effective border security.

- The Center for Maritime, Island and Remotes and Extreme Environment Security (MIREES), led by the University of Hawaii and Stevens Institute of Technology, focuses on developing robust research and education programs addressing maritime domain awareness to safeguard populations and properties in geographical areas that present significant security challenges.
- The Coastal Hazards Center of Excellence (CHC), led by the University of North Carolina at Chapel Hill and Jackson State University in Jackson, MS, performs research and develops education programs to enhance the nation's ability to safeguard populations, properties, and economies from catastrophic natural disaster.
- The National Transportation Security Center of Excellence (NTSCOE) was established in accordance with HR1, Implementing the Recommendations of the 9/11 Commission Act of 2007, in August 2007. The NTSCOE will develop new technologies, tools and advanced methods to defend, protect, and increase the resilience of the nation's multimodal transportation. It comprises seven institutions:
  - Connecticut Transportation Institute at the University of Connecticut
  - Tougaloo College
  - Texas Southern University
  - National Transit Institute at Rutgers—the State University of New Jersey
  - Homeland Security Management Institute at Long Island University
  - Mack Blackwell National Rural Transportation Study Center at the University of Arkansas
  - Mineta Transportation Institute at San José State University
- The Center of Excellence in Command, Control and Interoperability (C2I) led by Purdue University (visualization sciences co-lead) and Rutgers University (data sciences co-lead) will create the scientific basis and enduring technologies needed to analyze massive amounts of information to detect security threats.

In the coming years, technology will replace the human person in carrying out the mission of DHS in many cases, hopefully for the better. While controversial in many circles, many plane and helicopter applications are poised be replaced with drones for use in border security, surveillance, law enforcement, and search and rescue operations (Figure 12.4).

FIGURE 12.4 Air Force drone.

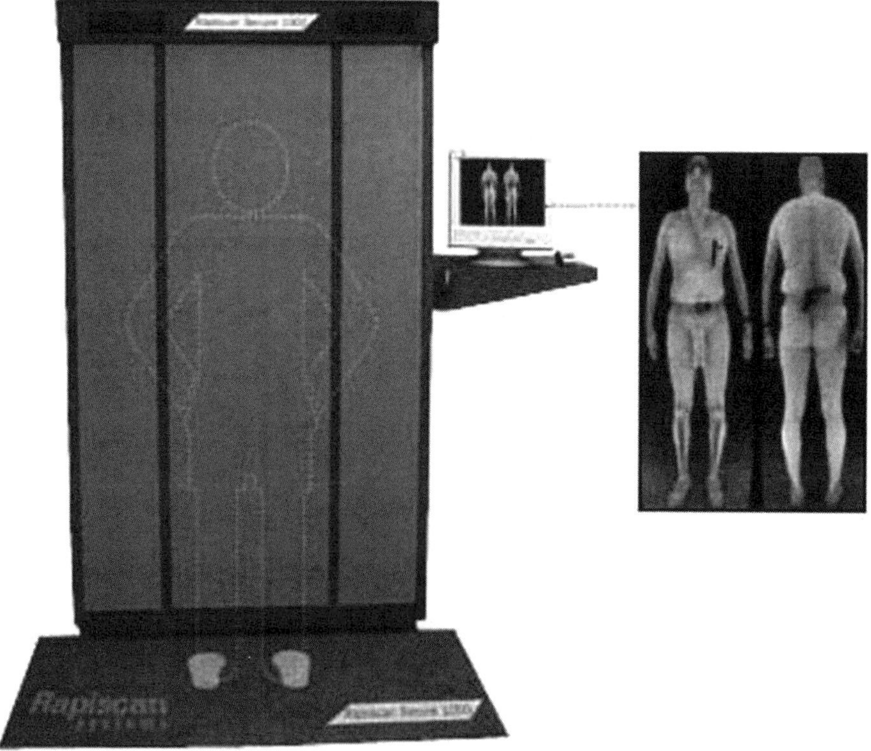

FIGURE 12.5 Millimeter wave.

TSA employees, who presently search bags and laptops, will be helped by new and emerging technologies (Figure 12.5).

DHS and its Science and Technology Directorate know keenly where the winds are blowing—to science and the role of technology securing the country. DHS committed substantial funding to science and technology in the 2011 cycle. See Figure 12.6.

This trend will continue into the long-term future. With new products and designs to track cargo, to sniff out explosives, to detect biological agents, and to prevent IED explosions, the role of technology will only increase in the years to come.

Budget Request (Dollars in Thousands)								
	FY 2009 Revised Enacted		FY 2010 Enacted		FY 2011 Pres. Budget		FY 2011 +/FY 2010	
	FTE	$000	FTE	$000	FTE	$000	FTE	$000
Management and Administration	257	$132,100	278	$143,200	317	$151,959	39	$8759
Border and Maritime	—	33,050	—	44,181	—	39,936	—	(4245)
Chemical and Biological	—	200,408	—	206,800	—	200,863	—	(5937)
Command, Control and Interoperability	—	74,890	—	81,764	—	74,832	—	(6932)
Explosives	—	96,149	—	120,809	—	120,809	—	—
HSI	—	5000	—	—	—	—	—	—
Human Factors	—	12,460	—	16,087	—	13,435	—	(2652)
Infrastructure and Geophysical	—	75,816	—	74,958	—	36,122	—	(38,836)
Innovation	—	33,000	—	44,000	—	44,000	—	—
Laboratory Facilities	124	161,940	130	150,188	130	122,000	—	(28,188)
Radiological and Nuclear	—	—	—	—	—	109,000	—	109,000
Test and Evaluations, Standards	—	28,674	—	29,000	—	23,174	—	(5826)
Transition	—	28,830	—	46,134	—	42,134	—	(4000)
University Programs	—	50,270	—	49,350	—	40,000	—	(9350)
Total Budget Authority	**381**	**$932,587**	**408**	**$1,006,471**	**447**	**$1,018,264**	**39**	**$11,793**
Prior Year Rescission	—	—	—	–[6944]	—	—	—	—

FIGURE 12.6 DHS budget allotments 2011.

Other areas in need of innovation and creative upgrade are surveillance practice, sensor capacity, robotics in hazardous situations, and new methods and protocols in all aspects of information technology. The DHS of the future will rely on technology in a much more substantial way than today.

12.6 The Need for a New Way of Thinking—Jump Out of the Box

Much of what has and continues to take place in homeland security, has taken place with limited to little objection. It is hard to argue that terrorism is a growing global and domestic threat and that it makes sense to take efforts to ensure the country's safety and security. However, it would be wise to take a step back, assess, and consider what we are doing and what needs to be done by way of homeland security. I mean this in three different senses.

First, why do we do what we do in so many cases? Is the threat real as described? If the threats were as real and meaningful as the experts indicate, would these events not occur with greater regularity? Is it really necessary to check passengers in airports as presently done? Is there some proof, if we choose not to frisk and search people, that terrorism would rise without resistance? More people die in suicide and car crashes each year, though no programs to deal with these tragedies have come around the bend. I do not make light of these things. I only point out that one wonders about assumptions. Do more procedures automatically translate to greater security? There has yet to be one event of terrorism involving aircraft since 9/11 though not for lack of trying (refer to the Christmas Day Bomber mentioned in Chapter 2). A party could conclude that this state of affairs results from such a diligent and enlightened security program. Others might argue sheer coincidence or luck. Thus, the question remains whether the TSA investment, as it currently stands, is justified given the paucity of events. Or have we ever considered that our fears are disproportionate to the potential risk or harm? Why do we assume these fears are properly correlated?

Benjamin Freidman's *Managing Fear: The Politics of Homeland Security*,[11] forces this sort of examination—begging whether fear can be justified in its present form. He is particularly piercing when he engages the threat of bioterrorism.

> Eight years later and counting, with plenty of conventional terrorism abroad and almost none in the United States, evidence is mounting that these trends are overstated or wrong—that September 11 was more an aberration than a harbinger of an age of deadlier terrorism. Terrorism using biological or

nuclear weapons should still worry us, but the common claim that these sorts of attacks are virtually inevitable is an overstatement.[12]

Freidman goes on to further argue that our fears may be "inflated" and given this reality, it is just the place for a bureaucrat to finds a comfy nest.[13]

Thinking outside any box is not an easy task, and thinking outside a governmental box is almost an impossibility. Yet, this is what must happen in order for DHS to thrive into the next century. It cannot use law enforcement techniques suitable for the twentieth century when technology can substitute. Homeland professionals of the future should not accept the status quo and need to look beyond the holiday and the personal day. Leap out of the box and do things differently than the traditional way of doing task and function. A few examples of this thinking might be:

- Target terrorists through behavioral profiling
- Have random rather than mandatory checkpoints at air and transportation facilities
- Allow frequent fliers to skip security systems; this has been done for registered flyers on an increasing basis
- Allow local police authorities to assume some homeland functions
- Insist on a grant program that is not universally applied but targeted to localities and their needs
- Disburse budgetary allotments at the local level
- Return non-DHS functions to previous agencies
- Halt the onerous license requirements for American citizens
- Decentralize more DHS operations to the states and localities

These are representative suggestions for how DHS and its staff might think outside the usual constraints.

In general, the future of DHS largely depends on the demand due to circumstance, incident, and event, and whether the functions of response remain local or national responsibilities. Regardless, we know with certainty that terrorism is not going away and, as such, there seems to be a long-term place and need for DHS in the future.

Notes

1. W. V. Pelfrey, Sr. and W. V. Pelfrey, Jr., Sensemaking in a nascent field: A conceptual framework for understanding the emerging discipline of homeland security, *The Homeland Security Review*, 4 (2010): 161.
2. FEMA Strategic Plan, Fiscal Years 2011–2014 (FEMA P-806) February 2011, http://www.fema.gov/pdf/about/strategic_plan11.pdf.
3. U.S. Department of Homeland Security, One Team, One Mission, Securing Our Homeland, http://www.hsdl.org/?view&did = 235371.

4. U.S. Coast Guard, United States Post Guard 2011 Posture Statement, with 2012 Budget in Brief, February 2011
5. E. Beidel, Homeland Security Market "Vibrant" Despite Budgetary Concerns, National Defense 34 (September 2011); for a full view of Research and Development funds for DHS, see: Congressional Research Service, Federal Research and Development Funding: FY 2011 (March 25, 2011).
6. Homeland Security Act of 2002, P.L. 107–296, U.S. Statutes at Large 116 (2002): §101(b).
7. W. L. Waugh Jr., *Future of Homeland Security and Emergency Management*, http://www.training.fema.gov/EMIWeb/edu/emfuture.asp.
8. See M. Mayer, J. J. Carafano, and J. Zuckerman, Homeland security 4.0: Overcoming centralization, complacency, and politics, the Heritage Foundation special report #97 (August 23, 2011), http://www.heritage.org/research/reports/2011/08/homeland-security-4-0-overcoming-centralization-complacency-and-politics.
9. S. H. Clovis Jr., *Homeland Security Affairs* 2 (October 2006): 17.
10. U.S. Department of Homeland Security, *Science and Technology for a Safer Nation* (Washington, DC: U.S. Government Printing Office, 2008), 41.
11. B. York, *Washington Examiner*, 01/09/11, http://washingtonexaminer.com/politics/beltway-confidential/2011/01/journalists-urged-caution-after-ft-hood-now-race-blame-palin.
12. B. H. Friedman, Managing fear: The politics of homeland security, *Political Science Quarterly*, 126 (2011): 77, 80; see also M. Leitenberg, Assessing the threat of bioterrorism, in B. H. Friedman, J. Harper, and C. A. Preble, eds., *Terrorizing Ourselves: Why Counterterrorism is Failing and How to Fix it* (Washington, DC: Cato Institute, 2010), 162–163.
13. Friedman, *Managing Fear*, at 83.

Appendix A: United States Department of Homeland Security: Homeland Security Advisory Council Charter

A.1 Official Designation

Homeland Security Advisory Council (HSAC).

A.2 Authority

This charter establishes the Homeland Security Advisory Council (HSAC) under the authority of section 871 of the Homeland Security Act of 2002, 6 U.S.C. section 451. This committee shall operate in accordance with the provisions of the Federal Advisory Committee Act (FACA), 5 U.S.C. App.

A.3 Purpose, Objectives, and Scope of Activities

The HSAC exists to provide organizationally independent advice and recommendations to the Secretary of the Department aiding in the creation and expeditious implementation of critical and actionable policy and operational capacities across the spectrum of Homeland Security operations. The HSAC shall periodically report, as appropriate, to the Secretary on matters within the scope of that function. The HSAC serves as an advisory body with the goal of providing advice upon the request of the Secretary. The HSAC shall provide the Secretary advisory services as follows:

a. *Policy Development*: Recommendations on developing the implementation of comprehensive, compatible, objectively measurable, and executable national strategies and plans to secure the United States from terrorist threats, attacks, and/or national emergencies.
b. *Coordination*: Recommendations on coordinating the implementation of such comprehensive national strategies within the Department; among the Department's Federal Government partners; and among state, local, and tribal governments, first responders, the private sector, and experts within academia and the research communities.
c. *Implementation*: Recommendations on the feasibility and effectiveness of implementing specific measures to detect, prepare for, prevent, protect against, respond to, and recover from terrorist threats, attacks, or national emergencies within the United States.
d. *Implementation Evaluation*: Recommendations to the Secretary on ways to improve coordination, cooperation, and communication among federal, state, local, and tribal officials; the private sector; and other organizations through the evaluation of the Secretary's policies and plans in light of the actual implementation of those plans.
e. *Force Multiplication*: Providing a vital means for the Secretary to leverage and integrate into the Department's operations the nation's diverse expertise by collecting and analyzing scholarly research, technological advice, and "best practice" processes and organizational management techniques from federal, state, tribal, and local governments; the private sector; and other organizations throughout the nation.

A.4 Description of Duties

The duties of the HSAC are solely advisory in nature.

A.5 Official to Whom the Committee Reports

The HSAC reports to the Secretary of the Department of Homeland Security.

A.6 Agency Responsible for Providing Necessary Support

The Policy Directorate, Homeland Security Advisory Committee Office, shall be responsible for providing financial and administrative support to the HSAC.

A.7 Estimated Costs, Compensation, and Staff Support

The estimated annual operating costs for Fiscal Year 2007 are $1,410,000 which includes travel and per diem, operating and other administrative expenses and support for 8 FTE positions.

A.8 Designated Federal Officer

The Executive Director of the Homeland Security Advisory Council shall serve as the HSAC Designated Federal Officer (DFO). The DFO or her/his designee shall approve or call HSAC meetings, approve meeting agendas, attend all committee, subcommittee, and task force meetings, adjourn any meeting when the DFO determines adjournment to be in the public interest, and chair meetings in the absence of the Chair or Vice Chair or as directed by the Secretary.

A.9 Estimated Number and Frequency of Meetings

The HSAC will strive to meet quarterly, or as frequently as the Secretary desires. The HSAC and its components may meet in the form of standing subcommittees, in ad hoc task force entities, or working groups as HSAC functions require or as tasked by the Secretary.

A.10 Duration

This charter shall be in effect for 2 years from the date it is filed with Congress unless sooner terminated. The charter may be renewed at the end of this 2-year period in accordance with section 14 of FACA.

A.11 Membership, Officers, and Organization

The HSAC shall be composed of not more than 21 members and a number of voting ex officio members as appointed by and serving at the pleasure of the Secretary for specified terms as defined by the Secretary. All members shall serve as Special Government Employees as defined in section 202(a) of title 18 U.S.C. Term length shall be up to 3 years in order to promote membership continuity and currency of expertise. Effective February 28, 2009, the terms of all members who did not have clear term lengths established upon their appointment will expire.

Henceforth term lengths will be staggered to allow for rotation of one-third of membership each year. In the event the HSAC terminates, all appointments to the committee shall terminate.

In order for the Secretary to fully leverage broad-ranging education and experience, the HSAC must be professionally, technically, and culturally diverse. These members shall all be national leaders found within diverse and appropriate professions and communities. The membership shall be drawn from the following fields:

a. Police, Fire, Emergency Medical Services, and Public Works
b. Public Health and Hospital Managers
c. State, Local, and Tribal Officials
d. National Policy Makers
e. Experts in Academia and the Research Community
f. Private Sector Representatives
g. Owners and Operators of Critical Industries, Resources, and Infrastructure

In addition to its 21 members, the HSAC shall also include as ex officio members the Chair or, in consultation with the Executive Director, the Vice Chair of the following without concern to the term limitation designated above:

h. The National Infrastructure Advisory Council
i. The National Security Telecommunications Advisory Committee
j. The Panel on the Science and Technology of Combating Terrorism, President's Council of Advisors on Science and Technology

The Secretary shall designate a Chair and a Vice Chair from among the appointed members of the HSAC.

A.12 Subcommittees, Task Forces, and Working Groups

The HSAC Chair, with the concurrence of the Executive Director, may establish subcommittees, task forces, or working groups. Subcommittees shall be composed of a number of members to be determined by the Chair subject to the appointment to that position by the Secretary. The Executive Director, with the consultation of the HSAC Chair, shall designate a Chair and a Vice Chair for each of the subcommittees from among the HSAC's members. The Chair of each subcommittee, in consultation with or at the direction of the HSAC Chair and Executive Director, may establish task force or working group entities to exchange information with other entities and to advise the subcommittees or the HSAC.

HSAC may establish subcommittees for any purpose consistent with this charter subject to the approval of the Executive Director. Such subcommittees may not work independently of the HSAC and must report their recommendations and advice to the HSAC for full deliberation and discussion. Subcommittees have no authority to make decisions on behalf of the HSAC and may not report directly to the Federal government or any other entity.

All subcommittee members shall serve as Special Government Employees as defined in section 202(a) of title 18 U.S.C., with the exception of state and local officials appointed as representative members because of their leadership role within a relevant association. Term length shall be up to 3 years in order to promote membership continuity and currency of expertise. Effective from February 28, 2009, the terms of all members who did not have clear term lengths established upon their appointment will expire.

February 7, 2007
Agency Approval Date

February 6, 2007
GSA Consultation Date

February 20, 2007
Date Filed with Congress

Appendix B: Definitions

Accidental Hazard

Definition: Source of harm or difficulty created by negligence, error, or unintended failure.

Example: The chemical storage tank in the loading area without a concrete barrier may present an accidental hazard.

Adversary

Definition: Individual, group, organization, or government that conducts or has the intent to conduct detrimental activities.

Example: Al-Qaeda is considered an adversary of the United States.

Annotation:

1. An adversary can be hypothetical for the purposes of training, exercises, red teaming, and other activities.
2. An adversary differs from a threat in that an adversary may have the intent, but not the capability, to conduct detrimental activities, while a threat possesses both intent and capability.

Asset

Definition: Person, structure, facility, information, material, or process that has value.

Example: Some organizations use an asset inventory to plan protective security activities.

Extended Definition: Includes: contracts, facilities, property, records, unobligated or unexpended balances of appropriations, and other funds or resources, personnel, intelligence, technology, or physical infrastructure, or anything useful that contributes to the success of something, such as an organizational mission; assets are things of value or properties to which value can be assigned; from an intelligence standpoint, includes any resource—person, group, relationship, instrument, installation, or supply—at the disposal of an intelligence organization for use in an operational or support role.

Annotation: In some domains, capabilities and activities may be considered assets as well. In the context of the National Infrastructure Protection Plan, people are not considered assets.

Attack Method

Definition: Manner and means, including the weapon and delivery method, an adversary may use to cause harm on a target.

Example: Analysts have identified weaponization of an aircraft as an attack method that terrorists may use.

Annotation: Attack method and attack mode are synonymous.

Attack Path

Definition: Steps that an adversary takes or may take to plan, prepare for, and execute an attack.

Example: Part of the attack path for the car bombing involved dozens of individuals moving money, arms, and operatives from the terrorist safe haven to the target area.

Annotation: An attack path may include recruitment, radicalization, and training of operatives, selection and surveillance of the target, construction or procurement of weapons, funding, deployment of operatives to the target, execution of the attack, and related post-attack activities.

Capability

Definition: Means to accomplish a mission, function, or objective.

Example: Counterterrorism operations are intended to reduce the capability of terrorist groups.

Annotation: Adversary capability is one of two elements, the other being adversary intent, that is commonly considered when estimating the likelihood of terrorist attacks. Adversary capability is the ability of an adversary to attack with a particular attack method. Other communities of interest may use capability to refer to any organization's ability to perform its mission, activities, and functions.

Consequence

Definition: Effect of an event, incident, or occurrence.

Example: One consequence of the explosion was the loss of over 50 lives.

Annotation: Consequence is commonly measured in four ways: human, economic, mission, and psychological, but may also include other factors such as impact on the environment.

See Also: Human consequence, economic consequence, mission consequence, psychological consequence.

Consequence Assessment

Definition: Process of identifying or evaluating the potential or actual effects of an event, incident, or occurrence.

Example: The consequence assessment for the hurricane included estimates for human casualties and property damage caused by the landfall of the hurricane and cascading effects.

Countermeasure

Definition: Action, measure, or device that reduces an identified risk.

Example: Some facilities employ surveillance cameras as a countermeasure.

Annotation: A countermeasure can reduce any component of risk-threat, vulnerability, or consequence.

Deterrent

Definition: Measure that discourages an action or prevents an occurrence by instilling fear, doubt, or anxiety.

Example: Fear of lethal retaliation can serve as a deterrent to some adversaries.

Annotation: A deterrent reduces threat by decreasing the likelihood of an attempted attack.

Economic Consequence

Definition: Effect of an incident, event, or occurrence on the value of property or on the production, trade, distribution, or use of income, wealth, or commodities.

Example: The loss of the company's entire trucking fleet was an economic consequence of the tornado.

Annotation: When measuring economic consequence in the context of homeland security risk, consequences are usually assessed as negative and measured in monetary units.

Evaluation

Definition: Process of examining, measuring and/or judging how well an entity, procedure, or action has met or is meeting stated objectives.

Example: After increasing the number of sensors at the port, the team conducted an evaluation to determine how the sensors reduced risks to the facility.

Annotation: Evaluation is the step in the risk management cycle that measures the effectiveness of an implemented risk management option.

Function

Definition: Service, process, capability, or operation performed by an asset, system, network, or organization.

Example: A primary function of the aviation industry is the transportation of people and cargo over long distances.

Hazard

Definition: Natural or man-made source or cause of harm or difficulty.

Example: Improperly maintained or protected chemical storage tanks present a potential hazard.

Annotation:

1. A hazard differs from a threat in that a threat is directed at an entity, asset, system, network, or geographic area, while a hazard is not directed.
2. A hazard can be actual or potential.

Human Consequence

Definition: Effect of an incident, event, or occurrence that results in injury, illness, or loss of life.

Example: The human consequence of the attack was 20 fatalities and 50 injured persons.

Annotation: When measuring human consequence in the context of homeland security risk, consequence is assessed as negative and can include loss of life or limb, or other short-term or long-term bodily harm or illness.

Implementation

Definition: Act of putting a procedure or course of action into effect to support goals or achieve objectives.

Example: The implementation of the emergency evacuation plan involved the activation of additional response personnel.

Annotation: Implementation is one of the stages of the risk management cycle and involves the act of executing a risk management strategy.

Incident

Definition: Occurrence, caused by either human action or natural phenomena, that may cause harm and that may require action.

Example: The Department of Homeland Security plays a role in reducing the risk of a catastrophic incident in the United States.

Annotation:

1. Homeland security incidents can include major disasters, emergencies, terrorist attacks, terrorist threats, wildland and urban fires, floods, hazardous materials spills, nuclear accidents, aircraft accidents, earthquakes, hurricanes, tornadoes, tropical storms, war-related disasters, public health and medical emergencies, law enforcement encounters, and other occurrences requiring a mitigating response.
2. Harm can include human casualties, destruction of property, adverse economic impact, and/or damage to natural resources.

Integrated Risk Management

Definition: Incorporation and coordination of strategy, capability, and governance to enable risk-informed decision making.

Example: DHS uses a framework of integrated risk management to ensure a unified approach to managing all homeland security risks.

Intent

Definition: Determination to achieve an objective.

Example: The content of domestic extremist websites may demonstrate an intent to conduct acts of terrorism.

Annotation:

1. Adversary intent is the desire or design to conduct a type of attack or to attack a type of target.
2. Adversary intent is one of two elements, along with adversary capability, that is commonly considered when estimating the likelihood of terrorist attacks and often refers to the likelihood that an adversary will execute a chosen course of action or attempt a particular type of attack.

Intentional Hazard

Definition: Source of harm, duress, or difficulty created by a deliberate action or a planned course of action.

Example: Cyber-attacks are an intentional hazard that DHS works to prevent.

Likelihood

Definition: Estimate of the potential of an incident or event's occurrence.

Example: The likelihood of natural hazards can be estimated through the examination of historical data.

Annotation:

1. Qualitative and semi-quantitative risk assessments can use qualitative estimates of likelihood such as high, medium, or low, which may be represented numerically but not mathematically. Quantitative assessments use mathematically derived values to represent likelihood.
2. The likelihood of a successful attack occurring is typically broken into two related quantities: the likelihood that an attack occurs (which is a common mathematical representation of threat), and the likelihood that the attack succeeds, given that it is attempted (which is a common mathematical representation of vulnerability). In the context of natural hazards, likelihood of occurrence is typically informed by the frequency of past incidents or occurrences.

3. The intelligence community typically estimates likelihood in bins or ranges such as "remote," "unlikely," "even chance," "probable/likely," or "almost certain."
4. Probability is a specific type of likelihood. Likelihood can be communicated using numbers (e.g., 0–100, 1–5) or phrases (e.g., low, medium, high), while probabilities must meet more stringent conditions.

See Also: Probability (Mathematical).

Mission Consequence

Definition: Effect of an incident, event, operation, or occurrence on the ability of an organization or group to meet a strategic objective or perform a function.

Example: The city government's inability to ensure the public's access to clean drinking water was a mission consequence of the earthquake.

Annotation: Valuation of mission consequence should exclude other types of consequences (e.g., human consequence, economic consequence, etc.) if they are evaluated separately in the assessment.

Model

Definition: Approximation, representation, or idealization of selected aspects of the structure, behavior, operation, or other characteristics of a real-world process, concept, or system.

Example: To assess risk for over 400 events, analysts created a model based on only the most important factors.

Annotation: See also: Simulation.

Natural Hazard

Definition: Source of harm or difficulty created by a meteorological, environmental, or geological phenomenon or combination of phenomena.

Example: A natural hazard, such as an earthquake, can occur without warning.

Network

Definition: Group of components that share information or interact with each other in order to perform a function.

Example: Power plants, substations, and transmission lines constitute a network that creates and distributes electricity.

Annotation: Network is used across DHS to explain the joining of physical, cyber, and other entities for a particular purpose or function.

Probabilistic Risk Assessment

Definition: Type of quantitative risk assessment that considers possible combinations of occurrences with associated consequences, each with an associated probability or probability distribution.

Example: The engineers conducted a probabilistic risk assessment to determine the risk of a meltdown resulting from a series of compounding failures.

Annotation: Probabilistic risk assessments are typically performed on complex technological systems with tools such as fault and event trees, and Monte Carlo simulations to evaluate security risks and/or accidental failures.

Probability (Mathematical)

Definition: Likelihood that is expressed as a number between 0 and 1, where 0 indicates that the occurrence is impossible and 1 indicates definite knowledge that the occurrence has happened or will happen, where the ratios between numbers reflect and maintain quantitative relationships.

Example: The probability of a coin landing on "heads" is 1/2.

Annotation:

1. Probability (mathematical) is a specific type of likelihood estimate that obeys the laws of probability theory.
2. Probability is used colloquially as a synonym for likelihood.

Psychological Consequence

Definition: Effect of an incident, event, or occurrence on the mental or emotional state of individuals or groups resulting in a change in perception and/or behavior.

Example: A psychological consequence of the disease outbreak could include the reluctance of the public to visit hospitals for fear of infection, which may make it more difficult for experts to control the outbreak.

Annotation: In the context of homeland security, psychological consequences are negative and refer to the impact of an incident, event, or occurrence on the behavior or emotional and mental state of an affected population.

Qualitative Risk Assessment Methodology

Definition: Set of methods, principles, or rules for assessing risk based on nonnumerical categories or levels.

Example: The qualitative risk assessment methodology allows for categories of "low risk," "medium risk," and "high risk."

Quantitative Risk Assessment Methodology

Definition: Set of methods, principles, or rules for assessing risks based on the use of numbers where the meanings and proportionality of values are maintained inside and outside the context of the assessment.

Example: Engineers at the nuclear power plant used a quantitative risk assessment methodology to assess the risk of reactor failure.

Annotation: While a semi-quantitative methodology also involves the use of numbers, only a purely quantitative methodology uses numbers in a way that allows for the consistent use of values outside the context of the assessment.

Redundancy

Definition: Additional or alternative systems, sub-systems, assets, or processes that maintain a degree of overall functionality in case of loss or failure of another system, sub-system, asset, or process.

Example: A lack of redundancy in access control mechanisms is a vulnerability that can result in a higher likelihood of a successful attack.

Residual Risk

Definition: Risk that remains after risk management measures have been implemented.

Example: While increased patrols lessened the likelihood of trespassers, residual risk remained due to the unlocked exterior doors.

Resilience

Definition: Ability to resist, absorb, recover from or successfully adapt to adversity or a change in conditions.

Example: The county was able to recover quickly from the disaster because of the resilience of governmental support systems.

Extended Definition

1. Ability of systems, infrastructures, government, business, and citizenry to resist, absorb recover from, or adapt to an adverse occurrence that may cause harm, destruction, or loss of national significance.
2. Capacity of an organization to recognize threats and hazards and make adjustments that will improve future protection efforts and risk reduction measures.

Annotation: Resilience can be factored into vulnerability and consequence estimates when measuring risk.

Return on Investment (Risk)

Definition: Calculation of the value of risk reduction measures in the context of the cost of developing and implementing those measures.

Example: Although the installation of new detection equipment was expensive, the team concluded that the return on investment for the new equipment was positive because of the significant reduction in risk.

Risk

Definition: Potential for an unwanted outcome resulting from an incident, event, or occurrence, as determined by its likelihood and the associated consequences.

Example: The team calculated the risk of a terrorist attack after analyzing intelligence reports, vulnerability assessments, and consequence models.

Extended Definition: Potential for an adverse outcome assessed as a function of threats, vulnerabilities, and consequences associated with an incident, event, or occurrence.

Annotation:

1. Risk is defined as the potential for an unwanted outcome. This potential is often measured and used to compare different future situations.
2. Risk may manifest at the strategic, operational, and tactical levels.

Risk Acceptance

Definition: Explicit or implicit decision not to take an action that would affect all or part of a particular risk.

Example: After determining that the cost of mitigation measures was higher than the consequence estimates, the organization decided on a strategy of risk acceptance.

Annotation: Risk acceptance is one of four risk management strategies, along with risk avoidance, risk control, and risk transfer.

Risk Analysis

Definition: Systematic examination of the components and characteristics of risk.

Example: Using risk analysis, the community identified the potential consequences from flooding.

Annotation: In practice, risk analysis is generally conducted to produce a risk assessment. Risk analysis can also involve aggregation of the results of risk assessments to produce a valuation of risks for the purpose of informing decisions. In addition, risk analysis can be done on proposed alternative risk management strategies to determine the likely impact of the strategies on the overall risk.

Risk Assessment

Definition: Product or process which collects information and assigns values to risks for the purpose of informing priorities, developing or comparing courses of action, and informing decision making.

Example: The analysts produced a risk assessment outlining risks to the aviation industry.

Extended Definition: Appraisal of the risks facing an entity, asset, system, network, geographic area, or other grouping.

Annotation: A risk assessment can be the resulting product created through analysis of the component parts of risk.

Risk Assessment Methodology

Definition: Set of methods, principles, or rules used to identify and assess risks and to form priorities, develop courses of action, and inform decision making.

Example: The Maritime Security Risk Analysis Model (MSRAM) is a risk assessment methodology used to assess risk at our nation's ports.

Risk Assessment Tool

Definition: Activity, item, or program that contributes to determining and evaluating risks.

Example: A checklist is a common risk assessment tool that allows users to easily execute risk assessments in a consistent way.

Annotation: Tools can include computer software and hardware or standard forms or checklists for recording and displaying risk assessment data.

Risk Avoidance

Definition: Strategies or measures taken that effectively remove exposure to a risk.

Example: He exercised a strategy of risk avoidance by refusing to live in an area prone to tornadoes.

Annotation: Avoidance is one of a set of four commonly used risk management strategies, along with risk control, risk acceptance, and risk transfer.

Risk Communication

Definition: Exchange of information with the goal of improving risk understanding, affecting risk perception and/or equipping people or groups to act appropriately in response to an identified risk.

Annotation: Risk communication is practiced for both non-hazardous conditions and during incidents. During an incident, risk communication is intended to provide information that fosters trust and credibility in government and empowers partners, stakeholders, and the public to make the best possible decisions under extremely difficult time constraints and circumstances.

Example: As part of risk communication efforts, DHS provides information regarding the current threat level to the public.

Risk Control

Definition: Deliberate action taken to reduce the potential for harm or maintain it at an acceptable level.

Example: As a risk control measure, security guards screen suitcases and other packages to reduce the likelihood of dangerous articles getting inside of office buildings.

Risk Identification

Definition: Process of finding, recognizing, and describing potential risks.

Example: During the initial risk identification for the facility's risk assessment, explosives and seismic events were chosen as scenarios to consider because of their potentially high consequences.

Risk Management

Definition: Process of identifying, analyzing, assessing, and communicating risk and accepting, avoiding, transferring or controlling it to an acceptable level at an acceptable cost.

Annotation: The primary goal of risk management is to reduce or eliminate risk through mitigation measures (avoiding the risk or reducing the negative effect of the risk), but also includes the concepts of acceptance and/or transfer of responsibility for the risk as appropriate. Risk management principles acknowledge that, while risk often cannot be eliminated, actions can usually be taken to reduce risk.

Risk Management Alternatives Development

Definition: Process of systematically examining risks to develop a range of options and their anticipated effects for decision makers.

Example: After completing the risk management alternatives development step, the analysis team presented the mayor with a list of risk management options.

Annotation: The risk management alternatives development step of the risk management process generates options for decision-makers to consider before deciding on which option to implement.

Risk Management Cycle

Definition: Sequence of steps that are systematically taken and revisited to manage risk.

Example: Using the risk management cycle, the organization was able to understand and measurably decrease the risks it faced.

Risk Management Methodology

Definition: Set of methods, principles, or rules used to identify, analyze, assess, and communicate risk, and mitigate, accept, or control it to an acceptable level at an acceptable cost.

Example: The risk management methodology recommended by the Government Accountability Office consists of five steps.

Risk Management Plan

Definition: Document that identifies risks and specifies the actions that have been chosen to manage those risks.

Example: Businesses often have a risk management plan to address the potential risks that they might encounter.

Risk Management Strategy

Definition: Course of action or actions to be taken in order to manage risks.

Example: Mutual Aid Agreements are a risk management strategy used by some emergency response authorities to increase their capacity to respond to large scale incidents.

Extended Definition: Proactive approach to reduce the usually negative impacts of various risks by choosing within a range of options that include complete avoidance of any risk that would cause harm or injury, accepting the risk, controlling the risk by employing risk mitigation options to reduce impacts, or transferring some or all of the risk to another entity based on a set of stated priorities.

Risk Matrix

Definition: Tool for ranking and displaying components of risk in an array.

Example: The security staff devised a risk matrix with the likelihoods of various threats to the subway system in the rows and corresponding consequences in the columns.

Annotation: A risk matrix is typically displayed in a graphical format to show the relationship between risk components.

Risk Mitigation

Definition: Application of measure or measures to reduce the likelihood of an unwanted occurrence and/or its consequences.

Example: Through risk mitigation, the potential impact of the tsunami on the local population was greatly reduced.

Annotation: Measures may be implemented prior to, during, or after an incident, event, or occurrence.

Risk Mitigation Option

Definition: Measure, device, policy, or course of action taken with the intent of reducing risk.

Example: Medical professionals advised the risk mitigation option of inoculations to reduce the risk of a disease outbreak.

Risk Perception

Definition: Subjective judgment about the characteristics and/or severity of risk.

Example: The fear of terrorist attacks may create a skewed risk perception.

Annotation: Risk perception may be driven by sense, emotion, or personal experience.

Risk Profile

Definition: Description and/or depiction of risks to an asset, system, network, geographic area, or other entity.

Example: A risk profile for a hydroelectric plant may address risks such as structural failure, mechanical malfunction, sabotage, and terrorism.

Annotation: A risk profile can be derived from a risk assessment; it is often used as a presentation tool to show how risks vary across comparable entities.

Risk Reduction

Definition: Decrease in risk through risk avoidance, risk control or risk transfer.

Example: By placing vehicle barriers outside the facility, the security team achieved a significant risk reduction.

Annotation: Risk reduction may be estimated both during the decision and evaluation phases of the risk management cycle.

Risk Score

Definition: Numerical result of a semi-quantitative risk assessment methodology.

Example: By installing a surveillance system, the chemical plant was able to reduce its risk score when the next assessment was conducted.

Extended Definition: Numerical representation that gauges the combination of threat, vulnerability, and consequence at a specific moment.

Annotation: The application of risk management alternatives may result in a change of risk score.

Risk Tolerance

Definition: Degree to which an entity is willing to accept risk.

Example: After a major disaster, a community's risk tolerance may decrease significantly.

Risk Transfer

Definition: Action taken to manage risk that shifts some or all of the risk to another entity, asset, system, network, or geographic area.

Example: A risk transfer may occur after increasing security at one facility because it might make an alternate facility a more attractive target.

Annotation: Risk transfer may refer to transferring the risk from asset to asset, asset to system, or some other combination, or shifting the responsibility for managing the risk from one authority to another (e.g., responsibility for economic loss could be transferred from a homeowner to an insurance company).

Risk-Based Decision Making

Definition: Determination of a course of action predicated primarily on the assessment of risk and the expected impact of that course of action on that risk.

Example: After reading about threats and vulnerabilities associated with vehicle explosives downtown, the Mayor practiced risk-based decision making by authorizing the installation of vehicle barriers.

Annotation: Risk-based decision making uses the assessment of risk as the primary decision driver, while risk-informed decision making may account for multiple sources of information not included in the assessment of risk as significant inputs to the decision process in addition to risk information. Risk-based decision making has often been used interchangeably with risk-informed decision making.

Risk-Informed Decision Making

Definition: Determination of a course of action predicated on the assessment of risk, the expected impact of that course of action on that risk, as well as other relevant factors.

Example: The Mayor practiced risk-informed decision making in planning event security by considering both the results of the risk assessment and logistical constraints.

Annotation: Risk-informed decision making may take into account multiple sources of information not included specifically in the assessment of risk as inputs to the decision process in addition to risk information, while risk-based decision making uses the assessment of risk as the primary decision driver.

Scenario (Risk)

Definition: Hypothetical situation comprised of a hazard, an entity impacted by that hazard, and associated conditions including consequences when appropriate.

Example: The team designed a scenario involving a car bomb at the power plant to help assess the risk of vehicle-borne improvised explosive devices.

Annotation: A scenario can be created and used for the purposes of training, exercise, analysis, or modeling as well as for other purposes. A scenario that has occurred or is occurring is an incident.

Semi-Quantitative Risk Assessment Methodology

Definition: Set of methods, principles, or rules to assess risk that uses bins, scales, or representative numbers whose values and meanings are not maintained in other contexts.

Example: By giving the "low risk, "medium risk," and "high risk" categories corresponding numerical values, the assessor used a semi-quantitative risk assessment methodology.

Annotation: While numbers may be used in a semi-quantitative methodology, the values are not applicable outside of the methodology, and numerical results from one methodology cannot be compared with those from other methodologies.

Sensitivity Analysis

Definition: Process to determine how outputs of a methodology differ in response to variation of the inputs or conditions.

Example: The sensitivity analysis showed that the population variable had the largest effect on the output of the model.

Annotation:

1. When a factor considered in a risk assessment has uncertainty, sensitivity analysis examines the effect that the uncertainty has on the results.
2. A sensitivity analysis can be used to examine how individual variables can affect the outputs of risk assessment methodologies.
3. Alternatively, sensitivity analysis can show decision makers or evaluators the impact or predicted impact of risk management alternatives.

Simulation

Definition: Model that behaves or operates like a given process, concept, or system when provided a set of controlled inputs.

Example: The scientists designed a simulation to see how weather impacted the plume of smoke.
Annotation: See also: Model.

Subject Matter Expert

Definition: Individual with in-depth knowledge in a specific area or field.
Example: A subject matter expert was consulted to inform team members on improvised nuclear devices.
Annotation: Structured techniques for the elicitation of expert judgment are key tools for risk assessment. Subject matter experts are also used to supplement empirical data when needed, or to provide input on specialized subject areas for the purposes of designing and executing risk assessments.

System

Definition: Any combination of facilities, equipment, personnel, procedures, and communications integrated for a specific purpose.
Example: The collection of roads, tunnels, and bridges provided the country with the foundation for a useful transit system.

Target

Definition: Asset, network, system, or geographic area chosen by an adversary to be impacted by an attack.
Example: Analysts identified mass gatherings as one potential target of an attack.

Threat

Definition: Natural or man-made occurrence, individual, entity, or action that has or indicates the potential to harm life, information, operations, the environment and/or property.
Example: Intelligence suggested that the greatest threat to the building was from explosives concealed in a vehicle.
Annotation: Threat as defined refers to an individual, entity, action, or occurrence; however, for the purpose of calculating risk, the threat of an intentional hazard is generally estimated as the likelihood of an attack (that accounts for both the intent and capability of the adversary) being attempted by an adversary; for other hazards, threat is generally estimated as the likelihood that a hazard will manifest.

Threat Assessment

Definition: Process of identifying or evaluating entities, actions, or occurrences, whether natural or man-made, that have or indicate the potential to harm life, information, operations and/or property.

Example: Analysts produced a threat assessment detailing the capabilities of domestic and foreign terrorist organizations to threaten particular infrastructure sectors.

Uncertainty

Definition: Degree to which a calculated, estimated, or observed value may deviate from the true value.

Example: The uncertainty in the fatality estimate for the chemical attack was due to the unpredictable wind direction in the affected area.

Annotation:

1. Uncertainty may stem from many causes, including the lack of information.
2. The concept of uncertainty is useful in understanding that likelihoods and consequences can oftentimes not be predicted with a high degree of precision or accuracy.

Vulnerability

Definition: Physical feature or operational attribute that renders an entity open to exploitation or susceptible to a given hazard.

Example: Installation of vehicle barriers may remove a vulnerability related to attacks using vehicle-borne improvised explosive devices.

Extended Definition: Characteristic of design, location, security posture, operation, or any combination thereof, that renders an asset, system, network, or entity susceptible to disruption, destruction, or exploitation.

Annotation: In calculating risk of an intentional hazard, the common measurement of vulnerability is the likelihood that an attack is successful, given that it is attempted.

Vulnerability Assessment

Definition: Process for identifying physical features or operational attributes that render an entity, asset, system, network, or geographic area susceptible or exposed to hazards.

Example: The team conducted a vulnerability assessment on the ship to determine how it might be exploited or attacked by an adversary.

Annotation: Vulnerability assessments can produce comparable estimates of vulnerabilities across a variety of hazards or assets, systems, or networks.

Appendix C: Biological Incident Annex

Coordinating Agency	Cooperation Agencies
Department of Health and Human Services	Department of Agriculture
	Department of Commerce
	Department of Defense
	Department of Energy
	Department of Homeland Security
	Department of the Interior
	Department of Justice
	Department of Labor
	Department of State
	Department of Transportation
	Department of Veterans Affairs
	Environmental Protection Agency
	General Services Administration
	U.S. Agency for International Development
	U.S. Postal Service
	American Red Cross

C.1 Introduction

C.1.1 Purpose

The purpose of the Biological Incident Annex is to outline the actions, roles, and responsibilities associated with response to a human disease outbreak of known or unknown origin requiring federal assistance. In this document, a biological incident includes naturally occurring biological diseases (communicable and noncommunicable) in humans as well as terrorist events. This definition also includes those biological agents found in the environment, or diagnosed in animals, that have the potential for transmission to humans (zoonosis). Incidents that are restricted to animal, plant, or food health or safety are reviewed in other annexes. Actions described in this annex take place with or without a Presidential Stafford Act declaration or a public health emergency declaration by the Secretary of Health and Human Services (HHS). This annex outlines biological incident response actions including threat assessment notification procedures, laboratory testing, joint investigative/response procedures, and activities related to recovery.

C.1.2 Scope

The objectives of the Federal Government's response to a biological terrorism event or to a naturally occurring disease outbreak with a known or novel pathogen are to

- Detect the event through disease surveillance and environmental monitoring.
- Identify and protect the population(s) at risk.
- Determine the source of the disease.
- Assess the public health, law enforcement, and international implications.
- Control and contain any possible epidemic (including providing guidance to state, tribal, territorial, and local public health authorities).
- Augment and surge public health and medical services.
- Identify the cause and prevent the recurrence of any potential resurgence, additional outbreaks, or further spread of disease.
- Assess the extent of residual biological contamination and conduct response, restoration, and recovery actions as necessary.

The unique attributes of this response require separate planning considerations that are tailored to specific health concerns and effects of the disease (e.g., terrorism versus natural outbreaks, communicable versus noncommunicable, etc.).

Specific operational guidelines, developed by respective organizations to address the unique aspects of a particular biological agent or planning consideration, will supplement this annex and are intended as guidance to assist federal, state, tribal, territorial, and local public health and medical planners.

C.1.3 Special Considerations

Detection of a bioterrorism act against the civilian population may occur in several different ways and involve several different modalities

- An attack may be surreptitious, in which case the first evidence of dissemination of an agent may be the presentation of disease in humans or animals. This could manifest either in clinical case reports to domestic or international public health authorities or in unusual patterns of symptoms or encounters within domestic or international health surveillance systems.
- A terrorist-induced infectious disease outbreak initially may be indistinguishable from a naturally occurring outbreak; moreover, depending upon the particular agent and associated symptoms, several days could pass before public health and medical authorities even suspect that terrorism may be the cause. In such a case, criminal intent may not be apparent until some time after illnesses are recognized.
- Environmental surveillance systems, such as the BioWatch system, may detect the presence of a biological agent in the environment and trigger directed environmental sampling and intensified clinical surveillance to rule out or confirm an incident. If confirmed, the utilization of environmental surveillance systems may allow for mobilization of a public health, medical, and law enforcement response in advance of the appearance of the first clinical cases or a rapid response after the first clinical cases are identified.
- Other cooperating departments and agencies listed in this annex may detect acts of bioterrorism or biological incidents through their normal operations and surveillance efforts. Should this occur, notifications should be made according to approved interagency response protocols, consistent with the health and law enforcement assessment process described in this annex.

C.1.4 Policies

This annex supports policies and procedures outlined in the National Response Framework, Emergency Support Function (ESF) #8—Public Health and Medical Services Annex, ESF #10—Oil and Hazardous Materials Response Annex, ESF #11—Agriculture and Natural Resources

Annex, ESF #15—External Affairs Annex, the Terrorism Incident Law Enforcement and Investigation Annex, and the International Coordination Support Annex.

HHS serves as the Federal Government's primary agency for the public health and medical preparation and planning for and response to a biological terrorism attack or naturally occurring outbreak that results from either a known or novel pathogen, including an emerging infectious disease.

The Department of Agriculture (USDA) serves as the Government's primary agency for outbreaks and/or attacks that may occur in animals used in the commercial production of food. USDA may also serve as the Government's primary agency for attacks on food processing/slaughtering facilities under its regulatory purview. In the event of a food or animal event, HHS may provide additional public health and veterinary epidemiological assistance to USDA. Wildlife events will be placed under the purview of the Department of the Interior (DOI), while those involving marine animals will be managed and monitored by the Department of Commerce.

The Secretary of Homeland Security is the principal Federal official for domestic incident management. Pursuant to the Homeland Security Act of 2002, the Secretary is responsible for coordinating Federal operations within the United States to prepare for, respond to, and recover from terrorist attacks, major disasters, and other emergencies, including biological incidents.

State, tribal, territorial, and local governments are primarily responsible for detecting and responding to disease outbreaks and implementing measures to minimize the health, social, and economic consequences of such an outbreak.

The Attorney General has lead responsibility for criminal investigations of terrorist acts or terrorist threats by individuals or groups inside the United States, or directed at U.S. citizens or institutions abroad. Generally acting through the Federal Bureau of Investigation (FBI), the Attorney General, in cooperation with other Federal departments and agencies engaged in activities to protect our national security, shall also coordinate the activities of the other members of the law enforcement community to detect, prevent, preempt, and disrupt terrorist attacks against the United States. If any agency or government entity becomes aware of an overt threat involving biological agents or indications that instances of disease may not be the result of natural causes, the Department of Justice (DOJ) must be notified through the FBI's Weapons of Mass Destruction Operations Unit (WMDOU).

If the threat is deemed credible by the FBI in coordination with HHS or USDA, the FBI, in turn, immediately notifies the National Operations Center (NOC) and the National Counterterrorism Center (NCTC). The Laboratory Response Network (LRN) is used to test samples for the presence of biological threat agents. Any agency or organization that identifies an unusual or suspicious test result should contact the FBI to ensure coordination of appropriate testing at an LRN laboratory. Decisions on where to perform additional tests on samples are made by the FBI, in coordination with HHS or USDA. All relevant threat and public health assessments should be provided to the NOC. Test results on human samples from non-LRN facilities are considered a “first pass” or “screening” test.

Once notified of a credible threat or disease outbreak, HHS convenes a meeting of ESF #8 partners to assess the situation and determine appropriate public health and medical actions. The Department of Homeland Security (DHS) coordinates overall nonmedical support and response actions across all federal departments and agencies. HHS leads public health and medical emergency response efforts across all federal departments and agencies.

The FBI coordinates the investigation of criminal activities if such activities are suspected.

HHS provides guidance to state, tribal, territorial, and local authorities and collaborates closely with the FBI in the proper handling of any materials that may have evidentiary implications (e.g., LRN samples, etc.) associated with disease outbreaks suspected of being terrorist or criminal in nature. If evidentiary materials are shared with or procured from foreign governments, HHS and the FBI will coordinate and share information with the Department of State (DOS) as appropriate.

HHS will be supported by other federal agencies as appropriate during the various states of a biological incident response in the preparation, planning, and/or response processes and will perform the roles described in this annex in coordination with DHS and state partners. If the incident response progresses such that it requires multiagency participation, DHS will serve as the Incident Coordinator. HHS will serve as the coordinating agency for public health issues as will other agencies for their area of technical expertise.

If there is potential for environmental contamination, HHS collaborates with the Environmental Protection Agency (EPA) in developing and implementing sampling strategies and sharing results.

In the event of an outbreak of an agriculturally significant zoonotic disease or human foodborne pathogen, HHS collaborates with USDA during the preparation, planning, and/or response processes.

Given the dynamic nature of a biological incident, HHS, in collaboration with other departments and agencies, determines the thresholds for a comprehensive Federal Government public health and medical response. These thresholds are based on specific event information rather than predetermined risk levels.

Federal public announcements, statements, or press releases related to a threat or actual bioterrorism event will be coordinated with the DHS Office of Public Affairs consistent with ESF #15, if activated.

C.1.5 Planning Assumptions

In a biological incident, federal, state, tribal, territorial, and local officials require a highly coordinated response to public health and medical emergencies. The biological incident also may affect other countries, or be of international concern, and therefore involve extensive coordination with DOS and the international health community (e.g., notification to the World Health Organization [WHO] and other international health organizations under the International Health Regulations [IHR]).

Disease transmission may occur from direct contact with an infected individual or animal, an environmental reservoir (includes contaminated surface or atmospheric dispersion), an insect vector, or contaminated food and water. Indirect contact transmission may also occur where contaminated inanimate objects (fomites) serve as the vehicle for transmission of the agent. Hands may also play a role in indirect transmission.

A biological incident may be distributed across multiple jurisdictions simultaneously. This could require the simultaneous management of multiple "incident sites" from national and regional headquarters locations in coordination with multiple state, tribal, territorial, and local jurisdictions.

A response to contagious and noncontagious public health emergencies may require different planning assumptions or factors.

The introduction of biological agents, both natural and deliberate, is often first detected through clinical or hospital presentation. However, there are other methods of detection, including environmental surveillance technologies such as BioWatch, and medical and syndromic surveillance systems. Early detection of biological agents offers an opportunity to take proactive measures to mitigate the consequences of disease outbreak.

Routine fish and wildlife health and disease surveillance, including investigation of wildlife mortality events conducted on public lands and in public laboratories, provides the opportunity for early detection of biological agents and acts of bioterrorism. Animal health surveillance in the agriculture sector provides similar opportunities.

No single entity possesses the authority, expertise, and resources to act unilaterally on the many complex issues that may arise in response to a nonroutine disease outbreak and loss of containment affecting a multijurisdictional area. The national response requires close coordination between numerous agencies at all levels of government and with the private sector.

The Federal Government supports affected state, tribal, territorial, and local health jurisdictions as requested or required. The response by HHS and other federal agencies is flexible and adapts as necessary as the outbreak evolves.

The LRN provides analytical support to inform public health assessment of the potential for human illness associated with exposure and the scope of this kind of risk. The LRN also provides for definitive testing of both environmental and clinical samples, as well as limited supporting analysis of food samples that may be implicated as part of epidemiological investigations associated with incident response to cases of human illness. Early HHS, FBI, USDA, EPA, and DHS coordination enhances the likelihood of successful preventative and investigative activities necessary to neutralize threats and attribute the source of the outbreak. (The Food Emergency Response Network [FERN] is a complementary system that integrates the Nation's food-testing laboratories at the local, state, and federal levels into a network that is able to respond to emergencies involving biological, chemical, or radiological contamination of food. The FERN structure is organized to ensure federal and state interagency participation and cooperation in the formation, development, and operation of the network.)

Response to disease outbreaks suspected of being deliberate in origin requires consideration of special law enforcement and homeland security requirements as well as international legal obligations and requirements.

An investigation into intentional biological threats or incidents will likely require the initiation of a joint criminal and epidemiological investigation. The FBI would coordinate criminal investigative activities with appropriate state/local and federal partner agencies, such as DHS, HHS, and USDA.

C.2 Concept of Operations

C.2.1 Biological Agent Response

The key elements of an effective biological response include (in nonsequential order)

- Rapid detection of the outbreak or introduction of a biological agent into the environment.
- Rapid dissemination of key safety information, appropriate personal protective equipment, and necessary medical precautions.
- Swift agent identification and confirmation.
- Identification of the population at risk (to include animals, marine life, and plants).
- Determination of how the agent is transmitted, including an assessment of the efficiency of transmission.
- Determination of susceptibility to prophylaxis and treatment.
- Definition of the public health and medical services, human services, and mental health implications.
- Control and containment of the epidemic when possible, and use of mitigation strategies when containment is not possible (e.g., in the event of an influenza pandemic).

- Identification of the law enforcement implications/assessment of the threat.
- Augmentation and surging of local health and medical resources.
- Protection of the population through appropriate public health and medical actions.
- Dissemination of information to enlist public support and provide risk communication assistance to responsible authorities.
- Assessment of environmental contamination and cleanup/decontamination/proper disposal of bioagents that persist in the environment, and provision of consultation on the safety of drinking water and food products that may be derived from directly or environmentally exposed animals, crops, plants and trees, or marine life.
- Tracking and preventing secondary or additional disease outbreak.
- Administration of countermeasures when appropriate.

Primary Federal functions include supporting state, tribal, territorial, and local public health and medical capacities according to the policies and procedures detailed in the National Response Framework and its annexes (e.g., ESF #8).

C.2.2 Outbreak Detection

C.2.2.1 Determination of a Disease Outbreak

The initial indication of a biological incident may be the recognition by public health and medical authorities that a significantly increased number of people are becoming ill and presenting to local healthcare providers.

One tool to support this process is the National Biosurveillance Integration System (NBIS). NBIS leverages the individual capabilities of multiple surveillance systems by integrating and analyzing domestic and international surveillance and monitoring data collected from human health, animal health, plant health, and food and water monitoring systems. This integrated cross-domain analysis allows for enhanced situational awareness and potentially reduced detection time, thus enabling more rapid and effective biological incident response decision making.

As a result of the nature in which a disease outbreak may be recognized, critical decision making support requires integrated surveillance information, identification of the causative biological agent, a determination of whether the observations are related to a naturally occurring or deliberate outbreak, and identification of the population(s) at risk.

C.2.2.2 Laboratory Confirmation

During the evaluation of a suspected disease outbreak, laboratory samples are distributed to appropriate laboratories. During a suspected terrorist incident, sample information is provided to the FBI for investigative use and to public health and emergency response authorities for epidemiological use and agent characterization to facilitate and ensure timely public health and medical interventions, as well as environmental cleanup. If the incident begins as an epidemic of unknown origin detected through federal, state, tribal, territorial, or local health surveillance systems or networks, laboratory analysis is initiated through the routine public health or animal health laboratory systems.

C.2.2.3 Identification (Analysis and Confirmation)

The samples collected and the analyses conducted must be sufficient to characterize the causative agent of the outbreak. LRN and FERN laboratories fulfill the federal responsibility for rapid analysis of biological agents. In a suspected terrorism incident, sample collection activities and testing are coordinated with the FBI and LRN member(s).

C.2.2.4 Suspicious Substances

Since there is no definitive/reliable field test for biological agents of concern, all potential bioterrorism samples are transported to an LRN laboratory, where expert analysis is conducted using established federal protocols/reagents. A major component of this process is to establish and maintain the law enforcement chain of custody and arrange for transport.

The following actions occur if a positive result is obtained by an LRN on an environmental sample submitted by the FBI or other designated law enforcement personnel:

- The LRN immediately notifies the local FBI of the positive test result and informs the appropriate public health officials.
- The local FBI Field Office makes local notifications and contacts the FBI Headquarters WMDOU.
- FBI Headquarters convenes an initial threat assessment conference call with the local FBI, HHS, and appropriate federal, state, tribal, territorial, and local response officials to review the results, assess the preliminary information and test results, and arrange for additional testing.
- FBI Headquarters immediately notifies DHS of the situation. Situational updates will be provided, as appropriate.
- Original samples may be sent to HHS/Centers for Disease Control and Prevention for confirmation of LRN analyses. As appropriate, the FBI will direct additional forensic examination of biological materials and/or evidence.
- HHS provides guidance on protective measures such as prophylaxis, treatment, continued facility operation, and use of personal protective equipment.

- HHS, EPA, and cooperating agencies support the determination of the contaminated area. EPA will provide data to support the determination of the contaminated area and to assist with decisions regarding whether to shelter-in-place. EPA will also play a role in the decontamination of facilities and outdoor areas.

C.2.3 Notification

Any disease outbreak suspected or identified by an agency within HHS or through a federal, state, tribal, territorial, or local public health partner as having public health implications is brought to the immediate attention of HHS (as detailed in the ESF #8 Annex), in addition to the notification requirements contained in the National Response Framework.

Any potentially significant biological agent, disease outbreak, or suspected bioterrorism act affecting or involving animals, plant health, or wildlife should involve notifications to USDA (animals and plant health) and DOI (wildlife).

Following these initial notifications, the procedures detailed in the ESF #8 Annex are followed. Instances of disease that raise the "index of suspicion" of terrorist or criminal involvement, as determined by HHS or USDA (for animal and plant diseases), are reported to FBI Headquarters. In these instances, FBI Headquarters, in conjunction with HHS and/or USDA, examines available law enforcement and intelligence information, as well as the technical characteristics and epidemiology of the disease, to determine if there is a possibility of criminal intent. If the FBI, in conjunction with HHS or USDA, determines that the information represents a potential credible terrorist threat, the FBI communicates the situation immediately to the NCTC and NOC, which notifies the White House, as appropriate. If warranted, the FBI, HHS, and/or USDA and respective state, tribal, territorial, and/or local health officials will conduct a joint law enforcement and epidemiological investigation to determine the causative agent of the disease outbreak, the extent of the threat to public health and public safety, and the individual(s) responsible.

In the event of an environmental detection of a biological threat agent above established agency-specific thresholds, the responsible agency should contact HHS, the FBI, and the NOC within 2 hours of laboratory confirmation. The FBI and HHS, in conjunction with DHS, will convene an initial threat assessment conference call with appropriate federal, state, tribal, territorial, and local officials to examine the potential threat and public health risk posed by the detection. Coordination of assessment and response activities will involve officials from the impacted state, tribal, territorial, and local jurisdiction(s).

C.2.4 Activation

Once notified of a threat or disease outbreak that requires or potentially requires significant Federal public health and medical assistance, HHS requests activation of ESF #8 from FEMA and convenes a meeting of its internal components and the ESF #8 partner organizations to assess the situation and determine the appropriate public health and medical actions. DHS coordinates all nonmedical support, discussions, and response actions.

The immediate task following any notification is to identify the affected and vulnerable population and the geographic scope of the incident. The initial public health and medical response includes some or all of the following actions:

- Targeted epidemiological investigation (e.g., contact tracing).
- Dissemination of key safety information and necessary medical precautions.
- Intensified surveillance within healthcare settings for patients with certain clinical signs and symptoms.
- Intensified collection and review of potentially related information (e.g., contacts with nurse call lines, laboratory test orders, school absences, over-the-counter pharmacy sales, unusual increase in sick animals, wildlife deaths, decreased commercial fish yields).
- Organization and potential deployment of Federal public health and medical response assets (in conjunction with state, tribal, territorial, and local officials) to include personnel, medical and veterinary supplies, and materiel (e.g., the Strategic National Stockpile [SNS] and the National Veterinary Stockpile [NVS]).

If there is suspicion that the outbreak may be deliberate, the FBI may establish a Joint Operations Center (JOC), which may be integrated into the Joint Field Office structure, if established, to coordinate investigative and intelligence activities among federal, state, tribal, territorial, and local authorities. Within the JOC structure locally, and the FBI's Strategic Information and Operations Center in Washington, DC, responsible public health officials would be integrated into the established structures to coordinate the interaction between law enforcement and public health investigations.

C.3 Actions

C.3.1 Controlling the Epidemic

The following steps are required to contain and control an epidemic affecting large populations:

- HHS assists state, tribal, territorial, and local public health and medical authorities with epidemic surveillance and coordination.
- HHS assesses the need for increased surveillance in state, tribal, territorial, and local entities not initially involved in the outbreak and notifies the appropriate state, tribal, territorial, and local public health officials with surveillance recommendations should increased surveillance in these localities be needed.
- DHS coordinates with HHS and state, tribal, territorial, and local officials on the messages released to the public to ensure that communications are timely, consistent, accurate, and actionable. Messages should address anxieties, alleviate any unwarranted concerns or distress, and enlist cooperation with necessary control measures. Public health and medical messages to the public should be communicated by a recognized health authority (e.g., the U.S. Surgeon General). (See the Public Affairs Support Annex.)
- Consistent with the IHR, if the outbreak first arises within the United States, HHS, in coordination with DOS, immediately notifies and coordinates with appropriate international health agencies. Given the nature of many disease outbreaks, this notification and coordination may have occurred earlier in the process according to internal operating procedures. HHS advises the NOC when notifications are made to international health agencies.
- The public health system, starting at the local level, is required to initiate appropriate protective and responsive measures for the affected population, including first responders and other workers engaged in incident-related activities. These measures may include mass vaccination or prophylaxis for populations at risk and populations not already exposed, but who are at risk of exposure from secondary transmission or the environment.
- HHS evaluates the incident with its partner organizations and makes recommendations to the appropriate public health and medical authorities regarding the need for isolation, quarantine, or shelter-in-place to prevent the spread of disease.
- The Governor of an affected state or territory implements isolation and/or social-distancing requirements using state/local legal authorities. The tribal leader of a recognized tribe may also order a curfew, isolation, social distancing, and quarantine under tribal legal authorities. In order to prevent the import or interstate spread of disease, HHS may take appropriate federal actions using the authorities granted by title 42 of the U.S. Code, 42 CFR parts 70 and 71, and 21 CFR part 1240. These measures may include state, tribal, territorial, and local assistance with the implementation and enforcement of isolation and/or quarantine actions if federal authorities are invoked.

- Where the source of the disease outbreak has been identified as originating outside the United States, whether the result of terrorism or a natural outbreak, HHS works in a coordinated effort with DHS and other supporting agencies to identify and isolate persons, cargo, mail, or conveyances entering the United States that may be contaminated.
- The scope of the disease outbreak may require mass isolation or quarantine of affected or potentially affected persons. Depending on the type of event, food, animals, and other agricultural products may need to be quarantined to prevent further spread of disease. In addition, livestock or poultry may need to be vaccinated or depopulated, and the movement of animals and equipment on and off affected premises may be restricted. In this instance, HHS and USDA will work with state, tribal, territorial, and local health and legal authorities to recommend the most feasible, effective, and legally enforceable methods of isolation and quarantine. If interstate travel restrictions, including restrictions on arriving international travelers, are determined to be necessary, HHS will work closely with DOS, DHS, the Department of Transportation, and state, tribal, territorial, and local authorities to implement any recommended measures. In the event that foreign nationals are subject to isolation and/or quarantine, HHS will work through DOS to notify affected foreign governments.

C.3.2 Decontamination

For certain types of biological incidents (e.g., anthrax), it may be necessary to assess the extent of contamination and decontaminate victims, responders, animals, equipment, transportation conveyances, buildings, critical infrastructure, and large outdoor areas. Such decontamination and related activities take place consistent with the roles and responsibilities, resources and capabilities, and procedures contained in the ESF #8, ESF #10, ESF #11, and ESF #14—Long-Term Community Recovery Annexes, the Terrorism Incident Law Enforcement and Investigation Annex, and the Catastrophic Incident Annex. (Note: Chemicals used for biological decontamination [e.g., for inactivating highly infectious biological agents such as *Bacillus anthracis* spores] must be registered for that purpose by EPA under the Federal Insecticide, Fungicide, and Rodenticide Act. If, during an emergency, a response entity wants to use a chemical that has not been registered for inactivating the specific biological agent(s) of concern, a request for an emergency exemption from registration must be submitted to and granted by EPA.)

C.3.3 Special Issues

C.3.3.1 International Notification/Implications

A biological incident may involve internationally prescribed reportable diseases. In addition to case reporting, biological incidents with global public health significance must also be reported to international public health authorities. A biological incident may also have implications under the Biological Weapons Convention if it can be attributed to actions of a foreign party; DOS would manage the diplomatic aspects of any such case.

Per the IHR, once a positive determination is made of a biological incident determined to be of sufficient concern and to be a "public health event of international consequence," HHS, working with DOS and DHS, notifies WHO through the appropriate regional office, the Pan American Health Organization. HHS, in coordination with DOS, notifies other international health agencies as appropriate.

C.3.3.2 Allocation and Rationing

If critical resources for protecting human life are insufficient to meet all domestic needs, the Secretary of Health and Human Services makes recommendations to the Secretary of Homeland Security regarding the allocation of scarce Federal public health and medical resources.

C.4 Responsibilities

The procedures in this annex are built on the core coordinating structures of the *National Response Framework*. The specific responsibilities of each department and agency are described in the respective ESF and Incident Annexes.

Appendix D: Suggested Protective Measures

1.0 Information and Intelligence

Seq. No.	Protective Measure	Action Required
1.1	Develop and implement a threat and vulnerability assessment process to assure that (a) all transit system facilities, support systems, and surrounding areas are regularly assessed for security threats, including terrorist attacks, and vulnerabilities, and (b) all reasonable measures are identified to mitigate these vulnerabilities.	
1.2	Establish priorities for protective measures and mitigation; Organize measures into specific actions to be taken at the appropriate threat condition.	
1.3	Establish contact information with local and regional law enforcement and security intelligence units, state and federal regional offices.	
1.4	Identify available security planning informational resources such as the FTA's website.	
1.5	Develop, disseminate, and implement procedures for employees receiving information (e.g., phone calls, e-mails) that threaten harm to the transit system, employees, or customers.	

continued

Seq. No.	Protective Measure	Action Required
1.6	Designate a primary and an alternate Security Coordinator (SC) and provide their contact information to the Transportation Security Administration (TSA). Immediately notify TSA (sd.masstransit@dhs.gov) of changes in SCs or contact information, e.g., telephone number(s).	RSD # 1: Notification to TSA required for rail operators, per TSA SD Railpax-04-01
1.7	Designate responsibilities of primary and alternate SCs to: (a) serve as the transit agency's primary and immediate contact for intelligence information, security-related activities, and communications with TSA; (b) be available to TSA on a 24-hour basis; (c) review, as appropriate, all security-related functions to ensure they are effective and consistent with rail passenger security measures, including TSA's SD Railpax-0401; (d) upon learning of non-compliance with TSA-required security measures, immediately initiate corrective action; (e) coordinate implementation of security measures with other organizations involved in security operations, including but not limited to, third-party owners of rail passenger stations and freight railroads hosting the operations of parties to which TSA SD Railpax-04-01 applies. This includes follow up reporting on federal inquiries.	RSD # 2: Notification to TSA required for rail operators, per TSA SD Railpax-04-01
1.8	Report threats and security concerns to law enforcement authorities and to TSA's Transportation Security Operation Center (TSOC) at 1-703-563-3237 or TSOC.ST@dhs.gov.	RSD # 3: Reporting to TSA required for rail operators, per TSA SD Railpax-04-01
1.9	Via e-mail to sd.masstransit@dhs.gov, notify TSA of the date of the most recent vulnerability assessment. Provide TSA access to the vulnerability assessment and corresponding security plan (if available). If no vulnerability assessment has been conducted, so advise.	RSD # 4: Notification to TSA required for rail operators, per TSA SD Railpax-04-01
1.10	Network with local and regional law enforcement and security intelligence units, Joint Terrorism Task Force, and the area TSA Federal Security Director or Surface Transportation Security Inspector for assessments of current and security-related information.	
1.11	Review/re-issue procedures for employees reporting threatening communications (e.g., phone calls, e-mails).	
1.12	Include intelligence information in roll-call briefings of security and law enforcement units.	
1.13	Review security vulnerability assessments and update regularly or whenever a new asset (i.e., a new facility such as an administrative building, bus depot, rail yard, or new type of revenue service) is added.	

Seq. No.	Protective Measure	Action Required
1.14	Include security in special event planning to identify any unique requirements.	
1.15	Join/participate in FBI Joint Terrorism Task Force (JTTF), Surface Transportation Information Sharing and Analysis Center (ST-ISAC) and Homeland Security Information Network (HSIN).	
1.16	Actively seek relevant intelligence with DHS, FTA, JTTF, ISAC, HSIN, state and local authorities, and other transit agencies.	
1.17	Assess the threat's characteristics. Determine the additional Protective Measures required.	
Active Incident		
1.18	Advise TSA via the TSOC (1-703-563-3237 or TSOC.ST@dhs.gov) immediately of all known information regarding the nature of the attack so that TSA can provide assistance and immediately disseminate the information to other transit and governmental agencies.	
1.19	Identify attacker(s) to law enforcement and security personnel. As appropriate, use witnesses or surveillance for timely and relevant information.	
Recovery		
1.20	Guard against secondary attacks.	
1.21	Coordinate with external intelligence and information agencies to return to the appropriate HSAS threat level condition.	
1.22	Prepare an After Action Report—Determine circumstances that led to successful attack. Evaluate response performance. Identify and implement corrective measures. Document actions and lessons learned.	

2.0 Security and Emergency Management

Seq. No.	Protective Measure	Action Required
2.1	Develop system security and emergency response plans and standard and emergency operating procedures. In these plans and procedures, identify the responsibilities of employees by job function. Include preparedness for multiple concurrent events.	
2.2	Establish a security and emergency management team or task force, with designated alternates, that is responsible for implementing procedures appropriate to the emergency condition.	

continued

Seq. No.	Protective Measure	Action Required
2.3	Review security and emergency management technical guidance on FTA's website.	
2.4	Inventory emergency equipment and supplies. Verify that needed quantities at higher HSAS threat level conditions are adequately stocked and/or available.	
2.5	Establish priorities for all outstanding maintenance and capital projects that could affect the security of facilities.	
2.6	As part of the system security plan, develop and implement access control systems for employees, visitors, facilities, and vehicles. Develop access restrictions that allow for the implementation of recovery plans after an attack or emergency, but that prevent tampering with the incident scene. Implementation of access controls should be incremental in response to changing HSAS threat level conditions.	
2.7	As part of the system security plan, develop and implement a document control system to identify and protect sensitive security information.	
2.8	Direct that all personal, transit, and contractor vehicles be secured when not in use.	
2.9	Survey areas adjacent to and surrounding transit properties to determine activities that might increase security risks to the transit system (e.g., government buildings, airports, stadiums, convention centers, industrial plants, pipelines, railroads).	
2.10	Develop procedures for shutting down and evacuating facilities and/or the transit system.	
2.11	Review/update all plans and procedures to ensure that they provide adequate assistance to employees and customers with disabilities.	
2.12	Deploy neighborhood watch personnel, if available, for routine patrols.	
2.13	Determine, map, and disseminate emergency evacuation route plans for transit system vehicles.	
2.14	Determine and document factors that would require partial or full service shutdown	
2.15	Develop and implement a security and emergency management data collection system consistent with FTA national transit database reporting requirements. Use the system to analyze incidents and trends. Control sensitive security information per document control system (see sequence number 2.7).	

Seq. No.	Protective Measure	Action Required
2.16	Perform background checks on all employees and on contractors consistent with applicable law.	
2.17	Apply concepts of crime prevention through environmental design (CPTED) in reviews of facilities and in new designs and modifications.	
2.18	Insure transit agency employees have visible identification (and uniforms for designated job categories); and that on-site contractors and visitors are identifiable by an appropriate identification system, such as badges.	
2.19	Develop and implement policies and procedures for a key control management/inventory system.	
2.20	Develop the procedure for a full inspection of public and nonpublic facilities including lockers and storage areas at higher threat conditions.	
2.21	Train all employees in security awareness, response plans, and individual roles and responsibilities.	
2.22	Train all employees on the Homeland Security Advisory System (HSAS) and on specific Protective Measures that the agency will implement at higher HSAS threat level conditions.	
2.23	Plan and provide policing and security appropriate to DHS threat levels and threat advisories.	RSD # 14: Action is required for rail operators, per TSA SD Railpax-0401
2.24	Conduct emergency drills and exercises that include employees and customers with disabilities.	
2.25	Develop training and testing to assess employee proficiency (e.g., table top and field drills with outside responders). Base training and testing, in part, on FTA's "Immediate Actions for Transit Agencies" guidance. For all table top and field drills, include a process for system improvements based on after action reports.	
2.26	Participate in regional drills and exercises to support the response to attacks or other emergencies, such as natural disasters.	
2.27	Insure that existing physical security and emergency measures (e.g., fencing, lighting, locks) are in good working order and adequately maintained. Conduct regular tests of security and emergency management equipment (e.g., emergency generators, communication and notification systems, surveillance, and intrusion detection systems). Repair/replace any defective equipment.	

continued

Seq. No.	Protective Measure	Action Required
2.28	Insure coordination between the safety and the security departments (e.g., emergency procedures are regularly reviewed and updated as needed by a safety management team).	
2.29	Inspect all mail and package deliveries. Examine mail and packages for letter/parcel bombs and suspicious substances. Do not open suspicious letters or packages.	
2.30	Maintain accurate records for tracking all identification cards, badges, decals, and uniforms. Cancel access for any items lost or stolen. Require uniform vendors to verify identities of individuals seeking to purchase uniform articles.	
2.31	Conduct immediate inventory sweep for all revenue and nonrevenue vehicles, including contingency/spare vehicles. Search for any missing vehicles.	
2.32	Immediately re-check all security systems (e.g., lighting, CCTV, and intrusion alarms). Install additional, temporary lighting if needed to provide desired lighting for key areas (e.g., underground stations, transit centers, rail yard, and bus garage perimeters).	
2.33	Physically audit (at supervisory level)/enforce positive identification of all personnel. Make no exceptions.	
2.34	Identify and train employees who can assist as drivers of transit vehicles during emergencies.	
2.35	Insure coordination between the security department and the operations and maintenance departments (e.g., jointly develop and approve standard operating procedures).	
2.36	Confirm availability of outside security resources to assist with intensified or increased span of coverage during peak periods.	
2.37	Increase special patrols (e.g., foot patrols, bicycle patrols) and on-board vehicle patrols as appropriate.	
2.38	Reduce the number of access points for vehicles and personnel to minimum levels. Spot check contents of vehicles at access points. Watch for vehicles parked for long periods of time in or near any facility. Lock doors and check that all designated locked doors remain locked.	
2.39	Conduct frequent inspections of facilities, stations, terminals, and other critical assets, including public storage areas, for persons and items that do not belong.	RSD # 12: Action is required for rail operators, per TSA SD Railpax-0401

Seq. No.	Protective Measure	Action Required
2.40	At regular intervals, inspect each passenger vehicle for suspicious or unattended items.	RSD # 13: Action is required for rail operators, per TSA SD Railpax-0401
2.41	If equipped with locking mechanisms, lock all doors that allow access to the engineer's or operator's cab or compartment. The TSA SD is not intended to supersede safety regulations concerning locking of certain types of doors on cards under DOT/FRA/FTA regulations.	RSD # 15: Action is required for rail operators, per TSA SD Railpax-0401
2.42	Elevate the priority of security maintenance and repairs such as perimeter fencing, lighting, facility locks, and access points.	
2.43	Limit visitor access to critical security areas. Confirm that visitors are expected and have a valid need to be in the area.	
2.44	Change appearance (e.g., orange/yellow vests) and patrol deployment strategies to disrupt terrorist planning.	
2.45	Alert vendors and contractors to heighten security awareness and report suspicious activity. Inform vendors and contractors about heightened control measures, including access, parking, and identification.	
2.46	Increase security spot checks of persons (employees, contractors, and visitors) entering nonpublic facilities, including confirming identification and randomly checking bags.	
2.47	Secure all buildings and storage areas not in regular use. Increase frequency of inspections and patrols in these areas.	
2.48	Increase surveillance of critical infrastructure areas (e.g., control and communication centers, loading docks, parking lots and garages, bridges, tunnels, rights-of-way).	
2.49	Check designated unmanned and remote sites more frequently for signs of unauthorized entry, suspicious packages, and unusual activities.	
2.50	Check all deliveries to facility loading docks to insure that the items received are as ordered and expected. Refuse any unexpected deliveries.	
2.51	For passenger stations with identified, significant risks, to the extent practicable, remove trash receptacles and other nonessential containers, except for bomb-resistant receptacles and clear plastic containers. Install bomb-resistant receptacles to the extent that resources allow.	RSD # 8: Action is required for rail operators, per TSA SD Railpax-0401

continued

Seq. No.	Protective Measure	Action Required
2.52	Use explosive detection canine teams, if available.	RSD # 9: Action is required for rail operators, per TSA SD Railpax-0401
2.53	At any time or place, allow TSA-designated canine teams to conduct operations under the overall direction of the authority responsible for security of the transit property or operator.	RSD # 10: Action is required for rail operators, per TSA SD Railpax-0401
2.54	At any time or location, allow TSA/DHS-designated Security Partnership Teams to work with the transit agency's Security Coordinator to perform inspections, evaluations, or tests, including copying records, for Security Directive Railpax-04-01.	RSD # 11: Action is required for rail operators, per TSA SD Railpax-0401
2.55	Review standard operating procedures for heating, ventilation, and air conditioning (HVAC) operations in various emergency conditions.	
2.56	Maintain respiratory protection equipment immediately available to law enforcement and operations personnel while they are in the field.	
2.57	Increase the frequency with which law enforcement/security personnel perform ad hoc security checks and sweeps of transit vehicles at ends of lines.	
2.58	Consider random screening of passengers' bags, backpacks, briefcases, suitcases, etc. at station entrances. Provide overt warning to potential passengers prior to their entering stations.	
2.59	Review procedures and prepare to establish/activate the Command Center(s). Prepare to dispatch Mobile Command Centers in the event of an actual emergency. Prepare to initiate the incident command system.	
2.60	Put the Emergency Operations Center [EOC] on "Stand-By" status with all systems operational. Verify that all systems are functioning.	
2.61	Increase security postings and patrols to maximum sustainable levels.	
2.62	Increase inspections of public storage areas, including bike and bag lockers.	
2.63	Close and lock all gates and barriers except those needed for immediate entry and exit. Inspect perimeter fences on a frequent basis.	
2.64	Restrict visitors to essential business purposes. Require positive identification and inspect suitcases, packages, and other articles of significant size.	

Seq. No.	Protective Measure	Action Required
2.65	Limit access to designated facilities to personnel with a legitimate and verifiable need to enter.	
2.66	Implement higher threat level sweep and inspection procedures for transit vehicles in and out of facilities, and continue driver inspections of vehicles. Increase ad hoc security checks and sweeps of transit vehicles in revenue service (i.e., during revenue trips) by law enforcement/security personnel.	
2.67	Relocate authorized parked vehicles away from stations, terminals, and other critical buildings or areas, if possible. Consider implementing centralized parking and employee shuttle buses. Remove unauthorized parked vehicles.	
2.68	Place backup/offsite operations control center on standby status. Test/verify its capability/readiness.	
2.69	Erect barriers and obstacles to control traffic flows and protect stations, terminals, and other facilities and critical infrastructure from attack by parked or moving vehicles. Consider using company vehicles as barriers.	
2.70	Increase presence/visibility of security and law enforcement personnel through consistent appearance (e.g., all patrols and posted security wearing vests, transit police in full uniform).	
2.71	Protect onsite or adjacent auxiliary facilities and services (e.g., day care center, homeless shelter, food service vendor) consistent with the agency's protective measures.	
2.72	Postpone all nonvital construction work performed by contractors, or continuously monitor their work with agency personnel.	
2.73	Limit administrative employee travel.	
2.74	Close all public restrooms in underground stations.	
2.75	Require service workers to empty trash receptacles more frequently.	
2.76	Review security camera stored disks/tapes to detect possible indicators of pre-operational surveillance.	
2.77	Monitor and inspect elevators more frequently.	
2.78	Increase the frequency of late night/overnight security sweeps and inspections of key right-of-way infrastructure elements (e.g., underground rail lines, electrical substations).	
2.79	Implement transit emergency plans and procedures. Assign emergency response personnel, pre-position resources, and mobilize specially trained teams.	

continued

Seq. No.	Protective Measure	Action Required
2.80	Activate the transit system's EOC.	
2.81	Implement 100% sweep and inspection procedures for transit vehicles in and out of facilities in addition to the driver inspections. Implement 100% security inspection at out-of-service stops.	
2.82	Augment security forces to ensure control of key command, control, and communications centers and other potential target areas. Establish surveillance points and reporting procedures.	
2.83	Maximize patrols in areas without stationed security personnel. Conduct frequent checks of building exteriors and parking areas.	
2.84	Implement surveillance in support of guarded and patrolled areas.	
2.85	Reduce facility access points to an operational minimum and restrict access to essential personnel.	
2.86	At facility access points, inspect 100% of employee, contractor, and visitor briefcases, suitcases, bags, and other articles.	
2.87	Minimize/eliminate administrative employee leave/ travel.	
2.88	Close visitor and employee parking lots, as appropriate.	
2.89	Disable and lock out public storage areas such as bike and bag lockers.	
2.90	Physically verify that vehicle gates, garage and building doors, and other gates and doors designated to be closed and locked at the "red" threat level are actually closed and locked.	
2.91	Close all nonessential functions (e.g., sales offices, neighborhood outreach offices, onsite day care facilities).	
2.92	Transfer/deliver all mail and packages to a central remote location for inspection.	
2.93	Close all public restrooms.	
2.94	Consider implementing temporary revenue service restrictions and/or re-routes associated with serving higher-risk targets/icons (e.g., military bases, stadiums, convention centers).	
2.95	Consider restricting or suspending bicycle transport (e.g., not allowing bicycles with bags or backpacks affixed to them to be carried on vehicles).	
2.96	Remove all nonexplosive resistant trash cans (except clear plastic containers) at passenger facilities.	

Seq. No.	Protective Measure	Action Required
2.97	Deploy on-duty vehicle cleaners to terminal stations during peak revenue hours. Remove or secure unattended newspaper vending machines in selected locations.	
2.98	When operators exit their vehicles at an end-of-line layover point, require all riders to de-board. Secure/lock the vehicle. When operators return to vehicles, require them to conduct a sweep before allowing riders to board/re-board.	
2.99	Staff backup/offsite operations control center. Prepare to assume control from primary operations control center if needed.	
2.100	Perform Immediate Actions (IAs) for suspicious activities and imminent threats as necessary.	
Active Incident		
2.101	Perform Immediate Actions (IAs) for attacks as necessary.	
2.102	Designate the incident commander. Activate and operationalize the EOC. Implement emergency operating procedures to mitigate the effects of the attack.	
2.103	Provide security for the site and other transit system assets during the emergency. Be alert for possible secondary attacks.	
2.104	Mobilize and provide transit assets (communications links, equipment, facilities, and personnel) in support of the overall response effort.	
2.105	Assess immediate impacts of the attack on transit service and facilities, and reduce or cancel services as required.	
2.106	Assist with response to casualties, as needed/requested.	
2.107	Restrict/eliminate access to facilities by contractors, vendors, and visitors. Accept deliveries on a case-by-case basis only.	
2.108	Position/park vehicles to block entrances to facilities, as appropriate.	
2.109	Review security camera stored disks/tapes for operational activity.	
2.110	Provide security for the incident site. Allow access to incident area only to security, mitigation, and investigating personnel. Other access restrictions should allow the implementation of recovery plans, but prevent tampering with the incident scene until fully released.	

continued

Seq. No.	Protective Measure	Action Required
2.111	Activate "on-call" external contractors and other special support, as required.	
2.112	Implement plans to return to the appropriate threat level ("green" through "red").	
2.113	Inspect facilities and infrastructure for latent damage before reoccupying facilities or restoring operations.	
2.114	Continue secure access control around affected area(s).	
2.115	Identify short- and long-term capital replacement needs. Develop plans and detailed designs.	
2.116	Recover facilities, infrastructure, and vehicles. Restore transit system capabilities. Restore the scene of attack to functionality.	

3.0 Regional Coordination

Seq. No.	Protective Measure	Action Required
3.1	Participate in development and review of local and regional security and emergency response plans.	
3.2	Establish local, regional, and system-wide threat and warning dissemination processes (consistent with federal level information sharing per protective measures in 1.0 Information and Intelligence).	
3.3	Establish emergency communications capability and coordinate notifications to emergency response organizations.	
3.4	Coordinate with emergency response agencies (e.g., military, police, fire, HAZMAT, hospitals, federal agencies) to develop support systems to provide post-incident support to customers and employees.	
3.5	Establish memoranda of agreement (MOAs) and other mutual aid agreements, as needed, to assure adequate regional emergency response coordination.	
3.6	Participate in local and regional security and emergency response training, drills, and exercises. Coordinate transit system's role in local and regional emergency response. Include an after-action report-based process improvement system for all tabletop exercises and drills.	
3.7	Coordinate security and emergency response awareness materials for transit employees and the public consistent with other local and/or regional transit agencies.	

Seq. No.	Protective Measure	Action Required
3.8	Periodically communicate with military, law enforcement units, emergency response organizations, hospitals, and other agencies and organizations (including federal agencies), as appropriate.	
3.9	Identify and train other community personnel who can assist as drivers of transit vehicles during emergencies.	
3.10	Advise local agencies, law enforcement, security officials with an operational need to know, and TSA's Transportation Security Operation Center (TSOC) at 1-703-563-3237 or TSOC.ST@dhs.gov, that the transit agency is at Elevated Condition (Yellow) and advise the protective measures being employed.	
3.11	Coordinate emergency preparedness/response plans with nearby jurisdictions.	
3.12	Participate in daily/weekly regional briefings.	
3.13	Advise local agencies, law enforcement, security officials with an operational need to know, and TSA's Transportation Security Operation Center (TSOC) at 1-703-563-3237 or TSOC.ST@dhs.gov, that the transit system is at HSAS condition "orange," and advise them of the Protective Measures being employed.	
3.14	Consult with local authorities about control of public roads and access that could make the transit system more vulnerable.	
3.15	Take additional precautions at local and regional public events. Consider alternative venues or postponing or canceling the events.	
3.16	Implement regional emergency plans with nearby jurisdictions. Implement plans to assist in evacuations or respond to emergency management requests.	
3.17	Coordinate with local authorities on the possible closing of public roads and facilities and the removal of unattended vehicles.	
3.18	Advise local agencies, law enforcement, security officials with an operational need to know, and TSA's Transportation Security Operation Center (TSOC) at 1-703-563-3237 or TSOC.ST@dhs.gov, that the transit system is at HSAS condition "red," and advise them of the Protective Measures being employed.	

continued

Seq. No.	Protective Measure	Action Required
3.19	Implement regional emergency preparedness plans with nearby jurisdictions. Implement plans to assist in evacuations or respond to emergency management requests.	
3.20	Deploy liaisons to regional emergency operations centers (EOCs) to participate in unified command.	
Active Incident		
3.21	Report the attack immediately to all local, regional, state, and federal emergency response organizations, including TSA's Transportation Security Operation Center (TSOC) at 1-703563-3237 or TSOC.ST@dhs.gov (including those mentioned in protective measure 1.10).	
3.22	Designate the transit agency Incident Commander, as needed, and activate transit agency's EOC. Provide onsite technical support to the regional EOC's Incident Commander.	
3.23	Mobilize and provide transit assets (communications links, equipment, facilities and personnel) to support of the response, as requested by the Regional EOC Incident Commander.	
Recovery		
3.24	Coordinate local and regional plans to return to appropriate threat level ("green" though "red").	
3.25	Coordinate funding and other needs for transit system restoration with federal, state, and local agencies.	

4.0 Information Technology and Communication Systems

Seq. No.	Protective Measure	Action Required
4.1	Develop and implement hardware, software and communications security and disaster recovery/business continuity plans and procedures, including (a) data management; (b) access partitions and permissions; (c) external communication links; (d) internal activity monitoring; (e) configuration management (hardware, software, network descriptions, and locations); (f) vehicle control systems. Provide for incremental responses to changing threat level conditions. Coordinate with systems security plans. Develop and implement plans for business, operations, and security.	

Seq. No.	Protective Measure	Action Required
4.2	Inventory existing emergency response infrastructure, equipment, supplies and service contracts, and compare against current requirements. Assign work/prepare purchase orders based on the inventory. Consider: (a) frequency management (e.g., allocation and assignment of frequencies, license renewals, tower capacity); (b) contracts for backup communications systems (e.g., cell phones); (c) procurement and assignment of backup communications systems (e.g., distribution of phones and phone numbers to assigned personnel); (d) interoperability with local and/or regional emergency responder organizations (e.g., update/implementation of frequency management with responder organizations, purchase/acquisition of translation equipment). Purchase and/or install items needed to implement protective measures at higher threat levels.	
4.3	Limit transit operations data communications to outbound information only. Install firewalls and DMZ environment. Block or control internet access. Establish private networks.	
4.4	Use "push" technology for antivirus and software security updates.	
4.5	Develop a computer incident response plan and team that includes representatives from various user groups.	
4.6	Develop information technology (IT) administrative and operational procedures to identify and respond to IT and communications related incidents in a timely and controlled manner.	
4.7	Configure IT infrastructure to provide fault tolerances across physical locations and within a single physical location.	
4.8	Secure employee and customer information (e.g., personal information, account data, credit card information) from unauthorized electronic access.	
4.9	Assess the impact on transit agency operations if all essential computer system resources (command, control, and financial computer systems) are disconnected from the Internet and public access during higher HSAS threat level conditions. Manage external transit fare vending machines so that they cannot be compromised/hacked.	
4.10	Perform daily incremental and weekly full backups of electronic data required for security, payroll, scheduling, operations, and business continuity. Transport backup(s) to a secure remote location weekly or more often for critical data. Practice data file restoration on a regular basis, including retrieval from offsite storage and return to offsite storage. Practice full System restoration on an annual or more frequent basis.	
4.11	Test primary emergency communications and notification systems. Order maintenance as necessary. Update emergency communications frequencies for interoperability with emergency responders.	

continued

Seq. No.	Protective Measure	Action Required
4.12	Test the network, servers, databases, and web servers to ensure that they can handle increasing transaction loads.	
4.13	Test to assure that the IT infrastructure is protected against unauthorized manipulation of website applications.	
4.14	Test IT systems for single points of failure.	
4.15	Secure command, control, and financial IT systems and communication networks from outside tampering.	
4.16	Inspect and test all closed-circuit television (CCTV), video camera/recording equipment, intercoms, emergency telephones, radios, and satellite communication devices to assure that all communication equipment is in place and operational.	
4.17	Update system software (servers, switches, routers, firewalls, DMZs) for Information security protection. Enter all changes into the configuration management system.	
4.18	Test/exercise primary and backup communications equipment and procedures with essential personnel to ensure that an agency or facility response can be mobilized appropriate to an incident or increased security requirement.	
4.19	Test/exercise external communications equipment and procedures used with designated emergency response or command locations.	
4.20	Monitor all digital communications links for security. Test alternate paths.	
4.21	Perform daily incremental backups of electronic data required for security, payroll, scheduling, operations, and business continuity. Maintain copies on-site and transport backup(s) to secure remote location.	
4.22	Develop and implement a procedure to identify vulnerabilities and patches for known viruses and "denial of service" attacks.	
4.23	Provide and test redundancy in emergency communications to contact security officials, law enforcement agencies, and field incident commanders.	
4.24	Coordinate with all IT and communications vendors and contractors to heighten security awareness and reporting of suspicious activity. Inform vendors and contractors of control measures, including access, parking, and identification.	
4.25	Check that offsite, stored backups for "as built" facility drawings and related engineering and capital projects information that might be needed in an emergency are readily available.	
4.26	Implement and test backup hardware and software systems at the Emergency Operations Center (EOC). Implement and test emergency website and network links to alternate sites.	

Seq. No.	Protective Measure	Action Required
4.27	Check that current backup copies of critical operations software are available to load onto backup servers.	
4.28	Keep all essential personnel on call. Establish and verify primary and alternate phone numbers. Issue backup communications equipment to essential personnel. Implement the use of restricted frequencies for critical communications.	
4.29	Practice restoring capability for critical data weekly. Recall tapes, verify correct labeling, and implement restoration procedures on main and alternate systems for selected critical business files.	
4.30	Issue backup communications equipment to essential personnel.	
4.31	Implement the use of restricted frequencies for critical communications.	
4.32	Implement 100% sweep and inspection procedures for all IT vendor service vehicles and off-site backup tape delivery vehicles.	
4.33	Disconnect all command, control, and financial computer systems from the Internet and public access. Allow internal/intranet access, as appropriate.	
4.34	Apply intrusion detection tools to detect and deter outside attempts to access the private network.	
4.35	Activate emergency website from alternate, secure location.	
Active Incident		
4.36	Provide communication links and IT equipment resources to support the response effort.	
Recovery		
4.37	Replace damaged communication infrastructure and IT infrastructure elements.	
4.38	Discontinue use of emergency radio frequencies, as appropriate.	
4.39	Recall tapes, verify correct labeling, and implement restoration procedures on main and alternate systems for selected critical business and operations files.	
4.40	Perform system and critical file restoration for all essential computer systems. Verify that systems restorations are correct and complete.	

5.0 Employee and Public Communications

Seq. No.	Protective Measure	Action Required
5.1	Develop emergency communications plans and procedures (including announcement types, frequency, and message based on threat condition). Establish points of contact for all internal and external communications. Develop emergency evacuation plans as appropriate.	
5.2	Incorporate security and emergency preparedness information into employee, customer, and general public education programs. Use the intranet to inform employees and the Internet site to inform customers and the public of current conditions, awareness campaigns, and regional plans and activities. Refresh employee postings, public signs and broadcast messages at station platforms and on-board vehicles.	
5.3	Develop specific provisions for disabled individuals in plans and procedures (e.g., employee and customer communications, security and emergency preparedness awareness campaigns).	
5.4	Establish contingency plans to provide for the welfare of employees and their families, such as assistance with overnight shelter and food. Include contingency and continuity plan information, as appropriate, in employee communications.	
5.5	Develop a database of employee emergency contact information and next of kin for use during response and recovery activities.	
5.6	Provide resource materials (e.g., brochures, websites) to employees to help with family preparedness planning activities.	
5.7	Schedule periodic reviews/updates for all operations plans, personnel assignments, and logistics requirements that pertain to implementing employee, customer, and public communications activities.	
5.8	Periodically contact liaisons with each station or facility served to maintain lines of communication. Use transit police or security personnel to routinely patrol stations/facilities.	
5.9	Develop and disseminate emergency response, contingency and continuity, and security awareness materials.	
5.10	Periodically update and test contact databases, calling trees, notification/recall lists, and other communications lists used during emergencies and heightened threat condition levels. Verify primary and secondary employee telephone numbers.	
5.11	Review with all employees the elements of security and emergency management plans and personal safety pertaining to implementing increased security levels. Insure that all employees receive a security briefing regarding current and emerging threat conditions.	

Seq. No.	Protective Measure	Action Required
5.12	Periodically test public emergency communications plans using tabletop drills and exercises with regional emergency response partners.	
5.13	Develop and issue quick reference emergency guidelines pocket cards to all employees.	
5.14	Review U.S. Postal Service "Suspicious Mail Alert" and "Bombs by Mail" publications with all employees involved in receiving mail and package deliveries.	
5.15	Remind employees and on-site contractors to always lock/secure their vehicles and personal spaces (e.g., personal vehicles, company-assigned vehicles, personal storage lockers, tool chests).	
5.16	Notify all transit agency employees, via briefings, e-mail, voice mail or signage, of any changes in HSAS threat level conditions and Protective Measures. Reinforce employee and rider Transit Watch programs.	RSD # 5: Actions is required for rail operators, per TSA SD Railpax-0401 # 5
5.17	Direct employees to be alert and immediately report any suspicious activity or potential threat. To the extent resources allow, use surveillance systems to monitor for suspicious activity.	RSD # 6: Action is required for rail operators, per TSA SD Railpax-0401 # 6
5.18	Re-check adequacy of emergency evacuation signage posted on board vehicles and at stations, transit centers, and administrative and maintenance facilities. Post signs and/or make routine public announcements emphasizing the need for all passengers to closely control baggage and packages. Increase the frequency of announcements, especially during peak hours.	
5.19	Regularly inform staff and contractors of the general security situation and additional threat information as available. Provide periodic updates on security measures being implemented.	
5.20	Instruct employees working alone at remote locations or on the ROW to check-in on a periodic basis.	
5.21	Communicate information on heightened security measures to passengers in stations, where practicable, and on vehicles. Ask passengers to report unattended property or suspicious behavior to uniformed crew members and/or law enforcement personnel (suggested per Transit Watch—announcement frequency every 30 min). Increase the frequency of announcements and distribution of security awareness materials to passengers in stations and on-board revenue service vehicles.	RSD # 7: Action is required for rail operators, per TSA SD Railpax-0401 # 7

continued

Seq. No.	Protective Measure	Action Required
5.22	Implement leave restrictions as necessary so that staff required to implement security plans are readily available (on call). Insure that all essential personnel, including employees with access to building plans and area evacuation plans, are available at all times.	
5.23	Provide periodic updates to all staff on security measures being deployed.	
5.24	Brief the Board of Directors and executive management, as necessary, on possible emergencies and protective measures being taken per the threat level condition.	
5.25	Include Immediate Actions (IAs) for Transit Employees' guidance in procedures and protocols, and ensure that employees receive adequate IA training and testing.	
5.26	Limit number of employees working alone in nonpublic areas to minimum. Increase the frequency of call-ins for isolated assignments.	
5.27	Prepare and issue press releases to local media on transit system states of readiness, including restrictions related to carry-on articles, modifications to service or schedules, and other actions that may impact the riding public.	
5.28	Increase the frequency of public address announcements (suggested Transit Watch frequency is every 5–10 min). Increase distribution of security awareness materials to passengers and the public.	
5.29	Notify labor unions of threat level condition to assist/increase security coordination.	
5.30	Use “all calls” to vehicle operators (Bus Dispatch/Radio Room to Bus Operators, Rail Control to Rail Operators, Paratransit Dispatch to Paratransit Drivers) to inform operators of threat level condition and related security needs/measures.	
5.31	Make public address announcements and post signage to inform passengers that bags, packages, and other carry-on articles may be subject to inspection.	
5.32	Schedule announcements and responses to local/regional media inquiries, and issue press releases on transit system states of readiness.	
5.33	Inform/prepare employees to perform Immediate Actions [IAs] as needed.	
5.34	Increase frequency of public address announcements (suggested Transit Watch frequency is every 5 min).	
Active Incident		
5.35	Provide internal briefings and transit system status information to the public as soon as possible.	

Seq. No.	Protective Measure	Action Required
Recovery		
5.36	Use all available media to make frequent announcements about restoration of service, transit security, and the transit system's state of readiness.	
5.37	Work to restore public confidence by reporting available incident and law enforcement information.	

6.0 Contingency and Continuity Plans

Seq. No.	Protective Measure	Action Required
6.1	Develop contingency and business continuity plans that address changes in HSAS threat level conditions. Develop contingency plans for loss of electrical power and loss of communications systems. Develop plans for revenue service continuation/restoration/recovery.	
6.2	Identify alternative sites where the human resources department can adequately staff the agency, if necessary.	
6.3	Develop plans to provide for the welfare of employees and their families (e.g., assistance with overnight shelter and food) in case of attack or major emergency.	
6.4	Develop and implement training based on contingency and continuity plans.	
6.5	Prepare emergency response, continuity and contingency, and security awareness materials. Coordinate and disseminate materials within the transit agency.	
6.6	Conduct drills and exercises of emergencies that require execution of contingency and continuity plans and procedures.	
6.7	Implement contingency and continuity plans, as appropriate.	
6.8	Modify standard contract terms and conditions to reflect the necessity of suspension of work for higher HSAS threat level conditions, including special requirements for jobsite configuration during work and nonwork periods.	
6.9	Prepare to execute continuity of operations procedures, such as moving to an alternate site or dispersing the workforce.	
6.10	Prepare to execute specific contingency procedures (e.g., relocation of incident command or the Board of Directors' office to alternative sites, dispersion of the workforce).	
6.11	Activate alternative location for the Board of Directors' office.	

continued

Seq. No.	Protective Measure	Action Required
Active Incident		
6.12	Assess the immediate impacts of the attack/emergency on the transit system, and prepare to implement contingency, continuity, and recovery plans as needed.	
Recovery		
6.13	Activate contingency plan, disaster recovery, business continuity/recovery plan, and/or other continuity of operations plan(s), as needed.	

Appendix E: CDC Reporting Form for Loss, Release, or Theft of Agents or Toxins

REPORT OF THEFT, LOSS, OR RELEASE OF SELECT AGENTS AND TOXINS (APHIS/CDC FORM 3)

FORM APPROVED
OMB NO. 0579-0213
OMB NO. 0920-0576
EXP DATE 10/31/2014

INSTRUCTIONS

Detailed instructions are available at http://www.selectagents.gov/TLRForm.html. Answer all items completely and type or print in ink. This report must be signed and submitted to either APHIS or CDC:

Animal and Plant Health Inspection Service
Agricultural Select Agent Program
4700 River Road Unit 2, Mailstop 22, Cubicle 1A07
Riverdale, MD 20737
FAX: (301) 734-3652
Email: ASAP@aphis.usda.gov

Centers for Disease Control and Prevention
Division of Select Agents and Toxins
1600 Clifton Road NE, Mailstop A-46
Atlanta, GA 30333
FAX: (404) 718-2096
Email: form3@cdc.gov

Accession Number:

(For Program Use ONLY)

Submit completed form only once by either email, fax, or mail

SECTION 1 – TO BE COMPLETED BY ALL ENTITIES

1. Date of Incident:	2. Date of Immediate Notification:	3. Type of Immediate Notification: ☐ Email ☐ Fax ☐ Telephone
4. Name of Entity (entities registered with CDC or APHIS) or Name of Hospital or Laboratory (non-registered entities):		5. Entity registration number (For select agent registered entities only):

6. Physical Address:	7. City:	8. State:	9. Zip Code:

10. Responsible Official (registered) or Name of Laboratory Supervisor (non-registered):

11. Telephone #:	12. Fax #:	13. Email address:

14a: Type of Incident (Human Health): ☐ Theft ☐ Loss ☐ Release ☐ Lab Acquired Infection	15. Did the release result in a potential exposure? ☐ No ☐ Yes ☐ N/A (If Yes , explain in Blocks 28 or 30)
14b: Type of Incident (Animal and Plant Health): ☐ Unintended Animal Infection ☐ Unintended Plant Agent Release	If yes, has medical surveillance been initiated? ☐ No ☐ Yes ☐ N/A (If Yes , explain in Blocks 28 or 30)
14c: Transfer: ☐ Transfer incident (complete Sections 1 and 2 and Appendix B)	

16. Time incident occurred:	17. Location of incident (building and room #):	18. Location of incident within room (e.g., freezer, incubator, centrifuge):
19. Biosafety level: ☐ BSL2 ☐ BSL3 ☐ BSL4 ☐ ABSL2 ☐ ABSL3 ☐ ABSL4 ☐ PPQ Agent ☐ BSL3 Ag	20. Date of last inventory (for reporting loss only):	21. Name of Principal Investigator:

SECTION 2 – TO BE COMPLETED BY ALL ENTITIES

	22. Name of Select Agent or Toxin	23. Characterization of Agent (e. g. strain, ATCC #)	24. Quantity / Amount
A			
B			
C			

25. Provide a detailed summary of events including a timeline of what occurred. Whenever possible, conduct a risk assessment of the event and determine if the root cause can be identified. State specifically what personal protective equipment was worn and what, if any, medical surveillance was provided or planned. If incident involves a non-human primate, please state species.

Block 25. Continued: (Use Appendix A for continuation, if necessary)

SECTION 3 – TO BE COMPLETED BY ALL ENTITIES ONLY FOR RELEASE OF SELECT AGENTS AND TOXINS OR OCCUPATIONAL EXPOSURE

26. An internal review of laboratory procedures and policies has been initiated to lessen the likelihood of recurrences of theft, loss or release of select agents and toxins at this entity.

☐ No ☐ Yes If yes, please provide additional details.

27. What were the hazards posed to humans by the extent of the release or occupational exposure?

28. What is the estimated extent of the release or exposure in relation to the proximity of susceptible humans, animals and plants?

29. Provide a brief summary of how the laboratory and work surfaces were decontaminated after the release.

30. In select agents and toxins posing a risk to humans, please state how many laboratorians were potentially exposed and provide a brief summary of the medical surveillance provided (do not provide names or confidential information).

Certification: I hereby certify that the information contained on this form is true and correct to the best of my knowledge. I understand that if I knowingly provide a false statement on any part of this form, or its attachments, I may be subject to criminal fines and/or imprisonment. I further understand that violations of the select agent regulations may result in civil or criminal penalties, including imprisonment. 7 CFR 331, 9 CFR 121, 42 CFR 73.

Signature of Respondent: ______________________ Title: ______________________

Typed or printed name of Respondent: ______________________ Date Signed: ______________________

APPENDIX A

ADDITIONAL SHEET FOR CONTINUATION OF INFORMATION

Continue Form 3 comments here. State which block from the Form 3 the continuation is from.
(Example: The following statement is a continuation of block 25:)

☐ Continue on next page

APPENDIX B IF THE INCIDENT OCCURRED DURING TRANSFER, COMPLETE SECTIONS 1 AND 2 OF FORM 3 AND PROVIDE THE FOLLOWING INFORMATION (INCLUDE A COPY OF THE RELEVANT APHIS/CDC FORM 2)	
1. Transfer authorization number from APHIS/CDC Form 2:	2. Date Shipped:
3. Name of Carrier:	4. Airway bill number, bill of lading number, tracking number:
5. Package Description (size, shape, description of packaging including number and type of inner packages; attach additional sheets as necessary):	
6. Package with select agents and toxins received by requestor: ☐ No ☐ Yes If yes, date of receipt:	7. Package with select agents and toxins appears to have been opened: ☐ No ☐ Yes If yes, include explanation in box 5 above.
8. Sender was contacted regarding incident: ☐ No ☐ Yes	9. Carrier/courier was contacted regarding incident: ☐ No ☐ Yes

Certification: I hereby certify that the information contained on this form is true and correct to the best of my knowledge. I understand that if I knowingly provide a false statement on any part of this form, or its attachments, I may be subject to criminal fines and/or imprisonment. I further understand that violations of the select agent regulations may result in civil or criminal penalties, including imprisonment. 7 CFR 331, 9 CFR 121, 42 CFR 73.

Signature of Respondent: ______________________________ Title: ______________________

Typed or printed name of Respondent: ______________________ Date Signed: ____________________

Public reporting burden: Public reporting burden of providing this information is estimated to average 1 hour per response, including the time for reviewing instructions, searching existing data sources, gathering and maintaining the data needed, and completing and reviewing the collection of information. An agency may not conduct or sponsor, and a person is not required to respond to a collection of information unless it displays a currently valid OMB control number. Send comments regarding this burden estimate or any other aspect of this collection of information, including suggestions for reducing this burden to CDC/ATSDR Reports Clearance Officer; 1600 Clifton Road NE, MS D74, Atlanta, Georgia 30333; ATTN: PRA (0920-0576).

Index

Note: Page number followed by "n" denotes footnote

A

A&M-based program, *see* Air and Marine-based program (A&M-based program)
AARs, *see* After Action Reports (AARs)
Accessibility, 148, 153
Accidental hazard, 539
ACE, *see* American Council on Education (ACE); Automated Commercial Environment (ACE)
Acids, *see* Caustics (Acids)
ACS, *see* Automated Commercial System (ACS)
ACSD, *see* Advanced Container Security Device (ACSD)
Actions
  administration homeland security, post 9/11, 37
  Biological Incident Annex, 569–572
Activation, Biological Incident Annex, 569
Adjutant general, 263
Advanced Container Security Device (ACSD), 425
Advanced imaging technology (AIT), 47, 415
  machine, 415, 416
  safety information, 416
Advanced spectroscopic portal (ASP), 121
Adversary, 539
Advisory panels and committees, DHS, 65–68
AFG, *see* Assistance to Firefighters Grant (AFG)
Afghanistan
  Department of Defense, 280
  national and homeland security contrast, 273
  private sector security, 199
After Action Reports (AARs), 230
Agriculture and food safety, 474; *see also* Bioterrorism
  assessments, 485
  bioterrorism, 489
  Department of Agriculture, 479
  DHS vision and purpose, 479
  infectious animals, 485–489
  midwestern farm, 480
  Plum Island Facility, 486
  SPPA, 483–485
  USDA assessment protocol, 482–483
  USDA's participation, 481
Agroterrorism, 483
AI, *see* Avian flu (AI)
AIATP, *see* Antiterrorism Intelligence Awareness Training Program (AIATP)
Air and Marine-based program (A&M-based program), 380; *see also* U.S. Customs and Border Protection (CBP)
  services, 381

Air Force, 282
drone, 528
MQ-1 Predator, 284
Air Force Intelligence, 281
Air Force Intelligence, Surveillance, and Reconnaissance Agency, 282
Air National Guard, 276
ALB, *see* Albany International Airport (ALB)
Albany International Airport (ALB), 419
ALERT, *see* Awareness & Location of Explosives-Related Threats (ALERT)
All-hazards response, 321
Allies, 7
Allocation, Biological Incident Annex, 572
Allotments, 95, 96, 97, 529, *see* Homeland Security budgeting
Al Qaeda, 24
attack on U.S. warship, 24, 25
nuclear weapons, 156
American Airlines #77, 30
American Council on Education (ACE), 224
American intelligence community, 337
American Public Works Association (APWA), 224
American Society for Industrial Security (ASIS), 200
ASIS International Certification, 92
American Society of Civil Engineers (ASCE), 224
American Society of Engineering Management (ASEM), 224
America's agriculture and food system, 479
America's Shield Initiative, 111
Amnesty, 388, 389
Amtrak, 450; *see also* Rail and mass transit
Mobile Tactical Unit, 451
PASS, 451
security protocols, 450
Analytic risk assessment, 143
Animal and Plant Health Inspection Service (APHIS), 487
job openings, 488
logo, 488
Animals, infectious, *see* Infectious animals
Anthrax (*Bacillus anthracis*), 169; *see also* Biological agents
diagnosis of, 169
effects of, 170
emergency plan, 170
infection, 170
information for health providers, 491
Anthrax Vaccine Immunization Program (AVIP), 170
Deputy Secretary's Order, 171
Anticoagulants, long-acting, 177; *see also* Chemical agents
Antiterrorism Intelligence Awareness Training Program (AIATP), 63
Antiterrorism technology seller, registration as, 92, 93–94
Antivirus (AV), 191
APHIS, *see* Animal and Plant Health Inspection Service (APHIS)
Approval, facility alternative security programs (ASPS), 436
APWA, *see* American Public Works Association (APWA)
Armed Helicopter for Homeland Security Project, 111
Army Corps of Engineers, 298, 312
ASCE, *see* American Society of Civil Engineers (ASCE)
ASEM, *see* American Society of Engineering Management (ASEM)
ASFPM, *see* Association of State Flood Plain Managers (ASFPM)
Ashara, Shoko, 176, 180
ASIS, *see* American Society for Industrial Security (ASIS)
ASP, *see* Advanced spectroscopic portal (ASP)
ASPS, *see* Approval, facility alternative security programs (ASPS)
Assessment protocol, 481
Asset, 540
value, 142
Assistance to Firefighters Grant (AFG), 221
logo, 221
Association of State Flood Plain Managers (ASFPM), 224
ATR, *see* Automated Target Recognition (ATR)
Attack method, 540
Attack path, 540
Attorney General, 562
Aum Shinri-kyo cult, 180
Automated Commercial Environment (ACE), 386; *see also* U.S. Customs and Border Protection (CBP)
benefits, 388
program logo, 387
roles, 387
Automated Commercial System (ACS), 386
Automated Target Recognition (ATR), 417
AV, *see* Antivirus (AV)
Avian flu (AI), 485, 497; *see also* H5N1 virus; Pandemics
AVIP, *see* Anthrax Vaccine Immunization Program (AVIP)
Awareness & Location of Explosives-Related Threats (ALERT), 526

B

Bacillus anthracis, see Anthrax (*Bacillus anthracis*)
Backscatter technology, 416
Baggage screening, 404, 450
BARDA, *see* Biomedical Advanced Research and Development Authority (BARDA)
Barriers, natural, 376
BCE, *see* Bovine spongiform encephalopathy (BCE)
Beirut, Lebanon
  significant terrorist incidents, 23, 24
Berlin
  Airlift, 10
  Wall, 9
Best Practices (LLIS. gov), 228
Bin Laden, Osama, 24; *see also* Al Qaeda
Biodefense Knowledge Center, 526
Biological agents, 165
  anthrax, 169
  categories, 167
  characteristics, 166
  under high-powered microscope, 168
  list of actions and decisions to be considered, 174–175
  plague, 171–172
  response, 565–566
  smallpox, 172–173
Biological Incident Annex, 560
  actions, 569–572
  activation, 569
  allocation and rationing, 572
  biological response, 565–566
  bioterrorism modalities, 561
  controlling the epidemic, 569–571
  decontamination, 571
  Department of State, 563
  disease outbreak deduction, 566
  identification, 567
  international notification, 572
  laboratory confirmation, 566–567
  planning assumptions, 564–565
  policies, 561–563
  scope, 560–561
  Secretary of Homeland Security, 562
  suspicious substances, 567–568
Biological threats, *see* Bioterrorism
Biological WMD, 165–173
Biomedical Advanced Research and Development Authority (BARDA), 493
Biometrics, 417
  fingerprint device, 120, 418
  Paperless Boarding Pass program, 419, 420
  registered traveler program, 418–419
Bioterrorism, 165, 490–491
  anthrax information for health providers, 491
  biological attack effects, 489
  communicable diseases, 490
  DHA chemist, 492
  at DHS level, 491
  HPP, 492
  infectious diseases and, 489
  National Select Agent Registry Program, 496
  NPS, 495
  Project BioShield, 493–495
  risk assessment, 526
Biotoxins, 177; *see also* Chemical agents
  ricin, 177–180
BioWatch, 167
  generation 3 monitoring station, 167
Bird flu, 497; *see also* Pandemics
Black Panther Party, 20
Black Panthers, 15, 19
Blair, Dennis, 353
Blanco, Kathleen, 322
Blast Containment Receptacles, 92
Blister agents, 177; *see also* Chemical agents
Blood agents, 177; *see also* Chemical agents
Boarding officer, 442
Border Patrol, 370; *see also* U.S. Customs and Border Protection (CBP)
  agents number, 378
  U.S. Coast Guard on, 371
Border Protection, Anti-terrorism, and Illegal Immigration Control Act of 2005, 389
Borders and Marine Division, 424
Border security; *see also* U.S. Customs and Border Protection (CBP)
  funding for, 111
  policy solution, 519
  surveillance cameras, 376
Botulism, 168
Bovine spongiform encephalopathy (BCE), 485
Brucellosis, 169
Bubonic plague, 172; *see also* Plague (*Yersinia pestis*)
Budgeting, finance, and funding, *see* Homeland Security budgeting
Building Security Committee, 61
Bureau of Justice Assistance, 201
Bush, George W. (President), 84
  CIA restructuring, 347
  on DHS establishment, 252, 254
  tour in NTC, 105
Business Outreach Group, 203

C

C2I, *see* Command, Control and Interoperability (C2I)
C3, *see* Cyber Crimes Center (C3)
Cabinet-level agency, 95
Camp/Unit 731, 5, 6
CAMRA, *see* Center for Advancing Microbial Risk Assessment (CAMRA)
Canine explosive detection unit, 412
Canines, 412
CanScan project, 425
CAOCL, *see* Center for Advanced Operational Culture Learning (CAOCL)
Capability, 540–541
Cards, 181
Cargo Advanced Automated Radiography Systems, 116, 117
Cargo and Facilities Division, 436
Cargo ship, 106
Carnegie Mellon University, 192
Carter, Jimmy (President), 298
CARVER + Shock assessment tool, 148, 204; *see also* Risk management
  accessibility, 153
  criticality, 153
  discussion questions, 207
  effect, 153
  exercises, 208
  flow process possibilities, 149–150
  recognizability, 153
  recuperability, 153
  sample interview page, 152
  scoring criteria, 151
  shock, 153
  vulnerability, 153
Castor beans, 178
Catastrophic events, 306
  health events, 470
  hurricane Isabel, 318
  hurricane Katrina, 320
Caustics (Acids), 177; *see also* Chemical agents
CBP, *see* Customs and Border Patrol (CBP); U.S. Customs and Border Protection (CBP)
CBR contamination, *see* Chemical, biological, or radiological contamination (CBR contamination)
CBRNE, *see* Chemical, biological, radiological, nuclear and explosive (CBRNE)
CCITP, *see* Cyber Counterterrorism Investigations Training Program (CCITP)
CDC, *see* Centers for Disease Control and Prevention (CDC)
CDP, *see* Center for Domestic Preparedness (CDP)
Center for Advanced Operational Culture Learning (CAOCL), 285
Center for Advancing Microbial Risk Assessment (CAMRA), 525
Center for Combating WMD, 290
Center for Domestic Preparedness (CDP), 213, 221–222
Center for Risk and Economic Analysis of Terrorism Events (CREATE), 525
Centers for Disease Control and Prevention (CDC), 98, 167, 489
  law enforcement pandemic influenza planning checklist, 507, 508–510
  reporting form, 596, 597, 598, 599
  stockpiles, 496
Centers for Excellence, 525–527
Central Intelligence Agency (CIA), 288, 347; *see also* Intelligence
  core values, 349
  Crime and Narcotics Center, 350
  Directorate of Intelligence, 350–351
  Directorate of Science and Technology, 351–352
  mission, 348–349
  Office of Clandestine Services, 351
  Office of Support, 352
  parts, 350
  seal of, 349
  Weapons, Intelligence, Nonproliferation, and Arms Control Center, 350
Central MASINT Office (CMO), 345–346
Central U.S. Earthquake States, 219
CERT, *see* Computer Emergency Readiness Team (CERT)
CERTs, *see* Community Emergency Response Teams (CERTs)
CESP, *see* Covert Electronic Surveillance Program (CESP)
CETP, *see* Covert Electronic Tracking Program (CETP)
Chain of custody, 448
Change of mandate, 337
CHC, *see* Coastal Hazards Center of Excellence (CHC)
Chemical agents
  nerve agents, 180–184, 185
  ricin, 177–180
  typology of, 177
Chemical attack, 178
Chemical, biological, or radiological contamination (CBR contamination), 472
Chemical, biological, radiological, nuclear and explosive (CBRNE), 215
  CBRN response drill, 124
  risk assessment, 526
Chemical facilities, 90–91

Chemical, Ordnance, Biological, and Radiological Training Facility (COBRATF), 221
Chemical Security Analysis Center, 526
Chemical Stockpile Emergency Preparedness, 215
Chemical Terrorism Risk Assessment, 526
Chemical threats, 175
  response actions, 178
Chemical weapons in World War I, 176
Chemical WMD, 173–184, 185
Chemist's war, 175
CHER-CAP, *see* Community Hazards Emergency Response-Capability Assurance Process (CHER-CAP)
Chertoff, Michael, 45, 46
  on intelligence, 333
Children
  Carver + shock, 153
  Code Adam Alerts, 61
  crimes against, 339
  dialing 911, 316
  influenza strains, 501, 502
Choking agents, 177; *see also* Chemical agents
Churchill, Winston, 7
  speech, 8
CI, *see* Counterintelligence (CI); Critical infrastructure (CI)
CIA, *see* Central Intelligence Agency (CIA)
CIKRTP, *see* Critical Infrastructure Key Resource Protection Qualification Training Program (CIKRTP)
Cincinnati/Northern Kentucky International Airport (CVG), 419
CIPTP, *see* Critical Infrastructure Protection Training Program (CIPTP)
CIRTP, *see* Critical Incident Response Training Program (CIRTP)
CITAT, *see* Container Inspection Training and Assist Team (CITAT)
Citizen Corps, 272
  assortment of Citizen Corps programs, 274
  logo, 273
Citizenship and Immigration Service, *see* U.S. Citizenship and Immigration Services
Civil cooperation, 276–277
Civil hazard, 155; *see also* Hazard
Civil Maritime Intelligence Division, 281
Civil Support Teams (CSTs), 288, 289
Clandestine operations, 351
Clapper, James R., 354; *see also* Director of National Intelligence
CMC, *see* Commandant of the Marine Corps (CMC)
CMO, *see* Central MASINT Office (CMO)
CMTP, *see* Crisis Management Training Program (CMTP)
CNITP, *see* Computer Network Investigations Training Program (CNITP)
Coastal Hazards Center of Excellence (CHC), 527
Coast Guard, *see* U.S. Coast Guard (USCG)
COBRATF, *see* Chemical, Ordnance, Biological, and Radiological Training Facility (COBRATF)
Code Adam Alert, 61
  flyer, 62
Cold war, 7
  Berlin Airlift, 10
  Churchill's speech, 8
  expansionist motivations, 8
  internet exercise, 8, 9
  major events of, 11
  problems associated with, 10
  Russia after WWII, 7
  Soviet expansionism, 10
  timeline of, 9, 11
  Truman Doctrine, 9
Collaborative federalism, 524
Combatant zones, 275
Combinatorial Analysis Utilizing Logical Dependencies Residing on Networks tool, 526
Commandant of the Marine Corps (CMC), 284
Command, Control and Interoperability (C2I), 527
Commercial Vehicle Counterterrorism Training Program (CVCTP), 63
Common flu, *see* Seasonal flu
Common operating picture (COP), 119, 379
Communicable diseases, 490
Communism, 10
Communist Workers Party, 20
Community Emergency Response Teams (CERTs), 213, 231–232
Community Hazards Emergency Response-Capability Assurance Process (CHER-CAP), 232
Compliance standards, 234, 235–236
Computer Emergency Readiness Team (CERT), 192
  vulnerabilities reported and incidents handled, 193
Computer Network Investigations Training Program (CNITP), 63
CONR, *see* Continental U.S. NORAD Region (CONR)
Consequence, 541
  assessment, 541
  economic, 542
  human, 543
  mission, 545
  psychological, 546
Container inspection, 439

Container Inspection Training and Assist Team (CITAT), 437, 439
Container Security Device (CSD), 425
Container Security Initiative (CSI), 102, 384; *see also* U.S. Customs and Border Protection (CBP)
  core elements of, 103–104
  partner ports, 384
  ports, 384–385
Contamination, food, 479–480
Continental U.S. NORAD Region (CONR), 283, *see* North American Aerospace Defense Command (NORAD)
Contraband items, 425
COP, *see* Common operating picture (COP)
Cornerstone Initiative, 393
  targets of enforcement, 394
Counterfeit passport, 397
Counterintelligence (CI), 335, 356
Counterintelligence Center Analysis Group, 350
Countermeasure, 541
Counterterrorism; *see also* National Counterterrorism Center (NCTC)
  Coast Guard, 434
  domestic, 96
  FBI in, 33
  FLETC in, 65
  unit, 345
Covert Electronic Surveillance Program (CESP), 63
Covert Electronic Tracking Program (CETP), 65
Covert intelligence community, *see* Central Intelligence Agency (CIA)
CPTED, *see* Crime prevention through environmental design (CPTED)
Cream, Vivien, 58
CREATE, *see* Center for Risk and Economic Analysis of Terrorism Events (CREATE)
Crime and Narcotics Center, 350
Crime prevention through environmental design (CPTED), 577
Crisis Management Training Program (CMTP), 65
Critical Incident Response Training Program (CIRTP), 65
Critical infrastructure (CI), 194, 471
Critical Infrastructure Key Resource Protection Qualification Training Program (CIKRTP), 65
Critical Infrastructure Partnership Advisory Council, 66
Critical Infrastructure Protection Month, 79
Critical Infrastructure Protection Training Program (CIPTP), 65
Criticality, 148, 153
Cross-border crimes, 394
Cross lighting ceremony, 18
CSD, *see* Container Security Device (CSD)
CSI, *see* Container Security Initiative (CSI)
CSTs, *see* Civil Support Teams (CSTs)
CSXT, *see* CSX Transportation (CSXT)
CSX Transportation (CSXT), 451, 453–455; *see also* Rail and mass transit
  CSXT Network Operations Workstation, 453–454
  freight train, 454
  rail system map, 453
C-TPAT, *see* Customs Trade Partnership Against Terrorism (C-TPAT)
Cuban missile crisis, 11
Cultural Studies Program, 284; *see also* U.S. Marine Corps (USMC)
Customs, 370
Customs and Border Patrol (CBP), 399; *see also* U.S. Customs and Border Protection (CBP)
Customs and Border Protection, *see* U.S. Customs and Border Protection (CBP)
Customs Trade Partnership Against Terrorism (C-TPAT), 104, 385, 399; *see also* U.S. Customs and Border Protection (CBP)
  benefits of, 386
  goals of, 385–386
  theme of, 386
CVCTP, *see* Commercial Vehicle Counterterrorism Training Program (CVCTP)
CVG, *see* Cincinnati/Northern Kentucky International Airport (CVG)
Cyber cop portal, 194
Cyber Counterterrorism Investigations Training Program (CCITP), 65
Cyber Crimes Center (C3), 394–397
Cyber risk management, 194
Cyber security, 195
  intrusion report form, 197
Cyber Security Threats, 106, 190–191
  categories, 191
  internet exercise, 192
  security, 192
Cyberspace, 187
  infrastructure designation relating to, 194–195
Cyberspace Response System, 194
Cyber Storm, 194
Cyber threats, 205
Cyber Warning and Information Network, 192

D

Daisy chain, 185; *see also* Improvised explosive device (IED)
Dam Safety Program Management Tools, 311; *see also* National Dam Safety Program (NDSP)
Days of Rage protest march, 19
DCA, *see* Ronald Reagan Washington National Airport (DCA)
Decentralization, 292
Dedicated units, homeland security
  Center for Combating WMD, 290
  Defense Threat Reduction Agency, 290
  National Maritime Intelligence Center, 287, 288
  National Reconnaissance Office, 288
  WMD Civil Support Teams, 288, 289
Defend America, 280
Defense Attaché System, 362
Defense Civil Preparedness Agency, 298
Defense HUMINT Service, 362; *see also* Defense Intelligence Agency (DIA)
Defense Intelligence Agency (DIA), 360; *see also* Intelligence
  component of, 362
  intelligence, 362
  mission and vision, 361–362
  seal of, 362
Defense Intelligence Analysis Center, 362
Defense Threat Reduction Agency (DTRA), 290
  research, 291
  symbol at headquarters entrance, 291
Deliberative risk assessment, 143
DEN, *see* Denver International Airport (DEN)
Denial of Service (DoS), 191
Denver International Airport (DEN), 419
Department of Agriculture, 479
Department of Commerce, 404, 562
Department of Defense (DoD), 83, 277
  lead federal agency and, 278
  organization chart, 281
Department of Energy, 122
Department of Homeland Security (DHS), 29, 68, 74, 214, 404, 515, 563; *see also* Homeland security
  during 2001–2003, 36–38
  administration Homeland Security action, 37
  advisory panels and committees, 65–68
  agencies swept into DHS, 54
  agency relocations within, 55–56
  agenda for, 45–46
  areas of responsibility, 40
  barrier and border techniques, 118
  bioterrorism, 491
  Borders and Marine Division, 424
  border security policy solution, 519
  budget allotments, 95, 96, 529
  budgetary lines–2006, 111
  cargo ship at sea, 106
  chemical facilities, 90–91
  Cyber Storm participants, 50
  decentralization merits, 523–524
  departmental movements in history of, 522
  directorates, 49–52
  discussion questions, 69, 134–135
  evolution and change in, 38–43
  evolution of paradigm, 39
  exercises, 70, 135
  expansionism, 520–523
  Federal Law Enforcement Training Center, 61–65
  Federal Protective Service, 61
  funding 2003–2005, 104
  funding and aligned governmental agency funding, 97
  genesis of, 31
  Goal 1 performance, 517
  growth, 518–520
  hallmarks of, 42
  health and security, 470
  high-value assets determined by, 144
  initiatives, 526
  internet exercise, 42
  Management Directorate organizational chart, 53
  mission, 38, 39–40, 520–521
  monitoring system, 107
  National infrastructure bank, 42
  new way of thinking, 530–531
  NIMS, 108
  NTAS alert, 103
  Office of the Secretary, 45–48
  offices, 52–53
  organizational chart, 41, 44, 253
  performance budget overview, 109
  performance goals for, 110
  Private Sector Office, 202–203
  programs, 214
  radiation monitor, 105
  REAL ID program, 88
  reorganization and evolution of, 43–45
  risk assessment model, 143
  risk concept, 141
  risk formula, 142
  SAFECOM program, 112
  significance, 36, 516–518
  technology rise, 525–530
  USA Patriot Act, 85
  U.S. Coast Guard, 56–58
  U.S. Secret Service, 59–60
  vision and purpose in food and agriculture sector, 479

Department of Justice (DOJ), 562
Department of State (DOS), 563
Department of the Interior (DOI), 562
Designated Federal Officer (DFO), 535
Deterrent, 541
DF, *see* Direction finding (DF)
DFO, *see* Designated Federal Officer (DFO)
DFTO, *see* Disaster Field Training Organization (DFTO)
DHA chemist, 492
DHS, *see* Department of Homeland Security (DHS)
DHS challenges, 252, 292
  Air Force Intelligence, 281
  Center for Combating WMD, 290
  Civil Support Teams, 288, 289
  dedicated units, homeland security, 287
  Defense Threat Reduction Agency, 290
  Department of Defense, 277–280, 281
  discussion questions, 293–294
  exercises, 294
  funding and local initiatives, 271
  fusion centers, 269–271
  intelligence gathering and sharing, 280
  national and homeland security, 273
  National Maritime Intelligence Center, 287, 288
  of national policy, 254
  National Reconnaissance Office, 288
  national vs. homeland security, 273
  Office of Naval Intelligence, 281
  U.S. Army, 285
  U.S. Marine Corps, 284
DHS directorates, 49; *see also* Federal Law Enforcement Training Center (FLETC); Federal Protective Service; Office of—Secretary of DHS; U.S. Coast Guard (USCG); U.S. Secret Service
  Directorate for Management, 52
  Directorate for National Protection and Programs, 49–51
  Directorate for Science and Technology, 51–52
DIA, *see* Defense Intelligence Agency (DIA)
Digital Library, 303
Direction finding (DF), 113
Directorate for Management, 52
Directorate for National Protection and Programs, 49
  Cyber Storm participants, 50
  infrastructure sectors, 51
  internet exercises, 50
  sectors, 50
Directorate for Science and Technology, 51–52, 351–352; *see also* Central Intelligence Agency (CIA)
Directorate of Intelligence, 350; *see also* Central Intelligence Agency (CIA)
  prominent sections, 350–351
Director of National Intelligence, 347; *see also* Office of the Director of National Intelligence (ODNI)
Dirty bomb, 162, 163; *see also* Radiological dispersal device (RDD); Weapons of mass destruction (WMD)
  and disaster drills, 165
  mock exercise on, 348
  secondary and cultural effects of, 164
Disaster
  natural, 61, 155, 519
  preparedness, 231
  response skills, 231
Disaster Field Training Organization (DFTO), 224
Disaster Operations and Recovery courses, 223
Discussion-based exercises, 227
Disease outbreak; *see also* Biological Incident Annex
  confirmation, 566–567
  deduction, 566
  determination, 566
Disease transmission, 564
DLSGP, *see* Driver's License Security Grant Program (DLSGP)
DNDO, *see* Domestic Nuclear Detection Office (DNDO)
Document fraud, 396
DoD, *see* Department of Defense (DoD)
DOI, *see* Department of the Interior (DOI)
DOJ, *see* Department of Justice (DOJ)
Domestic counterterrorism, 96
Domestic Nuclear Detection Office (DNDO), 54, 109, 157–158; *see also* Nuclear facility
  objectives of, 109, 111
  organization chart, 159
Domestic Outreach Plan, 424
Domestic terrorism, 17
  before 9/11 events, 18
  cross lighting ceremony, 18
  Kaczynski, Ted, 21, 22–23
  motivations, 21
  State Department bombing, 19
  Weather Underground, 19–20
  World Trade Center bombing, 20, 21
Domestic Terrorism and Hate Crimes Training Program (DTHCTP), 65
DoS, *see* Denial of Service (DoS)
DOS, *see* Department of State (DOS)
Drill, 227

Driver's License Security Grant Program (DLSGP), 217
DTHCTP, *see* Domestic Terrorism and Hate Crimes Training Program (DTHCTP)
DTRA, *see* Defense Threat Reduction Agency (DTRA)

E

E&T, *see* Education and training (E&T)
EAS, *see* Emergency Alert System (EAS)
Economic consequence, 542
Economics Group, 203
Education and training (E&T), 446
Einstein, 196
  data collection infrastructure and process, 198
Ellis Island, New Jersey, 389
Emergency Alert System (EAS), 114
Emergency Management Institute (EMI), 208, 222
  course offerings, 222–223
  critical infrastructure and key resources, 225
  firefighters in training at, 224
Emergency Management Performance Grants (EMPG), 218
Emergency Operations Center (EOC), 580, 581, 583, 586
  Grant Program, 217
Emergency Preparedness Directorate (EPD), 160
Emergency Preparedness Project Office (EPPO), 160
Emergency Response Plan (ERP), 473
Emergency Support Function (ESF), 561
EMI, *see* Emergency Management Institute (EMI)
EMPG, *see* Emergency Management Performance Grants (EMPG)
Encephalitis, 169, 490
Engaging Private Security to Promote Homeland Security, 201
Environmental Protection Agency (EPA), 470, 563
EOC, *see* Emergency Operations Center (EOC)
EPA, *see* Environmental Protection Agency (EPA)
EPD, *see* Emergency Preparedness Directorate (EPD)
Epidemics
  controlling, 486, 569–571
  flu, 498
EPPO, *see* Emergency Preparedness Project Office (EPPO)
Epsilon toxin, 169
Equipment list, approved, 218–219
ERP, *see* Emergency Response Plan (ERP)
ESF, *see* Emergency Support Function (ESF)
Espionage, 345, 357
Evaluation, 542
E-Verify logo, 125
Executive branch
  in funding, 92
  view of infrastructure, 79
Executive order, *see* Homeland Security executive orders
Exemplary program, 316
Exercise Evaluation and Improvement Planning, 226
Exercise Planning and Conduct, 226
Exercises, *see* Training and exercises in Homeland Security
Exigent circumstances, 84
Expansionism, curbing, 520–523
Explosive detection system, 116
Explosive devices, traditional, 185; *see also* Improvised explosive device (IED)

F

FAA, *see* Federal Aviation Administration (FAA)
Facility security plans (FSPs), 436
FBI, *see* Federal Bureau of Investigation (FBI)
FCC, *see* Federal Communications Commission (FCC)
FDA, *see* U.S. Food and Drug Administration (FDA)
FE, *see* Functional exercise (FE)
Federal Air Marshals, 410
Federal Air Marshal Service, 111, 410, 411
Federal Aviation Administration (FAA), 404
Federal broadcast system, 298
Federal Building, Oklahoma City, 21; *see also* McVeigh, Timothy
Federal Bureau of Investigation (FBI), 96, 228, 337, 562; *see also* Intelligence
  analysis of intelligence, 346
  benefits of active collaboration, 346
  education, 347
  investigations, 338
  investigators at work, 338
  JTTFs, 340–342
  mock exercise on dirty bomb, 348
  NSB, 343–346
  seal, 338
Federal Communications Commission (FCC), 114
Federal disaster assistance administration, 298

Federal Emergency Management Agency (FEMA), 55, 123, 298, 326; *see also* Office of G&T
biological agent categorization, 165
construction guidelines, 314
cycle of preparedness, 304
debris removal in Louisiana, 320
Digital Library, 303
directorates, 301
Disaster Relief Act of 1974, 328n2
discussion questions, 327
duration estimates for emergency events, 307
exemplary program, 316
exercises, 327
extensive grant programs and, 215
flood events, 313
FloodSmart program, 315, 316
flood threats, 312
hazard forms cross-references, 305
HAZUS, 307
historical foundation for, 298
initiatives, 311
internet exercise, 301, 304, 312, 314, 315
MAP MOD program, 315
mission, 299
mitigation role in preparedness model, 309–318
mitigation teams, 318
National Advisory Council, 301
national chemical stockpile, 306
national response framework, 320–325
natural disaster and, 519
organization chart, 300
Paramount in San Francisco, 311
philosophy of operation, 299
post-9/11, 299–303
pre-9/11, 298–299
and preparedness, 303–309
regions, 302
repetitive loss update worksheet, 317
response and recovery, 319–320
risk concept, 141
risk management series, 310
risk reductions, 315
after storm cleanup, 306
strategic goals and GPDs alignment, 216
Federal Flight Deck Officer (FFDO), 411
Federal Highway Administration, 404
Federal Law Enforcement Training Center (FLETC), 54, 232, 393
in Glynco, 63
internet resource, 65
organizational chart, 64
strategic goals of, 62
trainee in gear ready for exercise at, 64
training exercise, 63
training provided in, 65
Federal Preparedness Agency, 298
Federal Protective Service (FPS), 49, 61, 145
Federal Railroad Administration, 447
FEMA, *see* Federal Emergency Management Agency (FEMA)
Fence, border, 117, 118, 375, 376, 519
FERN, *see* Food Emergency Response Network (FERN)
FFDO, *see* Federal Flight Deck Officer (FFDO)
Fiery cross, 18
Final Solution, 3
Finance, *see* Budgeting, finance, and funding
Fire Prevention and Safety (FP&S), 221
FirstDefenderRMTM, 92
FISA, *see* Foreign Intelligence Surveillance Act (FISA)
Fish and wildlife health and disease surveillance, 564
FLETC, *see* Federal Law Enforcement Training Center (FLETC)
Flood Map Center, 315
FloodSmart program, 315, 316
Flow process, 148
CARVER + Shock flow process possibilities, 149–150
FMD, *see* Foot and mouth disease (FMD)
FOF, *see* Force on Force (FOF)
Food and Drug Administration, *see* U.S. Food and Drug Administration (FDA)
Food Emergency Response Network (FERN), 565
Food Safety and Inspection Service (FSIS), 484
Food safety officers, 484
Foot and mouth disease (FMD), 485
Force on Force (FOF), 161
NRC Force on Force training, 161
Foreign Intelligence Surveillance Act (FISA), 32
FP&S, *see* Fire Prevention and Safety (FP&S)
FPS, *see* Federal Protective Service (FPS)
Freight carriers, 447
Freight Rail Security Grant Program (FRSGP), 218
FRSGP, *see* Freight Rail Security Grant Program (FRSGP)
FSE, *see* Full-scale exercise (FSE)
FSIS, *see* Food Safety and Inspection Service (FSIS)
FSPs, *see* Facility security plans (FSPs)
Fugitive Operations Program, 392
Fugitive operations team, 393
Full-scale exercise (FSE), 227
Function, 542
Functional exercise (FE), 227
Funding, *see* Budgeting, finance, and funding
Fusion centers, 269, 292

fusion process as continuous cycle, 270
Massachusetts Fusion Center logo, 271
Future of Homeland Security and Emergency Management, The, 521

G

G&T, *see* Grants and Training (G&T)
Game, 227
GD, *see* Soman
Geographic information system (GIS), 307, 315
Germany
deportations to extermination camps, 6
invasion of Western Europe, 4
Secure Freight Initiative, 122
Third Reich assault, 2, 3, 4
troops, 3
GIS, *see* Geographic information system (GIS)
Giuliani, Mayor Rudolph W., 322
Glanders, 169
Global Maritime Intelligence Integration Plan, 424
Global Terrorism Database, 526
Global Trade Exchange (GTX), 383
Gorbachev, Mikhail, 14
GPT, *see* Gulfport-Biloxi International Airport (GPT)
Grants and Training (G&T), 213
Great Wave, 388; *see also* U.S. Citizenship and Immigration Services
mission of, 215, 249n1
Ground-based radar, 282
GTX, *see* Global Trade Exchange (GTX)
Gulfport-Biloxi International Airport (GPT), 419

H

H1N1 virus, 497, 501, 503
H5N1 virus, 497, 500; *see also* Avian flu (AI); Pandemics
Haitian Refugee Immigration and Fairness Act (HRIFA), 389
Hamas, 24
Hantavirus, 169, 490
Hassan, Major Nidal Malik, 355, 356
Hazard, 141, 151, 542; *see also* Weapons of mass destruction (WMD)
civil, 155
deaths from natural disasters, 155
local, 157
mitigation planning, 147, 209n11
natural, 154
people affected by natural disasters, 155
HAZUS, 307
MH data extractor, 307
process flowchart, 308
software updates, 308
Headquarters of the Marine Corps (HQMC), 284
Health and Human Services (HHS), 97, 560
Healy, 518; *see also* U.S. Coast Guard (USCG)
Heating, ventilation, and air conditioning (HVAC), 580
Heydrich, Reinhard, 5
Hezbollah, 24
HHS, *see* Health and Human Services (HHS)
High-threat urban areas (HTUA), 452
High-value geographic target regions, 144
Hijackings, 26
HITRAC, 146
HLT, *see* Hurricane Liaison Team (HLT)
Homeland security, 1, 36, 74; *see also* Department of Homeland Security (DHS)
advisory system levels, 101
chemical facilities, 90–91
collaborative federalism for, 524
future, 515
Homeland Security Act of 2002, 80
laws, 85–90
Office of US-VISIT, 88–90
private sector and, 198
REAL ID Program, 86–88
SAFETY Act, 91–92
USA Patriot Act, 83–85
Homeland Security Act of 2002, 43, 80, 99
internet exercises, 43
and Posse Comitatus, 82–83
table of contents of, 81–82
Homeland Security Advisory Council (HSAC), 66, 533
agency responsible for providing support, 534
authority, 533
charter duration, 535
coordinating strategy implementation, 534
designated federal officer, 535
duties of, 534
force multiplication, 534
implementation evaluation, 534
implementing specific measures, 534
meeting frequency, 535
members, 66–67
membership, officers, and organization, 535–536
operating costs, 535
in policy development, 534
reporting to, 534
subcommittees, task forces, and working groups, 536–537
Homeland Security and public health, 470; *see also* Agriculture and food safety
discussion questions, 511–512

Homeland Security and public health (*continued*)
- exercises, 512
- pandemic threats, 497–507
- water, 470–474

Homeland Security budgeting, 92
- budget growth: 2006–2008, 119
- budget year: 2003, 94–95
- budget year: 2004, 95–102
- budget year: 2005, 102–109
- budget year: 2006, 109–113
- budget year: 2007, 113–117
- budget year: 2008, 118–123
- budget years: 2009–2010, 123–125
- budget years: 2011–2012, 125–133
- high dollar overpayments, 126–128
- total budget authority, 129, 130–131

Homeland Security executive orders, 74
- on critical infrastructure protection, 78
- DHS establishment, 75–78
- executive order 13493 of January 22, 2009, 79
- executive order 13567 of March 7, 2011, 80
- internet resources, 79
- origin of DHS, 74
- protection of infrastructure, 74–79

Homeland Security Exercise and Evaluation Program (HSEEP), 213, 225
- discussion-based exercises, 227, 228
- intent of, 226
- key component of, 225
- operations-based exercises, 227
- planning team members, 227–228, 229
- program management cycle, 226
- volumes, 226

Homeland Security Grants, 123

Homeland Security Operations Center (HSOC), 113, 114

Homeland Security Research Corporation, 199, 211n49

Homeland Security Science and Tech Advisory Committee, 66

Homeland threats, 2, 25–26
- cold war experience, 7–15
- discussion questions, 27
- domestic terrorism, 17–23
- exercises, 27
- international terrorism, 23–25
- internet exercise, 16
- protest against Vietnam War, 16
- revolution, riot, and rightful demonstration, 15
- terroristic activities by event type, 17
- twentieth-century military movements, 2–7

Homeport, *see* Operation Homeport

Hospital Preparedness Program (HPP), 492

HPN, *see* Westchester County Airport (HPN)

HPP, *see* Hospital Preparedness Program (HPP)

HQMC, *see* Headquarters of the Marine Corps (HQMC)

HRIFA, *see* Haitian Refugee Immigration and Fairness Act (HRIFA)

HSAC, *see* Homeland Security Advisory Council (HSAC)

HSEEP, *see* Homeland Security Exercise and Evaluation Program (HSEEP)

HSOC, *see* Homeland Security Operations Center (HSOC)

HTUA, *see* High-threat urban areas (HTUA)

Human consequence, 543

Human-induced hazards, 157; *see also* Hazard

Human intelligence (HUMINT), 345

HUMINT, *see* Human intelligence (HUMINT)

Hurricane; *see also* Catastrophic events
- Isabel, 318
- Katrina, 320

Hurricane Liaison Team (HLT), 312

Hussein, Saddam, 7, 180, 489

HVAC, *see* Heating, ventilation, and air conditioning (HVAC)

Hybrid Composite Container project, 425

I

IACET, *see* International Association for Continuing Education and Training (IACET)

IAD, *see* Washington Dulles International Airport (IAD)

IAEM, *see* International Association of Emergency Managers (IAEM)

IALEETP, *see* Intelligence Awareness for Law Enforcement Executives Training Program (IALEETP)

IATP, *see* Intelligence Analyst Training Program (IATP)

IBMLTP, *see* International Banking and Money Laundering Training Program (IBMLTP)

IBSGP, *see* Intercity Bus Security Grant Program (IBSGP)

ICANN, *see* Internet Corporation for Assigned Names and Numbers (ICANN)

ICE, *see* Immigration and Customs Enforcement (ICE)

ICS, *see* Incident Command System (ICS)

IED, *see* Improvised explosive device (IED)

IEMS, *see* Integrated Emergency Management System (IEMS)

IHR, *see* International Health Regulations (IHR)

IIATP, *see* Introductory Intelligence Analyst Training Program (IIATP)

IIRIRA, *see* Illegal Immigrant Reform and Immigrant Responsibility Act (IIRIRA)
IITP, *see* Internet Investigations Training Program (IITP)
Illegal Immigrant Reform and Immigrant Responsibility Act (IIRIRA), 389
Illegal immigration, 375, 519
Illinois Terrorism Task Force (ITTF), 264
  members, 264
Imagery intelligence (IMINT), 345
IMINT, *see* Imagery intelligence (IMINT)
Immigrant, 388
Immigration, 388
Immigration and Customs Enforcement (ICE), 54, 61, 392
  Child Exploitation Unit, 395
  member at work, 396
  most wanted Homeland Security fugitives, 393
  Operation Predator program, 395–396
  red flag indicators, 395
Immigration and Naturalization Service (INS), 390, *see* U.S. Citizenship and Immigration Services (USCIS)
Immigration Reform and Control Act (IRCA), 388
Implementation, 543
Importer Self-Assessment Program (ISA), 386
Import surveillance liaison officer, 484
Improvised explosive device (IED), 185
  daisy chain, 185
  delivery methods, 185, 186
  health impacts, 186–187
  IE fuels, 186
  level of harm, 187
Incapacitating agents, 177; *see also* Chemical agents
Incident, 543
  site, 564
Incident Command System (ICS), 234, 323, 249n13; *see also* National Incident Management System (NIMS)
  characteristics of, 234, 236, 249n13
  credential program, 236–237
  in NIMS publication, 241
  organization chart, 240
Incident Management Systems Integration Division, 232
IND, *see* Indianapolis International Airport (IND)
Independent Study (IS), 224
Indianapolis International Airport (IND), 419
Infectious animals, 485
Infectious disease, 489
Influenza, 498, 501; *see also* Pandemics
  awareness, 499
  law enforcement pandemic influenza planning checklist, 507
  outbreak severity, 498
  planning and response, 504–506
  prevention and response program, 500, 514n33
  timeline, 497, 514n27
  timeline of influenza A cases, 497
  WHO on, 498, 514n31
Information infrastructure, 188
Information Operations Center Analysis Group, 350
Infrastructure, 40
  critical, 142
  protection, 74
  sectors, 50
Infrastructure Protection Program, 272
INS, *see* Immigration and Naturalization Service (INS)
INSCOM, *see* Intelligence and Security Command (INSCOM)
Inspection and Compliance Directorate, 435, 436
Inspection authority, rail transit, 449
Integrated Emergency Management System (IEMS), 299
Integrated Risk Management, 543–544
Intellectual property rights (IPR), 394
Intelligence, 252, 332, 363–364; *see also* Central Intelligence Agency (CIA); Defense Intelligence Agency (DIA); Federal Bureau of Investigation (FBI); Office of the Director of National Intelligence (ODNI)
  around 9/11, 335
  agencies, 335
  American intelligence community, 337
  cycle, 332
  disciplines, 333
  discussion questions, 364–365
  exercises, 365–366
  gathering matrix, 333
  organizations, 40
  sharing, 356
Intelligence Analyst Training Program (IATP), 65
Intelligence and Security Command (INSCOM), 285
  subordinate commands, 286–287
Intelligence Awareness for Law Enforcement Executives Training Program (IALEETP), 65
Intelligence community, 66
  American, 337
  covert, 349
  Office of the Executive, 357

Intelligence gathering and sharing, 280
  Air Force Intelligence, 281–284
  ONI, 281
  U.S. Army, 285
  USMC, 284
Intent, 544
Intentional Hazard, 544
Interagency cooperation, 158, 241
  in maritime threat affairs, 420
Interagency Coordinating Council on Emergency Preparedness and Individuals with Disabilities, 66
Intercity Bus Security Grant Program (IBSGP), 218
Intercity Passenger Rail Program (IPR-Amtrack Program), 218
International Association for Continuing Education and Training (IACET), 224
International Association of Emergency Managers (IAEM), 224
International Banking and Money Laundering Training Program (IBMLTP), 65
International Health Regulations (IHR), 564
International Outreach and Coordination Strategy, 423
International Standards Organization (ISO), 425
Internet Corporation for Assigned Names and Numbers (ICANN), 67
Internet exercises and resources
  ACE program, 388
  advisory panels and committees, 67
  AFG grants, 221
  Army Intelligence Service, 287
  ASIS, 200
  biological weapons, 173
  biometric applications, 419
  careers, 410, 456, 485
  CARVER software, 151
  chemical facility registration process, 122
  chemical threats, 177
  CHER-CAP, 232
  Citizen Corps, 273
  cold war, 8, 9
  collaboration and partnerships course, 204
  C-TPAT membership, 386
  cutting-edge practices, 308
  cyber threats, 192
  DHA, 42
  DHS fact sheet, 398
  DIA, 361, 362
  Directorate for National Protection and Programs, 49
  Directorate for Science and Technology, 52
  DTRA, 291
  EAS system, 115
  EMI, 225
  executive orders, 79
  FBI, 339
  Federal Law Enforcement Training Center, 65
  Federal Protective Service, 61
  FEMA, 301, 314
  flu epidemics, 498
  fusion center, 270, 271
  HITRAC, 146
  Homeland Security Act of 2002, 43
  Homeland threats, 16
  Homeport functions, 437
  HTUAs, 452
  ICE, 396
  immigration history, 390
  language of the act, 422
  marine interdiction agent job announcement, 380
  NAC biographies, 301
  National Dam Safety Program, 311
  National Vulnerability Center, 196
  NBACC, 100
  neighborhood's flood potential, 315
  NIMS plan, 233, 241
  NRC fact sheet, 165
  ODNI's electronic reading room, 354
  Office of US-VISIT, 90
  passport fraud, 397
  PASS program, 451
  plague, 172
  RASCAL, 162
  ricin contamination, 180
  SAFETY Act, 91
  SAR program, 429
  search and rescue tutorial, 232
  Southwest Border Fence, 376
  survival steps, 164
  2006 budget, 113
  USA Patriot Act, 85
  USCIS, 102
  U.S. Secret Service, 60
  US-VISIT program, 398
  VIPR teams, 132
  vulnerability assessments of chemical facilities, 180
Internet Investigations Training Program (IITP), 65
Internet Protocol Camera Program (IPCP), 65
Introductory Intelligence Analyst Training Program (IIATP), 65
IPCP, *see* Internet Protocol Camera Program (IPCP)
IPR, *see* Intellectual property rights (IPR)
IPR-Amtrack Program, *see* Intercity Passenger Rail Program (IPR-Amtrack Program)

Iraq
- biological agents, 489
- Department of Defense, 280
- national and homeland security contrast, 273
- private sector security, 200, 206
- significant terrorist incidents, 180

IRCA, *see* Immigration Reform and Control Act (IRCA)
Iron Curtain, 8
IS, *see* Independent Study (IS)
ISA, *see* Importer Self-Assessment Program (ISA)
Isabel, hurricane, 318
Islamic Jihad, 26
ISO, *see* International Standards Organization (ISO)
ITTF, *see* Illinois Terrorism Task Force (ITTF)

J

Jacksonville International Airport (JAX), 419
Jacobs, John, 19
Japanese imperialism, 5
JAX, *see* Jacksonville International Airport (JAX)
Jihad and jihadists, 26
JITF-CT, *see* Joint Intelligence Task Force for Combating Terrorism (JITF-CT)
JOC, *see* Joint Operations Center (JOC)
Joint Chiefs of Staff, 277
Joint Intelligence Task Force for Combating Terrorism (JITF-CT), 362
Joint Operations Center (JOC), 569
Joint Terrorism Task Forces (JTTFs), 340, 575; *see also* Federal Bureau of Investigation (FBI)
- Albany, 342
- duration estimates for emergency events, 342

JTTFs, *see* Joint Terrorism Task Forces (JTTFs)

K

Kaczynski, Ted, 21, 22–23
Katrina, hurricane, 319–321
- Post-Katrina Emergency Reform Act of 2006, 215

Kennedy, John F. (President), 11
Khobar Towers bombing, 24
Khrushchev, Nikita, 12
King, Dr. Martin Luther, Jr., 15
KKK, *see* Ku Klux Klan (KKK)
Korean War, 11
Ku Klux Klan (KKK), 15, 28n4
- jihadist contrast, 2
- terror, 17

Ku Klux Klansman, 2

L

Laboratory Response Network (LRN), 562
Lackawanna Six, 341
Law enforcement officers, 411
Law Enforcement Terrorism Prevention Program (LETPP), 272
Laws, *see* Homeland security—laws
Lebanon, *see* Beirut, Lebanon
Legal authority, 74
Legal Immigration Family Equity Act (LIFE), 389
Lessons Learned Information Sharing (LLIS. gov), 228
- homepage, 230
- types of, 230
- webpage, 231

LETPP, *see* Law Enforcement Terrorism Prevention Program (LETPP)
LIFE, *see* Legal Immigration Family Equity Act (LIFE)
Lighted cross, 18
Likelihood, 544–545
Line of bearing (LOB), 113
LIT, *see* Little Rock National Airport (LIT)
Little Rock National Airport (LIT), 419
LLIS. gov, *see* Best Practices (LLIS. gov); Lessons Learned Information Sharing (LLIS. gov)
LOB, *see* Line of bearing (LOB)
Location tracking, rail transit, 448
Long-range radar technology, 111
Louisiana State Homeland Security strategy, 263
LRN, *see* Laboratory Response Network (LRN)
Lung agents, *see* Choking agents

M

Mad Cow Disease, 485
Malicious software, 191
Man-made disasters, 61
MAP MOD program, 315
Marine Asset Tag Tracking System (MATTS), 425, 426
Marine Operations Coordination Plan (MOC), 420
Maritime Commerce Security Plan, 423
Maritime Infrastructure Recovery Plan, 423

Maritime, Island and Remotes and Extreme Environment Security (MIREES), 527
Maritime Law Enforcement Academy, 431
  patch, 432
Maritime Operational Threat Response (MOTR), 420
Maritime Security, 420; *see also* U.S. Coast Guard (USCG)
  Borders and Marine Division, 424–426
  Coast Guard role in, 426
  maritime domain, 421
  maritime plans, 423–424
  MOC plan, 420
  MTS Security Plan, 424
  National Plan to Achieve Maritime Domain Awareness, 424
  national strategy for, 422–423
Maritime Security Response Team (MSRT), 434
Maritime Security Transportation Act of 2002, 421
Maritime Transportation System Security Plan (MTS Security Plan), 424
MASINT, *see* Measurement and signatures intelligence (MASINT)
Massachusetts Fusion Center logo, 271
Massachusetts Homeland Security regions, 269
Mass transit, *see* Rail and mass transit
Master Exercise Practitioner Program (MEPP), 222
Master Trainer Program courses, 222–223
MATs, *see* Mitigation Assessment Teams (MATs)
MATTS, *see* Marine Asset Tag Tracking System (MATTS)
McGinley, Ian Patrick, 201, 211n53
MCO, *see* Orlando International Airport (MCO)
McVeigh, Timothy, 21, 26
  federal building bombing, 21
  VBIED attack, 87
Measurement and signatures intelligence (MASINT), 345
Medical response, 569
Megaports, 383
Memoranda of agreement (MOAs), 584
MEPP, *see* Master Exercise Practitioner Program (MEPP)
Metropolitan area, 268
Metropolitan Medical Response System (MMRS), 227
Military/defense units, specialized, 287
  NMIC, 287
  NRO, 288
  WMD and DTRA, 290
  WMD CSTs, 288
Military tactic, 278
Millimeter wave, 528
  imaging technology, 416
MIREES, *see* Maritime, Island and Remotes and Extreme Environment Security (MIREES)
Missile and Space Intelligence Center, 362
Mission consequence, 545
Mitigation, 309
  planning, 315
Mitigation Assessment Teams (MATs), 312
Mitigation Branch courses, 223
MMRS, *see* Metropolitan Medical Response System (MMRS)
MOAs, *see* Memoranda of agreement (MOAs)
Mobile tactical unit, 450, 451; *see also* Amtrak
MOC, *see* Marine Operations Coordination Plan (MOC)
Model, 545
MOTR, *see* Maritime Operational Threat Response (MOTR)
MQ-1 Predator, 284
MSRT, *see* Maritime Security Response Team (MSRT)
MTS Security Plan, *see* Maritime Transportation System Security Plan (MTS Security Plan)
Mueller III, Robert S., 339, 340
Mutual Aid Agreement, 244, 552

N

NACARA, *see* Nicaraguan Adjustment and Central American Relief Act (NACARA)
Nagin, Ray, 320, 322
Napolitano, Janet, 46–47
National Advisory Council, 301
National and homeland security, 273
  army personnel in Afghanistan, 280
  civil cooperation, 276–277
  DoD and homeland security, 277–280
  intelligence gathering and sharing, 280
  military assistance, 276
  rates of civilian deaths, 279
  specialized military/defense units, 287
  strategic objectives and critical areas of concern, 279
National Biodefense Analysis and Countermeasures Center (NBACC), 100
  interim capability, 100
  internet resources, 100
  safety measures, 100–101
National Bioforensics Analysis Center, 526
National Biosurveillance Integration System (NBIS), 566

National Capital Region Air Defense program, 115
National Capital Region Coordination, 215
National Center for Border Security and Immigration (NCBSI), 526–527
National Center for Food Protection and Defense (NCFPD), 525
National Center for Medical Intelligence, 362
National Clandestine Service (NCS), 351
National Commission on 9/11, 31
National Counterterrorism Center (NCTC), 355–356, 562; *see also* Counterterrorism; Office of the Director of National Intelligence (ODNI)
  mission of, 354
  seal, 355
National Cyber Alert System, 189
National Cyber Response Coordination Group, 194
National Cyber Security Awareness Month, 108
National Cyber Security Center, 43
National Cyber Security Division (NCSD), 106, 192, 205
  Cyberspace Response System, 194
  fundamental objectives, 193
  US-CERT, 195
National Cyberspace Response System, 193
National Dam Safety Program (NDSP), 311
National defense, 57, 427
National Defense Industrial Association (NDIA), 202, 211n56
National Domestic Preparedness Consortium logo, 218
National Earthquake Hazards Reduction Plan (NEHRP), 309, 310
National Emergency Management Association (NEMA), 224
National Emergency Responder Credentialing System, 236
National Emergency Training Center (NETC), 224
National Exercise Program (NEP), 219
National fire prevention control office, 298
National Flood Insurance Program (NFIP), 318
  flood events covered by, 313
National Foreign Intelligence Program, 288, 289
National Fugitive Operations Program (NFOP), 392
  fugitive operations teams, 393
National Guard, 274
National Hurricane Program (NHP), 312
National Incident Management System (NIMS), 106, 108, 123, 192, 213, 232; *see also* Incident Command System (ICS)
  certification, 242–243
  class list, 240
  compliance mandates, 237–239
  compliance standards of 2008, 235–236
  implementation activity schedule, 246–247
  incident radio communications plan, 245
  interagency cooperation, 241
  mandate, 233
  mutual aid agreement, 241, 244
  organization chart, 233
  program components, 234
National Infrastructure Advisory Council, 66
National infrastructure bank, *see* National Infrastructure Reinvestment Corporation (NIRC)
National Infrastructure Protection Plan (NIPP), 123, 272, 446, 484
National Infrastructure Reinvestment Corporation (NIRC), 42
National Institute of Health, 500
National Integration Center (NIC), 232
  organization chart, 233
National Intelligence Council (NIC), 358; *see also* Office of the Director of National Intelligence (ODNI)
  NIO, 359, 361
  responsibilities, 358–359
  2025 projected global landscape, 360
National intelligence estimates (NIEs), 359
National intelligence officers (NIOs), 359
  functions for, 359
  recruitment announcement, 361
National Intelligence program (NIP), 353
National Intelligence Strategy, 356
National Inventory of Dams, 311
National Level Exercise (NLE), 219
Nationally recognized professional emergency management and related organizations, 224
National Maritime Intelligence Center (NMIC), 287
  threats, 288
National Operations Center (NOC), 562
National Performance of Dams Program, 311
National Pharmaceutical Stockpile (NPS), 98, 495
  CDC stockpiles, 496
National Plan to Achieve Maritime Domain Awareness, 424
National Policy, challenge of, 254
  Citizen Corps, 272
  funding and local initiatives, 271
  fusion centers, 269–271
  FY2010 enacted and FY2011 budget request, 265
  Louisiana State Homeland Security strategy, 263

National Policy, challenge of *(continued)*
  Massachusetts Homeland Security regions, 269
  Pennsylvania Homeland Security regions, 268
  regional program, 268
  structure at local level, 268–269
  structure at state level, 254–268
National Preparedness Directorate (NPD), 303
National Preparedness Goal, 123
National Preparedness Guidelines, 271
National Preparedness Integration Program, 114
National Reconnaissance Office (NRO), 288, 289
National Response Framework (NRF), 222, 271–272, 320
  command structure, 323
  internet exercise, 320, 324
  response doctrine key principles, 320
  response plan, 324, 325
National Response Plan (NRP), 123
National Security Agency, 286
National Security Agency/Central Security Service Georgia (NSA/CSS Georgia), 286
National Security Branch (NSB), 343; *see also* Federal Bureau of Investigation (FBI)
  initiatives, 343
  mission and vision of, 343
  organizational chart, 344
  TSC, 345
National Select Agent Registry Program, 496
  CDC reporting form, 596, 597, 598, 599
National Special Security Event (NSSE), 60
National stockpile, 98
National Strategy for Maritime Security, 422–423
  implementation, 463
National Strategy for Pandemic Influenza, 501
National Strategy to Secure Cyberspace, 192
National Targeting Center (NTC), 105, 374
National Terrorism Advisory System (NTAS), 102
  alert, 103
National Threat Assessment Center (NTAC), 60
National Transportation Security Center of Excellence (NTSCOE), 527
National Vessel Documentation Center, 440
National Vulnerability Center, 196
Natural barriers, 376
Natural disasters, 61, 155, 519
Natural hazard, 545
Naturalization self-test, 391
NBACC, *see* National Biodefense Analysis and Countermeasures Center (NBACC)
NBIS, *see* National Biosurveillance Integration System (NBIS)
NCBSI, *see* National Center for Border Security and Immigration (NCBSI)
NCFPD, *see* National Center for Food Protection and Defense (NCFPD)
NCS, *see* National Clandestine Service (NCS)
NCSD, *see* National Cyber Security Division (NCSD)
NCTC, *see* National Counterterrorism Center (NCTC)
NDIA, *see* National Defense Industrial Association (NDIA)
NDSP, *see* National Dam Safety Program (NDSP)
Negroponte, John, 353
NEHRP, *see* National Earthquake Hazards Reduction Plan (NEHRP)
Nellis Air Force Base, 163
NEMA, *see* National Emergency Management Association (NEMA)
NEP, *see* National Exercise Program (NEP)
Nerve agents, 177, 180; *see also* Chemical agents
  sarin, 180
  soman, 180, 181
  tabun, 180–181, 182–184
  VX, 180, 181
NETC, *see* National Emergency Training Center (NETC)
Network, 545–546
Network Operations Workstation (NOW), 454
New York Police Department (NYPD), 322
NFIP, *see* National Flood Insurance Program (NFIP)
NFOP, *see* National Fugitive Operations Program (NFOP)
NGO, *see* Nongovernmental organization (NGO)
NHP, *see* National Hurricane Program (NHP)
NIC, *see* National Integration Center (NIC); National Intelligence Council (NIC)
Nicaraguan Adjustment and Central American Relief Act (NACARA), 389
NIEs, *see* National intelligence estimates (NIEs)
NII, *see* Nonintrusive inspection system (NII)
NIMS, *see* National Incident Management System (NIMS)
9/11 Commission, 39, 349
NIOs, *see* National intelligence officers (NIOs)
NIP, *see* National Intelligence program (NIP)
Nipah virus, 169
NIPP, *see* National Infrastructure Protection Plan (NIPP)
NIRC, *see* National Infrastructure Reinvestment Corporation (NIRC)
Nixon, Richard, 11, 13
NLE, *see* National Level Exercise (NLE)

NMIC, *see* National Maritime Intelligence Center (NMIC)
NOC, *see* National Operations Center (NOC)
Nongovernmental organization (NGO), 202, 237
Nonintrusive inspection system (NII), 425
Nonprofit Security Grant Program (NSGP), 217
NORAD, *see* North American Aerospace Defense Command (NORAD)
Normandy fencing, 377
Norman Mineta San Jose International Airport (SJC), 419
North American Aerospace Defense Command (NORAD), 282
  command center, 282
  geographic regions, 283
  mission, 283
NORTHCOM, *see* United States Northern Command (USNORTHCOM, or NORTHCOM)
NOW, *see* Network Operations Workstation (NOW)
NPD, *see* National Preparedness Directorate (NPD)
NPS, *see* National Pharmaceutical Stockpile (NPS)
NRC, *see* Nuclear Regulatory Commission (NRC)
NRF, *see* National Response Framework (NRF)
NRO, *see* National Reconnaissance Office (NRO)
NRP, *see* National Response Plan (NRP)
NSA/CSS Georgia, *see* National Security Agency/Central Security Service Georgia (NSA/CSS Georgia)
NSB, *see* National Security Branch (NSB)
NSGP, *see* Nonprofit Security Grant Program (NSGP)
NSIR, *see* Nuclear Security and Incident Response (NSIR)
NSSE, *see* National Special Security Event (NSSE)
NTAC, *see* National Threat Assessment Center (NTAC)
NTAS, *see* National Terrorism Advisory System (NTAS)
NTC, *see* National Targeting Center (NTC)
NTSCOE, *see* National Transportation Security Center of Excellence (NTSCOE)
Nuclear facility, 160; *see also* Domestic Nuclear Detection Office (DNDO)
  nuclear power plant, 158
  nuclear specialist at Nellis Air Force base, 163
  nuclear terrorism, 160
  protection officer at, 160
  security program for, 160–161
Nuclear Regulatory Commission (NRC), 158, 205
  Force on Force training, 161
  interface with DHS, 162
Nuclear Security and Incident Response (NSIR), 160
Nuclear terrorism, 160
Nuclear weapon, 156
  WMD, 156–162
NYPD, *see* New York Police Department (NYPD)

O

OAK, *see* Oakland International Airport (OAK)
Oakland International Airport (OAK), 419
ODNI, *see* Office of the Director of National Intelligence (ODNI)
Office of
  Asian Pacific, Latin American, and African Analysis, 350
  Chief Procurement, 123
  Civil Rights and Civil Liberties, 48
  Clandestine Services, 351; *see also* Central Intelligence Agency (CIA)
  Near Eastern and South Asian Analysis, 350–351
  General Counsel, 48
  Health, 52
  Innovation, 122, 350
  Intelligence and Analysis, 253, 335, 336
  Intelligence Czar, 363; *see also* Office of the Director of National Intelligence (ODNI)
  Iraq Analysis, 350
  Legislative Affairs, 48
  Management and Budget, 96
  Operations Coordination, 54
  Policy, 52, 202
  Policy Support, 351
  Russian and European Analysis, 351
  Secretary of DHS, 45–48
  Support, 352; *see also* Central Intelligence Agency (CIA)
  Terrorism Analysis, 351
  Transnational Issues, 351
Office of G&T, 215; *see also* Federal Emergency Management Agency (FEMA)
  equipment purchase funding, 218–219
  mission, 215
  strategy implementation chart, 217
  TOPOFF, 219, 220
  2011 grant cycle, 217

Office of Homeland Security (OHS), 471; *see also* Homeland security
Office of Naval Intelligence (ONI), 281
Office of Strategic Trade's (OST), 386
Office of the Director of National Intelligence (ODNI), 352; *see also* Intelligence
  authorities and duties, 353
  mission of, 354
  NCTC, 355–356
  NIC, 358–360
  ONCIX, 356
  seal of, 355
Office of the Inspector General (OIG), 196
Office of the National Counterintelligence Executive (ONCIX), 356; *see also* Office of the Director of National Intelligence (ODNI)
  intelligence community, 357–358
  organizational chart, 358
  poster, 357
OHS, *see* Office of Homeland Security (OHS)
OIG, *see* Office of the Inspector General (OIG)
Oklahoma City bombing, 187, 299, 339
ONCIX, *see* Office of the National Counterintelligence Executive (ONCIX)
ONI, *see* Office of Naval Intelligence (ONI)
Open-source intelligence (OSINT), 346
Operation Homeport, 437; *see also* U.S. Coast Guard (USCG)
  container inspection, 439
  inspection, 438
  port and harbor facilities, 437
  vessel inspection, 440–443
Operation Noble Eagle, 435
Operations-based exercises, 227
Operations Directorate, 117
Operations Security for Public Safety Agencies Counterterrorism Training Program (OPSACTP), 65
OPSACTP, *see* Operations Security for Public Safety Agencies Counterterrorism Training Program (OPSACTP)
Organizational chart
  DHS, 41, 44, 253
  FLETC, 64
  Management Directorate organizational chart, 53
  NSB, 344
  Office of Intelligence and Analysis, 253, 336
  ONCIX, 358
Organizational excellence, 38
Orlando International Airport (MCO), 419
OSINT, *see* Open-source intelligence (OSINT)
OST, *see* Office of Strategic Trade's (OST)

P

PACER, *see* Preparedness and Catastrophic Event Response (PACER)
Pan American Health Organization, 572
Pandemic flu, 497; *see also* Pandemics
  human flu pandemics, timeline of, 501–503
  seasonal flu vs., 498
Pandemics, 497, 498; *see also* Influenza
  categories, 497
  creating awareness, 499
  federal government response stages, 505
  global pandemic phases, 505
  H1N1timeline, 497
  H5N1 virus, 500
  human flu pandemics, timeline of, 501–503
  influenza planning checklist, 507, 508–510
  influenza viruses, 498
  planning and response, 500–507
Paperless Boarding Pass program, 419, 420
Paramount in San Francisco, 311
Partner ports, 384
Partners for Amtrak Safety and Security Program (PASS), 451
PASS, *see* Partners for Amtrak Safety and Security Program (PASS)
Passenger screening, 451
Passive radiation detection, 383
Patriot Act, *see* USA Patriot Act
Pennsylvania Homeland Security regions, 268
Pentagon, 33, 273, 275
PHMRF, *see* Precast Hybrid Movement Resistant Frame (PHMRF)
PHOTINT, *see* Photo intelligence (PHOTINT)
Photo intelligence (PHOTINT), 345
PIH, *see* Poisonous by inhalation materials (PIH)
Plague (*Yersinia pestis*), 171
  kinds of, 172
Plum Island Animal Disease Center, 487
Plum Island Facility, 486
Pneumonic plague, 172; *see also* Plague (*Yersinia pestis*)
POEs, *see* Ports of Entry (POEs)
Poisonous by inhalation materials (PIH), 452
Portland Seven, 341
Port Security Grant Program (PSGP), 218
Ports of Entry (POEs), 378
Posse Comitatus Act, 82–83; *see also* Homeland Security Act of 2002
Post-9/11 developments; *see also* September 11, 2001 (9/11)
  advisory panels and committees, 65–68
  Department of Homeland Security, 29, 68
  directorates, 49–52
  discussion questions, 69
  evolution and change, 38–43

exercises, 70
Federal Emergency Management Agency, 298
Federal Law Enforcement Training Center, 54
Federal Protective Service, 61
Office of the Secretary of DHS, 45–48
2001–2003, 36–38
U.S. Coast Guard, 54
U.S. Secret Service, 54
Post-Katrina Emergency Reform Act of 2006, 215
Potsdam Convention, 7
Prairie Fire, 20
Pralidoxime chloride (2-PAM), 181
Pre-9/11 developments; *see also* September 11, 2001 (9/11)
domestic terrorism, 18
Federal Emergency Management Agency, 298
international terrorism, 23–25
Precast Hybrid Movement Resistant Frame (PHMRF), 311
Predator B UAV, 375
Predator drone, 282
Preparedness and Catastrophic Event Response (PACER), 525–526
President's Daily Brief, 350
Prevention, 38
of future terrorist attacks, 456
Privacy Office, 48
Private sector, 198
business and commercial sectors, 199
constitution of committee, 204
Economics Group, 203
facet of, 199
and law enforcement coordination, 201–202
NDIA, 202
office, 202, 203
Outreach Group, 203
Private Sector Office, 202–203
public–private partnerships, 202
security personnel with Iraqi citizens, 200
Private sector justice, 74, 199, 200, 201
Privatization, 200; *see also* Private sector
Probabilistic Risk Assessment, 546
Probability, 546
Process flow diagram, 148
Project BioShield, 493
acquisition activity, 495
goals of, 493
medical countermeasure programs, 494
Project impact, 299
Project Shield America, 390
exported technology types, 390–391
logo, 392
Protective measures, 573
contingency and continuity plans, 593–594
employee and public communications, 590–593
information and intelligence, 573–575
information technology and communication systems, 586–589
regional coordination, 584–586
security and emergency management seq., 575–584
Protective services, 59
PSGP, *see* Port Security Grant Program (PSGP)
PSIC Grant Program, *see* Public Safety Interoperable Communications Grant Program (PSIC Grant Program)
Psittacosis, 169
Psychological Consequence, 546
Public health, *see* Homeland Security and public health
Public Health Security and Bioterrorism Preparedness and Response Act of 2002, 471
Public–private partnership, 203
Public Safety Interoperable Communications Grant Program (PSIC Grant Program), 272
Public water systems (PWS), 471
Pulmonary agents, *see* Choking agents
Push Packages, 99
Putin, Vladimir (President), 14
PWS, *see* Public water systems (PWS)

Q

Q fever, 169
Qualitative Risk Assessment Methodology, 547
Quantitative Risk Assessment Methodology, 547

R

R&D, *see* Research and development (R&D)
Radiation detection monitors, 105
Radiation exposure; *see also* Weapons of mass destruction (WMD)
determination of effects of, 163
pathways, 164
Radiation monitor, 105
Radiation portal monitor, 383
Radio frequency (RF), 416
Radiography, 383
advanced, 116
image of truck, 117

Radiological Assessment System for Consequence Analysis (RASCAL), 162
Radiological dispersal device (RDD), 162
Radiological Emergency Preparedness Program, 215, 304
Radiological WMD, 162–165
Rail and mass transit, 443; *see also* Transportation Security Administration (TSA)
  Amtrak, 450–451
  CSX, 451–455
  DHS rules, 448–449
  discussion questions, 464–465
  high-speed passenger train, 444
  initiatives in, 449–450
  mass transit security training program, 458–461
  railroads, 452
  railway route map, 456
  representative security programs for, 449
  rules on rail shipments, 452
  SEPTA, 455–457
  TSA recommendations, 445–447
  types of goods delivered by, 448
Rail secure area, 452
Rail security coordinator (RSC), 448
Rail security sensitive material, 452
Rail transit system, *see* Rail and mass transit
RAMP, *see* Risk Assessment and Management Program (RAMP)
RASCAL, *see* Radiological Assessment System for Consequence Analysis (RASCAL)
Rationing, 572
Raytheon, 121
RCPSP, *see* Regional Catastrophic Preparedness Grant Program (RCPSP)
RDD, *see* Radiological dispersal device (RDD)
Readiness courses, 223
Reagan, Ronald (President), 12, 13, 14
REAL ID program, 86
  driver's license security implementation, 89
  myths and facts, 86–87
Recognizability, 148, 153
Reconstruction finance corporation, 298
Recuperability, 148, 153
Redundancy, 547
Refugees, 388
Regional Catastrophic Preparedness Grant Program (RCPSP), 217
Regional planning council, 269
Registered Traveler program (RT program), 418
  agencies in, 418–419
Regulations, *see* Homeland security—laws
Religious fanaticism, 20
Reno/Tahoe International Airport (RNO), 419
Reorganization Plan #3, 298
Repetitive loss program, 315
Repetitive loss update worksheet, 317
Report from the Task Force on State and Local Homeland Security Funding, 252, 294n1
Rescue 21, 112, 113, 136n27
Research and development (R&D), 472
Residual Risk, 547
Resilience, 547–548
Response and recovery, *see* Federal Emergency Management Agency (FEMA)
Responsibilities, 572
Return on Investment, 548
RF, *see* Radio frequency (RF)
Ricin, 177; *see also* Biotoxins
  clues indicating presence of, 179–180
  delivery methods, 179
  exercise conducted by U.S. Army, 179
Ridge, Thomas, 45
Riot control agents, 177; *see also* Chemical agents
Risk, 140, 204, 548
  acceptance, 548–549
  analysis, 549
  assessment, 143–147
  avoidance, 550
  based decision making, 554
  communication, 550
  control, 550
  critical infrastructure, 142
  decision making, 554
  DHS, 141, 142
  discussion questions, 207
  exercises, 208
  FEMA, 141
  identification, 550
  matrix, 552
  mitigation, 552
  nature of, 141–143
  perception, 552–553
  profile, 553
  quantification, 142
  reduction, 553
  score, 553
  theory analysis, 140
  tolerance, 553
  transfer, 554
Risk assessment, 143–147, 549
  methodology, 549
  tool, 549–550
Risk Assessment and Management Program (RAMP), 145–146
Risk management, 140, 551
  alternatives development, 551

asset-based vs. geographically-based risk analysis, 145
CARVER + Shock assessment tool, 148–153
cycle, 551
hazard mitigation planning, 147
high-value geographic target regions, 144
methodology, 551
nature of risk, 141–143
plan, 551
possible hazards and emergencies risk abatement, 146
risk assessment, 143–147
strategy, 552
RNO, *see* Reno/Tahoe International Airport (RNO)
Robbins, Terry, 19
Ronald Reagan Washington National Airport (DCA), 419
Routine emergency, 307, 342
Roving wiretaps, 83, 85
RSC, *see* Rail security coordinator (RSC)
RT program, *see* Registered Traveler program (RT program)
Russia, *see* Soviet system

S

S&T Directorate, 122
SAFECOM program, 112
SAFER, *see* Staffing for Adequate Fire and Emergency Response (SAFER)
SAFETY Act, *see* Support Antiterrorism by Fostering Effective Technologies Act of 2002 (SAFETY Act)
Salmonella, 169
Salt Lake City International Airport (SLC), 419
San Francisco International Airport (SFO), 419
Sarin, 180, 205
SAR team, *see* Search and rescue team (SAR team)
SBI, *see* Secure Border Initiative (SBI)
SBInet program, 119, 378
goals of, 379
SBMTP, *see* Suicide Bomber Mitigation Training Program (SBMTP)
SC, *see* Security Coordinator (SC)
Scenario, 555
SDS, *see* Students for a Democratic Society (SDS)
Seaport Security Antiterrorism Training Program (SSATP), 65
Search and rescue team (SAR team), 428; *see also* U.S. Coast Guard (USCG)
team member, 429
Seasonal flu, 498; *see also* Pandemics
vs. pandemic flu, 498
Secretary of Homeland Security, 562
Secret Service, *see* U.S. Secret Service
Sector-Specific Agencies (SSA), 446
Secure Border Initiative (SBI), 374; *see also* U.S. Customs and Border Protection (CBP)
barriers, 376
border security surveillance cameras, 376
goals of, 374–375
Normandy fencing, 377
Predator B UAV, 375
SBInet program, 378–379
Secure Carton project, 426
Secure data portal account, 387
Secure Flight, 119–120
Secure Freight Initiative (SFI), 382; *see also* U.S. Customs and Border Protection (CBP)
scan, 383
x-ray image at SFI location, 383
Secure Freight program, 122
in Hamburg, 122
SECURE™ (Systems Efficacy through Commercialization, Utilization, Relevance, and Evaluation), 446
Secure Wrap project, 426
Security Coordinator (SC), 574
Security threat assessment (STA), 418
Seminar, 227
Semi-Quantitative Risk Assessment Methodology, 555
Sensitivity Analysis, 555
SEPTA, *see* Southeastern Pennsylvania Transit Authority (SEPTA)
September 11, 2001 (9/11); *see also* World Trade Center bombing
event chronology, 34
Pentagon, 33, 275
pre-9/11 world, 298
security of a nation, 31, 70n3
SVBIED attack, 187
United Flight 93 in Shanksville, 33
Septicemic plague, 172; *see also* Plague (*Yersinia pestis*)
SFI, *see* Secure Freight Initiative (SFI)
SFI scan, 383
SFO, *see* San Francisco International Airport (SFO)
Shazhad, Faisal, 343
Shock, 153; *see also* CARVER + Shock assessment tool
SHSP, *see* State Homeland Security Program (SHSP)
SIGINT, *see* Signals intelligence (SIGINT)
Signals intelligence (SIGINT), 345

Simplification, *see* Expansionism, curbing
Simulation, 555–556
Sino-Soviet, 11
SJC, *see* Norman Mineta San Jose International Airport (SJC)
SLC, *see* Salt Lake City International Airport (SLC)
SLGCP, *see* State and Local Government Coordination and Preparedness (SLGCP)
SLTT, *see* State, local, tribal, and territorial (SLTT)
SLTTGCC, *see* State, Local, Tribal, and Territorial Government Coordinating Council (SLTTGCC)
Smallpox, 172
  rash and body lesions, 173
  Variola, 172
Sneak and peek warrants, 84
SNS, *see* Strategic National Stockpile (SNS)
Socialist Workers Party, *see* Communist Workers Party
Somalia, 24
Soman, 180, 181
Southeastern Pennsylvania Transit Authority (SEPTA), 455; *see also* Rail and mass transit
  railway route map, 456
Soviet system
  expansionism, 10
  missile assembly in Cuba, 12
  rally against election fraud in Moscow, 15
SPBIED, *see* Suicide Pedestrian-Borne Improvised Explosive Device (SPBIED)
Special Weapons and Tactics (SWAT), 227
Spectroscopic portal, 121–122
Speer, Albert, 181
Spore, 169
SPPA, *see* Strategic Partnership Program on Agroterrorism (SPPA)
Spy agencies, 11
SSA, *see* Sector-Specific Agencies (SSA)
SSATP, *see* Seaport Security Antiterrorism Training Program (SSATP)
STA, *see* Security threat assessment (STA)
Staffing for Adequate Fire and Emergency Response (SAFER), 221
Stalin, Joseph, 7
START, *see* Study of Terrorism and Responses to Terrorism (START)
State and Local Government Coordination and Preparedness (SLGCP), 112
State Department bombing, 19
State Homeland Security Office contacts, 256–262
State Homeland Security Program (SHSP), 217
State, local, tribal, and territorial (SLTT), 446
State, Local, Tribal, and Territorial Government Coordinating Council (SLTTGCC), 254
  membership criteria, 254
  working groups, 255
ST-ISAC, *see* Surface Transportation Information Sharing and Analysis Center (ST-ISAC)
Strategic Command of WMD, *see* Defense Threat Reduction Agency (DTRA)
Strategic Information and Operations Center, 569
Strategic National Stockpile (SNS), 99, 569
Strategic Partnership Program on Agroterrorism (SPPA), 483
  assessments, 484–485
  objectives of, 483–484
Strengthen Operational Capability, 114
Students for a Democratic Society (SDS), 15
Study of Terrorism and Responses to Terrorism (START), 525
Subject Matter Expert, 556
Sudetenland assault, 3
Suicide Bomber Mitigation Training Program (SBMTP), 65
Suicide Pedestrian-Borne Improvised Explosive Device (SPBIED), 186
Suicide Vehicle-Borne Improvised Explosive Device (SVBIED), 186
Support Antiterrorism by Fostering Effective Technologies Act of 2002 (SAFETY Act), 91
  approved products and services, 92
  internet resources, 91, 92
  registration as antiterrorism technology seller, 93–94
  technologies protected by, 91
Surface Transportation Information Sharing and Analysis Center (ST-ISAC), 575
SVBIED, *see* Suicide Vehicle-Borne Improvised Explosive Device (SVBIED)
SWAT, *see* Special Weapons and Tactics (SWAT)
System, 556

T

Tabletop exercise (TTX), 227
Tabun, 180–181
  card, 182–184
Target, 556
Targeted violence, 60
Task force, 20
  FBI-led, 22
  on Secure Communities, 67
Task Force on New Americans, 66

TBML, *see* Trade-based money laundering (TBML)
Tear gas, *see* Riot control agents
Ted Kaczynski, 21, 22
  cabin, 23
Templehof Airport, 10
Tennessee
  Office of Homeland Security, 264
  suspicious letter risk assessment and sample submission guidelines, 266–267
Terror, 17
Terrorism, 155; *see also* Cold war; Hazard
  acts of, 155
  attack in Lebanon, 24
  Bin Laden, Osama, 24
  domestic, 17–23
  high-risk targets for, 155
  and information infrastructure, 188
  international, 23
Terrorist, 2, 156
  aboard Flight #77, 30
Terrorist Screening Center (TSC), 345
Terrorist Threat Integration Center (TTIC), 334
  goal, 335
  logo, 334
Third Reich, 2, 3; *see also* Germany
Threats, 151, 556; *see also* Weapons of mass destruction (WMD)
  analysis, 472
  assessment, 557
  chemical, 175
  Cyber Security, 190–191
  local, 157
  rating, 142
  scheme for categorizing, 154
  types, 154–155
THSGP, *see* Tribal Homeland Security Grant Program (THSGP)
TIH, *see* Toxic by inhalation materials (TIH)
Tokyo, terrorism in, 175, 180
TOPOFF, *see* Top officials (TOPOFF)
Top officials (TOPOFF), 219
  exercises and programs, 219–221
Toxic alcohols, 177; *see also* Chemical agents
Toxic by inhalation materials (TIH), 452
Trace portal, 414, 415
Trade-based money laundering (TBML), 394
Training, 214
Training and exercises in Homeland Security, 214
  best practices, 228
  CDP, 221–222
  CERT, 231–232
  discussion questions, 248
  EMI, 222–225
  exercises, 248–249
  HSEEP, 225–228
  NIMS, 232–241, 242–243, 244, 245, 246–247
  Office of G&T, 215–221
Transit Security Grant Program (TSGP), 217
Transportation Security Administration (TSA), 404, 462, 575
  AIT, 415
  ATR, 417
  biometrics, 417–420
  canine explosive detection unit, 412–413
  canine officer, 412
  canine searching for contraband, 413
  core values, 405
  discussion questions, 464–465
  exercises, 465
  Federal Air Marshals, 410
  FFDO, 411
  law enforcement officers, 411
  millimeter wave imaging technology, 416
  mission, 407, 408
  officer at security checkpoint, 407
  organization chart, 406
  public relations campaign, 405
  puppy breeding program recruits, 413
  responsibilities, 408
  risk management programs, 413–414
  scope of jurisdiction, 407
  seal of, 410
  technology and innovation, 414
  trace portals, 414, 415
  U.S. aviation security layers, 409
Transportation Security Agency (TSA), 54, 98
  AIT, 47
  Napolitano, Janet, 47
  VIPR member, 132
Transportation Security Operation Center (TSOC), 574, 585
Tribal Homeland Security Grant Program (THSGP), 217
Truman Doctrine, 9
Truman, Harry S. (President), 7, 8
TSA, *see* Transportation Security Administration (TSA); Transportation Security Agency (TSA)
TSC, *see* Terrorist Screening Center (TSC)
TSGP, *see* Transit Security Grant Program (TSGP)
TSOC, *see* Transportation Security Operation Center (TSOC)
TTIC, *see* Terrorist Threat Integration Center (TTIC)
TTX, *see* Tabletop exercise (TTX)
Tularemia, 169
Turf
  battles, 354
  issues, 35, 39

Twentieth-century military movements, 2
Camp 731, 6
German invasion, 3, 4
internet exercise, 5
Japanese imperialism, 5
Twin Towers disaster, *see* World Trade Center bombing
2-PAM, *see* Pralidoxime chloride (2-PAM)
Typhus fever, 169

U

UAE, *see* United Arab Emirates (UAE)
UASI, *see* Urban Areas Security Initiative (UASI)
UASs, *see* Unmanned aircraft systems (UASs)
UAV, *see* Unmanned aerial vehicle (UAV)
UCC, *see* Unified Combatant Command (UCC)
UNABOM, 22
Unabomber, *see* Kaczynski, Ted
Uncertainty, 557
Unified Combatant Command (UCC), 83
Unified command, 274, 275, 323–324
Unit/Camp 731, 6
United Arab Emirates (UAE), 385
United Nations, 173
United States Computer Emergency Readiness Team (US-CERT), 188, 194, 205
cyber threats, 191
discussion questions, 207
events qualified for reporting, 196
mission, 191
NCSD, 195
OIG assessment, 196
operations, 194
responsibility, 195
United States Department of Agriculture (USDA), 562
FSIS, 484
participation in Homeland Security, 481
site visits, 486
structure for homeland protection and food safety, 481
United States Northern Command (USNORTHCOM, or NORTHCOM), 83, 275
Unmanned aerial vehicle (UAV), 375
Unmanned aircraft systems (UASs), 380
Unmanned drones, 380
Urban Areas Security Initiative (UASI), 217
Grant Program, 272
U.S. Agency for International Development, 559
Usama, *see* Bin Laden, Osama
USAMRIID, *see* U.S. Army Medical Research Institute of Infectious Diseases (USAMRIID)
USA Patriot Act, 83–85
discussion questions, 134
exercises, 135
internet resources, 85
U.S. Armed Forces WMD strategy, 290
U.S. Army, 285
U.S. Army Medical Research Institute of Infectious Diseases (USAMRIID), 100
U.S. aviation security layers, 409
U.S. Border Patrol, 116
staffing, 124
USCENTCOM, *see* U.S. Central Command (USCENTCOM)
U.S. Central Command (USCENTCOM), 275
US-CERT, *see* United States Computer Emergency Readiness Team (US-CERT)
USCG, *see* U.S. Coast Guard (USCG)
USCIS, *see* U.S. Citizenship and Immigration Services (USCIS)
U.S. Citizenship and Immigration Services (USCIS), 54, 390, 399
cornerstone initiative, 393–394
counterfeit passport, 397
Cyber Crimes Center, 394–397
discussion questions, 400
exercises, 401
functions of, 390
internet resources, 102
naturalization self-test, 391
NFOP, 392–393
Project Shield America Initiative, 390–392
US-VISIT Program, 397–398
U.S. Coast Guard (USCG), 54, 463, 517; *see also* Maritime Security; U.S. Customs and Border Protection (CBP)
application for inspection of U.S. vessel by, 441
approaching cargo ship, 56
on border patrol, 371
cargo and ports, 435
Deepwater logo, 98
deficiencies in facility inspections, 438
discussion questions, 464–465
drug removal statistics, 430
emergency safety, 427–430
exercises, 465
facility security and vulnerability measures, 439
Healy, 518
HH65 Coast Guard helicopter, 115
homeland security functions, 57
Inspection and Compliance Directorate, 436
mission of, 57

over New Orleans, 428
Operation Homeport, 437–443
Operation Noble Eagle, 435
patrol vehicles, 427
Rescue 21, 113
responsibilities, 434
role in Maritime Security, 426
SAR team member, 429
search and rescue patch, 429
security and law enforcement, 430–435
at work, 59, 112
U.S. Customs and Border Protection (CBP), 54, 104, 119, 369, 370, 398; *see also* Automated Commercial Environment (ACE); Container Security Initiative (CSI); Customs Trade Partnership Against Terrorism (C-TPAT); Secure Freight Initiative (SFI)
A&M-based program, 379–381
activities, 373–374
agent, 377
Border Patrol, 370
border protection, 373–374
cargo, 382–388
discussion questions, 400
exercises, 401
national targeting center, 374
officer, 378
organization chart, 372
patrol boat, 380
patrol plane, 381
portal observation tower, 370
SBI, 374–379
targeting systems, 104
and trade and commerce facilitation, 381
trade strategy, 382
USDA, *see* United States Department of Agriculture (USDA)
USEUCOM, *see* U.S. European Command (USEUCOM)
U.S. European Command (USEUCOM), 275
U.S. Fire Administration, 215, 232
U.S. Food and Drug Administration (FDA), 148
site visits, 486
USG, *see* U.S. government (USG)
U.S. government (USG), 484
U.S. Marine Corps (USMC), 284
CAOCL, 285
distance education techniques, 285
USMC, *see* U.S. Marine Corps (USMC)
U.S.–Mexico border, 120, 516
USNORTHCOM, *see* United States Northern Command (USNORTHCOM, or NORTHCOM)
U.S. Pacific Command (USPACOM), 275
USPACOM, *see* U.S. Pacific Command (USPACOM)
USS *Cole*, 24, 25
U.S. Secret Service, 54, 58
agents on duty, 59
goal, 60
internet exercise, 60
role, 58–59
USSOUTHCOM, *see* U.S. Southern Command (USSOUTHCOM)
U.S. Southern Command (USSOUTHCOM), 275
U.S. Strategic Command, 290
U.S. Treasury Department, 273
U.S. visa-issuing post, 398
US-VISIT, *see* U.S. Visitor and Immigrant Status Indicator Technology (US-VISIT)
U.S. Visitor and Immigrant Status Indicator Technology (US-VISIT), 88, 397
biometric information, 90
exercises, 135
goals of, 398
guiding principles of, 90
internet resources, 90
logo, 398
Program's first phase, 104
Utility security, 474

V

VACTP, *see* Vehicle Ambush Countermeasures Training Program (VACTP)
VAs, *see* Vulnerability assessments (VAs)
VBIED, *see* Vehicle-Borne Improvised Explosive Device (VBIED)
Vehicle Ambush Countermeasures Training Program (VACTP), 65
Vehicle-Borne Improvised Explosive Device (VBIED), 186
Vendor managed inventory (VMI), 99
Vesicants, *see* Blister agents
Vessel inspection, 440–443
VGT, *see* Virtual Global Taskforce (VGT)
Vietnam War, 11, 16
VIPR Teams, *see* Visual Intermodal Prevention and Response Teams (VIPR Teams)
Viral encephalitis, 169
Viral hemorrhagic fevers, 169
Virtual Global Taskforce (VGT), 395
Visual Intermodal Prevention and Response Teams (VIPR Teams), 132, 408; *see also* Transportation Security Administration (TSA)
at subway, 409

VMI, *see* Vendor managed inventory (VMI)
Vomiting agents, 177; *see also* Chemical agents
Vulnerability, 557
  rating, 141, 142
Vulnerability assessments (VAs), 469, 471, 557–558
VX, 180
  palate, 185
  symptom, 181

W

Warrants, 84
Washington Dulles International Airport (IAD), 419
Water safety, 470
  EPA vulnerability guidelines, 475–478
  oft-cited methodology, 472
  recommendation for utility security, 474
  self-assessment program, 473
  water facts, 471
  WSD, 471–472
Water Security Division (WSD), 471, 472
Waterways, 421, 422
Waugh, William L, Jr., 521, 532n7
Weapons, Intelligence, Nonproliferation, and Arms Control Center, 350
Weapons of mass destruction (WMD), 111, 155, 156, 205, 346; *see also* Dirty bomb; Hazard; Threats
  biological, 165–173
  chemical, 173–184, 185
  Civil Support Teams, 288, 289
  CSTs, 288
  directorate, 346
  discussion questions, 207
  and DTRA, 290
  improvised explosive devices, 185–187
  nuclear, 156–162
  radiological, 162–165
  scale of threat, 347
  U.S. Armed Forces WMD strategy, 290
Weapons of Mass Destruction Operations Unit (WMDOU), 562
Weapons of Mass Destruction Training Program (WMDTP), 65
Weatherman, *see* Weather Underground
Weather Underground, 16, 19–20; *see also* Students for a Democratic Society (SDS)
Westchester County Airport (HPN), 419
WHO, *see* World Health Organization (WHO)
Wildlife health and disease surveillance, 564
WIRe, *see* World Intelligence Review (WIRe)
Wiretaps, 83–84
WMD, *see* Weapons of mass destruction (WMD)
WMDOU, *see* Weapons of Mass Destruction Operations Unit (WMDOU)
WMDTP, *see* Weapons of Mass Destruction Training Program (WMDTP)
Working group, 254, 255, 536
Workshop, 227
World Health Organization (WHO), 504, 564
World Intelligence Review (WIRe), 350
World map with military commanders' areas of responsibility, 275
World Trade Center bombing, 20, 21; *see also* September 11, 2001 (9/11), 28n9
  Coast Guard approaching disaster site, 58
  impact of, 30
  National Guard members at disaster site, 32
  New York City police department, 322
  Twin Towers rubble, 31
  workers in rubble, 35
World War II (WWII), 2
  Nazi onslaught of, 3
WSD, *see* Water Security Division (WSD)
WWII, *see* World War II (WWII)

Y

Yemen, 24, 25
Yersinia pestis, *see* Plague (*Yersinia pestis*)

Z

ZADD, *see* Zoonotic and Animal Disease Defense (ZADD)
Zoonotic and Animal Disease Defense (ZADD), 525